S0-CDX-820

Programming Microsoft®
Windows® 2000

Mickey Williams

201 West 103rd Street, Indianapolis, Indiana 46290

SAMS

Unleashed

Programming Microsoft® Windows® 2000 Unleashed

Copyright © 1999 by Sams Publishing

All rights reserved. No part of this book shall be reproduced, stored in a retrieval system, or transmitted by any means, electronic, mechanical, photocopying, recording, or otherwise, without written permission from the publisher. No patent liability is assumed with respect to the use of the information contained herein. Although every precaution has been taken in the preparation of this book, the publisher and author assume no responsibility for errors or omissions. Neither is any liability assumed for damages resulting from the use of the information contained herein.

International Standard Book Number: 0-672-31486-X

Library of Congress Catalog Card Number: 98-87346

Printed in the United States of America

First Printing: June 1999

00 99   4 3 2 1

Trademarks

All terms mentioned in this book that are known to be trademarks or service marks have been appropriately capitalized. Sams Publishing cannot attest to the accuracy of this information. Use of a term in this book should not be regarded as affecting the validity of any trademark or service mark.

Windows is a registered trademark of Microsoft Corporation.

Warning and Disclaimer

Every effort has been made to make this book as complete and as accurate as possible, but no warranty or fitness is implied. The information provided is on an "as is" basis. The authors and the publisher shall have neither liability nor responsibility to any person or entity with respect to any loss or damages arising from the information contained in this book or from the use of the CD-ROM or programs accompanying it.

EXECUTIVE EDITOR
Brad Jones

ACQUISITIONS EDITOR
Chris Webb

DEVELOPMENT EDITOR
Matt Purcell

MANAGING EDITOR
Jodi Jensen

PROJECT EDITOR
Heather Talbot

COPY EDITOR
Bart Reed

INDEXER
Bruce Clingaman

PROOFREADERS
Donna Martin
Carl Pierce

TECHNICAL EDITOR
Greg Guntle

SOFTWARE DEVELOPMENT SPECIALIST
Michael Hunter

INTERIOR DESIGNER
Gary Adair

COVER DESIGNEER
Aren Howell

COPY WRITER
Eric Borgert

LAYOUT TECHNICIANS
Brandon Allen
Stacey DeRome
Staci Somers

Overview

Contents

About the Authors

Mickey Williams is the co-author *of Programming Windows NT 4.0 Unleashed*, and the author of *Teach Yourself Visual C++ in 24 Hours* and *Essential Visual C++*. Mickey is the founder of Codev Technologies, a provider of tools and consulting for Win32 development. Mickey is a member of the Association for Computing Machinery, and lives in Laguna Hills, California, with his wife and two daughters. Mickey can be reached at mickey.williams@codevtech.com.

Christian Gross is a professional programmer, author, and consultant who speaks regularly at professional developers conferences around the world, including the Visual C++ Developers Conference, Microsoft DevDays, TechEd, and Software Development. You can also find Christian's work in professional journals such as *The Visual C++ Developer* journal. As an IT consultant, Christian has advised such companies as the National Westminster Bank, Magna International, Standard Life, and the Union Bank of Switzerland.

Dedication

For the three Amigas: Rene', Ali, and Mackenzie.

—Mickey

Acknowledgments

As usual, there is a large number of people who deserve my heartfelt thanks.

First, a big thanks to Manny Aggarwal for reminding me where I could find an operating cluster when mine broke down in the middle of writing about Microsoft Cluster Server.

Thanks also to Simon Brown, with whom I worked for a time while this book was in the planning stages, and who provided a great deal of help in selecting topics for this second edition. Unfortunately, I took Simon sailing just before I actually started writing and he decided to move across the country to take a job working for IBM. I'm still not entirely sure if it was the prospect of a better job, or the fear of more sailing excursions that served as his primary motivating factor in moving.

Thanks to Shlomo Wygodny from Mutek Solutions for his help in getting me an evaluation of BugTrapper, which I think is one of the coolest tools I've seen in years.

Thanks also to Bob O'Brien from the Compuware NuMega Lab for his help in getting me information, evaluation products, and cool NuMega boxer shorts.

A big thanks to Christian Gross for writing the chapters on COM+ and MTS— specifically, Chapters 1 and 21–25.

At Macmillan, thanks to Matt Purcell, Heather Talbot, Vince Mayfield, and Bart Reed. I'd also like to thank Brad Jones and Chris Webb, who helped keep me on track during the writing process. Or, at least as on track as I can be while writing.

—Mickey Williams

Tell Us What You Think!

As the reader of this book, *you* are our most important critic and commentator. We value your opinion and want to know what we're doing right, what we could do better, what areas you'd like to see us publish in, and any other words of wisdom you're willing to pass our way.

As an Associate Publisher for Sams Publishing, I welcome your comments. You can fax, email, or write me directly to let me know what you did or didn't like about this book—as well as what we can do to make our books stronger.

Please note that I cannot help you with technical problems related to the topic of this book, and that due to the high volume of mail I receive, I might not be able to reply to every message.

When you write, please be sure to include this book's title and authors as well as your name and phone or fax number. I will carefully review your comments and share them with the authors and editors who worked on the book.

Fax:	317-581-4770
Email:	adv_prog@mcp.com
Mail:	Associate Publisher
	Sams Publishing
	201 West 103rd Street
	Indianapolis, IN 46290 USA

Introduction

The information in this book is based on Beta software. Because this information was made public before the final release of Windows 2000, there may be some changes to the product before final release. After the final product has begun shipping, we encourage you to visit our Web site, www.samspublishing.com, for updates.

Additionally, you can always get up-to-the-minute information about Windows 2000 from the MSDN Web site at msdn.microsoft.com.

Windows 2000 carries on the tradition started by Microsoft when Windows NT 3.1 was publicly released to developers in 1992. Windows NT 3.1 was designed to meet the following criteria:

- Portability between platforms
- Extensibility as market requirements change
- Multiprocessing and scalability
- Reliability and robustness (in other words, the system should protect itself)
- Distributed computing
- POSIX compliance
- Government-certifiable security
- Compatibility with prior Microsoft software
- Performance (as fast as possible given these criteria)

Since that initial release, Windows NT has been constantly refined:

- Windows NT 3.5 brought speed improvements and support for OpenGL.
- Windows NT 3.51 introduced support for the PowerPC and COM.
- Windows NT 4.0 included support for the new shell introduced in Windows 95.

Microsoft has made Windows 2000 its most ambitious upgrade to Windows NT to date. Here are some of the new features included in Windows 2000:

- *Active Directory*. AD is an enterprisewide, scalable directory service. Active Directory supports the industry-standard LDAP protocol as well as ADSI, the COM-based directory management protocol introduced recently for NT 4.0.

- *COM*. Two major enhancements have been made to COM. The first is COM+, a runtime service supplement to COM that supports building component-based distributed applications. The second is asynchronous COM, a facility that enables asynchronous method calls to be made between client and server.
- *Improved security*. Windows 2000 now supports SSL, Kerberos, and public-key encryption. In addition, Windows 2000 introduces new API functions that simplify security programming.
- *VLM*. Applications can now address up to 28GB of data using the Very Large Memory model. VLM is initially supported only for the Alpha processor.

In addition, many features that were introduced into Windows NT 4.0 through service packs or the NT 4.0 Option Pack are now integrated into Windows 2000. Features such as Microsoft Message Queue Server are now tightly integrated into the operating system.

The Developer

This book is written for the intermediate-to-advanced level C/C++ programmer—someone who is developing commercial applications and needs to know the new features of Windows 2000. It's also written for corporate developers whose users are asking for new features and want full access to the power of Windows 2000. This is a developer-based book.

Some examples in the book are presented in Visual Basic as well as C and C++, when appropriate. For example, some message queue examples are presented using VB in order to demonstrate how a developer can take advantage of the VB support for message queues using very little code.

The Code

In the examples in this book, you'll see code snippets developed using primarily Visual C++. We have tried to give you useful examples rather than large code dumps to fill pages. The accompanying CD-ROM contains the full projects referenced in the text.

The Layout

The first step in writing this book was to develop a table of contents, building from my previous Windows NT 4 book. This new edition of the book has been substantially rewritten, with new coverage of COM and COM+ features. This book also discusses topics rarely addressed in other books, such as Microsoft Cluster Server and Microsoft Message Queue Server.

Part I: Windows 2000 Core Technologies

Part I discusses the basic concepts needed to create distributed applications using Windows 2000. The first chapter provides an overview of creating Windows DNA–style applications, followed by nine chapters that cover topics such as Windows 2000 process and thread management, distributed security, DLLs, and writing services.

Part II: User Interaction/Desktop

Part II covers topics associated with the Windows 2000 desktop. The two chapters in this section discuss advanced GSI topics such as handling 256-color bitmaps and using owner-draw and custom-draw functions.

Part III: COM and ActiveX

Part III discusses COM and ActiveX. COM is now an integral part of the operating system, and it's difficult to imagine writing a Windows 2000 application without taking advantage of COM in some way. The initial chapters in this section serve as an introduction to COM; subsequent chapters discuss creating custom COM components and ActiveX controls and using asynchronous COM.

Part IV: COM+

Part IV covers COM+ services, a new technology built on COM and released for the first time in Windows 2000. COM+ marries COM and Microsoft Transaction Server to enable the development of scalable, component-based, distributed applications.

Part V: Distributed Windows 2000 Services

Part V finishes the book by discussing Windows 2000 programming topics that support developing distributed systems. Chapters in this section discuss Microsoft Cluster Server, Active Directory, and Message Queue Server.

Conventions Used in This Book

This book uses different typefaces to differentiate code and regular English, and also to help you identify important concepts.

Text that you type and text that should appear on your screen is presented in `monospace` type.

```
It will look like this to mimic the way text looks on your screen.
```

Placeholders for variables and expressions appear in *`monospace italic`* font. You should replace the placeholder with the specific value it represents.

This arrow (➥) at the beginning of a line of code means that a single line of code is too long to fit on the printed page. Continue typing all characters after the ➥ as though they were part of the preceding line.

> **NOTE**
>
> A Note presents interesting pieces of information related to the surrounding discussion.

> **TIP**
>
> A Tip offers advice or teaches an easier way to do something.

> **CAUTION**
>
> A Caution advises you about potential problems and helps you steer clear of disaster.

 The CD-ROM icon alerts you to information or items that appear on the CD-ROM that accompanies this book.

Windows 2000 Core Technologies

PART

I

IN THIS PART

Windows DNA Overview

This chapter will explain how Windows 2000 fits into the Windows Distributed Internet Applications Architecture (Windows DNA). The entire concept of Windows DNA can be a bit nebulous. The following note provides a nutshell definition.

> **NOTE**
>
> Windows DNA is the realization of an operating system that exposes a various number of services and facilities that make it possible to build applications using a logical design process.

In this definition there are three important aspects. The first is an operating system. The operating system is a fundamental aspect of the computer system. It provides the basis of your entire framework. This operating system should be fast, stable, and scalable. The second aspect is that this operating system has a series of services and facilities. These services make it possible to do certain tasks, such as transaction processing or messaging. And finally, the operating system and services should be combined such that applications can be developed from it. And the process of application development should be a logical process.

This chapter outlines what Windows DNA is and explains the various services and facilities in detail.

History of Windows and Windows NT

To understand Windows DNA, you need a context of where Windows has been. The context is important because you will be able to understand the evolution of Windows DNA. So, let's step back in time and consider the history of Windows:

- *Windows 3.*x. The Windows family began in earnest with the release of Windows 3.0. What made this version of Windows popular was the rich user interface; however, Windows 3.*x* brought something more important to the table: a common user interface and device driver model. Before Windows, device drivers had to be custom-fitted to each DOS application. This was tedious. Applications with custom drivers have custom memory requirements and customization problems. Windows changed all that and made it possible for a customer to ask for Windows device drivers. The user interface and application tasking were good as well, because they allowed for a consistent user interface for accomplishing certain tasks.

- *Windows NT*. The problem with Windows 3.*x* was its stability. Windows NT was a new operating system intended for the enterprise. In a way, it was a stable version Windows 3.*x*. It included integrated networking and server components, such as services. However, the server service aspect was not enough for writing server-side applications because it didn't provide transactions, messaging, and so on. When Windows NT was introduced, there were three versions. However, on a technical level the three different operating systems did not differ, other than client access privilege count.

- *Windows 95/98*. The Windows family kept on growing, with Windows 95 and 98 as the Windows 3.*x* replacement. Windows 95 and 98 are 32-bit operating systems. However, they differ in perspective from Windows NT. Windows 95/98 are consumer operating systems. Here, the requirement is for devices to autoconfigure themselves, making it easier to manage the client machine. This is a formidable task because there are over a hundred million machines running Windows programs. The focus for Windows 95/98 is to make it easier to navigate the Web and perform the specific tasks required of it.

- *NT Option Pack*. Windows NT provided the foundation for a stable and scalable operating system. However, it did not provide the services required. The NT Option Pack has added that capability. The Option Pack contains the IIS, MSMQ, and MTS services, and more. This add-on marked an additional aspect of Microsoft development—it marked the distinction between the independent software developer and the enterprise application developer who require these services.

- *Windows 2000*. The release of Windows 2000 brings more services and a more consistent and elegant COM+. Windows 2000 is the operating system that can handle the large tasks that involve thousands of concurrent users.

Windows DNA in Detail

From looking at the context, the problem has been how to develop robust scalable applications. These two attributes indicate that Windows DNA is all about the server. This is incorrect, because Windows DNA is about the client, server, and any other machine. It is about a more generic solution, which can be defined as follows:

- It can interact with the user via a keyboard, screen, and/or mouse.

- It can potentially use other input devices, such as a touch screen and pen device, or it can even be voice activated.

- It can connect to other machines via networking concepts.

- It provides a reliable and consistent environment in which multiple machines can share data.
- It easily manages itself and its environment.

This type of solution is a huge change in requirements from the classical Windows API era. In this era, a developer was concerned about how cool his or her user interface was and what button images to draw. This has changed because the computer has become a daily part of our lives. And, as such, it must solve more tasks and be able to interact with other machines and environments. People want things to just happen, like a toaster or microwave oven.

The Solution

Windows DNA provides a solution by having the capability to implement all the requirements using a series of services and facilities. Because the requirements seem enormous, is Windows DNA only for the corporate client? The answer is a flat no. The reason for this answer is simple. It has been shown in the past that when a strategy was only for a specific corporate size, it tended to fail. An example is EDI—while being accepted by the large corporations, it is not even close to be being accepted by small corporations. Therefore, Windows DNA must address the small corporations, large corporations, and the consumer.

The Guiding Principles of Windows DNA

The Windows DNA platform is a multitiered distributed application model. (I'll talk in detail about the platform in the next section.) It provides a set of services and facilities that are part of the operating system infrastructure. These services combine functionality from personal computers, mainframes, Internet, client/server, and so on.

By mixing all these technologies, the operating system could be considered bloated. However, this is not the case, because you can pick and choose the services you require. You do this by picking the appropriate Windows 2000 tier and installing the required services. However, this aspect is beyond the scope of this book. Instead, this book will focus on all the services and facilities.

The guiding principles of Windows DNA are as follows:

- *Internet ready.* Internet technologies such as TCP/IP, HTTP, FTP, and so on are integrated into the operating system. This makes it possible for applications to assume Internet availability.

- *Faster time to market.* Developing vertical applications is not simple. (A *vertical application* is one that's very customer oriented. An example is a banking application.) Solutions developed in this industry tend to be specific to the client and to the industry. In the past, vertical market software developers tended to focus on plumbing, which cost precious development time. With Windows DNA, the plumbing (system services such as transactions, messaging) is provided to the solution developer, meaning more time to focus on the application.

- *Interoperability.* Cross-platform programming is a complicated issue. There are no easy solutions. One way of achieving almost the same thing is to *interoperate.* Interoperability uses open protocols and open standards to make sure a solution will work with multiple vendors.

- *Less complexity.* Creating an installation program is not a difficult program. What is difficult and complicated is having to deal with programs that install different versions of the same program. Consider the situation of a program released in 1996 and a program released in 1999. Both programs have some shared libraries. And chances are the program in 1999 cannot cope with the 1996 shared components. Quite a few of these problems were due to the fact that operating system components were not released with the operating system. Windows 2000 solves this by integrating the services within the operating system. And future services will be released with the operating system. This will make the operating system releases and program installations easier.

- *Language tool independence.* The basis of the Windows platform is to enable third-party developers to choose their own development environment. This makes it possible for you to choose the language that will best solve the business problem.

- *Lower total cost of ownership.* The last principle is to make the application simpler to deploy, manage, and iterate over time. This can be achieved by simplifying the installation and version control processes.

The Architecture of Windows DNA

The Windows DNA architecture, which is used to build multitier applications, has three tiers (see Figure 1.1). These three tiers are Presentation, Business Logic, and Data. This architecture does not represent a physical architecture. Instead, it represents an abstract concept. It's possible for multiple physical tiers to exist within one of the abstract tiers.

FIGURE **1.1**

*The Windows DNA
architecture.*

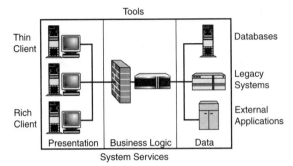

Windows DNA
The development model for Windows

COM Everywhere

In order for the entire architecture to work, the objects must be able to communicate with each other. This communication happens via a technology called COM (Component Object Model). COM is a vtable-based technology that makes it possible for two pieces of code to exchange information.

COM is a binary technology. Figure 1.2 shows an interface, which is a vtable. This vtable is a series of function pointers to some code. The vtable definition can exist on any platform. It's generated in a platform-neutral manner. The interface then points to some implementation that performs the action. The implementation has traditionally been binary and platform specific. However, with the advent of Visual J++, this isn't necessarily the case. Visual J++ generates Java code that can be executed on any platform. The only condition is that the COM runtime (implements the COM system API and system object model) must exist on the destination platform.

FIGURE **1.2**

*A COM interface
and implementa-
tion technique.*

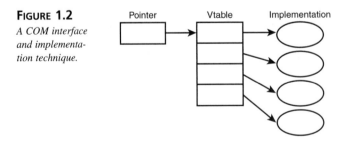

When developing Windows DNA applications, you'll most likely start with an interface definition. The interface is an intention of what it wants to achieve. An implementation will then implement intention specific to the domain. It may implement one or multiple interfaces. With a separation of the interface and implementation, it's possible for the COM runtime to dynamically query which implementation can be consumed.

Windows DNA exploits COM by exposing the services as a set of COM objects. This is in contrast to previous versions of Windows NT, where the majority of services were exposed using APIs. Examples of services include security, transaction, message queuing, and hardware support.

So why use COM? Besides the technical reasons, COM is by far the largest component strategy currently in use. This is the reason DNA is based on COM. Breaking compatibility is not a possibility. With COM, you can build software components that can be executed and deployed on any of the tiers. The COM runtime provides support for packaging, partitioning, and other multitier issues.

Presentation Tier

The presentation tier is where the application interacts with the user. This is a necessary tier, because humans do not have the capacity to comprehend the bits and bytes on the hard disk in an efficient manner. At this tier, the data is represented in a manner that users can understand. Currently, this is largely keyboard, screen, and mouse oriented. However, this will change in the future to provide better facilities for the handicapped—for example, voice and gesture facilities.

In the current version of Windows DNA, the focus of the presentation tier is to promote access—any time, anywhere, any how. This is made possible using Internet integration tools such as a browser and dial-up and networking facilities. This tier is challenging because the types of clients vary dramatically. In the Windows DNA architecture, the client is not just Windows based—it can include UNIX, Macintosh, and other operating systems.

To be able to support the various platforms, the presentation tier is graded from a rich client to a thin client. Don't think of a thin client in terms of bytes to download, because a thin client may include an image that could be several hundred megabytes. The varying parameter is the amount of functionality that can be executed on the client side.

Figure 1.3 presents an abstraction of how to build the presentation tier. On the right side are the various technologies, represented by a series of cogs. Using these technologies, you can build two types of clients: EXE-based and page-based. These types of clients can be further divided into the four types of subclients. These four types vary from a thin client to a rich client.

FIGURE **1.3**

*Presentation tier
details.*

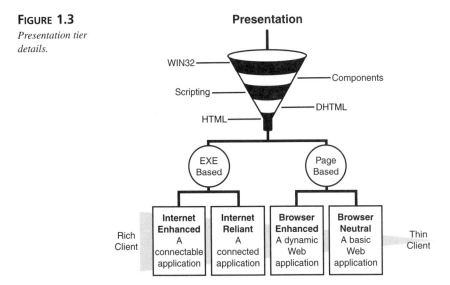

Page-based Solutions

A thin client is a type of page-based client. This means that the client is connected to the network and downloads content as required. In other words, it does not download an entire application, only pages of it.

Specifically, a thin client is *thin* because it presents to the presentation tier a static information set. The user can then fill out a few text boxes, set some check boxes, and submit it for processing. This type of functionality is very similar to batch form processing from the mainframe days. The only difference is that the terminal can be anywhere on the Internet. Typically, this type of client is a Web browser. A static Web browser approach ensures that your application has the broadest support. This type of application is called a *browser-neutral application*. In this solution, the client determines the runtime environment. Typically, the runtime environment is a Web browser.

If more functionality is required, a dynamic Web application is needed. In this situation, a more advanced user interface is used. This makes the application more interactive. However, the cost of this interaction is that fewer Web browsers can decipher the content. For example, it's possible to develop content that will function only on Internet Explorer or only on Netscape Navigator. However, the advantage of this extra functionality is a more versatile application. Typical applications would be a Web browser-based intranet or extranet application. Usually in this situation, you'll know which browser is used.

EXE-based Solutions

The next two types of solutions require quite a bit of functionality on the client side. These applications are executable based. This means that some application is installed on the client machine.

An Internet-reliant application is one that uses a mixture of the underlying operating system and the network for content. These applications require the functionality of the operating system because of the complex tasks being processed. In this situation, the browser, which may be embedded, does not provide the richness. Instead, as in the browser-based solution, it must be connected to the Internet to receive its content. An example of this is a data warehousing application. When sifting through a data warehouse, you typically generate complex pivot tables. These tables can be graphed and compared. From that information you could make some kind of decision. Because of the graphing and complex processing involved, an operating system graphic subsystem is required. You need to be connected to the network because you don't download a data warehouse to your desktop. The processing power required would be immense.

The last type of rich client is one that uses only the client machine and never interacts with the Internet. The application may be a single-user application that exists on its own. These types of applications are becoming fewer and fewer. The reason is that users want to exchange information. Client applications include Microsoft Word and Microsoft Excel. These applications do not explicitly require the Internet, but they can be used for collaboration purposes.

This type of client is also breeding a new hybrid client application. The hybrid client application uses the Internet when it needs to, but it does so invisibly, without the user noticing. An example is Microsoft Money. This application is installed on the client machine and can, for the most part, exist in isolation. However, when you want to retrieve your banking statements from your bank, you must go online. An embedded browser starts up and connects to your bank. From there, it downloads your statements and displays them. During this entire process, you never type in a URL or give any network commands. The only exception is connecting to the Internet. So, in other words, the hybrid client makes seamless use of the Internet.

The Various Technologies

For you to understand the various client types, the core technologies need to be outlined:

- *HTML*. Hypertext Markup Language is the user interface language of the Web. When only the term HTML is mentioned, typically it is Version 3.2 or more recently Version 4.0. Both versions are a plain vanilla variety, which support forms-based processing. This technology has the broadest reach among all technologies. This technology would typically be used in the thin client.

- *DHTML*. Dynamic HTML is the more advanced Web browser user interface. Dynamic HTML differs from HTML in that it supports a full-fledged object model. Every part of the user interface can be dynamically addressed, removed, or added. This makes the user interface incredibly powerful. However, there are fewer browsers that support this feature.

- *Scripting*. Within the DHTML object model, a scripting interface is defined. So it would seem questionable as to why scripting is considered a technology. The reason why it is considered a technology is because with scripting it is possible to control any type of client. For example, Microsoft Excel can be scripted to perform certain tasks. Scripting applies to all clients. The major benefit of scripting is that it provides application customizability, without requiring complex programming skills.

- *Components*. DHTML, scripting, and most other things on the client would not be possible without components. Not much more can be said, because most has been said.

- *Win32*. The Win32 API is a way of interacting with the operating system. This technology is appropriate for those clients that need the special graphics or high performance. The Win32 API is specific to Windows. It is not a similar programming model to HTML or Dynamic HTML.

Firewall Tier

This tier is not directly a tier, but it is something significant that needs to be mentioned. The firewall tier is erected between the presentation tier and the business logic tier. A firewall is a security feature that ensures the data on the inside of the firewall is not compromised.

It may seem that a firewall is only a service within the overall framework. This is the case in general architecture, but this is not the case with Windows DNA. Windows DNA is different from most operating systems in that it moves the security to the business logic tier.

There are several advantages to this setup. The first advantage is that there's a consistent security-verification mechanism. Consider the example of a castle. Using current security mechanisms, a rider could make his way into the castle anonymously. Then, depending on the service, a security verification would be required. The problem is that as the rider moves through the castle, he has to keep verifying his identity. Also, what happens if one service was not as secure as the others? A rider could become evil and cause destruction. With each service asking for identification, it's not easy to keep a consistent security policy. For example, the rider could be kicked out of one pub only. However, the rider should be kicked out of *all* pubs in the castle, but this does not happen.

If the firewall is the central security authority, anyone accessing any service will be known. The user will be assigned a specific set of rights and privileges, and if he abuses those rights, he can be revoked in an easy and consistent manner. In the end, this makes for a faster and simpler security framework.

Business Logic Tier

The business logic tier is the heart of an application. It processes and manipulates the data. (The business process rules and workflow procedures handle this.) This tier is very important, and you'll need to spend the most programming effort on this tier. This tier includes high-volume processing, transaction support, large-scale deployment, messaging, and possibly the Web. In other words, this middle tier is very complex.

The business logic tier has three major services: COM+, MSMQ, and IIS. Of course, there are other services, such as Microsoft Exchange and Microsoft SQL Server, but they're not part of the Windows 2000 distribution. The sample architecture can be illustrated as follows:

FIGURE **1.4**

Architecture of the business logic tier.

Business Logic

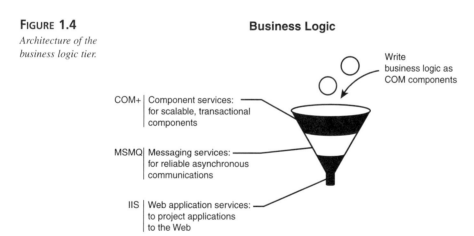

Write business logic as COM components

COM+ | Component services: for scalable, transactional components

MSMQ | Messaging services: for reliable asynchronous communications

IIS | Web application services: to project applications to the Web

Each service performs a specific task. COM+ is responsible for the basic COM and transaction functionality. IIS (Internet Information Server) is responsible for Internet services such as SMTP (Simple Mail Transfer Protocol), FTP (File Transfer Protocol), and HTTP (Hypertext Transfer Protocol). MSMQ (Microsoft Message Queue) is responsible for messaging. Each service can use other services to create new services. An example would be queued components, which use COM+ and MSMQ to create a new service.

COM+

The next generation of COM is COM+. COM+ extends COM by adding services that make it usable for the enterprise. Am I saying that COM is not usable for the enterprise? No, not at all. However, COM provides only the component framework. In order for COM components to have transaction capabilities, additional services are required. This is the purpose of COM+.

COM+ and transaction services first came to life in SQL Server. SQL Server 6.5 distributed a service called the Distributed Transaction Coordinator (DTC). This service was responsible for SQL Server transaction management. Then, the DTC was re-released with a simpler wrapper called Microsoft Transaction Server (MTS). MTS made it possible to write COM objects that perform business processes and control transactions. COM+ takes the transaction aspect and ingrains it into the COM runtime and operating system. MTS is embedded into the operating system; however, an MTS object can bypass MTS. The loopholes are closed in COM+, making it more consistent and elegant. From a programming point of view, COM+ enables all server-side COM objects to take advantage of transactions to make their applications more reliable.

TIP Integration

COM+ uses OLE transactions to manage the transaction-processing environment. However, this is specific only to the Windows 2000 platform. Using TIP (Transaction Internet Protocol), it's possible for COM objects to participate in other transaction-processing (TP) environments. These transactions can be managed by the TP system. This is different from the previous version in MTS. In that version, the transaction had to be managed by MTS and the DTC.

Enhanced Security

In the section on the firewall tier, I explained that Windows 2000 enhances the security model. Quite a bit of this work is part of the COM+ environment. COM+ security involves either role-based security or process access permissions. *Role-based security* is a mechanism whereby the user is part of a large group that has a role. Roles can be managers, employees, and so on. Roles make it simpler to manage users who have different security privileges, depending on their domain. A example is an accounting person who has high security access to the accounting processes but low security access to the manufacturing processes. An extension of role-based security in COM+ is the ability to apply security at the method level for the COM objects.

Centralized Administration

In the previous version of Windows NT, the COM components were managed using the MTS Explorer. To manage any DCOM settings, DCOMCNFG would be used. In Windows 2000, both these tools are replaced with the Component Services Explorer. It combines and extends the administration of the COM+ objects. Tasks include deploying, managing, and monitoring the COM+ application.

IMDB (In-memory Database)

One service that's new in Windows 2000 is IMDB. IMDB is an in-memory database that keeps tables in RAM memory. Many applications today require high performance. For those applications, much of the data is read-mostly. An example is the retrieval of a product catalog. This table changes, but very slowly. Most of the time it's read, and it can be cached. This is where IMDB serves its purpose. With it, you can cache the product catalog tables to make them high-speed access tables.

IMDB is not a general service. It serves a specific purpose and functionality which need to be determined by the programmer.

Queued Components

DCOM (Distributed COM) is used to allow a COM object to be called between two different machines. DCOM is a synchronous protocol. When a call originates from one machine, the receiver must be available. If that receiver is not available, the call fails and any operation also fails. If that operation was executing within the context of a transaction, the transaction fails as well. You must then implement a fail and retry mechanism.

In Windows 2000, an easier solution is to use queued components. Queued components make it possible to call another component on another machine asynchronously. Queued components use MSMQ as the underlying messaging architecture. Therefore, if the connection or call fails, it can retry until it succeeds.

Event Services

In Windows NT 4.*x*, connecting events to components is not easy. You could use a technology called COM connection points, but it's very limiting. What's needed is a technology that permits loosely coupled events, where the event receiver may be active or not active.

This event mechanism, available in Windows 2000, is called COM+ events. Using COM+ events, you can make unicast or multicast calls. The receiver of the event connects to the client using a subscription technique.

The publish-and-subscribe mechanism is where the publisher informs the COM+ event services that it has information it wants to distribute. A receiver that's interested in this information indicates its interest to the COM+ event service using a subscription. Then, when the publisher has any information that's changing, COM+ event services will propagate the changes to the various subscribers.

Dynamic Load Balancing

With the release of Windows 2000, you can now dynamically load-balance a COM+ object. *Dynamic load balancing* is the technique of evenly distributing the processing load over a set of machines. Load balancing a server-oriented process occurs transparently with respect to the client making the server call.

Internet Services

The Internet Information Server (IIS) provides various Internet services. Included are the following:

- *HTTP*. This is the protocol of the Web. It serves up Web pages and any content a Web browser requests.
- *FTP*. This is the protocol used on the Internet to transfer files. It's specifically geared toward file transfer and is therefore very efficient.
- *SMTP*. This is the protocol used to transfer mail messages from one machine to another. It can be used in conjunction with POP protocol, which is used to retrieve email.
- *Gopher*. This protocol existed in previous editions of IIS but is now obsolete. Gopher has been superseded by HTTP.

What makes IIS special with respect to other Internet servers is its integration with transactions. When a request is made to IIS, it's a transaction request. By using transactions as the basis for handling requests, you can realize all the benefits of COM+. It also makes it more flexible when the transaction or business process needs to be dynamically load-balanced or optimized.

To build content for IIS, you can use ISAPI (Internet Server API) or, typically, ASP (Active Server Pages). ASP technology is a scripting environment in which logic is executed from scripts. The scripting language is neutral and totally dynamic. It's used in conjunction with the COM+ object to provide a full-featured business application. ASP can be used to generate DHTML or XML. Although not part of Windows 2000, the process of creating ASP, DHTML, and XML applications can be handled using Visual InterDev.

Messaging Services

Asynchronous messages are handled using MSMQ (Microsoft Message Queue Server). Messaging involves a totally different way of writing code. It assumes that the connection between the client and server does not exist. It assumes that eventually the operation will be carried out. This eventuality model makes it possible for you to write applications that function over unreliable networks or in unreliable conditions.

MSMQ is an event-driven architecture. The data is pushed to the server, and then the server must react to the event being called. Event-driven architecture is nothing new— Windows, itself, is event driven. However, with event-driven architecture, application programming must be different from the norm, because it is an asynchronous programming model.

Interoperating with Existing Systems, Applications, and Data

Windows 2000 is not only Internet ready, it's also ready to integrate with legacy systems. Legacy systems work and do their tasks well enough; therefore, replacing these systems is not an option. Instead, they must be integrated into the overall architecture.

Windows 2000 can integrate with the following legacy technologies:

- *MSMQ integration.* Messaging integration is provided for MSMQ using various products. To connect from the Windows platform to the MQSeries product, SNA Server can be used. To connect from other platforms (UNIX, MVS, OS/2, and so on) to the MSMQ FalconMQ client, Level8 can be used.

- *COM Transaction Integrator.* Using this interface, you can extend CICS and IMS transactions as a series of COM objects. In the COM Transaction Integrator is a series of development and business logic tools that wrap the IBM mainframe transaction. Windows SNA Server handles the communication to the IBM transaction.

- *Universal Data Access.* This layer has not yet been discussed—it's known as the *database access layer.* By using native drivers, you can connect to resources that reside on the other platform's side.

- *DCOM on UNIX/mainframe.* This is a technology that makes it possible to write COM objects on platforms other than Windows. Software AG provided the first port to Solaris. However, this has been extended to include the mainframe platform and currently extends to a full architecture called EntireX iNTegrator.

- *TIP/XA transaction integration.* Several transaction protocol standards exist. TIP has already been discussed. Another standard is the XA protocol. Its integration is provided through a resource dispenser/manager.

Some Final Words

The business logic tier is a very important tier. It contains, by far, the largest number of COM objects that provide specific services. This flexibility is required to build world-class enterprise applications that can receive, process, and send back data from the data tier.

Data Tier

The last tier is the data tier. It's the resource management tier. In contrast to the business logic tier, the data tier performs no processing of data. Instead, the task of managing the huge amount of data is defined in the data tier. Databases and resources are getting bigger every day, and this task is becoming more and more difficult.

The UDA (Universal Data Access) strategy is a bit different from strategies used by other vendors. UDA stores and manipulates data. A question that must be asked is: What kinds of data exist? The answer is an infinite amount of different data. Some data is in a spreadsheet, some in a word processing document, and other data is in a relational database. To be able to store this data, you could write your own routines, but then sharing among different packages will become difficult. Or, another situation is to use one database and then store it within. The typical way to do this has been to use a blob. However, that makes things centralized and requires an additional software dependency and costs.

Now consider the situation of references within documents. One transaction creates a two-way relation between two documents. And another transaction changes the reference of one of the documents. When the other document attempts to use the reference, it may generate a GPF.

The solution to this problem or the varying data storage problem cannot be easily solved. The approach that UDA takes is in the definition of another data layer object model. Although this may seem drastic, it is necessary. The previous data access layer, ODBC, is great for relational data, but requires a large amount of tweaking for other data. In this data layer, each resource writes its own data format. But access to that data format is handled by the object layer.

An example of this working is the query processor within UDA. The query processor has the ability to retrieve data from various resources and make it appear like one query. In the end, this makes it possible to slice and dice data as needed from the various sources.

The UDA object model is called the *OLE DB object model* (see Figure 1.5). This is a low-level data access model that includes the specifications for how transactions and row sets are defined. The OLE DB object operates at very high speeds using raw interfaces with complex data types. This means that writing to OLE DB requires quite a bit of legwork. Although it's not part of the Windows 2000 distribution, Visual C++ has a thin template layer on top called *OLE DB Consumer templates*. This serves to simplify OLE DB, without making it slower or less efficient.

FIGURE 1.5
Universal data access.

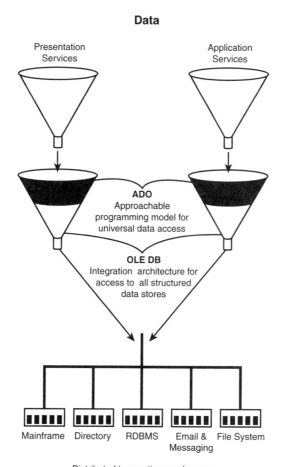

Data

The advantage of the OLE DB object model is that it's not limited. There's a specific subset that must be implemented. Nothing stops a vendor from extending the object model to provide fine-tuned access to its data. This, again, is like the presentation tier, where broad reach versus rich functionality must be traded off.

Because of the low-level nature of OLE DB, Visual Basic and script writers cannot use it directly. A simpler model known as ADO (Active Data Objects) has been created. This object model is a very small but powerful object that allows access to most of the features of OLE DB. One question that must be answered is how OLE DB exposes this rich functionality and blobs? The answer is as other COM objects. This is why ADO does not need to be big to handle all the various data formats. It's the responsibility of the provider to generate the COM objects.

Summary

Windows 2000 is a part of Windows DNA. It is the operating system that provides the facilities needed to write complex vertical market applications.

It starts at the client machine, which can be simple handheld computing devices or high-end workstations. The client machine is responsible for displaying the data and interacting with the user. In the middle tier, the business logic is executed. The services required include transactions and messaging. By integrating these various services into the operating system, the entire system becomes more stable and more scalable. Finally, the data is stored in the data services tier. Here, another set of services relating to data storage is exposed.

Windows DNA is not about only services and Windows 2000. This book will discuss the details regarding the various services and facilities. However, there is also a methodology, which is beyond the scope of this book.

Virtual Memory and Memory Management

This chapter discusses memory management functions offered by Windows 2000. You'll learn about the virtual memory management functions, which enable you to directly manage virtual memory addresses. You'll also see a sample program that illustrates how virtual memory is used; this is provided on the accompanying CD-ROM.

You'll also learn about the Windows 2000 *Heap Memory API*, a set of functions that provide higher-level management of virtual memory in Windows 2000. You'll see an example of using the Heap API to manage memory privately in C++ classes as well.

Using Virtual Memory

Virtual memory enables you to allocate and use a much larger range of memory addresses than you have available on your computer. Windows 2000 makes extensive use of virtual memory; every application behaves as though it's running on a machine that contains 4GB of memory address space, regardless of how much RAM is actually installed on the computer.

The 4GB address space is divided into two sections: Typically the upper 2GB are used by the operating system, and the lower 2GB are available to the application, as shown in Figure 2.1.

FIGURE 2.1
The Windows 2000 address space.

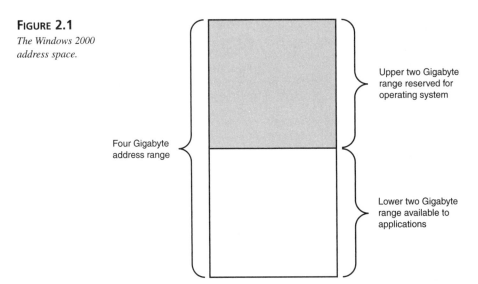

The Advanced Server of Windows 2000 for the Intel family of processors includes *RAM Tuning*, which allows you to reserve an extra 1GB of address space for applications, leaving only 1GB for the operating system, as shown in Figure 2.2.

FIGURE 2.2

RAM Tuning allots up to 3GB of RAM to Windows 2000 applications.

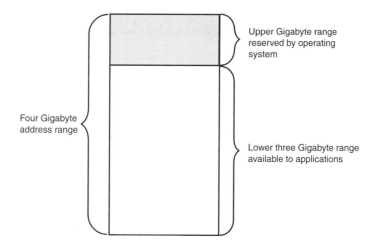

Upper Gigabyte range reserved by operating system

Four Gigabyte address range

Lower three Gigabyte range available to applications

2

VIRTUAL MEMORY AND MEMORY MANAGEMENT

NOTE

RAM Tuning is not available for the Alpha processor versions of Windows 2000. Very Large Model (or VLM) addressing is used for the Alpha processor, and it includes 64-bit addressing. This is a much more powerful facility for addressing large amounts of memory than RAM Tuning. Using the VLM APIs is discussed later in this chapter.

Obviously, the 4GB range of virtual memory addresses is not directly mapped to actual memory hardware. Instead, a Windows 2000 application works with virtual addresses, which can be moved to different physical locations in memory or out to page file storage on the hard disk.

Windows 2000 deals with virtual memory in pages. Each page is a fixed size, which can be determined by calling the GetSystemInfo function. The GetSystemInfo function fills a SYSTEM_INFO structure; the dwPageSize member will contain the virtual memory page size, as shown in this code:

```
SYSTEM_INFO inf;
GetSystemInfo(&inf);
_tprintf(_T("Page size = %d\n"), inf.dwPageSize);
```

Deciding When to Use Virtual Memory

Virtual memory is ideal in situations in which you're not sure how much memory will be used. If you implement a private heap, you actually allocate memory from Windows 2000. With virtual memory, you can reserve a large range of addresses and only allocate, or commit, the pages you actually use.

Virtual memory also is useful when you're implementing a sparse memory data structure. A sparse memory scheme reserves a large range of virtual memory and uses only a few pages at a time. This is an easy way to implement grid- or spreadsheet-based applications, because you can reserve a large virtual address range that represents the entire grid and then commit only the pages that represent cells that actually are used (see Figure 2.3).

FIGURE 2.3

Sparse memory allocation in a spreadsheet.

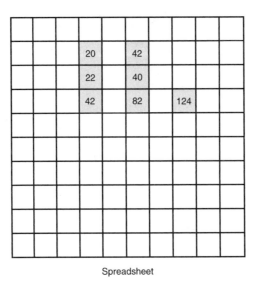

Spreadsheet

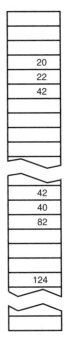

Virtual address space

Figure 2.3 shows a typical sparse memory data structure used to implement a spreadsheet. When a grid initially is used, the page used by that grid is committed. Until a page is committed, no memory is actually allocated by Windows 2000.

If you've programmed for 16-bit Windows, you might be familiar with the older heap management functions. These functions still are supported in 32-bit versions of Windows, but their use is discouraged. When programming under Windows 2000, you use Win32 Heap API functions to manage the heap. These functions are discussed in the next few sections.

Reserving a Range of Virtual Memory

The first step in using virtual memory in your Windows 2000 application is to allocate a range of addresses. The `VirtualAlloc` function returns a pointer to the base of a range of virtual memory that has been reserved for your application:

```
pMem = VirtualAlloc(NULL, cAllocSize, MEM_RESERVE, PAGE_NOACCESS);
```

The first parameter passed to `VirtualAlloc` is the base address of the virtual memory range. That's right—in Windows 2000, you actually can specify the virtual memory address that the system should return to you. If Windows 2000 cannot allocate memory at that address, NULL is returned. In most cases, you pass NULL as the base address, which allows Windows 2000 to select an address for you.

If you pass an address to `VirtualAlloc`, it's rounded down to the first useable address. If you're reserving a block of memory, the address is rounded down to a 64KB boundary. If you're committing a page, as will be discussed later, the address is rounded down to a page boundary.

The second parameter passed to `VirtualAlloc` is the size of the requested memory reservation. In most cases, you should ask for as much memory as you are likely to use. The time required for reserving a large number of pages doesn't vary in relation to the amount of memory requested; there's no advantage to being thrifty here.

The MEM_RESERVE flag is passed as the third parameter to `VirtualAlloc`. MEM_RESERVE is one of four memory allocation flags you can use with `VirtualAlloc`; it's used to reserve memory. The other three flags follow:

- MEM_COMMIT. Commits a range of virtual memory. If this is combined with MEM_RESERVE, the virtual memory range is reserved and then committed during the same function call.

- MEM_RESET. Indicates that the address range is no longer to be used as part of the virtual address space. The memory will not be written to, or read from, the paging file.

- MEM_TOP_DOWN. Specifies that the virtual memory should be allocated from the top of the virtual memory address range. You can combine the MEM_TOP_DOWN and MEM_RESERVE flags.

The fourth parameter is the page-access flag, which enables you to set the access permission for virtual memory pages. Here's a list of the eight page-access flags:

- `PAGE_READONLY`. Allows read access to the committed region of pages. An attempt to write to the committed region results in an access violation.
- `PAGE_READWRITE`. Allows both read and write access to the committed region of pages.
- `PAGE_EXECUTE`. Allows execute access to the committed region of pages for systems that differentiate between read and execute access. An attempt to read or write to the committed region results in an access violation.
- `PAGE_EXECUTE_READ`. Allows both execute and read access to the committed region of pages. An attempt to write to the committed region results in an access violation.
- `PAGE_EXECUTE_READWRITE`. Allows execute, read, and write access to the committed region of pages.
- `PAGE_GUARD`. Specifies that pages in the region are guard pages. A *guard page* can be used as a boundary page when you're using virtual memory. An exception is raised when a page with this attribute is initially accessed. (Using guard pages is discussed later in this chapter.)
- `PAGE_NOACCESS`. Specifies that no attempts to read, write, or execute the specified pages is allowed. Any access attempts will result in an exception.
- `PAGE_NOCACHE`. Specifies that no caching of the committed regions of virtual memory is allowed. This generally is used only when writing device drivers.

The page-access flags only apply after a page is committed. If a page is free or reserved, any attempt at access causes an access violation exception to be raised.

Committing a Page of Virtual Memory

After you reserve a range of the virtual memory address space, you must commit it before you actually can use it. You must commit virtual memory in multiples of the virtual memory page size; even if you need only part of a page, the entire page is committed. To commit a page of virtual memory, use the `VirtualAlloc` function with the `MEM_COMMIT` flag:

```
pv = VirtualAlloc(pMem, cPageSize, MEM_COMMIT, PAGE_READWRITE);
```

In this code, the `PAGE_READWRITE` flag indicates that the page is now both readable and write enabled. It's also possible to use the `PAGE_NOACCESS` flag to prevent the page from being written to or used. If you use this flag, you must change the access rights to a different page-access value before using the page.

The idea behind reserving a range of virtual memory addresses and committing them as needed is simple enough, but deciding on a mechanism for committing new pages is difficult. You can commit new pages in one of three ways:

- Keep track of the number of allocated pages manually and increase the allocation when needed. This involves a lot of bookkeeping, because you need to remember how you've committed objects into the committed virtual memory space. This approach adds processing costs to every virtual memory access.

- Use guard pages as boundary markers in your virtual memory and commit more pages when a guard page is touched and a structured exception is raised. This approach works well for some types of applications (it's discussed later in the chapter).

- Use Windows 2000 structured exception handling to help determine which pages should be committed. Write your code so that all your pages are assumed to be committed and then catch access exceptions. Inside the access exception handler, commit the page and repeat whatever access was made on the page.

One of the fastest methods for committing pages involves using structured exception handling.

Using Exceptions

Win32 structured exception handling is discussed in detail in Chapter 5, "Structured Exception Handling." If you're unfamiliar with structured exceptions, it's enough for now for you to know a few basic things about Win32 exceptions:

- If an exception is raised inside a __try block, the operating system will transfer execution to the associated __except block.

- The __except block is never executed unless an exception is raised by the operating system.

- You can determine the specific exception that's raised by calling the GetExceptionCode function.

A simple approach to using structured exceptions is very useful in sparse memory schemes. The basic idea is to attempt to write to a page and, if an access violation exception is raised by the operating system, to commit the page and then write to the page again. Listing 2.1 shows an example of this.

2

VIRTUAL MEMORY
AND MEMORY
MANAGEMENT

LISTING 2.1 ALLOCATING VIRTUAL MEMORY AS NEEDED USING STRUCTURED EXCEPTIONS

```
_ _try
{
    g_ptrGridArray[nGridIndex] = pGrid;
}
_ _except(GetExceptionCode() == EXCEPTION_ACCESS_VIOLATION)
{
    VirtualAlloc(g_rgGridArray + nGridIndex * sizeof(CGridItem*),
                 sizeof(CGridItem),
                 MEM_COMMIT,
                 PAGE_READWRITE);
    g_ptrGridArray[nGridIndex] = pGrid;
}
```

In Listing 2.1, a pointer to a CGridItem object is stored in the g_ptrGridArray array. If the requested page has not been committed, Windows 2000 generates an EXCEPTION_ACCESS_VIOLATION exception. The exception handler commits the page and stores a pointer to the object on the new page. This approach is very fast because it doesn't require you to track the currently committed pages.

Using Guard Pages

Another approach to committing pages in virtual memory is useful when the memory is used from the "bottom up." This type of allocation model can take advantage of virtual memory *guard pages*, which generate exceptions when they are used. Figure 2.4 shows an example of virtual memory using guard pages.

FIGURE 2.4

Virtual memory using guard pages.

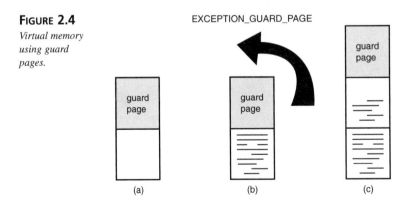

In Figure 2.4, section A shows a new virtual memory area with two pages committed, one of which is a guard page. Storage is used from the bottom of the committed address space, as shown in section B, and when the first access is made on the guard page in section C, an EXCEPTION_GUARD_PAGE exception is raised by Windows 2000. At this point, your application has two choices:

- Allocate additional pages
- Stop using virtual memory before the storage on the guard page is exhausted

The EXCEPTION_GUARD_PAGE exception is raised only for the first access made to a guard page. After the exception is raised, no more exceptions are raised for that page, no matter how many times it's accessed. Listing 2.2 shows an example of using guard pages.

LISTING 2.2   USING GUARD PAGES TO EFFICIENTLY COMMIT VIRTUAL MEMORY

```
#include <windows.h>
#include <tchar.h>

TCHAR* g_rgChar = NULL;
const int nAllocLimit = 0x100000 * sizeof(TCHAR);
int main()
{
    SYSTEM_INFO  inf;
    GetSystemInfo(&inf);

    g_rgChar = (TCHAR*)VirtualAlloc(NULL,
                                    nAllocLimit,
                                    MEM_RESERVE,
                                    PAGE_READWRITE);
    _tprintf(_T("Reserved range based at %p\n"), g_rgChar);
    // Commit the first page in the virtual address space,
    // and mark it as a guard page.
    VirtualAlloc(g_rgChar,
                 inf.dwPageSize,
                 MEM_COMMIT,
                 PAGE_READWRITE | PAGE_GUARD);
    int nPagesCommitted = 1;
    int nIndex;
    for(nIndex = 0; nIndex * sizeof(TCHAR)< nAllocLimit; nIndex++)
    {
        _ _try
        {
            g_rgChar[nIndex] = (nIndex%26)+'A';
        }
        _ _except(GetExceptionCode() == EXCEPTION_GUARD_PAGE)
        {
            // A guard page has been touched, commit a new one.
            g_rgChar[nIndex] = (nIndex%26)+'A';
```

continues

LISTING 2.2 CONTINUED

```
            void* pvNewPage;
            pvNewPage = g_rgChar +
                        nPagesCommitted * inf.dwPageSize/
                        sizeof(TCHAR);
            int n = nPagesCommitted*inf.dwPageSize;
            if(pvNewPage < g_rgChar + nAllocLimit)
            {
                void* pv = VirtualAlloc(pvNewPage,
                                        inf.dwPageSize,
                                        MEM_COMMIT,
                                        PAGE_READWRITE|PAGE_GUARD);
                _tprintf(_T("Committed a new page at %p\n"), pv);
                nPagesCommitted++;
            }
        }
    }
    VirtualFree(g_rgChar, nAllocLimit, MEM_RELEASE);
    return 0;
}
```

The console mode program in Listing 2.2 reserves 100KB of virtual address space and then commits one page at a time. Each page is committed as a guard page. The first time the guard page is accessed, an EXCEPTION_GUARD_PAGE exception is raised and an additional guard page is committed.

Locking a Page of Virtual Memory

Normally, you should let the virtual memory management functions built into Windows 2000 determine which pages are loaded into RAM or swapped out to a page file. Sometimes, however, it's necessary to guarantee that a page always is loaded in RAM for performance reasons. You can lock a page of virtual memory by using the VirtualLock function. Here's an example:

```
VirtualLock(pvPageAddr, inf.dwPageSize);
```

The VirtualLock function takes two parameters:

- The address that marks the beginning of the locked region of virtual memory
- The number of bytes that should be locked

The VirtualLock function affects your virtual memory in one-page chunks, but the values passed to VirtualLock can specify any address—not necessarily a page boundary.

Here are some things to remember about locking pages of virtual memory:

- If you lock a range of virtual memory, you prevent that range of data from being swapped out. If the system needs to free up physical RAM, you have increased the chance that code will be swapped out. This causes total system performance to decrease in many cases.

- If you lock a large range of virtual memory, other applications are more likely to be swapped out, and total system performance decreases in many cases.

Most of the time, the Virtual Memory Manager makes intelligent choices about which pages currently should be loaded. Unless you're writing device drivers or other time-critical software, the pain is probably not worth the gain.

Freeing a Page of Virtual Memory

Freeing sparse pages of virtual memory is quite a bit more difficult than efficiently committing memory. Fortunately, the virtual memory swapping algorithm used by Windows 2000 swaps out unused pages to the hard disk. Once swapped out, these pages are made active only when they're accessed. In almost all cases, this is sufficient for most applications. Typically, you can defer free virtual memory until the entire range is no longer needed and then use the `VirtualFree` function:

```
VirtualFree(pvAddr, dwSize, MEM_RELEASE);
```

The `VirtualFree` function is called with three parameters: the base address of the memory to be released, the size of the range to be released, and a release flag (in this case, `MEM_RELEASE`).

If you need to "decommit" virtual memory, you can explicitly decommit pages of virtual memory by using the `VirtualFree` function with the `MEM_DECOMMIT` flag:

```
VirtualFree(pvAddr, dwSize, MEM_DECOMMIT);
```

Virtual memory that has been uncommitted still is marked as reserved and is available to be committed.

Allocating Memory for Other Processes

Normally, it's not possible for one process to allocate memory for another process. However, the virtual memory APIs include the following functions to allow you to do just that:

- `VirtualAllocEx`. Similar to `VirtualAlloc`, except it allocates virtual memory for another process

- `VirtualFreeEx`. Similar to `VirtualFree`, except it frees virtual memory allocated for another process

After allocating memory for the other process, you can use the `WriteProcessMemory` and `ReadProcessMemory` functions to access the block of memory. Allocating memory for other processes is discussed in more detail in Chapter 3, "Threads and Processes."

Looking at an Example That Uses Virtual Memory

As an example of how the virtual memory functions can be used, the CD-ROM that accompanies the book includes a sample project named VMGrid. VMGrid uses an ActiveX grid control to display the status of a range of virtual memory.

If you're building the VMGrid project from scratch, use AppWizard to create a dialog-based project named VMGrid that supports ActiveX controls.

Figure 2.5 shows the main dialog box, `IDD_VMGRID_DIALOG`.

FIGURE 2.5
The main dialog box from the VMGrid example.

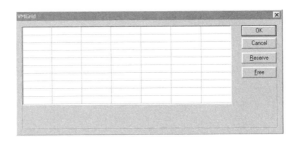

The dialog box has two additional pushbutton controls and one grid control from the Component Gallery. Table 2.1 contains the resource IDs for the new controls.

TABLE 2.1 CONTROL PROPERTIES FOR VMGRID'S MAIN DIALOG BOX

Control	Resource ID
Free pushbutton	`IDC_FREE`
Reserve pushbutton	`IDC_RESERVE`
Microsoft FlexGrid control	`IDC_GRID`

If you've never added an ActiveX control to a Visual C++ project, follow these steps, which assume you're using Visual C++ 6.0 (other versions of Visual C++ are similar):

1. Select Project, Add To Project, Components and Controls from the menu. The Component and Controls Gallery dialog box is displayed.

2. Select Registered ActiveX Controls from the list box. The ActiveX controls registered on your computer are displayed.

3. Select the Microsoft FlexGrid Control icon and then click the Insert button. A Confirm Classes dialog box is displayed.

4. Click the OK button on the Confirm Classes dialog box. The ActiveX grid control is added to your project and inserted into the control palette displayed when editing a dialog box resource.

5. Close the Component Gallery by clicking the Close button.

To add a grid control to the dialog box resource, just drag it from the control palette and drop it on the dialog box, just like any other control. Table 2.2 contains the properties for the grid control. All properties not listed should be set to their default values.

TABLE 2.2   PROPERTIES FOR THE GRID CONTROL USED IN VMGRID

Property	Value
Rows	10
Cols	10
FixedRows	0
FixedCols	0
BorderStyle	0 - None
ScrollBars	3 - Both
Highlight	0 - Never

The CVMGridDlg class has new member variables associated with controls that were added to the dialog box. Information that you can use to add the variables to CVMGridDlg using ClassWizard is shown in Table 2.3.

TABLE 2.3   VALUES USED TO ADD MEMBER VARIABLES FOR *CVMGridDlg*

Control ID	Variable Name	Category	Type
IDC_FREE	m_btnFree	Control	CButton
IDC_RESERVE	m_btnReserve	Control	CButton
IDC_GRID	m_grid	Control	CMSFlexGrid

Three message-handling functions must be added to the `CVMGridDlg` class, as shown in Table 2.4:

- `OnMouseDownGrid` is a handler for the `MouseDown` message from the grid control. When the user clicks the mouse over a grid cell, the grid location will be determined and the virtual memory page that contains that cell will be committed.
- `OnFree` is a handler for the `IDC_FREE` pushbutton control. When this button is pressed, all the reserved virtual memory for the grid is freed.
- `OnReserve` is a handler for the `IDC_RESERVE` pushbutton control. When this button is pushed, virtual memory for the grid control will be reserved.

The added message-handling functions for the `IDC_GRID`, `IDC_FREE`, and `IDC_RESERVE` controls are listed in Table 2.4.

TABLE 2.4 ADDING MESSAGE-HANDLING FUNCTIONS FOR THE MAIN DIALOG BOX

Object ID	Message	Class	Function
IDC_GRID	MouseDown	CVMGridDlg	OnMouseDownGrid
IDC_FREE	BN_CLICKED	CVMGridDlg	OnFree
IDC_RESERVE	BM_CLICKED	CVMGridDlg	OnReserve

A `CGridItem` structure is used to represent chunks of virtual memory used by VMGrid. The actual size of each `CGridItem` depends on the size of `TCHAR`. In Unicode builds, each `CGridItem` is a 2KB chuck of virtual memory. In non-Unicode builds, it's a 1KB chuck of virtual memory. The class definition provided in Listing 2.3 is part of the `VMGridDlg.cpp` file, before any `CVMGridDlg` class member functions.

LISTING 2.3 THE *CGridItem* STRUCTURE USED BY VMGRID

```
#define CHUNK_LENGTH 1024
struct CGridItem
{
    TCHAR m_chData[CHUNK_LENGTH];
};
```

The VMGrid application uses `VirtualAlloc` to reserve a 100KB range of addresses when it's initialized. The source code shown in bold in Listing 2.4 has been added to the `CVMGrid::OnInitDialog` function to reserve this range of addresses.

LISTING 2.4 CHANGES MADE TO THE *CVMGridDlg::OnInitDialog* FUNCTION

```
BOOL CVMGridDlg::OnInitDialog()
{
    .
    // existing code
    .
    .
    .
    // TODO: Add extra initialization here
    m_pVirtualAlloc = (TCHAR*)VirtualAlloc(NULL,
                                100 * sizeof(CGridItem),
                                MEM_RESERVE,
                                PAGE_NOACCESS);
    ASSERT(m_pVirtualAlloc);
    m_btnReserve.EnableWindow(FALSE);
    UpdateGrid();
    return TRUE;
}
```

After the Free button is clicked, all the virtual memory is released by the VMGrid application through the VirtualFree function. After the Reserve button is clicked, the 100KB range of virtual memory addresses is reserved, just as in OnInitDialog. Listing 2.5 shows the source code for the OnFree and OnReserve functions.

LISTING 2.5 RESERVING AND FREEING VIRTUAL MEMORY IN VMGRID

```
void CVMGridDlg::OnReserve()
{
    ASSERT(m_pVirtualAlloc == NULL);
    if(m_pVirtualAlloc == NULL)
    {
        m_pVirtualAlloc = (TCHAR*)VirtualAlloc(NULL,
                                    100 * sizeof(CGridItem),
                                    MEM_RESERVE,
                                    PAGE_NOACCESS);
        ASSERT(m_pVirtualAlloc);
        m_btnFree.EnableWindow();
        m_btnReserve.EnableWindow(FALSE);
        UpdateGrid();
    }
}

void CVMGridDlg::OnFree()
{
    ASSERT(m_pVirtualAlloc != NULL);
    if(m_pVirtualAlloc != NULL)
    {
        VirtualFree(m_pVirtualAlloc, 0, MEM_RELEASE);
```

continues

LISTING 2.5 CONTINUED

```
            m_pVirtualAlloc = NULL;
            m_btnFree.EnableWindow(FALSE);
            m_btnReserve.EnableWindow();
            UpdateGrid();
        }
    }
}
```

After a range of virtual memory is reserved, the user can commit a page of virtual memory by clicking a grid cell. Each cell represents a chunk of virtual memory. Because virtual memory is managed in pages, clicking an uncommitted cell results in several cells being committed. Listing 2.6 shows the source code that handles mouse clicks reported from the grid control.

LISTING 2.6 HANDLING MOUSE CLICKS IN THE GRID CONTROL

```
void CVMGridDlg::OnMouseDownGrid(short Button, short Shift, long x, long
y)
{
    if(m_pVirtualAlloc != NULL)
    {
        int nIndex = m_grid.GetRow() * 10 + m_grid.GetCol();
        CommitAt(nIndex);
        UpdateGrid();
    }
}
```

Two new member functions for the CVMGridDlg class must be added manually:

- CommitAt. Copies a string to a section of virtual memory, committing the page if needed.

- UpdateGrid. Runs through the virtual address space reserved by VMGrid and displays the status of the memory addresses represented by the grid.

Listing 2.7 contains the source code for these functions.

LISTING 2.7 MEMORY-HANDLING AND REPORTING FUNCTIONS FOR THE *CVMGridDlg* CLASS

```
void CVMGridDlg::CommitAt(int index)
{
    _ _try
    {
        // Try a simple access to test if the page is committed.
        TCHAR chTest = *(m_pVirtualAlloc + index * CHUNK_LENGTH);
        // The page is committed, just do a string copy
```

```
        lstrcpy(m_pVirtualAlloc + index * CHUNK_LENGTH,
                _T("Committed"));
    }
    _ _except(GetExceptionCode() == EXCEPTION_ACCESS_VIOLATION)
    {
        VirtualAlloc(m_pVirtualAlloc + index*CHUNK_LENGTH,
                    sizeof(CGridItem),
                    MEM_COMMIT,
                    PAGE_READWRITE);
        lstrcpy(m_pVirtualAlloc + index*CHUNK_LENGTH,
                _T("Committed"));
    }
}

void CVMGridDlg::UpdateGrid()
{
    MEMORY_BASIC_INFORMATION  mbi;
    VOID* pAddr = m_pVirtualAlloc;

    TRACE(_T("updategrid -- \n"));
    TRACE(_T("m_pVirtualAlloc at %X\n"), m_pVirtualAlloc);

    do{
        int cQuery = VirtualQuery(pAddr, &mbi, sizeof(mbi));
        if(cQuery != sizeof(MEMORY_BASIC_INFORMATION))
            break;
        if(mbi.AllocationBase == 0)
            break;
        // Change the status of the grid control
        LPTSTR   pszMsg;
        switch(mbi.State)
        {
        case MEM_RESERVE:
            pszMsg = _T("Res");
            break;
        case MEM_COMMIT:
            pszMsg = _T("Com");
            break;
        case MEM_FREE:
            pszMsg = _T("Free");
            break;
        default:
            pszMsg = _T("Unk");
            break;
        }

        TRACE(_T("vm info - allocation starts at %X\n"),
mbi.AllocationBase);
        TRACE(_T("vm info - base at %X\n"), mbi.BaseAddress);
        TRACE(_T("vm info - region size is %X\n"), mbi.RegionSize);
        TRACE(_T("vm info - state is %s\n"), pszMsg);
```

continues

LISTING 2.7   CONTINUED

```
        ULONG delta = (char*)mbi.BaseAddress - (char*)mbi.AllocationBase;
        ULONG nGridStart =  delta/sizeof(CGridItem);
        int cGrids = mbi.RegionSize/sizeof(CGridItem);
        int nFoo = mbi.RegionSize;

        TRACE(_T("Grid start is %d, grid count is %d\n"), nGridStart,
cGrids);

        while(cGrids != 0 && nGridStart < 100)
        {
            int nCol = nGridStart%10;
            int nRow = nGridStart/10;
            m_grid.SetRow(nRow);
            m_grid.SetCol(nCol);
            m_grid.SetText(pszMsg);
            nGridStart++;
            cGrids--;
        }

        // Get the next Chunk O' RAM
        if(nGridStart < 100)
            pAddr = (char*)mbi.BaseAddress + mbi.RegionSize;
        else
            break;

    } while(pAddr);
    m_grid.SetRow(0);
    m_grid.SetCol(0);
}
```

The CommitAt function provided in Listing 2.7 tries to access an address represented by a grid location clicked by a user. It starts by trying to access the first address represented by the cell; if the cell is not committed, an EXCEPTION_ACCESS_VIOLATION exception is raised. The exception handler first commits the page and then copies a string at the address.

The UpdateGrid function uses VirtualQuery to walk through the virtual address range used by VMGrid. Each call to VirtualQuery returns the status of a single block of virtual memory. This block may be as small as a page or as large as the entire range. UpdateGrid calculates the grid cell that represents each 1KB chunk of memory and labels the grid with the virtual memory status.

As the final step, add the UpdateGrid and CommitAt member functions to the CVMGridDlg class declaration. At the same time, declare a new member variable, m_pVirtualAlloc, which will serve as a pointer to the block of virtual memory used by VMGrid. These changes are shown in bold in Listing 2.8.

LISTING 2.8   MODIFICATIONS (IN BOLD) TO THE *CVMGridDlg* CLASS DECLARATION

```
class CVMGridDlg : public CDialog
{
    .
    .
    .
// Implementation
protected:
    HICON m_hIcon;
    void UpdateGrid();
    void CommitAt(int index);
    TCHAR* m_pVirtualAlloc;
    .
    .
    .
};
```

Compile and run the VMGrid application; then experiment by clicking different cells in the grid control. Each click commits one page's worth of cells in the grid. For Intel platforms, each click changes four cells. Figure 2.6 shows the VMGrid main dialog box after several cells have been clicked.

FIGURE 2.6

The VMGrid application after several pages of virtual memory have been committed.

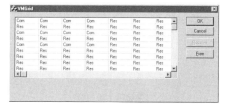

Windows 2000 Advanced Server for computers equipped with Alpha processors offers a facility for accessing up to 64GB of RAM. This facility, known as the *Very Large Memory* model (or VLM), allows you to address substantially more than the 4GB addressing on other versions of Windows 2000.

Here's a list of the virtual memory functions that have been expanded for use with VLM:

- VirtualAllocVlm
- VirtualFreeVlm
- VirtualProtectVlm
- VirtualQueryVlm

Each of these functions is similar to other virtual memory functions, with their parameters and return values modified to work with 64-bit addresses. Each of the functions accepts a process handle to enable you to allocate VLM memory in another process.

`VirtualAllocVlm` returns a 64-bit pointer to void:

```
PVOID64 pMem = VirtualAllocVlm(hProcess,
                               NULL,
                               cAllocSize,
                               MEM_RESERVE,
                               PAGE_NOACCESS);
```

`VirtualAllocVlm` has five parameters:

- A handle to the process that the virtual memory is accessed for.
- The base address for the range of virtual memory to be allocated. As with `VirtualAlloc`, the operating system will choose a base address for you if you pass `NULL` for this parameter.
- The amount of memory to be allocated. Unlike `VirtualAlloc`, this parameter is a `DWORDLONG` (a 64-bit unsigned value).
- A flag that specifies the allocation type, same as with `VirtualAlloc`.
- A flag that specifies the protection type, same as with `VirtualAlloc`.

`VirtualFreeVlm` decommits, or frees, a range of virtual VLM memory. Here's an example:

```
BOOL fFree = VirtualFree(hProcess,
                         pMemBase,
                         nAllocLimit,
                         MEM_RELEASE);
```

`VirtualFreeVlm` has four parameters:

- A handle to the process that owns the virtual memory.
- The base address for the range of virtual memory to be free or decommitted.
- The amount of memory to be freed. Unlike `VirtualFree`, this parameter is a `DWORDLONG` (a 64-bit unsigned value).
- The type of free operation to be performed, same as with `VirtualFree`.

`VirtualProtectVlm` allows you to change the protect flags on a range of virtual VLM memory:

```
BOOL fProtect = VirtualProtectVlm(hProcess,
                                  pMemBase,
                                  cProtectSize,
                                  PAGE_READWRITE,
                                  &oldProtect);
```

`VirtualProtectVlm` has five parameters:

- A handle to the process that owns the virtual memory.

- The address of the first address that will have its protection flag changed.

- The amount of memory that will have its protection flag changed. Unlike `VirtualProtect`, this parameter is a `DWORDLONG` (a 64-bit unsigned value).

- The new protection flag for the range of memory.

- The address of a `DWORD` variable that will be filled with the first virtual memory page's old protection flag.

`VirtualQueryVlm` returns the status of a range of virtual VLM memory:

```
DWORD cQuery = VirtualQueryVlm(hProcess,
                               pAddr,
                               &mbi,
                               sizeof(mbi));
```

`VirtualQueryVlm` has four parameters:

- A handle to the process that owns the virtual memory.

- The base address for the range of virtual memory to be freed or decommitted.

- A pointer to a `MEMORY_BASIC_INFORMATION_VLM` structure, which is similar to the `MEMORY_BASIC_INFORMATION` structure used by `VirtualQuery`.

- The size of the `MEMORY_BASIC_INFORMATION_VLM` structure.

2

VIRTUAL MEMORY AND MEMORY MANAGEMENT

> **NOTE**
>
> When a range of virtual memory is allocated using the VLM APIs, the memory is never paged out. This improves performance if enough memory is present, but it can greatly decrease performance if enough physical RAM is not present.

Using Windows 2000 Heap Functions

Unlike 16-bit versions of Windows, under Windows 2000, there is no difference between the local and global heap. When accessing the heap, you always get access to the (usually) 2GB virtual address space maintained by Windows 2000 for your application. Although many of the heap management functions available under 16-bit Windows also are available in Windows 2000, you should use the newer heap API functions introduced specifically for Win32.

If your application allocates and frees small amounts of data, runs for a relatively short lifetime, or has only moderate demands on its performance, you'll be very happy using the default memory allocation offered by your C or C++ compiler. The runtime libraries included with your compiler include memory suballocation schemes that effectively manage the heap in most cases.

These built-in memory allocation schemes are created for general-purpose computing; however, you might have needs that are not addressed by the default compiler libraries. You might constantly allocate and free small objects of different sizes, for example. This often causes heap fragmentation and poor performance using most default suballocation schemes. Using the heap management API functions offered by Windows 2000 can help you solve this and many other memory-management problems.

Performing Heap Management Under Windows 2000

Windows 2000 offers a set of memory functions that allows for a higher level of memory management than the virtual memory APIs, while still allowing for a great deal of control over heap-allocated memory. The Windows 2000 heap-management APIs include functions that create, manage, and destroy private heaps.

Every process has a default heap provided by the operating system. The handle to this heap can be retrieved via the GetProcessHeap function:

```
HANDLE hDefaultHeap = GetProcessHeap();
```

The only difference between this heap and a heap created dynamically is that this one is created for you based on link information embedded in your executable file. The default heap is used for C++ runtime library malloc and new allocations. You can use this default heap or create one or more dynamic heaps.

Creating a Heap

To create a dynamic heap, you use the HeapCreate function:

```
HANDLE hHeap = HeapCreate(HEAP_GENERATE_EXCEPTIONS,
                          0x01000,
                          0);
```

The HeapCreate function has three parameters:

- Options for the dynamic heap. In this case, HEAP_GENERATE_EXCEPTIONS is used.
- The initial size for the heap, which is rounded up to the next page boundary. In this case, 4KB is allocated for the heap.

- The maximum size for the heap. In this case, 0 is used, which indicates that the heap is limited only by the amount of virtual memory that can be committed by Windows 2000.

You can use two option flags when a dynamic heap is created:

- HEAP_GENERATE_EXCEPTIONS. Specifies that the heap should generate Win32 structured exceptions instead of returning NULL in error conditions.
- HEAP_NO_SERIALIZE. Specifies that the heap should not synchronize access. This flag should be used with care because unsynchronized access to a heap by multiple threads corrupts the heap. Use this flag only if you're sure that two threads will not attempt to manipulate the heap at the same time.

Allocating from a Heap

The HeapAlloc function is used to allocate memory from a heap. You can use this function with default or dynamic heaps, because the first parameter is a heap handle that specifies the heap used to allocate the memory. HeapAlloc returns a pointer to the memory allocated from the heap, as shown in this code:

```
TCHAR pszName = HeapAlloc(hHeap,
                         HEAP_GENERATE_EXCEPTIONS,
                         cName);
```

The HeapAlloc function has three parameters:

- A handle to the heap that's servicing the allocation request.
- Optional flags used to specify how the memory is allocated. In this example, HEAP_GENERATE_EXCEPTIONS is used. Other values for this parameter follow.
- The size of the requested memory allocation.

Three heap-allocation flags are used for HeapAlloc:

- HEAP_GENERATE_EXCEPTIONS. Specifies that Windows 2000 should use exceptions to indicate error conditions instead of returning NULL.
- HEAP_NO_SERIALIZE. Indicates that the heap does not need to synchronize this call to the heap with other heap-management functions. This flag should be avoided unless you can guarantee that multiple threads will not access the heap at the same time.
- HEAP_ZERO_MEMORY. Tells the heap to initialize the contents of the allocated memory to 0.

As with HeapCreate, you can pass a value of 0 to indicate that no flags are used, or you can combine two or more flags together if more than one option is needed.

Freeing Heap Memory

To release a block of memory allocated with HeapAlloc, use the HeapFree function. HeapFree takes only three parameters: the heap handle, an optional flag, and a pointer to the memory to be freed. Here's an example:

```
BOOL fFreed = HeapFree(hHeap, 0, pszName);
```

The second parameter passed to HeapFree can be 0, as in this example, or HEAP_NO_SERIALIZE. As in the previously discussed heap functions, you should use this flag only if you're certain that only one thread will attempt to manage the heap at any given time.

Using Private Heaps in C++ Classes

As an example of how you can use dynamic heaps to manage private memory heaps in C++ programs, the CD-ROM included with this book includes a console mode project named PrivHeap. The PrivHeap application creates a simple linked list using C++ classes that manage their own private heaps so that the main application doesn't need to perform any memory management.

As shown in Figure 2.7, two classes are used to implement the linked list used by PrivHeap. The CVMListNode class is a *payload* class that's stored in the linked list. The CVMList class maintains a link to one CVMListNode object and a link to the next CVMList object in the list.

FIGURE 2.7
The relationship between CVMList and CVMListNode objects.

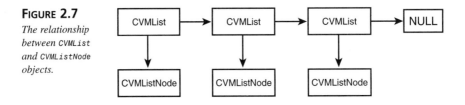

The CVMList and CVMListNode objects are different sizes. If you create a database that allocates and frees these objects at random for a long period of time, the heap becomes fragmented, as shown in Figure 2.8.

FIGURE 2.8

Fragmentation of heap memory.

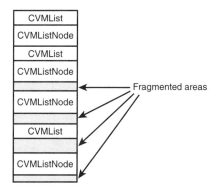

By allowing each class to manage a private dynamic heap in which the allocations are always the same size, fragmentation is avoided.

The C++ language allows a class to provide an implementation of the new operator, which allows a class to control how memory is allocated before the constructor is called. The classes used in PrivHeap include specialized versions of the new operator and follow this basic scheme:

- If a private heap is not created, create one and initialize a reference counter
- Allocate the number of requested bytes from the heap
- Increment the reference counter

In addition, the C++ language allows a class to define how memory is released by implementing an operator delete function. The classes used in PrivHeap use the following method for operator delete:

- Release the requested memory block to the heap
- Decrement the reference counter
- If the reference counter is 0, destroy the heap

Using the CVMListNode Class

The CVMListNode class is very simple; it only stores one integer as its data. Most of the work done by the class concerns memory management. Listing 2.9 shows the CVMListNode class declaration. You can find this class on the CD-ROM as listnode.h in the PrivHeap project directory.

LISTING 2.9   THE CVMListNode CLASS DECLARATION

```
class CVMListNode
{
    int         m_n;
    static HANDLE  m_hHeap;
    static int     m_nRef;
public:
    CVMListNode() {};
    CVMListNode(int n) : m_n(n) {};
    virtual ~CVMListNode() {};
    void* operator new(size_t s);
    void  operator delete(void* p);

    virtual int Get() const { return m_n; };
    virtual void Set(int n){ m_n = n; };
};
```

Listing 2.10 provides the implementation of the CVMListNode class. This file is located on the accompanying CD-ROM as listnode.cpp in the project directory.

LISTING 2.10   THE IMPLEMENTATION OF THE CVMListNode CLASS

```
#include <windows.h>
#include <tchar.h>
#include "listnode.h"
#ifndef UNICODE
    #include <stdio.h>
#endif

HANDLE CVMListNode::m_hHeap = NULL;
int    CVMListNode::m_nRef = 0;

void* CVMListNode::operator new(size_t size)
{
    void* p;
    if(m_hHeap == NULL)
    {
        SYSTEM_INFO inf;
        GetSystemInfo(&inf);
        m_hHeap = HeapCreate(0, inf.dwAllocationGranularity ,0);
        _tprintf(_T("List Node: Private heap allocated"));
    }
    if((p = HeapAlloc(m_hHeap, 0, size)) != NULL)
    {
        m_nRef++;
        _tprintf(_T("List Node: Allocated %d bytes\n", size));
    }
    return p;
```

```
}

void CVMListNode::operator delete(void* p)
{
    if(HeapFree(m_hHeap, 0, p) != FALSE)
    {
        m_nRef--;
        _tprintf(_T("List Node: Released one chunk\n"));
    }
    if(m_nRef == 0)
    {
        HeapDestroy(m_hHeap);
        m_hHeap = NULL;
        _tprintf(_T("List Node: Heap destroyed\n"));
    }
}
```

Listing 2.11 shows the implementation of the CVMList class. This file is located on the accompanying CD-ROM as list.cpp in the project directory.

LISTING 2.11   THE IMPLEMENTATION OF THE CVMList CLASS

```
#include <windows.h>
#include <tchar.h>
#include "listnode.h"
#include "list.h"
#ifndef UNICODE
    #include <stdio.h>
#endif


HANDLE CVMList::m_hHeap = NULL;
int    CVMList::m_nRef = 0;

CVMList::CVMList():m_pNext(0)
{
    m_pNode = new CVMListNode(0);
}
CVMList::CVMList(int n) : m_pNext(0)
{
    m_pNode = new CVMListNode(n);
}
CVMList::~CVMList()
{
    delete m_pNext;
    delete m_pNode;
}
CVMList* CVMList::Insert(int n)
{
```

continues

LISTING 2.11   CONTINUED

```
    CVMList* pTemp = NULL;
    pTemp = new CVMList(n);
    if(m_pNext != NULL)
    {
        pTemp->m_pNext = m_pNext->m_pNext;
    }
    pTemp->m_pNext = m_pNext;
    m_pNext = pTemp;
    return pTemp;
}
void* CVMList::operator new(size_t size)
{
    void* p;
    if(m_hHeap == NULL)
    {
        SYSTEM_INFO inf;
        GetSystemInfo(&inf);
        m_hHeap = HeapCreate(0, inf.dwAllocationGranularity ,0);
        _tprintf(_T("List: Private heap allocated"));
    }
    if((p = HeapAlloc(m_hHeap, 0, size)) != NULL)
    {
        m_nRef++;
        _tprintf(_T("List: Allocated %d bytes\n", size));
    }
    return p;
}

void CVMList::operator delete(void* p)
{
    if(HeapFree(m_hHeap, 0, p) != FALSE)
    {
        m_nRef--;
        _tprintf(_T("List: Released one chunk\n"));
    }
    if(m_nRef == 0)
    {
        HeapDestroy(m_hHeap);
        m_hHeap = NULL;
        _tprintf(_T("List: Heap destroyed\n"));
    }
}
```

Listing 2.12 shows the main function for the PrivHeap program; you can find this on the accompanying CD-ROM as main.cpp in the project directory.

LISTING 2.12   THE main FUNCTION FOR PRIVHEAP

```
#include <windows.h>
#include <tchar.h>
```

```
#include "listnode.h"
#include "list.h"

int main()
{
    CVMList    listHead;

    listHead.Insert(5);
    listHead.Insert(3);
    listHead.Insert(2);

    return 0;
}
```

In the main function, a CVMList object is created, and several items are added to the list. The first CVMList object is created on the stack frame, and all other CVMList and CVMListNode objects are created using private dynamic heaps.

Using the CVMList Class

The CVMList class is a simple linked list; again, most of the work done by the class is concerned with memory management. Listing 2.13 shows the CVMList class declaration. This class is included on the accompanying CD-ROM as list.h in the PrivHeap project directory.

LISTING 2.13 THE CVMList CLASS DECLARATION

```
class CVMList
{
    CVMListNode*    m_pNode;
    CVMList*        m_pNext;
    static HANDLE   m_hHeap;
    static int      m_nRef;
public:
    int Get() { return m_pNode->Get(); }
    CVMList* Next() {return m_pNext;}
    void Set(int n) {m_pNode->Set(n);}

    CVMList();
    CVMList(int n);
    virtual ~CVMList();

    void* operator new(size_t s);
    void  operator delete(void* p);

    CVMList* Insert(int n);
};
```

Summary

In this chapter, you looked at the virtual memory management functions used when programming for Windows 2000. You also examined an example showing how virtual memory is used to implement a sparse memory array in an application. You learned about the Windows 2000 Heap Memory API and how you can use it to create dynamic heaps in your applications. Finally, an example of using heaps to implement private memory management in C++ classes was presented in a small example.

Threads and Processes

This chapter covers how processes and threads are created and managed, as well as how they're used in developing multithreaded applications in Windows 2000.

A major portion of this chapter is used to discuss synchronization between threads and processes. Windows 2000 provides a number of ways to efficiently synchronize your multithreaded applications, and this chapter discusses them all.

As always, this chapter also includes a number of sample projects that can be found on the accompanying CD-ROM. These projects illustrate the concepts of multithreading and synchronization.

Processes and Threads

A process is started by Windows 2000 when an application is launched. The process owns the memory, resources, and threads of execution associated with that particular instance of running an executable program. When a process is started, a primary thread is started as well. As long as at least one thread is associated with a process, the process will continue to run.

A thread, sometimes called a *thread of execution*, is the smallest unit of execution in Windows 2000. A thread is always associated with a process and always lives within a particular process. Although many processes have only a single thread that lasts for the life of the process, it's not unusual for a process to have many threads over its lifetime, as shown in Figure 3.1.

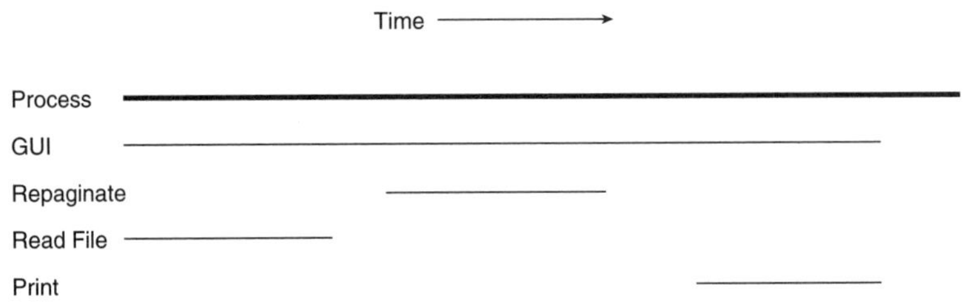

FIGURE 3.1

A typical Windows 2000 process has many threads over its lifetime.

Threads are scheduled according to their priority, and within a certain priority, in a circular (or *round-robin*) fashion. There are 31 different priority levels, as shown in Figure 3.2.

FIGURE 3.2

Windows 2000 has 31 different priority levels available.

31	
30	
29	
28	
27	
26	
25	
24	REALTIME_PRIORITY_CLASS
23	
22	
21	
20	
19	
18	
17	
16	
15	
14	
13	HIGH_PRIORITY_CLASS
12	
11	
10	
9	NORMAL_PRIORITY_CLASS (Foreground)
8	
7	NORMAL_PRIORITY_CLASS (Background)
6	
5	
4	IDLE_PRIORITY_CLASS
3	
2	
1	

3

THREADS AND PROCESSES

A thread can be in one of six states:

- Waiting
- Ready
- Running
- Standby
- Terminated
- Transition

The last three states in the preceding list are really "substates." In these substates, the thread is either waiting, as in the case of a thread in the standby state, or running, in the case of the transition state. A thread in the terminated state has finished executing, and is about to be removed from the process.

At any given time, only one thread per system processor is in the running state. All other threads are either waiting or ready. A running thread is allowed to run until one of the following actions occur:

- It exceeds its maximum allotted execution time, known as a *quantum*.
- A higher priority thread marked as waiting becomes waiting.
- The running thread decides to wait for an event or object.

When a thread exceeds its time quantum, Windows 2000 marks the thread as ready and looks for the highest priority ready thread in the system. If there are other ready threads with the same priority level as the previously running thread, the next thread is marked as running, and it starts executing. In this way, threads at the same priority level are serviced in a circular (round-robin) sort of queue. If a thread is waiting for an I/O event or for some other object to be signaled, another thread is selected to run using the same scheduling process.

In order to make Windows-based applications appear more responsive, the thread that owns the foreground window is normally boosted by two priority levels. This boost only applies if the thread is running at the usual priority class. If a thread has an idle, high, or real-time priority class, switching to the foreground does not affect its priority level.

When a thread is prevented from running due to a large number of higher-priority work, it's said to be *starved*. Threads that have an extremely low priority are occasionally given a "boost" in their priority that enables them to be scheduled for one execution cycle. This is enough, in most cases, to guarantee that all threads get at least some chance to compete for CPU cycles.

Managing Processes

The most common ways to start a process are to launch it from the Windows 2000 Explorer, launch it from the Start menu, or launch it by typing the name of the program at the console command line. Windows 2000 also includes a number of functions that can be used to create and manage processes.

Using the `CreateProcess` Function

A process can be started in many ways, such as launching it from the Windows 2000 Start menu or clicking an icon. To start a process from within another Windows 2000 application, you must call the `CreateProcess` function:

```
STARTUPINFO si;
ZeroMemory(&si, sizeof(STARTUPINFO));
si.cb = sizeof(STARTUPINFO);
PROCESS_INFORMATION pi;
BOOL fCreated = CreateProcess(_T("C:\\foo.exe"),
                              NULL,
                              NULL,
```

```
                            NULL,
                            FALSE,
                            CREATE_NEW_CONSOLE,
                            NULL,
                            _T("C:\\"),
                            &si,
                            &pi);
HANDLE hProcess = pi.hProcess;   // Process handle
```

The `CreateProcess` function has 10 parameters:

- The path to the executable file that's to be started. If this parameter is NULL, the next parameter is used to determine the filename.

- The command line used to start the process. This parameter can be NULL if no command-line arguments are passed to the new process.

- A pointer to a `SECURITY_ATTRIBUTES` structure that specifies the security attributes for the new process. Using NULL for this parameter causes the operating system to give the new process a default security descriptor.

- A pointer to a `SECURITY_ATTRIBUTES` structure that specifies the security attributes for the primary thread created by the new process. A NULL value causes a default security descriptor to be used.

- A flag that specifies whether the new process will inherit the handles owned by the current process—in this case FALSE.

- A flag that specifies how the process will be created and its priority level—in this case, the flag is CREATE_NEW_CONSOLE. Other possible values for this flag are discussed later.

- A pointer to an environment block used by the new process or NULL if the new process will use the environment block of the parent process.

- The current drive and directory for the new process or NULL if the new process will use the same drive and current directory as the parent process.

- A pointer to a `STARTUPINFO` structure, which can be used to set various attributes for the new process, such as its title and window position. The `STARTUPINFO` structure should be initialized as shown in the example, particularly the cb member, which must be initialized with the size of the `STARTUPINFO` structure.

- A pointer to a `PROCESS_INFORMATION` structure, which will be filled in by Windows 2000 while creating the new process.

The "create" flag parameter has one or more of the following values:

- `CREATE_DEFAULT_ERROR_MODE` prevents the new process from inheriting the error mode set by the parent process.

- `CREATE_NEW_CONSOLE` gives the new process its own console, instead of inheriting the one owned by the parent process. This flag cannot be used with the `DETACHED_PROCESS` flag.

- `CREATE_NEW_PROCESS_GROUP` specifies that the new process is the root member of a new process group.

- `CREATE_SEPARATE_WOW_VDM` is used when you're creating a 16-bit process. This flag specifies that the new process is given its own Windows on Windows (WOW) Virtual DOS Machine.

- `CREATE_SHARED_WOW_VDM` is used when you're creating a 16-bit process. This flag specifies that the new process will share a Windows on Windows (WOW) Virtual DOS Machine.

- `CREATE_SUSPENDED` specifies that the primary thread of the new process is created in a suspended state.

- `CREATE_UNICODE_ENVIRONMENT` specifies that the environment block uses Unicode instead of ANSI characters.

- `DEBUG_PROCESS` specifies that the parent process is interested in receiving debug events generated from the new process.

- `DEBUG_ONLY_THIS_PROCESS` is used to specify that the new process should not be debugged using the same debugger used for the parent process.

- `DETACHED_PROCESS` prevents the new process from accessing the console window of the parent process. This flag cannot be used with the `CREATE_NEW_CONSOLE` flag.

- `IDLE_PRIORITY_CLASS` specifies that the threads owned by the process only run when the system is idle.

- `BELOW_NORMAL_PRIORITY_CLASS` specifies that threads owned by the process should run at a priority level between `IDLE_PRIORITY_CLASS` and `NORMAL_PRIORITY_CLASS`. This is a more fine-grained option that was not available prior to Windows 2000.

- `NORMAL_PRIORITY_CLASS` is used to specify a process without special scheduling requirements. This thread priority value should be used for almost all cases.

- `ABOVE_NORMAL_PRIORITY_CLASS` specifies that threads owned by the process should run at a priority level between `NORMAL_PRIORITY_CLASS` and `HIGH_PRIORITY_CLASS`. This is a more fine-grained option that was not available prior to Windows 2000.

- `HIGH_PRIORITY_CLASS` specifies that the threads in the process need to perform delay-sensitive tasks that must be executed with a minimum amount of delay. This flag should be used with care, because it will causes the thread to preempt most other threads in the system. This priority level will not be inherited by child processes.

- REALTIME_PRIORITY_CLASS specifies that the threads owned by the process must be given the highest possible priority. Threads running at this level literally outrun parts of the operating system. Because threads with this attribute execute faster than the virtual memory management system and other internal processes, they may become deadlocked and cause the system to behave erratically. This priority level will not be inherited by child processes.

The CreateProcess function returns TRUE if it was able to begin launching the new process. If the process cannot be started, it's usually considered a fault in the new process; as far as CreateProcess is concerned, its work is finished.

The PROCESS_INFORMATION structure contains information about the new process and its primary thread. The PROCESS_INFORMATION structure has four members:

- hProcess is a handle for the new process.
- hThread is a handle to the primary thread of the new process.
- dwProcessId is an ID number for the new process. Take care when using this value—it's only valid as long as the process is running, and Windows 2000 may reassign it to a new process immediately after this process is finished.
- dwThreadId is an ID number for the primary thread of the new process.

Ending a Process

There are three ways to end a process. The preferred way is to call the ExitProcess function from within one of the threads executing the process:

```
ExitProcess(NO_ERROR);
```

Calling ExitProcess enables a process to perform an orderly exit—such as calling the DLL entry point functions for any DLLs that the process has loaded, signaling threads that may be waiting for it to finish, and closing all the object handles owned by the process.

After the process has ended, the GetExitCodeProcess function returns the value passed as a parameter to ExitProcess. If the GetExitCodeProcess function is called before the process ends, the return value is STILL_ACTIVE.

Another way to end a process is to call TerminateProcess, passing the handle of the process to be ended:

```
TerminateProcess(hProcess, NO_ERROR);
```

This method should be avoided when possible, because it does not unload DLLs and perform other types of system cleanup that are normally performed when a process ends.

The third way to kill a process is to terminate all the threads owned by the process. This is the method used by most Win32 programs—after all the threads associated with a program have finished their work, the process is terminated.

Managing Threads

Unlike many popular multithreaded operating systems, Windows 2000 offers true threads. Most multithreaded operating systems require you to create a new process when creating a new path of execution. However, a Windows 2000 thread is much less expensive to create than a typical UNIX process, in terms of computing resources, and offers a wide range of management options. The next few sections discuss how threads are created and managed in a Windows 2000 application.

Creating Threads

A thread can be created in four ways:

- By launching a new process
- By calling the Win32 `CreateThread` API function
- By calling the C runtime library function `_beginthread`
- By calling the C runtime library function `_beginthreadex`

When you're launching a new process with the `CreateProcess` function, the thread ID is found in the `dwThreadId` member of the `PROCESS_INFORMATION` structure that's filled after the function call returns. The thread handle can be found in the `hThread` member of the same structure.

Using `CreateThread` to Start a New Thread

A thread is created by calling the `CreateThread` function. Here's an example:

```
long WINAPI ThreadEntry(LPARAM lparam)
{
    // ...
}
unsigned long nThreadID;
HANDLE hThread = CreateThread(NULL,
                              0,
                              (LPTHREAD_START_ROUTINE)ThreadEntry,
                              (void*)szHello,
                              0,
                              &nThreadID);
```

The CreateThread function takes six parameters:

- A pointer to a SECURITY_ATTRIBUTES structure that specifies the security attributes for the new thread. Using NULL for this parameter causes the operating system to give the new thread a default security descriptor.

- The initial stack size for the new thread. If 0 is passed as this parameter, the new thread is given a stack the same size as the primary thread. This is usually a good value to use as a default, because Windows 2000 will increase the size of the stack if necessary.

- The address of a start function where the thread begins executing.

- A 32-bit parameter passed to the new thread's start function. The new thread begins executing in this function; when the thread exits this function, it's terminated.

- A flag that specifies how the thread is created. This flag can either be CREATE_SUSPENDED, which creates the flag in a suspended state, or 0, which enables the thread to begin executing. A thread that's suspended does not execute until the ResumeThread function has been called for it.

- The address of a 32-bit variable that's filled with the thread ID when CreateThread returns.

If your thread uses C runtime library functions, you should not use CreateThread. In some cases, using it will result in small memory leaks when the thread terminates, due to the way CreateThread interacts with the C runtime library. If you must use C runtime library functions, you should use _beginthread or _beginthreadex, as discussed in the next section.

Using the C Runtime Library Thread Functions

The Visual C++ compiler offers two extensions to the C runtime library for creating threads:

- _beginthread
- _beginthreadex

NOTE

These functions require you to use one of the multithreaded versions of the C runtime library. If you're using the Visual C++ IDE, you can specify the runtime library by selecting Settings from the Project menu to display the Project Settings dialog box. Click the C++ tab and then select the Code Generation category from the drop-down list. You can select the runtime library your project will use from the Use Runtime Library drop-down list.

Both functions enable you to create a thread that can safely interact with the C runtime library. Of the two functions, _beginthread is the simplest function to use, as shown in Listing 3.1.

LISTING 3.1   USING _beginthread TO LAUNCH A WORKER THREAD

```
/* Compile this listing using the multi-threaded C runtime library */
#include <windows.h>
#include <tchar.h>
#include <process.h>
#ifndef UNICODE
    #include <stdio.h>
#endif

void threadFunc(void* pv);

int _tmain()
{
    ULONG tid = 0;
    _tprintf(_T("Hello from the main thread\n"));
    tid = _beginthread(threadFunc, 0, NULL);
    if(tid == -1)
    {
        /* handle error */
    }
    WaitForSingleObject((HANDLE)tid, INFINITE);
    _tprintf(_T("Goodbye from the main thread\n"));
    return 0;
}

void threadFunc(void* pv)
{
    _tprintf(_T("Hello from the worker thread\n"));
    _tprintf(_T("Work, work, work\n"));
    _tprintf(_T("Goodbye from the worker thread\n"));
}
```

As shown in Listing 3.1, _beginthread has three parameters:

- The address of a thread's start function where the new thread will start executing
- The size of the stack for the new thread or 0 if the C runtime library should automatically manage the stack
- A void* that can optionally contain an argument to be passed to the thread's start function

The _beginthread function returns a handle to the thread that was started or -1 if the thread could not be launched.

The _beginthread function does not provide many of the options available with
CreateThread, such as the ability to create a thread in the suspended state and the ability
to provide a security descriptor for the new thread.

The _beginthreadex function, shown in Listing 3.2, is somewhat more complicated than
_beginthread, but it more closely models the Win32 CreateThread function.

LISTING 3.2   USING _beginthreadex TO LAUNCH A WORKER THREAD

```
#include <windows.h>
#include <tchar.h>
#include <process.h>
#ifndef UNICODE
    #include <stdio.h>
#endif

unsigned __stdcall threadFunc(void* pv);

int _tmain()
{
    ULONG hThread = 0;
    unsigned threadId = 0;

    /* Initialize security descriptor for worker thread */
    SECURITY_DESCRIPTOR* psd;
    psd = (SECURITY_DESCRIPTOR*)LocalAlloc(LPTR,
                            SECURITY_DESCRIPTOR_MIN_LENGTH);
    InitializeSecurityDescriptor(psd,SECURITY_DESCRIPTOR_REVISION);
    SetSecurityDescriptorDacl(psd, TRUE, NULL, FALSE);

    _tprintf(_T("Hello from the main thread\n"));
    /* Create thread in a suspended state */
    hThread = _beginthreadex(psd,
                        0,
                        threadFunc,
                        NULL,
                        CREATE_SUSPENDED,
                        &threadId);
    if(!hThread)
    {
        /* handle error */
    }
    /* Wake up the worker thread */
    ResumeThread((HANDLE)hThread);
    WaitForSingleObject((HANDLE)hThread, INFINITE);
    _tprintf(_T("Goodbye from the main thread\n"));

    CloseHandle((HANDLE)hThread);
    LocalFree(psd);
```

continues

LISTING 3.2   CONTINUED

```
    return 0;
}

unsigned _ _stdcall threadFunc(void* pv)
{
    _tprintf(_T("Hello from the worker thread\n"));
    _tprintf(_T("Work, work, work\n"));
    _tprintf(_T("Goodbye from the worker thread\n"));
    return NO_ERROR;
}
```

As shown in Listing 3.2, _beginthreadex has six parameters:

- A pointer to a SECURITY_DESCRIPTOR structure for the new thread or NULL to use a default security descriptor.
- The size of the stack for the new thread or 0 if the C runtime library should automatically manage the stack.
- The address of a thread's start function where the new thread will start executing
- A pointer to a list of arguments to be passed to the thread or NULL if no arguments are used.
- The initial startup state of the thread—either CREATE_SUSPENDED to create the thread in a suspended state or 0 to create the thread in an immediately runnable state.
- The address of an unsigned int variable that will be filled with the thread ID for the new thread.

The _beginthread function returns a handle to the thread that was started or 0 if the thread could not be launched.

Ending a Thread

There are three ways to end a thread. The "normal" way to end a thread is to call the ExitThread function from within the thread that's ending. When ExitThread is called, a thread exit code is passed as a parameter:

```
ExitThread(NO_ERROR);
```

The second method is to allow the thread to exit its thread function. The ExitThread function is called implicitly when you exit from the thread's start function. For example, the following thread function executes a for loop five times and then returns NO_ERROR as the thread's exit code:

```
long WINAPI ThreadFunc(long lParam)
{
    for(int n = 0; n < 5; n++)
    {
        // Work with thread
    }
    return NO_ERROR;
}
```

The third, and least preferred, method to end a thread is to use `TerminateThread`. Calling `TerminateThread` does not give a thread a chance to clean up any partially completed work; the thread may own critical sections that are not released, or it may have partially completed work that cannot be concluded. The call to `TerminateThread` looks like this:

```
HANDLE hThread = CreateThread(....);
.
.
.
TerminateThread(hThread, NO_ERROR);
```

The `TerminateThread` function has two parameters: the thread handle and an exit code for the thread.

If any of these methods is used to kill the last remaining thread owned by a process, the process terminates.

The exit code for a thread can be retrieved by calling `GetExitCodeThread`:

```
DWORD dwResult;
GetExitCodeThread(hThread, &dwResult);
if(dwResult != NO_ERROR)
{
    // Handle error case
}
```

The `GetExitCodeThread` function has two parameters: the thread handle and the address of a 32-bit variable that will be filled with the thread's exit code. If the `GetExitCode` thread is called for a thread that has not yet exited, the return value is `STILL_ACTIVE`.

Fetching and Changing a Thread's Priority

Windows 2000 enables you to dynamically change the priority of a thread. You should take extreme care when changing the priority of a thread—it's easy to severely impact the performance of your entire system by raising a thread's priority too high.

Windows 2000 offers six process priority classes:

- `IDLE_PRIORITY_CLASS`
- `BELOW_NORMAL_PRIORITY_CLASS`

- `NORMAL_PRIORITY_CLASS`

- `ABOVE_NORMAL_PRIORITY_CLASS`

- `HIGH_PRIORITY_CLASS`

- `REALTIME_PRIORITY_CLASS`

Every thread can be set to run within a range of five priority levels, regardless of its priority class:

- `THREAD_PRIORITY_LOWEST` is two steps below the priority class assigned to the process.

- `THREAD_PRIORITY_BELOW_NORMAL` is one step below the priority class assigned to the process.

- `THREAD_PRIORITY_NORMAL` is the same as the priority class assigned to the process.

- `THREAD_PRIORITY_ABOVE_NORMAL` is one step above the priority class assigned to the process.

- `THREAD_PRIORITY_HIGHEST` is two steps above the priority class assigned to the process.

In addition, two special priority levels can be passed to `SetThreadPriority`:

- `THREAD_PRIORITY_IDLE` always sets the thread's priority level to 1, unless the process priority class is `REALTIME_PRIORITY_CLASS`, in which case it's set to 16.

- `THREAD_PRIORITY_TIME_CRITICAL` always sets the thread's priority to 15, unless the process priority class is `REALTIME_PRIORITY_CLASS`, in which case it is set to 31. This is the only way a thread can run at priority level 31.

Thread-local Storage

Automatic variables, such as the variables declared inside a function body, are created in the context of the currently running thread. This means that every thread has its own copy of every automatic variable. This is normally a good thing, because you don't need to synchronize access to variables created on the stack.

When it's necessary to use global variables, threads tend to complicate your life quite a bit. First, access to the variable must be synchronized so that multiple threads don't attempt to modify the variable at the same time. Second, a normal global variable is shared between all threads—unless you use an array, there's no way to store data on a per-thread basis.

Windows 2000 has a specific way of dealing with this problem. *Thread-local storage* enables you to create variables that are maintained on a per-thread basis, with very little bookkeeping or maintenance required on your part. There are two types of thread-local storage:

- Static thread-local storage
- Dynamic thread-local storage

The advantages of both methods are discussed in the next two sections.

Using Static Thread-local Storage

Static thread-local storage is very easy to use. There are no functions to call, no special precautions to take, and no weird compiler switches to set.

Static thread-local storage lives in a special memory section named `.tls`, created in the address space of your process. When a new thread is created, Windows 2000 makes a new copy of the thread-local storage for the new thread and destroys the block of memory when the thread is killed. A thread can only access the thread-local variables used for its thread.

To declare a thread-local storage variable, use `__declspec(thread)` as part of the variable's declaration:

```
_ _declspec(thread) int nMeals = 0;
```

To make your code more readable, you can also use a `typedef`:

```
typedef _ _declspec(thread) TLS;
TLS int nMeals = 0;
```

A thread-local storage variable is used just like any other variable. You can read to it, write to it, or take its address, just as you can with other global variables. You don't need to synchronize access to it, because only one thread can touch it.

A thread-local storage variable can be declared in global scope or as a static variable in a function. It can never be declared as a plain automatic variable.

Using Dynamic Thread-local Storage

Dynamic thread-local storage is created and used at runtime by your application. Although it's slightly more complex than static thread-local storage, dynamic thread-local storage is much more flexible, because it can be allocated and freed as needed.

Windows 2000 maintains the dynamic thread-local storage, and each process accesses the thread-local storage using indexes, as shown in Figure 3.3.

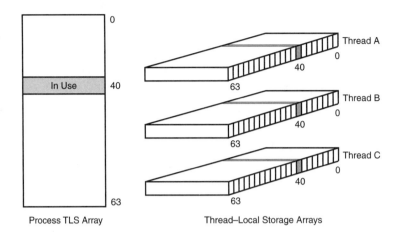

FIGURE 3.3
Thread-local storage uses indexes maintained by Windows 2000.

Process TLS Array   Thread–Local Storage Arrays

Each thread in a process has its own copy of the thread-local storage. Windows 2000 maintains a status flag for each thread-local storage index and allocates a new one for any process requesting a new storage index. There are four functions used to manage the thread-local storage:

- `TlsAlloc` is used to request a new thread-local storage index from Windows 2000.
- `TlsSetValue` is used by a thread to store a 32-bit value in its copy of the thread-local storage.
- `TlsGetValue` is used by a thread to retrieve a 32-bit value previously stored in thread-local storage.
- `TlsFree` is used to notify Windows 2000 that a process no longer needs a particular thread-local storage index.

Each thread in the process has access to its own copy of the thread-local storage. It cannot change the values used by any other threads.

Determining a Thread's Identifier

When a thread is created, the operating system will assign a thread identifier to it. The thread ID uniquely identifies the thread for the entire system—no two processes will contain threads with the same thread ID. The thread ID is a useful tag that's used in many thread-centric API calls.

There are two ways to determine the thread identifier:

- Store the thread ID returned to you when the thread is created using the `CreateThread`, `_beginthread`, or `_beginthreadex` function.
- Use the `GetCurrentThreadId` function.

If you're only interested in the thread ID for a small number of worker threads, it's fairly easy to store the thread ID when the thread is created. However, this approach will not help you determine the thread ID of the primary thread for the process. It may also require a substantial amount of bookkeeping if you have a lot of worker threads.

GetCurrentThreadId has no parameters and returns the thread ID used to identify the thread that made the function call:

```
DWORD dwThreadID = GetCurrentThreadId();
```

You can also retrieve a pseudohandle for your own thread by calling the GetCurrentThread function:

```
HANDLE hThread = GetCurrentThread();
```

A *pseudohandle* is not really a thread handle, but it will serve as a placeholder for any functions that require an actual thread handle. Also, a pseudohandle never needs to be closed.

You can retrieve a pseudohandle for the current process with the GetCurrentProcess function:

```
HANDLE hProcess = GetCurrentProcess();
```

Working with Thread Affinity

Thread affinity is the association between a particular thread and another object. Later, in Chapter 16, "COM Threading Models," thread affinity for COM objects will be covered. In this chapter, thread affinity toward particular CPUs is discussed.

Windows 2000 allows you to specify thread affinity for a process or thread so that it's allowed to run on a subset of available processors. Setting the thread affinity for a thread or process, *in some cases*, can improve performance by optimizing the usage of your CPU cache.

The thread and process affinity APIs only work with multiprocessor systems—if you're working with a single CPU machine, all your threads are bound to a single CPU. Keep in mind that on an SMP machine, the thread affinity defined for your threads or processes does not prevent other threads from using your preferred CPUs—used improperly, the thread and processor affinity APIs can cause the performance of your application to suffer.

The thread affinity mask is a DWORD variable, with bit zero (the least-significant bit) used for the first CPU, bit one used for the second CPU, and so on.

You can set the affinity mask for the entire process or for a particular thread in the process. To set the thread affinity for a thread, call `SetThreadAffinityMask`, as shown in Listing 3.3.

LISTING 3.3   FORCING A THREAD TO RUN ON THE SECOND CPU

```
#include <windows.h>
#include <tchar.h>

int _tmain()
{
    // Get pseudo handle for thread
    HANDLE hThread = GetCurrentThread();
    DWORD dwAffinity = 0x02; // run on second processor only!
    DWORD dwOldAffinity = SetThreadAffinityMask(hThread, dwAffinity);
    _tprintf(_T("Old affinity mask was %x\n"), dwOldAffinity);
    .
    .
    .
    return 0;
}
```

The `SetThreadAffinityMask` function has two parameters:

- A handle to the thread that will have its affinity mask changed
- The new affinity mask

The `SetThreadAffinityMask` function returns the thread's previous affinity mask.

You can set the affinity mask for all the threads in a process with the `SetProcessAffinityMask` function, as shown in Listing 3.4.

LISTING 3.4   FORCING A PROCESS TO RUN ON THE SECOND CPU

```
#include <windows.h>
#include <tchar.h>

int _tmain()
{
    // Get pseudo handle for process
    HANDLE hProcess = GetCurrentProcess();
    DWORD  dwAffinity = 0x02;  // run on second processor only!
    BOOL fSetAffinity = SetProcessAffinityMask(hProcess,
                                                dwAffinity);
    .
    .
    .
    return 0;
}
```

The SetProcessAffinityMask function has two parameters:

- A handle to the process that will have its affinity mask changed
- The new affinity mask

The SetProcessAffinityMask function returns FALSE upon failure and nonzero upon success—it does not return the previous affinity mask. To retrieve the affinity mask for the process, you must call the GetProcessAffinityMask function:

```
DWORD dwProcAffinity;
DWORD dwSysAffinity;
HANDLE hProcess = GetCurrentProcess();
BOOL fGetAffinity = GetProcessAffinityMask(hProcess,
                                           &dwProcAffinity,
                                           &dwSysAffinity);
```

The GetProcessAffinityMask function has three parameters:

- A handle to the process you're interested in.
- A pointer to a DWORD that will be filled with the current process affinity mask.
- A pointer to a DWORD that will be filled with the affinity mask for the system. Every available processor will have its bit set in this affinity mask.

As discussed earlier, locking a thread or process to a particular processor can negatively affect performance. Even if a processor is available, your thread will be prevented from running if the affinity mask allows none of the available processors to run your thread.

The SetThreadIdealProcessor function gives you a means to indicate your preferred processor for a thread. Your thread won't be prevented from running, but it will be scheduled to run on the specified processor whenever possible. You can't set a mask of preferred processors—you must specify a single processor as your ideal processor:

```
HANDLE hProcess = GetCurrentThread();
DWORD  dwPreferredProc = 0x02;  // Prefer processor 3
DWORD  dwPrevious = SetThreadIdealProcessor(hProcess,
                                            dwPreferredProc);
if(dwPrevious == -1)
    ReportError();
```

The SetThreadIdealProcessor function has two parameters:

- A handle to the thread that will have its affinity mask changed
- The preferred processor for the thread

The SetThreadIdealProcessor function returns the previous preferred processor or MAXIMUM_PROCESSORS if no preferred processor was previously specified. If an error occurs, the function returns -1.

Getting Multiple Threads to Cooperate

The need to manage threads and processes in an application is not something unique to Windows 2000. Once you break an application into more than one thread, you may need to handle problems you never knew existed under single-threaded programming.

For example, the simple act of reading and writing to a global variable must be properly synchronized. Often, seemingly innocent code fragments can hide danger areas:

```
/* global variable */
int g_nRequestsOutstanding;

void QueueNewRequest(void)
{
    ++g_nRequestsOutstanding;
    DoSomethingInterestingToQueueRequest();
}

void SatisfyRequest(void)
{
    RemoveOutstandingRequestInAnEfficientManner();
    - -g_nRequestsOutstanding;
}
```

This code fragment shows two different functions that write to the same variable, g_nRequestsOutstanding. If two (or more) threads attempt to change the value of a variable at the same time, the variable will be corrupted. There are actually two different types of failure scenarios:

- On multiprocessor machines, it's very easy for a multithreaded process to have two threads executing simultaneously. If your code does not employ synchronization techniques for controlling access to variables accessed by multiple threads, it will definitely fail.

- On single-processor machines, multiple threads in a process cannot run at the same time. However, it's possible for a thread to be interrupted at any point during the execution of your program. If it's interrupted while executing the several instructions required to write to a variable, another thread may write to the variable while the first thread is waiting to run.

Listing 3.5 contains an example of a program that is not thread safe. The BadCount console mode application can be found on the CD-ROM that accompanies this book. BadCount creates two threads that attempt to increment a global variable to 50,000 by splitting the work between the two threads.

LISTING 3.5   THE BADCOUNT PROGRAM SHOWS THE WRONG WAY TO SHARE
GLOBAL DATA

```c
/*
 * BadCount.c - unsynchronized access to a global variable through
 * two threads. Compile with the Multi-threaded runtime library.
 */
#include <windows.h>
#include <tchar.h>
#ifndef UNICODE
    #include <stdio.h>
#endif

/* Global counter */
int  g_nTheCounter = 0;
void IncCounter();

DWORD WINAPI threadFunc(LPVOID);
int _tmain()
{
    DWORD dwThreadId;
    /* Create worker thread for half the work */
    HANDLE hThread = CreateThread(NULL,
                                  0,
                                  threadFunc,
                                  NULL,
                                  0,
                                  &dwThreadId);
    if(!hThread) return 0;
    /*
     * Increment global variable 25,000 times, then wait for
     * the worker thread to finish executing.
     */
    IncCounter();
    WaitForSingleObject(hThread, INFINITE);
    /*
     * Display the value of the global variable, after it has
     * been incremented 50,000 times.
     */
    _tprintf(_T("The value of the global counter is %d\n"),
             g_nTheCounter);
    return 0;
}

/*
 * Worker thread function - increments the global variable
 * 25,000 times, and exits.
 */
DWORD WINAPI threadFunc(LPVOID lpv)
{
```

3

THREADS AND
PROCESSES

continues

LISTING 3.5 CONTINUED

```
        IncCounter();
        return NO_ERROR;
}

/*
 * Common function used by both threads to increment the global
 * counter variable.
 */
void IncCounter()
{
    int n;
    for(n = 0; n < 25000; ++n)
    {
        ++g_nTheCounter;
    }
}
```

How bad is BadCount? It depends on the machine. On my SMP machine, an IBM 704 with dual Pentium Pro CPUs, the reported count at the end of the program is usually around 30,000 or so. However, on another workstation I have with a single Alpha CPU, the result is usually the expected value of 50,000. The problem still appears on the single-CPU system, it just happens rarely. These differing results illustrate a few points about multithreading:

- Just because a program runs on your machine doesn't mean that it isn't broken.
- SMP machines are great testing tools.
- Synchronization problems can be very difficult to track down.

Any operating system that supports multiple threads of execution must provide some way for you to handle these synchronization issues. What makes Windows 2000 unique is its large number of management options. Windows 2000 is chockfull of methods to help you manage threads and processes. These methods are discussed in detail in the section titled "Synchronization," later in this chapter.

When to Create a Thread

Several problems are easily solved by splitting an application into two or more threads. Your application is probably a good candidate for multithreading if it meets one of the following criteria:

- It spends a lot of time testing to check for completed I/O.
- It has a number of "background" tasks to perform asynchronously.
- It has other tasks that can be performed independently without much synchronization.

Using multiple threads tends to make applications with these properties easier to program. However, it's easy to go overboard when using threads for the first time. Consider the next section.

When Not to Create a Thread

Some types of applications are not good candidates for becoming multithreaded. Your application may not be a great candidate for multithreading if it meets one of the following criteria:

- It's basically monolithic.
- It doesn't consume existing computing resources.
- It has complex synchronization issues.
- It has many dependencies between tasks.

Remember, adding multiple threads to your application may solve some of your problems, but it will create new issues, such as synchronization, thread and object lifetime, and increased complexity during testing. Also, remember this: Your program will not, in most cases, run any faster on a single CPU machine. In fact, it will often run slower.

Synchronization

As discussed earlier, when two or more threads use a common variable, problems can result. If multiple threads attempt to read a variable, there's no problem. If, however, one thread attempts to modify a common variable, access to that variable must be synchronized.

A *synchronization primitive* is an object that helps you manage a multithread application. Five basic types of synchronization primitives are available in Windows 2000:

- *Events* are objects created by you and are used to signal that a variable or routine is available for access.
- *Critical sections* are areas of code that can be accessed by a single thread at any given time.
- *Mutexes* are Windows 2000 objects used to ensure that only a single thread has access to a protected variable or code.
- *Semaphores* are similar to mutexes but behave like counters, allowing a specified number of threads access to a protected variable or code.
- *API-level atomic operations* are provided by Windows 2000 to enable you to increment, decrement, or exchange the contents of a variable in a single operation.

3

THREADS AND
PROCESSES

Each of these synchronization primitives is useful in certain situations. Each is discussed in the next few sections.

Using Win32 Interlocked Operations

The simplest synchronization primitives are used to manipulate or test the value of one or two variables. The Win32 API includes seven functions that are guaranteed to be atomic and thread safe, even in the presence of multiple CPUs:

- `InterlockedIncrement` increments a 32-bit variable and returns the new value.
- `InterlockedDecrement` decrements a 32-bit variable and returns the new value.
- `InterlockedExchange` changes the value of a 32-bit variable to a new value and returns the previous value.
- `InterlockedExchangeAdd` increments the value of a 32-bit variable by a specified amount and returns the previous value.
- `InterlockedExchangePointer` changes the value of a 32-bit variable to a new value and returns the previous value. In 64-bit versions of Windows 2000, the parameters will be 64 bits.
- `InterlockedCompareExchange` conditionally sets the value of a 32-bit variable to a new value and returns the initial value.
- `InterlockedCompareExchangePointer` conditionally sets the value of a 32-bit variable to a new value and returns the initial value. In 64-bit versions of Windows 2000, the parameters will be 64 bits.

Variables passed to these functions must be 32-bit aligned on Intel SMP systems. When running on 64-bit versions of Windows 2000, variables passed to `InterlockedExchangePointer` and `InterlockedCompareExchangePointer` must be 64-bit aligned.

The most commonly used of these functions are `InterlockedIncrement` and `InterlockedDecrement`. Listing 3.6 contains GoodCount, a new version of the BadCount example provided in Listing 3.5. GoodCount uses `InterlockedIncrement` to atomically increment the global variable, and it runs correctly on all Windows 2000 systems.

LISTING 3.6 THE GOODCOUNT PROGRAM SHOWS THE RIGHT WAY TO SHARE GLOBAL DATA

```
/*
 * GoodCount.c - synchronized access to a global variable through
 * two threads. Compile with the Multi-threaded runtime library.
 */
```

```c
#include <windows.h>
#include <tchar.h>
#ifndef UNICODE
    #include <stdio.h>
#endif

/* Global counter */
long g_nTheCounter = 0;
void IncCounter();

DWORD WINAPI threadFunc(LPVOID);
int _tmain()
{
    DWORD dwThreadId;
    /* Create worker thread for half the work */
    HANDLE hThread = CreateThread(NULL,
                                  0,
                                  threadFunc,
                                  NULL,
                                  0,
                                  &dwThreadId);
    if(!hThread) return 0;
    /*
     * Increment global variable 25,000 times, then wait for
     * the worker thread to finish executing.
     */
    IncCounter();
    WaitForSingleObject(hThread, INFINITE);
    /*
     * Display the value of the global variable, after it has
     * been incremented 50,000 times.
     */
    _tprintf(_T("The value of the global counter is %d\n"),
            g_nTheCounter);
    return 0;
}

/*
 * Worker thread function - increments the global variable
 * 25,000 times, and exits.
 */
DWORD WINAPI threadFunc(LPVOID lpv)
{
    IncCounter();
    return NO_ERROR;
}

/*
 * Common function used by both threads to increment the global
 * counter variable. This version of IncCounter uses the
 * InterlockedIncrement function.
```

continues

LISTING 3.6   CONTINUED

```
*/
void IncCounter()
{
    int n;
    for(n = 0; n < 25000; ++n)
    {
        InterlockedIncrement(&g_nTheCounter);
    }
}
```

Critical Sections

A *critical section* is a section of code that must be used by only one thread at any given time. If two or more threads attempt to access a critical section at the same time, only one thread will be allowed control of the critical section, and all other threads are *blocked*, or kept waiting, until the critical section is free, as shown in Figure 3.4.

FIGURE 3.4

A critical section enables only one thread at a time to execute.

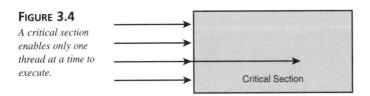

Critical Section

When compared with the other synchronization methods that will be discussed later in this chapter, creating a critical section is very inexpensive in terms of computing resources. However, unlike other Windows 2000 synchronization primitives, a critical section can only be used within a single process.

A critical section is guarded by a CRITICAL_SECTION variable. This variable must be initialized before it is used, and it must be in scope for every thread that uses it. It must not be allowed to go out of scope while in use; for this reason, critical section variables are often given global scope.

The InitializeCriticalSection function is used to initialize the CRITICAL_SECTION variable:

```
CRITICAL_SECTION cs;
InitializeCriticalSection(&cs);
```

To take possession of a critical section, a thread must call the EnterCriticalSection function:

```
EnterCriticalSection(&cs);
```

If the critical section is not in use, it's marked as busy, and the thread immediately continues execution. If the critical section is already in use, the thread is blocked until the section is free.

When a thread has finished working with the protected variable or function, the critical section is released by calling LeaveCriticalSection:

```
LeaveCriticalSection(&cs);
```

One thread blocked on this CRITICAL_SECTION variable is able to take control of the variable.

A single CRITICAL_SECTION variable can protect many related variables or functions. Later in this chapter, a single CRITICAL_SECTION variable is used to ensure that only one of eight threads is working with the controls in a dialog box.

Once a thread takes control of a critical section, it will prevent other threads from taking control of the critical section. For best results, it's important for threads to hold a critical section for as small an interval as possible.

Every call to EnterCriticalSection must be balanced with a call to LeaveCriticalSection. If you forget to call LeaveCriticalSection, threads waiting to enter the critical section are blocked forever, or until the process ends, whichever comes first. Unless the work performed inside a critical section is very simple, it's a good idea to use _ _try and _ _finally blocks to make sure your calls to EnterCriticalSection and LeaveCriticalSection are balanced, as shown here:

```
void DoSomething()
{
    _ _try
    {
        EnterCriticalSection(&csOutput);
        .
        .
        // Do some interesting work here
        .
    }
    _ _finally
    {
        LeaveCriticalSection(&csOutput);
    }
}
```

In this code fragment, the LeaveCriticalSection function is always called, even if an exception is thrown while executing inside the critical section. Another approach is to wrap a critical section inside a C++ class that guarantees that the critical section will be properly initialized and destroyed.

A single thread is permitted to call EnterCriticalSection multiple times using the same CRITICAL_SECTION variable. This is because it can be difficult to determine all the possible nested critical sections in a large application. For example, the following code calls the EnterCriticalSection function twice with the same CRITICAL_SECTION variable:

```
void CIsdnTerminal::HandleKeyPress()
{
    EnterCriticalSection(&m_csAction);
    if(ReceivedRelease() == FALSE)
        TranslateKey();
    LeaveCriticalSection(&m_csAction);
}
BOOL CIsdnTerminal::ReceivedRelease()
{
    BOOL fResult;
    EnterCriticalSection(&m_csAction);
    if(m_state == CLEARING)
        fResult = TRUE;
    else
        fResult = m_fReleaseStored;
    LeaveCriticalSection(&m_csAction);
    return fResult;
}
```

In this example, each call to EnterCriticalSection is balanced with a call to LeaveCriticalSection. When a thread that owns a CRITICAL_SECTION variable calls EnterCriticalSection with the same variable, an internal counter is incremented, and the thread is allowed to continue without blocking. When the internal counter decrements to zero, other threads are allowed to take control of the critical section.

When the critical section is no longer needed, the resources used by the critical section are freed by calling DeleteCriticalSection:

```
DeleteCriticalSection(&cs);
```

In addition to the critical section management functions listed in this section, Windows 2000 also allows you to test the state of a critical section without blocking, with the TryEnterCriticalSection function:

```
BOOL fAcquired = TryEnterCriticalSection(&cs);
```

```
if(fAcquired)
{
    // Write to protected variables
    nAgeAlexandria = 6;
    nAgeMackenzie = 2;
}
else
{
    // Couldn't acquire critical section
}
```

TryEnterCriticalSection returns TRUE if your thread has control over the critical section, or it returns FALSE if another thread already has possession of the critical section.

The TryEnterCriticalSection function allows you to take a crack at acquiring the critical section—if the critical section is available, your thread takes ownership of it. If the critical section is not available, TryEnterCriticalSection returns FALSE, and your thread is free to handle other work.

Managing Events

Critical sections are useful when you're protecting data or functions from multiple threads. However, in a multithreaded application, sometimes you need to notify another thread that an event has occurred. With Windows 2000, this is done by creating events.

An *event* is a Windows 2000 synchronization object that's managed by the operating system. Each event can have an associated name; this allows multiple processes to share the same event handle.

Events are used when one thread must wait for another thread to complete a task, or when a thread must sleep and wait for another thread to indicate that an event has occurred.

Once created, an event can be in one of two states:

- *Signaled*. A wait request on this event will be satisfied.
- *Not signaled*. A wait request on this thread will not be satisfied, and the waiting thread will be blocked.

Typically, an event is used to indicate a particular task is completed. A thread waiting for this task to be completed waits until the event is signaled and then continues processing, as shown in Figure 3.5.

Normally, an event that's signaled is immediately reset to the not-signaled state in an atomic operation. This prevents another thread from reusing the event. Manual-reset events that stay signaled, even after a wait request has been satisfied, are discussed later in this chapter.

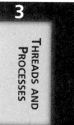

3

THREADS AND PROCESSES

FIGURE 3.5
Multiple threads using events for synchronization.

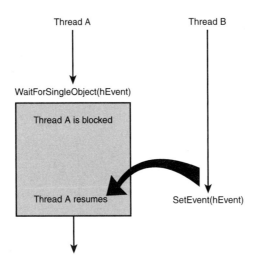

Creating and Closing Event Handles

The CreateEvent function is used to create an event:

```
HANDLE hEvent = CreateEvent(NULL, FALSE, FALSE, "EventName");
```

The CreateEvent function takes four parameters:

- A pointer to a SECURITY_ATTRIBUTES structure. If you aren't concerned about security issues, you can use NULL for this parameter.
- A flag that indicates whether this is to be a manual-reset event. Manual-reset events are described in detail later; this parameter is normally FALSE.
- A flag that indicates the initial state of the event. If this parameter is TRUE, the event is signaled; a value of FALSE indicates that this event should be placed into a not-signaled state.
- An optional name for the event. Keep in mind that all event, mutex, and file-mapping objects use the same namespace, so you must take care not to reuse names accidentally. In most cases, this value is NULL, especially when you're not sharing events across process boundaries.

If the event is successfully created, a handle to the event is returned. If an error occurs, NULL is returned.

Event handles are Windows 2000 objects, much like file, thread, and process handles. When you're finished using an event handle, the `CloseHandle` function is used:

```
CloseHandle(hEvent);
```

Signaling and Resetting Event Handles

To change the state of an event handle to signaled, the `SetEvent` function is used:

```
SetEvent(hEvent);
```

The `SetEvent` function takes a handle as its only parameter.

Once signaled, an auto-reset event handle is reset after it's used to satisfy a wait request. Manual-reset events must be explicitly reset using the `ResetEvent` function:

```
ResetEvent(hEvent);
```

Auto-reset events are often used when you're performing initializations or other events that must be broadcast to a number of threads. In this case, it makes sense to leave a thread signaled, even though it has been used to satisfy a wait request. This enables all waiting threads to be satisfied by setting a single event.

When you're using manual-reset events to signal a group of threads, it can be difficult to determine when all waiting threads have been released. Windows 2000 includes a `PulseEvent` function for this very purpose:

```
PulseEvent(hEvent);
```

The `PulseEvent` function signals the event handle and resets it after all the waiting threads have been released.

Waiting on a Handle

When a thread needs to wait for a handle to be signaled, there are several different ways to do so. Two functions can be used to put a thread into a wait state while waiting for a handle to be signaled:

- `WaitForSingleObject` is used when the thread is waiting for one handle to be signaled.
- `WaitForMultipleObjects` is used for testing an array of handles.

`WaitForSingleObject` tests a handle passed to it as a parameter and returns immediately if the handle is signaled:

```
DWORD dwResult = WaitForSingleObject(hEvent, INFINITE);
```

The `WaitForSingleObject` function takes two parameters:

- The handle to be tested
- A timeout value, in milliseconds, or `INFINITE` for no timeout limit

The event remains signaled for a manual-reset event handle, even after the first thread's wait request has been satisfied. All other events are set to their nonsignaled state by `WaitForSingleObject` after satisfying a wait request.

Here are the three possible return values for `WaitForSingleObject`:

- `WAIT_OBJECT_0` is returned when the handle is signaled. Note that the last character of this symbol is a zero, not the letter *O*.
- `WAIT_TIMEOUT` is returned when the handle is not signaled and the timeout limit has expired.
- `WAIT_ABANDONED` is returned only when a thread is waiting on a mutex handle.

Beware of nested calls to `WaitForSingleObject`. At times, a thread may need to wait for several handles to become signaled. Using nested calls to `WaitForSingleObject` can be risky in cases where multiple threads are contending for multiple objects, as shown in Figure 3.6.

In Figure 3.6, both thread A and thread B have one of the resources needed to continue.

FIGURE 3.6

An example of deadlock.

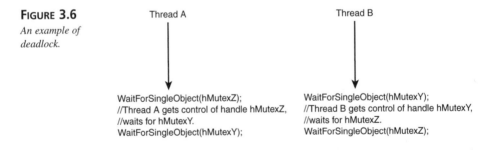

Unfortunately, neither can continue unless the other thread relinquishes the resource it has already taken possession of. Fortunately, Windows 2000 enables you to wait for several synchronization objects at the same time, as discussed in the next section.

Waiting on Multiple Handles

The `WaitForMultipleObjects` function is similar to `WaitForSingleObject`, except that it works with an array of handles. All handles are supervised at the same time, and none are favored with respect to the others. The call to `WaitForMultipleObjects` looks like this:

```
HANDLE hEvents[2];
.
.
.
DWORD dw = WaitForMultipleObjects(2, hEvents, TRUE, INFINITE);
```

WaitForMultipleObjects has four parameters:

- The number of object handles to be tested.
- The base address of the handle array.
- A flag that specifies whether all handles must be signaled or just one. In this case, TRUE indicates that all event handles must be signaled.
- A timeout value, in milliseconds, or INFINITE for no timeout limit.

If TRUE is specified as the third parameter to WaitForMultipleObjects, no event handle has its state altered unless all handles are available. This is necessary to prevent deadlock conditions that might occur if threads were allowed to take control of a subset of the threads needed to continue.

The return values for WaitForMultipleObjects are slightly more complex than those WaitForSingleObject:

- WAIT_OBJECT_0 through WAIT_OBJECT_0 + (number of handles –1) is returned when the handle is signaled. The return value indicates the index of the lowest numbered handle that has become signaled.
- WAIT_TIMEOUT is returned when the handle is not signaled and the timeout limit has expired.
- WAIT_ABANDONED_0 through WAIT_ABANDONED_0 + (number of handles –1) is returned only when a thread is waiting on a mutex handle.

If you're interested in exactly which handle has been signaled, use a code fragment like this:

```
HANDLE rghEvents[63];
.
.
.
DWORD dw = WaitForMultipleObjects(63, rghEvents, FALSE, 0x10000);

if((dw >= WAIT_OBJECT_0)&&(dw <= WAIT_OBJECT_0 + 63))
{
    int ndx = dw - WAIT_OBJECT_0;
    HANDLE hSignaled = rghEvents[ndx];
    .
    // Use hSignaled
    .
}
```

3

THREADS AND
PROCESSES

Using Event Handles Across a Process Boundary

As discussed earlier, you can use event handles between processes. An event handle can be inherited, passed to a new process during CreateProcess, or duplicated using DuplicateHandle.

In addition, if an event object was created with an optional name, you can use CreateEvent or OpenEvent to get a handle to that event object from another process. For example, assume that an event object was created with the name "Shared":

```
HANDLE hEvent = CreateEvent(NULL, FALSE, FALSE, "Shared");
```

Another process can get a handle to the same event by calling CreateEvent with the same parameters. The OpenEvent function also can be used by another process:

```
HANDLE hEvent = OpenEvent(EVENT_ALL_ACCESS, FALSE, "Shared");
```

Two small console mode applications on the CD-ROM provide examples of using an event handle across process boundaries. The WaitEvent project creates an event handle and waits for it to be signaled. The SigEvent project opens a copy of this event handle and signals it, thus allowing WaitEvent to complete its execution.

The complete source code for WaitEvent is provided in Listing 3.7.

LISTING 3.7   THE WAITEVENT PROGRAM

```
#include <windows.h>
#include <tchar.h>
#ifndef UNICODE
    #include <stdio.h>
#endif

int _tmain()
{
    HANDLE hEvent = CreateEvent(NULL, FALSE,
                                FALSE, _T("WaitEvent"));

    _tprintf(_T("Waiting for SigEvent\n"));
    WaitForSingleObject(hEvent, INFINITE);
    _tprintf(_T("Caught event handle, all done.\n"));
    CloseHandle(hEvent);
    return 0;
}
```

The complete source code for SigEvent is provided in Listing 3.8.

LISTING 3.8 THE SIGEVENT PROGRAM

```c
#include <windows.h>
#include <tchar.h>
#ifndef UNICODE
    #include <stdio.h>
#endif

int _tmain()
{
    HANDLE hEvent = OpenEvent(EVENT_ALL_ACCESS,
                              FALSE, _T("WaitEvent"));
    _tprintf(_T("Signaling WaitEvent handle\n"));
    SetEvent(hEvent);
    return 0;
}
```

Compile both programs. Run the WaitEvent program first. The console displays the following:

```
Waiting for SigEvent
```

Launching the SigEvent program in a different console window displays the following:

```
Signaling WaitEvent handle
```

The SigEvent program signals the event handle and enables the WaitEvent program to finish. The WaitEvent console window displays the following:

```
Caught event handle, all done
```

Figure 3.7 shows two console mode windows used to run these two programs at the same time.

FIGURE 3.7

Running the WaitEvent and SigEvent programs.

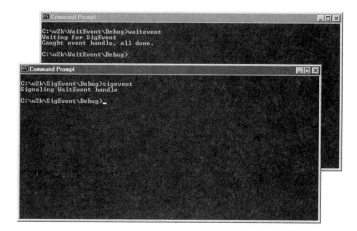

Mutexes and Mutual Exclusion

A *mutex* is a Windows 2000 object used as a mutual exclusion primitive. As is the case with critical sections, only one thread can have possession of a mutex object. However, unlike critical sections, mutexes are Windows 2000 objects and are managed by the operating system. They can also be named and shared between processes.

To take possession of a mutex, a thread must perform a wait on the mutex handle. A mutex is considered "signaled" when available and "not signaled" when in use.

A common synchronization example that illustrates mutual exclusion is the "dining philosophers" problem. Several philosophers are sitting at a table, with one chopstick between each philosopher. A philosopher must have possession of two chopsticks before eating and must put down both chopsticks before thinking. Each philosopher will spend an arbitrary amount of time thinking and eating.

The problem is to design the program such that these conditions are met:

- No philosopher goes hungry or, literally, is starved for both CPU cycles and food.
- No philosopher is forced to eat continuously and is prevented from thinking.
- Most importantly, no deadlock condition is created.

The mutual exclusion part of the dining philosophers problem occurs when two philosophers attempt to gain control of the same chopstick. Mutual exclusion can be used to ensure that only one of the philosophers can grab a free chopstick.

When you're designing an algorithm for selecting a chopstick, care must be taken to avoid deadlocks. If the philosophers are able to grab one chopstick and wait for the other chopstick to become free, every philosopher could have one chopstick and a deadlock situation could occur.

One solution to the dining philosophers problem has been included on the CD-ROM. The Philo project is a console mode program that uses mutex objects to represent the chopsticks used by the dining philosophers. When a philosopher wants to eat, WaitForMultipleObjects is used to wait for both mutex handles at the same time. Because neither mutex is acquired until both are ready, deadlock conditions are avoided.

The source code for the solution on the CD-ROM is provided in Listing 3.9. This version of the source code models 63 philosophers. You can change the number of philosophers by changing the value of nMaxPhil.

LISTING 3.9 THE DINING PHILOSOPHERS PROBLEM USING WINDOWS 2000
SYNCHRONIZATION PRIMITIVES

```c
#include <windows.h>
#include <tchar.h>
#ifndef UNICODE
    #include <stdio.h>
#endif

long  g_fDone = FALSE;
typedef struct tagCPhilosopher
{
    int     m_nID;
    HANDLE  m_hSticks[2];
    int     m_nMeals;
}CPhilosopher;

#define nMaxPhil 63

void SayEat(CPhilosopher* pPhilo)
{
    _tprintf(_T("Philosopher %d eats a while\n"), pPhilo->m_nID);
    pPhilo->m_nMeals++;
}

void SayThink(int nPhilo)
{
    _tprintf(_T("Philosopher %d thinks a while\n"), nPhilo);
}

void SayDone(CPhilosopher* pPhilo)
{
    _tprintf(_T("Philosopher %d had %d meals\n"),
            pPhilo->m_nID,
            pPhilo->m_nMeals);
}

long WINAPI WaitToEat(long lParam)
{
    CPhilosopher* pPhilo = (CPhilosopher*)lParam;
    DWORD dwEatTime = 1000 + GetCurrentThreadId();

    _tprintf(_T("Philosopher %d is alive!\n"), pPhilo->m_nID);
    while(g_fDone == FALSE)
    {
        // Wait for my two chopsticks.
        WaitForMultipleObjects(2,
                               pPhilo->m_hSticks,
                               TRUE,
                               INFINITE);
        //
```

3

THREADS AND
PROCESSES

continues

LISTING 3.9   CONTINUED

```
            // Wait satisfied - I have both chopsticks
            SayEat(pPhilo);
            Sleep(dwEatTime);
            SayThink(pPhilo->m_nID);
            // Release both chopsticks.
            ReleaseMutex(pPhilo->m_hSticks[1]);
            ReleaseMutex(pPhilo->m_hSticks[0]);
        }
        return 0;
}

int _tmain()
{
    unsigned long  nThread;
    unsigned int   ndxStick;
    unsigned int   ndxPhilo;

    HANDLE         rghSticks[nMaxPhil];
    CPhilosopher   rgPhilos[nMaxPhil];

    for(ndxStick = 0; ndxStick < nMaxPhil; ndxStick++)
        rghSticks[ndxStick] = CreateMutex(NULL,FALSE,NULL);

    // Kick off the philosopher threads, using WaitToEat
    // as the thread function.
    for(ndxPhilo = 0; ndxPhilo < nMaxPhil; ndxPhilo++)
    {
        HANDLE hThread;
        rgPhilos[ndxPhilo].m_nID = ndxPhilo;
        rgPhilos[ndxPhilo].m_nMeals = 0;
        rgPhilos[ndxPhilo].m_hSticks[0] = rghSticks[ndxPhilo];
        if(ndxPhilo < nMaxPhil-1)
          rgPhilos[ndxPhilo].m_hSticks[1] = rghSticks[ndxPhilo+1];
        else
          rgPhilos[ndxPhilo].m_hSticks[1] = rghSticks[0];
        hThread = CreateThread(NULL,
                               0,
                               (LPTHREAD_START_ROUTINE)WaitToEat,
                               (void*)&rgPhilos[ndxPhilo],
                               0,
                               &nThread);
        CloseHandle(hThread);
    }
    Sleep(100000);  // Run for ~ 100 seconds
    g_fDone = TRUE;
    Sleep(8000);    // Wait ~ 8 seconds for thread completion.

    for(ndxPhilo = 0; ndxPhilo < nMaxPhil; ndxPhilo++)
    {
```

```
        SayDone(&rgPhilos[ndxPhilo]);
        CloseHandle(rghSticks[ndxPhilo]);
    }
    return 0;
}
```

Semaphores

The *semaphore* was one of the first synchronization primitives described in computer science literature. Semaphores were invented by Edsger Dijkstra (pronounced *Dike-stra*) as a tool to be used in multithreaded computing, which was a new field in the mid-1960s. A semaphore is like a counter that acts as a guardian over a section of code or a resource. In fact, semaphores are sometimes referred to as *Dijkstra counters*.

The semaphore maintains an internal counter that's decremented or incremented as operations are performed on the semaphore. If the semaphore's internal counter reaches zero, any new thread attempting to decrement the counter must wait until another thread increments it. Two operations can be performed on a semaphore:

- *P*, sometimes called *DOWN*, is used to indicate that a resource is not available. P is short for ""proberen te verlagen," a Dutch phrase that roughly translates to ""attempt to decrease."

- *V*, sometimes called *UP*, is used to indicate that a resource has become available. P is short for ""verhogen," a Dutch word that translates to "increase."

Semaphores and Wait Functions

Before using a resource guarded by a semaphore, a thread must always perform a wait on the semaphore's handle. This enables the thread to be blocked if the semaphore is not signaled. It also enables the semaphore's internal counter to be decremented after the thread's wait is completed. This is the "P" or "attempt to decrease" function described in the previous section.

When a thread is finished using a controlled resource, the semaphore is released by calling the `ReleaseSemaphore` function. This function increases the semaphore's internal counter and enables another waiting thread to take control of the semaphore. This is the "V" or "increase" function described in the preceding section.

Figure 3.8 illustrates how a semaphore is initialized, used, and released.

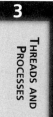

3

THREADS AND
PROCESSES

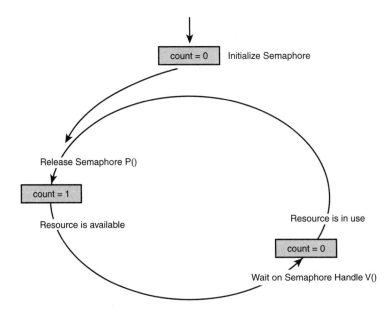

FIGURE 3.8

Using a semaphore to control resources.

A semaphore can be used with either of the wait functions discussed earlier in this chapter. A semaphore is considered to be signaled when its counter is greater than zero; it's not signaled as long as the count equals zero.

The semaphore's internal counter should always reflect the number of resources available for consumption. Any threads that take possession of a resource controlled by a semaphore must perform a wait function on the semaphore object. If the semaphore counter is zero, no resources are available, and the thread is blocked until it times out or a resource becomes available.

Applications for Semaphores

A semaphore is more flexible than a critical section because it enables a quantity of resources to be guarded, rather than enabling a single thread's access to a certain part of the code. For example, a typical exercise in multithreaded computing deals with allocating scarce resources to a group of consumers, as shown in Figure 3.9.

In Figure 3.9, a group of barbers is controlled using a semaphore. Initially, this semaphore is set with a maximum value of 3, to indicate that three barber resources are available. As customers enter the barber shop, the semaphore is decremented (see Figure 3.10).

FIGURE 3.9

Three available barbers controlled by a semaphore.

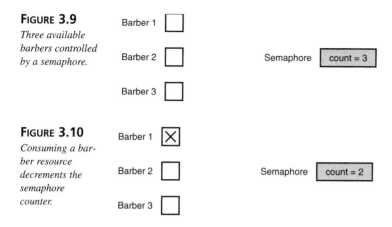

FIGURE 3.10

Consuming a barber resource decrements the semaphore counter.

As the semaphore is decremented for each new customer, eventually the semaphore's internal counter reaches zero, indicating that no barbers are available, as shown in Figure 3.11.

FIGURE 3.11

Blocking access to the barbers using a semaphore.

As a barber finishes with a customer, that customer releases the semaphore, thus allowing the internal counter to increase and one more customer to be served, as shown in Figure 3.12.

FIGURE 3.12

Releasing a semaphore enables a new customer to be served.

These are the basic steps in the lifecycle of a producer/consumer application. The barbers are "producing" haircuts, and the customers in line are "consuming" them. Later in this chapter, a dialog-based application that uses semaphores in a similar manner is introduced.

3

THREADS AND
PROCESSES

Creating Semaphores

A semaphore is created by calling CreateSemaphore:

```
HANDLE hsemBarbers = CreateSemaphore(NULL,
                                     0,
                                     5,
                                     NULL);
if(hsemBarbers == NULL)
{
    // Handle Error
}
```

The call to CreateSemaphore has four parameters:

- A pointer to a SECURITY_ATTRIBUTES structure. Using this structure is discussed later in this chapter.
- An initial value for the semaphore's counter. This value must be greater than or equal to zero.
- A maximum value for the semaphore's counter. This value must be at least 1; it must also be at least as large as the initial value for the counter.
- An optional name for the semaphore. Keep in mind that all event, mutex, and file-mapping objects use the same namespace, so you must take care not to reuse names. In most cases, this value is NULL.

Returning Semaphore-controlled Resources

When a semaphore-controlled resource becomes available, the resource counter must be incremented by calling ReleaseSemaphore:

```
BOOL fReleased = ReleaseSemaphore(hSemBarbers,
                                  1,
                                  NULL);
if(fReleased == FALSE)
{
    // Handle Error
}
```

The call to ReleaseSemaphore has three parameters:

- A handle to the semaphore to be released
- The number of steps the semaphore counter is to be incremented by
- An optional pointer to a long variable to hold the previous counter value (otherwise, NULL)

Using Semaphores and Critical Sections in an Application

As an example of using semaphores in a Windows 2000 application, a program named SkiLift can be found on the CD-ROM accompanying this book. SkiLift is a dialog-based application that displays the status of a group of skiers using a ski lift.

A semaphore controls access to the ski lift, enabling a maximum of four skiers at a time to use the lift. After reaching the top of the mountain, each skier takes a semi-random amount of time to enter the lift line at the base of the mountain. For the purposes of this demonstration, there's no shortcut line for the ski patrol. Figure 3.13 shows the SkiLift application in use.

FIGURE 3.13

The SkiLift application uses semaphores to control lift access.

The main dialog box for the SkiLift project contains two pushbutton controls and 20 checkbox controls, as shown in Figure 3.14.

FIGURE 3.14

Adding controls to the main dialog box for the SkiLift project.

Properties for the checkbox and pushbutton controls are listed in Table 3.1. All properties that aren't listed should be set to the default values. The checkbox controls must be assigned sequentially, with `IDC_CHECK1` through `IDC_CHECK8` in the first column, `IDC_CHECK9` through `IDC_CHECK12` in the middle column, and `IDC_CHECK13` through `IDC_CHECK20` in the last column.

TABLE 3.1 PROPERTY VALUES FOR CONTROLS IN THE SKILIFT MAIN DIALOG BOX

Control	*Resource ID*	*Caption*
Start button	`IDC_STARTSTOP`	`&Start Lift`
Status static control	`IDC_STATUS`	
Checkbox buttons	`IDC_CHECK1` through `IDC_CHECK20`	empty

The `SkiLift.h` file serves as the header file for the SkiLift project; it's provided in Listing 3.10.

LISTING 3.10 THE `SkiLift.h` HEADER FILE

```
struct CSkier
{
    int  m_nID;
    HWND m_hWnd;
};

BOOL InitApplication(HINSTANCE hInst);
BOOL InitInstance(HINSTANCE hInst, int nCmdShow);
LRESULT CALLBACK WndProc(HWND    hWnd,
                         UINT    uMsg,
                         WPARAM  wParam,
                         LPARAM  lParam);

BOOL CALLBACK DialogProc(HWND    hWndDlg,
                         UINT    uMsg,
                         WPARAM  wParam,
                         LPARAM  lParam);
void  OnStart();
DWORD WINAPI SkiThread(PVOID pv);
DWORD WINAPI Cleaner(PVOID pv);
void  WaitForLift(CSkier* pSkier);
void  GetOnLift(CSkier* pSkier);
void  SkiAWhile(CSkier* pSkier);
void  SetCheckBoxArray(UINT low, UINT high, BOOL fSet);
```

The main source file for the SkiLift project is found in `SkiLift.cpp`. The most relevant parts of this source file are shown in Listing 3.11.

LISTING 3.11 THE SKILIFT MULTITHREADED WINDOWS APPLICATION

```
BOOL        g_fLiftStopped = FALSE;
CSkier      g_rgSkier[8];
HANDLE      g_hChairLift = NULL;
HINSTANCE   g_hInstance = NULL;
HWND        g_hWnd = NULL;
LPCTSTR     g_szAppName = _T("SkiLift");

CRITICAL_SECTION g_cs;
    .
    .
    .
    .

void OnStart()
{
    HWND hWndStart = GetDlgItem(g_hWnd, IDC_STARTSTOP);
    if(g_fLiftStopped)
    {
        // It's time to open the lift - perform some
        // initializations
        g_fLiftStopped = FALSE;
        const int nMaxOnLift = 4;
        const int nMaxSkiers = 8;
        srand( (unsigned)time( NULL ) );
        SetWindowText(hWndStart, _T("&Stop Lift"));
        // Initialize the critical section used for the GUI,
        // and create a semaphore with four slots used for
        // the ski lift.
        InitializeCriticalSection(&g_cs);
        g_hChairLift = CreateSemaphore(NULL,
                                       0,
                                       nMaxOnLift,
                                       _T("ChairLift"));
        // Create eight skiers, each with its own thread.
        // Each of the skiers knows its skier number and
        // window handle.
        for(int n = 0; n < nMaxSkiers; n++)
        {
            g_rgSkier[n].m_nID = n;
            g_rgSkier[n].m_hWnd = g_hWnd;
            DWORD dwThreadId;
            HANDLE hThread;
            hThread = CreateThread(NULL,
                                   0,
                                   (LPTHREAD_START_ROUTINE)SkiThread,
                                   (void*)&g_rgSkier[n],
```

3

THREADS AND
PROCESSES

continues

LISTING **3.11**   CONTINUED

```
                                        0,
                                        &dwThreadId);
                CloseHandle(hThread);
        }
        // After all of the skiers have been created, release
        // all of the semaphore resources.
        ReleaseSemaphore(g_hChairLift, nMaxOnLift, NULL);
    }
    else
    {
        // We are stopping the lift. Create a "cleaner" thread
        // which will clean up all of the synchronization
        // resources. The start/stop button is disabled until
        // the cleanup process is completed.
        DWORD dwThreadId;
        g_fLiftStopped = TRUE;
        EnableWindow(hWndStart, FALSE);
        SetWindowText(hWndStart, _T("&Start Lift"));
        HANDLE hCleanThread;
        hCleanThread = CreateThread(NULL,
                                    0,
                                    (LPTHREAD_START_ROUTINE)Cleaner,
                                    (void*)g_hWnd,
                                    0,
                                    &dwThreadId);
        CloseHandle(hCleanThread);
    }
}


DWORD WINAPI SkiThread(PVOID pv)
{
    CSkier* pSkier = (CSkier*)pv;
    while(g_fLiftStopped == FALSE)
    {
        WaitForLift(pSkier);
        GetOnLift(pSkier);
        SkiAWhile(pSkier);
    }
    return NO_ERROR;
}

DWORD WINAPI Cleaner(PVOID pv)
{
    Sleep(10000);
    CloseHandle(g_hChairLift);
    // Restore the start button, and clean up the
    // status window.
    HWND hWndStart = GetDlgItem(g_hWnd, IDC_STARTSTOP);
```

CARMEN
MUSATESCU

```
        EnableWindow(hWndStart, TRUE);
        HWND hWndLabel = GetDlgItem(g_hWnd, IDC_STATUS);
        SetWindowText(hWndLabel, _T(""));
        DeleteCriticalSection(&g_cs);
        return NO_ERROR;
}

void WaitForLift(CSkier* pSkier)
{
        TCHAR szMsg[256];
        wsprintf(szMsg,
                _T("Skier %d starts waiting in line"),
                pSkier->m_nID);
        // Update status window with information about this skier, and
        // put a check mark in the lift line column.
        EnterCriticalSection(&g_cs);
        SetCheckBoxArray(IDC_CHECK1, IDC_CHECK8, TRUE);
        SetDlgItemText(g_hWnd, IDC_STATUS, szMsg);
        Sleep(100);
        LeaveCriticalSection(&g_cs);
        // Wait on the chair lift semaphore. If a resource is not yet
        // available, the thread will block here until one is ready.
        // If a chair is ready, it will be allocated to this thread,
        // and execution continues in the GetOnLift function.
        WaitForSingleObject(g_hChairLift, INFINITE);
}

void GetOnLift(CSkier* pSkier)
{
        TCHAR szMsg[256];
        wsprintf(szMsg,
                _T("Skier %d gets on lift"),
                pSkier->m_nID);
        // Update status window with information about this skier,
        // remove a check from the lift line column, and put a check
        // mark in the lift column.
        EnterCriticalSection(&g_cs);
        SetCheckBoxArray(IDC_CHECK1, IDC_CHECK8,  FALSE);
        SetCheckBoxArray(IDC_CHECK9, IDC_CHECK12, TRUE);
        SetDlgItemText(g_hWnd, IDC_STATUS, szMsg);
        Sleep(100);
        LeaveCriticalSection(&g_cs);
        // Spend a short (fixed) amount of time on the chair lift, then
        // return one chair lift resource. Execution continues in the
        // SkiAWhile function.
        Sleep(2000);

        EnterCriticalSection(&g_cs);
        SetCheckBoxArray(IDC_CHECK9, IDC_CHECK12,  FALSE);
        LeaveCriticalSection(&g_cs);
        ReleaseSemaphore(g_hChairLift, 1, NULL);
```

3

THREADS AND
PROCESSES

continues

LISTING 3.11 CONTINUED

```c
}

void SkiAWhile(CSkier* pSkier)
{
    TCHAR szMsg[256];
    wsprintf(szMsg,
            _T("Skier %d starts downhill"),
            pSkier->m_nID);
    // Move a skier from the lift line check boxes to the
    // skiing checkboxes. After updating the status display, hold
    // the status window for 100 milliseconds so it can be read.
    EnterCriticalSection(&g_cs);
    SetCheckBoxArray(IDC_CHECK13, IDC_CHECK20, TRUE);
    SetDlgItemText(g_hWnd, IDC_STATUS, szMsg);
    Sleep(100);
    LeaveCriticalSection(&g_cs);
    // Simulate skiing by sleeping a random amount of time
    // between 0 and 1999 milliseconds.
    Sleep( rand() % 2000 );
    // Finished skiing, clear one of the skiing checkboxes.
    EnterCriticalSection(&g_cs);
    SetCheckBoxArray(IDC_CHECK13, IDC_CHECK20, FALSE);
    LeaveCriticalSection(&g_cs);
}

void SetCheckBoxArray(UINT low, UINT high, BOOL fSet)
{
    UINT nResIndex;
    if(fSet)
    {
        // We are setting a check mark, find a clear checkbox.
        for(nResIndex = low; nResIndex <= high; nResIndex++)
            if(!IsDlgButtonChecked(g_hWnd, nResIndex))
                break;
    }
    else
    {
        // Clearing a check mark
        for(nResIndex = high; nResIndex >= low; nResIndex--)
            if(IsDlgButtonChecked(g_hWnd, nResIndex))
                break;
    }
    CheckDlgButton(g_hWnd, nResIndex, fSet);
}
```

Listing 3.10 defines a structure named CSkier, which represents each skier in the SkiLift project. In Listing 3.11, an array of eight CSkier structures are used in the SkiLift project. In addition, a CRITICAL_SECTION variable is used to synchronize control of dialog items. A semaphore handle is used to control access to the chair lift so that only four skiers are permitted to use the ski lift at any given time. Finally, a flag is used to indicate when the ski lift is running. When the ski lift is stopped, g_fLiftStopped is set to TRUE, and all running threads stop using the ski lift.

A total of seven functions control the multithread aspects of the user interface. The SkiThread function is used as a "thread start" function. This function is called by threads that represent skiers in the SkiLift project. These threads cycle through calling the WaitForLift, GetOnLift, and SkiAWhile functions. The SetCheckBoxArray function is used to check or clear checkboxes that indicate the current status of the application.

The Cleaner function is used to clean up the application before exiting.

Compile and run the SkiLift application. Click the Start Lift button. Eight checkmarks appear in the left column, representing eight skiers waiting in line for a ski lift. Four of the checkmarks immediately move to the center column, representing four skiers who enter the ski lift. When these skiers reach the top of the mountain, four more skiers enter the ski lift.

Each skier thread takes a random amount of time to reenter the ski lift line. After a few cycles of the lift line, the load balances out; however, the ski lift will always tend to be a bottleneck, just as in real life.

Using Job Objects

Windows 2000 introduces a new process-control primitive known as a *job object*. A job object is a collection of one or more processes that can be managed as a single entity. As you'll see in an example, you can set quotas for total execution time and processor time, as well as control scheduling options for the job object. You can also set processor affinity, control how processes in the job may interact with the Clipboard, and define security parameters for the job object.

Each job object is created by calling the CreateJobObject function:

```
HANDLE hJobs = CreateJobObject(NULL, _T("MyJobObject"));
```

CreateJobObject has two parameters:

- A pointer to a SECURITY_ATTRIBUTE structure, which can be NULL if you don't want child processes to inherit the job object.

- The name of the job object. This name can't duplicate any other kernel objects, such as events, mutexes, semaphores, file-mapping objects, and waitable timers.

After you've created a job object, other processes can obtain a handle to the job object through the `OpenJobObject` function:

```
HANDLE hJobs = OpenJobObject(MAXIMUM_ALLOWED, FALSE, _T("MyJobObject"));
```

`OpenJobObject` has three parameters:

- The desired level of access toward the job object. In this case, `MAXIMUM_ACCESS` requests full access rights. Other possible values are listed later.
- A flag that specifies whether the job object handle should be inheritable by child processes.
- The name of the job object.

Here are the possible access levels when a job object is being opened:

- `MAXIMUM_ALLOWED` requests the full access rights that are valid for the caller.
- `JOB_OBJECT_ASSIGN_PROCESS` requests rights to allow the caller to assign processes to the job object.
- `JOB_OBJECT_SET_ATTRIBUTES` requests rights to allow the caller to set attributes for the job object.
- `JOB_OBJECT_QUERY` requests rights to allow the caller to query job object attributes.
- `JOB_OBJECT_TERMINATE` requests rights to allow the caller to terminate the job object.
- `JOB_OBJECT_SET_SECURITY_ATTRIBUTES` requests rights to allow the caller to assign security attributes for the job object.
- `JOB_OBJECT_ALL_ACCESS` requests full access rights to the job object.

Processes are assigned to a job object after it's created with the `AssignProcessToJobObject` function:

```
BOOL fAssigned = AssignProcessToJobObject(hJob, hProcess);
```

`AssignProcessToJobObject` has two parameters:

- A handle to the job object
- A handle to the process to be added to the job object

Controlling Job Object Attributes

Each job object has a large number of attributes that you can control. All attributes for job objects are set via the `SetInformationJobObject` function:

```
BOOL fSet = SetInformationJobObject(g_hJobs,
                                    JobObjectBasicLimitInformation,
                                    &jbli,
                                    sizeof(jbli));
```

The `SetInformationJobObject` function has four parameters:

- A handle to the job object.
- An enumerated value that indicates which of five different sets of job object attributes you would like to change (options for this value are discussed later).
- A pointer to a structure that contains attribute information for the job object. This structure is one of seven different types, as discussed later.
- The size of the structure passed as the third parameter.

There are five different sets of job object information that can be changed; each of these sets is represented by a specific enumerated value that's passed as the second parameter in `SetInformationJobObject`. Each of the five information types also has a specific structure that must be filled in and passed as the third parameter:

- `JobObjectAssociateCompletionPortInformation`. Attribute information about associating the job object with an I/O completion port is passed in a `JOBOBJECT_ASSOCIATE_COMPLETION_PORT` structure.
- `JobObjectBasicLimitInformation`. Attribute information about quotas, processor affinity, and scheduling is passed in a `JOBOBJECT_BASIC_LIMIT_INFORMATION` structure.
- `JobObjectBasicUIRestrictions`. Attribute information about Clipboard use, access to user handles, and the ability to call certain Windows API functions is passed in a `JOBOBJECT_BASIC_UI_RESTRICTIONS` structure.
- `JobObjectEndOfJobTimeInformation`. Attribute information about the actions to be taken when the job object exceeds its time limit is passed in a `JOBOBJECT_END_OF_JOB_TIME_INFORMATION` structure.
- `JobObjectSecurityLimitInformation`. Attribute information about security limitations is passed in a `JOBOBJECT_SECURITY_LIMIT_INFORMATION` structure.

3

THREADS AND
PROCESSES

A Job Object Example

As an example of using job objects in Windows 2000, a project named JobObj can be found on the CD-ROM. JobObj is a console mode application that creates a job object containing Solitaire and FreeCell. JobObj receives feedback about the status of the job object through an I/O completion port.

The source code for the main source file in the JobObj project is provided in Listing 3.12.

LISTING 3.12 `Main.cpp`—THE MAIN SOURCE FILE FOR THE JOBOBJ PROJECT

```cpp
#define _WIN32_WINNT 0x500
#include <windows.h>
#include <tchar.h>
#ifndef UNICODE
    #include <stdio.h>
#endif

HANDLE CreateSolitaireProcess(void);
HANDLE CreateFreecellProcess(void);
void AssociateJobAndCompletionPort(void);
void SetJobLimits(void);

HANDLE      g_hCompletionPort;
OVERLAPPED  g_ov;
HANDLE      g_hJobs = NULL;

int _tmain()
{
    g_hJobs = CreateJobObject(NULL, _T("Unleashed JobObj"));
    AssociateJobAndCompletionPort();
    SetJobLimits();

    HANDLE hSolitaire = CreateSolitaireProcess();
    HANDLE hFreecell = CreateFreecellProcess();

    DWORD dwCurrentProcesses = 0;
    AssignProcessToJobObject(g_hJobs, hSolitaire);
    AssignProcessToJobObject(g_hJobs, hFreecell);

    /* Display messages for completion events.*/
    bool done = false;
    while(!done)
    {
        DWORD dwMsgId, dwKey;
        LPOVERLAPPED pov;
        LPCTSTR psz;
        GetQueuedCompletionStatus(g_hCompletionPort,
```

```
                                    &dwMsgId,
                                    &dwKey,
                                    &pov,
                                    INFINITE);
        switch(dwMsgId)
        {
            case JOB_OBJECT_MSG_END_OF_JOB_TIME:
                psz = _T("JOB_OBJECT_MSG_END_OF_JOB_TIME");
            break;
            case JOB_OBJECT_MSG_END_OF_PROCESS_TIME:
                psz = _T("JOB_OBJECT_MSG_END_OF_PROCESS_TIME");
            break;
            case JOB_OBJECT_MSG_ACTIVE_PROCESS_LIMIT:
                psz = _T("JOB_OBJECT_MSG_ACTIVE_PROCESS_LIMIT");
            break;
            case JOB_OBJECT_MSG_ACTIVE_PROCESS_ZERO:
                psz = _T("JOB_OBJECT_MSG_ACTIVE_PROCESS_ZERO");
                done = true;
            break;
            case JOB_OBJECT_MSG_NEW_PROCESS:
                psz = _T("JOB_OBJECT_MSG_NEW_PROCESS");
                dwCurrentProcesses++;
            break;
            case JOB_OBJECT_MSG_EXIT_PROCESS:
                psz = _T("JOB_OBJECT_MSG_EXIT_PROCESS");
                dwCurrentProcesses—;
                if(!dwCurrentProcesses) done = true;
            break;
        }
        _tprintf(_T("Job completion message - %s\n"), psz);
    }
    CloseHandle(g_hJobs);
    CloseHandle(g_hCompletionPort);
    MessageBox(NULL, _T("Finished"), _T("JobObj"), MB_OK);
    return 0;
}


/*
 * Creates a process for the Solitaire game, and returns
 * the process handle.
 */
HANDLE CreateSolitaireProcess(void)
{
    TCHAR     lpszSolitairePath[_MAX_PATH];
    PROCESS_INFORMATION pi;
    STARTUPINFO          si;

    ZeroMemory(&si, sizeof(STARTUPINFO));
    si.cb = sizeof(STARTUPINFO);

    GetSystemDirectory(lpszSolitairePath, _MAX_PATH);
```

3

THREADS AND
PROCESSES

continues

Windows 2000 Core Technologies

LISTING 3.12   CONTINUED

```c
    lstrcat(lpszSolitairePath, _T("\\SOL.EXE"));

    CreateProcess(lpszSolitairePath,
                    NULL,
                    NULL,
                    NULL,
                    FALSE,
                    0,
                    NULL,
                    NULL,
                    &si,
                    &pi);
    return pi.hProcess;
}


/*
 * Creates a process for the FreeCell game, and returns
 * the process handle.
 */
HANDLE CreateFreecellProcess(void)
{
    TCHAR   lpszFreecellPath[_MAX_PATH];
    PROCESS_INFORMATION pi;
    STARTUPINFO         si;

    ZeroMemory(&si, sizeof(STARTUPINFO));
    si.cb = sizeof(STARTUPINFO);

    GetSystemDirectory(lpszFreecellPath, _MAX_PATH);
    lstrcat(lpszFreecellPath, _T("\\FREECELL.EXE"));

    CreateProcess(lpszFreecellPath,
                    NULL,
                    NULL,
                    NULL,
                    FALSE,
                    0,
                    NULL,
                    NULL,
                    &si,
                    &pi);
    return pi.hProcess;
}

/*
 * Associate the job object handle with an I/O completion port, and
 * set an end of job action to post a notification to the
 * completion port.
```

```
     */
void AssociateJobAndCompletionPort(void)
{
    JOBOBJECT_ASSOCIATE_COMPLETION_PORT jacp;
    g_hCompletionPort= CreateIoCompletionPort(INVALID_HANDLE_VALUE,
                                              NULL,
                                              0x42,
                                              0);
    jacp.CompletionKey = NULL;
    jacp.CompletionPort = g_hCompletionPort;

    ZeroMemory(&g_ov, sizeof(OVERLAPPED));
    SetInformationJobObject(g_hJobs,
                    JobObjectAssociateCompletionPortInformation,
                    &jacp,
                    sizeof(jacp));

    JOBOBJECT_END_OF_JOB_TIME_INFORMATION  jeot;
    jeot.EndOfJobTimeAction = JOB_OBJECT_POST_AT_END_OF_JOB;
    SetInformationJobObject(g_hJobs,
                    JobObjectEndOfJobTimeInformation,
                    &jeot,
                    sizeof(jeot));
}

/*
 * Set a (very small) time limit for the processes in the job
 * object. In this case, 500,000 nano-seconds, which is about
 * two minutes in dog-years.
 */
void SetJobLimits(void)
{
    JOBOBJECT_BASIC_LIMIT_INFORMATION jbli;
    ZeroMemory(&jbli, sizeof(jbli));

    jbli.PerJobUserTimeLimit.QuadPart = 500000;
    jbli.LimitFlags = JOB_OBJECT_LIMIT_JOB_TIME;

    BOOL f0 = SetInformationJobObject(g_hJobs,
                    JobObjectBasicLimitInformation,
                    &jbli,
                    sizeof(jbli));
}
```

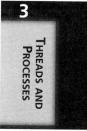

Compile and run the JobObj application from a command prompt. The job object will launch the Solitaire and FreeCell applications. As the processes are started, information messages will be displayed in the console window. You'll also see messages when the job object's time limit expires, as well as when the Solitaire or FreeCell processes are terminated.

Summary

This section discussed thread, synchronization, and security primitives. It also covered the methods used to create and manage threads and processes, as well as the pros and cons of creating multithreaded applications.

Finally, a few sample projects were used to demonstrate how threads and synchronization primitives are used together to create Windows 2000 applications.

Files

IN THIS CHAPTER

This chapter discusses how files are used in applications written for Windows 2000. You'll learn about the basics of file input and output (I/O) and then move on to more advanced topics, such as asynchronous file I/O and using file I/O completion routines. This chapter also discusses searching for files and subscribing to notifications about file system changes.

In addition, this chapter discusses the Encrypting File System, which is new in Windows 2000; it allows you to encrypt files on your hard drive.

 Along the way, several sample programs included on this book's CD-ROM will be presented, including examples that demonstrate how to use the Encrypting File System, asynchronous file I/O, file searching, and the file-notification functions.

Using Windows 2000 File Systems

Windows 2000 supports several types of file systems. Unlike some operating systems, each of these systems can be used on the same Windows 2000 installation. Also, the OS/2 High Performance File System (HPFS) no longer is supported. The file systems included with Windows 2000 are as follows:

- *The File Allocation Table file system (FAT).* Included for backward compatibility with MS-DOS and Windows files. FAT offers no security and has poor performance with large volumes. Also, minor errors can wipe out your entire volume. It has recently had several iterations of enhancements to make it more useful with today's larger disk sizes, but it's still the FAT file system.

- *The New Technology File System (NTFS).* Developed for Windows 2000. NTFS has excellent performance for large volumes. It also has excellent security and recovery functions. Windows 2000 includes new enhancements such as encryption and file quotas.

- *The Compact Disc File System (CDFS).* Included to support CD-ROMs, which are used in most Windows 2000 installations. In fact, most development tools, including Visual C++, are delivered on CD-ROM.

Performing General File Operations

Windows 2000 has a rich set of functions used to interact with files. The most basic of these functions create, open, read, write, and delete files. The next few sections cover these functions and how they are used.

Collecting Volume Information

Windows 2000 includes many different types of file systems. Each of these file systems has a different set of capabilities and features. In fact, just knowing the type of file system does not give you enough information to determine the features available on a specific volume. NTFS, the native file system used by Windows 2000, has been updated over the years to offer more features. Also, Windows 2000 systems can be configured to restrict features such as compression and file encryption.

To discover all sorts of information about a disk volume, including whether a particular feature is supported, you can call the GetVolumeInformation function:

```
BOOL fInfo = GetVolumeInformation(pszVolumePath,
                                  szVolumeName,
                                  _MAX_PATH,
                                  &dwSerialNo,
                                  &dwMaxComponent,
                                  &dwFileSysFlags,
                                  szFileSystemName,
                                  _MAX_PATH);
```

GetVolumeInformation has eight parameters:

- The path to the root of the volume.
- The address of a buffer that GetVolumeInformation will fill with the volume's label. If you're not interested in the volume name, you can pass NULL as this parameter.
- The size of the buffer passed in the second parameter (in characters, not bytes). This parameter is ignored if NULL is passed as the second parameter.
- The address of a DWORD that will be filled with the volume's serial number. If you aren't interested in the serial number, pass NULL as this parameter.
- The address of a DWORD that will be filled with the maximum size of filename components. This indicates the maximum size of text elements that make up a filename. If you aren't interested in the maximum component size, pass NULL as this parameter.
- The address of a DWORD that contains flags specifying the capabilities of the file system installed on the volume. The different values for the file system flags are provided in the following section. As with the other parameters, you can pass NULL as this parameter if you're not interested in this information.

- The address of a buffer that the function will fill with the name of the file system. As with the other parameters, you can pass NULL as this parameter if you're not interested in this information.
- The size of the previous parameter, in characters. This parameter is ignored if the previous parameter was NULL.

File System Flags

The following file system flags are returned from a call to GetVolumeInfo to indicate features available in the file system:

- FS_CASE_IS_PRESERVED. Files stored in the file system retain their original case.
- FS_CASE_SENSITIVE. Files can be stored with mixed-case names.
- FS_UNICODE_STORED_ON_DISK. Filenames are stored in Unicode on disk.
- FS_PERSISTENT_ACLS. ACLs are stored (and enforced) in the file system.
- FS_FILE_COMPRESSION. Individual files in the file system can be compressed.
- FS_VOL_IS_COMPRESSED. The volume is compressed.
- FILE_SUPPORTS_ENCRYPTION. Files stored in the file system can be encrypted.
- FILE_SUPPORTS_OBJECT_IDS. Object IDs can be stored in the file system.
- FILE_SUPPORTS_REPARSE_POINTS. Reparse points are supported by the file system.
- FILE_SUPPORTS_SPARSE_FILES. Sparse files are supported.
- FILE_VOLUME_QUOTAS. Disk quotas are supported.

Example

Listing 4.1 contains the source code for VolInfo, a console mode program that displays information about drive volumes accessible from your computer.

LISTING 4.1 THE VOLINFO PROGRAM DISPLAYS VOLUME INFORMATION

```
/*
 * VolInfo.c
 *
 * Retrieves volume information for a root directory passed on the
 * command line. For example, to check drive C:, use:
 *
 *    VolInfo C:\
 *
 * This example program is from "Programming Windows 2000
 * Unleashed", by Mickey Williams.
 */
```

```
#include <windows.h>
#include <tchar.h>
#ifndef UNICODE
    #include <stdio.h>
#endif

LPTSTR pszVolumePath;
TCHAR szVolumeName[_MAX_PATH];
TCHAR szFileSystemName[_MAX_PATH];
DWORD dwSerialNo;
DWORD dwMaxComponent;
DWORD dwFileSysFlags;

VOID Usage(VOID);

/*
 * A structure that defines file system flags and simple
 * descriptions. There is also a table that contains all
 * of the current flags.
 */
typedef struct tagVOL_FLAGS{
    DWORD dwFlag;    // File system flag
    LPCTSTR szDesc;  // Description of the flag
}VOL_FLAGS;

#define VOL_FLAG_COUNT 11

VOL_FLAGS flagTable[VOL_FLAG_COUNT] = {
    FS_CASE_IS_PRESERVED,_T("FS_CASE_IS_PRESERVED"),
    FS_CASE_SENSITIVE,_T("FS_CASE_SENSITIVE"),
    FS_UNICODE_STORED_ON_DISK,_T("FS_UNICODE_STORED_ON_DISK"),
    FS_PERSISTENT_ACLS,_T("FS_PERSISTENT_ACLS"),
    FS_FILE_COMPRESSION,_T("FS_FILE_COMPRESSION"),
    FS_VOL_IS_COMPRESSED,_T("FS_VOL_IS_COMPRESSED"),
    FILE_SUPPORTS_ENCRYPTION,_T("FILE_SUPPORTS_ENCRYPTION"),
    FILE_SUPPORTS_OBJECT_IDS,_T("FILE_SUPPORTS_OBJECT_IDS"),
    FILE_SUPPORTS_REPARSE_POINTS,_T("FILE_SUPPORTS_REPARSE_POINTS"),
    FILE_SUPPORTS_SPARSE_FILES,_T("FILE_SUPPORTS_SPARSE_FILES"),
    FILE_VOLUME_QUOTAS,_T("FILE_VOLUME_QUOTAS")
};

int _tmain(int argc, TCHAR* argv[])
{
    int ndx;
    BOOL fVolInfo = FALSE;

    if(argc != 2)
    {
        Usage();  // display usage information
        return 1;
```

4

FILES

continues

LISTING 4.1 CONTINUED

```
    }
    else
        pszVolumePath = argv[1];

    fVolInfo = GetVolumeInformation(pszVolumePath,
                                    szVolumeName,
                                    _MAX_PATH,
                                    &dwSerialNo,
                                    &dwMaxComponent,
                                    &dwFileSysFlags,
                                    szFileSystemName,
                                    _MAX_PATH);

    if(fVolInfo == FALSE)
    {
        DWORD dwError = GetLastError();
        _tprintf(_T("Failed due to Win32 error %X\n"), dwError);
        return 1;
    }

    _tprintf(_T("Information for %s:\n\n"), pszVolumePath);
    _tprintf(_T("The volume's name: %s\n"), szVolumeName);
    _tprintf(_T("The serial number: %X\n"), dwSerialNo);
    _tprintf(_T("The file system: %s\n"), szFileSystemName);
    _tprintf(_T("Filename component size: %X\n"), dwMaxComponent);
    _tprintf(_T("These file system flags have been set:\n"));

    for(ndx = 0; ndx < VOL_FLAG_COUNT; ndx++)
    {
        if(dwFileSysFlags & flagTable[ndx].dwFlag)
            _tprintf(_T("\t%s\n"), flagTable[ndx].szDesc);
    }
    return 0;
}

VOID Usage(VOID)
{
    _tprintf(_T("Invalid number of parameters \n\n"));
    _tprintf(_T("To check drive C:, use:\n"));
    _tprintf(_T("\tVolInfo C:\\ \n\n"));
}
```

To use VolInfo, pass a path as a command-line parameter. For example, to check drive C, use this:

```
VolInfo C:\
```

Information about the volume, such as the serial number, file system, and file system flags, will be displayed.

Opening, Closing, and Deleting Files

You open files by using the `CreateFile` function. You can use `CreateFile` to open existing files as well as new files. To open an existing file, you use the `OPEN_EXISTING` flag, as Listing 4.2 shows.

LISTING 4.2   USING `CreateFile` TO OPEN AN EXISTING FILE

```
TCHAR  szFile[255] = ("TestFile.txt");
HANDLE   hReadFile = CreateFile( szFile,
                                 GENERIC_READ,
                                 0,
                                 (LPSECURITY_ATTRIBUTES)NULL,
                                 OPEN_EXISTING,
                                 FILE_ATTRIBUTE_NORMAL,
                                 (HANDLE)NULL );
```

The return value from `CreateFile` is a file handle that identifies the created file.

> **NOTE**
>
> It's possible for a valid handle to have a value of 0; therefore, you must test the returned handle against `INVALID_FILE_HANDLE`, rather than 0 or `NULL`.

The parameters used by `CreateFile` specify the following:

- The name of the file (`TestFile.txt`, in the example in Listing 4.2).
- The read and write attributes for the file; in this case, the file is opened as read-only. Other values for this parameter are discussed later.
- The share mode attributes for this file; in this case, 0 prevents any file sharing. Other values for this parameter are discussed later.
- The security descriptor for this access of the file. This parameter has no effect when used on file systems that don't support security (such as FAT and CDFS, for example).
- A flag that states how the file should be opened; in this case, the call to `CreateFile` will open only existing files. Other values for this parameter are discussed later.
- A flag that specifies the file-level attributes for the file (in this case, `FILE_ATTRIBUTE_NORMAL`). Other values for this parameter are discussed later.
- An optional handle to a template file that specifies extended attributes for the file.

4

FILES

The parameter used to specify read and write permissions can be one or both of the following values:

- GENERIC_READ. Opens the file with read access
- GENERIC_WRITE. Opens the file with write access

If a value of 0 is used, the file is created or opened without read or write permission, and the file handle can be used to collect information about the file. Note that GENERIC_WRITE does not imply automatic read access. If you want both read and write access, you must specify GENERIC_READ¦GENERIC_WRITE.

The share attributes for the file can be 0, indicating that file sharing is not allowed, or one or all of the following flags:

- FILE_SHARE_READ. Indicates that other read operations can be performed on the file
- FILE_SHARE_WRITE. Indicates that other write operations can be performed on the file
- FILE_SHARE_DELETE. Indicates that any other attempts to open the file will fail unless delete access is requested

The most flexible of the CreateFile parameters are the flags that specify how the file will be created. Table 4.1 lists the possible values for CreateFile.

TABLE 4.1   PARAMETERS FOR CreateFile

Flag	Function
CREATE_ALWAYS	Creates a new file and overwrites the specified file if it exists.
CREATE_NEW	Creates a new file. This flag fails if the specified file already exists.
OPEN_ALWAYS	Opens the file, creating it first, if necessary.
OPEN_EXISTING	Opens the specified file. This flag fails if the specified file does not exist.
TRUNCATE_EXISTING	Opens the file and truncates its size to 0 bytes. The file must have been opened with write access.

The file attribute parameter can be a combination of one or more of the values shown in Table 4.2.

TABLE 4.2   FILE ATTRIBUTE PARAMETER VALUES

Parameter	Function
FILE_ATTRIBUTE_ARCHIVE	Indicates that the file is an archive file.
FILE_ATTRIBUTE_ENCRYPTED	Indicates that the file is encrypted, unless FILE_ATTRIBUTE_SYSTEM is also set, in which case this flag is ignored. For directories, this flag indicates that files are encrypted by default.
FILE_ATTRIBUTE_HIDDEN	Creates a hidden file or directory.
FILE_ATTRIBUTE_NORMAL	Used when no other flags apply. This flag is ignored if it's combined with any other flags.
FILE_ATTRIBUTE_OFFLINE	Indicates that the file data is located in offline storage that's not immediately available.
FILE_ATTRIBUTE_READONLY	Creates a read-only file.
FILE_ATTRIBUTE_SYSTEM	Marks a file as used by the operating system.
FILE_ATTRIBUTE_TEMPORARY	Marks the file as being used for temporary storage. Windows 2000 will try to cache the file in RAM.
FILE_FLAG_BACKUP_SEMANTICS	Used during backups or restore operations. An application also can set this flag to obtain a handle to a directory, which can be passed to some Win32 functions in place of a file handle.
FILE_FLAG_DELETE_ON_CLOSE	Notifies the operating system that it must delete the file immediately after all its handles have been closed.
FILE_FLAG_NO_BUFFERING	Specifies that the file must be opened with no intermediate buffering or caching, which can improve performance. If this flag is used, you must access the file in multiples of the file's sector size. You can get the sector size used by a volume with the GetDiskFreeSpace function.
FILE_FLAG_OPEN_NO_RECALL	Indicates that data should remain in remote storage, rather than being moved to the local drive in the case of Hierarchical Storage Management (HSM) file systems. An HSM file system moves infrequently accessed files to long-term storage and retrieves them as needed.
FILE_FLAG_OPEN_REPARSE_POINT	Immediately returns a file handle without involving the filter that controls the reparse point.

4

FILES

continues

TABLE 4.2 CONTINUED

Parameter	Function
FILE_FLAG_OVERLAPPED	Indicates that ReadFile and WriteFile operations will use an OVERLAPPED structure, and asynchronous file I/O will be performed using this file. This topic is covered in detail later in this chapter.
FILE_FLAG_POSIX_SEMANTICS	Indicates that the file will be accessed according to POSIX rules, which include case sensitivity on file systems that support case-sensitive naming. Files created with this flag might not be accessible by applications written for Windows 2000.
FILE_FLAG_RANDOM_ACCESS	Indicates that the file will be accessed randomly. This flag gives Windows 2000 a chance to optimize file caching.
FILE_FLAG_SEQUENTIAL_SCAN	Indicates that the file is to be accessed sequentially from beginning to end. This flag gives Windows 2000 a chance to optimize file caching.
FILE_FLAG_WRITE_THROUGH	Indicates that the operating system must write through any intermediate cache and write directly to the file. The file might be cached, but the file can't be placed into a lazy cache—bits must actually be touched out on the disk.

To close a file, use the CloseHandle function, like this:

```
CloseHandle(hReadFile);
```

After all open handles for a file have been closed, you can delete the file using the DeleteFile function:

```
DeleteFile(_T("Foo.txt"));
```

Writing to Files

You use the WriteFile function to write to files. Here's an example of using the WriteFile function:

```
WriteFile(hWriteFile, szBuff, dwRead, &dwWritten, NULL);
```

WriteFile has five parameters:

- The file handle to be written to.
- The address of a buffer containing the data to be written.

- The number of bytes to be written.

- A pointer to a DWORD that will contain the number of bytes actually written after WriteFile returns.

- An optional OVERLAPPED structure used for asynchronous write requests. (This parameter is discussed later in this chapter.)

In addition to WriteFile, Windows 2000 also offers the WriteFileEx function, which is used exclusively for asynchronous file output. The WriteFileEx function is discussed in the section titled "Using File-Completion Routines."

Reading from Files

You use the ReadFile function to read data from files. Listing 4.3 shows you how to use the ReadFile function.

LISTING 4.3   USING ReadFile TO READ DATA FROM A FILE

```
#define BUFFERSIZE = 0x1000;
BYTE buffer[BUFFERSIZE];
DWORD dwRead;
do{
    BOOL fRead = ReadFile(hReadFile,
                          buffer,
                          BUFFERSIZE,
                          &dwRead,
                          NULL);
    if(fRead == FALSE)
    {
        // Handle error
    }
    else if(fRead && dwRead)
    {
        // use data from file
    }
    else
    {
        // end of file detected
    }
}while(dwRead == BUFFERSIZE);
```

ReadFile has five parameters:

- The file handle to be read from

- The address of a buffer that will receive the transferred data

- The maximum number of bytes to be read

- A pointer to a `DWORD` that will contain the number of bytes actually read after `ReadFile` returns

- An optional `OVERLAPPED` structure used for asynchronous read requests. (This parameter is discussed later in this chapter.)

In addition to `ReadFile`, Windows 2000 also offers the `ReadFileEx` function, which is used exclusively for asynchronous file output. The `ReadFileEx` function is discussed later in the section titled "Using File-Completion Routines."

The console mode program shown in Listing 4.4 is an example of opening a file and reading its contents. After prompting a user for a pathname, the file is opened and its contents are displayed in the Console window.

LISTING 4.4   READING A FILE USING ReadFile UNDER WINDOWS 2000

```
#include <windows.h>
#include <tchar.h>
#ifndef UNICODE
    #include <stdio.h>
#endif

#define  BUFFERSIZE 0x1000
void DisplayError(LPCTSTR pszTitle);

int _tmain(int argc, TCHAR* argv[])
{
    // Get path name to file from user, and open
    // file as read-only.
    TCHAR   szFile[_MAX_PATH];
    HANDLE  hReadFile;

    _tprintf(_T("File name:"));
    _getts(szFile);

    hReadFile = CreateFile(szFile,
                           GENERIC_READ,
                           0,
                           (LPSECURITY_ATTRIBUTES)NULL,
                           OPEN_EXISTING,
                           FILE_ATTRIBUTE_NORMAL,
                           (HANDLE)NULL);
    if(hReadFile == INVALID_HANDLE_VALUE)
    {
        DisplayError(argv[0]);
    }
    else
    {
        // Read the file, one 4K chunk at a time, and display it
        // on the console.
```

```
            BYTE  buffer[BUFFERSIZE];
            DWORD dwRead;
            do{
                BOOL fRead = ReadFile(hReadFile,
                                      buffer,
                                      BUFFERSIZE,
                                      &dwRead,
                                      NULL);
                if(fRead == FALSE)
                {
                    // Handle error
                    DisplayError(argv[0]);
                    break;
                }
                else if(dwRead == 0)
                {
                    // Display eof
                    _tprintf(_T("\nEOF detected\n"));
                    break;
                }
                else
                {
                    // display data
                    DWORD ndx;
                    for(ndx = 0; ndx < dwRead; ndx++)
                    {
                        _tprintf(_T("%c [%#2.2hx]\t"),
                                 buffer[ndx],
                                 (USHORT)buffer[ndx]);
                    }
                }
            }while(dwRead == BUFFERSIZE);
        }
    CloseHandle(hReadFile);
    return 1;
}

/*
 * Displays an error message describing the last system error
 * message, along with a title passed as a parameter.
 */
void DisplayError(LPCTSTR pszTitle)
{
    LPVOID pv;
    FormatMessage(FORMAT_MESSAGE_ALLOCATE_BUFFER|
                  FORMAT_MESSAGE_FROM_SYSTEM,
                  NULL,
                  GetLastError(),
                  MAKELANGID(LANG_NEUTRAL,SUBLANG_DEFAULT),
                  (LPTSTR)&pv,
                  0,
```

4

FILES

continues

LISTING 4.4 CONTINUED

```
                NULL);
    MessageBox(NULL, pv, pszTitle, MB_ICONHAND);
    LocalFree(pv);
}
```

Searching for Files

Windows 2000 also allows you to search for files and directories located in the file system. Using these functions, you can perform powerful searches that can locate files and directories based on portions of their names or attributes.

Obviously, locating a specific file is much easier if you know its exact name and location, but there are times when a file search is useful. Some examples of applications that might need to search for a file are

- A utility that allows a user to search for a misplaced file.
- A program that searches for all instances of a particular type of file (files that have the TXT file extension, for example).
- A utility that looks for files that haven't been updated for a long period of time.

The Windows 2000 file-searching functions can be used to solve each of these problems.

Using FindFirstFile, FindNextFile, and FindClose

Three basic functions are used to locate files in a Windows 2000 application:

- FindFirstFile
- FindNextFile
- FindClose

FindFirstFile is used to find the first occurrence of a file that matches a particular search string. The function takes two parameters: the search pattern used to perform the search and the address of a structure that receives the search result. The function returns a handle that can be used to continue the search:

```
WIN32_FIND_DATA wfd;
HANDLE hSearch = FindFirstFile(_T("C:\\*.*"), &wfd);
```

If the search is successful, a valid handle is returned that can be used to continue the search. Information about the first file that matched the search string is placed into the WIN32_FIND_DATA structure that was passed as a parameter.

FindNextFile is used to continue a search that was started with FindFirstFile. The function takes two parameters: the handle returned from FindFirstFile and the address of a WIN32_FIND_DATA structure that will be filled if the search is successful. The function returns nonzero if the search succeeded or FALSE otherwise:

```
if(FindNextFile(hSearch, &wfd) != FALSE)
    _tprintf(_T("%s\n"),wfd.cFileName);
```

FindClose is used to close a handle that was opened using FindFirstFile:

```
FindClose(hSearch);
```

Listing 4.5 shows an example of how FindFirstFile, FindNextFile, and FindClose can be used. In this listing, a console mode program uses these functions to list all files with the .c extension in the C:\ directory.

LISTING 4.5   USING FindFirstFile TO SEARCH FOR FILES

```
#include <windows.h>
#include <tchar.h>
#ifndef UNICODE
    #include <stdio.h>
#endif

void DisplayError(LPCTSTR pszTitle);

int _tmain(int argc, TCHAR* argv[])
{
    WIN32_FIND_DATA wfd;
    HANDLE hSearch = FindFirstFile(_T("C:\\*.c"), &wfd);
    if(hSearch != INVALID_HANDLE_VALUE)
    {
        _tprintf(_T("%s\n"),wfd.cFileName);
        while(FindNextFile(hSearch, &wfd))
            _tprintf(_T("%s\n"),wfd.cFileName);
        FindClose(hSearch);
    }
    else
    {
        //File not found or other error
        DisplayError(argv[0]);
    }
    return 0;
}

void DisplayError(LPCTSTR pszTitle)
{
    LPVOID pv;
    FormatMessage(FORMAT_MESSAGE_ALLOCATE_BUFFER|
```

continues

LISTING 4.5   CONTINUED

```
                        FORMAT_MESSAGE_FROM_SYSTEM,
                        NULL,
                        GetLastError(),
                        MAKELANGID(LANG_NEUTRAL,SUBLANG_DEFAULT),
                        (LPTSTR)&pv,
                        0,
                        NULL);
    MessageBox(NULL, pv, pszTitle, MB_ICONHAND);
    LocalFree(pv);
}
```

As you can see in Listing 4.5, if a search is successful, the FindFirstFile and FindNextFile functions fill in a WIN32_FIND_DATA structure with information about files that were found. The WIN32_FIND_DATA structure is defined as this:

```
typedef struct _WIN32_FIND_DATA {
    DWORD     dwFileAttributes;
    FILETIME  ftCreationTime;
    FILETIME  ftLastAccessTime;
    FILETIME  ftLastWriteTime;
    DWORD     nFileSizeHigh;
    DWORD     nFileSizeLow;
    DWORD     dwReserved0;
    DWORD     dwReserved1;
    TCHAR     cFileName[MAX_PATH];
    TCHAR     cAlternateFileName[14];
} WIN32_FIND_DATA;
```

As shown here, the WIN32_FIND_DATA structure has 11 members:

- dwFileAttributes. One or more flags combined to indicate the attributes of the file or directory returned in the search result. The possible values for this parameter are discussed later.

- ftCreationTime. A FILETIME variable that indicates when the file was created. The FILETIME type stores time in UTC format and is discussed later in this section.

- ftLastAccessTime. The time the file was last accessed (stored as a FILETIME).

- ftLastWriteTime. The time the file was last written to (stored as a FILETIME).

- nFileSizeHigh. The upper 32 bits of the file size.

- nFileSizeLow. The lower 32 bits of the file size.

- dwReserved0. The reparse point tag, if one exists.

- dwReserved1. Not used.

- cFileName. The name of the file or directory found in the search.

- cAlternateFileName. The 8.3 name of the file or directory found in the search.
- dwAfileAttributes. Filled with one or more of the following file attribute flags (some of the following flags were discussed earlier in Table 4.2):
    - FILE_ATTRIBUTE_ARCHIVE. The file is an archive file.
    - FILE_ATTRIBUTE_COMPRESSED. The file or directory is compressed. If the search result is a directory, this flag means that, by default, all files stored in it are compressed.
    - FILE_ATTRIBUTE_DIRECTORY. The search result is a directory.
    - FILE_ATTRIBUTE_ENCRYPTED. The file is encrypted. For directories, this flag indicates that files are encrypted by default.
    - FILE_ATTRIBUTE_HIDDEN. The search result is a hidden file or directory.
    - FILE_ATTRIBUTE_NORMAL. This attribute is set when no other flags apply.
    - FILE_ATTRIBUTE_OFFLINE. The file data for this file is located in storage that isn't immediately available.
    - FILE_ATTRIBUTE_READONLY. The search result is a read-only file or directory.
    - FILE_ATTRIBUTE_REPARSE_POINT. The search result has a reparse point.
    - FILE_ATTRIBUTE_SPARSE_FILE. The search result is a sparse file.
    - FILE_ATTRIBUTE_SYSTEM. The search result is part of the operating system, or it's a file or directory used only by the operating system.
    - FILE_ATTRIBUTE_TEMPORARY. The file is being used for temporary storage. Windows 2000 will try to cache the file in RAM.

> **NOTE**
>
> You can use the FindFirstFile function to convert from an old-style 8.3 file-name into the true filename. Just call FindFirstFile with the 8.3 filename as the search pattern. Windows will return the full file name in the WIN32_FIND_DATA structure's cFileName member variable.

A Hint of Things to Come: `FindFirstFileEx`

You may be interested in searching for files based on information other than the file-name. For example, you may want to apply additional search criteria to a file search, such as returning only files that match a certain set of attributes.

The good news is that Windows 2000 includes `FindFirstFileEx`, a function that has extra parameters for additional control over filename searches. The bad news is that the function isn't completely implemented. By examining `FindFirstFileEx`, you can see that Windows 2000 will eventually allow powerful searches based on file attributes. However, in the current prerelease of Windows 2000 used when writing this book (beta 3), it's just a complex version of `FindFirstFile`:

```
HANDLE hSearch = FindFirstFileEx(_T("C:\\*.*"),
                                 FindExInfoStandard,
                                 &wfd,
                                 FindExSearchLimitToDirectories,
                                 NULL,
                                 FIND_FIRST_EX_CASE_SENSITIVE);
```

`FindFirstFileEx` has six parameters:

- The search pattern used in the search.
- A value that specifies the information level for the result returned in the search. The value must be taken from the `FINDEX_INFO_LEVELS` enumeration. The only value currently in the enumeration is `FindExInfoStandard`.
- The address of a buffer that will hold the search result. The function defines this parameter as a `PVOID`, with the actual type determined by the type of information requested in the second parameter. For `FindExInfoStandard`, this parameter is a pointer to a `WIN32_FIND_DATA` structure.
- The type of filtering to perform on the search, taken from the `FIND_SEARCH_OPS` enumeration. Possible values for this parameter are discussed later.
- A pointer to information that may be used in the future to pass detailed information about the type of filtering that must be performed on the search result. At the present time, this parameter must be `NULL`.
- Additional flags that can be applied to the search. Currently, the only defined flag is `FIND_FIRST_EX_CASE_SENSITIVE`, which is used to perform a case-sensitive search. If you want the default case-insensitive search, pass 0 here.

At the present time, only three possible `FIND_SEARCH_OPS` values can be passed as the fourth parameter:

- `FindExSearchNameMatch` performs the default search based solely on the search pattern passed as the first parameter.

- `FindExSearchLimitToDirectories` returns only directories that match the pattern passed as the first parameter. If the file system doesn't support directory filtering, you'll receive search results for all matching files; therefore, it's a good idea to check the attributes of returned filenames if you're not certain that the file system supports this operation.

- `FindExSearchLimitToDevices` is not currently supported.

Using the `FILETIME` Structure

As discussed earlier, the `WIN32_FIND_DATA` structure uses the `FILETIME` structure to hold times used in the file system. The `FILETIME` structure is used to track time in the file systems used by Windows 2000. A `FILETIME` instance tracks time according to Coordinated Universal Time (or UTC). Internally, `FILETIME` uses two `DWORD` variables to track the time in 100-nanosecond intervals since January 1, 1601:

```
typedef struct _FILETIME {
    DWORD dwLowDateTime;
    DWORD dwHighDateTime;
} FILETIME;
```

To convert the UTC time returned from `FindFirstFile` or `FindFirstFileEx` into a `FILETIME` structure that's normalized with your local machine time, call the `FileTimeToLocalFileTime` function:

```
FileTimeToLocalFileTime(&wfd.ftCreationTime, &ftLocal);
```

To reverse the conversion process and move from local time to UTC time, call the `LocalFileTimeToFileTime` function:

```
LocalFileTimeToFileTime(&ftLocal, &ftUtc);
```

To convert a `FILETIME` structure into easy-to-use date and time formats, use the `FileTimeToSystemTime` function, which moves the date and time information into a `SYSTEMTIME` structure:

```
SYSTEMTIME st;
FileTimeToSystemTime(&ftLocal, &st);
```

Listing 4.6 extends the example presented earlier in Listing 4.5 by using the `FILETIME` and `SYSTEMTIME` structures to display the creation date for each filename returned in the search.

LISTING 4.6   USING THE FILETIME STRUCTURE TO RETRIEVE THE FILE CREATION TIME AND DATE

```
#define _WIN32_WINNT 0x0400
#define WINVER      0x0400

#include <windows.h>
#include <tchar.h>
#ifndef UNICODE
    #include <stdio.h>
#endif

void DisplayError(LPCTSTR pszTitle);
void DisplayFileWithTimeAndDate(WIN32_FIND_DATA* pwfd);


int _tmain(int argc, TCHAR* argv[])
{
    WIN32_FIND_DATA wfd;
    HANDLE hSearch = FindFirstFileEx(_T("C:\\*.*"),
                                     FindExInfoStandard,
                                     &wfd,
                                     FindExSearchLimitToDirectories,
                                     NULL,
                                     FIND_FIRST_EX_CASE_SENSITIVE);
    if(hSearch != INVALID_HANDLE_VALUE)
    {
        DisplayFileWithTimeAndDate(&wfd);
        while(FindNextFile(hSearch, &wfd))
        {
            DisplayFileWithTimeAndDate(&wfd);
        }
        FindClose(hSearch);
    }
    else
    {
        //File not found or other error
        DisplayError(argv[0]);
    }
    return 0;
}

/*
 * Display file name and time information in a variety of
 * formats.
 */
void DisplayFileWithTimeAndDate(WIN32_FIND_DATA* pwfd)
{
    FILETIME   ftLocal;
    SYSTEMTIME st;

    if(!pwfd) return;
```

```
FileTimeToLocalFileTime(&pwfd->ftCreationTime, &ftLocal);
FileTimeToSystemTime(&ftLocal, &st);

_tprintf(_T("%s\n"), pwfd->cFileName);
_tprintf(_T("\tUTC time = %I64X\n"), pwfd->ftCreationTime);
_tprintf(_T("\tLocal time = %I64X\n"),ftLocal);
_tprintf(_T("\tSystem date = %2.2hd/%2.2hd/%4.4hd\n"),
            (WORD)st.wMonth,
            (WORD)st.wDay,
            (WORD)st.wYear);
_tprintf(_T("\tSystem time = %2.2hd:%2.2hd:%2.2hd\n"),
            (WORD)st.wHour,
            (WORD)st.wMinute,
            (WORD)st.wSecond);
}

void DisplayError(LPCTSTR pszTitle)
{
    LPVOID pv;
    FormatMessage(FORMAT_MESSAGE_ALLOCATE_BUFFER|
                FORMAT_MESSAGE_FROM_SYSTEM,
                NULL,
                GetLastError(),
                MAKELANGID(LANG_NEUTRAL,SUBLANG_DEFAULT),
                (LPTSTR)&pv,
                0,
                NULL);
    MessageBox(NULL, pv, pszTitle, MB_ICONHAND);
    LocalFree(pv);
}
```

Performing Other File Operations

Windows 2000 offers other file operations; the most commonly used are covered in this section. These include functions that copy files, set the current position of the file pointer, and get file size information.

Using CopyFile

You use the CopyFile function to copy the contents of a file from one location to another:

```
CopyFile(szSourcePath, szDestPath, TRUE);
```

CopyFile has three parameters:

- The pathname of the existing file.

- The pathname of the new file.
- A flag that indicates whether the function should fail if the destination already exists. If this flag is FALSE, the destination is overwritten. If this flag is TRUE, the function fails.

Using MoveFile

You use the MoveFile function to move a file from one location to another. You can rename a file using this function by specifying a new filename while keeping the same directory path:

```
MoveFile(szOldPath, szNewPath);
```

MoveFile takes two parameters:

- The current pathname for the file to be moved
- The pathname to the location the file is to be moved to

The MoveFile function fails if you attempt to move a file to a different volume.

Using SetFilePointer

In situations in which you use random file access, such as accessing a disk-based database, you must change the position of the file pointer. To move the file pointer to a new position, you use the SetFilePointer function, as shown in Listing 4.7.

LISTING 4.7   USING THE SetFilePointer FUNCTION

```
DWORD dwPos = SetFilePointer(hFile, dwOffset, NULL, FILE_BEGIN);
if( dwPos != 0xffffffff )
{
    // seek succeeded
}
```

In Listing 4.7, SetFilePointer is used to move to a known offset from the beginning of the file. SetFilePointer has four parameters:

- The handle to the file.
- The number of bytes to move the file pointer. If the value is positive, the pointer moves forward; a negative value moves it backward. Internally, Windows 2000 uses 64-bit values to move the file pointer. If the file pointer is moved more than 2^{31} bytes in one direction, you must use the next parameter for the higher 32-bit portion of the total 64-bit distance value.

- A pointer to an optional higher order word to move the file pointer. If this value is NULL, the previous 32-bit value is used to move the file pointer. If this value is not NULL, it's used as the higher 32-bit part of a 64-bit quantity used to move the file pointer. This is useful in cases in which your file sizes exceed 2^{32} bytes.

- A move method for the seek request—in this case, FILE_BEGIN, which moves the file pointer to a position measured from the beginning of the file.

Three values are possible for the move method:

- FILE_BEGIN. Specifies that the file pointer should be moved to a new position measured from the beginning of the file.

- FILE_CURRENT. Specifies that the file pointer is moved to a new position measured from its current location.

- FILE_END. Specifies that the file pointer is moved to a new location measured from the end of the file.

SetFilePointer returns 0xffffffff on failure. You can determine the cause of the error by calling GetLastError. When SetFilePointer is successful, the return value is the new file position. If the upper 32-bit parameter is not NULL, the DWORD variable pointed to by this parameter is filled with the higher order word for the new file position.

A special case can occur when you're dealing with file sizes greater than 2^{32}—sometimes 0xffffffff really is a valid value. When the 32-bit higher order word is used, GetLastError returns NO_ERROR if the return value is 0xffffffff and there is no error. Listing 4.8 demonstrates how to handle this case.

LISTING 4.8   PROPER HANDLING OF RETURN VALUES FROM SetFilePointer

```
DWORD dwLow = SetFilePointer(hFile, dwOffset, &dwHigh, FILE_BEGIN);
if(dwPos == 0xffffffff)
{
    if(GetLastError() != NO_ERROR)
    {
        // Handle error
        return;
    }
}
__int64 cFilePos = dwHigh;
cFilePos << 32;
cFilePos += dwLow;
```

If you use this function in a multithreaded application or with asynchronous I/O, you must be careful not to change the pointer while it's being used. Protect your calls to SetFilePointer using a CriticalSection or Mutex if necessary.

Using `GetFileSize`

You use the `GetFileSize` function to retrieve the size of a file:

```
DWORD cFile = GetFileSize(hFile, NULL);
```

`GetFileSize` has two parameters:

- A file handle
- An optional pointer to a `DWORD`, which stores the upper 32 bits of the file size if the file size can't be stored in a 32-bit value

`GetFileSize` returns the size of the file unless the file size cannot be stored in a 32-bit variable. If you're working with very large files that require 64-bit file sizes, you must pass a pointer to a `DWORD` that stores the higher order 32-bit value of the file size, if needed, and then convert the two `DWORD`s to a 64-bit quantity, as Listing 4.9 shows.

LISTING 4.9 HANDLING LARGE FILE SIZES WITH `GetFileSize`

```
DWORD dwHigh;
DWORD dwLow = GetFileSize(hFile, &dwHigh);
if(dwLow == 0xffffffff)
{
    if(GetLastError() != NO_ERROR)
    {
        // Handle error here
        return;
    }
}
__int64 cFileSize = dwHigh;
cFileSize << 32;
cFileSize += dwLow;
```

Using Asynchronous Input and Output

The one bottleneck that most Windows 2000 applications have in common is input and output. Unless you have a very simple application that never needs to read or write to a file, your application probably spends at least some of its time waiting for file I/O to be completed.

With Windows 2000, you can take advantage of asynchronous file routines that enable your application to continue working while the operating system handles your input and output. Under 16-bit Windows and MS-DOS, a call to an input or output function was blocked or had to wait until the request was satisfied. Because disk I/O is much slower than memory access, this means your program has to wait, as shown in Figure 4.1. This is known as *synchronous I/O*.

FIGURE 4.1

Synchronous file input and output.

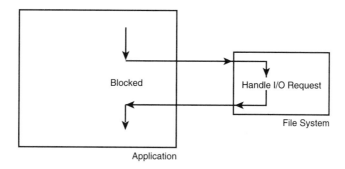

If you use the Windows 2000 asynchronous file routines, your application can continue to do other work while the operating system satisfies your I/O request, as shown in Figure 4.2.

FIGURE 4.2

Asynchronous file input and output.

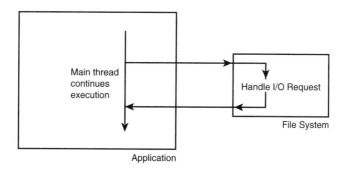

You'll achieve better overall performance by using asynchronous I/O because you'll use your processing power more efficiently.

Using Overlapped Input and Output

Windows 2000 offers an easy way for you to spin off asynchronous file input and output and perform other work while waiting for the I/O work to be completed. This sort of file I/O is called *overlapped I/O*, because other work can be performed while the operating system handles your I/O request.

Using overlapped I/O is useful in situations in which you know that data must be read to or written from a file, and you can structure your code so that other work can be done while waiting for the I/O to be completed.

Using the OVERLAPPED Structure

You use the OVERLAPPED structure to manage overlapped I/O. Because multiple reads and writes can be requested and can remain pending for relatively long periods of time, it can be difficult to keep track of the file location and other information related to the I/O request. You use the OVERLAPPED structure to track this information. The OVERLAPPED structure has five members:

- Offset. The lower 32-bit value specifying the read or write location.
- OffsetHigh. The upper 32-bit value specifying the read or write location.
- hEvent. An event handle that's alerted when the I/O request is satisfied. This enables you to create an event that is associated with this OVERLAPPED structure, instead of waiting on the file handle associated with the file. This approach allows multiple overlapped reads or writes to be performed at the same time.
- Internal. Reserved for operating system use.
- InternalHigh. Reserved for operating system use.

Two common mistakes are made when using overlapped I/O:

- Allowing the OVERLAPPED variable to go out of scope before the I/O request is satisfied.
- Failing to set OffsetHigh to a value. If this member is not used, it must be set to 0.

Looking at an Overlapped I/O Example

You need to follow five steps to use overlapped I/O:

1. Create a file handle using the FILE_FLAG_OVERLAPPED attribute.
2. Initialize an OVERLAPPED structure.
3. Perform a ReadFile or WriteFile function.
4. Sleep or wait for the file handle to be alerted.
5. Get the result of the I/O operation.

These steps are demonstrated in the console mode application provided in Listing 4.10.

LISTING 4.10 USING OVERLAPPED I/O IN A CONSOLE MODE PROGRAM

```c
#include <windows.h>
#include <tchar.h>
#ifndef UNICODE
    #include <stdio.h>
#endif

#define BUFFERSIZE 0x1000

int _tmain(int argc, TCHAR* argv[])
{
    TCHAR       szFile[_MAX_PATH];
    HANDLE      hReadFile;
    OVERLAPPED  ov;
    BYTE        buffer[BUFFERSIZE];
    DWORD       dwRead;

    // Get path name to file from user, and open
    // file as read-only.
    _tprintf(_T("File name:"));
    _getts(szFile);

    hReadFile = CreateFile(szFile,
                           GENERIC_READ,
                           0,
                           (LPSECURITY_ATTRIBUTES)NULL,
                           OPEN_EXISTING,
                           FILE_FLAG_OVERLAPPED,
                           (HANDLE)NULL);
    if(hReadFile == INVALID_HANDLE_VALUE)
    {
        MessageBox(NULL,
                   _T("Can't Open File"),
                   _T("Console File"),
                   MB_ICONHAND );
        return 1;
    }
    // Read the file, one 4K chunk at a time, and display it
    // on the console.
    ov.Offset = 0;
    ov.OffsetHigh = 0;
    ov.hEvent = NULL;
    do{
        BOOL fReadStarted = ReadFile(hReadFile,
                                     buffer,
                                     BUFFERSIZE,
                                     NULL,
                                     &ov);
        if(fReadStarted)
```

continues

LISTING 4.10   CONTINUED

```
        {
            DWORD ndx;
            for(ndx = 0; ndx < 10; ndx++)
                _tprintf(_T("Lah te dah\n"));
            // Wait for handle to be signaled
            WaitForSingleObject(hReadFile, INFINITE);
            GetOverlappedResult(hReadFile,
                                &ov,
                                &dwRead,
                                TRUE);
            // display data
            for(ndx = 0; ndx < dwRead; ndx++)
            {
                _tprintf(_T("%c [%#2.2hx]\t"),
                          buffer[ndx],
                          (USHORT)buffer[ndx]);
            }
        }
        ov.Offset += dwRead;
    }while(dwRead == BUFFERSIZE);

    CloseHandle(hReadFile);
    return 1;
}
```

The console mode program provided in Listing 4.10 opens an existing file using a name that's supplied by a user. Unlike the file I/O example shown in Listing 4.3, in this example the FILE_FLAG_OVERLAPPED attribute is used to open the file with an overlapped file handle.

Next, an OVERLAPPED structure is created and initialized. In this case, the file is read from the beginning—that is, stating offset 0. The OVERLAPPED structure and its offset information are updated after every iteration of the do/while loop.

The do/while loop has four parts:

- A call to ReadFile, in which the overlapped structure is passed to Windows 2000 and the file read is started.
- Work that's done while the operating system handles the file request (in this case, a few calls to _tprintf).
- A call to WaitForSingleObject, in which the thread waits for the file handle to become signaled. (A file handle becomes signaled when a pending I/O request is satisfied.)
- A call to GetOverlappedResult that returns the result of the file read.

Note that the call to ReadFile passes NULL instead of a pointer to a variable to hold the number of bytes read. This is because an overlapped call to ReadFile returns almost immediately, and the number of bytes read hasn't been determined. The call to GetOverlappedResult includes a parameter that determines the number of bytes actually read.

Using File-Completion Routines

A more sophisticated form of asynchronous I/O involves completion routines. A *completion routine* is a function that you specify to be called when your asynchronous I/O request is satisfied. When the thread that made the I/O request sleeps or waits in an "alertable" state, the completion routine is called to handle the completion of the I/O request. Figure 4.3 shows how this works in a typical Windows 2000 application.

FIGURE 4.3

Alertable file input and output using completion routines.

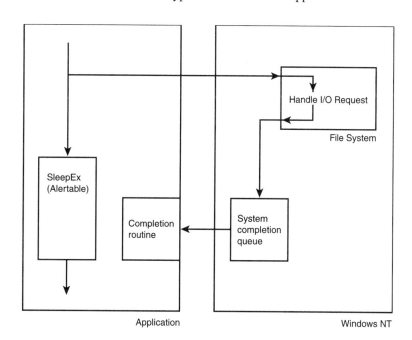

The completion routine is a callback function that follows the general form shown in Listing 4.11.

LISTING 4.11 TYPICAL FORMAT FOR FILE COMPLETION ROUTINES

```
void WINAPI ReadComp(DWORD dwErr, DWORD dwBytes, OVERLAPPED* pOv)
{
    if(dwErr == 0)
        // Handle completed I/O
    else if(dwErr == ERROR_HANDLE_EOF)
        // Handle end-of-file
    else
        // Handle error
}
```

Three parameters are required for a completion routine:

- An error code for the I/O request, if any. This variable is 0 if no error exists.

- The number of bytes written or read during the I/O request.

- A pointer to the OVERLAPPED structure passed to ReadFileEx or WriteFileEx.

To take advantage of completion routines, you must use ReadFileEx and WriteFileEx in place of the ReadFile and WriteFile functions. These functions accept an extra parameter that's used for the address of the completion routine:

```
BOOL fWrite = ReadFileEx(hWriteFile,
                    szBuffer,
                    dwWrite,
                    pOverlapped,
                    ReadCompletion);
```

Except for the extra parameter, the behavior of ReadFileEx and WriteFileEx is exactly like that for overlapped I/O using ReadFile and WriteFile.

Looking at an Example Using File-Completion Routines

As an example of using file-completion routines, this book's CD-ROM includes a sample program named AsynchCopy that copies a file using ReadFileEx and WriteFileEx. This program works exactly like the CopyFile function, but it shows how you can use file-completion routines and asynchronous I/O in a Windows 2000 application.

You can open this project as is, or you can create the project yourself using the steps presented in the next few sections.

Modifying the Main Dialog Box

AsynchCopy is a dialog box–based project with a progress control and three pushbutton controls added to the main dialog box, as shown in Figure 4.4.

FIGURE 4.4

The main dialog box for the AsynchCopy application.

Table 4.3 lists the resource IDs used by the main dialog box controls. The `Visible` property is cleared for the progress control; all other control attributes are set to their default values.

TABLE 4.3   CONTROLS USED BY THE MAIN DIALOG BOX

Control	Resource ID
Source button	IDC_SOURCE
Destination button	IDC_DEST
Copy button	IDC_COPY
Source label	IDC_LABEL_SRC
Destination label	IDC_LABEL_DEST
Progress control	IDC_PROGRESS

The `CAsynchCopyDlg` class has one new member variable that's associated with the progress control, as shown in Table 4.4.

TABLE 4.4   VALUES FOR THE CAsynchCopyDlg MEMBER VARIABLE

Resource ID	Category	Type	Name
IDC_PROGRESS	Control	CProgressCtrl	m_progressCtrl

Adding Message-handling Functions

There are three message-handling functions for the `CAsynchCopyDlg` class—one for each of the three button controls added to the dialog box. The values in Table 4.5 describe these message-handling functions.

TABLE 4.5   VALUES FOR NEW MEMBER FUNCTIONS IN CAsynchCopyDlg

Object ID	Class Name	Message	Function
IDC_SOURCE	CAsynchCopyDlg	BN_CLICKED	OnSource
IDC_DEST	CAsynchCopyDlg	BN_CLICKED	OnDest
IDC_COPY	CAsynchCopyDlg	BN_CLICKED	OnCopy

4

FILES

Modifying the `CAsynchCopyDlg` Class

The `CAsynchCopyDlg` has several new member variables and member functions that are used to implement the actual copying operations. These new members are shown in bold in Listing 4.12. Unchanged parts of the class declaration have been removed to save space.

LISTING 4.12 NEW CAsynchCopyDlg MEMBER VARIABLES

```
class CAsynchCopyDlg : public CDialog
{
    .
    .
    .
// Implementation
private:
    CString         m_szSourcePath;
    CString         m_szDestPath;
    HANDLE          m_hReadFile;
    HANDLE          m_hWriteFile;
    BOOL            m_fDone;
    DWORD           m_dwReadChunk;
    BYTE            m_buffer[4096];
    MY_OVERLAPPED m_overlapped;
    void WriteBuffer(DWORD dwWrite, OVERLAPPED* pOverlapped);
    void ReadBuffer(OVERLAPPED* pOverlapped);
    static void WINAPI ReadCompletion(DWORD dwErr,
                                      DWORD dwBytes,
                                      OVERLAPPED* pOv);
    static void WINAPI WriteCompletion(DWORD dwErr,
                                       DWORD dwBytes,
                                       OVERLAPPED* pOv);
protected:
    .
    .
    .
};
```

One of the variables in Listing 4.12, m_overlapped, is a MY_OVERLAPPED variable. MY_OVERLAPPED is a structure that has an OVERLAPPED structure as its first member. The second member of MY_OVERLAPPED is a pointer to the CAsynchCopyDlg object that "owns" the structure. This is necessary because you'll use static member functions as file-completion routines. By passing a pointer to MY_OVERLAPPED instead of OVERLAPPED to Windows 2000, you'll be able to find your way back to the instance of CAsynchCopyDlg performing the I/O.

Listing 4.13 provides the definition of MY_OVERLAPPED. This declaration is part of the project's AsynchCopyDlg.h file, located just before the class declaration.

LISTING 4.13 THE MY_OVERLAPPED STRUCTURE DEFINITION

```
struct MY_OVERLAPPED
{
    OVERLAPPED ov;
    CWnd* pWnd;
};
```

Three pushbuttons must handle user clicks in the main dialog box, and each of these buttons has a member function associated with it:

- OnSource. Creates a File Open common dialog box and collects a filename to be used as a source file for the copy operation.
- OnDest. Creates a File Open common dialog box and collects a file name to be used as a destination file in the copy operation.
- OnCopy. Opens the source and destination files and starts the copy process.

Listing 4.14 provides the source code for these three functions.

LISTING 4.14 MESSAGE-HANDLING FUNCTIONS FOR THE CAsynchCopyDlg CLASS

```
void CAsynchCopyDlg::OnDest()
{
    CFileDialog     fileDlg(FALSE);
    if(fileDlg.DoModal() == IDOK)
    {
        m_szDestPath = fileDlg.GetPathName();
        CWnd* pWnd = GetDlgItem(IDC_LABEL_DEST);
        ASSERT(pWnd);
        CString szTitle = fileDlg.GetFileTitle();
        szTitle += "." + fileDlg.GetFileExt();
        pWnd->SetWindowText(szTitle);
    }
}

void CAsynchCopyDlg::OnSource()
{
    CFileDialog     fileDlg(TRUE);
    if(fileDlg.DoModal() == IDOK)
    {
        m_szSourcePath = fileDlg.GetPathName();
        CWnd* pWnd = GetDlgItem(IDC_LABEL_SRC);
        ASSERT(pWnd);
```

4

FILES

continues

LISTING 4.14 CONTINUED

```
        CString szTitle = fileDlg.GetFileTitle();
        szTitle += "." + fileDlg.GetFileExt();
        pWnd->SetWindowText( szTitle );
    }
}

void CAsynchCopyDlg::OnCopy()
{
    m_hReadFile = CreateFile(m_szSourcePath,
                            GENERIC_READ,
                            0,
                            (LPSECURITY_ATTRIBUTES)NULL,
                            OPEN_EXISTING,
                            FILE_FLAG_OVERLAPPED,
                            (HANDLE)NULL );
    m_hWriteFile = CreateFile(m_szDestPath,
                            GENERIC_WRITE,
                            0,
                            (LPSECURITY_ATTRIBUTES)NULL,
                            CREATE_ALWAYS,
                            FILE_FLAG_OVERLAPPED,
                            (HANDLE)NULL);
    if(m_hReadFile == INVALID_HANDLE_VALUE)
    {
        AfxMessageBox(_T("Can't Open Source File"));
        return;
    }
    if(m_hWriteFile == INVALID_HANDLE_VALUE)
    {
        AfxMessageBox(_T("Can't Open Destination File"));
        CloseHandle(m_hReadFile);
        return;
    }

    m_progressCtrl.SetRange(0, 100);
    m_progressCtrl.ShowWindow(SW_SHOW);

    m_fDone = FALSE;
    m_overlapped.ov.hEvent = NULL;
    m_overlapped.pWnd = this;
    m_dwReadChunk = 4096;
    m_overlapped.ov.OffsetHigh = 0;
    m_overlapped.ov.Offset = 0;

    ReadBuffer((OVERLAPPED*)&m_overlapped);
    while(m_fDone == FALSE)
        SleepEx(INFINITE, TRUE);
```

```
    m_progressCtrl.ShowWindow(SW_HIDE);
    CloseHandle(m_hReadFile);
    CloseHandle(m_hWriteFile);
}
```

The OnSource and OnDest functions are straightforward; they use the Open File common dialog box to get source and destination filenames from the user and store the filenames in member variables.

The OnCopy member function is slightly more complicated. It attempts to open the source and destination files with the overlapped file flag. If the files are opened successfully, OnCopy initializes the progress control and makes it visible.

Next, m_overlapped is initialized, and the copy process is kicked off by a call to the ReadBuffer member function, followed by a call to SleepEx. The main thread sleeps until alerted by a completed I/O function. If the m_fDone flag is still FALSE, SleepEx is called again. This process continues until m_fDone is set to TRUE.

Several member functions are involved in the I/O processing in the AsynchCopy project, as shown in Figure 4.5.

Figure 4.5

Member functions used to process I/O in AsynchCopy.

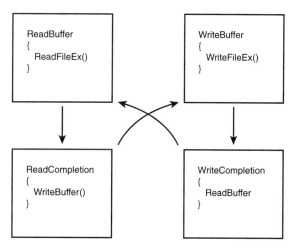

The ReadBuffer function calls ReadFileEx to read a buffer from the source file and specifies ReadCompletion as its completion routine. If the read is successful, ReadCompletion calls WriteBuffer to write the buffer contents. WriteBuffer calls WriteFileEx and uses WriteCompletion as its completion routine. WriteCompletion calls ReadBuffer, and the entire process starts again. If, at any time, an end-of-file marker is detected, the m_fDone flag is raised and I/O stops.

Listing 4.15 provides the source code for the remaining I/O functions.

LISTING 4.15   ALERTABLE FILE I/O FUNCTIONS FROM THE CAsynchCopyDlg CLASS

```
void CAsynchCopyDlg::ReadBuffer(OVERLAPPED* pOverlapped)
{
    int nPos = pOverlapped->Offset * 100;
    nPos /= GetFileSize(m_hReadFile, NULL);
    m_progressCtrl.SetPos(nPos);
    BOOL fRead = ReadFileEx(m_hReadFile,
                            m_buffer,
                            sizeof(m_buffer),
                            pOverlapped,
                            ReadCompletion);
    if(fRead == FALSE)
    {
        if(GetLastError() == ERROR_HANDLE_EOF)
        {
            // End of file
            m_fDone = TRUE;
        }
        else
        {
            TRACE(_T("ReadBuffer error = %l\n"), GetLastError());
            // Some other error
        }
    }
}

void CAsynchCopyDlg::WriteBuffer(DWORD dwWrite, OVERLAPPED* pOverlapped)
{
    BOOL fWrite = WriteFileEx(m_hWriteFile,
                              m_buffer,
                              dwWrite,
                              pOverlapped,
                              WriteCompletion );
    if(fWrite == FALSE)
    {
        if(GetLastError() == ERROR_HANDLE_EOF)
        {
            // End of file
            m_fDone = TRUE;
        }
        else
        {
            // Some other error
            TRACE(_T("WriteBuffer error = %l\n"), GetLastError());
```

```
        }
    }
}

void WINAPI CAsynchCopyDlg::ReadCompletion(DWORD dwErr,
                                           DWORD dwBytes,
                                           OVERLAPPED* pOv)
{
    MY_OVERLAPPED* pOverlapped = (MY_OVERLAPPED*)pOv;
    CAsynchCopyDlg* pDlg = (CAsynchCopyDlg*)pOverlapped->pWnd;

    ASSERT(pDlg);

    if(dwErr == 0)
        pDlg->WriteBuffer(dwBytes, pOv);
    else if(dwErr == ERROR_HANDLE_EOF)
        pDlg->m_fDone = TRUE;
    else
        AfxMessageBox(_T("Error in Read Completion"));
}

void WINAPI CAsynchCopyDlg::WriteCompletion(DWORD dwErr,
                                            DWORD dwBytes,
                                            OVERLAPPED* pOv)
{
    MY_OVERLAPPED* pOverlapped = (MY_OVERLAPPED*)pOv;
    CAsynchCopyDlg* pDlg = (CAsynchCopyDlg*)pOverlapped->pWnd;

    ASSERT(pDlg);

    if(dwErr == 0)
    {
        pOverlapped->ov.Offset += pDlg->m_dwReadChunk;
        pDlg->ReadBuffer((OVERLAPPED*)pOverlapped);
    }
    else if(dwErr == ERROR_HANDLE_EOF)
        pDlg->m_fDone = TRUE;
    else
        AfxMessageBox(_T("Error in Write Completion"));
}
```

Compile and run the AsynchCopy project. Select the source and destination files and copy a file to a new location. You might need to choose very large files; on my machine, anything smaller than 1MB barely shows the progress control. Figure 4.6 shows the AsynchCopy dialog box copying a file.

FIGURE 4.6

Copying a file with AsynchCopy.

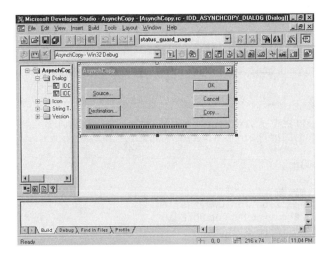

Taking Advantage of the Encrypted File System

One of the new features in Windows 2000 is the Encrypted File System (or EFS). EFS uses the Win32 Crypto API to encrypt the contents of a file so that they can't be viewed by an unauthorized person.

There are a couple of limitations to using EFS:

- EFS is not enabled unless there's a recovery key defined for the system. This makes it a little bit more difficult to encrypt a file and then forget how to recover it.
- EFS is only supported for the NTFS file system. If you're using one of the many flavors of the FAT file system, you're out of luck.

To create a file that's encrypted, use `CreateFile` with the `FILE_ATTRIBUTE_ENCRYPTED` flag. To encrypt a file that's already created, call `EncryptFile`:

```
BOOL fEncrypted = EncryptFile(pszTargetFile);
```

NTFS file compression and encryption are mutually exclusive. If you try to encrypt a compressed file, it will be automatically uncompressed.

There are two ways to determine whether a file is encrypted: You can check the file attributes by calling `GetFileAttributes`, or you can use the more direct `FileEncryptionStatus` function:

```
BOOL fStatus = FileEncryptionStatus(pszTargetFile, &dwStatus);
```

`FileEncryptionStatus` has two parameters:

- The file pathname
- The address of a `DWORD` that will be set to an encryption status value

The following values can be returned for the file encryption status:

- `FILE_ENCRYPTABLE`. The file can be encrypted but is not.
- `FILE_IS_ENCRYPTED`. The file is encrypted.
- `FILE_SYSTEM_ATTR`. The file is part of the operating system and can't be encrypted.
- `FILE_ROOT_DIR`. The file is a root directory and can't be encrypted.
- `FILE_SYSTEM_DIR`. The file is the system directory and can't be encrypted.
- `FILE_UNKNOWN`. The file has an unknown status.
- `FILE_SYSTEM_NOT_SUPPORT`. The file can't be encrypted because the file system doesn't support encryption.
- `FILE_USER_DISALLOWED`. This value is not currently returned but is reserved for future use.
- `FILE_READ_ONLY`. The file cannot be encrypted because it's read-only.

 As an example of how the file encryption functions are used, this book's CD-ROM includes Crypt, a console mode application that encrypts, decrypts, and checks the status of files.

The source code for `crypt.c` is provided in Listing 4.16.

LISTING 4.16 A CONSOLE MODE PROGRAM THAT USES THE ENCRYPTING FILE SYSTEM

```
/*
 * Crypt.c
 *
 * Allows a user to encrypt, decrypt, or query the encryption
 * status for files on an NTFS volume.
 *
 * Usage:
 *    Crypt {C|D|Q} filename
 *           C = Encrypt file
 *           D = Decrypt file
 *           Q = Query file encryption status
 *
 *
 * This example program is from "Programming Windows 2000
 * Unleashed", by Mickey Williams.
 */
```

continues

LISTING 4.16   CONTINUED

```c
#include <windows.h>
#include <tchar.h>
#ifndef UNICODE
    #include <stdio.h>
#endif

LPTSTR pszTargetFile;
TCHAR  chAction;        // see ACTION_*

#define ACTION_ENCRYPT 'C'
#define ACTION_DECRYPT 'D'
#define ACTION_QUERY   'Q'

VOID Usage(VOID);

#ifdef _UNICODE
#define TOUPPER(x) towupper(x)
#else
#define TOUPPER(x) toupper(x)
#endif


int _tmain(int argc, TCHAR* argv[])
{
    if(argc != 3)
    {
        Usage();  // display usage information
        return 1;
    }

    chAction = TOUPPER(*argv[1]);
    pszTargetFile = argv[2];

    switch(chAction)
    {
        case ACTION_ENCRYPT:
            if(!EncryptFile(pszTargetFile))
            {
                _tprintf(_T("EncryptFile failed!\n"));
                return 1;
            }
            _tprintf(_T("Encryption succeeded\n"));
            break;

        case ACTION_DECRYPT:
            if(!DecryptFile(pszTargetFile, 0))
            {
                _tprintf(_T("DecryptFile failed!\n"));
                return 1;
```

```
        }
        _tprintf(_T("Decryption succeeded\n"));
        break;

    case ACTION_QUERY:
    {
        DWORD  dwStatus;
        LPTSTR psz;
        if(!FileEncryptionStatus(pszTargetFile, &dwStatus))
        {
            _tprintf(_T("FileEncryptionStatus failed!"));
            return 1;
        }
        switch(dwStatus)
        {
            case FILE_ENCRYPTABLE:
            psz = _T("can be encrypted.");
            break;

            case FILE_IS_ENCRYPTED:
            psz = _T("is encrypted.");
            break;

            case FILE_SYSTEM_ATTR:
            psz = _T("is not encryptable - system file.");
            break;

            case FILE_ROOT_DIR:
            psz = _T("is not encryptable - root directory.");
            break;

            case FILE_SYSTEM_DIR:
            psz = _T("is not encryptable - system directory");
            break;

            case FILE_UNKNOWN:
            psz = _T("has unknown encryption status.");
            break;

            case FILE_SYSTEM_NOT_SUPPORT:
            psz = _T("is not encryptable - no FS support.");
            break;

            case FILE_READ_ONLY:
            psz = _T("is a read-only file.");
            break;

            default:
            psz = _T("has unknown encryption status.");
        }
```

4

FILES

continues

LISTING 4.16   CONTINUED

```
            _tprintf(_T("The file %s\n"), psz);
            break;
        }
        default:
        _tprintf(_T("Unknown action request. Must be C, D, or Q\n"));
        Usage();
    }
    return 0;
}

VOID Usage(VOID)
{
    _tprintf(_T("Invalid number of parameters \n\n"));
    _tprintf(_T("Usage:\n"));
    _tprintf(_T("\tCrypt {C¦D¦Q} filename \n\n"));
    _tprintf(_T("\tC = Encrypt\n"));
    _tprintf(_T("\tD = Decrypt\n"));
    _tprintf(_T("\tQ = Query encryption status\n"));
}
```

Compile and run `crypt.c`. You can encrypt, decrypt, or determine a file's encryption status by passing two parameters to Crypt on the command line:

- A command character—either C (for encryption), D (for decryption), or Q (for a query).
- The file or directory's pathname.

Using File-Notification Functions

Windows 2000 also allows you to request to be notified when files or directories are erased, updated, or created. When you request to be notified, Windows 2000 returns a handle. You can use this handle to determine when the notification has been made.

Three functions are used to implement file notifications:

- FindFirstChangeNotification
- FindNextChangeNotification
- FindCloseChangeNotification

FindFirstChangeNotification is used to open a handle to control the notification process:

```
HANDLE hNotify = FindFirstChangeNotification(szRootDir,
                                             fIncludeSubdirs,
                                             dwFilter);
```

FindFirstChangeNotification has three parameters:

- The pathname to the directory that will cause a notification to be created.
- A BOOL that specifies if subdirectories are included in the directories that are watched for changes. If this parameter is FALSE, only changes to the specified directory will result in a notification.
- A DWORD consisting of one or more filter values that specify events that will result in a notification.

Six flags can be used as filter values:

- FILE_NOTIFY_CHANGE_FILE_NAME. A filename in the directory has changed.
- FILE_NOTIFY_CHANGE_DIR_NAME. A directory name has changed.
- FILE_NOTIFY_CHANGE_ATTRIBUTES. A file or directory attribute has changed.
- FILE_NOTIFY_CHANGE_SIZE. The size of a file has changed.
- FILE_NOTIFY_CHANGE_LAST_WRITE. The last-write date for a file has changed.
- FILE_NOTIFY_CHANGE_SECURITY. A file security descriptor has changed.

If FindFirstFileNotification fails, it returns INVALID_HANDLE_VALUE. If it succeeds, it returns a handle that will be signaled when the notification occurs. If you're not familiar with WaitForSingleObject and WaitForMultipleObjects, it's enough for now to know that they allow you enter a low-cost wait state to wait for a handle to change its state to signaled:

```
WaitForSingleObject(hNotify, INFINITE);
```

WaitForMultipleObjects is used in a similar way, except that it allows you to wait for an array of handles. These functions are discussed in gory detail in Chapter 9, "Threads and Processes."

After you're notified about a change in the file system and you return from the wait function, you'll not automatically be notified about future changes unless you call FindNextChangeNotification:

```
BOOL fNotify = FindNextChangeNotification(hNotify);
```

FindNextChangeNotification resets the file change notification handle so that you'll be notified after the next change.

After you're finished using a file change notification handle, you must release it by calling FindCloseChangeNotification:

```
BOOL fClosed = FindCloseChangeNotification(hNotify);
```

4

FILES

The FileChange project builds a console-based application that watches for changes on the C:\ drive and all of its subdirectories. The complete source code for FileChange is provided in Listing 4.17.

LISTING 4.17   A CONSOLE MODE APPLICATION THAT DISPLAYS CHANGES TO THE C:\ FILE SYSTEM

```c
/*
 *  FileChange.c
 *
 *  Demonstrates file system change notification functions.
 *
 *  This example is from Programming Windows 2000 Unleashed
 *  by Mickey Williams.
 */

#include <windows.h>
#include <tchar.h>
#ifndef UNICODE
    #include <stdio.h>
#endif
#include "FileChange.h"

/*
 * Define a table that contains all of the file notifications
 * and descriptions.
 */
FN_ATTRIBUTES g_ntfyTable[NOTIFICATION_COUNT] =
{
    FILE_NOTIFY_CHANGE_FILE_NAME,
    _T("A file name has changed\n"),

    FILE_NOTIFY_CHANGE_DIR_NAME,
    _T("A directory name has changed\n"),

    FILE_NOTIFY_CHANGE_ATTRIBUTES,
    _T("A file or directory attribute has changed\n"),

    FILE_NOTIFY_CHANGE_SIZE,
    _T("The size of a file has changed\n"),

    FILE_NOTIFY_CHANGE_LAST_WRITE,
    _T("The last-write date for a file has changed\n"),

    FILE_NOTIFY_CHANGE_SECURITY,
    _T("A file security descriptor has changed\n")
};

HANDLE g_hndlTable[NOTIFICATION_COUNT];
TCHAR  g_szRootDir[] = _T("C:\\");
```

```
BOOL    g_fSubdirs = TRUE;

/*
 * Main program loop - initialize the change notification
 * handles, and hang in a loop waiting for notifications
 * to be signaled.
 */
int _tmain(int argc, TCHAR* argv[])
{
    __try
    {
        int ndx;
        ZeroMemory(g_hndlTable, sizeof(g_hndlTable));
        for(ndx = 0; ndx < NOTIFICATION_COUNT; ndx++)
        {
            SetFirstNotification(ndx);
        }

        while(1)
        {
            DWORD dwWait;
            dwWait = WaitForMultipleObjects(NOTIFICATION_COUNT,
                                            g_hndlTable,
                                            FALSE,
                                            INFINITE);
            if(dwWait != WAIT_FAILED)
            {
                int ndx = dwWait - WAIT_OBJECT_0;
                OnFileNotification(ndx);
                SetNextNotification(ndx);
            }
        }
    }
    __finally
    {
        FreeNotifications();
    }
    return 0;
}

/*
 * Subscribe to file notifications for a particular filter type.
 * The index to the filter type is passed as a parameter.
 * g_szRootDir contains the root directory for the notification,
 * and g_fSubdirs is TRUE if subdirectories are to be included
 * in the notification.
 */
void SetFirstNotification(int ndx)
{
```

4

FILES

continues

LISTING 4.17   CONTINUED

```c
        g_hndlTable[ndx] = FindFirstChangeNotification(
                            g_szRootDir,
                            g_fSubdirs,
                            g_ntfyTable[ndx].dwFilter);
        if(g_hndlTable[ndx] == INVALID_HANDLE_VALUE)
        {
            DisplayError(_T("SetFirstNotification: Invalid Handle"));
        }
}

/*
 * Re-subscribe to file notifications for a particular filter
 * type by passing the handle to FindNextChangeNotification.
 */
void SetNextNotification(int ndx)
{
    BOOL fNotify = FindNextChangeNotification(g_hndlTable[ndx]);
    if(fNotify == FALSE)
    {
        DisplayError(_T("SetNextNotification: FindNext failed"));
    }
}

/*
 * Release handles used for file change notifications.
 */
void FreeNotifications(void)
{
    int ndx;
    for(ndx = 0; ndx < NOTIFICATION_COUNT; ndx++)
        FindCloseChangeNotification(g_hndlTable[ndx]);
}

/*
 * Prints the description for a particular index in the file
 * change notification table.
 */
void OnFileNotification(int ndx)
{
    _tprintf(g_ntfyTable[ndx].szDesc);
}

/*
 * Displays an error message describing the last system error
 * message, along with a title passed as a parameter.
 */
void DisplayError(LPCTSTR pszTitle)
{
    LPVOID pv;
```

```
FormatMessage(FORMAT_MESSAGE_ALLOCATE_BUFFER¦
              FORMAT_MESSAGE_FROM_SYSTEM,
              NULL,
              GetLastError(),
              MAKELANGID(LANG_NEUTRAL,SUBLANG_DEFAULT),
              (LPTSTR)&pv,
              0,
              NULL);
    MessageBox(NULL, pv, pszTitle, MB_ICONHAND);
    LocalFree(pv);
}
```

Compile and run the FileChange project. If you move files on the C:\ drive, the changes will be displayed in the console window.

Summary

In this chapter, you learned how files are manipulated in Windows 2000 applications. You learned about creating, moving, and copying files. The functions used to search for files were also discussed. In addition, this chapter discussed file change notifications, which you can use to be notified when part of the file system is changed.

Synchronous and asynchronous file input and output was discussed, along with an MFC-based example that demonstrated how asynchronous I/O can be used as a method to improve program performance.

4

FILES

Structured Exception Handling

This chapter explains how you can use exception handling to make your Windows 2000 applications more robust. You'll learn about structured exception handling (SEH) offered by Windows 2000 as well as ANSI C++ standard exception handling. You'll also see how ANSI C++ exception handling and Windows 2000 SEH can be integrated with each other.

Looking at the Exception-handling Basics

Handling errors and special cases is a major cause of frustration for many programmers. Much of the code presented in examples in programming books or in sample programs deals with the *normal case*—code executed when a program is executed as expected. Adding source code that checks for errors often clutters a listing and makes it less clear. Listing 5.1 tests the return values of all function calls and handles errors by displaying a message to the user.

LISTING 5.1   HANDLING ERRORS BY TESTING RETURN VALUES

```
int ConcatStrings(TCHAR* pszDest, TCHAR* pszSrc, int cDest)
{
    TCHAR* pResult = NULL;
    if(pszDest && pszSrc)
    {
        int nDest = lstrlen(pszDest);
        int nSrc = lstrlen(pszSrc);
        if((nDest + nSrc) < cDest)
            pResult = lstrcat(pszDest, pszSrc);
    }
    if(pResult)
        return lstrlen(pResult);
    else
        return 0;
}
```

The general term *exception handling* refers to using mechanisms that separate error-handling code from source code executed in the normal case. These mechanisms help separate source code used for normal processing from the source code executed to recover from errors. Listing 5.2 shows an example of exception handling using Windows 2000 structured exception handling to deal with error conditions.

LISTING 5.2 DEALING WITH ERRORS USING STRUCTURED EXCEPTION HANDLING

```
int ConcatStrings(TCHAR* pszDest, TCHAR* pszSrc, int cDest)
{
    _ _try
    {
        TCHAR* pResult = lstrcat(pszDest, pszSrc);
        return lstrlen(pResult);
    }
    _ _except(EXCEPTION_EXECUTE_HANDLER)
    {
        return 0;
    }
}
```

As you can see, exception handling is useful because it helps preserve the flow of the essential source code by moving the error-handling code into a separate block. The second version of ConcatStrings will catch every error caught by the first version, but it uses less code and has a simpler construction.

When programming for Windows 2000, you have three exception-handling options:

- Use structured exception handling offered by the Windows 2000 operating system.
- Use ANSI C++ exception handling offered by your C++ compiler.
- Integrate the exception handling between Windows 2000 and your C++ compiler.

All three approaches are discussed in this chapter.

Understanding How SEH Works

When an exception is detected by Windows 2000, the executing thread is suspended immediately and processing shifts from User mode to Kernel mode. Control is transferred to the *exception dispatcher*, which is responsible for finding a way to handle the new exception.

If an exception handler isn't available for the exception, the exception dispatcher transfers control to a system-wide exception handler, which displays a dialog box similar to the one shown in Figure 5.1.

FIGURE 5.1

The standard dialog box displayed for unhandled exceptions.

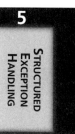

On the other hand, if an exception handler can be found, control is passed to it. Then the application, if it's coded to take advantage of exception handling, can handle the error gracefully. Even if you choose to terminate your application, catching exceptions enables you to

- Clean up data in external databases.
- Restore allocated resources.
- Send detailed information to the event log.
- Provide detailed failure information to the user to help debug the problem.

Any of these options is much better than displaying an application error dialog box to the user.

Using Termination Handlers

The most basic form of structured exception handling offered by Windows 2000 is the termination handler. A *termination handler* is a block of code that is guaranteed to be executed. Termination handlers often are used in situations in which memory or other resources must be freed before a function returns. Listing 5.3 shows how a termination handler is used to ensure that heap memory is released inside a function.

LISTING 5.3   USING A TERMINATION HANDLER TO GUARANTEE MEMORY IS RELEASED

```
BOOL SomeFunc()
{
    int*   p = 0;
    _ _try
    {
        // Use p in here
    }
    _ _finally
    {
        delete [] p;
    }
    return fReturn;
}
```

Here are the SEH keywords in the code fragment:

- _ _try. Marks the beginning of an exception try block.
- _ _finally. Marks the beginning of a termination-handler block.

The _ _try and _ _finally keywords are prefixed with double underscores, and are C/C++ language extensions. Other compilers may offer different keywords to take advantage of Win32 SEH.

Note that in Listing 5.3, the `return` statement is outside the _ _try and _ _finally blocks. This is good coding practice, and it encourages an easy-to-follow structure for your code. You can include `return` and `goto` statements inside a _ _try block, but the path of execution can become difficult to trace and your code's performance will suffer.

Listing 5.4 shows an example of source code that exits prematurely from a _ _try block.

LISTING 5.4 AN EXAMPLE OF THE WRONG WAY TO EXIT FROM A _ _try BLOCK

```
long CalcAndLogFactorial(int n)
{
    long  lResult;
    _ _try
    {
        if(n > 2)
        {
            for(lResult = 1; n > 1; n--)
                lResult *= n;
        }
        else
            return (long)n;
    }
    _ _finally
    {
        // Store result in log file.
    }
    return lResult;
}
```

If `CalcAndLogFactorial` is called with a parameter of 2 or less, the parameter value is returned from the function. For a larger value of n, the factorial is calculated as the sum of the product of all integers from 1 to n.

If the value of n is greater than 2, the factorial is calculated and execution flows through to the body of the _ _finally block. After the _ _finally block is executed, the factorial is returned by the `return lResult` statement. The flow of execution is more complicated for cases in which the value of n is 2 or less. First, the return value is stored; then the code inside the termination handler is executed. After the termination handler executes, control returns to the `return` statement, and the value of n is returned to the caller.

Whenever a premature exit from a _ _try block is detected, the termination block must be called. If the premature exit occurs due to a `return`, the `return` value is stored until after the termination handler executes.

This can lead to even more complex cases. Listing 5.5 shows a case in which the last `return` statement is inside the termination handler.

LISTING 5.5 USING return INSIDE A TERMINATION HANDLER

```
long CalcAndLogFactorial(int n)
{
    long  lResult;
    _ _try
    {
        if(n > 2)
        {
            for(lResult = 1; n > 1; n--)
                lResult *= n;
        }
        else
            return (long)n;
    }
    _ _finally
    {
        return lResult;
    }
}
```

In Listing 5.5, the return statement inside the _ _try block causes the termination handler to be called. The termination handler also contains a return, however. In this case, the return value from the _ _finally block is returned to the caller.

Obviously, all these twists and turns, caching and retrieving, come at a performance penalty. If possible, avoid premature exits from _ _try–_ _finally blocks.

Using_ _leave to Exit a_ _try Block

If you must exit a _ _try block, Windows 2000 offers a controlled way that's more efficient than using return. The _ _leave keyword enables you to make a controlled jump to the termination handler without incurring the extra overhead that results in a goto or return. The syntax is very simple:

```
_ _try
{
    ...
    _ _leave;
    ...
}
```

After a _ _leave is encountered, execution continues at the exception handler.

Using Normal and Abnormal Termination

When executing the code in a termination handler, you may need to know whether the termination handler was called due to an error or as a result of normal processing. There are basically two ways to reach a termination handler:

- The _ _try block was executed normally, and execution continued into the _ _finally block.

- An abnormal exit occurred due to a premature exit from the _ _try block, such as an exception or a goto or return statement.

The AbnormalTermination function returns FALSE if the termination handler was reached via normal execution. If an abnormal exit from the _ _try block was detected, AbnormalTermination returns a non-zero value. If the _ _try block was exited due to a _ _leave statement, AbnormalTermination returns FALSE, as shown in the console mode program provided in Listing 5.6.

LISTING 5.6   A CONSOLE MODE PROGRAM THAT TESTS FOR AN ABNORMAL EXIT USING AbnormalTermination

```
#include <windows.h>
#include <tchar.h>

int main()
{
    _ _try
    {
        _ _leave;
        _tprintf(_T("never\n"));
    }
    _ _finally
    {
        if(AbnormalTermination() != FALSE)
            _tprintf(_T("Abnormal termination\n"));
        else
            _tprintf(_T("Normal termination\n"));
    }
    return 0;
}
```

The program in Listing 5.6 displays Normal termination. If the _ _leave statement is replaced by return or goto, the program displays Abnormal termination.

The only way for you to avoid a termination handler is if you kill the currently executing thread. If abort is called inside a _ _try block, for example, the process is killed and the termination handler is never called.

Using Exception Handlers

Of course, the real highlight of structured exception handling is handling errors encountered while executing your program. SEH uses exception filters to determine how errors detected in your application should be handled. Two keywords are used when building an exception handler:

- _ _try. Marks the beginning of a guarded block, much as it is used in termination handlers discussed earlier in this chapter.
- _ _except. Marks the beginning of an exception filter that may be capable of handling an exception.

The syntax for an exception handler is similar to that used by termination handlers. In Listing 5.7, using *p generates an access violation, and control immediately is passed to the _ _except block. The string "Never got here" is not sent to cout.

LISTING 5.7   HANDLING AN ACCESS VIOLATION WITH AN EXCEPTION HANDLER

```
_ _try
{
    char *p = NULL;
    *p = 'A';
    _tprintf(_T("Never got here\n"));
}
_ _except(EXCEPTION_EXECUTE_HANDLER)
{
    _tprintf(_T("Caught exception\n"));
}
```

The value used with _ _except—in this case, EXCEPTION_EXECUTE_HANDLER—is an *exception filter* and is discussed in the next section.

Using Exception Filters

An *exception filter* indicates how your application will handle an exception. The filter is evaluated when control is passed to the _ _except clause in order to determine how the exception will be handled. The filter can have one of three values:

- EXCEPTION_EXECUTE_HANDLER. Indicates that the exception handler should pass control to the _ _except block, which takes responsibility for handling the exception. This symbol is equivalent to using a value of 1.
- EXCEPTION_CONTINUE_SEARCH. Indicates that this particular exception handler is not interested in handling the exception. The exception dispatcher should look further for an exception handler. This symbol is equivalent to using a value of 0.

- EXCEPTION_CONTINUE_EXECUTION. Indicates that the exception handler will handle the exception, and execution should resume at the instruction following the instruction that generated the exception. This symbol is equivalent to using a value of –1.

CAUTION

Take extreme care with EXCEPTION_CONTINUE_EXECUTION as an exception filter. In practice, it's often impossible to predict exactly what is "next" after the instruction that generates an exception.

Remember that Windows 2000 determines the next instruction, not the programming language you're currently using. Many assembly instructions may be generated for a single statement, particularly if you're using languages such as C++ or Visual Basic.

Handling Specific Exception Codes

One way to use exception handling is to just catch every possible exception raised in a particular function or even the entire application. It's much more likely, however, that you're interested in catching and applying some specific handling to a few specific exceptions. If you're interested in specific exception codes, you can use the GetExceptionCode function to retrieve the value of the current exception being handled, as shown in Listing 5.8.

LISTING 5.8 USING GetExceptionCode TO DETERMINE THE CURRENT EXCEPTION VALUE

```
_ _except(GetExceptionCode() == EXCEPTION_ACCESS_VIOLATION)
{
    _tprintf(_T("Caught access violation exception\n"));
}
```

This sample exception filter expression is TRUE for access violations. The exception filter expression evaluates TRUE as equal to EXCEPTION_EXECUTE_HANDLER.

The GetExceptionCode function can be called only from the exception filter expression, as shown in Listing 5.8, or from within the body of an exception handler.

If you're interested in testing for more complicated criteria when deciding whether to handle an exception, you must create a *filter function* and then call the filter function from inside the _ _except clause, like this:

```
_ _try
{
    // some guarded code here
```

5

STRUCTURED
EXCEPTION
HANDLING

```
}
_ _except(ExceptionFilter(GetExceptionCode()))
{
    // exception-handling code here
}
```

An example of an exception filter function that tests for access violations and divide-by-zero exceptions is shown in Listing 5.9.

LISTING 5.9 AN EXAMPLE OF AN EXCEPTION FILTER FUNCTION

```
int ExceptionFilter(int nException)
{
    int nReturn;
    switch(nException)
    {
    case EXCEPTION_ACCESS_VIOLATION:
        nReturn = EXCEPTION_EXECUTE_HANDLER;
        break;

    case EXCEPTION_INT_DIVIDE_BY_ZERO:
        nReturn = EXCEPTION_EXECUTE_HANDLER;
        break;

    default:
        nReturn = EXCEPTION_CONTINUE_SEARCH;
    }
    return nReturn;
}
```

Understanding the Exception Record Information

In addition to the exception code, you can to determine a wide range of information about the exception currently being handled. You can use the GetExceptionInformation function to return all the information you could ever need about an exception.

You can call the GetExceptionInformation function only from within the exception filter expression. The return value from GetExceptionInformation is a pointer to an EXCEPTION_POINTERS structure. This value usually is passed to a filter function that returns a value to be used by the exception filter expression.

The EXCEPTION_POINTERS structure is defined like this:

```
typedef struct _EXCEPTION_POINTERS {
    PEXCEPTION_RECORD ExceptionRecord;
    PCONTEXT          ContextRecord;
} EXCEPTION_POINTERS;
```

The EXCEPTION_POINTERS structure contains two pointers:

- ExceptionRecord. A pointer to an EXCEPTION_RECORD structure. This structure contains information about the exception currently being handled.

- ContextRecord. A pointer to a CONTEXT structure, which contains information about the CPU state. This structure is dependent on the CPU. Intel and PowerPC CPUs, for example, generate CONTEXT structures with different semantics.

The EXCEPTION_RECORD structure is defined as follows:

```
typedef struct _EXCEPTION_RECORD {
    DWORD ExceptionCode;
    DWORD ExceptionFlags;
    struct _EXCEPTION_RECORD *ExceptionRecord;
    PVOID ExceptionAddress;
    DWORD NumberParameters;
    DWORD ExceptionInformation[EXCEPTION_MAXIMUM_PARAMETERS];
} EXCEPTION_RECORD;
```

The EXCEPTION_RECORD structure has the following members:

- ExceptionCode. Indicates the reason the exception occurred. Possible values for the exception code are discussed in the next section.

- ExceptionFlags. Indicates whether the exception is "continuable." If this flag is 0, the exception is continuable. If this flag is EXCEPTION_NONCONTINUABLE, the exception cannot be continued. If you attempt to resume after a "noncontinuable" exception, an EXCEPTION_NONCONTINUABLE_EXCEPTION is raised.

- ExceptionRecord. Points to another EXCEPTION_RECORD structure that is chained to this record. This typically is done in case of nested exceptions.

- ExceptionAddress. Indicates the address where the exception occurred.

- NumberParameters. Contains the number of elements in the ExceptionInformation array.

- ExceptionInformation. An array of 32-bit values that describe the exception. Only one exception from Windows 2000 uses this array. If the exception code is EXCEPTION_ACCESS_VIOLATION, the first element of the array indicates whether a read or write operation caused the exception. A value of 0 indicates a read, and a value of 1 indicates a write.

The CONTEXT structure is defined as different structures for each type of processor that Windows 2000 runs on. Different versions of this structure exist for MIPS, Alpha, Intel, and PowerPC processors. If you're interested in the actual structure, you can find all four definitions in the winnt.h header file.

5

STRUCTURED EXCEPTION HANDLING

In practice, the CONTEXT structure rarely is used. It's so processor dependent that using it requires an in-depth knowledge of the CPU on which your application is actually running. The different versions of the CONTEXT structure are very long—they serve to document the state of the processor when the exception was raised.

Using Exception Codes

The following list of exception codes can be raised by Windows 2000 while your application is executing:

- EXCEPTION_ACCESS_VIOLATION. Indicates that the thread attempted to read from or write to a virtual address without the appropriate access.
- EXCEPTION_BREAKPOINT. Indicates that a debugging breakpoint was encountered while executing the program. This exception is only useful to debuggers.
- EXCEPTION_DATATYPE_MISALIGNMENT. Raised when a thread attempts to read or write misaligned data. On some non-Intel processors, data must be properly aligned. For example, a long integer may be required to be aligned on an even address boundary. Because Windows 2000 automatically fixes alignment errors for you (although at a large performance cost), you won't see this exception.
- EXCEPTION_SINGLE_STEP. Indicates that a trace trap or other single-instruction mechanism signaled that one instruction was executed.
- EXCEPTION_ARRAY_BOUNDS_EXCEEDED. Thrown when a thread attempts to access an array element that's out of bounds when using hardware that supports bounds checking.
- EXCEPTION_FLT_DENORMAL_OPERAND. Indicates that one of the operands in a floating-point operation is too small to represent as a standard floating-point value.
- EXCEPTION_FLT_DIVIDE_BY_ZERO. Indicates that the thread attempted to divide a floating-point value by a floating-point divisor of zero.
- EXCEPTION_FLT_INEXACT_RESULT. Indicates that the result of a floating-point operation cannot be represented exactly as a decimal fraction.
- EXCEPTION_FLT_INVALID_OPERATION. Indicates that a floating-point exception (other than the types listed here) has occurred.
- EXCEPTION_FLT_OVERFLOW. Indicates that the exponent of a floating-point operation is greater than the magnitude allowed by the corresponding type.
- EXCEPTION_FLT_STACK_CHECK. Indicates that the stack overflowed or underflowed due to a floating-point operation.
- EXCEPTION_FLT_UNDERFLOW. Indicates that the exponent of a floating-point operation is less than the magnitude allowed by the corresponding type.

- EXCEPTION_INT_DIVIDE_BY_ZERO. Indicates that the thread attempted to divide an integer value by 0.

- EXCEPTION_INT_OVERFLOW. Indicates that the result of an integer operation caused an overflow in the result register. The processor's "carry flag" will contain the most significant bit of the result.

- EXCEPTION_PRIV_INSTRUCTION. Indicates that the thread attempted to execute an instruction for which the operation is not allowed in the current machine mode.

- EXCEPTION_NONCONTINUABLE_EXCEPTION. Indicates that the thread attempted to continue execution after a noncontinuable exception occurred.

Handling Floating-Point Exceptions

By default, floating-point exceptions are not raised. Instead, predefined error values, such as NAN and INFINITY, are returned when error cases are detected. To enable floating-point exceptions, you must use the _controlfp function. The following code, for example, enables EXCEPTION_FLT_DIVIDE_BY_ZERO exceptions:

```
int n = _controlfp(0,0);
n &= ~EM_ZERODIVIDE;
_controlfp(n, MCW_EM);
```

> **NOTE**
>
> There's also a _control87 function, which is much like _controlfp, except it's specific to the Intel *x*86 processor. If you're writing portable code, you should use _controlfp instead of _control87.

Table 5.1 lists the five flags for enabling floating-point exceptions.

TABLE 5.1   FLAGS USED TO ENABLE FLOATING-POINT EXCEPTIONS

Flag	*Enables*
EM_OVERFLOW	EXCEPTION_FLT_OVERFLOW
EM_UNDERFLOW	EXCEPTION_FLT_UNDERFLOW
EM_INEXACT	EXCEPTION_FLT_INEXACT_RESULT
EM_ZERODIVIDE	EXCEPTION_FLT_DIVIDE_BY_ZERO
EM_DENORMAL	EXCEPTION_FLT_DENORMAL_OPERAND

To use more than one of these flags, you can combine them using the ¦ operator.

When a floating-point exception is caught, you must use the _clearfp function to clear the floating-point exception flag. You must clear this flag before you perform any additional floating-point calculations. Listing 5.10 shows an example of enabling and handling floating-point exceptions.

LISTING 5.10   ENABLING AND HANDLING FLOATING-POINT EXCEPTIONS

```
double CalcAverageRate(double* pdTotal, double* pdTime)
{
    double dResult;

    int n = _controlfp(0,0);
    n &= ~EM_ZERODIVIDE;
    _controlfp(n, MCW_EM);

    __try
    {
        dResult = *pdTotal / *pdTime;
    }
    __except(EXCEPTION_EXECUTE_HANDLER)
    {
        dResult = 0.0;
        _clearfp();
    }
    return dResult;
}
```

C++ Exception Handling

So far, this chapter has focused on the structured exception handling offered in Windows 2000. If you're using C++ to write your applications, you also can take advantage of the exception-handling capabilities that are part of the C++ language specification.

Using Exceptions to Detect Errors

The general idea behind C++ exception handling is similar to that of structured exception handling: A section of code that fails can throw (or raise) an exception that can be caught by an exception handler. The simplest example is when an exception is handled within a single function, as Listing 5.11 shows.

LISTING 5.11 THROWING AND CATCHING A C++ EXCEPTION INSIDE A SINGLE FUNCTION

```
int Divide(int n1, int n2)
{
    int nReturn = 0;
    try
    {
        if(!n2) throw range_error();
        nReturn = n1/n2;
    }
    catch(range_error& e)
    {
        cout << "Caught divide by zero attempt" << endl;
    }
    return nReturn;
}
```

The try keyword marks the beginning of a try block. Inside a try block, any exceptions that are thrown are handled by exception handlers that follow the try block. An exception handler specifies the exceptions that it handles by using the catch keyword. A single try block may throw several types of exceptions, as Listing 5.12 shows.

LISTING 5.12 THROWING MULTIPLE EXCEPTIONS FROM A SINGLE try BLOCK

```
try
{
    if(nIndex < 0)
        throw range_error();
    else if(nIndex >= m_cbText)
        throw range_error();
    else if(check_lock(nIndex) == CL_LOCKED)
        throw "Element is locked";


    .
    . Normal processing
    .
}
catch(const char* psz)
{
    cout << *pszErr << endl;
}
catch(logic_error& e)
{
    cout << e.what() << endl;
}
```

In Listing 5.12, a pointer to char is thrown to the exception handler. The result of the throw expression is used to evaluate which catch clause should be used to resume processing.

Normally, a function throws exceptions intended to be caught by the calling function. If no suitable `catch` expression can be found in the calling function, the next higher-level function is checked for a `try` block and a suitable exception handler. If no exception handler can be found, a special high-level function named `terminate` is called. This function normally terminates the program.

A `catch` expression matches the thrown exception if it's an exact match for the thrown object. The standard conversions also are allowed; for example, a pointer to a base class catches a pointer to a derived class. A `catch` expression that contains an ellipsis (…) catches all exceptions. The block of code following a `catch` expression is called a `catch` block and must be enclosed in curly braces.

Using Exceptions to Clean Up After Errors Are Detected

When an exception is thrown, any objects that have been fully constructed are guaranteed to be destroyed properly. This is potentially one of the big benefits of using exception handling, because it ensures that your program cleans up properly, even in error conditions.

However, if you use old-fashioned C-style pointers to point to other dynamically created objects, the dynamic objects will not be automatically released when an exception is detected. For example, the code in Listing 5.13 will result in a memory leak.

LISTING 5.13   THE WRONG WAY TO HANDLE DYNAMIC DATA WITH C++ EXCEPTIONS

```
void CreateSomeMemoryLeaks()
{
    try
    {
        CFoo* pFoo = new CFoo;
        CBar* pBar = new CBar;
        CreateException(); // exceptions created here!
        delete pFoo;
        delete pBar;
    }
    catch(...)
    {
        // Cleanup here
    }
}
```

If the `CreateException` function creates an exception, the calls to delete the dynamic objects that `pFoo` and `pBar` point to will be bypassed. From the C++ language's point of view, pFoo and pBar are not objects—instead, they are simply pointers to objects. The pointers do not have destructors and will not be automatically cleaned up if an exception occurs.

In order to avoid this problem, the C++ standard library includes the auto_ptr class, a "smart pointer" class that mimics a pointer. Because auto_ptr is a C++ class, it will be destroyed at the appropriate time in the presence of exceptions. In turn, the auto_ptr destructor will delete any dynamic objects that auto_ptr points to.

Using auto_ptr also reduces the amount of code you need to write. Because the auto_ptr destructor automatically deletes its dynamic objects, you don't need to explicitly call delete. As the auto_ptr goes out of scope, its destructor will be called, and any dynamically created object will be freed.

Rewriting the previous example to use auto_ptr, as shown in Listing 5.14, results in less code as well as a function that is guaranteed to release its dynamic data, even if an exception occurs.

LISTING 5.14   USING auto_ptr TO AVOID MEMORY LEAKS

```
void DontCreateMemoryLeaks()
{
    try
    {
        auto_ptr<CFoo> pFoo = new CFoo;
        auto_ptr<CBar> pBar = new CBar;
        CreateException(); // exceptions created here!
    }
    catch(...)
    {
        // Cleanup here
    }
}
```

Using the Standard Exception Library

The Standard Exception Library is part of the ANSI C++ Draft Standard. It defines a hierarchy of exception types that can be thrown to indicate an exception condition. The only mandatory exception is bad_alloc, which is thrown to indicate a failed request for memory allocation. The ANSI draft requires a conforming implementation of C++ to throw bad_alloc instead of returning 0 for the allocation request.

Other than bad_alloc, there is no requirement that these exception types be used; as shown in earlier examples, any type of object can be thrown as an exception. A standard set of exceptions helps to provide an easy way to handle exceptions thrown by code written by others, however. Figure 5.2 shows the ANSI C++ exception hierarchy.

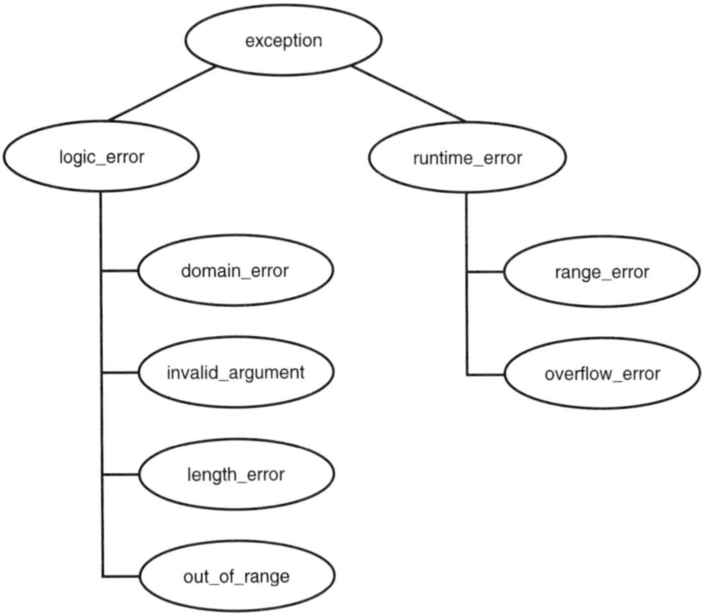

Figure 5.2

*The ANSI C++
Standard
Exception Library.*

The standard exception hierarchy is divided into two sections:

- Runtime errors. Indicate problems that are not possible to predict—for example, lack of memory or hardware failure.
- Logic errors. Indicate a problem with function processing, such as illegal function parameter values or other preconditions.

Using Runtime Exceptions

Runtime exceptions normally are used to indicate problems that have occurred outside the program's control. Problems with hardware, lack of memory, or other resources are examples of runtime errors. These problems generally are difficult, if not impossible, to predict when the program is compiled.

When a runtime error is encountered, it's often possible to take some sort of alternative action without terminating the current process. If memory cannot be allocated, it may be possible to process an operation differently. Likewise, if a disk is full, you might want to ask the user to take some action and then try the operation again.

All runtime exception classes included in the Standard Exception Library are derived from `runtime_error`. Any runtime exception can be caught by specifying `runtime_error` in the `catch` expression, as shown in Listing 5.15.

LISTING 5.15   THROWING AND CATCHING A runtime_error EXCEPTION

```
void SomeFunc()
{
    try
    {
        char szDest[] = "Hello";
        char szSrc[] = "World";
        Concatenate(szDest, sizeof(szDest), szSrc);
    }
    catch(runtime_error e)
    {
        cout << e.what() << endl;
    }
}

void Concatenate(char szDest[], int nSize, char szSrc[])
{
    int nStrlen = lstrlen(szSrc) + lstrlen(szDest);
    if(nStrlen < nSize)
        lstrcat(szDest, szSrc);
    else
        throw range_error("Concatenate:Destination too small");
}
```

Using Logic Exceptions

Logic exceptions normally are used to indicate a problem in the coding or logic used in the program. A parameter that's out of range, for example, is a logic error. Logic errors are difficult to recover from because they often result from a misunderstanding about how a particular object or function is meant to be used.

All logic error exception classes included in the Standard Exception Library are derived from the logic_error class. Four classes are used to throw logic error exceptions:

- domain_error. Indicates an internal processing error.

- invalid_argument. Indicates that a faulty parameter argument has been detected.

- length_error. Indicates an attempt to create or use an object of illegal size.

- out_of_range. Indicates that a parameter is out of range.

Any logic error exception can be handled by specifying logic_error in the catch expression, as Listing 5.16 shows.

LISTING 5.16   THROWING AND CATCHING `logic_error` EXCEPTIONS

```
void SomeFunc()
{
    try
    {
        CMySafeArray     ar;
        int nVal = ar[5];
    }
    catch(logic_error e)
    {
        cout << e.what() << endl;
    }
}

int CMySafeArray::operator[](int nIndex)
{
    if(nIndex < 0)
        throw domain_error("Negative index");
    else
        return m_nData[nIndex];
}
```

Detecting Errors During Construction

As discussed earlier, one of the reasons exceptions were added to the C++ language was to handle errors that occur inside constructors. Because a constructor does not have a return value, there are only two ways to handle errors during construction if exceptions are not used:

- Using *two-stage construction*, in which only "safe" operations that cannot fail are performed during construction. A separate `Create` or `Init` function then is used to complete construction of the object.

- Using a *test function* that returns an error code if construction failed.

Each of these methods has drawbacks. Two-stage construction results in code that is difficult to read and write. One of the advantages of using constructors is that initialization is done automatically inside the constructor. When two-stage construction is used, this benefit is reduced. Also, two-stage construction cannot be used for copy constructors and doesn't work well with assignment operators; therefore, those operations must be handled in other ways.

The primary difficulty with using a function to determine whether construction was successful is that a great deal of extra source code must be added. There's also a problem using copy constructors and assignment operators, because it might not always be obvious when a test function should be called.

Exception handling is easier to use than either of these methods. As shown in the console mode program in Listing 5.17, the `try` block should enclose all objects that might throw exceptions when they're constructed.

LISTING 5.17 THROWING AND CATCHING ERRORS DURING CONSTRUCTION

```
CSafeArray::CSafeArray(int nArraySize)
{
    try
    {
        m_nData = new int[nArraySize];
        m_pLogger = new CLog;
    }
    catch(...)
    {
        cout << "Error constructing CSafeArray" << endl;
        throw;
    }
}
```

Using `throw` with no argument inside a `catch` block rethrows the currently executing exception, just as if it had not been handled. This allows the expression to be caught and handled by an enclosing set of `try` and `catch` blocks.

Integrating Win32 SEH with C++ Exception Handling

Using C++ exceptions and structured exception handling together requires a small amount of planning on your part. The basic problems with mixing these two exception-handling mechanisms follow:

- Using SEH can cause an object's destructor to be bypassed.

- Failing to handle SEH exceptions makes your application less robust. If you're writing mission-critical applications, you must handle SEH exceptions.

- Many ANSI Standard Library functions throw C++ exceptions when they fail. If your compiler doesn't support this yet, it will—it's part of the standard.

Fortunately, there's a way to integrate SEH with C++ exceptions. Windows 2000 provides the `_set_se_translator` function, which enables you to define a function that translates SEH exceptions into C++ exceptions. The new translation function must use an `unsigned int` and a pointer to an `EXCEPTION_POINTERS` structure as parameters:

```
void new_xlation_func(unsigned int nCode,
                EXCEPTION_POINTERS* pEx);
```

These values are used exactly as if they were returned from GetExceptionCode and GetExceptionInformation.

The _set_se_translator function takes one parameter—the address of the new translation function:

```
_se_translator_function  fnOld;
fnOld = _set_se_translator(new_xlation_func);
```

The return value from _set_se_translator is the address of the current translation function, if any. You should restore the previous value when exiting your exception-handling code.

Inside the translation function, you can throw a C++ exception using information about the structured exception that has been raised. You can simply throw a char string or any of the Standard Exception Library exception objects.

Listing 5.18 contains the source code for the CWin32Except class, which I use when translating a structured exception into a C++ exception.

LISTING 5.18   THE CWin32Except CLASS

```
#include <eh.h>
class CWin32Except
{
    unsigned int m_nCode;
public:
    CWin32Except(unsigned int nCode) : m_nCode(nCode) {};
    unsigned int Code() const { return m_nCode; };
};
```

Listing 5.19 shows an example of using this code in a console mode program. First, a translation function is defined that throws a CWin32Except object. When an SEH exception is sent to this function, the exception code is stored in the CWin32Except object and is caught by a catch expression that specifies a CWin32Except object.

LISTING 5.19   USING THE CWin32Except CLASS TO HANDLE STRUCTURED EXCEPTIONS

```
#include <iostream>
#include <windows.h>
#include "w32ex.h"
using namespace std;

void SEH_TransFunc(unsigned int nCode, EXCEPTION_POINTERS* pExp)
{
    throw CWin32Except(nCode);
}
```

```
void DoAccessViolation()
{
    int* p = 0;
    *p = 42;
}

int main()
{
    // Set the translation function, and save
    // the previous function address as fnOld.
    _se_translator_function  fnOld;
    fnOld = _set_se_translator(SEH_TransFunc);
    try
    {
        DoAccessViolation();
    }
    catch(CWin32Except& e)
    {
        cout.flags(ios::hex);
        cout << "Caught a _ _try exception with CWin32Except." << endl;
        cout << "Exception number " << e.Code() << endl;
    }
    // Restore the previous translation function
    _set_se_translator(fnOld);
}
```

Before any code in the main function starts executing, the translation function is enabled using the _set_se_translation function. When the access violation occurs, it's translated into a C++ exception and is caught and handled in the program.

Summary

In this chapter, you learned how you can use exception handling to improve the readability and robustness of programs written for Windows 2000. This chapter also discussed using Windows 2000 structured exception handling to create termination and exception handlers, as well as the exception handling built into the C++ language. The Standard Exception Library included in the ANSI Draft C++ Standard also was discussed.

Dynamic Link Libraries

In this chapter, you'll learn about dynamic link libraries (DLLs) and how you can use them to write programs for Windows 2000. Different approaches for writing and using DLLs are presented, and several examples are provided, including examples that demonstrate how to use DLLs when programming with C++ classes that are shared across a DLL boundary. This chapter also discusses thunking—a topic that's useful when you're moving a 16-bit application to Windows 2000.

Understanding Libraries

Simply put, a *library* is a file that contains functions or other resources available for use in applications. These resources are usually general-purpose, allowing many different applications to share the same code or resources easily.

Libraries used in Windows applications come in two basic flavors: *static link libraries* and *dynamic link libraries*. Figure 6.1 illustrates the difference between these two types.

FIGURE 6.1

Calling a function in a static link library versus calling a function in a dynamic link library.

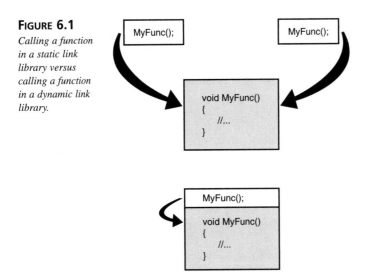

Static link libraries are groups of reusable functions that are linked with a Windows 2000 application. The static link library is part of the application's executable file and is not shared with other applications that may be using the same functions. Static linking is very easy to implement, and it's very easy to distribute an application that uses static link libraries. However, updating a static link library requires that the program be relinked with the updated library.

DLLs are often used for common functions used by several applications simultaneously. For example, the runtime code for the Microsoft Foundation Classes (MFC) is contained in a DLL. The first MFC-based application started by Windows 2000 loads the DLL. Once the MFC library DLL is loaded by Windows 2000, launching another application that uses the DLL proceeds much more quickly.

Only one instance of a DLL is actually loaded at any particular time. If a DLL is already loaded and in use by another process, the DLL is simply mapped into the address space of the new process that depends on it. A DLL can be easily updated without modifying the programs that depend on it, as long as the interfaces supported by the DLL are not changed.

Examining Static Link Libraries

Static link libraries normally are reserved for relatively small, stable function libraries such as the standard C library, which provides functions such as `strlen` and `mktime`. Static link libraries are often used for small libraries due to the cost of creating and maintaining a DLL. A static link library is easy to create and maintain, and it's a good distribution choice for a small library that's not likely to be updated.

Examining Dynamic Link Libraries

Dynamic link libraries are executable files that contain functions, data, or resources available to other applications. As the name suggests, a DLL is loaded when needed—at load time or while an application is running. This is in contrast to static linking, in which a library is added to an executable when it's compiled and linked.

Dynamic link libraries are useful when functions or other resources may be used by multiple processes on a single machine. The contents of each DLL loaded by an application are mapped into the calling application's process address space and linked as the DLL is loaded. A good example of a DLL used in Windows 2000 is `MFC42.dll`, which is used by C++ programs built using the Microsoft Foundation Classes. Most of the MFC code in a typical MFC-based application actually is located in this DLL. Because `MFC42.dll` is a shared DLL, many MFC applications can use it simultaneously.

If an application needs a DLL that is already loaded, two things happen:

- It maps the DLL into the address space of the new process.
- It increases a reference counter kept by Windows 2000 for this DLL. If this counter drops to 0, Windows 2000 unloads the DLL.

> **NOTE**
>
> The path to a DLL is part of its identity. As Windows 2000 loads a DLL, it uses the path to decide if the DLL is currently loaded. If multiple copies of a DLL are located on your machine, it's possible for each copy to be loaded separately by the operating system.

Unlike 16-bit versions of Windows, under Windows 2000, a DLL is loaded in the address space of the calling process instead of a global address space. This protects the DLL from faulty applications, because only the calling process has access to the DLL. It also changes the way in which DLLs are used, however. If you're accustomed to using DLLs in 16-bit versions of Windows, you'll need to make some changes in the way you use DLLs in your applications.

The biggest change in the way that DLLs are used is that, by default, all data in a DLL is mapped into the address space of the calling process, as shown in Figure 6.2.

FIGURE 6.2

DLLs use data in the context of the process that loaded the DLL.

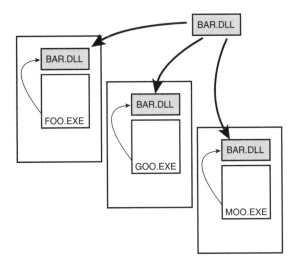

This means the process that loaded the DLL gets its own copy of global data. Any heap memory allocation made by the DLL is made in the context of the process that loaded the DLL and is "owned" by that process. In addition, the DLL uses the process's stack (unlike 16-bit Windows, in which each DLL allocates a private stack).

Later in this chapter, you'll learn some methods for sharing variables in a DLL.

Looking at the Advantages of Using DLLs

Most nontrivial Windows 2000 applications use one or more DLLs. There are four main advantages to using DLLs in a Windows 2000 application:

- Executable code size can be reduced, because several applications can use the same library.

- A central code base isolated in a library is more economical to develop than similar functions used in multiple projects. Reusing code contained in DLLs can look very attractive when several projects need similar functionality.

- Large projects can be broken up into smaller, easier-to-manage subprojects.

- DLLs make it easy to implement new functions: You just release a new version of the DLL. As long as the existing interface doesn't change, you can add new functions without recompiling existing clients.

Looking at the Disadvantages of Using DLLs

The advantages of using DLLs don't come without a price. You should consider a few issues before you break your project into hundreds of tiny DLLs:

- Using DLLs results in more deliverables. Your main EXE may be smaller, but now you need to track more than one binary file.

- DLLs increase project complexity. DLLs must be released and maintained throughout the development and testing processes. These intraproject dependencies grow exponentially with the number of DLLs if you don't plan your project carefully.

- You must deal with version issues with a DLL. Because a DLL is a compiled product, you should use version resources to mark your DLLs. This is discussed later, in the section titled "Using Version Control with DLLs."

If any of these issues apply to your project, you should consider using static libraries.

Creating and Using Dynamic Link Libraries

Dynamic link libraries usually are created using your C or C++ compiler, although you can use other development tools to create DLLs. In this section, you'll learn the steps required to create a DLL using Visual C++. Tools from other vendors are similar; see your documentation for the exact details.

The next few sections cover several issues involved in creating and using DLLs:

- Initializing a DLL
- Exporting functions and data from a DLL
- Loading a DLL when an application starts
- Loading a DLL during runtime
- Using version control with a DLL
- Using shared memory in a DLL

Following these general topics, sample projects are developed that demonstrate each of these subjects.

Understanding DLL Initialization

In 16-bit Windows, separate entry and exit points are defined for each DLL. LibMain is called when the DLL is loaded, and WEP is called when the DLL is freed. The world of 16-bit DLL programming is a strange place—for example, under some degenerate error conditions, the WEP exit function could be called without an associated call to LibMain.

Under Windows 2000, you can define the name of the DLL's main entry point. By convention, the name of this function is DllMain, but you can use any name you like. This entry point is a function called by the operating system at the following times:

- When a process calls the DLL for the first time
- When a new thread is created by a process attached to a DLL
- When a thread owned by a process attached to a DLL is destroyed
- When a process releases a DLL

If you're using Visual C++ 6.0, you can change the entry point for the DLL by following these steps in the Developer Studio IDE:

1. Choose Settings from the Project menu.
2. Click the Link tab.
3. Select Output from the Category drop-down list.
4. Enter a new name as the entry-point symbol. This will be the function name called when the DLL is loaded.

If you're using a makefile, the DLL entry point is specified using the /entry: switch in the linker's command line.

Changing the DLL entry point requires you to manually manage the construction of global objects, as well as the initialization of the C runtime library.

Listing 6.1 shows a typical example of a DLL entry-point function.

LISTING 6.1   A GENERIC DLL ENTRY-POINT FUNCTION

```
BOOL DllMain(HINSTANCE  hLibInstance,
             DWORD      dwReason,
             LPVOID     lpvReserved)
{
    BOOL fResult = FALSE;
    switch(dwReason)
    {
        case DLL_PROCESS_ATTACH:
        // A process has loaded the library
        // Set fResult to TRUE if initialization
        // is successful.
        break;

        case DLL_PROCESS_DETACH:
        // A process has unloaded the library
        break;

        case DLL_THREAD_ATTACH:
        // A new thread has loaded the library
        break;

        case DLL_THREAD_DETACH:
        // A thread has unloaded the library
        break;

        default:
        break;
    }
    return fResult;
}
```

In Listing 6.1, the DLL_THREAD_ATTACH and DLL_THREAD_DETACH labels will be reached when a new thread is started in a process that's already attached to the DLL. It's not necessary for the new thread to perform any housekeeping; the call is made by the operating system. Also, note that there's no generic method that the DLL can use to determine how many threads the calling process has launched before it has attached to the DLL.

If you don't care to be called every time a process spins up a thread, you can get a small performance increase by calling the DisableThreadLibraryCalls function when the process is attached to the DLL to block these notifications.

If your DLL has no global data or initialization or cleanup functions that must be performed when it's loaded or unloaded, you can safely omit the DllMain function from your DLL. If you don't create an entry point, the compiler and linker conspire together to generate a default version that returns TRUE for every case.

If you're using Visual C++ 6.0, the wizard used to create Win32 DLLs will optionally create a skeleton DllMain function for you.

Exporting and Importing DLL Functions and Data

By default, no functions or data located in a DLL are visible to the process that loads the DLL. All functions, data, and resources must be explicitly exported from the DLL using one of these methods:

- Placing the names of the exported items in the EXPORTS section of the library's .def file

- Using a tool-specific method, such as the __declspec(dllexport) keyword used by Visual C++

Once upon a time, when wheels were made of stone and real programmers used C but preferred assembler, all the symbols exported from a library were entered into a library's definition (DEF) file. You can still use this method. In fact, the MFC Library explicitly lists every exported symbol in the DLL version of the MFC Library. If you're using a newer compiler, however, you don't even need a DEF file—in many cases, you can just use the __declspec method to export symbols.

Examining the Module Definition File

In 16-bit Windows development, the DEF file has a much more central role than it does in 32-bit Windows. For one thing, you can omit the DEF file in most cases. For a 32-bit DLL, there are at least two entries in a DEF file, if it exists:

- LIBRARY. Specifies the name of the DLL

- EXPORTS. Marks the beginning of a list of exported symbols

A minimal DEF file that exports no symbols looks like this:

```
LIBRARY     "FOO"
EXPORTS
            ; No exports
```

Exporting Symbols in a DEF File

Every symbol that's exported from the DLL must appear after an EXPORTS label in the DEF file. For example, the following DEF file exports two functions:

```
LIBRARY        "FOO"
EXPORTS

                GetData
                SetData
```

Beware of C++ name mangling. If the DLL is compiled with a C++ compiler, you have two options if you want to use the EXPORTS section of the DEF file:

- Compile the DLL as a C project in order to turn off name mangling.
- Determine the mangled names for each of your exported functions and enter these names in the EXPORTS portion of the DEF file.

In order to determine the mangled names for C++ symbols included in your DLL, build the DLL with no exports and have the linker generate a MAP file. To create a MAP file using Visual C++ 6.0, follow these steps:

1. Choose Settings from the Projects menu.
2. Click the Link tab.
3. Select General from the Category drop-down list.
4. Click the Generate Mapfile checkbox.

If you're using a makefile, the name of the map file is specified using the /map switch on the linker command line:

```
/map:"myDll.map"
```

A map file is fairly large, even for small C++ programs. The section you're interested in looks something like this:

```
Address          Publics by Value          Rva+Base   Lib:Object

0001:00000000    ??2CVMListNode@@SAPAXI@Z   00401000 f listnode.obj
0001:000000b2    ??3CVMListNode@@SAXPAX@Z   004010b2 f listnode.obj
0001:000001f0    ??0CVMList@@QAE@XZ         004011f0 f list.obj
```

The symbol names in the Publics by Value column are the mangled C++ names used by this C++ application.

If you're exporting a large number of symbols from your DLL, you should export your them *by ordinal*, meaning that they are referenced by ordinal number instead of name. This slightly speeds up the search for individual symbols in a library; this approach is used in the MFC DLLs.

To export by ordinal, add an "at" sign (@) followed by an ordinal number after every symbol in the EXPORTS portion of the DEF file:

```
LIBRARY     "FOO"
EXPORTS
            GetData  @1
            SetData  @2
```

The linker generates export and import libraries that use the associated ordinal instead of the name to reference each symbol. The numbers used as ordinals must begin with 1, and they must be consecutive.

Using __declspec, dllimport, and dllexport

As you can see, managing the DEF file can be a big headache. If you're using a current C++ compiler, you can probably avoid dealing with the EXPORTS section of the DEF file altogether. Visual C++ uses the __declspec keyword, for example, to add extra attributes when declaring a function or variable name:

```
int __declspec(dllexport) foo();
```

The __declspec keyword is specific to Visual C++, and it has many possible parameter values. The following two values are useful when you're declaring DLLs:

- dllexport. Declares a function or variable as exported from a DLL
- dllimport. Declares a function or variable as imported from a DLL

In some cases, using dllexport and dllimport enables the compiler to generate more efficient code than using a DEF file, because the compiler can identify which symbols are exported and imported from the DLL, rather than forcing the linker to perform all the work independently.

A slight amount of complexity is added to your declarations when using __declspec. Consider a DLL that exports a function named foo:

```
int foo(int)
{
    // Does something useful...
    return 1216;
}
```

When building the DLL, foo is declared using dllexport:

```
int __declspec(dllexport) foo(int);
```

When importing the DLL, foo is declared using dllimport:

```
int __declspec(dllimport) foo(int);
```

At first glance, this seems to require two header files—one file used when building the DLL and another header file used by clients of the DLL. This approach is certainly possible, but it will result in a great deal of work when the DLL is modified. Instead of using two header files, the examples in this chapter use conditional compilation to ensure that the proper declaration is used, as Listing 6.2 demonstrates.

LISTING 6.2 A HEADER FILE USING __declspec WITH CONDITIONAL COMPILATION

```
// Conditional compilation for DLL declarations

#ifdef ESPRESSO_DLL
// export function from library
#define FUNC_DECL  __declspec(dllexport)
#else
// import function from library
#define FUNC_DECL  __declspec(dllimport)
#endif

int  FUNC_DECL GetLatteFoamDensity(void);
void FUNC_DECL SetLatteFoamDensity(int nDensity);
```

In the DLL implementing these functions, ESPRESSO_DLL is defined before the header file is included, resulting in __declspec(dllexport) being used for the declarations. When this header is used without defining ESPRESSO_DLL, the __declspec(dllimport) declaration is used.

Loading a DLL at Load Time

An executable can contain information about the DLLs it needs to have loaded. This information is placed into the EXE file by the linker and is used by Windows 2000 when an application is launched.

When the EXE is started, Windows 2000 is responsible for locating the DLLs needed by the application and resolving the address for each of the references made to the DLL. This type of loading is call *implicit loading*, because it occurs automatically when the EXE is launched.

Windows 2000 searches for DLLs in the following order:

- The directory containing the EXE file that owns the process
- The current directory
- The Windows 2000 system directory
- The Windows 2000 directory
- The directories listed in the PATH environment variable

If any of the DLLs associated with an application cannot be found or fails to load for any other reason, the application terminates.

Every DLL that's found is treated like a memory-mapped file, and its contents are mapped into the process of the starting application. Because it's treated like a memory-mapped file, only the parts of the DLL that actually are used are loaded into physical memory.

As discussed earlier in the chapter, if a DLL used by an application is already in use by another process, Windows 2000 creates another mapping for the new process and increments a reference count stored internally by the operating system. This counter is incremented when processes attach to a DLL, and it's decremented when processes detach or are terminated. When this counter reaches 0, the DLL is released.

To notify the linker that your application depends on a DLL, you must link your application with an import library created for the DLL. Visual C++ creates an import library automatically when building DLL projects created by AppWizard.

Loading a DLL at Runtime

The second method you can use to load a DLL is *runtime* or *dynamic loading*. With this method, you can attempt to explicitly load a DLL using LoadLibrary, as Listing 6.3 shows.

LISTING 6.3 USING LoadLibrary TO LOAD A DLL AT RUNTIME

```
typedef int(*PFUNC)(void);
.
.
.
HINSTANCE   hLibInstance;
hLibInstance = LoadLibrary(_T("FuncDll"));
if(hLibInstance != NULL)
{
    PFUNC pFunc = (PFUNC)GetProcAddress(hLibInstance,
                                    _T("GetUltimateAnswer"));
    if(pFunc != NULL)
    {
        int n = pFunc();
        _tprintf(_T("The answer is %d\n"), n);
    }
    FreeLibrary(hLibInstance);
}
else
{
    _tprintf(_T("Couldn't load library\n"));
}
```

The LoadLibrary function returns an instance handle that refers to the DLL. If LoadLibrary is not successful, NULL is returned. In order to use any functions exported by the DLL, you must call GetProcAddress with the library's instance handle and the name of the function:

```
pFunc = (PFUNC)GetProcAddress(hLibInstance, _T("GetUltimateAnswer"));
```

The function name must be spelled exactly as it is exported. Alternatively, you can use the ordinal export value, if one exists, like this:

```
pFunc = (PFUNC)GetProcAddress(hLibInstance, MAKEINTRESOURCE(1));
```

The return value from GetProcAddress is typed as a FARPROC. In most cases, you must cast it to the proper type, as shown in the preceding example.

After you get the address, you use it like any other function pointer:

```
int n = pFunc();
```

After you finish using the library, you should release it by calling FreeLibrary:

```
FreeLibrary(hLibInstance);
```

When using LoadLibrary, you don't need to link your application with an import library for the DLL. Because you don't explicitly call any of the DLL functions, the linker doesn't complain about missing references.

This method is extremely useful in situations in which a DLL may not exist on a particular installation. You can use LoadLibrary to load a DLL containing optional resources or functions; if it's not found, you can take some alternative action.

The Win32 API also contains LoadLibraryEx, a function that can offer improved performance in special cases. For example, if you're loading a resource-only DLL, LoadLibraryEx can be called with flags that indicate that the operating system need not initialize the DLL or call the DllMain function.

Using Version Control with DLLs

One of the types of resources that can be bound to Win32 executable files and fonts is the *version resource*. The version resource tags the executable files and font resources with the company name, filename, and other version information. Other programs can use this information to compare files to determine the revision level of the file. Windows 2000 offers version control functions that can be used to query standard version resources.

Adding version information to a DLL project is easy and takes only a few minutes. To take advantage of the standard version control functions, you must define a version resource for your project. Figure 6.3 shows a version resource being edited inside the Visual C++ Developer Studio IDE.

FIGURE 6.3

*Using Visual C++
Developer Studio
to edit a version
resource.*

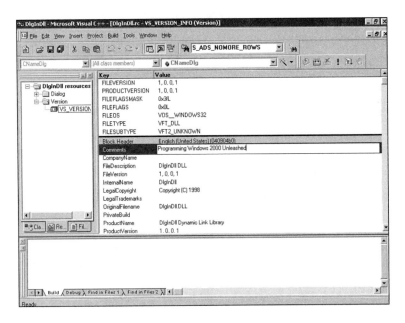

If you use Developer Studio to edit your version resource, the individual fields are conveniently displayed for editing. Just fill in the relevant information and rebuild the DLL project.

That's all there is to marking your files with version information. You can see this information easily by using the Windows 2000 Explorer and displaying the file properties. Figure 6.4 shows an example of version information for a DLL.

FIGURE **6.4**

Displaying version information for a DLL.

Creating Shared Memory for a DLL

It's sometimes necessary for processes that use a DLL to share information. In 16-bit versions of Windows, this usually is done through shared memory owned by the DLL. Because the DLL in 16-bit Windows is mapped into the global address space, all applications have access to data owned by the DLL, so this scheme is easy to implement.

In Windows 2000, where each DLL is mapped into the address space of the process that loaded the DLL, any memory used by the DLL is actually in the address space of the calling process. You can still share memory—it just takes a little more work.

A section of memory used by a DLL is defined as sharable by using the SECTIONS keyword in a module definition file. Listing 6.4 defines a section named .shared as a readable, writable, and shared section of memory. Windows 2000 memory sections always begin with a dot (.), but you can give them any name you want.

LISTING 6.4 A DEF FILE DEFINING A SHARED DATA SECTION

```
LIBRARY       "ESPRESSODLL"
DESCRIPTION   'ESPRESSODLL Windows Dynamic Link Library'

SECTIONS
   .shared  READ WRITE SHARED

EXPORTS
   ; Explicit exports can go here
```

After you define a memory section, you must place your shared memory into that section and initialize it. Only initialized data can be shared using this method; uninitialized data is not placed into the shared memory section. If you're using Visual C++, the `data_seg` pragma is used to mark the beginning and end of a data segment, as Listing 6.5 shows.

LISTING 6.5   USING THE `data_seg` PRAGMA TO MARK A DATA SEGMENT

```
#pragma data_seg(".shared")
int nServedLattes = 42;
#pragma data_seg()

int GetLatteCount( void )
{
    return ++nServedLattes;
}
```

The code fragment in Listing 6.5 creates a data segment named `.shared` that contains one variable: `nServedLattes`. When this code is used in a DLL, every process will share the `nServedLattes` variable. When `GetLatteCount` is called, `nServedLattes` is incremented and the new value is returned.

When this code is run on a Windows 2000 installation with one processor, it works as expected. On a machine with multiple processors, however, it has a fatal flaw. It's possible for more than one CPU to attempt to change the value of `nServedLattes`, thus resulting in undefined results.

As discussed in Chapter 3, "Threads and Processes," data that's shared between threads may be corrupted if multiple threads access the data simultaneously. A similar problem exists when multiple processes access shared memory sections exposed by a DLL. If you're using shared memory in a DLL, beware of using nonatomic operations on data or functions that may be used by multiple threads or processes simultaneously.

As discussed in Chapter 3, the `InterlockedIncrement` function safely increments a variable stored at an address passed to it as a parameter:

```
InterlockedIncrement(&nServedLattes);
```

Listing 6.6 shows an improved version of `GetLatteCount`. Using a test driver, this version of `GetLatteCount` compiles into a DLL, which runs without losing any transactions.

LISTING 6.6   A MULTIPROCESSOR-SAFE VERSION OF GetLatteCount

```
#pragma data_seg(".shared")
int nServedLattes = 0;
#pragma data_seg()

int GetLatteCount(void)
{
    InterlockedIncrement(&nServedLattes);
    return nServedLattes;
}
```

Looking at a Simple DLL Example

To show you how DLLs are used in Windows 2000 applications, several sample programs have been included on the CD-ROM accompanying with this book. These examples range from simple examples involving console mode applications to MFC-based DLLs.

The first sample program demonstrates how different applications can use a DLL as a "function warehouse." The FuncDll project creates a DLL that exports a single function; later, shared memory is added. This DLL is also used later in the chapter by a console mode program and a dialog-based MFC application.

Each version of the DLL and its clients are included on the CD-ROM. You can use those projects or create them from scratch by following the steps presented here.

Creating the FuncDll DLL Project

The first version of the FuncDll project exports a single function: GetCounter. The AppWizard included with Visual C++ 6.0 was used to create FuncDll as a Win32 dynamic link library project.

Two files are used in the first version of the project:

- FuncDll.c. Contains the DLL source code
- FuncDll.h. Contains the declarations for FuncDll.c

Listing 6.7 provides the source code for the FuncDll.h source file.

LISTING 6.7 THE FuncDll.h HEADER FILE USED BY FUNCDLL

```
#ifdef __cplusplus
extern "C" {
#endif
// Define FUNC_DECL to be either an imported or exported
// library symbol, depending on whether we are building the
// DLL or using it in a client.
#ifdef FUNCDLL_DLL
// export function from library
#define FUNC_DECL  __declspec(dllexport)
#else
// import function from library
#define FUNC_DECL  __declspec(dllimport)
#endif
int FUNC_DECL GetCounter(void);
#ifdef __cplusplus
}
#endif
```

The FuncDll.h header file is used by the FuncDll.c source file, as well as by any applications that use load-time or implicit linking to the DLL. When used in FuncDll.c, the symbol FUNCDLL_DLL is defined, causing GetCounter to be exported. All other users of the header file do not define this symbol, so GetCounter is imported.

Listing 6.8 contains the FuncDll.c source file. This is the main source file used by the FuncDll project. Enter the source code as shown here and save it in the project directory. After saving the file, add it to the project.

LISTING 6.8 THE FuncDll.c SOURCE FILE USED BY FUNCDLL

```
#define  FUNCDLL_DLL
#include "funcdll.h"

int GetCounter(void)
{
    return 42;
}
```

FuncDll.c defines no DLL entry point because no initialization is performed. All FuncDll does is export a simple function from a DLL.

If you compile the project using Visual C++, the compiler will create the DLL and LIB files and store them in the project's Debug subdirectory.

Using FuncDll in a Console Mode Application

The simplest type of Windows 2000 program that can use a DLL is a console mode application. The CD-ROM includes a console mode project named CallFunc that demonstrates how to use a DLL in a console mode application.

The CallFunc project directory includes two files from the FuncDll project: the FuncDll.h header file and the FuncDll.LIB import library, which is used by the linker to generate a list of DLLs on which CallFunc depends. You must add the FuncDll.LIB file to the project in order to call functions in the DLL.

Only one source file exists in the CallFunc project. Listing 6.9 provides the source code for CallFunc.c.

LISTING 6.9 THE CallFunc.c SOURCE FILE USED BY CALLFUNC

```c
#include <windows.h>
#include <tchar.h>
#include "funcdll.h"
#ifndef UNICODE
    #include <stdio.h>
#endif

int main()
{
    int nCounter = GetCounter();
    _tprintf(_T("The counter is %d\n"), nCounter);
    return 0;
}
```

Build the CallFunc project. If there are no errors, you can start the CallFunc application. You first must copy the FuncDll into the CallFunc project's Debug subdirectory, however. This ensures that FuncDll is found when the application is started.

Open an MS-DOS console and change to the CallFunc project's Debug subdirectory. Start the application by typing **CallFunc** at the DOS prompt. If everything goes as planned, the following output appears:

```
The counter is 42
```

Using FuncDll in an MFC Application

Using a DLL such as FuncDll in an MFC application is very simple. In fact, you follow exactly the same steps used in the console mode example. If your DLL does not use any of the MFC Class Library, just use exactly the same steps outlined in the earlier sections. Situations in which you need access to the MFC Class Library in your DLL are covered later in this chapter, in the section titled "Using MFC and DLLs."

Adding Shared Memory Functions to FuncDll

A second version of FuncDll demonstrates how shared memory can be added to a DLL, as discussed earlier in this chapter. The new version of FuncDll stores a global counter in a shared memory section named .shared that's incremented every time the GetCounter function is called.

Listing 6.10 contains a module definition file for FuncDll, including the necessary declarations for a shared memory section.

LISTING 6.10 THE MODULE DEFINITION FILE FOR FUNCDLL

```
LIBRARY      "FUNCDLL"
DESCRIPTION  'FUNCDLL Windows Dynamic Link Library'

SECTIONS
    .shared  READ WRITE SHARED

EXPORTS
    ; Explicit exports can go here
```

In addition, the FuncDll.c source file must be edited. Listing 6.11 shows the new version of FuncDll.c.

LISTING 6.11 THE NEW VERSION OF FuncDll.c

```
#include <windows.h>
#define   FUNCDLL_DLL
#include "funcdll.h"

#pragma data_seg(".shared")
int nCounter = 0;
#pragma data_seg()

int GetCounter(void)
{
    InterlockedIncrement(&nCounter);
    return nCounter;
}
```

Build the new version of the FuncDll project and copy the DLL and LIB files into the CallFunc Debug subdirectory. To test the new version of FuncDll, start several instances of the CallFunc project created earlier. Every time GetCounter is called, it returns a higher value. You can also modify the CallFunc project to call GetCounter repeatedly, like this:

```
int i = 0;
for(i = 0; i < 5000; ++i)
{
    int nCounter = GetCounter();
    _tprintf(_T("The counter is %d\n"), nCounter);
}
```

Several versions of CallFunc modified in this way are shown running in Figure 6.5.

FIGURE 6.5

*Several instances
of CallFunc using
shared memory in
FuncDll.*

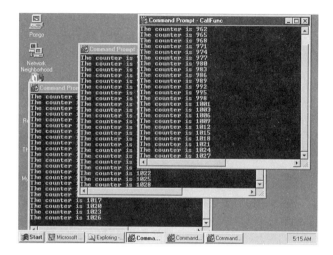

Using C++ and DLLs

The previous DLL examples export C functions because they are the simplest functions to export. You can also export C++ classes and member functions from a DLL, however. If you use a C++ interface in your DLL, be warned: A DLL that exports classes created with Visual C++ cannot be used by applications created with a compiler that uses different object-management or name-mangling schemes.

When exporting class or member function symbols, you use __declspec much the same as you do for standard C functions. To export a class, you follow the class keyword with __declspec:

```
class __declspec(dllexport) CLatte {
// class info here
};
```

To export an individual function from a class, you include __declspec in the function declaration:

```
class CLatte{
public:
    int __declspec(dllexport) GetFoamDensity() const;
};
```

Examining a Payroll Record Class Stored in a DLL

As an example of exporting a C++ class from a DLL, the CD-ROM includes a project named ClassDll. The ClassDll project builds a DLL that exports CPayrollRec—a C++ class that represents a payroll record.

Listing 6.12 shows the CPayrollRec class declaration, which can be found in the payrec.h header file in the project directory.

LISTING 6.12   THE CLASS DECLARATION FOR CPayrollRec

```
#pragma once
#ifdef PAYREC_DLL
#define CLASS_DECL __declspec(dllexport)
#else
#define CLASS_DECL __declspec(dllimport)
#endif

class CLASS_DECL CPayrollRec
{
public:
    CPayrollRec();
    CPayrollRec( double dRate, double dHours = 0.0 );
    double GrossPay() const;
private:
    double m_dRate;
    double m_dHours;
};
```

Listing 6.13 contains the source code for the CPayrollRec function definitions, which can be found in the payrec.cpp source file in the project directory.

LISTING 6.13 THE CLASS DEFINITION FOR CPayrollRec

```cpp
#define PAYREC_DLL
#include "payrec.h"

CPayrollRec::CPayrollRec(): m_dRate(0.0), m_dHours(0.0)
{
}

CPayrollRec::CPayrollRec(double dRate, double dHours)
            :m_dRate(dRate), m_dHours(dHours)
{
}

double CPayrollRec::GrossPay() const
{
    return m_dRate * m_dHours;
}
```

Compile the ClassDll project. Visual C++ creates a DLL and an import LIB file for ClassDll.

Using the ClassDll Example in an Application

The CD-ROM also includes Payroll, a project that demonstrates how you can use ClassDll in a Windows 2000 application. The Payroll project is a console mode application that creates and uses a CPayrollRec object defined in ClassDll.

Only one source file exists in the Payroll project, in addition to the ClassDll.lib file and payrec.h header file. Listing 6.14 provides the source code for Payroll.cpp.

LISTING 6.14 THE SOURCE CODE FOR Payroll.cpp

```cpp
#include <windows.h>
#include <tchar.h>
#ifndef UNICODE
    #include <stdio.h>
#endif
#include "payrec.h"

int main()
{
    CPayrollRec   theRec(2.5, 42.00);
    _tprintf(_T("Current gross pay is $%.2f\n"), theRec.GrossPay());
    return 0;
}
```

Build the Payroll project. As is the case with the earlier examples, you first must copy the DLL `ClassDll.dll` into the Payroll project's `Debug` subdirectory. This ensures that the DLL is found when the application is started.

Open an MS-DOS console and change to the Payroll project's `Debug` subdirectory. Start the application by typing `Payroll` at the DOS prompt. If everything goes as planned, the following output appears:

```
Current gross pay is $105
```

As you can see, using a C++ class exported by a DLL is almost exactly like using a standard C function exported from a DLL.

Using MFC and DLLs

Three basic ways exist to mix MFC and DLLs with your Windows 2000 application:

- Your application uses a DLL that uses MFC internally, and the DLL is linked to the MFC DLL dynamically. In MFC terminology, the DLL is known as a *dynamically linked regular DLL*.

- Your application uses a DLL that uses MFC internally, and the DLL is statically linked to the MFC Library. In MFC terminology, the DLL is known as a *statically linked regular DLL*.

- Your application uses a DLL that extends the MFC Library by exposing classes that are derived from the MFC Class Library. In MFC terminology, the DLL is known as an *extension DLL*.

When a Windows application uses MFC, the default behavior is to use MFC in a shared DLL, as shown in Figure 6.6. This helps reduce the size of your application and helps your application load faster if another MFC application is already running.

FIGURE 6.6

An MFC application using the MFC core code from the shared MFC DLL.

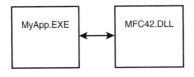

As discussed earlier, another way to use the shared MFC DLL is by creating a regular DLL that uses the MFC DLL. The main application does not have to be MFC-based. In fact, it's possible to use a C interface between the main application and the DLL. Figure 6.7 illustrates this sort of interface.

FIGURE 6.7

*Non-MFC appli-
cations using
MFC code via a
DLL.*

The most common way to use MFC in a DLL is with an extension DLL, as shown in Figure 6.8. An *extension DLL* uses the shared MFC Library and is called by an MFC-based application.

FIGURE 6.8

*Using an exten-
sion DLL in an
MFC application.*

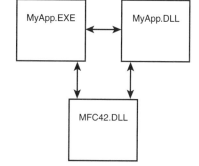

The next few sections discuss the steps required to create and use MFC extension DLLs.

Initializing an MFC Extension DLL

Every MFC extension DLL must perform some initialization in its DLL entry-point function. Listing 6.15 provides an example of a typical DLL entry point for an extension DLL. Actually, this function was created by AppWizard as part of an extension DLL project.

LISTING 6.15 SOURCE CODE CREATED BY APPWIZARD FOR MFC EXTENSION DLLs

```
static AFX_EXTENSION_MODULE theDLL = { NULL, NULL };
extern "C" int APIENTRY
DllMain(HINSTANCE hInstance, DWORD dwReason, LPVOID lpReserved)
{
    if (dwReason == DLL_PROCESS_ATTACH)
    {
```

continues

LISTING 6.15 CONTINUED

```
        TRACE0("DLGINDLL.DLL Initializing!\n");
        // Extension DLL one-time initialization
        AfxInitExtensionModule(theDLL, hInstance);
        // Insert this DLL into the resource chain
        new CDynLinkLibrary(DlgInDllDLL);
    }
    else if (dwReason == DLL_PROCESS_DETACH)
    {
        TRACE0("DLGINDLL.DLL Terminating!\n");
    }
    return 1;
}
```

Even if you don't use AppWizard to create your extension DLL project, you should copy this function because it shows exactly how an extension DLL must be started and registered with the MFC framework.

When a process is attached to an extension DLL, the global AFX_EXTENSION_MODULE variable is used to track classes and other objects used in the DLL. A CDynLinkLibrary object is created on the heap; this object is inserted into a list that's searched when resources are required by the process that loaded the DLL.

Creating an Extension DLL

In this section, an MFC extension DLL project named DlgInDll that exports a dialog box resource and an associated CDialog-based class used to manage it are created. Like the earlier projects in this chapter, the complete project can be found on the accompanying CD-ROM. You can use that project, or you can follow along with the steps presented here to create the project from scratch.

To get started on the DlgInDll project, use AppWizard to create an MFC extension DLL. First, select MFC AppWizard (dll) as the project type, as shown in Figure 6.9.

After clicking OK, a Wizard page appears, as shown in Figure 6.10. Select MFC Extension DLL (using shared MFC DLL).

Using Developer Studio, add a dialog resource type to the project. Give this dialog box a resource ID of IDD_EXT_NAME. Add an Edit control to the dialog box, as shown in Figure 6.11.

FIGURE **6.9**

*Using AppWizard
to create a DLL
that uses MFC.*

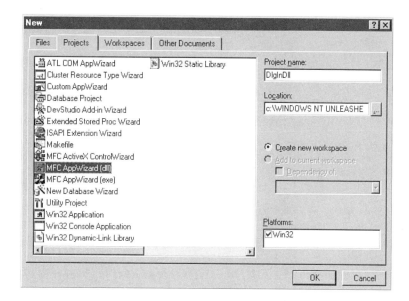

FIGURE **6.10**

*Selecting MFC
Extension DLL as
the project type.*

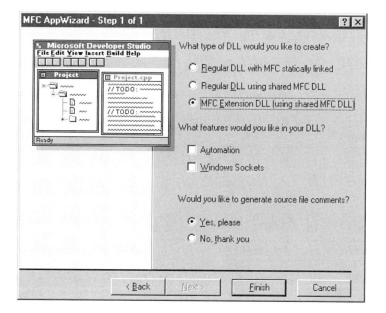

FIGURE **6.11**

Adding an Edit control to the DlgInDll dialog box.

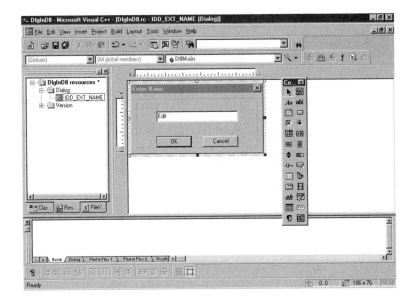

Table 6.1 provides the resource ID used by the Edit control. Use ClassWizard to associate a member variable with the Edit control, using the values from the same table.

TABLE **6.1** EDIT CONTROL RESOURCE INFORMATION

Control Name	Resource ID	Category	Type	Variable
Name edit	IDC_NAME	Value	CString	m_strName

Using ClassWizard, create a class derived from CDialog named CNameDlg to manage the new dialog resource. Use the values in Table 6.2 to create the new class.

TABLE **6.2** VALUES USED FOR THE DIALOG BOX

Control	Value
Name	CNameDlg
Base class	CDialog
File	NameDlg.cpp
Dialog ID	IDD_EXT_NAME
Automation	None

In order to export the `CNameDlg` class from the library, you must edit the `CNameDlg` class declaration. Listing 6.16 shows the changes made to the `NameDlg.h` header file in bold.

LISTING 6.16   THE `CNameDlg` CLASS DECLARATION

```
#ifndef _AFXEXT
#define IDD_EXT_NAME 129
#else
#include "resource.h"
#endif

class AFX_EXT_CLASS CNameDlg : public CDialog
{
// Construction
public:
    CNameDlg(CWnd* pParent = NULL);

// Dialog Data
    //{{AFX_DATA(CNameDlg)
    enum { IDD = IDD_EXT_NAME };
    .
    .
    .
};
```

Two changes are made in the `NameDlg.h` header file:

- The symbol used to define the dialog box is hard-coded in the header. This resource symbol is hard-coded because there's a dependency between the class declaration and the `IDD_EXT_NAME` symbol. If you use Visual C++ and follow the steps described, this value should be correct. You can always determine the actual value by selecting Resource Symbols from the Developer Studio View menu.

- The `AFX_EXT_CLASS` symbol is used in the `CNameDlg` class declaration. This symbol is used exactly as other placeholders used in previous examples. When an MFC extension DLL is built, the `AFX_EXT_CLASS` symbol expands to `__declspec (dllexport)`. For all other builds, it expands to `__declspec(dllimport)`.

Compile the DlgInDll project. Visual C++ creates a DLL and an import LIB file for DlgInDll.

Looking at an Example Using an Extension DLL

As an example of using an MFC extension DLL, the CD-ROM includes the Hello project, which uses the DlgInDll DLL project created in the preceding section.

Once again, you can open this project and follow along as the project is described, or you can create the project yourself using the steps presented in the next few sections. To begin, create a dialog-based project named Hello using ClassWizard.

Modifying the Main Dialog Box

Using Developer Studio, add a new pushbutton control to the main dialog box, as shown in Figure 6.12.

FIGURE 6.12

Adding controls to the main dialog box for the Hello application.

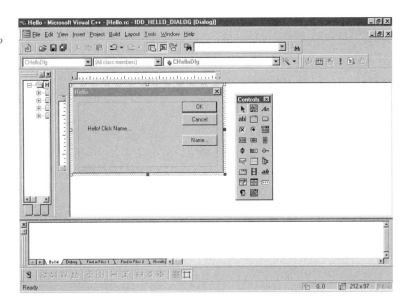

Table 6.3 shows the resource IDs used by the main dialog box controls. Note that the static control has a new resource ID and caption.

TABLE 6.3   CONTROLS USED BY THE MAIN DIALOG BOX

Control	Resource ID	Caption
Name button	IDC_NAME	&Name...
Static control	IDC_NAME_LABEL	Hello! Click Name...

Using ClassWizard, add a message-handling function for the CHelloDlg class. Use the values from Table 6.4 when adding this message-handling function.

TABLE 6.4 VALUES FOR NEW MEMBER FUNCTIONS IN CHelloDlg

Object ID	Class Name	Message	Function
IDC_NAME	CHelloDlg	BN_CLICKED	OnBtnName

Using ClassWizard, associate a CStatic member variable named m_wndNameLabel with the IDC_NAME_LABEL static control.

Listing 6.17 provides the source code for the CHelloDlg::OnBtnName function.

LISTING 6.17 CALLING A DIALOG BOX CLASS LOCATED IN AN EXTENSION DLL

```
void CHelloDlg::OnBtnName()
{
    CNameDlg    dlg;
    if(dlg.DoModal() == IDOK)
    {
        CString strHello = _T("Hello ");
        m_wndNameLabel.SetWindowText(strHello + dlg.m_strName);
    }
}
```

Remember to add the following code to the top of the HelloDlg.cpp source file, just after the standard #include files:

```
#include "NameDlg.h"
```

Before compiling the Hello project, copy DlgInDll.lib, the import library, from the DlgInDll project into the Hello project directory. Also copy the NameDlg.h header file into the Hello project directory.

Add the import library from the DlgInDll DLL to the Hello project by following these steps:

1. Choose Build and then Settings from the main menu.
2. Click the Link tab.
3. Select Input from the Category drop-down list control.
4. Enter DlgInDll.lib in the Object/Library module's Edit control.
5. Close the Settings dialog box.

Build the Hello project. As is the case with the earlier examples, you must copy the DlgInDll DLL into the Hello project's Debug subdirectory before running the application. This ensures that the DLL is found when the application is started.

Start the Hello application. If you click the Name button, the dialog box from the DlgInDll DLL is displayed, as shown in Figure 6.13. After entering a name in the dialog box, the static label in the main dialog box is updated.

FIGURE 6.13

The Hello application after the Name dialog box has been created.

Using Generic Thunks

Over the years, many complex applications have been written for the 16-bit versions of Windows. Microsoft recognizes that complex systems may need to be migrated to Windows 2000 in multiple steps. For this reason, a facility has been added to Windows 2000 that allows a 16-bit application to access and use components such as DLLs that are written for Windows 2000. This facility is known as *thunking*.

Thunking is a term that was originally used to describe how a specific type of function call was made using the ALGOL programming language. There aren't many ALGOL programs still in use today, but the word *thunk* lives on.

There are three types of thunks used in Win32:

- A *generic thunk* allows 16-bit code to call 32-bit DLLs. This is useful in the case where a 16-bit EXE or DLL needs to call a 32-bit DLL that has been written to take advantage of Windows 2000. It can also be used to allow 16-bit binaries to call Windows 2000 API functions directly. Generic thunks are available on Windows 2000 and Windows 9*x*.

- A *universal thunk*, contrary to what you might expect from its name, is used only for Win32s. A universal thunk allows a Win32 application running on Win32s to load a 16-bit DLL when running on Windows 3.1.

- A *flat thunk* is used in Windows 9*x* to allow 32-bit applications to call 16-bit DLLs and to allow 16-bit applications to call 32-bit DLLs.

> **NOTE**
>
> The availability and performance of thunking depend on the platform and operating system.
>
> Windows 2000 does not provide any way for a 32-bit executable to thunk to a 16-bit DLL. This facility is provided in Windows 95 and Windows 98 with the *flat thunk* mechanism, but it's not provided in Windows 2000.
>
> Also, unlike Windows 2000, Windows 95 and Windows 98 do not allow a DLL that's called via a thunk from a 16-bit client to create threads. If you require compatibility with Windows 95 or Windows 98, beware of this restriction.

Generic Thunking Architecture

Using a Windows 2000 generic thunk to load a 32-bit DLL from a 16-bit application is similar to the runtime loading of DLLs discussed earlier in the chapter. The generic thunking mechanism allows the 16-bit process to use the Windows 2000 *Virtual DOS Machine* (or VDM) as a proxy that actually loads the DLL, as shown in Figure 6.14.

FIGURE 6.14

Generic Thunking uses the Windows 2000 VDM to load the 16-bit DLL.

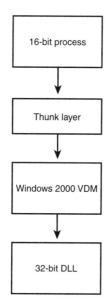

As you might expect, this arrangement brings up some interesting debugging issues. After all, half your application is running in the 16-bit space, and half is running in the 32-bit space. Debugging strategies for generic thunks are discussed later in the chapter.

Generic Thunking Functions

Nearly two dozen functions are used for generic thunks. Here are the most commonly used:

- `LoadLibraryEx32W` is used to load a 32-bit DLL so that a 16-bit binary can call functions located in the library.
- `FreeLibrary32W` releases a DLL previously loaded with `LoadLibraryEx32W`.
- `GetVDMPointer32W` converts a pointer used in the 16-bit address space so that it can be used by a 32-bit DLL.
- `CallProc32W` is used to call a function in a 32-bit DLL from a 16-bit binary.
- `CallProcEx32W` is used to call a function in a 32-bit DLL from a 16-bit binary; unlike `CallProc32W`, it uses the `cdecl` calling convention.

Each of these functions is discussed in more detail in the following sections. The 16-bit compiler does not document these functions; they are actually part of Windows 2000 and are (partially) documented in the Win32 SDK. The best SDK documentation is actually found in two header files:

- `wownt16.h` is the header file for 16-bit generic thunk functions.
- `wownt32.h` is the header file for 32-bit generic thunk functions.

Your 16-bit application must explicitly import any generic thunking functions imported from the kernel—there is no import library. The Client16 example provided later in this chapter includes a DEF file that imports the necessary functions from the kernel.

Loading and Freeing 32-bit Libraries

A 16-bit binary cannot directly load a 32-bit DLL using the standard `LoadLibrary` or `LoadLibraryEx` API call. The `LoadLibraryEx32W` function is exposed by the kernel so that a 16-bit application can load a 32-bit DLL for thunking:

```
DWORD hDll = LoadLibraryEx32W("dll32.dll", 0L, 0L);
```

The `LoadLibraryEx32W` function takes three parameters:

- The name of the DLL.
- A reserved parameter that's set to zero or `NULL`.
- A `DWORD` that can contain multiple flags; this value is usually zero. Check the SDK documentation for some special cases where the flags may be useful.

The library must be released by calling the `FreeLibrary32W` function:

```
BOOL fFreed = FreeLibrary32W(hDll);
```

The `FreeLibrary32W` function has one parameter—the `DWORD` handle returned from `LoadLibraryEx32W`.

Adjusting 16-bit Segmented Pointers

Pointers and other addresses that are passed to the 32-bit DLL must be converted from their native segmented format into a flat 32-bit address format. As discussed in the next section, pointers passed as parameters can be converted during the `CallProc32W` and `CallProcEx32W` function calls.

If you prefer to convert the address before performing the function call, or if an address is passed as an embedded pointers inside a structure, you can use the `GetVDMPointer32W` function:

```
int n16 = 0;
DWORD dw32BitPtrToInt = GetVDMPointer32W(&n16, 1);
```

The `GetVDMPointer32W` function has two parameters:

- The 16:16 address that's to be converted to a flat address

- A flag that's set if the 16:16 address is a protected-mode address or cleared if it's a real-mode address

Calling 32-bit Functions with `CallProc32W` and `CallProcEx32W`

The call to the 32-bit function is performed by calling the `CallProc32W` or `CallProcEx32W` function. These two functions are similar, differing only in their calling convention and parameter order.

The Client16 sample program uses the `CallProc32W` function. Later in the next section, you'll see that the Client16 sample program defines `CallProc32W` as this:

```
DWORD FAR PASCAL CallProc32W(DWORD, LPVOID fnProcAddress,
                             DWORD dwBitMask, DWORD nParams);
```

As defined here, `CallProc32W` has four parameters:

- A parameter passed to the 32-bit function.

- The address of the 32-bit function, which is determined by calling `GetProcAddress32W`.

- A bitmask that specifies the information about the 32-bit function. (This parameter is discussed in more detail later.)

- The number of parameters passed to the 32-bit function.

The `CallProc32W` function can have up to 32 parameters. Due to limitations of the
`PASCAL` calling convention, you cannot use a variable number of parameters with
`CallProc32W`. You must declare it once, and use that number of arguments throughout
your application.

The bitmask passed as the third parameter is used to indicate which parameters are pointers that require conversion from segmented 16:16 values to flat 0:32 values. This parameter is zero when no conversion is required. In Client16, this parameter is always
zero—when a pointer is passed, the conversion is performed using `GetVDMPointer32W`.
The first bit in the bitmask must be set if the last parameter requires conversion; the second bit is set for the next-to-last parameter, and so on.

The final parameter is the number of parameters to be passed to the 32-bit function. If
the 32-bit function you're thunking to uses the `cdecl` calling convention, you must combine the symbol `CPEX_DEST_CDECL` with the number of parameters, using the C/C++ "or"
function, |, like this:

```
DWORD dwParams = 2|CPEX_DEST_CDECL;
```

In a real application, the functions you call will likely use a varying number of parameters. One option is to use `CallProcEx32W`, which uses the `cdecl` calling convention:

```
DWORD dwRet = CallProcEx32W(2, 0, pFunc, nSetVal1, nSetVal2);
```

The parameters passed to `CallProcEx32W` are used exactly like `CallProc32W`, except that
they appear in reverse order:

- The number of parameters passed to the 32-bit function, optionally combined with
the `CPEX_DEST_CDECL` symbol if the 32-bit function uses the `cdecl` calling conven-
tion.
- The address conversion bitmask, which is reversed when compared to
`CallProc32W`. The first bit in the bitmask refers to the first parameter, the second
bit refers to the second parameter, and so on.
- The address of the 32-bit function.
- One or more parameters to be passed to the 32-bit function.

A Generic Thunking Example

To illustrate how generic thunks are used in Windows 2000, two sample projects have
been included on the CD-ROM accompanying the book:

- *Client16*. A 16-bit project built with Visual C++ 1.52
- *Dll32*. A 32-bit DLL project

The Client16 application uses generic thunks to call functions located in the 32-bit DLL.

The Client16 Project

The Client16 project is based on the Generic project from the 16-bit Windows SDK. Client16 has menu items that generate function calls via generic thunks into the Dll32 32-bit DLL, which will be built later in this chapter.

To conserve space, the majority of the source code is not presented here. Only the relevant parts of the source files are shown in the listings for these two projects.

The main window procedure for Client16 is provided in Listing 6.18. When WM_CREATE is sent to Client16, the 32-bit DLL is loaded by calling LoadLibraryEx32W. When WM_DESTROY is received, the DLL is unloaded with FreeLibrary32W.

LISTING 6.18 THE MAIN WINDOW PROCEDURE FOR CLIENT16

```
long CALLBACK __export MainWndProc(HWND    hWnd,
                                   UINT    message,
                                   WPARAM  wParam,
                                   LPARAM  lParam)
{
    switch(message)
    {
        case WM_COMMAND:
            return OnCommand(hWnd, message, wParam, lParam);

        case WM_CREATE:
            g_hDll = LoadLibraryEx32W("dll32.dll", 0L, 0L);
            return 0;

        case WM_DESTROY:
            FreeLibrary32W(g_hDll);
            PostQuitMessage(0);
            break;

        default:
            return DefWindowProc(hWnd, message, wParam, lParam);
    }
    return 0L;
}
```

As discussed earlier, four menu commands are translated into function calls to the 32-bit DLL. The menu resource portion of the RC file for Client16 is shown in Listing 6.19.

LISTING 6.19 THE MENU RESOURCE USED BY CLIENT16

```
GENERICMENU MENU DISCARDABLE
BEGIN
    POPUP "&File"
    BEGIN
        MENUITEM "E&xit",              ID_FILE_EXIT
    END
    POPUP "&Test"
    BEGIN
        MENUITEM "GetPascalVar",       ID_TEST_GETPASCALVAR
        MENUITEM "SetPascalVar",       ID_TEST_SETPASCALVAR
        MENUITEM "GetPascalVarRet",    ID_TEST_GETPASCALVARRET
        MENUITEM "SetPascalVarRet",    ID_TEST_SETPASCALVARRET
    END
    POPUP "&Help"
    BEGIN
        MENUITEM "&About Client 16...",  IDM_ABOUT
    END
END
```

Command handling for each menu item is distributed in the OnCommand function, which is provided in Listing 6.20.

LISTING 6.20 COMMAND HANDLING USED BY CLIENT16

```
long __pascal OnCommand(HWND    hWnd,
                        UINT    message,
                        WPARAM wParam,
                        LPARAM lParam)
{
    switch(wParam)
    {
        case IDM_ABOUT:
            DialogBox(hInst, "AboutBox", hWnd, About);
            break;

        case ID_TEST_GETPASCALVAR:
            CallDllGetVal(hWnd, "16-bit client");
            break;

        case ID_TEST_SETPASCALVAR:
            CallDllSetVal(hWnd, "16-bit client");
            break;

        case ID_TEST_GETPASCALVARRET:
            CallDllGetValRet(hWnd, "16-bit client");
            break;
```

```
    case ID_TEST_SETPASCALVARRET:
        CallDllSetValRet(hWnd, "16-bit client");
        break;

    default:
        return DefWindowProc(hWnd, message, wParam, lParam);
    }
    return 0L;
}
```

Listing 6.21 shows Thunk.c, the file that contains the guts of the generic thunk code in
the Client16 project. There are four functions—one function for each menu item command. Each function determines the address of the targeted function by calling
GetProcAddress32W. If necessary, a local pointer is converted using GetVDMPointer32W.
Finally, the 32-bit function is called using CallProc32W.

LISTING 6.21   THUNK-HANDLING ROUTINES IN CLIENT16

```
/*
 * Thunk.c - Client16 project.
 *
 * Function-handling routines used by the 16-bit
 * client. This example program is part of "Programming
 * Windows 2000 Unleashed", by Mickey Williams.
 *
 */

#include "stdinc.h"

extern DWORD g_hDll;
long nLastDllVal = 0;

int CallDllGetVal(HWND hWnd, LPSTR pszCaption)
{
    long   nRet = 0;
    if(!g_hDll)
    {
        MessageBox(hWnd,
                    "Can't load 32-bit DLL",
                    pszCaption,
                    MB_OK|MB_ICONHAND);
    }
    else
    {
        PFUNC3 pFunc  = (PFUNC3)GetProcAddress32W(g_hDll,
                                                    "GetPascalVar");
        if(pFunc)
        {
```

continues

LISTING 6.21 CONTINUED

```
                //* convert 16:16 to 0:32 *
                DWORD dwPtrToRet = GetVDMPointer32W(&nRet, 1);
                CallProc32W(dwPtrToRet, pFunc, 0, 1);
                nLastDllVal = nRet;
        }
    }
    return (int)nRet;
}

int CallDllSetVal(HWND hWnd, LPSTR pszCaption)
{
    long nSetVal = nLastDllVal + 1;
    long nRet = 0;

    if(!g_hDll)
    {
        MessageBox(hWnd,
                    "Can't load 32-bit DLL",
                    pszCaption,
                    MB_OK¦MB_ICONHAND);
    }
    else
    {
        PFUNC4 pFunc = (PFUNC4)GetProcAddress32W(g_hDll,
                                            "SetPascalVar");
        if(pFunc)
        {
            CallProc32W(nSetVal, pFunc, 0, 1);
            nRet = 1;
        }
    }
    return (int)nRet;
}

int CallDllGetValRet(HWND hWnd, LPSTR pszCaption)
{
    long nRet = 0;
    long nFuncRet = 0;

    if(!g_hDll)
    {
        MessageBox(hWnd,
                    "Can't load 32-bit DLL",
                    pszCaption,
                    MB_OK¦MB_ICONHAND);
    }
    else
    {
```

```
        PFUNC1 pFunc = (PFUNC1)GetProcAddress32W(g_hDll,
                                        "GetPascalVarRet");
        if(pFunc)
        {
            //* convert 16:16 to 0:32 *
            DWORD dwPtrToRet = GetVDMPointer32W(&nRet, 1);
            nFuncRet = CallProc32W(dwPtrToRet, pFunc, 0, 1);
            nLastDllVal = nRet;
        }
    }
    return (int)nFuncRet;
}

int CallDllSetValRet(HWND hWnd, LPSTR pszCaption)
{
    long nRet = nLastDllVal + 1;

    if(!g_hDll)
    {
        MessageBox(hWnd,
                    "Can't load 32-bit DLL",
                    pszCaption,
                    MB_OK|MB_ICONHAND);
    }
    else
    {
        PFUNC2 pFunc = (PFUNC2)GetProcAddress32W(g_hDll,
                                        "SetPascalVarRet");
        if(pFunc)
        {
            nRet = CallProc32W(nRet, pFunc, 0, 1);
            nLastDllVal = nRet;
        }
    }
    return (int)nRet;
}
```

You can build and run the Client16 project "as is." However, you cannot execute any of the menu commands found under the Test menu until you've built the Dll32 project. The Dll32 project is discussed in the next section.

The Dll32 Project

The Dll32 project creates a simple 32-bit DLL that exposes four functions:

- SetPascalVar. A function that accepts an integer as a parameter; the value is stored inside the DLL for later use. The function returns void.

- GetPascalVar. A function that accepts a pointer to int as a parameter, filling the int with a value passed into the DLL previously with SetPascalVar or SetPascalVarRet. The function returns void.

- SetPascalVarRet. Identical to SetPascalVar, except it has a return value of int.

- GetPascalVarRet. Identical to GetPascalVar, except it has a return value of int.

The DEF file for the Dll32 project, Dll32.def, is shown in Listing 6.22.

LISTING 6.22   THE DEF FILE USED BY DLL32

```
LIBRARY      "DLL32"
DESCRIPTION  'Generic Thunk Example DLL'

EXPORTS
  GetPascalVar
  SetPascalVar
  GetPascalVarRet
  SetPascalVarRet
```

The header file for the Dll32 project, Dll32.h, is provided in Listing 6.23.

LISTING 6.23   THE Dll32.h HEADER FILE

```
/*
 * Dll32.h
 *
 * Declarations for functions in the Dll32 project.
 * This example program is part of "Programming
 * Windows 2000 Unleashed", by Mickey Williams.
 *
 */
#pragma once

void __stdcall GetPascalVar(int* pn);
void __stdcall SetPascalVar(int n);
int  __stdcall GetPascalVarRet(int* pn);
int  __stdcall SetPascalVarRet(int n);
```

The functions in the Dll32 project are implemented in one file, Dll32.c, which is provided in Listing 6.24. The functions are very simple—most of the code in Listing 6.24 is devoted to displaying message boxes to trace program execution.

LISTING 6.24   THE IMPLEMENTATION OF DLL32 FUNCTIONS IN Dll32.c

```
/*
 * Dll32.c
 *
 * Definitions for functions in the Dll32 project.
 * This example program is part of "Programming
 * Windows 2000 Unleashed", by Mickey Williams.
```

```
 *
 */

#include <windows.h>
#include "dll32.h"

int  g_nSimple = 42;

BOOL APIENTRY DllMain( HANDLE hModule,
                       DWORD ul_reason_for_call,
                       LPVOID lpReserved )
{
    switch(ul_reason_for_call)
    {
        case DLL_PROCESS_ATTACH:
            MessageBox(NULL, "Proc Attach", "dll32.c", MB_OK);
            DisableThreadLibraryCalls(hModule);
            break;

        case DLL_PROCESS_DETACH:
            MessageBox(NULL, "Proc Detach", "dll32.c", MB_OK);
            break;
    }
    return TRUE;
}

void __stdcall GetPascalVar(int* pn)
{
    if(pn)
    {
        char szMsg[80];
        wsprintf(szMsg,
                "GetPascalVar - Returning %d as parameter value",
                g_nSimple);
        MessageBox(NULL, szMsg, "dll32.c", MB_OK);
        *pn = g_nSimple;
    }
}

void __stdcall SetPascalVar(int n)
{
    char szMsg[80];
    wsprintf(szMsg,
            "SetPascalVar - Received %d as parameter value",
            n);
    MessageBox(NULL, szMsg, "dll32.c", MB_OK);

    g_nSimple = n;
}
```

continues

LISTING 6.24   CONTINUED

```c
int __stdcall GetPascalVarRet(int* pn)
{
    int  nRet = 0;
    char szMsg[80];
    if(pn)
    {
        wsprintf(szMsg,
                "GetPascalVarRet - Returning %d as parameter value",
                g_nSimple);
        MessageBox(NULL, szMsg, "dll32.c", MB_OK);

        *pn = g_nSimple;
        nRet = 21;
    }
    wsprintf(szMsg,
            "GetPascalVarRet - Returning %d as return value",
            nRet);
    MessageBox(NULL, szMsg, "dll32.c", MB_OK);
    return nRet;
}

int __stdcall SetPascalVarRet(int n)
{
    char szMsg[80];
    wsprintf(szMsg,
            "SetPascalVarRet - Received %d as parameter value",
            n);
    MessageBox(NULL, szMsg, "dll32.c", MB_OK);

    g_nSimple = n;
    return n;
}
```

To successfully test the Client16 project, follow these steps:

1. Build the Client16 project using Visual C++ 1.5.

2. Build the Dll32 project using a 32-bit version of Visual C++.

3. Copy Dll32.dll into a directory where Client16 can find it—for example, the same directory as the Client16 executable file.

4. Run Client16 and select items from its Test menu. As you select items on the Test menu, message boxes will display the progress of the generic thunk.

Debugging a Generic Thunk

Debugging a generic thunk can be difficult, because the 16-bit application runs as a 16-bit process, and the DLL is running as a 32-bit process called by the Windows 2000 VDM. Debugging is made more difficult due to the following factors:

- Different tools must be used to debug your application.
- The debugging tools used to debug a thunk are made for different platforms— additionally, 16-bit tools are rather primitive when compared to recent 32-bit tools.
- You can't step directly from a 16-bit client app into a 32-bit DLL.
- As the process is launched by the VDM, the normal DLL debugging procedures don't apply.

The best approach is to debug normally when required in the 16-bit app. You can lay a trap inside the 32-bit DLL by following these steps:

1. Add a call to DebugBreak inside your DLL. A good place to add this call is inside an initialization function that's called when the DLL is first launched.

2. When the DebugBreak statement is executed, the operating system will cause a debugger exception. A dialog box similar to a just-in-time debugging dialog box will be displayed. Elect to launch the debugger.

3. Once the debugger is launched, continue execution. As the debugger now has control over the VDM, you can debug your 32-bit DLL by setting breakpoints as required, just as you would debug any other DLL.

Summary

This chapter discussed many of the issues involved with building and using DLLs when programming for Windows 2000. The differences between DLLs written for 16-bit versions of Windows and Windows 2000 were also discussed.

Several projects were provided to illustrate how to export standard C functions, C++ classes, and MFC objects. An example illustrating how to avoid synchronization problems in shared DLL memory was also presented.

A discussion about generic thunking included two projects—a 16-bit client and a 32-bit DLL. The project demonstrates how a 16-bit application can call a 32-bit DLL in Windows 2000.

Distributed Security

CHAPTER 7

This chapter discusses distributed security in Windows 2000. Security has been a key part of Windows NT programming since the operating system was introduced to developers in 1992. Although the original security manipulation functions were very low-level and difficult to use, security programming became much easier with the release of Windows NT 4.0, which included high-level functions for access control. Windows 2000 extends these functions to offer support for security when interacting with non-Windows operating systems.

This chapter includes a number of sample functions you can use to simplify your security programming. It also includes an example that illustrates how a server can use impersonation to properly handle the access of securable objects on behalf of a client.

Windows 2000 Security Overview

Windows 2000 security has two aspects: authorization and authentication. *Authentication* is the process used by the operating system to ensure that you are who you say you are. *Authorization* is the process used by the operating system to allow access to objects or tasks based on the security credentials of a user.

Although authentication and authorization are two sides of the same coin (and work closely together), they are not two names for the same topic. Authentication is involved only with guaranteeing the identity of a user and does not concern itself with access control. Similarly, authorization is concerned only with granting or denying access to an authenticated user.

Prior to Windows 2000, Windows NT used the Windows NT LAN Manager (NTLM) protocol as its sole network authentication protocol. Windows 2000 has expanded its horizons somewhat and uses the industry-standard Kerberos version 5 protocol as its default authentication protocol. Kerberos has many advantages over NTLM, such as the ability to authenticate both client and server. Authentication via NTLM is still available when interacting with NT 4.0 and earlier machines. Windows 2000 also supports the Crypto API, Secure Sockets Layer (SSL), and public key encryption as additional authentication tools.

Before a user is allowed access to any resources, the Windows 2000 logon process must authenticate the user. As will be discussed later, access tokens that describe the user's security information are associated with the user and can be used to identify the user on the computer and network.

After a user has been authenticated, Windows 2000 will allow or deny access to securable objects, based on comparisons between the access rights granted to the user and the access control lists attached to the securable objects. Windows 2000 performs these checks automatically; there's usually no need for you to test access permissions programmatically in your code.

Server applications that perform work on behalf of clients use an operating system feature known as *impersonation*. Impersonation enables the server thread to assume the security identity of the client in order to access securable objects. Later in the chapter, you'll see an example of a named pipe server that uses impersonation to provide the proper security access to clients.

Fundamental Security Data Structures

Several data structures are used constantly in Windows 2000 security programming. Many of the data structures are often referred to by abbreviated names—which doesn't simplify your life if you're a newcomer to security programming. Here are a few of the most commonly used security structures:

- SID. Short for *security identifier*. This is a structure that uniquely identifies a user or group.
- ACE. Short for *access control entry*. This is a structure that defines how a SID can interact with securable objects. An ACE may allow or deny access to a particular SID. It may also define security-auditing parameters for a SID.
- ACL. Short for *access control list*. This is an array of zero or more ACEs. An ACL may contain both access-allowed and access-denied ACEs.
- DACL. Short for *discretionary access control list*. This is an ACL that's used to allow or deny access to a securable object.
- SACL. Short for *system access control list*. This is an ACL that's used to audit access to a securable object.
- SECURITY_DESCRIPTOR. A structure that contains security information for an object. This information includes the DACL and SACL associated with the object, as well as information about its owner and group membership.

These structures interact with each other as shown in Figure 7.1.

Figure 7.1

The relationships between basic low-level security structures.

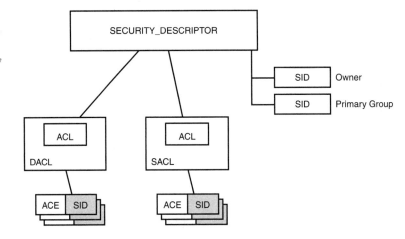

Understanding Process and Thread Security Tokens

When a thread or process is created, it's provided with an *access token*. The access token describes the security attributes associated with the process or thread. The access token is normally obtained from the owner of the process. Later in the chapter, you'll see how the access token can be adjusted programmatically.

An access token caries information that can be used to determine the privileges and rights for a process or thread. In Windows 2000, privileges and rights refer to the capabilities of a user to perform certain actions, but they are different concepts. Here's an explanation of each:

- A *privilege* is the ability to perform a system-level action, such as the ability to modify the system time, and is granted by a system administrator.
- A *right* is the ability to access a securable object and is allowed or denied by the DACL associated with the object.

Access tokens carry a great deal of information about the user. Here's a list of the most commonly used information:

- The SID for the user's account
- The SID for the user's primary group
- SIDs for groups that the user belongs to
- A logon SID that identifies the logon session

- A list of privileges held by the user and the user's groups
- A DACL, known as the *default DACL*, that's assigned to objects created without a security descriptor

Every process has a primary access token. In addition, each thread has an impersonation token that's used when a server impersonates a client in order to assume the security context of the calling process. During impersonation, Windows 2000 uses the impersonation token when authorizing access to resources.

Manipulating Process and Thread Access Tokens

Several Windows 2000 functions are used to interact with access tokens. Here are four commonly used functions:

- OpenProcessToken. Returns an access token handle
- OpenThreadToken. Returns an impersonation token handle that identifies a client
- GetTokenInformation. Returns security information stored in the access token
- SetTokenInformation. Modifies security information stored in the access token

Modifying Token Privileges

Various Win32 and Windows 2000 functions require that the caller have certain privileges enabled. If the access token of the calling process does not possess the required set of privileges, the function call will be rejected by the operating system.

Two functions are used to modify the privileges of an access token:

- LookupPrivilegeValue. Returns a locally unique identifier (LUID) that's used to identify a specific privilege
- AdjustTokenPrivileges. Enables or disables privileges in an access token

For example, some security functions require that the calling process have the SE_SECURITY_NAME privilege. Although a user in an administrator group may enable this privilege, it's not normally enabled by default; the calling process must adjust its access token. Listing 7.1 contains an example of a function that enables or disables the SE_SECURITY_NAME privilege for the calling process.

LISTING 7.1 A FUNCTION THAT ADJUSTS THE SE_SECURITY_NAME PRIVILEGE ON A PROCESS TOKEN

```
/*
 * Enables or disables the SE_SECURITY_NAME privilege for the
 * current process.  This privilege must be explicitly enabled
```

continues

LISTING 7.1   CONTINUED

```
 * in order to access some security information. Returns FALSE
 * if the privilege was adjusted, or TRUE otherwise.
 */
BOOL EnableSecurityNamePrivilege(BOOL fEnable)
{
    HANDLE hProcess = GetCurrentProcess();
    HANDLE hToken;

    if(!OpenProcessToken(hProcess, TOKEN_ALL_ACCESS, &hToken))
        return FALSE;

    TOKEN_PRIVILEGES tpNew;
    BOOL fLookup = LookupPrivilegeValue(NULL,
                                        SE_SECURITY_NAME,
                                        &tpNew.Privileges[0].Luid);
    if(!fLookup)
        return FALSE;

    if(fEnable)
        tpNew.Privileges[0].Attributes = SE_PRIVILEGE_ENABLED;
    else
        tpNew.Privileges[0].Attributes = 0;
    tpNew.PrivilegeCount = 1;

    BOOL fAdjusted = AdjustTokenPrivileges(hToken,
                                           FALSE,
                                           &tpNew,
                                           0,
                                           NULL,
                                           NULL);
    if(!fAdjusted)
        return FALSE;
    return TRUE;
}
```

In Listing 7.1, the EnableSecurityNamePrivilege function begins by obtaining a pseudohandle for the current process by calling GetCurrentProcess. Next, calling OpenProcessToken retrieves a handle to the process access token.

The LookupPrivilegeValue function is then called to determine the LUID used to identify the SE_SECURITY_NAME privilege. This LUID is passed to the AdjustTokenPrivileges function in order to enable or disable the SE_SECURITY_NAME privilege for the process's access token.

Understanding the Security Identifier

The security identifier structure, or `SID`, is used to uniquely identify a user or group in a Windows 2000 domain. In general, you should not manipulate a `SID` directly; however, it is instructive to take a look at a `SID` in order to get some understanding about how it's put together.

A security identifier contains the following items:

- The revision level of the `SID`.
- The 48-bit identifier for the Windows 2000 domain that issued the `SID`.
- A list of subauthority or relative identifiers (`RID`s) that uniquely identify the `SID`. This list is guaranteed to be unique within a Windows 2000 domain.

A `SID` will always uniquely identify a user or group. In the event that two users or groups have identical rights, the list of `RID`s is guaranteed to be unique.

Converting `SID`s to Strings

The `SID` is stored as a binary value that shouldn't be examined directly. You can, however, convert the `SID` into a format that's easily displayed with the `ConvertSidToStringSid` function:

```
BOOL fConverted = ConvertSidToStringSid(pSid, ppszSidString);
```

The `ConvertSidToStringSid` function has two parameters:

- A pointer to the `SID` to be converted.
- A pointer to a string buffer that will be allocated and filled with the string representation of the `SID`. This buffer must be freed using the `LocalFree` function.

The string representation of a `SID` follows a specific format, known as *S-R-I-S*. Each `SID` string is composed of four or more elements:

- *S*. The letter S
- *R*. A number that represents the revision level
- *I*. An identifier for the authority that issued the `SID`
- *S*. One or more subauthority values or relative identifiers

As an example of a `SID`, here's the current value of the `mickeyw` security identifier in the `codevtech.com` domain:

```
S-1-5-21-854245398-515967899-1417001333-1105
```

The `ConvertStringSidToSid` function is used to convert a `SID` from a string format into its native binary format:

```
BOOL fConverted = ConvertStringSidToSid(pszSidString,
                                        &pSid);
```

The `ConvertStringSidToSid` function has two parameters:

- A pointer to the `SID`, in string form, to be converted.
- The address of a pointer to a `SID` that will be allocated and filled with the binary form of the `SID`. This buffer must be freed using the `LocalFree` function.

A *well-known* `SID` is a security identifier that specifies a commonly used, generic user or group. Well-known `SID`s include the Everyone group, the Local Administrators group, and the Local System group.

Retrieving a `SID` for a User or Group

The `LookupAccountName` function is used to retrieve a `SID` for a particular user or group:

```
BOOL fRet = LookupAccountName(_T("amigas.com"),
                              _T("ali"),
                              pSid,
                              &cbSid,
                              lpszRefDomain,
                              &cbRefDomain,
                              &sne);
```

The `LookupAccountName` function has seven parameters:

- The name of the system where the lookup will take place (or `NULL` to specify the local system).
- The account name you're searching for.
- A pointer to a `SID` that will receive the account's security identifier.
- A pointer to a `DWORD` that contains the length, in bytes, of the `SID` buffer. If he buffer is too small, the function will fail with a return code of `ERROR_INSUFFICIENT_BUFFER`, and this parameter will be filled with the minimum required size for the `SID` buffer.
- The address of a string buffer that will be filled with the account's domain name.
- A pointer to a `DWORD` that contains the length, in bytes, of the previous parameter. If the buffer is too small, the function will fail with a return code of `ERROR_INSUFFICIENT_BUFFER`, and this parameter will be filled with the minimum required size for the domain name.
- The address of a `SID_NAME_USE` variable that will be filled with a value from the `SID_NAME_USE` enumeration that defines the type of account.

Typically, you'll call `LookupAccountName` twice—the first time with the `SID` buffer size set to zero in order to determine the size of the account's `SID`, and the second time with a properly sized `SID` buffer to retrieve the `SID`. Listing 7.2 contains a wrapper function around the `LookupAccountName` function that retrieves the `SID` for a specified account and then converts the `SID` into string form.

LISTING 7.2 A FUNCTION THAT RETRIEVES SIDS IN STRING FORM

```
void AccountNameToSidString(LPCTSTR  lpszSystem,
                            LPCTSTR  lpszAccountName,
                            LPTSTR   pszSidBuffer,
                            DWORD    cbSidBuffer)
{
    PSID  pSid = NULL;
    DWORD cbSid = 0;
    TCHAR lpszRefDomain[256];
    DWORD cbRefDomain = 256;
    SID_NAME_USE sne;

    BOOL fRet = LookupAccountName(lpszSystem,
                                  lpszAccountName,
                                  pSid,
                                  &cbSid,
                                  lpszRefDomain,
                                  &cbRefDomain,
                                  &sne);
    /* First call is expected to fail */
    if(fRet != FALSE)
    {
        HandleError(_T("LookupAccountName returned invalid val"));
        return;
    }
    DWORD dwErr = GetLastError();
    if(dwErr == ERROR_INSUFFICIENT_BUFFER)
    {
        pSid = LocalAlloc(LPTR, cbSid);
        if(!pSid)
        {
            HandleError(_T("LocalAlloc for SID failed"));
            return;
        }
        fRet = LookupAccountName(lpszSystem,
                                 lpszAccountName,
                                 pSid,
                                 &cbSid,
                                 lpszRefDomain,
                                 &cbRefDomain,
                                 &sne);
```

continues

7

DISTRIBUTED SECURITY

LISTING 7.2   CONTINUED

```
        if(fRet == FALSE)
        {
            HandleError(_T("LookupAccountName #2 failed"));
            LocalFree(pSid);
            return;
        }
    }
    else
    {
        HandleError(_T("GetLastError returned invalid val"));
        return;
    }

    LPTSTR pszSidString = NULL;

    ConvertSidToStringSid(pSid, &pszSidString);
    lstrcpyn(pszSidBuffer, pszSidString, cbSidBuffer);
    LocalFree(pszSidString);
    LocalFree(pSid);
}
```

In Listing 7.2, the `AccountNameToSidString` function begins by calling `LookupAccountName` with a SID buffer that has a length of zero. The function is expected to fail with an error code of `ERROR_INSUFFICIENT_BUFFER`. The SID buffer is allocated using the minimum buffer length returned in the `cbSid` parameter, and the `LookupAccountName` function is called again to retrieve the account's SID.

After the SID is obtained, it's converted into a string using the `ConvertSidToStringSid` function and then copied into the caller's string buffer.

A simple wrapper for the `LookupAccountName` function is provided in Listing 7.3. The `AccountNameToSid` function dynamically allocates a SID for a user passed as a parameter to the function.

LISTING 7.3   A FUNCTION THAT CREATES A SID BASED ON A USER NAME

```
PSID AccountNameToSid(LPCTSTR  lpszAccountName)
{
    PSID  pSid = NULL;
    DWORD cbSid = 0;
    TCHAR lpszRefDomain[256];
    DWORD cbRefDomain = 256;
    SID_NAME_USE sne;
```

```
        BOOL fRet = LookupAccountName(NULL,
                                      lpszAccountName,
                                      pSid,
                                      &cbSid,
                                      lpszRefDomain,
                                      &cbRefDomain,
                                      &sne);
        /* First call is expected to fail */
        if(fRet != FALSE)
        {
            return NULL;
        }
        DWORD dwErr = GetLastError();
        if(dwErr == ERROR_INSUFFICIENT_BUFFER)
        {
            pSid = LocalAlloc(LPTR, cbSid);
            if(!pSid)
            {
                return NULL;
            }
            fRet = LookupAccountName(NULL,
                                     lpszAccountName,
                                     pSid,
                                     &cbSid,
                                     lpszRefDomain,
                                     &cbRefDomain,
                                     &sne);
            if(fRet == FALSE)
            {
                LocalFree(pSid);
                return NULL;
            }
        }
        else
        {
            return NULL;
        }
        return pSid;
}
```

In Listing 7.3, the AccountNameToSid function works in much the same way as the
AccountNameToSidString function presented in Listing 7.2. The only difference is that
instead of converting the SID into string form, the AccountNameToSid function passes the
dynamically allocated SID back to the caller.

Understanding ACE, DACL, and SACL Structures

The ACE, DACL, and SACL structures form the heart of Windows 2000 security. The next few sections discuss how these structures are used.

The ACE Structure

An ACE, or *access control entry* structure, is used to specify a type of action to be taken for a particular user or group with respect to security. Each ACE contains a SID that identifies a security trustee and a set of masks that contain the rights for the trustee.

Here are the six different types of ACE structures:

- ACCESS_ALLOWED_ACE. An ACE that specifies a user or group that's allowed access to a securable object.
- ACCESS_DENIED_ACE. An ACE that specifies a user or group that's denied access to a securable object.
- SYSTEM_AUDIT_ACE. An ACE that specifies a user or group that causes a security audit event to be generated.
- ACCESS_ALLOWED_OBJECT_ACE. An ACE used in Active Directory that's similar to the ACCESS_ALLOWED_ACE structure. It adds information that controls the inheritance of the ACE by child objects.
- ACCESS_DENIED_OBJECT_ACE. An ACE used in Active Directory that's similar to the ACCESS_DENIED_ACE structure. It adds information that controls inheritance of the ACE by child objects.
- SYSTEM_AUDIT_OBJECT_ACE. An ACE used in Active Directory that's similar to the ACCESS_ALLOWED_ACE structure. It adds information that controls inheritance of the ACE by child objects.

All ACE structures have a similar format. Figure 7.2 shows the memory layout for an ACCESS_ALLOWED_ACE structure.

The DACL and SACL Structures

Every securable object may have two ACLs, or *access control lists*, associated with it:

- A DACL, or *discretionary access list*, which specifies the users and groups permitted access to the object
- A SACL, or *system access control list*, which specifies the conditions that cause a security audit event to be generated for the object

FIGURE 7.2

The layout of an ACCESS_ALLOWED_ACE.

ACCESS_ALLOWED_ACE

Both DACLs and SACLs are arrays of ACE structures, beginning with an ACL structure used as a header for the list. A SACL contains only system audit ACE structures, and a DACL contains only access-allowed or access-denied ACE structures. ACEs in a DACL must be arranged in proper order: ACEs that deny access must come before ACEs that allow access.

Determining the Size Required for an ACL

Occasionally, you may need to copy or add an entry to an ACL. Because an ACL is a variable-length structure, you'll need to determine the size of the ACL and allocate a new buffer that's large enough to store the (possibly larger) new ACL.

The size of an ACL is determined by adding the size of the ACL structure to the size of all ACLs contained in the list. The simplest way to determine the size is to call the GetAclInformation function, as shown in the following wrapper function:

```
BOOL GetAclSize(PACL pacl, LPDWORD pdw)
{
    ACL_SIZE_INFORMATION info;
    BOOL fInfo = GetAclInformation(pacl,
                                   &info,
                                   sizeof(info),
                                   AclSizeInformation);
    if(fInfo)
        *pdw = info.AclBytesInUse;
    return fInfo;
}
```

The GetAclInformation function has four parameters:

- A pointer to an ACL
- The address of either an ACL_SIZE_INFORMATION structure, if you're retrieving the size of an ACL, or an ACL_REVISION_INFORMATION structure, to retrieve revision information about the ACL
- The size of the structure in the previous parameter
- Either AclSizeInformation, to retrieve size information from the ACL, or AclRevisionInformation, to retrieve revision information

7

DISTRIBUTED SECURITY

Adding an Access-allowed ACE to a DACL

An access-allowed ACE is added to a DACL using the AddAccessAllowedAceEx function:

```
BOOL AllowUserAccessThroughAcl(PACL pacl, LPCTSTR lpszUser)
{
    PSID pSid = AccountNameToSid(lpszUser);
    if(!pSid) return FALSE;

    BOOL fAdded = AddAccessAllowedAceEx(pAcl,
                                        ACL_REVISION,
                                        0,
                                        GENERIC_ALL,
                                        pSid);
    LocalFree(pSid);
    return fAdded;
}
```

As shown in this code fragment, you don't need to create the ACCESS_ALLOWED_ACE yourself; you simply pass a SID to the AddAccessAllowedAceEx function. AddAccessAllowedAceEx has five parameters:

- A pointer to the ACL.
- The revision level of the ACL. This parameter is ACL_REVISION_DS when working with ACLs in Active Directory. Otherwise, this parameter is ACL_REVISION.
- Zero or more flags that specify the inheritance characteristics of the new ACE. Possible values for this parameter are discussed later.
- One or more flags that specify the access rights affected by this ACL. Possible values for this parameter are discussed later.
- A pointer to the SID that will be added to the ACL as an access-allowed ACE.

For DACLs that are applied to containers (such as Registry keys, directories, and printers), child objects may inherit ACEs. The following inheritance flags control the type of inheritance allowed:

- CONTAINER_INHERIT_ACE. Enables the ACE to be inherited by child objects that are container objects, such as directories, printers, and Registry keys.
- INHERIT_ONLY_ACE. Specifies that the ACE does not apply to this object. However, child objects can inherit it.
- INHERITED_ACE. Specifies an inherited ACE for use in operations on child objects.
- NO_PROPAGATE_INHERIT_ACE. Inhibits the OBJECT_INHERIT_ACE and CONTAINER_INHERIT_ACE flags from being copied to an inherited ACE.
- OBJECT_INHERIT_ACE. Enables the ACE to be inherited by noncontainer child objects, such as files, Registry values, and printer shares.

The access rights controlled by the ACL are a combination of one or more of the following flags:

- DELETE. The ACE affects the right to delete the object.
- READ_CONTROL. The ACE affects the right to read non-SACL security descriptor information.
- SYNCHRONIZE. The ACE affects the right to use the object for process and thread synchronization.
- WRITE_DAC. The ACE affects the right to modify the object's DACL.
- WRITE_OWNER. The ACE affects the right to change the owner in the object's security descriptor.

To simplify things, here are a number of constants that combine one or more of the preceding flags:

- STANDARD_RIGHTS_ALL. Combines all rights from the previous list
- STANDARD_RIGHTS_EXECUTE. Same as READ_CONTROL
- STANDARD_RIGHTS_READ. Same as READ_CONTROL
- STANDARD_RIGHTS_REQUIRED. Combines all flags except SYNCHRONIZE
- STANDARD_RIGHTS_WRITE. Same as READ_CONTROL

There's also a set of generic rights that can be applied to securable objects in Windows 2000. You can use the following generic rights with an ACE in place of the preceding flags:

- GENERIC_ALL. Includes read, write, and execute access.
- GENERIC_EXECUTE. Execute access only.
- GENERIC_READ. Read access only.
- GENERIC_WRITE. Write access only.

The AddAccessDeniedAceEx function works just like AddAccessAllowedAceEx, except that it adds an access-denied ACE to the end of the DACL. Both functions may result in a DACL that contains ACE structures in the wrong order. When using low-level security functions such as AddAccessAllowedAceEx and AddAccessDeniedAceEx, you need to make sure that all access-denied entries are located before any access-allowed entries. If necessary, you must manually reorder the list.

The AddAccessAllowedAceEx function does not allocate new storage for an ACL—it simply adds the new ACE to the end of an existing ACL. You must calculate the required size of your new ACL and allocate a new ACL if necessary. In cases where you're adding an ACE to an existing ACL, it's easier to use a newer TRUSTEE-based access control function, such as SetEntriesInAccessList. These functions will be discussed later in this chapter.

7

DISTRIBUTED SECURITY

Security Descriptors

The SECURITY_DESCRIPTOR structure is used to store security information for a securable object. The security descriptor for an object includes the following items:

- An optional DACL that specifies access rights for the object
- An optional SACL that specifies what type of access results in security audit events
- An owner SID that identifies the owner of the object
- A group SID that identifies group membership of the object

There are two basic types of security descriptors:

- A security descriptor in *absolute form* contains pointers to the SID and ACL information. SID and ACL information is usually not located in the same contiguous chunk of memory as the SECURITY_DESCRIPTOR structure.
- A security descriptor in *self-relative form* contains the SID and ACL information in the same contiguous chunk of memory as the SECURITY_DESCRIPTOR structure. Instead of pointers, the structure contains offsets to the SID and ACL information. This type of security descriptor is useful in COM, because it can easily be transmitted to another machine on the network.

Figure 7.3 illustrates the difference between absolute and self-relative security descriptors.

FIGURE 7.3

The layout of self-relative and absolute security descriptors.

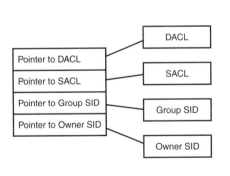

| Offset to DACL |
| Offset to SACL |
| Offset to Group SID |
| Offset to Owner SID |
| DACL |
| SACL |
| Owner SID |
| Group SID |

Absolute Format   Self-Relative Format

The process of creating a security descriptor begins by initializing it. Listing 7.4 contains a wrapper function that illustrates how to allocate and initialize an empty security descriptor.

LISTING 7.4 CREATING AN EMPTY SECURITY DESCRIPTOR

```
PSECURITY_DESCRIPTOR CreateEmptySecurityDescriptor()
{
    PSECURITY_DESCRIPTOR psd = NULL;

    psd = LocalAlloc(LPTR, SECURITY_DESCRIPTOR_MIN_LENGTH);
    if(psd)
    {
        BOOL fInit = InitializeSecurityDescriptor(psd,
                                    SECURITY_DESCRIPTOR_REVISION);
        if(!fInit)
        {
            LocalFree(psd);
            psd = NULL;
        }
    }
    return psd;
}
```

In Listing 7.4, the CreateEmptySecurityDescriptor function begins by allocating a buffer with a length of SECURITY_DESCRIPTOR_MIN_LENGTH. This is the size of a security descriptor that does not include SID or DACL information in the same memory block as the SECURITY_DESCRIPTOR structure. Next, the security descriptor is initialized into an empty state with the InitializeSecurityDescriptor function. Note that the security descriptor returned from the function in Listing 7.4 is allocated using LocalAlloc. Any function that calls this function must free the returned security descriptor using LocalFree.

The SetSecurityDescriptorDacl function is used to add a DACL to a security descriptor:

```
BOOL fAdded = SetSecurityDescriptorDacl(psd, TRUE, pAcl, FALSE);
```

The SetSecurityDescriptorDacl function has four parameters:

- A pointer to a security descriptor
- A flag that indicates whether a DACL is included in the security descriptor
- A pointer to the ACL to be used as the security descriptor's DACL
- A flag that's set to TRUE if the DACL is a default DACL

To create a security descriptor that contains a DACL, you need to allocate and initialize the security descriptor and ACL and then use SetSecurityDescriptorDacl to add the ACL to the security descriptor. Listing 7.5 is an example of a function that creates a security descriptor that grants access to a specific user.

LISTING 7.5 CREATING A SECURITY DESCRIPTOR THAT ALLOWS ACCESS TO A SPECIFIC USER

```
PSECURITY_DESCRIPTOR CreateAllowedSDForUser(LPCTSTR lpszUser)
{
    PSECURITY_DESCRIPTOR psd = NULL;

    psd = CreateEmptySecurityDescriptor();
    if(!psd) return NULL;

    PSID  pSid = AccountNameToSid(lpszUser);
    if(!pSid || !IsValidSid(pSid))
    {
        LocalFree(pSid);
        LocalFree(psd);
        return NULL;
    }

    DWORD cbSid = GetLengthSid(pSid);
    PACL pAcl = NULL;
    DWORD cbAcl = sizeof(ACL) + sizeof(ACCESS_ALLOWED_ACE) + cbSid;
    pAcl = (PACL)LocalAlloc(LPTR, cbAcl);

    BOOL fAdded = AddAccessAllowedAceEx(pAcl,
                                       ACL_REVISION,
                                       0,
                                       GENERIC_ALL,
                                       pSid);
    LocalFree(pSid);
    SetSecurityDescriptorDacl(psd, TRUE, pAcl, FALSE);

    return psd;
}
```

In Listing 7.5, the `CreateAllowedSDForUser` function begins by calling the
`CreateEmptySecurityDescriptor` function presented earlier in Listing 7.4. Next, a SID
for the specified user is created using the `AccountNameToSid` function. The SID is then
added to a new ACL, and the ACL is added to the security descriptor before the security
descriptor is returned to the caller.

Retrieving a Security Descriptor

Retrieving an existing security descriptor is much easier than creating a new security
descriptor. To retrieve a security descriptor, use the `GetNamedSecurityInfo` function:

```
DWORD GetNamedSecurityInfo(LPTSTR pObjectName,
                           SE_OBJECT_TYPE ObjectType,
                           SECURITY_INFORMATION SecurityInfo,
                           PSID *ppsidOwner,
```

```
                       PSID *ppsidGroup,
                       PACL *ppDacl,
                       PACL *ppSacl,
                       PSECURITY_DESCRIPTOR *ppSecurityDescriptor);
```

The `GetNamedSecurityInfo` function has eight parameters:

- A string that identifies the securable object. For a file, this parameter is the path to the file. Each type of securable object has a different name format. For details about specific types, consult the online documentation.

- An identifier for the object type. Possible values for this parameter are listed later.

- One or more flags that specify the type of information to be returned by the function. Possible values for this parameter are listed later.

- The address of a pointer to a `SID` that will be set to the address of the owner `SID` contained in the security descriptor. This parameter can be `NULL` if the `OWNER_SECURITY_INFORMATION` flag is not included in the third parameter.

- The address of a pointer to a `SID` that will be set to the address of the group `SID` contained in the security descriptor. This parameter can be `NULL` if the `GROUP_SECURITY_INFORMATION` flag is not included in the third parameter.

- The address of a pointer to an `ACL` that will be set to the address of the `DACL` contained in the security descriptor. This parameter can be `NULL` if the `DACL_SECURITY_INFORMATION` flag is not included in the third parameter.

- The address of a pointer to an `ACL` that will be set to the address of the `SACL` contained in the security descriptor. This parameter can be `NULL` if the `SACL_SECURITY_INFORMATION` flag is not included in the third parameter.

- The address of a pointer to a `SECURITY_DESCRIPTOR` structure that will be set when the function returns. This structure is dynamically allocated and must be freed using `LocalFree` when the structure is no longer needed.

The object type identifier is used to indicate the type of object named in the first parameter. Here are the possible values for this parameter:

- `SE_FILE_OBJECT`. The object is a file or directory.
- `SE_SERVICE`. The object is a Windows 2000 service.
- `SE_PRINTER`. The object is a printer.
- `SE_REGISTRY_KEY`. The object is a Registry key.
- `SE_LMSHARE`. The object is a network share.
- `SE_KERNEL_OBJECT`. The object is a Windows 2000 kernel object, such as a pipe, mutex, waitable timer, or similar object.

- SE_WINDOW_OBJECT. The object is a window station or desktop object.
- SE_DS_OBJECT. The object is an Active Directory object. The object can also be a property or property set of an Active Directory object.
- SE_DS_OBJECT_ALL. The object is an Active Directory object that includes all its property sets and properties.
- SE_PROVIDER_DEFINED_OBJECT. The object is a user-defined object.

The following security information flags are combined to specify the types of information returned by the function:

- OWNER_SECURITY_INFORMATION. A pointer to the owner SID will be returned.
- GROUP_SECURITY_INFORMATION. A pointer to the group SID will be returned.
- DACL_SECURITY_INFORMATION. A pointer to the DACL will be returned.
- SACL_SECURITY_INFORMATION. A pointer to the SACL will be returned.

An example of a function that returns a security descriptor for a given filename is provided in Listing 7.6. The GetFileSecurityDescriptor function returns a pointer to a SECURITY_DESCRIPTOR structure that must be freed using LocalFree.

LISTING 7.6 A FUNCTION THAT RETRIEVES A SECURITY DESCRIPTOR FOR A FILE

```
PSECURITY_DESCRIPTOR GetFileSecurityDescriptor(LPTSTR pszPath)
{
    PSID psidOwner = NULL;
    PSID psidGroup = NULL;
    PACL pAcl = NULL;
    PACL pSacl = NULL;
    PSECURITY_DESCRIPTOR psd = NULL;

    GetNamedSecurityInfo(pszPath,
                    SE_FILE_OBJECT,
                    OWNER_SECURITY_INFORMATION|
                    GROUP_SECURITY_INFORMATION|
                    DACL_SECURITY_INFORMATION,
                    &psidOwner,
                    &psidGroup,
                    &pAcl,
                    &pSacl,
                    &psd);
    return psd;
}
```

Using the Security Attributes Structure

The SECURITY_ATTRIBUTES structure is used by most Win32 functions that create or access securable objects. For example, CreateFile, CreateNamedPipe, and CreateMutex (just to name three), all accept a pointer to a SECURITY_ATTRIBUTES structure as a parameter.

It's a common practice to pass NULL in place of a pointer to a valid SECURITY_ATTRIBUTES structure. When a securable object is created using a NULL security attributes structure, the default security attributes from the creator's access token are used.

The SECURITY_ATTRIBUTES structure is very straightforward:

```
typedef struct _SECURITY_ATTRIBUTES
{
    DWORD  nLength;
    LPVOID lpSecurityDescriptor;
    BOOL   bInheritHandle;
}SECURITY_ATTRIBUTES;
```

Here are the three member variables in the SECURITY_ATTRIBUTES structure:

- nLength. The size of the SECURITY_ATTRIBUTES structure

- lpSecurityDescriptor. A pointer to a SECURITY_DESCRIPTOR structure

- bInheritHandle. A flag that's set to True to allow the handle to the created object to be inherited

As you can see, the SECURITY_ATTRIBUTES structure is basically just a wrapper around a SECURITY_DESCRIPTOR pointer.

Trustee-based Access Control

Trustee-based access control was originally introduced in Windows NT 4.0, where it was commonly known as *Windows NT 4.0 Access Control*. Windows 2000 has extended the trustee-based access control functions to include support for Active Directory objects as well as support for alternate security providers. In Windows 2000, you can also interact with securable objects on non-Windows systems.

The structures used in trustee-based access control are nested several layers deep, as shown in Figure 7.4.

Windows 2000 Core Technologies

FIGURE 7.4

*The structures
used in Windows
2000 access
control.*

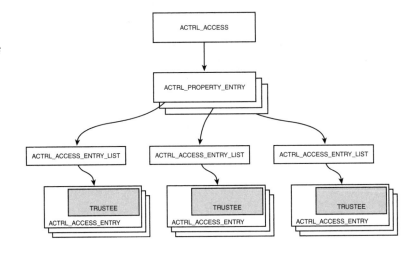

As shown in Figure 7.4, five structures are used in Windows 2000 access control:

- TRUSTEE. A structure that represents a trustee or security principal. A trustee may be a user, group, or login session.

- ACTRL_ACCESS_ENTRY. A structure that contains access control information about a single TRUSTEE, including a mask of the rights that are controlled by the TRUSTEE as well as whether those rights are allowed or denied. This structure includes a TRUSTEE as one of its member variables.

- ACTRL_ACCESS_ENTRY_LIST. A structure that represents the actual access control list. This structure hosts an array of zero or more ACTRL_ACCESS_ENTRY structures.

- ACTRL_PROPERTY_ENTRY. Manages a collection of ACTRL_ACCESS_ENTRY_LIST structures for an object. In a typical simple case where an object does not offer management of individual properties, there's one ACTRL_PROPERTY_ENTRY per ACTRL_ACCESS structure.

- ACTRL_ACCESS. A structure that contains access control lists for an object. A new feature in Windows 2000 is the ability to set attributes for properties located on some objects. This structure contains a pointer to an array of ACTRL_ACCESS_ENTRY_LIST structures, with one structure for each managed property.

Using the TRUSTEE Structure

The TRUSTEE structure is used to identify a security principal, and it can easily be initialized using either the security principal's name or a SID that refers to the principal.

The TRUSTEE structure is defined as follows:

```
typedef struct _TRUSTEE
{
    PTRUSTEE                    pMultipleTrustee;
    MULTIPLE_TRUSTEE_OPERATION  MultipleTrusteeOperation;
    TRUSTEE_FORM                TrusteeForm;
    TRUSTEE_TYPE                TrusteeType;
    LPTSTR                      ptstrName;
} TRUSTEE;
```

Here are the members of the TRUSTEE structure:

- pMultipleTrustee. Reserved for future use. Must be set to NULL.

- MultipleTrusteeOperation. The only valid value for this member is
  NO_MULTIPLE_TRUSTEE.

- TrusteeForm. Indicates whether the TRUSTEE structure contains a SID or the name
  of a security principal. If the structure contains a SID, the value of this member
  is TRUSTEE_IS_SID; if the structure contains a principal name, the value of this
  member is TRUSTEE_IS_NAME. A value of TRUSTEE_BAD_FORM indicates that neither
  member is valid.

- TrusteeType. Indicates the type of trustee identified by the structure. Values for
  this member are discussed later.

- ptstrName. A pointer to a SID or security principal name. If TrusteeForm is
  TRUSTEE_IS_SID, this member is a pointer to the trustee's SID. If TrusteeForm is
  TRUSTEE_IS_NAME, this member is a pointer to the trustee's name.

The following values can be used for the TrusteeType member variable:

- TRUSTEE_IS_UNKNOWN. The trustee has an unknown trustee type.

- TRUSTEE_IS_USER. The trustee is a user account.

- TRUSTEE_IS_GROUP. The trustee is a group account.

- TRUSTEE_IS_DOMAIN. The trustee is a domain.

- TRUSTEE_IS_ALIAS. The trustee is an alias account.

- TRUSTEE_IS_WELL_KNOWN_GROUP. The trustee is a well-known group, such as
  Everyone.

- TRUSTEE_IS_DELETED. The trustee refers to a deleted account.

- TRUSTEE_IS_INVALID. The trustee is an invalid trustee type.

Although you're free to manipulate the TRUSTEE structure directly, Windows 2000 includes two functions that make it easy to initialize a TRUSTEE structure:

- BuildTrusteeWithName. Initializes a TRUSTEE structure from a trustee's name
- BuildTrusteeWithSid. Initializes a TRUSTEE structure from a trustee's SID

The BuildTrusteeWithName function properly initializes a TRUSTEE structure from a trustee's name:

```
TRUSTEE trustee;
BuildTrusteeWithName(&trustee, _T("codevtech.com\\mickeyw"));
```

The BuildTrusteeWithName function has two parameters:

- The address of the TRUSTEE structure to be initialized
- A pointer to a string that contains the trustee name

The BuildTrusteeWithName function doesn't allocate any data for the TRUSTEE structure, particularly the ptstrName member variable. The string passed to the function must remain valid for the lifetime of the TRUSTEE structure; otherwise, you'll have unpredictable results. Functions such as the one in Listing 7.7 must be avoided.

LISTING 7.7 IMPROPER USE OF THE BuildTrusteeWithName FUNCTION

```
void BuildBadTrusteeStruct(TRUSTEE* pTrustee)
{
    LPTSTR pTempString = _T("codevtech\\ali");
    BuildTrusteeWithName(pTrustee, pTempString);
}
```

Inside BuildBadTrusteeStruct, the address of a variable with local scope, pTempString, is used to initialize the TRUSTEE structure. The pTempString variable is allocated on the thread's stack; when the function returns to the caller, the variable will be discarded. Any attempt to use the TRUSTEE structure will result in difficult-to-trace faults.

The proper way to use BuildBadTrusteeStruct is to allocate a buffer that exists for the lifetime of the TRUSTEE structure.

The BuildTrusteeWithSid function is similar to the BuildTrusteeWithName function, except that it uses a trustee's SID to initialize the structure:

```
TRUSTEE trustee;
BuildTrusteeWithSid(pTrustee, psid);
```

The BuildTrusteeWithSid function has two parameters:

- The address of the TRUSTEE structure to be initialized
- A pointer to the trustee's SID

The SID passed as a parameter to BuildTrusteeWithSid must be valid for the lifetime of the TRUSTEE structure—as is the case with the BuildTrusteeWithName function discussed earlier, the BuildTrusteeWithSid function does not allocate data for the TRUSTEE member variables.

Windows 2000 also provides functions that can be used to extract information from a TRUSTEE structure, thus saving you the trouble of picking the structure apart explicitly. Each of these functions accepts a TRUSTEE pointer as a parameter and returns the value of a TRUSTEE member variable:

- GetTrusteeForm
- GetTrusteeSid
- GetTrusteeType

The ACTRL_ACCESS_ENTRY Structure

The ACTRL_ACCESS_ENTRY structure contains access control information for a specific trustee. The ACTRL_ACCESS_ENTRY structure is similar to the ACE structure discussed earlier in the chapter, except it has the ability to work with provider-independent security functions.

The ACTRL_ACCESS_ENTRY structure is defined as follows:

```
typedef struct _ACTRL_ACCESS_ENTRY
{
    TRUSTEE         Trustee;
    ULONG           fAccessFlags;
    ACCESS_RIGHTS   Access;
    ACCESS_RIGHTS   ProvSpecificAccess;
    INHERIT_FLAGS   Inheritance;
    LPCTSTR         lpInheritProperty;
} ACTRL_ACCESS_ENTRY;
```

Here are the members of the ACTRL_ACCESS_ENTRY structure:

- Trustee. A TRUSTEE structure that identifies the trustee represented by this structure.
- fAccessFlags. Contains flags that specify how access control is to be applied to the trustee. Values for this member are discussed later.

- `Access`. Contains one or more flags that specify the access rights controlled by the access entry. You must use the provider-independent flags, such as `ACTRL_FILE_WRITE`. Commonly used flags are discussed later.

- `ProvSpecificAccess`. Usually set to zero but can optionally contain flags that are passed directly to the security provider.

- `Inheritance`. One or more flags that specify the inheritance characteristics of the access entry. This value is set to `NO_INHERITANCE` unless the secured object is stored in Active Directory.

- `lpInheritProperty`. A string that specifies the type of objects that can inherit the access entry (or `NULL` if inheritance is not used).

The value of `fAccessFlags` must be one of the following values:

- `ACTRL_ACCESS_ALLOWED`. Rights are granted to the trustee.

- `ACTRL_ACCESS_DENIED`. Rights are denied to the trustee.

- `ACTRL_AUDIT_FAILURE`. Audit messages are generated for failed attempts to use the rights.

- `ACTRL_AUDIT_SUCCESS`. Audit messages are generated for successful attempts to use the rights.

The value of the `Access` member variable must be taken from the provider-independent flags defined in the `AccCtrl.h` header file. A complete list of values is provided in the Platform SDK online Help. Here are some common flags used with the Windows 2000 file system:

- `ACTRL_FILE_EXECUTE`. Controls the right to execute a binary file

- `ACTRL_FILE_READ`. Controls the right to read a file

- `ACTRL_FILE_WRITE`. Controls the right to write to a file

- `ACTRL_DIR_CREATE_OBJECT`. Controls the right to create a file

Listing 7.8 contains a function that loads an `ACTRL_ACCESS_ENTRY` structure so that any user or group name passed as a parameter has file-access rights.

LISTING 7.8   AN EXAMPLE OF FILLING IN AN `ACTRL_ACCESS_ENTRY` STRUCTURE

```
VOID FillAccessEntry(PACTRL_ACCESS_ENTRY pae, LPTSTR pszName)
{
    ZeroMemory(pae, sizeof(ACTRL_ACCESS_ENTRY));
    BuildTrusteeWithName(&pae->Trustee, pszName);
```

```
      pae->Inheritance = NO_INHERITANCE;
      pae->fAccessFlags = ACTRL_ACCESS_ALLOWED;
      pae->Access = ACTRL_FILE_WRITE¦ACTRL_FILE_READ¦
                 ACTRL_FILE_EXECUTE¦ACTRL_FILE_APPEND¦
                 ACTRL_FILE_READ_ATTRIB¦ACTRL_FILE_WRITE_ATTRIB¦
                 ACTRL_FILE_READ_PROP¦ACTRL_FILE_WRITE_PROP;
}
```

The ACTRL_ACCESS_ENTRY_LIST Structure

The ACTRL_ACCESS_ENTRY_LIST structure acts as a list header for ACTRL_ACCESS_ENTRY structures. The ACTRL_ACCESS_ENTRY_LIST is declared as follows:

```
typedef struct _ACTRL_ACCESS_ENTRY_LIST
{
    ULONG                 cEntries;
    PACTRL_ACCESS_ENTRY   pAccessList;
}ACTRL_ACCESS_ENTRY_LIST;
```

The ACTRL_ACCESS_ENTRY_LIST structure has two members:

- cEntries is the number of ACTRL_ACCESS_ENTRY structures pointed to by pAccessList.

- pAccessList is an array of ACTRL_ACCESS_ENTRY structures that define the access-control characteristics.

If you use API functions to manipulate access-control lists, you'll rarely need to manipulate an ACTRL_ACCESS_ENTRY_LIST structure directly. However, handling the structure directly is useful if you want to deny access to an object to all users. If cEntries is set to 0 and pAccessList is set to NULL, access will be denied to all users and groups.

The ACTRL_PROPERTY_ENTRY Structure

The ACTRL_PROPERTY_ENTRY structure is introduced in Windows 2000 to enable objects to manage security for multiple properties located on a securable object. The ACTRL_PROPERTY_ENTRY structure is defined as follows:

```
typedef struct _ACTRL_PROPERTY_ENTRY
{
    LPCTSTR                    lpProperty;
    PACTRL_ACCESS_ENTRY_LIST   pAccessEntryList;
    ULONG                      fListFlags;
} ACTRL_PROPERTY_ENTRY;
```

The ACTRL_PROPERTY_ENTRY structure has three members:

- lpProperty is used only when specifying security for properties located on an object. This member variable is a pointer to a string containing a GUID that identifies the property. In the more common case where the structure refers to an object, this member variable is NULL.

- pAccessEntryList is a pointer to an ACTRL_ACCESS_ENTRY_LIST structure that contains the access entry list for the object or property.

- fListFlags is a flag that specifies characteristics for the access control list. Currently, this variable has one documented value: ACTRL_ACCESS_PROTECTED, which is used to prevent the property or object from inheriting entries from its parent when used with objects stored in Active Directory.

As with the ACTRL_ACCESS_ENTRY_LIST structure, you'll rarely need to access ACTRL_PROPERTY_ENTRY structure directly if you build your access control lists using Windows 2000 API functions. However, you can grant access to an object for all users if you set pAccessEntryList to NULL.

The ACTRL_ACCESS Structure

The ACTRL_ACCESS structure is the most commonly used structure for programming security using access control lists in Windows 2000. The structure itself is very simple, and it's defined as follows:

```
typedef struct _ACTRL_ALIST
{
    ULONG                       cEntries;
    PACTRL_PROPERTY_ENTRY       pPropertyAccessList;
}ACTRL_ACCESS;
```

There are only two members in the ACTRL_ACCESS structure:

- cEntries. Contains the number of ACTRL_PROPERTY_ENTRY structures in the array pointed to by pPropertyAccessList.

- pPropertyAccessList. Points to an array of ACTRL_PROPERTY_ENTRY structures. Each member of the array specifies access control for the entire object or for a property found on the object.

Several functions make use of the ACTRL_ACCESS structure. Here are some of the most commonly used ones:

- SetEntriesInAccessList
- GetNamedSecurityInfoEx
- ConvertAccessToSecurityDescriptor

These functions are discussed in the following section.

Using `SetEntriesInAccessList` to Create and Modify Access Control Lists

Earlier in the chapter, the `AddAccessAllowedAceEx` function was used to add an `ACE` to the end of an `ACL`. This function, like many of the low-level Windows security functions, requires you to manage the order and size of the access control list. When using trustee-based security, you can often eliminate the need to manage the low-level details of the access control list.

For example, the `SetEntriesInAccessList` function is used to add, modify, or remove the entries in an access control list:

```
DWORD SetEntriesInAccessList(ULONG                cEntries,
                             PACTRL_ACCESS_ENTRY  pAccessEntryList,
                             ACCESS_MODE          AccessMode,
                             LPCTSTR              lpProperty,
                             PACTRL_ACCESS        pOldList,
                             PACTRL_ACCESS*       ppNewList);
```

The `SetEntriesInAccessList` function returns zero when it's successful and the Win32 error code when it fails. `SetEntriesInAccessList` has six parameters:

- The number of `ACTRL_ACCESS_ENTRY` elements in the array passed as the next parameter.

- An array of `ACTRL_ACCESS_ENTRY` structures that each define the access control for a single trustee.

- An `ACCESS_MODE` value that defines how the new array of `ACTRL_ACCESS_ENTRY` structures is to be applied to the current access list. Possible values for this structure are discussed later.

- An optional string parameter used when the access control list is applied to a property on the object. This parameter is set to `NULL`, when the access control list is applied to the object, or to a string that contains the property's `GUID`.

- A pointer to the current `ACTRL_ACCESS` structure that contains the access control list, if any. This parameter is optional if you're creating a new access control list. It's required if you're removing an entry from the list or if you're merging new entries into an existing list.

- The address of a pointer to an `ACTRL_ACCESS` structure that will receive the new access control list. The `ACTRL_ACCESS` structure and access control list will be dynamically allocated and must be freed using the `LocalFree` function.

7

DISTRIBUTED
SECURITY

The `ACCESS_MODE` can be one of the following values:

- `GRANT_ACCESS`. Adds new access control entries to the front of the access control list without removing any existing entries

- `REVOKE_ACCESS`. Removes access control entries from the access control list for any trustees passed in the access entry list array

- `SET_ACCESS`. Adds new access control entries to the front of the access control list and removes any existing entries for the same trustees

Using `GetNamedSecurityInfoEx` to Retrieve Security Information

The `GetNamedSecurityInfoEx` function is used to retrieve access control information for Active Directory objects, Registry keys, kernel objects, and other Windows 2000 named objects. This function is similar to the `GetNamedSecurityInfo` function discussed earlier in the chapter, except that it adds support for property-level security and works with trustee-based access control structures:

```
DWORD GetNamedSecurityInfoEx(LPCTSTR lpObject,
                             SE_OBJECT_TYPE ObjectType,
                             SECURITY_INFORMATION SecurityInfo,
                             LPCTSTR lpProvider,
                             LPCTSTR lpProperty,
                             PACTRL_ACCESS *ppAccessList,
                             PACTRL_AUDIT *ppAuditList,
                             LPTSTR *lppOwner,
                             LPTSTR *lppGroup);
```

The `GetNameSecurityInfoEx` function returns zero when it's successful and a Win32 error code when it fails. This function has nine parameters:

- A string that identifies the securable object. As with the `GetNamedSecurityInfo` function discussed earlier, each type of securable object has a different name format. For details about specific types, consult the online documentation.

- An identifier for the object type that uses the same values as the `GetNamedSecurityInfo` function.

- One or more flags that specify what sort of information is to be returned by the function, using the same values as the `GetNamedSecurityInfo` function.

- A string that specifies the name of the security provider that will handle the request. You normally pass `NULL` for this parameter, which causes Windows 2000 to select the proper security provider for you.

- A string that identifies the child object or property this function is requesting information about. In the most common case, where you're interested in retrieving information for the object, you pass `NULL` as this parameter.

- The address of a pointer to an `ACTRL_ACCESS` structure that contains access control information for the object. This parameter can be `NULL` if the `DACL_SECURITY_INFORMATION` flag is not included in the third parameter.
- The address of a pointer to an `ACTRL_AUDIT` structure that contains audit control information for the object. This parameter can be `NULL` if the `SACL_SECURITY_INFORMATION` flag is not included in the third parameter.
- The address of a pointer to a string that will be set to point to the object's owner. This parameter can be `NULL` if the `OWNER_SECURITY_INFORMATION` flag is not included in the third parameter.
- The address of a pointer to a string that will be set to point to the object's group. This parameter can be `NULL` if the `GROUP_SECURITY_INFORMATION` flag is not included in the third parameter.

Using the `ConvertAccessToSecurityDescriptor` Function

The process of converting an access control list into a security descriptor has been simplified in Windows 2000. If you're using trustee-based access control lists, you can simply call the `ConvertAccessToSecurityDescriptor` function to create a security descriptor that contains access control list, owner, and group information that you pass as parameters.

The `ConvertAccessToSecurityDescriptor` function is declared as follows:

```
DWORD ConvertAccessToSecurityDescriptor(PACTRL_ACCESS pAccessList,
                      PACTRL_AUDIT pAuditList,
                      LPCTSTR lpOwner,
                      LPCTSTR lpGroup,
                      PSECURITY_DESCRIPTOR *ppSecDescriptor);
```

`ConvertAccessToSecurityDescriptor` has five parameters:

- A pointer to a `PACTRL_ACCESS` structure that will be used to create the DACL of the security descriptor.
- A pointer to a `PACTRL_AUDIT` structure that will be used to create the SACL of the security descriptor.
- A string that contains the owner's name for the security descriptor.
- A string that contains the primary group name for the security descriptor.
- The `ConvertAccessToSecurityDescriptor` function returns zero, if successful, or a Win32 error code upon failure.

An example of using the `ConvertAccessToSecurityDescriptor` and other trustee-based access control functions is provided in Listing 7.9. The function in Listing 7.9 creates a security descriptor for a named pipe that denies access to the author.

LISTING 7.9   CREATING A SECURITY DESCRIPTOR FOR A NAMED PIPE

```c
/*
 * Create a security descriptor that restricts the author from
 * accessing a named pipe. The caller must use LocalFree to release
 * the memory used by the security descriptor.
 */
PSECURITY_DESCRIPTOR CreateAntiAuthorSecurityDescriptor(void)
{

    ACTRL_ACCESS_ENTRY   ae;
    PACTRL_ACCESS        pal = NULL;
    PSECURITY_DESCRIPTOR psd = NULL;
    DWORD                dwErr = 0;

    __try
    {
        ZeroMemory(&ae, sizeof(ae));
        BuildTrusteeWithName(&ae.Trustee,
                             _T("codevtech.com\\mickeyw"));

        ae.Inheritance = NO_INHERITANCE;
        ae.fAccessFlags = ACTRL_ACCESS_DENIED;
        ae.Access = ACTRL_FILE_CREATE_PIPE;
        dwErr = SetEntriesInAccessList(1,
                                       &ae,
                                       SET_ACCESS,
                                       NULL,
                                       NULL,
                                       &pal);
        if(dwErr) __leave;
        dwErr = ConvertAccessToSecurityDescriptor(pal,
                                                  NULL,
                                                  NULL,
                                                  NULL,
                                                  &psd);

        if(dwErr) __leave;
    }
    __finally
    {
        if(dwErr)
            HandleError(_T("Security"));
        if(pal) LocalFree(pal);
        return psd;
    }
}
```

In Listing 7.9, the function starts by calling the `BuildTrusteeWithName` function to initialize an `ACTRL_ACCESS_ENTRY` structure. Next, an `ACTRL_ACCESS` structure is created.

Then it's converted into a security descriptor with the
`ConvertAccessToSecurityDescriptor` function.

Impersonating a Client

As discussed at the beginning of this chapter, servers typically impersonate a client in
order to access secured objects. During the impersonation process, the server's impersonation token will assume the security characteristics of the client. This simplifies the security model, because Windows 2000 will simply use the thread's impersonation token to
perform access checks.

To begin impersonation, the server calls one of the following impersonation functions:

- `ImpersonateNamedPipeClient`. Used when the client and server are connected via
  a named pipe
- `ImpersonateLoggedOnUser`. Used when the client is the currently logged-on user

After a server has finished accessing resources on behalf of the client, it stops impersonating the client by calling the `RevertToSelf` function.

As an example of how a server process uses impersonation to use the client's security
context, the CD-ROM that accompanies this book includes the following projects:

- `FilePipeServer`. A console mode application that hosts a named pipe and attempts
  to open files on behalf on clients that connect to the pipe.
- `FilePipeClient`. A console mode application that connects to `FilePipeServer`
  through a named pipe and sends it the names of files that should be opened using
  its access token.

If you don't understand how named pipes work, don't worry. Named pipes are discussed
in detail in Chapter 26, "Pipes." The only function in the `FilePipeServer` project that
relates to security is provided in Listing 7.10. In the `TestFileForAccess` function, the
server impersonates the named-pipe client and attempts to open a filename passed as a
parameter.

LISTING 7.10 A FUNCTION THAT IMPERSONATES A CLIENT BEFORE ATTEMPTING FILE
ACCESS

```
BOOL TestFileForAccess(HANDLE hPipe, LPCTSTR szFileName)
{
    HANDLE hFile;
    BOOL   fAllowed = FALSE;
```

continues

LISTING 7.10   CONTINUED

```
    // impersonate the client
    ImpersonateNamedPipeClient(hPipe);

    // Open file for reading and writing
    hFile = CreateFile(szFileName,
                       GENERIC_READ¦GENERIC_WRITE,
                       0,
                       NULL,
                       OPEN_EXISTING,
                       FILE_ATTRIBUTE_NORMAL,
                       NULL);
    if(hFile != INVALID_HANDLE_VALUE)
    {
        fAllowed = TRUE;
        CloseHandle(hFile);
    }

    // Revert to primary access token
    RevertToSelf();
    return fAllowed;
}
```

In Listing 7.10, the `TestFileForAccess` function begins by impersonating the client located on the other end of the named pipe. Next, the function attempts to open the file using the filename passed as a parameter. The file is accessed using the client's access token rather than the server's. Before returning, the function calls `RevertToSelf` to start using the server's access token rather than the impersonation token.

It's very easy to run the `FilePipeServer` and `FilePipeClient` programs. You can run these programs on the same computer or on separate computers on a network. Start the `FilePipeServer` program first, then the `FilePipeClient`. The `FilePipeClient` will prompt you for the name of the remote server and the name of the file to be opened. The server will then try to open the file, and the client and server programs will display the results. When you're finished, enter `Quit` when prompted for a filename by the client.

Summary

This chapter has discussed Windows 2000 security, including both the traditional low-level security structures and functions and the newer trustee-based access control functions offered by Windows 2000. This chapter also included an example of how a server can use impersonation to properly handle access requests from a client.

Windows 2000 Debugging

IN THIS CHAPTER

This chapter discusses debugging tools and strategies that are available to you as a Windows 2000 developer. You probably already have most of the tools discussed in this chapter, because many of them are supplied by Microsoft with Visual Studio and the Platform SDK. This chapter also discusses some of the more popular third-party development tools, such as the SoftIce debugger from NuMega.

Windows Debugging Strategies

You can debug a software application in many ways. The best debugging and testing tips, however, apply to activities that occur before a bug is discovered. There are a few software quality, testing, and debugging tips that most experienced developers are aware of. Here are some of my favorite software quality tips:

- It's much better to find a bug early in the development process than later. A bug discovered after a product is released is expensive to correct and will cost you (or your organization) customer goodwill. It also eats up time better spent developing new products.

- A bug found early is easier to detect, trap, and correct. On your development station, you probably have the Visual C++ compiler and integrated debugger. If you have the Platform SDK, you also have the Microsoft kernel debuggers and other bug-trapping tools. If you develop products commercially, you may have already invested in third-party tools. Any bugs found on your development station are much easier to analyze and correct than bugs found on machines without debugging tools.

- Good development and testing tools make a difference. Third-party testing and debugging tools such as BoundsChecker, Visual Test, SoftIce, and BugTrapper may each cost more than your C++ compiler, but they can pay for themselves many times over by enabling you to discover bugs early—while they're still on your development station.

- Understand the amount of code coverage you achieve during your testing. It's not unusual for applications to have a great deal of untested code, unless a code-coverage tool is used to identify portions of your source code that have not been tested. Who should execute that code first, you or your customer?

Making Your Code More Easily Debuggable

The most important step you can take to improve your debugging efficiency is to develop applications that are easily debuggable. You can do this by taking advantage of application-level support that's built into the operating system to enable your application to communicate with the debugger. You can also take advantage of the support in your development tools in order to catch bugs early—before they cause a problem for one of your customers.

Debugging Support for Windows 2000

Windows 2000 offers a number of functions that an application can use to communicate with a debugger:

- `OutputDebugString`. Sends a string to the debugger, which can display the string in an output window.
- `DebugBreak`. Creates a user breakpoint exception, causing the debugger to stop at the line that calls `DebugBreak`.
- `IsDebuggerPresent`. Returns `TRUE` if the current process is running in the context of a debugger.

The `OutputDebugString` function is used to send display information to the debugger. Messages sent to the debugger typically include trace information about the internal state of the program as well as diagnostic information about errors that occur at runtime.

The `OutputDebugString` function has one parameter—the string to be passed to the debugger:

```
OutputDebugString(_T("Can't find Po"));
```

If a debugger isn't attached to the process, the function is ignored.

The `DebugBreak` function is used to create a hard-coded breakpoint in your application. If you're running in the debugger, it will halt inside a call to `DebugBreak`. If you're not running in the debugger, a message box similar to the one shown in Figure 8.1 will be displayed.

FIGURE 8.1

A call to
DebugBreak *will
cause the just-in-
time debugging
message box to be
displayed.*

Clicking OK terminates the application. Clicking Cancel attaches the default debugger to
the process. DebugBreak will cause a breakpoint exception even in non-debug builds.

The IsDebuggerPresent function is used to determine whether the application is running
in a debugger. If the application is not attached to a debugger, IsDebuggerPresent
returns FALSE. If the application is running in a debugger, the function returns a nonzero
value.

MFC Support for Debugging

If you're writing applications using MFC, you can take advantage of three macros to
help you test and debug your code:

- The ASSERT macro is used to test an assumption in your code that should be true.
  The ASSERT macro is only evaluated in debug MFC builds; the macro has no effect
  when compiling a release build.

- The VERIFY macro is used to test the result of an expression. The expression contained inside the VERIFY macro is included in both release and debug builds.
  However, the macro takes no action in release builds.

- The TRACE macro is used to send messages to the debug terminal and is basically a
  sophisticated C++ macro wrapped around a call to OutputDebugString.

The ASSERT and VERIFY macros are used to verify whether expressions are true. If an
expression inside an ASSERT or VERIFY macro isn't true, a message box similar to the one
shown in Figure 8.2 is displayed.

FIGURE 8.2

*A failed expres-
sion inside an*
ASSERT *macro will
cause a message
box to be dis-
played.*

Use the ASSERT macro whenever a statement will only be tested in debug builds. Any statements included inside an ASSERT macro are removed for release builds, so you can be generous with ASSERT macros and still have a slimmed-down executable as your final release.

The VERIFY statement is used when you want to test the return value from a function that's necessary in a release build. The VERIFY macro is typically applied to functions that return BOOL or HANDLE values, such as the CDC::FromHandle member function:

```
CDC* pdcTemp;
VERIFY(pdcTemp = CDC::FromHandle(hDC));
```

If pdcTemp is NULL in a debug build, the VERIFY macro will take the same action as a failed ASSERT macro—the Failed Assertion message box will be displayed to the user.

Understanding the Difference Between VERIFY and ASSERT

If you're building a non-debug version of your application, all ASSERT macros are removed by the compiler's preprocessor when the project is built. In non-debug builds, VERIFY macros are left untouched, although the expression inside the macro is not tested as it is in non-debug builds.

Be sure you understand the difference between the ASSERT and VERIFY macros. For example, the following line of code will be removed in non-debug compilations, thus leading to disaster if the pWnd variable is used later:

```
ASSERT(pWnd = GetDlgItem(IDC_TREE));
```

You have two options if you want to perform an assertion test on a variable such as pWnd in the preceding example. One way is to test the return value on a separate line:

```
pWnd = GetDlgItem(IDC_TREE);
ASSERT(pWnd);
```

The other option is to use the VERIFY macro:

```
VERIFY(pWnd = GetDlgItem(IDC_TREE));
```

Both methods cost the same in terms of program execution. The method that's right for you depends on your preferred coding style. Remember, when you use the ASSERT macro, the expression included in the macro must not include the function call unless you want the function call removed for non-debug builds.

8

WINDOWS 2000
DEBUGGING

Launching the Debugger on ASSERT or VERIFY Failures

If you're executing a debug build and an expression inside an ASSERT or VERIFY macro evaluates to False, the message box presented earlier in Figure 8.2 will be displayed. This message box presents you with three options:

- *Abort.* Causes the application to call AfxAbort, which terminates the process.

- *Retry.* Causes AfxDebugBreak to be called.

- *Ignore.* Causes the ASSERT or VERIFY macro to be bypassed. Execution will continue at the next line following the macro.

If you click Retry, nothing is actually retried. What really happens is that AfxDebugBreak is immediately called. If your process is not running in the context of the debugger, the message box shown earlier in Figure 8.1 is displayed.

At this point, you can click Cancel to launch the debugger. The debugger will load the necessary symbols and source code for your application and take you to the offending line in your application, as shown in Figure 8.3.

FIGURE 8.3

The Visual C++ debugger running after an ASSERT failure.

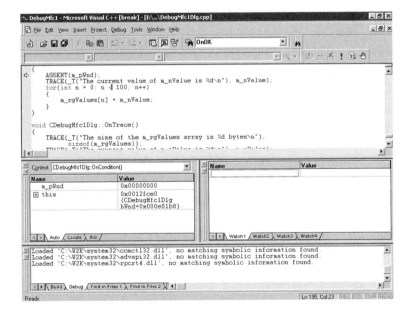

Windows 2000 Debugging Overview

Several tools are available for you to use in debugging your Windows 2000 applications. (You probably already have a number of these tools.) This chapter will also touch on a number of third-party tools that can be used to debug your code.

Understanding Symbolic Debug Information

Before you debug your application, you should install the Windows 2000 debug symbols. This is the symbolic debug information for Windows 2000, stripped out into a collection of separate files. The symbolic information is supplied in both DBG and PDB files for each module. You must explicitly install the symbolic information from the support directory on your Windows 2000 CD-ROM—the files are not installed as part of the normal operating system installation process in order to save space.

You must install the symbolic debug information to reliably debug your Windows 2000 applications. Due to the way recent versions of the Visual C++ compiler optimize stack management, it's not always possible for the debugger to display the proper call stack if the symbolic information has not been installed.

In order to be useful, the debug symbols must precisely match the version of Windows you're using. Don't try to install the Windows NT debug symbols found on your Visual C++ CD-ROM.

Microsoft's Debugging Tools

Microsoft supplies four debuggers that can be used for Windows 2000 debugging:

- The Visual Studio debugger is the simplest debugger to use, and it's the most widely used debugger simply because it's integrated with Visual C++.

- The GUI-based Windows kernel debugger is included with the Platform SDK. This debugger is sometimes called *WindBag* because of its filename, WINDBG.EXE.

- The command-line Windows 2000 kernel mode debugger, KD, is also supplied. This debugger's executable file is I386KD.EXE on Intel systems and ALPHAKD.EXE on systems that use the Alpha processor. This debugger is often used in device-driver development, but it's difficult to use for application debugging.

- The command-line Windows 2000 symbolic debugger, NTSD, provides a minimal command-line interface and is also difficult to use for application debugging.

The last two debuggers in this list are normally used with two computers connected by a serial communications cable. One computer hosts the debugger, and the other computer hosts the target executable. Because this book doesn't discuss kernel-mode device-driver development, the last two debuggers aren't discussed further in this chapter.

Third-party Debugging Tools

In addition to the debugging tools available from Microsoft, a number of third-party debugging tools are available for testing and debugging your applications. Here's a list of some of the more popular tools:

- *BoundsChecker*. A tool that detects misuse of memory and API calls.
- *SoftIce*. Widely regarded as the best debugger for Windows development.
- *Purify*. A tool that detects misuse of memory.
- *Visual Test*. An automated testing tool for Windows applications.
- *BugTrapper*. A tool that records the steps leading up to a fault so that they can be replayed for debugging.

Several of these programs are discussed later in the chapter. Also, contact information for the companies that provide these tools is provided at the end of this chapter.

Using the Visual C++ Integrated Debugger

The debugger that's integrated into Visual Studio is very easy to use. By default, your project's initial build configuration will create an executable that's ready to be debugged. To start a debug session, simply press F5 on your keyboard, select the Go icon from the toolbar, or select Start Debug, Go from the Build menu.

As with all debuggers, the Visual C++ debugger has a special relationship with the program being debugged, also known as the *debuggee*. When an interesting event occurs in the debuggee, Windows 2000 will send events to the debugger in the form of notification events. Here are some examples of events a debugger is interested in:

- If the debuggee calls OutputDebugString, the debugger is notified so that the text string can be displayed.
- If the debuggee executes an instruction that's marked as a breakpoint, the debugger is given the opportunity to halt execution of the debuggee.
- Exceptions that occur in the debuggee are passed to the debugger. Even exceptions that will be handled by an exception handler are initially passed to the debugger.

The Win32 interfaces and events used to implement basic debuggers are documented in the Platform SDK in the chapter titled "Debug and Error Handling," located in the "Base Services" section. You won't be able to write a competitor to SoftIce using these interfaces, but you may be able to gain an understanding into the partnership that's established between the operating system and the debugger.

Visual C++ Debugger Basics

Running your program in the context of the Visual C++ debugger offers the following advantages over running your program normally from Explorer or a command prompt:

- If your program crashes while running in the debugger, the debugger will attempt to stop at the offending source line. The values of variables and the call stack are available. These often give you enough information to correct the problem.

- If you detect a fault, you may be able to use the Visual C++ Edit and Continue feature to recompile your application and continue debugging without needing to restart your debugging session. Edit and Continue is discussed later in this chapter.

- Trace and debug statements are available in the Debug tab of the output window. You can use these statements to trace the execution of your program, even if you aren't manually stepping through your source code.

Setting a Breakpoint

A *breakpoint* is a location in your application that causes the debugger to stop running your program. When the debugger stops at a breakpoint, all threads in your application are suspended. There are two basic types of breakpoints:

- Unconditional breakpoints
- Conditional breakpoints

An *unconditional breakpoint* always causes the debugger to halt. You can set an unconditional breakpoint in one of several ways:

- Click the breakpoint icon in the toolbar. A breakpoint will be added to your source code at the current cursor position.

- Right-click in your source code window and select Insert/Remove Breakpoint from the context menu.

- Press the F9 key. A breakpoint will be added to your source code at the current cursor position.

Regardless of which method you use to set your breakpoint, the location of the breakpoint is indicated by a red dot in the left margin of the source code.

A *conditional breakpoint* causes the debugger to halt when the breakpoint is executed *and* a specific condition is true. For example, you may want to skip a breakpoint location 100 times before executing the break, or you may want to wait until a variable is set to a specific value.

To set a conditional breakpoint, you must open the Breakpoints dialog box by pressing Ctrl+B or by selecting Breakpoints from the Edit menu. The Breakpoints dialog box is shown in Figure 8.4.

FIGURE 8.4

The Breakpoints dialog box is used to set conditional breakpoints.

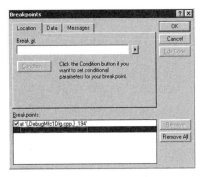

To select the line number for the breakpoint, click the right arrow located next to the edit control. The current line number will be displayed as a menu item. Select the line number, and the edit control will be filled in properly.

After selecting a line number for the breakpoint, you can specify an additional condition that must be true in order for the break to be executed. Clicking the Conditions button brings up the Breakpoint Condition dialog box, as shown in Figure 8.5.

FIGURE 8.5

The Breakpoint Condition dialog box allows you to set additional criteria for the breakpoint.

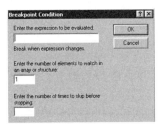

In the Breakpoint Condition dialog box, you can enter an expression that must be evaluated as true in order for the break to occur. You can also specify the number of times a breakpoint will be skipped before the break occurs.

Stepping Through Program Statements

If your program is stopped at a breakpoint, you have several options for continuing execution:

- You can step to the next source line by pressing the F10 key.
- If the next line is a function call, you can step into the function by pressing F11.
- You can continue executing the current function and return to the calling function by pressing Shift+F11.
- You can run to the cursor position by pressing Ctrl+F10.

Each of these options is also available in the Debug menu.

Using DataTips

The Visual C++ debugger will display the value for many variables in a DataTip window if you hover the mouse cursor over the variable. The DataTip window is similar to a ToolTip, except it displays the value of the variable. In the case of commonly used structures, such as `CRect` or `CString`, a DataTip is displayed that provides information about the most commonly used members of the class or structure.

The DataTip will not be displayed for invalid values. Also, the debugger will not display a DataTip for structures and classes that it doesn't recognize. However, displaying DataTip information for your own data types is discussed later in this chapter.

Changing the Next Line to Be Executed

There will be times when you need to change the flow of execution for your program. Typically, you're single-stepping in the debugger, and you want to skip over a line of source code or return to the top of a function.

To change the next line to be executed, right-click the line you want to execute and select Set Next Statement from the context menu.

Using Edit and Continue

Edit and Continue is one of the really cool features introduced in Visual C++ 6.0. Edit and Continue enables you to make small changes to your source code and continue debugging without relaunching your application.

When Edit and Continue is enabled, the compiler is automatically launched when you step to the next instruction after you've made changes to the source code. If Edit and

Continue can update your executable, messages similar to the following one will be displayed in the compiler's Build output window:

```
Compiling...
DebugMfc1Dlg.cpp
Applying Code Changes...

Edit and Continue - 0 error(s), 0 warning(s)
```

You can also elect to invoke Edit and Continue by Selecting Apply Code Changes from the Debug menu.

Changing the Value of a Variable

When debugging an application, you can change the values of any registers or nonconstant variables. Variables can be changed in the Watch or Variables window simply by clicking the value of the variable and entering a new value.

What's in a Window?

If you've only used the Visual C++ debugger for stepping through your code, you may not be aware of many of the features available in the debugger. A number of dockable windows can be used to display all sorts of information about the current state of your program. These windows include the following:

- *Watch window.* Displays the values of variables and expressions. This window allows you to change the values of variables.
- *Call Stack window.* Displays the current call stack. Each entry in the Call Stack window represents a nested function call to reach the current instruction. You can follow the path used to execute the current instruction by clicking entries in the call stack.
- *Memory window.* Displays a range of memory. This tab is useful when you're looking at blocks of data.
- *Variables window.* Displays variables in use. The Local tab displays variables that are in scope in the current function. The Auto tab displays variables used in the previous and current lines. The This tab displays variables accessed through the current `this` pointer.
- *Registers window.* Displays the current contents of the machine's registers.
- *Disassembly window.* Displays the current program in assembly mode. By default, the display of assembly code is annotated with your source code.

Figure 8.6 shows the Visual C++ debugger with the Call Stack, Watch, and Variables windows displayed.

8

WINDOWS 2000
DEBUGGING

FIGURE 8.6

*The Visual C++
Debugger with
several debug
windows in use.*

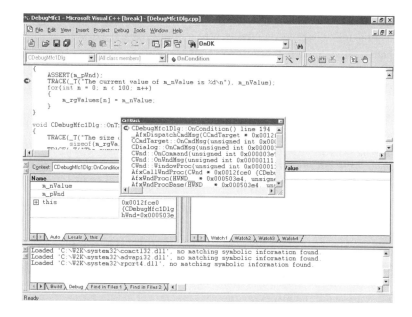

Visual C++ Debugger Tricks

All the windows that are available during debugging have extra functionality that might not be obvious at first glance. Most of the windows are editable, and you can use drag-and-drop and cut-and-paste techniques, just as if they were text-editing windows.

For example, if you're having problems with a particular ASSERT or VERIFY macro, it's easy to copy the information from the Call Stack window into a text file for later use.

Another trick you can do with the Call Stack window is to set a breakpoint inside the window. This enables you to easily return to a point listed inside the Call Stack window just by pressing F5 or clicking the Debug icon on the toolbar.

Another cool integration feature allows you to drag and drop variables from your source file directly into the Watch window. If you've ever struggled to accurately type m_pAfxSomeThingOrOther into a Watch window at 3 A.M., you'll appreciate this feature.

As discussed earlier in this chapter, the current value of a variable is displayed in a DataTip if you place the cursor over a variable in your source code while debugging. This works great if the variable is an int, DWORD, LPSTR, or other simple type. The Visual C++ debugger also displays the members of commonly used structures and classes, such as RECT and CRect. Although it isn't well documented, you can easily extend DataTips to include the classes and structures you're interested in.

The Visual C++ debugger uses a file named AUTOEXP.DAT to control how variables are automatically expanded when viewed in the debugger. The AUTOEXP.DAT file contains both the type information for the variable and formatting properties that control the contents of the DataTip. The AUTOEXP.DAT file is found in the MsDev98\Bin subdirectory in your Visual C++ installation directory. By default, the path is

```
C:\Program Files\Microsoft Visual Studio\MsDev98\Bin\AUTOEXP.DAT
```

This path may be different on your machine, depending on your installation directory.

What little documentation that exists for automatic expansion is located at the top of the AUTOEXP.DAT file. To add an entry for a new type, follow this format:

```
type = [optional text] <member varname[,optional format]>...
```

The entry begins with the name of the type to be added to the file, such as SailBoat, followed by a mandatory =. Optional text is followed by a list of one or more member variables that are included in the DataTip. Each member variable is enclosed in angle brackets and may include optional formatting information, which is used to help format the contents of the member variable correctly.

The following are examples of valid entries in the version of AUTOEXP.DAT that's included with Visual C++ 6.0:

```
CPaintDC =<,t> hWnd=<m_hWnd>
_bstr_t=<m_Data->m_wstr,su> (<m_Data->m_RefCount,u>)
CTime =time=<m_time>
```

As you can see, some entries in AUTOEXP.DAT provide formatting information, and some do not. In general, the formatting information is ignored by the debugger, which uses the formatting options set for the Watch window and Variables window. In any case, the documented values for formatting information are prided in Table 8.1.

TABLE 8.1 VALUES FOR AUTO-EXPANDING FORMATTING INFORMATION

Data Type	Description	Example
d, i	Signed int	-5, 20000
u	Unsigned int	234345
o	Unsigned octal int	0324563
x	Lowercase hex	0x3a
X	Uppercase hex	0X3ADE
l	Long prefix	0x32454345
h	Short prefix	0xABCD

Data Type	Description	Example
f	Signed floating point	-1.32
e	Signed scientific notation	5.300000e+000
g	Shorter of either f or e	5.3
c	Single character	a
s	String	"Ali"
su	Unicode string	"Kenzie"
st	Generic string	"Ace"

As an example of an entry that you might add for your own types, consider the following structure:

```
// Listing information for a sailboat
struct SailBoat{
    LPTSTR pszName;  // name of the boat
    int    length;   // length of the boat
    int    sailArea; // sail area
};
```

Normally, the Visual C++ debugger would not display any information about a SailBoat variable. Adding the following line to AUTOEXP.DAT enables the Visual C++ debugger to provide a DataTip for SailBoat variables as well as automatically display additional information in the Watch and Variables windows:

```
Boat = name=<pszName,st> length=<length,d> sail area=<sailArea,d>
```

After modifying the value of the AUTOEXP.DAT file, you must quit and restart Visual C++ to take advantage of any changed entries.

Using WINDBG, the Windows Debugger

WINDBG is a GUI-based debugger that ships with the Platform SDK. In many ways, it resembles the Visual Studio debugger:

- It can be used to debug at the source level.

- Memory, Watch, Variable, and Call Stack windows are displayed as MDI client windows.

- You can set a variety of breakpoints.
- You can single-step through your code using the same functions and key combinations that the Visual C++ debugger uses.

However, unlike the Visual C++ debugger, WINDBG allows you to use kernel debugger commands while debugging. Unfortunately, these commands are not well documented. Some documentation exists in the WINDBG online Help, but it's not complete.

Using SoftIce to Debug Programs

SoftIce is a third-party debugger that can be used to debug both kernel mode drivers and application programs. Unlike the kernel mode debuggers supplied by Microsoft in the Platform SDK, SoftIce does not require you to dedicate a second computer for debugging—you can debug in kernel mode using a single computer.

SoftIce allows you to define when it's loaded. The choice you make depends on the type of debugging support you require from SoftIce. The options are as follows:

- *Boot.* SoftIce is loaded immediately after all boot drivers. This is the earliest possible load option for SoftIce.
- *System.* SoftIce is loaded after all system drivers have been loaded.
- *Automatic.* SoftIce is loaded during the last phases of system startup. Use this option if you aren't debugging core device drivers but need to debug drivers or services.
- *On Demand.* SoftIce is launched as needed. This mode is typically used when you don't need to use SoftIce while the system is booting.

SoftIce has a number of features that make it the Ferrari of debugging tools. Here are some of my favorite features:

- You can step into Windows 2000 components just as though you were debugging your own code.
- It contains debugging commands that aren't offered in the Platform SDK debuggers—for example, one-shot breakpoints, which are breakpoints that are automatically removed after they're used once.
- Best of all, SoftIce comes with a great tutorial and command reference, unlike the tools provided with the Platform SDK.

If you're using SoftIce with a Beta version of Windows 2000, check out the NuMega Web site at www.numega.com to determine the proper version of SoftIce to use with your particular build of Windows 2000. SoftIce is tightly coupled to the operating system, and service packs and new operating system releases require an updated copy of SoftIce.

Using Dr. Watson to Find the Cause of Crashes

Dr. Watson is a tool that has long been shipped with Windows operating systems. Dr. Watson is used to generate trace information that can be used to determine the cause of an application crash.

On Windows 2000 installations that do not have development tools installed, Dr. Watson is installed as the default debugger. When an application crashes, Dr. Watson is launched as the just-in-time debugger, and it creates a log file that contains a number of useful pieces of information, such as information about currently running applications, threads running in the failing process, and call stack information for the calling process.

To install Dr. Watson as the default debugger on a development station, use the following command in a DOS window:

```
drwtsn32 -i
```

In order to get the maximum benefit from a Dr. Watson trace, you must first install the Windows 2000 debug symbol tree. Otherwise, it can be difficult to interpret call stack information.

The CD-ROM that accompanies the book includes a console mode project named Crash1, which contains functions such as the one provided in Listing 8.1.

LISTING 8.1 ONE OF THE BAD FUNCTIONS FROM THE CRASH1 PROJECT

```
int BadFunc1()
{
    int *p = 0;
    *p = 42;
    p[45] = 42;
    return 0;
}
```

When the BadFunc1 function in Listing 8.1 is called, a NULL pointer is referenced, thus causing an access violation.

Dr. Watson can be configured to collect different types of information. Figure 8.7 shows the Dr. Watson main dialog box, which is displayed by launching Dr. Watson from a DOS window using this command:

```
drwtsn32
```

FIGURE 8.7

*Dr. Watson can be
configured to log
several types of
information after
an application
crashes.*

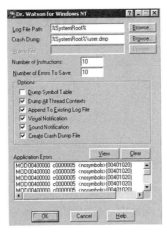

In order to use Dr. Watson, your executable must include debug information in the Common Object File Format (COFF). You can include COFF symbols in release mode builds, as well as debug builds, by modifying the Linker's debug settings in the Project Settings dialog box in Visual C++ 6.0.

The Crash1 project is configured to generate the proper debug information in release and debug builds. Running the Crash1 program on a Windows 2000 machine that has Dr. Watson configured as the default debugger causes Dr. Watson to make an appearance, as shown in Figure 8.8.

FIGURE 8.8

*The message box
displayed as a Dr.
Watson log is gen-
erated.*

Dr. Watson logs are placed in the Windows 2000 root directory in a file named `drwt-sn32.log`. Listing 8.2 contains excerpts from a Dr. Watson log file generated by running Crash1.

LISTING 8.2 EXCERPTS FROM A DR. WATSON LOG FILE

```
Application exception occurred:
        App: Release/crash1.exe (pid=2128)
        When: 3/4/99 @ 00:49:14.984
        Exception number: c0000005 (access violation)

*----> System Information <----*
```

```
Computer Name: SLARTIBARTFAST
User Name: Administrator
Number of Processors: 2
Processor Type: x86 Family 6 Model 1 Stepping 9
Windows Version: 5.0
Current Build: 1946
Service Pack: None
Current Type: Multiprocessor Free
Registered Organization: codev technologies
Registered Owner: Mickey Williams

*----> Task List <----*
   0 Idle.exe
   8 System.exe
 120 smss.exe
 152 csrss.exe
 172 winlogon.exe
2156 MSDEV.exe
2128 crash1.exe
2200 drwtsn32.exe
   0 _Total.exe



function: BadFunc1
        00401029 55                  push    ebp
        0040102a 8bec                mov     ebp,esp
        0040102c 51                  push    ecx
        0040102d c745fc00000000      mov     dword ptr [ebp+0xfc]
        00401034 8b45fc              mov     eax,[ebp+0xfc]
FAULT ->00401037 c7002a000000        mov     dword ptr [eax],0x2a
        0040103d 8b4dfc              mov     ecx,[ebp+0xfc]


*----> Stack Back Trace <----*

FramePtr ReturnAd Param#1  Param#2  Param#3  Function Name
0012FF44 00401020 0012FFC0 004011C2 00000001 crash1!BadFunc1
0012FF4C 004011C2 00000001 00312368 00312A68 crash1!main
0012FFC0 77EDE388 77F818A2 00140E68 7FFDF000 crash1!mainCRTStartup
0012FFF0 00000000 004010DF 00000000 00000000 kernel32!CreateProcessW
```

A number of lines have been removed in Listing 8.2 for clarity. Also, several of the lines were shortened to allow them to fit on the printed page. A full copy of the Dr. Watson log file is included in the Crash1 project directory.

One of the great things about Dr. Watson logs is that an access violation actually places an arrow pointing at the line of assembly code that caused the fault. This is often a great help, as is the stack trace that's included in the Dr. Watson log.

Using BugTrapper to Find the Cause of Crashes

The biggest limitation of a Dr. Watson log is that it's a snapshot rather than a full description of the problems that led up to the fault. When debugging a fault that has resulted in a Dr. Watson log, you must give an accurate accounting of the steps that led up to the crash. However, even with accurate reporting, it can be difficult to reproduce faults that occur on different machines or configurations.

BugTrapper is a product developed by Mutek Solutions that solves the shortcomings of a Dr. Watson log by recording the steps that led up to an application failure. The steps can be played back later, much like a debugging session, so that you can determine exactly how you arrived at a state that caused your application to crash.

BugTrapper works by modifying the binary image of your executable, so there's no need for you to modify your existing source code.

BugTrapper also can be used to generate reports of crashes that occur at a remote site, such as at a customer's location. The resulting log file can be sent back to you so that it can be replayed for debugging. If you've ever had to drop everything in the middle of a development project in order to debug a problem at a remote customer site, you can appreciate a tool such as BugTrapper.

Sources for Third-party Tools

The following companies supply third-party tools for testing and debugging. Most of these companies offer limited-time demonstration versions of their products on their Web sites.

Compuware NuMega Lab

NuMega Technologies has been an innovator in advanced tools for debugging Windows applications. The original version of SoftIce was released for debugging under DOS. NuMega is now part of Compuware and sells a number of tools for the Windows developer. NuMega also has a number of tools that are suitable for use with Visual Basic and Java. You can reach NuMega on the Web at www.numega.com.

Products available from NuMega include the following:

- *SoftIce*. As discussed earlier in this chapter, SoftIce is the ultimate debugger for Windows. If you're doing serious development work—especially if you're working with services or device drivers—do yourself a favor and pick up a copy of SoftIce.

- *BoundsChecker.* This is a great tool for validating your calls to the Win32 API as well as for testing for common memory access and heap errors. BoundsChecker will detect buffer overruns, writing through invalid pointers, and releasing buffers that have already been freed.

- *TrueCoverage.* This tool enables you to determine which parts of your code have been executed during testing. A great feature of TrueCoverage is its ability to merge coverage information from multiple users or sessions so that an entire development team can add to your coverage data.

Mutek Solutions Ltd.

Mutek Solutions Ltd. develops products in the U.S. and Israel and has introduced BugTrapper as its first product. Evaluation copies of Mutek's products as well as whitepapers can be downloaded from its Web site at www.mutek.com.

Rational

Rational Software is best known for its line of design tools, such as Rational Rose. Rational is the home of Grady Booch, Ivar Jacobson, and James Rumbaugh, the three leaders in the field of object-oriented system design. You can reach Rational on the web at www.rational.com.

Tools for debugging and testing that are offered by Rational include the following:

- *Visual Test.* The industry-standard testing tool for Windows-based applications. Visual Test was originally developed by Microsoft and transferred to Rational a few years ago. Visual Test is a great way to use automated, hands-off testing for your applications.

- *Purify.* A tool that tests for memory problems, such as overrunning buffers, memory leaks, and invalid pointers.

Summary

This chapter has discussed various debugging tools available to you as a Windows 2000 developer. This chapter covered some of the tools provided with Visual C++ and the Platform SDK, such as the debugger that's integrated with Visual C++. This chapter also discussed some third-party debugging tools, such as SoftIce and BugTrapper.

Writing Windows 2000 Services

This chapter covers Windows 2000 services. A *service* is a special executable that runs under Windows 2000 but doesn't interact with the user or other applications as most processes do. Services usually run in a different security context than the logged-on user, and they often run even if no interactive user is present.

Developing a service poses new issues for you as a developer. How do you interact and control a process that can't assume that you're logged on? How can you determine if your service is running correctly? This chapter answers these questions and more.

Understanding Services

Services are special executables that run under Windows 2000. Unlike normal executables, services don't normally run as processes that are run under the account of the logged-on user. Instead, a service usually runs in a special account known as *local system* or in an account that's specially configured for the service. Services are normally used to control hardware attached to the computer or supply resources that must be available at all times.

Interacting with Windows 2000 Services

In general, a service written for Windows 2000 does not interact directly with the desktop. There are ways for a service to communicate directly with an interactive user, but, in general, services have no direct contact with the user's desktop.

Services don't interact with users at all—instead, they interact with the Windows 2000 *Service Control Manager*, or *SCM*. The SCM stores information about every service installed on the computer and tracks each service's state as it's launched, run, and stopped.

In fact, many Windows 2000 users have no idea services are running on their machine at all. The first indication that many users have that a service is even installed is the message box shown in Figure 9.1, notifying the user that a service or device driver has failed.

FIGURE 9.1

The dialog box displayed when a service or device driver fails to start.

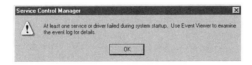

By the way, a service is nothing like a device driver, but Windows 2000 displays the same message box for drivers and services. The burden is placed on the user or help desk to narrow down the problem further.

Controlling Windows 2000 Services

User interaction with a service is done in two ways. The *Microsoft Management Console*, or *MMC*, includes a Services snap-in that enables simple management of all services registered on a computer. Prior to Windows 2000, services were managed through a common Control Panel applet found in Windows NT. Beginning with Windows 2000, the MMC is a common tool for all administrative functions (except for the MSCS Clustering Service).

The MMC Services snap-in is shown in Figure 9.2.

FIGURE 9.2
The MMC snap-in used to manage system services in Windows 2000.

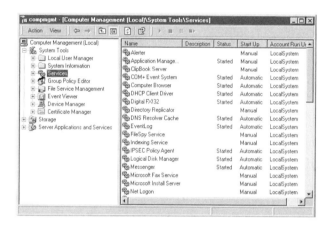

Services can also be controlled with specialized Control Panel applets. Control Panel applets are special DLLs that are launched by the user through the Control Panel. Writing Control Panel applets that control services is discussed in Chapter 10, "Controlling Windows 2000 Services."

Services and the Windows 2000 Event Log

Like almost all programs, services encounter error conditions from time to time. Unlike most programs, a service can't assume that a user is currently logged in. This means that the service can't reliably and easily interact with the user by displaying a dialog box or other message. For this reason, services use the Windows 2000 event log as a storage location for messages that may be useful to an administrator or user.

9

WRITING
WINDOWS 2000
SERVICES

As shown in Figure 9.3, the Windows 2000 event log stores messages from operating system components and services in one of three predefined event logs:

- The System log is used by device drivers.
- The Security log is used by the system to store audit success and failure results when security auditing is turned on.
- The Application log is used by services and normal applications.

FIGURE 9.3

The Windows 2000 event log stores information in three predefined log files.

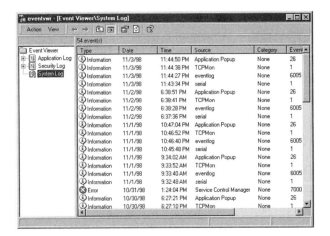

You can extend the event-logging mechanism by adding your own event logs. Unless you need this added functionality, it's much easier to send your events to the Application log. You can also create your own event log viewer that provides specific features that aren't included with the standard event log viewer shown in Figure 9.3.

Later in this chapter, the sample service updates the application event log with its status.

Windows 2000 Services and System Security

As discussed earlier, a service is usually associated with a machine rather than a particular user. Users may come and go, but services are expected to stay running, even when no user is logged onto a machine. Windows 2000 allows services to survive user logons and logoffs by allowing their security information to be specified in the Service Control Manager's database.

When you create your service and register it with the Service Control Manager, you must include information that tells the SCM under which security context the service is to be run. The SCM uses the account information from the database when the service is started.

Three different types of accounts are used by Windows 2000 services:

- The local system account
- The account of the current interactive user
- A specified account in the system

The pros and cons of these three approaches are discussed in the following sections.

Using the Local System Account

Many services run in the security context of the local system account, also known as the *system account*. Here are the advantages to using the local system account for your service:

- You don't need to administer account information for the service because the local system account is a built-in account.
- The local system account is very powerful—by default, it has complete control over the entire machine.
- A service running under the local system account will not be interrupted when interactive users establish or end sessions on the machine.

The main disadvantage of the local system account is that it has very little power in a domain. Beginning with Windows 2000, you can assign default privileges to the machine; these credentials will be used by the local system account in the network. If your service does not need specific rights that aren't granted to all local system users, this approach will work for you.

> **NOTE**
>
> In previous releases of Windows NT, a service with local system credentials could not establish any sort of securable network connection. You could tweak a Registry key to allow connections to be made to the local system account, but this introduced large, gaping holes into the network's security configuration.

9

WRITING
WINDOWS 2000
SERVICES

Using the Interactive User Account

When a service runs as the interactive user, it runs in the security context of the currently logged-on user. Here are the advantages of using the interactive user account:

- The service is somewhat easier to debug.
- You don't need to configure a special account for the service because the service will be run under an existing user account.

Here are the disadvantages of configuring a service to run as the interactive user:

- The service will terminate when the interactive user logs off. Typically, a service is meant to run between user sessions, so this is a major drawback.
- The service will have a variable set of user rights, depending on the interactive user. If the interactive user is an administrator, the service may have a large number of access rights. When the interactive user is a guest account, the permissions may differ.
- Finally, the service can't be launched if there's no interactive user.

Just about the only time you'll ever configure a service to run as the interactive user is during development. After the service is complete, you'll want to select another account option.

Using a Specific Account

The third option for your service is to run it as a specific account. This is the option used by services that require specific permissions.

Here are the advantages of running a service in a specific dedicated account:

- The system administrator can control the service by adjusting its privileges.
- The service can easily be allowed access to domain resources, such as other computers, without opening a security hole as is needed with the local system account.

This is the preferred method to use when developing a service meant for distribution in the enterprise. The only disadvantage of using a dedicated account for a service is that it requires a small amount of administration. However, in return, the service can participate fully in the Windows 2000 security model.

Programming a Windows 2000 Service

As discussed earlier, the service interacts with the Service Control Manager throughout its lifetime. The service is launched by the Service Control Manager, and it must keep the Service Control Manager informed whenever its status changes. This interaction is not difficult, but it is different from most Windows applications you may be accustomed to writing.

For example, the Service Control Manager must be notified in the following situations:

- When the service is in the process of being started or stopped.
- When the service reaches a running state.
- When the service is paused.
- When the service stops.

In addition, you must register the service and its configuration information into the Service Control Manager's database so that the Service Control Manager can launch the service. The details of registering a service are discussed in Chapter 10.

As you'll see in the following sections, a series of steps must be followed when you're running your service; otherwise, you'll find yourself fighting the operating system rather than working with it.

Updating the Service Control Manager with the Service Status

As discussed earlier, the Service Control Manager must be kept up-to-date with the status of the service. At a minimum, the Service Control Manager must be updated when the status changes; in addition, the Service Control Manager should be updated at regular intervals during transitions that take a long time, such as starting or stopping the service.

The service notifies the Service Control Manager of its state by calling the `SetServiceStatus` function:

```
SetServiceStatus(hStatus, &ssStatus);
```

The `SetServiceStatus` function has two parameters:

- A `SERVICE_STATUS_HANDLE`, which is returned from a successful call to `RegisterServiceCtrlHandler` or `RegisterServiceCtrlHandlerEx`
- A pointer to a `SERVICE_STATUS` structure

The `SERVICE_STATUS` structure is defined as follows:

```
typedef struct _SERVICE_STATUS {
    DWORD dwServiceType;
    DWORD dwCurrentState;
    DWORD dwControlsAccepted;
    DWORD dwWin32ExitCode;
    DWORD dwServiceSpecificExitCode;
    DWORD dwCheckPoint;
    DWORD dwWaitHint;
} SERVICE_STATUS, *LPSERVICE_STATUS;
```

9

WRITING
WINDOWS 2000
SERVICES

Each member variable in the SERVICE_STATUS structure is used to provide a different type of feedback about the service's state to the Service Control Manager:

- dwServiceType specifies the type of the service. (Possible values for the service type are provided later.)

- dwCurrentState is the current state of the service. This value is set to indicate whether the service is running, stopped, paused, or another state. (Possible values are listed later in this section.)

- dwControlsAccepted indicates which control message will be accepted by the service. It's interesting that this value is not set when the service is registered with the Service Control Manager—this makes it possible for you to be very flexible with your service. For example, you can update this value depending on the state or capabilities of the hardware your service controls. (Possible values for this member variable are listed later in this section.)

- dwWin32ExitCode is used to notify the Service Control Manager that an error has occurred while starting or stopping the service. This member variable should contain a Win32 error code such as a value retrieved using the GetLastError function. If you want to return an error code that's unique to the service, set this member variable to ERROR_SERVICE_SPECIFIC_ERROR and place the error value in dwServiceSpecificExitCode. If no error has occurred, this variable must be set to NO_ERROR.

- dwServiceSpecificExitCode is ignored unless dwWin32ExitCode is set to ERROR_SERVICE_SPECIFIC_ERROR. This member variable is set to a service-specific error value that's returned to the Service Control Manager.

- dwCheckPoint is a number that's incremented as the service is being started, stopped, paused, or restarted.

- dwWaitHint indicates the amount of time, in milliseconds, the Service Control Manager should expect to wait for the next status update. If this time passes with no update from the service, the Service Control Manager marks the service as failed.

The dwServiceType member variable contains the service's type; it can be either SERVICE_WIN32_OWN_PROCESS if the service runs in its own process or SERVICE_WIN32_SHARE_PROCESS if the service runs in a process with other services. There are also other values used for device drivers, but these are the only values used for services. As discussed earlier, if you want your service to be able to communicate directly with the interactive user, you must combine one of the two service types with SERVICE_INTERACTIVE_PROCESS.

The dwCurrentState member variable contains the current state of the service, chosen from the following values:

- SERVICE_START_PENDING is used when the service is processing a start request from the Service Control Manager.

- SERVICE_RUNNING indicates that the service is running.

- SERVICE_PAUSE_PENDING is used when the service is processing a pause request from the Service Control Manager.

- SERVICE_PAUSED indicates that the service is paused.

- SERVICE_CONTINUE_PENDING is used when the service is processing a continue request from the Service Control Manager.

- SERVICE_STOP_PENDING is used when the service is processing a stop request from the Service Control Manager.

- SERVICE_STOPPED indicates that the service is not running.

The dwControlsAccepted member variable contains a combination of zero or more of the following values:

- SERVICE_ACCEPT_STOP indicates that the service can be stopped, and the service's control handler will accept the SERVICE_CONTROL_STOP value from the Service Control Manager.

- SERVICE_ACCEPT_PAUSE_CONTINUE indicates that the service can be paused and restarted. The service's control handler will accept the SERVICE_CONTROL_PAUSE and SERVICE_CONTROL_CONTINUE values from the Service Control Manager.

- SERVICE_ACCEPT_SHUTDOWN specifies that the service needs to be notified when the system is shutting down, and the service's control handler will accept the SERVICE_CONTROL_SHUTDOWN value from the Service Control Manager.

- SERVICE_ACCEPT_PARAMCHANGE indicates that the service is capable of reading its startup parameters without being stopped and restarted. The service's control handler will accept the SERVICE_CONTROL_PARAMCHANGE value from the Service Control Manager.

- SERVICE_ACCEPT_NETBINDCHANGE indicates that the service is a network component that can accept changes in its binding without being stopped and restarted. The service's control handler will accept the SERVICE_CONTROL_NETBINDADD, SERVICE_CONTROL_NETBINDREMOVE, SERVICE_CONTROL_NETBINDENABLE, and SERVICE_CONTROL_NETBINDDISABLE values from the Service Control Manager.

9

WRITING
WINDOWS 2000
SERVICES

- `SERVICE_ACCEPT_HARDWAREPROFILECHANGE` indicates that the service wants to be notified when the computer's hardware profile has changed, and the service's control handler will accept the `SERVICE_CONTROL_HARDWAREPROFILECHANGE` from the Service Control Manager. This option is only available if the service has called the `RegisterServiceCtrlHandlerEx` function instead of the `RegisterServiceCtrlHandler` function.

- `SERVICE_ACCEPT_POWEREVENT` indicates that the service wants to be notified when the power status of the computer has changed, and the service's control handler will accept the `SERVICE_CONTROL_POWEREVENT` value from the Service Control Manager. This option is only available if the service has called the `RegisterServiceCtrlHandlerEx` function instead of the `RegisterServiceCtrlHandler` function.

The Life Cycle of a Windows 2000 Service

The life cycle of a Windows 2000 service can be broken down into three main phases:

- Starting a service
- Pausing a service
- Stopping a service

Starting a Windows 2000 Service

The startup sequence for a Windows 2000 service is shown in Figure 9.4.

FIGURE 9.4

The startup sequence for a Windows 2000 service.

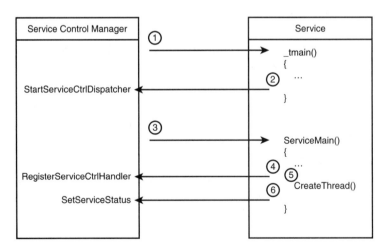

Here are the steps shown in Figure 9.4:

1. The Service Control Manager calls the main entry point for the registered executable that contains the service.

2. The service calls back to the operating system's `StartServiceCtrlDispatcher` function.

3. The Service Control Manager calls the service's `ServiceMain` function.

4. The service registers its service control handler using the `RegisterServiceCtrlHandler` function.

5. The service typically launches a thread that performs the work of the service.

6. The service notifies the Service Control Manager that the service has started.

In Figure 9.4, step 1 shows the Service Control Manager calling the service's entry point—`main`, `wmain`, or `WinMain`. The examples in this chapter use the `_tmain` macro, which evaluates to `wmain` in Unicode builds and `main` otherwise.

In response, the service is expected to call back to the Service Control Manager using the `StartServiceCtrlDispatcher` function, as shown in step 2 in Figure 9.4. This function has one parameter—an array of `SERVICE_TABLE_ENTRY` structures that contain the names of the services in this executable as well as the addresses of their `ServiceMain` functions. Listing 9.1 is a minimal version of a service's main function.

LISTING 9.1 A MINIMAL VERSION OF A WINDOWS 2000 main FUNCTION

```
int cdecl _tmain()
{
    SERVICE_TABLE_ENTRY ste[] =
    {
        _T("MyService"), MyServiceMain,
        NULL, NULL
    };
    StartServiceCtrlDispatcher(ste);
    return 0;
}
```

The `SERVICE_TABLE_ENTRY` structure has two members:

- The name of the service, which can be omitted if the service is registered as `SERVICE_WIN32_OWN_PROCESS`

- The address of the service's `ServiceMain` function

If the service module contains multiple services, you'll have more entries in the array. You must always have an extra entry that contains `NULL` for both values—the Service Control Manager tests for the double `NULL` values to find the end of the array.

The `StartServiceCtrlDispatcher` will return `TRUE` if the Service Control Manager attempts to start your service and `FALSE` otherwise. The unusual thing about this function is that it will return `TRUE` *after* the service has finished executing! For this reason, there shouldn't be any service-related code in `main` (or `_tmain` in this example) after the call to `StartServiceCtrlDispatcher`.

> **NOTE**
>
> With a small amount of work, you can make it possible to run your service from the command line. You may have noticed that Listing 9.1 looks like a perfectly reasonable console mode application. As you'll see later in this chapter's sample service, if the call to `StartServiceCtrlDispatcher` returns `FALSE`, your service can easily convert itself into a console mode application.

Continuing with Figure 9.4, the Service Control Manager will call the service's `ServiceMain` function. This function closely resembles a `main` or `wmain` function—it includes command-line parameter information that's created from information stored in the Service Control Manager's database. Listing 9.2 contains a minimal example of a `ServiceMain` function.

LISTING 9.2   AN EXAMPLE OF A WINDOWS 2000 `ServiceMain` FUNCTION

```
SERVICE_STATUS_HANDLE  ssh = 0L;
VOID WINAPI MyServiceMain(DWORD argc, TCHAR* argv[])
{
    ssh = RegisterServiceCtrlHandler(_T("MyService"),
                                     MyCtrlHandler);
    if(g_hSvcStatus == 0)
    {
        // Handle error
        return;
    }
    // Notify SCM that the service is starting.
    TellScmThatServiceIsStarting();
    // Initialize service
    InitService();
    // Notify SCM that the service is running.
    TellScmThatServiceHasStarted();
    // Run Service
    RunService();
    // Notify SCM that the service is finished.
    TellScmThatServiceHasStopped();
}
```

Although Listing 9.2 is a contrived example, it shows the basic sequence of steps that every ServiceMain function must follow:

1. The service control handler must be registered by calling the RegisterServiceCtrlHandler function.

2. As soon as possible, the Service Control Manager must be notified of the current state of the service.

3. The service should perform any necessary initializations after notifying the Service Control Manager that it's starting. If the initialization should fail, the service *must* notify the Service Control Manager that the service has stopped. Failure to do so will result in a confused Service Control Manager, and it will be difficult to control the service from the MMC. If the initialization is successful, the service must notify the Service Control Manager that it's running.

4. After the initialization is complete, the service should perform its work. Normally, this involves spinning up a worker thread that performs the actual work of the service. This concludes the work required to start the service.

Pausing and Continuing a Windows 2000 Service

The pause and continue sequence for a Windows 2000 service is shown in Figure 9.5.

FIGURE 9.5

The pause and continue sequence for a Windows 2000 service.

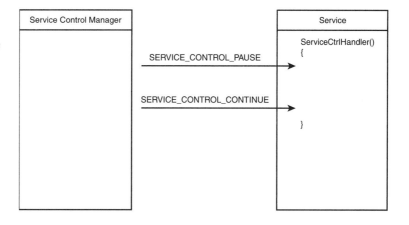

You can notify the Service Control Manager that services will accept these requests by including SERVICE_ACCEPT_PAUSE_CONTINUE as one of the services' supported command types when calling SetServiceStatus.

Services receive pause and continue command requests in their service control handlers, which are registered with the Service Control Manager using the `RegisterServiceCtrlHandler` or `RegisterServiceCtrlHandlerEx` function. A partial example of a service control handler is shown in Listing 9.3.

LISTING 9.3 A SIMPLIFIED SERVICE CONTROL HANDLER THAT MANAGES PAUSE AND CONTINUE COMMANDS

```
VOID WINAPI CtrlHandler(DWORD dwControl)
{
    switch(dwControl)
    {
        case SERVICE_CONTROL_PAUSE:
            PauseTheService();
            break;

        case SERVICE_CONTROL_CONTINUE:
            ResumeTheService();
            break;

        // other cases..
                    .
                    .
                    .
    }
}
```

As shown in Listing 9.3, when the Service Control Manager wants the service to pause, it will send a `SERVICE_CONTROL_PAUSE` message to the service control handler. When the Service Control Manager wants the service to continue, it sends a `SERVICE_CONTROL_CONTINUE` message to the service.

When the service is paused, it's expected that the service will enter a state where it seems to be stopped, but it remains loaded by the Service Control Manager. When a paused service receives a continue request, it can resume operation much faster than if it had been stopped and started.

NOTE

Most services don't support pause and continue requests. If you choose to support this service, be aware that you can receive other control messages while your service is paused. For example, the computer may be shut down or the service stopped.

Stopping a Windows 2000 Service

The shutdown sequence for a Windows 2000 service is shown in Figure 9.6.

FIGURE 9.6

The shutdown sequence for a Windows 2000 service.

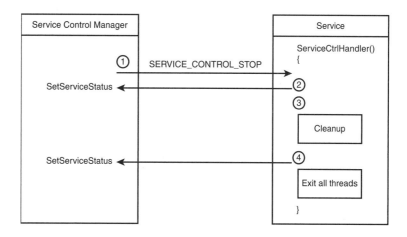

You can notify the Service Control Manager that services will accept a stop request by including SERVICE_ACCEPT_STOP as one of the services' supported command types when calling SetServiceStatus.

A service will receive stop command requests in its service control handler, which is registered with the Service Control Manager using the RegisterServiceCtrlHandler or RegisterServiceCtrlHandlerEx function. A partial example of a service control handler is shown in Listing 9.4.

LISTING 9.4 A PARTIAL EXAMPLE OF A SERVICE CONTROL HANDLER

```
VOID WINAPI CtrlHandler(DWORD dwControl)
{
    switch(dwControl)
    {
        case SERVICE_CONTROL_STOP:
            StopTheService();
            break;

        // Other cases
                .
                .
                .

    }
}
```

Figure 9.6 shows the steps that every service goes through as it is shut down:

1. The Service Control Manager sends a `SERVICE_CONTROL_STOP` message to the service control handler.

2. The service acknowledges the stop request by calling the `SetServiceStatus` function, with the service status set to `SERVICE_STOP_PENDING`.

3. The service cleans up resources that it has allocated and confirms that it has stopped by calling the `SetServiceStatus` function, with the service status set to `SERVICE_STOPPED`.

4. The service exits all running threads, including the `ServiceMain` function.

It's very important that your service shut down properly. If it doesn't manage this process correctly, it will be difficult for you to control the service using the MMC, because the Service Control Manager will not be able to determine the service's state.

Writing Data to the Windows 2000 Event Log

As discussed earlier, a Windows 2000 service must use the event log to store messages from the service when interesting events occur within the service. Here are some examples of interesting events:

- The service has started. A service should avoid this message if it's meant to run when the computer starts, because the event log will have an extra entry every time it's restarted.

- The service fails to start. When a service fails to start, the user is prompted to look in the event log for information. Services that place startup failure information in the event log make it easier for the end user to diagnose and correct the problem.

- The service begins to run out of a resource, such as a disk quota that's close to reaching its limit. Placing a warning in the event log is one way to notify a user or administrator that some corrective action must be taken.

- The service is running and encounters a problem that forces it to stop. In this case, placing as much information as possible into the event log is a very good idea. The user or administrator will probably look into the event log as soon as he or she discovers that the service is no longer running.

Specifying Event Attributes

Every event in the event log has a set of attributes that can be used by an administrator to filter or search for particular events:

- The event type indicates the severity or general nature of the event message.

- The event source is the service that generated the event log message.

- The category is an optional attribute that's specified by the event source. If provided, this value is displayed in the Event Viewer.
- The event ID is used when generating the event text.

You may assign one of the following event types to your message:

- *Information* is used for messages that convey some sort of non–error-related data, such as normal service startup or normal shutdown.
- *Warning* is used to indicate that a minor problem has occurred.
- *Error* is used for messages that indicate a major problem has occurred, such as a primary service function that could not be performed or a failed service.
- *Success audit* is used to indicate that a successful security audit event has occurred.
- *Failure audit* is used to indicate that an unsuccessful security audit event has occurred.

The event ID is used by Windows 2000 to determine how the message should be output to the event log. The event ID is used by Windows 2000 to determine how the message is to be formatted in the log.

The event log facility in Windows 2000 uses a very flexible mechanism to format and translate event messages into different languages. As you'll see in the next section, every service must have a message resource that contains an entry for each event ID. This entry specifies how the message is formatted for the event log, much like the specifiers used for `printf` or `wsprintf`.

Creating a Message Resource

If your service doesn't use a message resource file, messages placed into the event log won't be properly formatted. If an administrator uses the Event Log Viewer to view the message, it will look like Figure 9.7.

FIGURE 9.7

Viewing an event log message that isn't properly formatted.

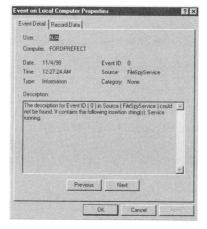

Think of the message file as containing a series of `printf` specifiers that describe how your message must be formatted. If you're only interested in supporting a single language, you need only one entry in your message resource, like this:

```
; //Message file for MyService
MessageID=0
Language=English
%1
.
```

In this example, `MessageID` is the same value as the event log event ID. This value is used to identify the message when it's generated by the service and sent to the event log.

In the example, `Language` is set as `English`. It's possible, even likely, to have different formatting specifications for different languages.

The `%1` found on the fourth line is the description string. This line describes how the event message from the service will be formatted. In this case, the entire event message string from the service will be output to the event log, with no text placed before or after the message. You could also have a description string like this one:

```
The myservice service would like you to know that %1
```

In this case, each event message would have a standard prefix.

The message file has an `.mc` file extension and is compiled into a message resource by being run through the message compiler included with the Platform SDK and Visual C++. To compile the `myservice.mc` message file, issue the following command:

```
mc myservice.mc
```

If the message file is successfully compiled into a message resource, the result is two files: a file with a `.bin` extension and a resource file with an `.rc` extension that uses the message resource (in this case, `myservice.rc`). This file must be bound to the service executable or to a DLL that the service is linked with.

Writing to the Event Log

A service must call three functions in order to write a message to the event log:

- `RegisterEventSource` is used to open a handle to an event source.
- `ReportEvent` is used to write a message to the event log, using the handle returned from `RegisterEventSource`.
- `DeregisterEventSource` is used to close a handle to an event source.

A short example that shows how these three functions can be used together is provided in
Listing 9.5.

LISTING 9.5 WRITING A MESSAGE TO THE WINDOWS 2000 EVENT LOG

```
HANDLE hEventSrc = RegisterEventSource(NULL, _T("MyService"));
if(hEventSrc)
{
    ReportEvent(hEventSrc, /* Source handle     */
                wType,     /* Message type      */
                0,         /* Category          */
                0,         /* Event ID          */
                NULL,      /* SID               */
                1,         /* Strings in array  */
                0,         /* Binary data size  */
                rgStr,     /* String array      */
                NULL);     /* Binary data       */
    DeregisterEventSource(hEventSrc);
}
```

The `RegisterEventSource` function has two parameters:

- A UNC path to the machine that hosts the event source, or `NULL` for the local
  machine
- The name of the event source that the handle will refer to

If the call to `RegisterEventSource` is successful, a handle to a message source is
returned. If an error occurs, `NULL` is returned.

The `ReportEvent` function has nine parameters:

- The handle to the message source opened by calling the `RegisterEventSource`
  function.
- The message type for the message to be added to the event log. This value is
  `EVENTLOG_ERROR_TYPE`, `EVENTLOG_WARNING_TYPE`, `EVENTLOG_INFORMATION_TYPE`,
  `EVENTLOG_AUDIT_SUCCESS`, or `EVENTLOG_AUDIT_FAILURE`.
- The category for the message or zero if no category is used.
- The event ID for the message.
- The security identifier for the process writing to the event log.
- The number of strings in the string array used to build the message.
- The size, in bytes, of the binary data attached to the message.
- An array of strings that contain the message.
- A pointer to binary data that will be appended to the message.

9

WRITING
WINDOWS 2000
SERVICES

If the message is written to the event log, `ReportEvent` returns `TRUE`; if an error occurs, `ReportEvent` returns `FALSE`.

The `DeregisterEventSource` has one parameter: the handle to the event source that's to be closed. If the handle can be closed, the function returns `TRUE`; otherwise, it returns `FALSE`.

An Example of a Windows 2000 Service

The remaining sections in this chapter present a sample service named FileSpy. The FileSpy service is an adaptation of the FileChange example presented in Chapter 4, "Files." The FileSpy service places information about changes into the event log. A Control Panel applet is included in the next chapter that enables a user to define the behavior of the service.

FileSpy: An Example of a Windows 2000 Service

The FileSpy project is used to build the FileSpy service. FileSpy is a service that can also be run as a console mode application from the command line.

There are a total of 10 files that play a part in the FileSpy project:

- `SvcMain.c` contains the core service functions and data that are generic for most services. Much of this source file can be reused in services you create.
- `SvcMain.h` contains declarations for `SvcMain.h`.
- `FSpy.c` contains functions that are specific to the FileSpy service. Although this file contains a great deal of code that's specific to the FileSpy service, you can use it as a skeleton for your own services.
- `FSpy.h` contains declarations for `FSpy.c`.
- `FSpy.rc` is a resource file for the FileSpy service. This file contains one resource—`MSG00001.bin`, the binary message resource file generated by the message compiler. In fact, the message compiler generates this resource file also. The source code for this file is not presented in this chapter because it's generated by the message compiler.
- `MSG00001.bin` is the binary message resource created by the message compiler, as discussed earlier. Because this is a binary file generated by the message compiler, the contents of this file aren't presented in this chapter.

- Reg.c contains reusable functions that are used to access the system Registry. This file is also used in the CtlFileSpy Control Panel applet presented later in this chapter.

- Reg.h contains declarations for Reg.c.

- Util.c contains reusable functions that are useful when writing services, such as functions that update the service's status with the SCM, write to the event log, and handle security structures.

- Util.h contains declarations for Util.c.

- FSpy.mc is not really part of the project, but it's the source file that's compiled using the message compiler. The output from the compilation includes the FSpy.rc and MSG00001.bin files.

The complete source files for FileSpy and other projects in this chapter are available on the CD-ROM. Due to the amount of source code in these projects, some source listings in this chapter are edited to conserve space.

The generic functions used in the FileSpy service, such as the service's main entry point, the ServiceMain function, and related functions, are found in SvcMain.c. Part of the source code for SvcMain.c is shown in Listing 9.6. The CD-ROM that accompanies this book contains the complete listing.

LISTING 9.6   THE GENERIC SERVICE FUNCTIONS USED IN THE FILESPY SERVICE

```
#include <windows.h>
#include <tchar.h>
#ifndef UNICODE
    #include <stdio.h>
#endif
#include "util.h"
#include "svcmain.h"
#include "fspy.h"

LPTSTR    g_szService = _T("FileSpyService");
HANDLE    g_hTerminate = NULL;
FN_PARAMS g_params;
HANDLE    g_hndlTable[FN_TABLESIZE];
BOOL      g_fRunningAsService;
SERVICE_STATUS_HANDLE  g_hSvcStatus = 0L;

/*
 * Main entry point for this service module. This is where
 * all of the action starts. If the SCM can't be contacted,
 * the process is run as a console-mode application.
 */
```

9

WRITING
WINDOWS 2000
SERVICES

continues

LISTING 9.6   CONTINUED

```c
int _cdecl _tmain(int argc, TCHAR* argv[])
{
    /*
     * Service table entry that specifies interfaces for the
     * services in this module.
     */
    SERVICE_TABLE_ENTRY ste[] =
    {
        g_szService, SvcMain,
        NULL, NULL
    };
    /*
     * Handle command-line arguments from the user.
     */
    if(argc > 1)
    {
        HandleCmdLine(argc, argv);
        return 0;
    }
    /*
     * By default, mark us as running as a service, and call the
     * SCM via StartServiceCtrlDispatcher. If the function returns
     * FALSE, then we're running in console-mode. We set the flag,
     * and avoid any service-specific code. We call ConsoleMain
     * directly since the SCM isn't directing traffic for us :)
     */
    g_fRunningAsService = TRUE;
    if(StartServiceCtrlDispatcher(ste) == FALSE)
    {
        DWORD dwErr = GetLastError();
        if(dwErr == ERROR_FAILED_SERVICE_CONTROLLER_CONNECT)
        {
            /* Couldn't connect to SCM because we're launched
             * from the command line.
             */
            g_fRunningAsService = FALSE;
            ConsoleMain();
        }
        else
        {
            /* Some other error has occurred. */
            WriteToEventLog(EVENTLOG_ERROR_TYPE,
                            _T("Couldn't start service"));
        }
    }
    return 0;
}

/*
 * The ServiceMain function for this service.
```

```
*/
VOID WINAPI SvcMain(DWORD argc, TCHAR* argv[])
{
    DWORD  dwError;
    HANDLE hSvcThread = NULL;
    SECURITY_ATTRIBUTES sa;
    DWORD dwThreadId;

    g_hSvcStatus = RegisterServiceCtrlHandler(g_szService,
                                              CtrlHandler);
    if(g_hSvcStatus == 0)
    {
        WriteToEventLog(EVENTLOG_ERROR_TYPE,
                        _T("RegisterServiceCtrlHandler failed"));
        return;
    }

    UpdateServiceStatus(g_hSvcStatus,
                        SERVICE_START_PENDING,
                        NO_ERROR,
                        FS_CTRL_INTERVAL);

    /*
     * Create event used to indicate that the service should
     * terminate the service main function.
     */
    g_hTerminate = CreateEvent(NULL, FALSE, FALSE, NULL);

    /* Call OnInit to initialize service. */
    if(OnInit(&dwError) == FALSE)
    {
        WriteToEventLog(EVENTLOG_ERROR_TYPE,
                        _T("Service Init failed"));
        UpdateServiceStatus(g_hSvcStatus,
                            SERVICE_STOPPED,
                            dwError,
                            FS_CTRL_INTERVAL);
        return;
    }
    /*
     * This is where things get interesting. The service has work
     * to do, but if we exit this function, the service will be
     * stopped.  At this point we will spin up a thread that will
     * handle the majority of the thread's work. If we can't init-
     * ialize the security attributes structure, or create the
     * thread, we must notify the SCM that the service is stopped,
     * and exit this function.

     * Note that the thread is started with CreateThread. If the
     * service uses the C runtime, this call should be changed to
     * _beginthreadex to avoid occasional memory leaks.
```

continues

9

LISTING 9.6   CONTINUED

```
    */
    __try
    {
        if(SetSimpleSecurityAttributes(&sa) == FALSE)
        {
            WriteToEventLog(EVENTLOG_ERROR_TYPE,
                            _T("Couldn't init security attributes"));
            __leave;
        }
        hSvcThread = CreateThread(&sa,
                                  0,
                                  fspymain,
                                  NULL,
                                  0,
                                  &dwThreadId);
        if(hSvcThread == NULL)
        {
            WriteToEventLog(EVENTLOG_ERROR_TYPE,
                            _T("Couldn't start worker thread"));
            __leave;
        }
        UpdateServiceStatus(g_hSvcStatus,
                            SERVICE_RUNNING,
                            NO_ERROR,
                            FS_CTRL_INTERVAL);
        WriteToEventLog(EVENTLOG_INFORMATION_TYPE,
                        _T("Service running"));

        /* Wait for termination event and worker thread to
         * spin down.
         */
        WaitForSingleObject(hSvcThread, INFINITE);
        WaitForSingleObject(g_hTerminate, INFINITE);
        WriteToEventLog(EVENTLOG_INFORMATION_TYPE,
                        _T("Service termination event signaled"));
    }
    __finally
    {
        /* Release resources */
        UpdateServiceStatus(g_hSvcStatus,
                            SERVICE_STOPPED,
                            NO_ERROR,
                            FS_CTRL_INTERVAL);

        CloseHandle(g_hTerminate);
        if(hSvcThread)
            CloseHandle(hSvcThread);
        FreeSecurityAttributes(&sa);
        OnUnInit();
```

```
            /* Elvis has left the building */
            UpdateServiceStatus(g_hSvcStatus,
                                SERVICE_STOPPED,
                                GetLastError(),
                                FS_CTRL_INTERVAL);
    }
}

/*
 * Service control handler function. The service handles two
 * commands - interrogate and stop.
 */
VOID WINAPI CtrlHandler(DWORD dwControl)
{
    WriteToEventLog(EVENTLOG_INFORMATION_TYPE,
                    _T("Service control handler called"));
    switch(dwControl)
    {
        case SERVICE_CONTROL_STOP:
            OnServiceStop();
            break;

        case SERVICE_CONTROL_INTERROGATE:
            OnServiceInterrogate();
            break;

    }
}
```

The main entry point for the service module is the _tmain function found in Listing 9.6. If this function can't connect to the Service Control Manager, the service runs as a console mode application by calling the ConsoleMain function. The global BOOL flag g_fRunningAsService is set to FALSE if the process is running as a console mode application. This greatly simplifies the work of debugging the application, because it's fairly simple to debug a console mode application running in your process.

Declarations for functions implemented in SvcMain.c are found in the SvcMain.h header file, which can be found in the FileSpy project directory on the CD-ROM that accompanies this book.

The FileSpy service functions that perform work specific to the service are found in the FSpy.c source file. This file is similar to the FileChange example from Chapter 4, except for the following features:

- It has been modified to present a user interface via the event log.
- It uses synchronization events to signal when the process should terminate.
- Parameters are collected from the system Registry.

Excerpts from the source code for FSpy.c is provided in Listing 9.7. The complete listing can be found on the CD-ROM accompanying this book.

LISTING 9.7   THE FSpy.c SOURCE FILE FROM THE FILESPY SERVICE

```c
#include <windows.h>
#include <tchar.h>

#include "fspy.h"
#include "util.h"
#include "svcmain.h"
#include "reg.h"

/*
 * Main program loop - initialize the change notification
 * handles, and hang in a loop waiting for notifications
 * to be signaled.
 */
DWORD WINAPI fspymain(void* pv)
{
    __try
    {
        while(1)
        {
            DWORD dwWait;
            dwWait = WaitForMultipleObjects(FN_TABLESIZE,
                                            g_hndlTable,
                                            FALSE,
                                            INFINITE);
            if(dwWait >= FN_MINWAIT && dwWait < FN_MAXWAIT)
            {

                // One of the file notification events was signaled
                int ndx = dwWait - WAIT_OBJECT_0;
                OnFileNotification(ndx);
                SetNextNotification(ndx);
            }
            else if(dwWait == FN_KILLEVENT)
            {
                /*
                 * The service is terminating. The control handler
                 * has already set the terminate event. We can just
                 * write to the event log, and break out of the
                 * loop.
                 */
                WriteToEventLog(EVENTLOG_INFORMATION_TYPE,
                                _T("Main loop terminating"));
                break;
            }
            else
```

```
        {
            /*
             * An error has occurred. We must write the error
             * to the event log, and set the terminate event
             * before breaking out of the loop.
             */
            WriteToEventLog(EVENTLOG_ERROR_TYPE,
                _T("Error while receiving file notifications"));
            UpdateServiceStatus(g_hSvcStatus,
                                    SERVICE_STOP_PENDING,
                                    GetLastError(),
                                    FS_CTRL_INTERVAL);
            SetEvent(g_hTerminate);
            break;
        }
    }
}
__finally
{
    /*
     * Cleanup resources, if any - in this case there are none.
     */
}
return 0;
}
```

Declarations for functions implemented in FSpy.c are found in the FSpy.h header file, which can be found on the CD-ROM.

The FileSpy service functions that work directly with the system Registry are located in the Reg.c source file. Reg.c includes functions that simplify commonly performed functions, such as retrieving Boolean or string variables from the registry. Some of the source code for this file is provided in Listing 9.8. The complete source is found on the CD-ROM that accompanies this book.

LISTING 9.8   REGISTRY ACCESS FUNCTIONS FOR THE FILESPY SERVICE

```
#include <windows.h>
#include <tchar.h>
#include "reg.h"

/*  Returns a handle to the Options key for the service in the
 *  Registry, given a handle to the service key as a parameter. If
 *  the Options key does not exist, it is created.
 */
HKEY GetRegParamKey(HKEY hKeyService)
{
```

continues

LISTING 9.8   CONTINUED

```
    HKEY  hKeyRet = NULL;
    DWORD dwDisposition;
    LONG lRet = RegCreateKeyEx(hKeyService,
                               _T("Options"),
                               0,
                               NULL,
                               REG_OPTION_NON_VOLATILE,
                               KEY_ALL_ACCESS,
                               NULL,
                               &hKeyRet,
                               &dwDisposition);
    if(lRet != ERROR_SUCCESS)
    {
        hKeyRet = NULL;
    }
    return hKeyRet;
}

/* Given a key handle, retrieve a named BOOL value. Returns FALSE
 * if an error occurs. If the value isn't present, it is added
 * with the default value.
 */
BOOL GetRegValBool(HKEY    hkey,
                   LPCTSTR pszValueName,
                   BOOL*   pfValue,
                   BOOL    fDefault)
{
    DWORD dwType;
    BOOL  fReturn = FALSE;
    DWORD dwSize = sizeof(BOOL);
    LONG  lQuery = RegQueryValueEx(hkey,
                                   pszValueName,
                                   NULL,
                                   &dwType,
                                   (LPBYTE)pfValue,
                                   &dwSize);

    if(lQuery == ERROR_SUCCESS)
        fReturn = TRUE;
    else if(lQuery == ERROR_FILE_NOT_FOUND)
    {
        LONG lSet = RegSetValueEx(hkey,
                                  pszValueName,
                                  0,
                                  REG_DWORD,
                                  (LPBYTE)&fDefault,
                                  dwSize);
        if(lSet == ERROR_SUCCESS)
        {
```

```
              // Copy default value to return value.
              *pfValue = fDefault;
              fReturn = TRUE;
          }
      }
      return fReturn;
}
```

Declarations for functions implemented in Reg.c are found in the Reg.h header file, which can be found on the CD-ROM that accompanies this book.

General-purpose functions that handle the event log, security attributes, and the current service status are located in the Util.c source file. The source code for this file is provided in Listing 9.9.

LISTING 9.9   GENERAL-PURPOSE FUNCTIONS FOR THE FILESPY SERVICE

```c
#include <windows.h>
#include <tchar.h>

#include "util.h"
#include "svcmain.h"

extern SERVICE_STATUS_HANDLE  g_hSvcStatus;
extern LPTSTR g_szService;
extern BOOL g_fRunningAsService;


/*
 * The service status is kept as a global so that it can be easily
 * re-sent if interrogated by the SCM.
 */
static SERVICE_STATUS  ss;

/*
 *  UpdateServiceStatus
 *  Sends the current service status to the SCM. Also updates
 *  the global service status structure.
 */
BOOL UpdateServiceStatus(SERVICE_STATUS_HANDLE hStatus,
                         DWORD dwStatus,
                         DWORD dwErrorCode,
                         DWORD dwWaitHint)
{
    BOOL            fReturn = FALSE;
    DWORD static    dwCheckpoint = 1;
    DWORD           dwControls = SERVICE_ACCEPT_STOP;
```

continues

LISTING 9.9 CONTINUED

```
    if(g_fRunningAsService == FALSE) return FALSE;

    ZeroMemory(&ss, sizeof(ss));
    ss.dwServiceType = SERVICE_WIN32;
    ss.dwCurrentState = dwStatus;
    ss.dwWaitHint = dwWaitHint;

    if(dwErrorCode)
    {
        ss.dwWin32ExitCode = ERROR_SERVICE_SPECIFIC_ERROR;
        ss.dwServiceSpecificExitCode = dwErrorCode;
    }
    // special cases that depend on the new state
    switch(dwStatus)
    {
        case SERVICE_START_PENDING:
            dwControls = 0;
            break;

        case SERVICE_RUNNING:
        case SERVICE_STOPPED:
            dwCheckpoint = 0;
            break;
    }
    ss.dwCheckPoint = dwCheckpoint++;
    ss.dwControlsAccepted = dwControls;

    return SetServiceStatus(hStatus, &ss);
}

/*
 * Sends the current service to the SCM.
 */
BOOL ReportCurrentServiceStatus(SERVICE_STATUS_HANDLE hStatus)
{
    return SetServiceStatus(hStatus, &ss);
}

/*
 * Sends a message to the event log.
 */
VOID WriteToEventLog(WORD wType, LPCTSTR pFormat, ...)
{
    TCHAR   szMsg[256];
    LPTSTR  rgStr[1];
    va_list pArg;

    va_start(pArg, pFormat);
     _vstprintf(szMsg, pFormat, pArg);
```

```
        va_end(pArg);

        rgStr[0] = szMsg;

        if(g_fRunningAsService)
        {
            HANDLE  hEventSrc = NULL;
            hEventSrc = RegisterEventSource(NULL, g_szService);
            if(hEventSrc == NULL) return;

            ReportEvent(hEventSrc,
                        wType,
                        0,
                        0,
                        NULL,
                        1,
                        0,
                        rgStr,
                        NULL);
            DeregisterEventSource(hEventSrc);
        }
        else
        {
            // output with CR at the end of string.
            _putts(szMsg);
        }
}
```

Declarations for functions implemented in Util.c are found in the Util.h header file, which can be found on the CD-ROM that accompanies this book.

The message resource file for the FileSpy service, FSpy.mc, is provided in Listing 9.10.

LISTING 9.10 THE FSpy.mc MESSAGE RESOURCE FILE

```
; //Message file for FileSpy
MessageID=0
Language=English
%1
.
```

The FSpy.mc message resource file is compiled using the message compiler and the following command line:

```
mc FSpy.mc
```

Several files are generated after the compilation, including MSG00001.bin and FSpy.rc. These files must be copied into the project directory and added to the FileSpy project.

After you've built the FileSpy project, it can't be launched from the MMC until the service is registered. To register the FileSpy service, launch the service using the following command line:

```
FileSpy /register
```

To unregister the service, launch the service using the following command line:

```
FileSpy /unregister
```

You can run the FileSpy project in console mode by launching it in the Visual C++ debugger or by running the executable from the command line.

NOTE

When a service executable is launched from the command line, there's a short delay until the Service Control Manager times out and the process continues as a console mode application.

Summary

This chapter discussed writing services for Windows 2000. This chapter also presented examples for a fully functional service.

Controlling Windows 2000 Services

CHAPTER 10

This chapter discusses how you can write programs that control Windows 2000 services. In the preceding chapter, you created the FileSpy service. In this chapter, you'll create a Control Panel applet that configures the Registry parameters used by the service. This chapter also examines the code used by FileSpy to handle self-registration.

Writing Service Control Programs

Service control programs are specialized programs that are used to control Windows 2000 services. Service control programs are traditionally written as Control Panel applets, but they can also be normal Windows 2000 executables.

Service control programs typically perform one or more of the following activities:

- Starting and stopping a service
- Registering and unregistering a service
- Changing the configuration parameters for a service in the Service Control Manager (SCM) database
- Changing configuration information used by the service (such as Registry keys)

Registering a Service with the Service Control Manager

Before the Service Control Manager can manage a service, the service must be registered in the SCM database. You can see the service database entries in the Registry, located under the following key:

```
HKEY_LOCAL_MACHINE\SYSTEM\CurrentControlSet\Services
```

For some reason, this key includes device drivers, as well as services. Don't attempt to tweak Registry entries directly; instead, use the APIs that have been developed specifically for registering services.

Typically, your service will be registered (and unregistered) in one of three ways:

- By the installation program used to install the service
- By a separate registration program that's launched by a script or other tool
- By a command-line switch, such as `myservice /register`, that's passed as a parameter to the service (as done by FileSpy in the preceding chapter)

No matter which approach you take, the service is installed by calling the

CreateService function:

```
SC_HANDLE sch = CreateService(schServiceCtrlMgr,
                              _T("MyTestService"),
                              _T("My Service"),
                              STANDARD_RIGHTS_REQUIRED,
                              SERVICE_WIN32_OWN_PROCESS,
                              SERVICE_AUTO_START,
                              SERVICE_ERROR_NORMAL,
                              _T("C:\\Projects\\nt2k\\myserv.exe"),
                              NULL,    // load-order group
                              NULL,    // group member tag
                              NULL,    // dependencies
                              NULL,    // account
                              NULL);   // password
if(sch == NULL)
{
    // handle error
}
```

As shown here, the CreateService function has 13 parameters:

- The SC_HANDLE for the Service Control Manager. This handle is returned when the SCM is opened using the OpenSCManager function.

- A name for the service. This name will be used to refer to the service in the Service Control Manager's database. This name is used as a key in the Services portion of the Registry.

- A user interface name for the service. This name is used when the service name is presented to a user or administrator, and it's usually a "friendlier" name for the service.

- The type of access you're requesting to the service. (Possible values for this parameter are discussed later.)

- The type of service process that's being created. (Possible values for this parameter are discussed later.)

- A flag that indicates how the service will be launched. The preceding example uses SERVICE_AUTO_START, which causes the service to be launched after Windows 2000 is loaded. (Other values are discussed later.)

- A flag that specifies what sort of action should be taken by the system if the service fails to start. SERVICE_ERROR_NORMAL is used in the preceding example; it causes the Service Control Manager to store the error in the system error log. (Other values are discussed later.)

- The path to the EXE module that contains the service.

- The load order group name or NULL if the service isn't part of a group.

- A pointer to a DWORD that contains a tag for this service's position in the load order group. Device drivers use this parameter, but this parameter is always NULL for services.

- A list of names of service or load order groups that the service depends on. Names on the list are separated by zeros, with the last name in the list double-zero terminated. Windows 2000 will start the listed services before this service is launched. If the service has no dependencies, pass NULL as this parameter.

- An optional account name for the service or NULL if the service will run as the local system.

- An optional password for the account or NULL if the service is running as the local system.

The fourth parameter in CreateService is used to specify the type of access you're requesting to the service. A large number of options are available for specifying the type of access required (see the Platform SDK documentation for details). The preceding example uses STANDARD_RIGHTS_REQUIRED, which, if granted, will allow you to delete the service from the SCM database, as well as query and modify security attributes for the service.

The fifth parameter is the service's process type. This parameter is set to SERVICE_WIN32_OWN_PROCESS for services that run in their own address space, or it's set to SERVICE_WIN32_SHARE_PROCESS if the service shares a process with other services. If the service can interact with the desktop, the process type is combined with SERVICE_INTERACTIVE_PROCESS.

The sixth parameter in CreateService indicates how the service is to be started. Here are the possible values:

- SERVICE_AUTO_START specifies that the service is started automatically when Windows 2000 is started.

- SERVICE_DEMAND_START specifies that the service will be started when requested by another application or via the MMC.

- SERVICE_DISABLED indicates that the service is not available for use.

The seventh parameter in CreateService indicates how the Service Control Manager should handle errors that occur when the service can't be launched. Here are the possible values:

- SERVICE_ERROR_IGNORE specifies that the SCM should log the error and continue trying to start the service.

- `SERVICE_ERROR_NORMAL` specifies that the SCM should log the error, display a message box to the user, and continue trying to start the service.

- `SERVICE_ERROR_SEVERE` specifies that the service performs an important operation. If the last-known good configuration is being started, the SCM will log the error and continue trying to start the service. In other cases, the SCM will log the error and restart the system with the last-known good configuration.

- `SERVICE_ERROR_CRITICAL` specifies that the service performs an operation that's absolutely critical. If the last-known good configuration is being started, the SCM will log the error if possible, and the startup will fail. In other cases, the SCM will log the error and restart the system with the last-known good configuration.

As discussed in the preceding chapter, the FileSpy service registers itself with the Service Control Manager when launched from the command line with the `/register` argument. The function that handles this task, `RegisterService`, is provided in Listing 10.1.

LISTING 10.1 THE `RegisterService` FUNCTION FROM THE FILESPY SERVICE

```
VOID RegisterService()
{
    TCHAR szServicePath[MAX_PATH];
    SC_HANDLE schScm = NULL;
    SC_HANDLE schSvc = NULL;

    GetModuleFileName(NULL, szServicePath, MAX_PATH);
    __try
    {
        schScm = OpenSCManager(NULL,
                               NULL,
                               SC_MANAGER_CREATE_SERVICE);
        if(schScm == NULL)
        {
            DisplayError(_T("Can't open SCM"));
            __leave;
        }
        schSvc = CreateService(schScm,
                               _T("FileSpyService"),
                               _T("FileSpy Service"),
                               SERVICE_ALL_ACCESS,
                               SERVICE_WIN32_OWN_PROCESS,
                               SERVICE_AUTO_START,
                               SERVICE_ERROR_NORMAL,
                               szServicePath,
                               NULL,    // load-order group
                               NULL,    // group member tag
```

continues

10

CONTROLLING WINDOWS 2000 SERVICES

LISTING 10.1   CONTINUED

```
                                    NULL,    // dependencies
                                    NULL,    // account
                                    NULL);   // password
        if(schSvc == NULL)
        {
            DisplayError(_T("Can't open service"));
            __leave;
        }
        MessageBox(NULL,
                    _T("Service installed"),
                    _T("FileSpy Service"),
                    MB_ICONINFORMATION);
    }
    __finally
    {
        if(schScm) CloseServiceHandle(schScm);
        if(schSvc) CloseServiceHandle(schSvc);
    }
}
```

The RegisterService function opens a handle to the Service Control Manager and then uses the CreateService function to add the FileSpy service to the SCM database. A message box is displayed with the status of the registration attempt.

Unregistering a Service

To unregister a service from the Service Control Manager's database, call the DeleteService function. You must open a handle to the service before deleting it, as shown in Listing 10.2.

LISTING 10.2   DELETING A SERVICE FROM THE SCM DATABASE

```
SC_HANDLE schScm = OpenSCManager(NULL,
                                    NULL,
                                    SC_MANAGER_CREATE_SERVICE);
if(schScm != NULL)
{
    SC_HANDLE schSvc = OpenService(schScm,
                                    _T("MyService"),
                                    SERVICE_ALL_ACCESS);
    if(schSvc != NULL)
    {
        if(DeleteService(schSvc))
        {
            // service deleted
```

```
        }
        CloseServiceHandle(schSvc);
    }
    CloseServiceHandle(schScm);
}
```

Listing 10.2 starts by opening a handle to the Service Control Manager. If the handle can be retrieved, calling the OpenService function opens a handle to the service. Finally, the service's handle is passed as a parameter to DeleteService, which removes the service from the Service Control Manager's database.

As discussed in the preceding chapter, the FileSpy service removes itself from the Service Control Manager's database when launched from the command line with the /unregister argument, much like the registration process described in the preceding section. The function that handles this task in FileSpy, UnregisterService, is provided in Listing 10.3.

LISTING 10.3   THE UnregisterService FUNCTION FROM THE FILESPY SERVICE

```
VOID UnregisterService()
{
    SC_HANDLE schScm = NULL;
    SC_HANDLE schSvc = NULL;
    __try
    {
        schScm = OpenSCManager(NULL,
                               NULL,
                               SC_MANAGER_CREATE_SERVICE);
        if(schScm == NULL)
        {
            MessageBox(NULL,
                       _T("Can't open SCM"),
                       _T("FileSpy Service"),
                       MB_ICONHAND);
            __leave;
        }
        schSvc = OpenService(schScm,
                             _T("FileSpyService"),
                             SERVICE_ALL_ACCESS);
        if(schSvc == NULL)
        {
            MessageBox(NULL,
                       _T("Can't open service"),
                       _T("FileSpy Service"),
                       MB_ICONHAND);
            __leave;
```

continues

10

CONTROLLING
WINDOWS 2000
SERVICES

LISTING 10.3 THE *UnregisterService* FUNCTION FROM THE FILESPY SERVICE

```
        }

        if(DeleteService(schSvc) == FALSE)
        {
            MessageBox(NULL,
                        _T("Can't delete service"),
                        _T("FileSpy Service"),
                        MB_ICONHAND);
            __leave;
        }
        MessageBox(NULL,
                    _T("Service deleted"),
                    _T("FileSpy Service"),
                    MB_ICONINFORMATION);
    }
    __finally
    {
        if(schScm) CloseServiceHandle(schScm);
        if(schSvc) CloseServiceHandle(schSvc);
    }
}
```

The UnregisterService function opens a handle to the Service Control Manager and then opens a handle to the FileSpy service. The DeleteService function is used to delete the FileSpy service from the SCM database.

Automatically Restarting Failed Services

In versions of Windows NT prior to Windows 2000, a service that crashed could not be restarted without manual intervention. A crashed service can be a major problem if other applications or even other services depend on it. Beginning with Windows 2000, you can specify the action to be taken if your service stops unexpectedly.

You can configure four options for the SCM to take if your service ends unexpectedly:

- *Do nothing*. This is the default action taken if no option is selected programmatically.
- *Restart the service*. This option attempts to relaunch the failed service.
- *Run a command*. The command will run in the same account as the service.
- *Reboot the computer*. This is a rather drastic step and should be undertaken only in the most extreme conditions.

You can also choose to escalate your recovery actions. For example, even if you have a service that's so important that the machine must be rebooted (if necessary), you'll probably want to initially run a command or restart the service.

> **NOTE**
>
> This facility makes it very important that you terminate your service correctly. The SCM will mark your service as terminating unexpectedly if the service doesn't report its service status as SERVICE_STOPPED. Because the administrator can also declaratively set these options via the MMC, a service that doesn't close correctly might be continuously restarted or even lead to the computer being rebooted.

You can programmatically change the actions to be taken upon service failure by using the ChangeServiceConfig2 function, as shown in the code fragment in Listing 10.4.

LISTING 10.4   CONFIGURING TWO LEVELS OF RECOVERY ACTIONS FOR A SERVICE

```
SC_ACTION rgActions[2] = {
    SC_ACTION_RESTART, 60000,
    SC_ACTION_RUN_COMMAND, 60000
};

SERVICE_FAILURE_ACTIONS sfa;
ZeroMemory(&sfa, sizeof(sfa));
sfa.dwResetPeriod = 9000; // 15 minutes
sfa.lpRebootMsg = NULL;
sfa.lpCommand = _T("C:\\Projects\\cleanup.exe");
sfa.cActions = sizeof(rgActions)/sizeof(rgActions[0]);
sfa.lpsaActions = rgActions;

ChangeServiceConfig2(schSvc,
                     SERVICE_CONFIG_FAILURE_ACTIONS,
                     &sfa);
```

ChangeServiceConfig2 has three parameters:

- A handle to the Service Control Manager.
- A DWORD that specifies the type of configuration to be changed. This parameter must be set to either SERVICE_CONFIG_DESCRIPTION, to change the service description, or SERVICE_CONFIG_FAILURE_ACTIONS, to change the action taken when the service fails.

10

CONTROLLING
WINDOWS 2000
SERVICES

- A pointer to a structure used to change the service configuration. If SERVICE_CONFIG_FAILURE_ACTIONS is specified in the second parameter, this parameter is the address of a SERVICE_FAILURE_ACTIONS structure.

The SERVICE_FAILURE_ACTIONS structure is defined as follows:

```
typedef struct _SERVICE_FAILURE_ACTIONS {
    DWORD         dwResetPeriod;
    LPTSTR        lpRebootMsg;
    LPTSTR        lpCommand;
    DWORD         cActions;
    SC_ACTION * lpsaActions;
} SERVICE_FAILURE_ACTIONS, *LPSERVICE_FAILURE_ACTIONS;
```

Here are the structure's five parameters:

- The reset period, in seconds, that marks a single failure period for escalation purposes. If the service fails, this timer is started. If the service fails again before the timer expires, the next action in the escalation procedure is taken.

- A pointer to a string sent to users as a broadcast message if the machine is rebooted. If you never reboot the machine as part of your recovery activity, or if you want to keep the current message, pass NULL as this parameter. If you want to erase the current message, send an empty string as this parameter.

- A pointer to a command-line string that will be executed if a command is executed as part of the recovery activity. As with the broadcast string, pass NULL to keep the current command line unchanged. Pass an empty string to remove the command line.

- A DWORD that provides a count of the number of recovery actions in the next parameter.

- An array of SC_ACTION structures, one for each new recovery action in an escalation sequence.

The SC_ACTION structure describes a recovery action and is defined as follows:

```
typedef struct _SC_ACTION {
    SC_ACTION_TYPE  Type;
    DWORD           Delay;
} SC_ACTION, *LPSC_ACTION;
```

In the SC_ACTION structure, the Delay member variable specifies the amount of time, in milliseconds, that the Service Control Manager should wait before taking the indicated action. The Type member variable contains one of the following action values:

- SC_ACTION_NONE specifies that no action should be taken by the SCM.

- SC_ACTION_RUN_COMMAND specifies that the command found in the SERVICE_FAILURE_ACTION structure should be run by the SCM.

- `SC_ACTION_RESTART` specifies that the service should be restarted.

- `SC_ACTION_REBOOT` specifies that the computer should be rebooted.

Writing Control Panel Applets

It's common practice to use a Control Panel applet to configure a service. Providing run-time access to Registry keys used by your service is much more convenient than forcing the user to edit Registry keys by hand or run the service installation program.

The Control Panel Applet Interface

Control Panel applets aren't standalone applications; instead, they're DLLs that expose the `CPlApplet` function as a consistent interface to the system. When a user opens the Control Panel folder or double-clicks the applet icon, the system will send the applet's `CPlApplet` messages, which signify events that should be acted upon by the applet. A typical `CPlApplet` function is shown in Listing 10.5.

LISTING 10.5   A SKELETON `CPlApplet` FUNCTION

```
LONG CALLBACK CPlApplet(HWND    hwnd,
                        UINT    msg,
                        LPARAM  lParam1,
                        LPARAM  lParam2)
{
    switch(msg)
    {
        // Handle individual CPL_XXX messages
           .
           .
           .
        default:
            break;
    }
    return 0;
}
```

Here are the eight messages that can be sent to the `CPlApplet` function:

- `CPL_INIT` is sent to the applet's DLL when it's initially loaded. It will not be sent again, unless the DLL is unloaded and `CPL_EXIT` is received by the applet. The applet should perform any global initializations required and return a nonzero value if the initialization is successful.

10

CONTROLLING
WINDOWS 2000
SERVICES

- CPL_GETCOUNT is sent after CPL_INIT is successfully processed by the applet's DLL. The DLL must return the number of applets supported by the DLL.

- CPL_INQUIRE is sent once for each applet to collect information about the applet, such as its description and icon. The applet number is passed as the first LPARAM; the second LPARAM is a pointer to a CPLINFO structure that must be filled in. Normally, Windows 2000 will attempt to cache information provided in response to this message. If your applet needs to change its visual identity based on its current status, process CPL_NEWINQUIRE instead of this message. The applet must return zero if this message is processed successfully.

- CPL_NEWINQUIRE is similar to CPL_INQUIRE, except that the second LPARAM points to a NEWCPLINFO structure. The data returned in response to this message is not cached. If your applet's visuals are static, handle CPL_INQUIRE instead of this message. The applet's message-handling function must return zero if it processes this message.

- CPL_DBLCLK is sent when a user is launching the Control Panel applet. The applet number is passed as the first LPARAM. The second LPARAM contains the lData value that was stored in the CPLINFO or NEWCPLINFO structure. In response to this message, the applet's message-handling function should display the applet's dialog box.

- CPL_STARTWPARAMS is similar to CPL_DBLCLK, except that the second LPARAM contains a help string that specifies additional information about how the applet should be launched.

- CPL_STOP is sent once for each applet. You can use this notification to free any dialog box resources that are allocated for the applet specified in the first LPARAM. You should return zero if this message is successfully processed.

- CPL_STOP is sent once for the entire DLL, just before the DLL is unloaded. You must free any global resources that have been allocated for the DLL. You should return zero if this message is processed successfully.

You must fill the CPLINFO structure in response to the CPL_INQUIRE message. The CPLINFO structure is defined like this:

```
typedef struct tagCPLINFO
{
    int idIcon;
    int idName;
    int idInfo;
    LONG lData;
} CPLINFO;
```

The data members inside CPLINFO are used to store information about the applet:

- idIcon is the resource identifier for the applet's icon.
- idName is the resource identifier for a string table entry that contains the name of the applet.
- idInfo is the resource identifier for a string table entry that contains a description for the applet.
- lData is a 32-bit variable that you can use to store information. This value is returned to you as part of the CPL_DBLCLK and CPL_STARTWPARAMS messages.

If you process the CPL_NEWINQUIRE message, you must fill in the contents of a NEWC-PLINFO structure. This structure is similar to the CPLINFO structure:

```
typedef struct tagNEWCPLINFO {
    DWORD dwSize;
    DWORD dwFlags;
    DWORD dwHelpContext;
    LONG  lData;
    HICON hIcon;
    TCHAR szName[32];
    TCHAR szInfo[64];
    TCHAR szHelpFile[128];
} NEWCPLINFO;
```

As with the previous structure, the data members inside NEWCPLINFO are used to store information about the applet:

- dwSize must be set to sizeof(NEWCPLINFO).
- dwFlags is not used.
- dwHelpContext is not used.
- lData is a 32-bit variable that you can use to store information. This value is returned to you as part of the CPL_DBLCLK and CPL_STARTWPARAMS messages.
- hIcon is a handle to an icon that the Control Panel will use to represent the applet.
- szName is a string that contains the name of the applet.
- szInfo is a string that contains a description for the applet.
- szHelpFile is not used.

In the next section, you'll see an example of a Control Panel applet that controls a sample service.

CtlFileSpy: A Control Panel Applet for FileSpy

As an example of how a Control Panel applet can be used to control a service, the CD-ROM includes the CtlFileSpy project. CtlFileSpy is a Control Panel applet that sets parameters used by the FileSpy service.

A total of 10 files is included in the CtlFileSpy project:

- CtlFileSpy.rc is the resource file used by CtlFileSpy.
- Resource.h is a header that contains resource symbol declarations.
- CplMain.c is a somewhat generic source file for Control Panel applets. Most of the source code in this file can be reused in other applets.
- CplMain.h contains declarations for CplMain.c.
- FileSpy.c is a source file that contains functions and data specific to this applet. You can use this source file as a skeleton for other applets.
- FileSpy.h contains declarations for FileSpy.c.
- Reg.c is used to interact with the system Registry. This file is identical to the Reg.c file used in the service presented earlier in this chapter; therefore, it isn't provided here.
- Reg.h contains declarations for Reg.c.
- FileSpy.def is the module definition file for the applet.
- FileSpy.ico is the icon displayed in the Control Panel.

The dialog box used by CtlFileSpy is shown in Figure 10.1.

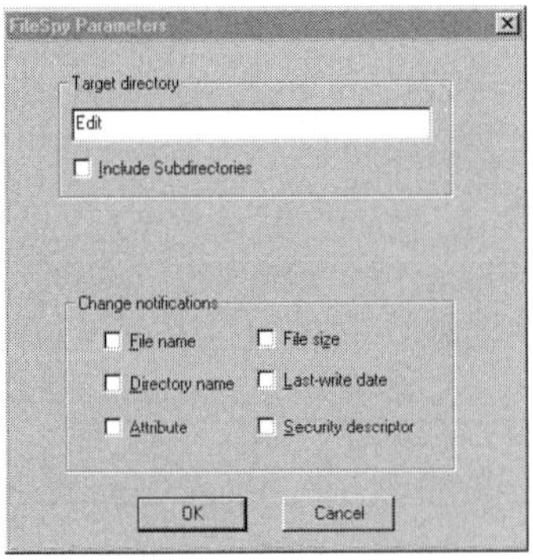

FIGURE 10.1

The main dialog box used by the CtlFileSpy applet.

The resource file for the CtlFileSpy project defines the dialog box in Figure 10.1, as well as the string table and icon resources used by the applet. The `CtlFileSpy.rc` resource file is provided in Listing 10.6.

LISTING 10.6 THE CtlFileSpy.rc RESOURCE FILE

```
#include "resource.h"
#include "windows.h"


IDI_FILESPY            ICON     DISCARDABLE     "filespy.ico"

IDD_FILESPY DIALOG DISCARDABLE  0, 0, 234, 206
STYLE DS_MODALFRAME | WS_POPUP | WS_CAPTION | WS_SYSMENU
CAPTION "FileSpy Parameters"
FONT 8, "MS Sans Serif"
BEGIN
    GROUPBOX        "Target directory",IDC_STATIC,23,13,179,51
    EDITTEXT        IDC_EDIT_DIRECTORY,29,27,164,14,ES_AUTOHSCROLL
    CONTROL         "&Include Subdirectories",IDC_CHK_SUBDIR,
                    "Button", BS_AUTOCHECKBOX | WS_TABSTOP,
                    30,47,83,10
    GROUPBOX        "Change notifications",IDC_STATIC,26,102,177,73
    CONTROL         "&File name",IDC_CHK_FILENAME,"Button",
                    BS_AUTOCHECKBOX | WS_TABSTOP,44,117,46,10
    CONTROL         "&Directory name",IDC_CHK_DIRNAME,"Button",
                    BS_AUTOCHECKBOX | WS_TABSTOP,44,134,63,10
    CONTROL         "&Attribute",IDC_CHK_ATTRIBUTE,"Button",
                    BS_AUTOCHECKBOX | WS_TABSTOP,44,152,42,10
    CONTROL         "File si&ze",IDC_CHK_FILESIZE,"Button",
                    BS_AUTOCHECKBOX | WS_TABSTOP,114,116,41,10
    CONTROL         "&Last-write date",IDC_CHK_LASTWRITE,"Button",
                    BS_AUTOCHECKBOX | WS_TABSTOP,114,133,62,10
    CONTROL         "&Security descriptor",IDC_CHK_SECURITY,
                    "Button", BS_AUTOCHECKBOX | WS_TABSTOP,
                    114,152,74,10
    DEFPUSHBUTTON   "OK",IDOK,59,185,50,14
    PUSHBUTTON      "Cancel",IDCANCEL,125,185,50,14
END

STRINGTABLE DISCARDABLE
BEGIN
    IDS_FILESPY             "FileSpy Control Applet"
    IDS_FILESPY_DESC        "Controls the FileSpy service."
END
```

Resource symbols used by the CtlFileSpy applet are found in the `resource.h` header file, which is shown in Listing 10.7.

LISTING 10.7 THE resource.h HEADER FILE USED BY CTLFILESPY

```
#define IDS_FILESPY                1
#define IDS_FILESPY_DESC           2
#define IDI_FILESPY                101
#define IDD_FILESPY                102
#define IDC_STATIC                 -1
#define IDC_CHK_SUBDIR             1000
#define IDC_CHK_FILENAME           1001
#define IDC_CHK_DIRNAME            1002
#define IDC_CHK_ATTRIBUTE          1003
#define IDC_CHK_FILESIZE           1004
#define IDC_CHK_LASTWRITE          1005
#define IDC_CHK_SECURITY           1006
#define IDC_BTN_BROWSE             1008
#define IDC_LAB_DIRECTORY          1009
#define IDC_EDIT_DIRECTORY         1010
```

The functions and interfaces common to most Control Panel applets are located in the
CplMain.c source file. A partial listing of this file is provided in Listing 10.8 (the
CD-ROM contains the full source).

LISTING 10.8 PART OF THE CONTENTS OF THE CplMain.c SOURCE FILE, WHICH CONTAINS
THE BASIC CONTROL PANEL APPLET INTERFACES

```
#include <windows.h>
#include <cpl.h>
#include <tchar.h>
#include "resource.h"

#include "cplmain.h"
#include "filespy.h"

HANDLE  g_hInstance = NULL;
LPCTSTR g_szService = _T("FileSpyService");
LPCTSTR g_szModuleName = _T("CtlFileSpy.CPL");
const   g_nAppletCount = 1;

LONG CALLBACK CPlApplet(HWND    hwnd,
                        UINT    msg,
                        LPARAM  lParam1,
                        LPARAM  lParam2)
{
    switch(msg)
    {
        case CPL_INIT:
            return OnCplInit();

        case CPL_GETCOUNT:
```

```
                    return OnCplGetCount();

            case CPL_INQUIRE:
                return OnCplInquire((UINT)lParam1, (LPCPLINFO)lParam2);

            case CPL_NEWINQUIRE:
                return OnCplNewInquire((UINT)lParam1,
                                        (LPNEWCPLINFO)lParam2);

            case CPL_DBLCLK:
                return OnCplDblClick(hwnd, (UINT)lParam1, (LONG)lParam2);

            case CPL_STOP:
                return OnCplStop();

            case CPL_EXIT:
                return OnCplExit();

            default:
                break;
        }
        return 0;
}

/*
 * The applet DLL has been loaded, save the global instance
 * handle, and perform any other global initializations that
 * are required.
 */
LONG WINAPI OnCplInit(void)
{
    g_hInstance = GetModuleHandle(g_szModuleName);
    return 1;
}

/*
 * Return the number of applets in this module.
 */
LONG WINAPI OnCplGetCount(void)
{
    return g_nAppletCount;
}

/*
 * Called once - information is cached. If the information needs to
 * change dynamically, set these values to CPL_DYNAMIC_RES. Control
 * Panel will not cache the information and will instead make
 * frequent calls via CPL_NEWINQUIRE.
```

continues

10

CONTROLLING WINDOWS 2000 SERVICES

LISTING 10.8   CONTINUED

```
 */
LONG WINAPI OnCplInquire(UINT uAppNo, LPCPLINFO pCplInfo)
{
    if(pCplInfo)
    {
        pCplInfo->idIcon = IDI_FILESPY;
        pCplInfo->idName = IDS_FILESPY;
        pCplInfo->idInfo = IDS_FILESPY_DESC;
        pCplInfo->lData = 0;
        return 0;
    }
    return 1;
}


/*
 * The user is launching the applet.
 */
LONG WINAPI OnCplDblClick(HWND hWndParent, UINT uAppNo, LONG lAppData)
{
    DialogBox(g_hInstance,
                MAKEINTRESOURCE(IDD_FILESPY),
                hWndParent,
                FileSpyDlgFcn);
    return 0;
}
```

The CplMain.h header file contains declarations of functions found in the CplMain.c source file. CplMain.h can be found on the CD-ROM that accompanies this book.

Functions that are unique to the CtlFileSpy applet are located in the FileSpy.c source file. This file includes functions that initialize the dialog box, as well as functions that read and write parameters to the Registry.

Listing 10.9 is a partial listing of the FileSpy.c source file. The complete source file can be found on this book's CD-ROM.

LISTING 10.9   A PARTIAL LISTING OF FileSpy.c FROM CTLFILESPY, THE CONTROL PANEL APPLET

```
#include <windows.h>
#include <tchar.h>

#include "filespy.h"
#include "reg.h"
#include "resource.h"
```

```
extern HANDLE  g_hInstance;
extern LPCTSTR g_szService;
extern LPCTSTR g_szModuleName;

/*
 * Names of parameters stored in the Registry.
 */
LPCTSTR rgszParamNames[FNPAR_COUNT] = {
    _T("FileNameChange"),
    _T("DirNameChange"),
    _T("AttributeChange"),
    _T("SizeChange"),
    _T("LastWriteDateChange"),
    _T("SecurityChange")
};

/*
 * Dialog box procedure for the applet. Commands are routed to
 * a command handler, and the OnInit handler takes care of
 * initializing the dialog box.
 */
BOOL CALLBACK FileSpyDlgFcn(HWND hDlg, UINT msg, WPARAM wParam,
                            LPARAM lParam)
{
    switch(msg)
    {
        case WM_INITDIALOG:
            OnInitDlg(hDlg);
            return TRUE;

        case WM_COMMAND:
            return OnFileSpyDlgCommand(hDlg, LOWORD(wParam));
    }
    return FALSE;
}

/*
 * Command handler for the applet. If the user clicks OK, the
 * contents of the dialog box are written to the Registry. If
 * the user clicks Cancel, we just close the dialog box.
 */
BOOL WINAPI OnFileSpyDlgCommand(HWND hDlg, WORD nCtlId)
{
    switch(nCtlId)
    {
        case IDOK:
            OnOkay(hDlg);
            EndDialog(hDlg, 0);
            return TRUE;
```

continues

LISTING 10.9   CONTINUED

```c
        case IDCANCEL:
            EndDialog(hDlg, 0);
            return TRUE;
    }
    return FALSE;
}

/*
 * Fill an FN_PARAMS struct with parameters from the Registry.
 */
BOOL LoadParamsFromRegistry(LPCTSTR pszServiceName,
                            FN_PARAMS* pParams)
{
    HKEY hParamsKey  = NULL;
    HKEY hServiceKey = NULL;
    int  ndx         = 0;
    BOOL fRegRead    = FALSE;
    BOOL fRetVal     = FALSE;

    /*
     * Use Win32 SEH to make sure that the Registry key handles
     * are properly cleaned up.
     */
    __try
    {
        hServiceKey = GetRegServiceKey(pszServiceName);
        if(!hServiceKey)
        {
            __leave;
        }
        hParamsKey = GetRegParamKey(hServiceKey);
        if(!hParamsKey)
        {
            __leave;
        }

        /*
         * Retrieve the file notification flag
         * parameters.
         */
        for(ndx = 0; ndx < FNPAR_COUNT; ndx++)
        {
            fRegRead = GetRegValBool(hParamsKey,
                                     rgszParamNames[ndx],
                                     &pParams->fLogChange[ndx],
```

```
                                    FALSE);
            if(!fRegRead)
                __leave;
    }
    /*
     * Retrieve the other service parameters.
     */
    fRegRead = GetRegValBool(hParamsKey,
                             _T("IncludeSubdirectories"),
                             &pParams->fSubdirs,
                             FALSE);
        if(!fRegRead)
            __leave;
        fRegRead = GetRegValSz(hParamsKey,
                               _T("RootDirectory"),
                               pParams->szRootDir,
                               _MAX_PATH,
                               _T("C:\\"));
        if(!fRegRead)
            __leave;
        fRetVal = TRUE;
    }
    __finally
    {
        if(hServiceKey)
            RegCloseKey(hServiceKey);
        if(hParamsKey)
            RegCloseKey(hParamsKey);
    }
    return fRetVal;
}
```

The declarations of functions found in FileSpy.c can be found in the FileSpy.h header
file, which is located in the FileSpy project directory on the CD-ROM that accompanies
this book.

Finally, the module definition file for the CtlFileSpy applet must export the following
three functions:

- CPlApplet
- FileSpyDlgFcn
- OnFileSpyDlgCommand

The module definition file for the CtlFileSpy project is provided in Listing 10.10.

LISTING 10.10 THE CTLFILESPY MODULE DEFINITION FILE

```
LIBRARY   CtlFileSpy
DESCRIPTION "FileSpy CPL Applet"
EXPORTS
    CPlApplet
    FileSpyDlgFcn
    OnFileSpyDlgCommand
```

Compile and run the CtlFileSpy Control Panel applet. The project included on the CD-ROM will build the DLL with a file extension of .cpl so that it will be recognized as a Control Panel applet. After the applet is compiled, you must copy it to the System32 subdirectory so that it will be loaded by the Control Panel. Figure 10.2 shows the CtlFileSpy icon inside the Control Panel.

FIGURE 10.2

The CtlFileSpy icon inside the Control Panel.

Figure 10.3 shows an example of CtlFileSpy running, with the current parameters used by the FileSpy service displayed.

FIGURE 10.3

A running example of the CtlFileSpy applet.

Summary

This chapter discussed managing services for Windows 2000. This chapter also presented complete examples of self-registration code for services and a Control Panel applet used to control a service.

10

CONTROLLING
WINDOWS 2000
SERVICES

User Interaction/ Desktop

PART

II

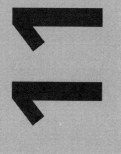

Advanced Graphical Device Interface Programming

CHAPTER 11

This chapter discusses the Graphical Device Interface (GDI) that's provided by Windows 2000. The basic differences between the GDI offered by Windows 9x and Windows 2000 are covered, as well as the various types of GDI objects offered by Windows 2000.

Most of this chapter covers 256-color bitmaps and the steps required to modify the system color palette to display 256-color bitmaps properly. A sample program that loads and displays 256-color bitmaps is provided; this application includes two reusable classes you can include in your own programs.

This chapter also covers using enhanced metafiles, which are used to store GDI functions for playback at a later time, and GDI paths, which can be used to draw irregular or unusual shapes. Sample programs for each of these topics are provided also.

GDI Basics

The Windows 2000 GDI is similar to the GDI offered in Windows 9x and earlier versions of 16-bit Windows. However, it also includes some enhancements that make Windows 2000 a preferred choice for some types of graphics applications.

> **NOTE**
>
> Many of the differences between the GDI offered by Windows 2000 and that offered by Windows 9x are a result of the generic desktop version of Windows needing to offer backward compatibility to applications that run on Windows 3.1. Too many Windows 3.1 applications rely on implementation details with regard to GDI objects, and these applications tend to break when these structures change. In addition, Microsoft made certain tradeoffs to reduce the memory footprint required by Windows 95—these tradeoffs were carried forward into Windows 98 and include some Win32 functions that aren't implemented in Windows 95 or Windows 98.
>
> In fact, much of the Windows 9x GDI is 16-bit code. Many parameters and values are truncated at 16 bits. Most of these issues are only minor problems for most people. Still, it's nice to know where possible problems are. Of course, this is only an issue if you write code that must run on Windows 9x and Windows 2000. A list of differences between the Windows 9x and Windows 2000 GDIs is provided in the following sections.
>
> Two major problems occur when you move GDI code between Windows 2000 and Windows 9x:
>
> - In Windows 9x, all coordinates are 16-bit values. If you use a 32-bit value, the least significant 16 bits are truncated.

- In Windows 9x, if you delete a GDI object that's selected into a device context (DC), the operation succeeds. The deleted object is still selected into the DC, but it's destroyed when the DC is deleted. However, in Windows 2000, the call to DeleteObject will fail, and you'll have a memory leak unless you deselect the GDI object and delete it again.

In addition to these issues, some GDI calls and options aren't supported between the two platforms. All these differences are documented, and there's always a way around the limitation. These differences will probably not cause you any trouble, in most cases.

Device Contexts

A *DC* is an important part of the Windows 2000 GDI. A DC is a structure maintained by Windows, which stores information needed when a Windows 2000 application must display output to a device. The DC stores information about the drawing surface and its capabilities. Before using any of the GDI output functions, you must create a DC for that device.

Windows 2000 and the MFC class library provide the following four different basic types of DCs. Although you use these DCs in different situations, the basic rules for their use are consistent:

- Display DCs are used to display information to a standard video terminal. These are the most commonly used DCs in a Windows program.
- Printer DCs are used to display output on a printer or plotter.
- Memory DCs, sometimes called *compatible DCs*, are used to perform drawing operations on a bitmap.
- Information DCs are used to collect information on a device. These DCs cannot be used for actual output. However, they're extremely fast and have little overhead and are therefore ideal for use when information is being collected.

With the exception of the information DCs, each of the different DC types is used for creating a different sort of output. That's why the MFC class library offers five classes that help encapsulate Windows 2000 DCs. These five classes are shown in Figure 11.1.

Here's a list of the DC classes provided by MFC:

- CDC is the base class for all the DC classes.
- CPaintDC performs some useful housekeeping functions that are needed when a window responds to WM_PAINT.

- `CMetaFileDC` is used when creating metafiles, which are records of GDI commands that can be used in place of bitmaps.
- `CClientDC` is used when a DC will be used only for output to a window's client area.
- `CWindowDC` is used when the entire window may be drawn on.

FIGURE 11.1

The relationships between MFC DC classes.

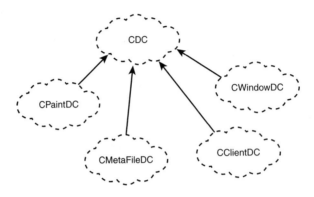

The GDI Map Modes

In Windows, you use *map modes* to define the size and direction of units used in drawing functions. As a Windows programmer, you have several different coordinate systems available. Map modes can use physical or logical dimensions, and they can start at the top, at the bottom, or at an arbitrary point on the screen.

A total of eight different map modes are available in Windows. You can retrieve the current map mode used by a DC using the `GetMapMode` function and set a new map mode using `SetMapMode`. Here are the available map modes:

- `MM_ANISOTROPIC` uses a viewport to scale the logical units to an application-defined value. The `SetWindowExt` and `SetViewportExt` member functions are used to change the units, orientation, and scaling.
- `MM_HIENGLISH`, where each logical unit is converted to a physical value of 0.001 inch. Positive x is to the right; positive y is up.
- `MM_HIMETRIC`, where each logical unit is converted to a physical value of 0.01 millimeter. Positive x is to the right; positive y is up.
- `MM_ISOTROPIC` (similar to `MM_ANISOTROPIC`), where logical units are converted to arbitrary units with equally scaled axes. This means that one unit on the x-axis is always equal to one unit on the y-axis. Use the `SetWindowExt` and `SetViewportExt` member functions to specify the desired units and orientation of the axes.

- MM_LOENGLISH, where each logical unit is converted to a physical value of 0.01 inch. Positive x is to the right; positive y is up.

- MM_LOMETRIC, where each logical unit is converted to a physical value of 0.1 millimeter. Positive x is to the right; positive y is up.

- MM_TEXT, where each logical unit is converted to one device pixel. Positive x is to the right; positive y is down.

- MM_TWIPS, where each logical unit is converted to 1/20 of a point. Because a point is 1/72 inch, a *twip* is 1/1440 inch. This mapping mode is useful when sending output to a printer. Positive x is to the right; positive y is up.

GDI Objects and Their Use

When a DC is created, it has a number of default GDI objects assigned to it, as shown in Figure 11.2. Each of the GDI objects shown in Figure 11.2 has a default value. For example, the bitmap is always a one-pixel monochrome bitmap. The pen is always a solid black pen. Before a DC can be used, it almost always needs to be massaged in some way.

FIGURE 11.2
A DC is created with a set of default GDI objects.

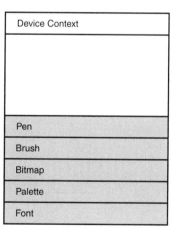

Each of these default objects can be replaced by calling SelectObject to replace the current GDI object with a new one. When a new GDI object is selected, the current object is passed back to the caller as a return value. Failure to return a DC to its original state is a common source of memory leaks. MFC code that selects a new object should always look something like this:

```
CBitmap* pbmpOld = dcMem.SelectObject(&bmpHello);
if(pbmpOld != NULL)
{
```

```
    // Use the bitmap...
    //
    // Return the old bitmap to the DC.
    dcMem.SelectObject(pbmpOld);
}
```

Notice that the pbmpOld value is checked to make sure that it isn't NULL. If the call to SelectObject fails, the original bitmap isn't returned. In that case, there's no need to return the original bitmap to the DC, because a new one was never selected.

Bitmaps

Every DC stores a handle to a bitmap as one of its attributes. As discussed earlier, this is a one-pixel monochrome bitmap that isn't useful for much; you'll almost always select a new bitmap rather than use the default bitmap.

DDBs Versus DIBs

Bitmaps come in two basic flavors: device-independent bitmaps (DIBs) and device-dependent bitmaps (DDBs). In early versions of 16-bit Windows, only DDBs were supported. Beginning with Windows 3.0, and on all versions of Windows NT, DIBs are also supported.

A DDB is tightly coupled to the device on which it's intended to be displayed. The memory that's used to store the bitmap is actually allocated by the device driver, and an application that needs to change the contents of the bitmap must do so indirectly—a slow and inefficient process. Figure 11.3 shows how a DDB is controlled by a device driver (the application has only indirect access to the bitmap).

FIGURE 11.3

A device-dependent bitmap is controlled by the device driver.

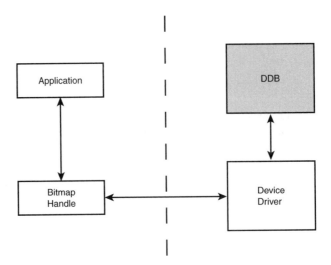

Advanced Graphical Device Interface Programming

CHAPTER 11

349

11

ADVANCED GRAPHICAL
DEVICE INTERFACE
PROGRAMMING

One of the problems with DDBs is that an application must supply bitmaps in a format supported by the device driver. The application must either store bitmaps in multiple formats, or be capable of converting a bitmap from one format into another. Either way, dealing with a DDB can be difficult and time-consuming.

The DIB Format

To get around these problems, all versions of Windows since the Jurassic era (Windows 3.0) support DIBs. A DIB has a known structure that can be converted easily into a DDB whenever necessary.

A DIB can exist in two formats: the Windows format and the OS/2 format. Because the OS/2 format is rarely used, examples in this chapter assume the DIB is in the Windows format. A DIB bitmap stored in a file consists of four sections, as shown in Figure 11.4.

FIGURE 11.4

DIBs contain four data structures.

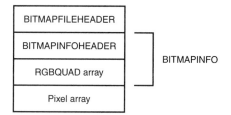

The BITMAPFILEINFO Structure

The BITMAPFILEINFO structure is used when a bitmap is located on a disk, and it's defined as follows:

```
typedef struct tagBITMAPFILEHEADER {
    WORD    bfType;
    DWORD   bfSize;
    WORD    bfReserved1;
    WORD    bfReserved2;
    DWORD   bfOffBits;
} BITMAPFILEHEADER;
```

The value of bfType is always 0x4D42, the ASCII value for the characters B and M. The value of bfSize is supposed to be the size of the bitmap file; however, in many bitmaps, this value is incorrect due to an early SDK documentation error. The value of bfOffBits is the distance to actual bitmap data and is rarely used. The remaining structure members are reserved and should always be set to 0.

The BITMAPFILEINFO structure is only used when the bitmap is read or stored to disk. When a DIB is manipulated in memory, the BITMAPFILEINFO structure is often discarded.

The remaining parts of the DIB structure follow the same format, whether they're located in RAM or in a disk file.

The BITMAPINFO **Structure**

The actual bitmap header consists of a BITMAPINFO structure that has the following members:

```
BITMAPINFOHEADER bmiHeader;
RGBQUAD          bmiColors[]; // contains zero or more palette values
```

The BITMAPINFO structure contains a BITMAPINFOHEADER and zero or more palette values for pixels stored in the bitmap. BITMAPINFOHEADER contains information about the dimensions, color format, and compression information for the bitmap.

The BITMAPINFOHEADER structure contains the following members:

DWORD	biSize
LONG	biWidth
LONG	biHeight
WORD	biPlanes
WORD	biBitCount
DWORD	biCompression
DWORD	biSizeImage
LONG	biXPelsPerMeter
LONG	biYPelsPerMeter
DWORD	biClrUsed
DWORD	biClrImportant

biSize is the size of the bitmap structure. Due to documentation errors in the early versions of the Windows SDK, this value can't always be trusted as accurate when reading a DIB off a disk file. If you're creating a DIB, you must set this value to sizeof(BITMAPINFOHEADER). If you're reading the bitmap from a file, biSize may also be set to sizeof(BITMAPV4HEADER) or sizeof(BITMAPV5HEADER).

biWidth and biHeight are the bitmap dimensions in pixels. If the height is a negative number, the bitmap is a "top-down" bitmap (see the following note). The value of biPlanes is the number of planes supported by the bitmap. This value is always 1 in Windows 2000.

Advanced Graphical Device Interface Programming

CHAPTER 11

351

11

ADVANCED GRAPHICAL
DEVICE INTERFACE
PROGRAMMING

> **NOTE**
>
> Until recently, all bitmaps were "bottom-up," meaning that the first pixel stored in the bitmap was the lower-left pixel in the displayed image. The pixels stored in a bottom-up bitmap are stored in order, with the last pixel representing the upper-right pixel in the displayed image.
>
> Top-down bitmaps reverse the order of the stored pixels. The first pixel in the bitmap refers to the top-left pixel in the displayed image, and the last pixel in the bitmap refers to the bottom-right pixel in the displayed image.

The value of `biBitCount` is the number of bits used to represent each pixel in the bitmap. This value must be 1, 4, 8, 16, 24, or 32.

The type of compression, if any, is determined by the value of `biCompression`. Top-down bitmaps are never compressed. `biCompression` has one of the following values:

- `BI_RGB` indicates that the bitmap is not compressed.

- `BI_RLE4` is an RLE format for bitmaps with four bits per pixel.

- `BI_RLE8` is a run-length encoded (RLE) format for bitmaps with eight bits per pixel.

- `BI_BITFIELDS` is used to specify that the bitmap isn't compressed, and the color table is made up of three RGB doubleword values for each pixel in the bitmap. This value is used when `biBitCount` is 16 or 32.

- `BI_JPEG` is used to indicate that the image is in the JPEG format. This value is only used in Windows 2000.

- `BI_PNG` is used to indicate that the image is in the PNG format. This value is only used in Windows 2000.

The size of the bitmap image in bytes is given in the `biSizeImage` member. If the value of `biCompression` is `BI_RGB`, this value may be 0. For images that are in the JPEG or PNG formats, this value is the size of the JPEG or PNG image buffer.

The values of `biXPelsPerMeter` and `biYPelsPerMeter` can be used to help an application select the most appropriate bitmap for a particular resolution, if multiple resources are available.

The value of `biClrUsed` specifies the number of valid entries in the bitmap's color table. If this value is 0, the maximum number of entries should be assumed, based on the value of `biBitCount`.

The number of colors considered "important" is stored in `biClrImportant`. If this value is 0, all colors are considered important. This information is never used by any of the GDI functions; rather, it's meant for use by applications. If an application is unable to create a palette that contains all the bitmap's colors, this value can be used to determine whether the result is acceptable.

> **NOTE**
>
> If your application is written for Windows NT 4.0 or Windows 2000, you can use the `BITMAPV4HEADER` and `BITMAPV5HEADER` structures. `BITMAPV4HEADER` was introduced beginning with Windows NT 4.0 and Windows 95; it supplied color-matching data that could be used with Image Color Management (ICM) functions. `BITMAPV5HEADER` can be used beginning with Windows 2000 and Windows 98, and it improves the ICM support. If you don't need these features, stick with the original `BITMAPINFOHEADER`.

The DIB's Color Table

After the `BITMAPINFOHEADER` structure, the `bmiColors` variable marks the beginning of the color table. This table is used if the bitmap is not a 16-, 24-, or 32-bit-per-pixel bitmap. The color table is an array of `RGBQUAD` structures, with each entry storing one of the colors used by the bitmap. Here are the members of the `RGBQUAD` structure:

```
BYTE    rgbBlue;
BYTE    rgbGreen;
BYTE    rgbRed;
BYTE    rgbReserved; // Always set to zero
```

The members of the `RGBQUAD` structure represent the red, green, and blue color intensity for a color stored in the color table. Each structure member has a range of 0–255. If all members have a value of 0, the color is black; if all members have a value of 255, the color is white.

The DIB Image Array

An array of pixel information follows the color table. Every pixel in the bitmap is represented by one element of this array. Each of the elements contains a value that represents one of the color map entries. For example, if the first element in the array has a value of 32, the first pixel in the bitmap will use the color found in color table entry number 32, as shown in Figure 11.5.

Advanced Graphical Device Interface Programming
CHAPTER 11

353

11
ADVANCED GRAPHICAL
DEVICE INTERFACE
PROGRAMMING

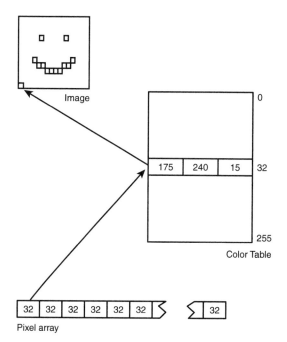

FIGURE 11.5
Every entry in the image array refers to a pixel in the displayed image.

If this is a 16-, 24-, or 32-bit-per-pixel bitmap, there is no color table, and each element of the array contains the RGB color for a single pixel. In effect, the palette has been moved out to the pixel array for these types of bitmaps.

16-Color DIBs

The CBitmap class is often used to manipulate monochrome and 16-color bitmaps. Loading and displaying a bitmap with the CBitmap class is easy and requires only a few lines of code. To display a bitmap with a resource ID of IDB_HELLO in a view, edit the view's OnDraw function, like this:

```
void CBitmapView::OnDraw(CDC* pDC)
{
    CBitmap     bmp;
    bmp.LoadBitmap( IDB_HELLO );
    // Calculate bitmap size using a BITMAP structure.
    BITMAP      bm;
    bmp.GetObject( sizeof(BITMAP), &bm );
    // Create a memory DC, select the bitmap into the
    // memory DC, and BitBlt it into the view.
    CDC         dcMem;
    dcMem.CreateCompatibleDC( pDC );
    CBitmap* pbmpOld = dcMem.SelectObject( &bmp );
```

```
pDC->BitBlt( 10,10, bm.bmWidth, bm.bmHeight,
             &dcMem, 0,0, SRCCOPY );
// Reselect the original bitmap into the memory DC.
dcMem.SelectObject( pbmpOld );
}
```

256-Color DIBs

You might think that manipulating a 256-color bitmap is just as easy as loading a 16-color bitmap. Unfortunately, that's not the case. When a 256-color DIB is displayed on a 256-color device, the colors are almost never correct because of the way Windows 2000 (as well as other Windows flavors) handles the color palette.

Before looking at the code used to display 256-color bitmaps, you may want to review how Windows 2000 determines the colors available to your application. When a bitmap is loaded, Windows 2000 doesn't make any special effort to make sure that color entries in the bitmap's color table are added to the system's color palette. The result is an ugly-looking bitmap. To display a 256-color bitmap, you must always create and manage a logical palette for your application.

An Overview of the Windows 2000 Palette

The Windows 2000 GDI uses palettes to manage color selection for 256-color devices. There are actually several different types of palettes, as shown in Figure 11.6.

FIGURE 11.6

The different types of color palettes used in Windows 2000.

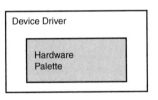

Device Driver

Hardware Palette

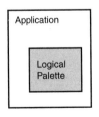

Application

Logical Palette

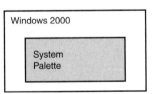

Windows 2000

System Palette

Device drivers that use palettes have an internal palette that stores the current set of colors available for display. This means that 256-color devices have 256 entries in the hardware palette.

Advanced Graphical Device Interface Programming

CHAPTER 11

355

11

ADVANCED GRAPHICAL
DEVICE INTERFACE
PROGRAMMING

The Windows 2000 palette manager maintains a system palette that (we hope) matches the hardware palette.

Every application can have one or more logical palettes. An application interacts with the system palette in order to control the colors that are currently available for display.

To maintain some level of consistency, Windows 2000 reserves the first and last 10 palette entries, leaving 236 palette entries for application use, as shown in Figure 11.7.

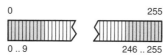

FIGURE 11.7
Windows 2000 makes 236 palette entries available to applications.

0   255

0 .. 9   246 .. 255

At first glance, it might seem unfair for 20 entries to be removed from the system palette. The reason that these entries are removed is to keep the basic window display predictable. The 20 reserved palette entries include the colors used by 16-color VGA devices. As long as these palette entries are available, Windows applications that don't use the palette are displayed as expected.

The System Palette

A palette is one of the attributes that belongs to a DC. Once you've decided to use a palette in your application, you must follow these basic steps:

1. Create a logical palette. This is the process of allocating space for the palette entries and describing the colors that will be included in the palette. As you'll soon see, this process is much easier than it sounds. In most cases, when you need to create a palette, you copy the colors from a bitmap or other object into the new palette. This step is usually performed once, and the logical palette is stored by the application so that it can be used whenever needed.

2. Select the palette into a DC. Unlike other GDI objects, `SelectObject` doesn't work for logical palettes. You must use the `SelectPalette` function.

3. Realize the palette. Basically, this means that the Windows 2000 palette manager is asked to add your palette to the system palette or map your palette to a reasonably close substitute. Selecting and realizing the palette always happen at the same time; there's no point in selecting a palette unless you intend to realize it immediately.

4. Use the palette. If the system palette is updated, the application should redraw itself. This is usually done by invalidating any windows that depend on palette entries.

5. Deselect the palette by selecting the previous palette back into the DC.

6. Delete the palette object. This step is usually performed only when you're sure the palette is no longer needed.

In addition, two messages related to palettes are sent to your application:

- When a window moves into the foreground, Windows 2000 sends it a WM_QUERYNEWPALETTE message. In response to this message, your application should realize its palette.

- If the system palette is changed, all windows in the background will receive a WM_PALETTECHANGED message. An application in the background should again realize its palette to attempt to reassert colors in the system palette. If no free positions in the system palette are available, the palette manager maps the requested color to the closest palette entry.

In any case, you should invalidate any parts of your application that depend on your logical palette if the system palette is updated.

The DIB Example

As an example of how 256-color bitmaps are displayed, the CD-ROM that accompanies this book includes an MFC sample project named Dib. The design of the Dib project uses a basic AppWizard SDI skeleton with these modifications:

- A class, CDIBitmap, that handles the display of DIBs
- A class, CBmpPalette, that handles creating a new 256-color palette
- Additional palette message-handling functions

The CDIBitmap Class

The CDIBitmap class does most of the work in the Dib project. The CDIBitmap class provides an easy-to-use interface for handling 256-color DIBs. The class interface for CDIBitmap is shown in Listing 11.1. It's also included in the Dib project as dib256.h.

LISTING 11.1 THE CDIBitmap CLASS INTERFACE

```
#ifndef DIBMP_UNLEASHED
#define DIBMP_UNLEASHED

class CDIBitmap
{
    friend class CBmpPalette;
//constructors
```

Advanced Graphical Device Interface Programming

CHAPTER 11

357

11

ADVANCED GRAPHICAL
DEVICE INTERFACE
PROGRAMMING

```
public:
    CDIBitmap();
    virtual ~CDIBitmap();
private:
    CDIBitmap(const CDIBitmap& dbmp);

//operations
public:
    inline BITMAPINFO* GetHeaderPtr();
    inline BYTE* GetPixelPtr();
    virtual void DrawDIB(CDC* pDC, int x, int y);
    virtual BOOL Load(CFile* pFile);
    virtual BOOL Load(HINSTANCE hInstance, UINT nResourceID);
    int GetPixelCount() const;

    RGBQUAD* GetColorTablePtr();

protected:
    int GetPalEntries() const;
    int GetPalEntries(BITMAPINFOHEADER& infoHeader) const;
    int GetWidth() const;
    int GetHeight() const;

//implementation
private:
    BITMAPINFO* m_pInfo;
    BYTE*       m_pPixels;
};
#endif
```

Note that CDIBitmap isn't derived from CBitmap, or CObject for that matter. The class itself consumes only a few bytes, requiring space for two pointers and a virtual function table.

CDIBitmap has six public functions:

- GetHeaderPtr returns a pointer to the BITMAPINFO structure.
- GetPixelPtr returns a pointer to the beginning of the pixel image array.
- DrawDIB draws the DIB at a specified location.
- A version of Load reads a DIB from an MFC CFile file associated with a BMP file and initializes the CDIBitmap object.
- Another version of Load reads a DIB from a bitmap resource and initializes the CDIBitmap object.
- GetColorTablePtr returns a pointer to the color table.

The source code for the implementation of CDIBitmap is provided in Listing 11.2. Remember, you don't actually have to type all this source code yourself, because it's located on the CD-ROM in the Dib project as dib256.cpp.

LISTING 11.2 THE IMPLEMENTATION OF THE CDIBitmap CLASS

```
#include "stdafx.h"
#include "dib256.h"

CDIBitmap::CDIBitmap()
{
    m_pInfo = 0;
    m_pPixels = 0;
}

CDIBitmap::~CDIBitmap()
{
    delete [] (BYTE*)m_pInfo;
    delete [] m_pPixels;
}

BOOL CDIBitmap::Load(HINSTANCE hInstance, UINT nResourceID)
{
    try
    {
        HRSRC hRes = FindResource(hInstance,
                                  MAKEINTRESOURCE(nResourceID),
                                  RT_BITMAP);
        if(hRes == NULL)
            throw TEXT("Error:Can't find resource.\n");

        HGLOBAL hGlob = LoadResource(hInstance, hRes);
        if(hGlob == NULL)
            throw TEXT("Error:Can't find load resource.\n");

        BYTE* pBitmapBlock = NULL;
        pBitmapBlock = reinterpret_cast<BYTE*>(LockResource(hGlob));
        if(pBitmapBlock == NULL)
            throw TEXT("Error:Can't find lock resource.\n");

        BITMAPINFOHEADER infoHeader;
        MoveMemory(&infoHeader, pBitmapBlock, sizeof(infoHeader));
        if(infoHeader.biSize != sizeof(infoHeader))
            throw TEXT("Error:OS2 PM BMP Format not supported\n");

        // Store the sizes of the DIB structures
        int cPaletteEntries = GetPalEntries(infoHeader);
        int cColorTable = 256 * sizeof(RGBQUAD);
        int cInfo = sizeof(BITMAPINFOHEADER) + cColorTable;
        int cPixels = 0;
```

Advanced Graphical Device Interface Programming

CHAPTER 11

359

11

ADVANCED GRAPHICAL
DEVICE INTERFACE
PROGRAMMING

```
        if(infoHeader.biSizeImage > 0)
            cPixels = infoHeader.biSizeImage;
        else if(infoHeader.biHeight > 0) // top down or bottom-up
            cPixels = infoHeader.biWidth * infoHeader.biHeight;
        else
            cPixels = infoHeader.biWidth * -infoHeader.biHeight;


        //
        // Allocate space for a new bitmap info header, and copy
        // the info header that was loaded from the resource table.
        m_pInfo = (BITMAPINFO*)new BYTE[cInfo];
        MoveMemory(m_pInfo, &infoHeader, sizeof(BITMAPINFOHEADER));

        pBitmapBlock += sizeof(infoHeader);
        MoveMemory(((BYTE*)m_pInfo) + sizeof(BITMAPINFOHEADER),
                    pBitmapBlock,
                    cColorTable);
        //
        // Allocate space for the pixel area, and load the pixel
        // info from the file.
        m_pPixels = new BYTE[cPixels];
        pBitmapBlock += cColorTable;
        MoveMemory(m_pPixels, pBitmapBlock, cPixels);
    }
    catch(TCHAR* psz)
    {
        TRACE(psz);
        return FALSE;
    }
    return TRUE;
}

BOOL CDIBitmap::Load(CFile* pFile)
{
    ASSERT(pFile);
    BOOL fReturn = TRUE;
    try
    {
        delete [] (BYTE*)m_pInfo;
        delete [] m_pPixels;
        m_pInfo = 0;
        m_pPixels = 0;
        DWORD      dwStart = pFile->GetPosition();
        //
        // Check to make sure we have a bitmap. The first two bytes must
        // be 'B' and 'M'.
        BITMAPFILEHEADER fileHeader;
        pFile->Read(&fileHeader, sizeof(fileHeader));
```

continues

LISTING 11.2   CONTINUED

```
        if( fileHeader.bfType != 0x4D42 )
            throw TEXT("Error:Unexpected file type, not a DIB\n");

        BITMAPINFOHEADER infoHeader;
        pFile->Read(&infoHeader, sizeof(infoHeader));
        if(infoHeader.biSize != sizeof(infoHeader))
            throw TEXT("Error:OS2 PM BMP Format not supported\n");

        // Store the sizes of the DIB structures
        int cPaletteEntries = GetPalEntries(infoHeader);
        int cColorTable = 256 * sizeof(RGBQUAD);
        int cInfo = sizeof(BITMAPINFOHEADER) + cColorTable;
        int cPixels = fileHeader.bfSize - fileHeader.bfOffBits;
        //
        // Allocate space for a new bitmap info header, and copy
        // the info header that was loaded from the file. Read the
        // file and store the results in the color table.
        m_pInfo = (BITMAPINFO*)new BYTE[cInfo];
        memcpy(m_pInfo, &infoHeader, sizeof(BITMAPINFOHEADER));
        pFile->Read(((BYTE*)m_pInfo) + sizeof(BITMAPINFOHEADER),
                    cColorTable);
        //
        // Allocate space for the pixel area, and load the pixel
        // info from the file.
        m_pPixels = new BYTE[cPixels];
        pFile->Seek(dwStart + fileHeader.bfOffBits, CFile::begin);
        pFile->Read(m_pPixels, cPixels);
    }
    catch(TCHAR* psz)
    {
        TRACE(psz);
        fReturn = FALSE;
    }
    return fReturn;
}

//
// DrawDib uses StretchDIBits to display the bitmap.
void CDIBitmap::DrawDIB(CDC* pDC, int x, int y)
{
    ASSERT(pDC);
    HDC     hdc = pDC->GetSafeHdc();
    if(m_pInfo)
        StretchDIBits(hdc,
                      x,
                      y,
                      GetWidth(),
                      GetHeight(),
                      0,
```

```
                    0,
                    GetWidth(),
                    GetHeight(),
                    GetPixelPtr(),
                    GetHeaderPtr(),
                    DIB_RGB_COLORS,
                    SRCCOPY);
}

BITMAPINFO* CDIBitmap::GetHeaderPtr()
{
    ASSERT(m_pInfo);
    ASSERT(m_pPixels);
    return m_pInfo;
}

RGBQUAD* CDIBitmap::GetColorTablePtr()
{
    ASSERT(m_pInfo);
    ASSERT(m_pPixels);
    RGBQUAD* pColorTable = 0;
    if(m_pInfo != 0)
    {
        int cOffset = sizeof(BITMAPINFOHEADER);
        pColorTable = (RGBQUAD*)(((BYTE*)(m_pInfo)) + cOffset);
    }
    return pColorTable;
}

BYTE* CDIBitmap::GetPixelPtr()
{
    ASSERT(m_pInfo);
    ASSERT(m_pPixels);
    return m_pPixels;
}

int CDIBitmap::GetWidth() const
{
    ASSERT(m_pInfo);
    return m_pInfo->bmiHeader.biWidth;
}

int CDIBitmap::GetHeight() const
{
    ASSERT(m_pInfo);
    return m_pInfo->bmiHeader.biHeight;
}

int CDIBitmap::GetPixelCount() const
{
```

continues

LISTING 11.2 CONTINUED

```
    ASSERT(m_pInfo);
    if(m_pInfo->bmiHeader.biSizeImage > 0)
        return m_pInfo->bmiHeader.biSizeImage;
    else
        return m_pInfo->bmiHeader.biHeight * m_pInfo->bmiHeader.biWidth;
}

int CDIBitmap::GetPalEntries() const
{
    ASSERT(m_pInfo);
    return GetPalEntries(*(BITMAPINFOHEADER*)m_pInfo);
}

int CDIBitmap::GetPalEntries(BITMAPINFOHEADER& infoHeader) const
{
    int nReturn;
    if(infoHeader.biClrUsed == 0)
    {
        nReturn = (1 << infoHeader.biBitCount);
    }
    else
        nReturn = infoHeader.biClrUsed;

    return nReturn;
}
```

Most of the work in the CDIBitmap class is done by the CDIBitmap::Load member functions. The first version of this member function takes a pointer to a CFile object as its only parameter. Depending on your application, you could modify this routine to accept a filename. However, in an MFC application, a CFile pointer is easy to get from the MFC framework during serialization.

After verifying that the CFile object refers to a Windows bitmap, the Load function reads each part of the bitmap data structure and creates a DIB dynamically. Note that there are actually two calls to the new operator; there's no requirement that the DIB exist in one solid chunk of memory. The BITMAPINFOHEADER is stored in one location, and the pixel image array is stored in another location.

The second version of the Load member function reads the bitmap from a resource file. The FindResource, LoadResource, and LockResource API functions are used to access the block of memory that contains the raw bitmap resource.

The CDIBitmap::DrawDIB member function calls StretchDIBits to display the DIB. Very little work is actually done in this function. For example, the width and height of the DIB are calculated using CDIBitmap member functions.

The remaining member functions are used to calculate various bits of information about the DIB. Only a pointer to the beginning of the BITMAPINFO structure and a pointer to the beginning of the pixel image array are stored; all other information is calculated as it's needed.

The CBmpPalette **Class**

The CBmpPalette class is used to create a logical palette that contains the colors used by a CDIBitmap object. Although the MFC class library includes a CPalette class, you must derive your own class from it in order to do any meaningful work. Listing 11.3 contains the class declaration for CBmpPalette. This class is included in the Dib project as dibpal.h.

LISTING 11.3 THE CBmpPalette CLASS INTERFACE

```
#ifndef BMP_PAL_UNLEASHED
#define BMP_PAL_UNLEASHED
class CBmpPalette : public CPalette
{
public:
    CBmpPalette(CDIBitmap* pBmp);
};
#endif
```

All the work done by CBmpPalette is done in the constructor; there are no member functions other than the functions inherited from CPalette. The CPalette class is always used together with CDIBitmap. A pointer to a CDIBitmap object is passed to CBmpPalette as a constructor parameter.

CBmpPalette allocates a logical palette with enough entries to store the palette required by the CDIBitmap object. After storing some basic palette information, the palette entries are filled in, using the values collected from the CDIBitmap object. After the palette is created, the logical palette is deleted. The implementation for CBmpPalette is provided in Listing 11.4 and is included in the Dib project as dibpal.cpp.

LISTING 11.4 THE IMPLEMENTATION OF THE CBmpPalette CLASS

```
#include "stdafx.h"
#include "dib256.h"
#include "dibpal.h"

CBmpPalette::CBmpPalette( CDIBitmap* pBmp )
{
```

continues

LISTING 11.4 CONTINUED

```
    ASSERT( pBmp );
    int cPaletteEntries = pBmp->GetPalEntries();
    int cPalette = sizeof(LOGPALETTE) +
                    sizeof(PALETTEENTRY) * cPaletteEntries;
    // Since the LOGPALETTE structure is open-ended, you
    // must dynamically allocate it, rather than using one
    // off the stack.
    LOGPALETTE* pPal = (LOGPALETTE*)new BYTE[cPalette];
    RGBQUAD*    pColorTab = pBmp->GetColorTablePtr();
    pPal->palVersion = 0x300;
    pPal->palNumEntries = cPaletteEntries;
    // Roll through the color table, and add each color to
    // the logical palette.
    for(int ndx = 0; ndx < cPaletteEntries; ndx++)
    {
        pPal->palPalEntry[ndx].peRed   = pColorTab[ndx].rgbRed;
        pPal->palPalEntry[ndx].peGreen = pColorTab[ndx].rgbGreen;
        pPal->palPalEntry[ndx].peBlue  = pColorTab[ndx].rgbBlue;
        pPal->palPalEntry[ndx].peFlags = NULL;
    }
    VERIFY(CreatePalette(pPal));
    delete [] (BYTE*)pPal;
}
```

CDibDoc **Class Changes**

In the Dib example, the CDibDoc class is responsible for the bitmap objects and has two new member functions:

- GetBitmap returns a pointer to a CDIBitmap object.
- GetPalette returns a pointer to a CBmpPalette object.

The CDibDoc class contains a CDIBitmap object and a pointer to a CBmpPalette object. The CDibDoc class header is shown in Listing 11.5, with changes in bold type.

LISTING 11.5 THE CDibDoc CLASS HEADER, WITH CHANGES IN BOLD TYPE

```
#include "dib256.h"
#include "dibpal.h"

class CDibDoc : public CDocument
{
protected: // create from serialization only
    CDibDoc();
    DECLARE_DYNCREATE(CDibDoc)
```

Advanced Graphical Device Interface Programming

CHAPTER 11

365

11

ADVANCED GRAPHICAL
DEVICE INTERFACE
PROGRAMMING

```
// Attributes
public:

// Operations
public:
    CDIBitmap* GetBitmap();
    CPalette*  GetPalette();
// Overrides
    // ClassWizard generated virtual function overrides
    //{{AFX_VIRTUAL(CDibDoc)
    public:
    virtual BOOL OnNewDocument();
    virtual void Serialize(CArchive& ar);
    //}}AFX_VIRTUAL

// Implementation
protected:
    CDIBitmap    m_dib;
    CBmpPalette* m_pPal;
public:
    virtual ~CDibDoc();
#ifdef _DEBUG
    virtual void AssertValid() const;
    virtual void Dump(CDumpContext& dc) const;
#endif

// Generated message map functions
protected:
    //{{AFX_MSG(CDibDoc)
    // NOTE - the ClassWizard will add and remove member functions here.
    //    DO NOT EDIT what you see in these blocks of generated code !
    //}}AFX_MSG
    DECLARE_MESSAGE_MAP()
};
```

The CDIBitmap object is loaded during serialization. After it has been loaded, the CBmpPalette object is created dynamically. m_pPal, the pointer to CBmpPalette, is initialized in the constructor and deleted in the destructor. The changes for the constructor, destructor, OnNewDocument, and Serialize member functions for the CDibDoc class are shown in Listing 11.6. All changed lines are marked in bold.

LISTING 11.6 CHANGES TO CDibDoc MEMBER FUNCTIONS, WITH CHANGES IN BOLD TYPE

```
CDibDoc::CDibDoc()
{
    m_pPal = 0;
}
```

continues

LISTING 11.6   CONTINUED

```
CDibDoc::~CDibDoc()
{
    delete m_pPal;
}

BOOL CDibDoc::OnNewDocument()
{
    if (!CDocument::OnNewDocument())
        return FALSE;
    delete m_pPal;
    m_pPal = 0;
    return TRUE;
}

void CDibDoc::Serialize(CArchive& ar)
{
    if (ar.IsStoring())
    {
        TRACE(TEXT("Storing a bitmap is not supported"));
        ASSERT(FALSE);
    }
    else
    {
        CFile* pFile = ar.GetFile();
        ASSERT( pFile );
        ar.Flush();
        BOOL fLoaded = m_dib.Load(pFile);
        if(fLoaded != FALSE)
        {
            delete m_pPal;
            m_pPal = new CBmpPalette(&m_dib);
            UpdateAllViews(NULL);
        }
        else
            AfxMessageBox(TEXT("Error Loading Bitmap"));
    }
}
```

As discussed earlier, the CDibDoc class has two new member functions to return pointers to the bitmap and palette data members. Add the source code provided in Listing 11.7 to the CDibDoc class.

LISTING 11.7   NEW CDibDoc MEMBER FUNCTIONS TO RETURN THE BITMAP AND PALETTE POINTERS

```
CDIBitmap* CDibDoc::GetBitmap()
{
```

```
    return &m_dib;
}

CPalette* CDibDoc::GetPalette()
{
    return m_pPal;
}
```

Main Frame Class Changes

When the Dib application receives a palette message, Windows 2000 actually sends the message to the application, where it will be routed to the CMainFrame class. Because the CMainFrame class has no knowledge about how the bitmap or palette is organized, it must forward these messages to the view class. When CMainFrame receives a palette message from Windows, it must determine the active view and send it the message.

ClassWizard was used to add message-handling functions for WM_PALETTECHANGED and WM_QUERYNEWPALETTE. The source code for the message-handling functions is shown in Listing 11.8.

LISTING 11.8   CMainFrame PALETTE MESSAGE-HANDLING FUNCTIONS

```
void CMainFrame::OnPaletteChanged(CWnd* pFocusWnd)
{
    CView* pView = GetActiveView();
    if( pView )
    {
        HWND hWndFocus = pView->GetSafeHwnd();
        pView->SendMessage( WM_PALETTECHANGED,
                            (WPARAM)hWndFocus,
                            (LPARAM)0 );
    }
}

BOOL CMainFrame::OnQueryNewPalette()
{
    CView* pView = GetActiveView();
    if( pView )
    {
        HWND hWndFocus = pView->GetSafeHwnd();
        pView->SendMessage( WM_QUERYNEWPALETTE,
                            (WPARAM)hWndFocus,
                            (LPARAM)0 );
    }
    return TRUE;
}
```

CDibView **Class Changes**

The CDibView class has two main functions: drawing the 256-color bitmap and responding to palette messages. The CDibView::OnDraw function must be modified to draw the bitmap, as shown in Listing 11.9.

LISTING **11.9** A NEW VERSION OF CDibView::*OnDraw*

```
void CDibView::OnDraw(CDC* pDC)
{
    CDibDoc* pDoc = GetDocument();
    ASSERT_VALID(pDoc);

    CPalette* pPal = pDoc->GetPalette();
    CPalette* pOldPal = pDC->SelectPalette( pPal, FALSE );
    pDC->RealizePalette();

    CDIBitmap* pBmp = pDoc->GetBitmap();
    pBmp->DrawDIB( pDC, 0, 0 );

    pDC->SelectPalette( pOldPal, FALSE );
}
```

OnDraw fetches pointers to the bitmap and palette from CDibDoc, using the new member functions added to the document class earlier. The palette is selected and realized and then the bitmap is drawn. After the bitmap is drawn, the previous palette is selected back into the DC.

The CMainFrame class forwards WM_PALETTECHANGED and WM_QUERYNEWPALETTE messages to the view class. However, there's one small problem—ClassWizard does not offer direct support for palette messages sent to child window classes such as CDibView. Therefore, some trickery is required. The following steps were used to convince ClassWizard to add palette message handling to the view class:

1. Open ClassWizard.
2. Select the CDibView class.
3. Select the Class Info tab.
4. In the Advanced Options group, click the Message Filter combo box and select Topmost Frame instead of Child Window.
5. Select the Message Map tab and add the message-handling functions for WM_PALETTECHANGED and WM_QUERYNEWPALETTE to the CDibView class.
6. Select the Class Info tab.

Advanced Graphical Device Interface Programming

CHAPTER 11

369

11

ADVANCED GRAPHICAL
DEVICE INTERFACE
PROGRAMMING

7. In the Advanced Options group, click the Message Filter combo box and select Child Window instead of Topmost Frame.

8. Close ClassWizard.

The source code for the palette message-handling functions is provided in Listing 11.10.

LISTING 11.10 NEW FUNCTIONS ADDED TO THE CDibView CLASS

```
// OnPaletteChanged - Handles WM_PALETTECHANGED, which is a
// notification that a window has changed the current palette. If
// this view did not change the palette, forward this message to
// OnQueryNewPalette so the palette can be updated, and redrawn
// if possible.
void CDibView::OnPaletteChanged(CWnd* pFocusWnd)
{
    if( pFocusWnd != this )
        OnQueryNewPalette();
}
// Notification that the view is about to become active,
// and the view should realize its palette.
BOOL CDibView::OnQueryNewPalette()
{
    CDibDoc* pDoc = GetDocument();
    ASSERT_VALID(pDoc);

    CBmpPalette* pPal = (CBmpPalette*)pDoc->GetPalette();
    if( pPal )
    {
        CDC*      pDC = GetDC();
        CPalette* pOldPal = pDC->SelectPalette( pPal, FALSE );
        UINT uChanges = pDC->RealizePalette();
        pDC->SelectPalette( pOldPal, FALSE );
        ReleaseDC( pDC );
        if( uChanges != 0 )
            InvalidateRect( NULL );
    }
    return TRUE;
}
```

In most cases, OnPaletteChanged calls the OnQueryNewPalette function directly. The only exception is when the WM_PALETTECHANGED message is sent because this view had updated the system palette. If this view is the foreground window, the Windows 2000 palette manager will give you first crack at setting the system's palette. If you're in the background, you only have access to the unused entries. If there's no more room in the palette, your palette will be mapped to the closest possible match.

Remember to include the declarations for the CDIBitmap class at the top of the dibView.cpp source file, after the other #include directives:

```
#include "dib256.h"
```

Compile and run the Dib example. If you have a 256-color display, load a 256-color bitmap. Notice that you get all of the colors. If you run several instances of the program using different 256-color bitmaps, you may notice the palette change if you switch between windows. Figure 11.8 shows the Dib example displaying the 256-color Windows 2000 Server logo.

FIGURE 11.8

The Dib sample program displaying a 256-color bitmap.

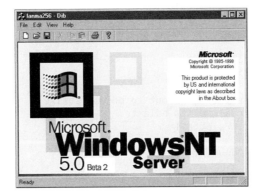

Paths

A *path* is a GDI object that was first introduced in Windows NT 3.1. It's a collection of figures or shapes that can be combined to draw other figures or shapes or to create irregular clipping regions. When you use a path to describe a shape, the Windows 2000 GDI can display the path in one operation instead of a series of small building blocks. Although Windows 95 and Windows 98 now support GDI paths, they only support a subset of the functions available to you as a Windows 2000 programmer.

A path is created by calling BeginPath, describing the path endpoints, and calling EndPath. This series of function calls is known as a *path bracket*. A sample path bracket is shown in Figure 11.9.

As shown in Figure 11.9, 21 functions can be called in a path bracket. By combining these functions in a path, you can create a wide range of complicated shapes.

Once you've created a path, you can draw its outline, fill its interior, or use it as a clipping region. To demonstrate using paths to create clipping regions, the CD-ROM includes an MFC sample project named Path.

FIGURE 11.9

An example of a path bracket.

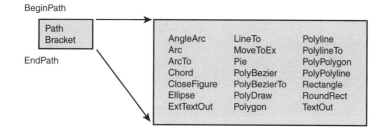

The Path example is a standard AppWizard SDI application. All the interesting work in this example is done in the CPathView::OnDraw function, shown in Listing 11.11.

LISTING 11.11 USING A PATH TO CREATE A CLIPPING REGION

```
void CPathView::OnDraw(CDC* pDC)
{
    // Calculate the size of the clipping area
    CRect rcClient;
    GetClientRect( rcClient );
    int xBorder = rcClient.Width()/4;
    int yBorder = rcClient.Height()/4;
    int cxRect  = rcClient.Width()/2;
    int cyRect  = rcClient.Height()/2;

    //
    // Create a large Arial font, and select it into
    // the device context. This font will be part of
    // the clipping path.
    CFont   fntClip;
    LOGFONT lf;
    memset( &lf, 0, sizeof(LOGFONT) );
    lstrcpy( lf.lfFaceName, "Arial" );
    lf.lfWeight = FW_BOLD;
    lf.lfHeight = yBorder;
    fntClip.CreateFontIndirect( &lf );
    CFont* pOldFont = pDC->SelectObject( &fntClip );

    // Create a path, and use it as a clipping area
    HDC hdcPath = pDC->GetSafeHdc();
    pDC->BeginPath();
        MoveToEx( hdcPath, xBorder, yBorder, NULL );
        LineTo( hdcPath, xBorder + cxRect, yBorder );
        LineTo( hdcPath, xBorder + cxRect, yBorder + cyRect );
        LineTo( hdcPath, xBorder, yBorder + cyRect );
        LineTo( hdcPath, xBorder, yBorder );
        DrawText( hdcPath, TEXT("NT"), 2, &rcClient,
```

continues

LISTING 11.11   CONTINUED

```
                   DT_CENTER | DT_SINGLELINE| DT_VCENTER );
pDC->EndPath();
pDC->SelectClipPath( RGN_COPY );
//
// Create red brushes and pens for the sun burst, and
// select them into the device context.
CBrush  brRed( RGB(255,0,0) );
CPen    penRed( PS_SOLID, 1, RGB(255,0,0) );
CBrush* pOldBrush = pDC->SelectObject( &brRed );
CPen*   pOldPen = pDC->SelectObject( &penRed );

CSize   sizeOfSun( cxRect/2, cxRect/2 );
CPoint  ptSun( cxRect + (xBorder/2), yBorder/2 );
CRect   rcSun( ptSun, sizeOfSun );
//
// Calculate the sin and cosine of one 90 degree
// quadrant.
double rgSin[90], rgCos[90];
const  double pi = 3.14159;
CPoint ptCenter( xBorder + cxRect, yBorder );
for( int nAngle = 0; nAngle < 90; nAngle++ )
{
    rgSin[nAngle] = sin( (((double)nAngle)/180.0) * pi );
    rgCos[nAngle] = cos( (((double)nAngle)/180.0) * pi );
}
//
// Starting from the upper-right corner of the rectangle,
// draw rays across the clipping path, then draw an ellipse
// centered in the upper-right corner.
double flSegment = (double)(rcClient.Width());
for( nAngle = 0; nAngle < 90; nAngle++ )
{
    pDC->MoveTo( ptCenter.x, ptCenter.y );
    int x = (int)(rgCos[nAngle] * flSegment);
    int y = (int)(rgSin[nAngle] * flSegment);
    pDC->LineTo( ptCenter.x - (int)(rgCos[nAngle]*flSegment),
                 ptCenter.y + (int)(rgSin[nAngle]*flSegment));

}
pDC->Ellipse( rcSun );

pDC->SelectObject( pOldBrush );
pDC->SelectObject( pOldPen );
pDC->SelectObject( pOldFont );
}
```

Listing 11.11 contains calls to the `sin` and `cos` functions; therefore, the following `#include` directive must be added to either `stdafx.h` or to the top of the `PathView.cpp` source file, after the other `#include` directives:

```
#include <math.h>
```

In Listing 11.11, a path is created that contains a rectangle, along with a text string. After the path is selected as a clipping region, all drawing functions are affected by it, as shown in Figure 11.10.

FIGURE 11.10

The Path example uses a path as a clipping region.

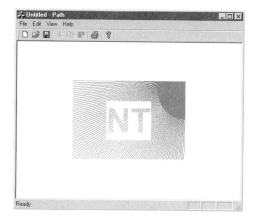

Metafiles

A *metafile* is a collection of GDI function calls that have been stored in a binary format. Windows 2000 uses *enhanced* metafiles, which have more capabilities than the ordinary metafiles used in 16-bit versions of Windows.

A metafile is often used to exchange drawing information via the Clipboard. In fact, a metafile is useful in any case where a bitmap image would take up too much storage. Although a metafile requires much less storage than a bitmap, it takes more time to display a metafile than to transfer a bitmap using the `BitBlt` function.

A metafile is constructed by creating a metafile DC and then drawing it just like any other DC. After the GDI calls have been drawn into the metafile DC, the metafile is "played" in order to display its contents.

The MFC class library includes the `CMetaFileDC` class, which can be used to simplify creating and playing both plain metafiles and enhanced metafiles. To create an enhanced metafile, the `CreateEnhanced` member function is used:

```
CMetaFileDC dcMetaFile;
dcMetaFile.CreateEnhanced( pDC ,
                           TEXT("C:\\FOO"),
                           NULL,
                           TEXT("Unleashed MetaFile Example") );
```

The `CreateEnhanced` function has four parameters:

- A reference DC that indicates the resolution and device units used by the current device.
- A filename, if any, that will store the metafile after it's closed. If a metafile is created by an application for temporary purposes, this parameter will be `NULL`, and the metafile will be destroyed when its handle is deleted.
- A bounding rectangle for the image stored in the metafile. If this value is `NULL`, an appropriate size will be selected, based on the size of the image drawn into the metafile.
- A description of the metafile image, if any. Otherwise, `NULL` is entered for this parameter.

After the metafile is created, it can be used just like any other DC, except that instead an image being drawn, the function calls are stored in the metafile. Here's an example:

```
dcMetaFile.MoveTo( rcDot.TopLeft() );
dcMetaFile.LineTo( rcDot.BottomRight() );
```

After all the required GDI function calls have been recorded in the metafile, the metafile is closed using the `CloseEnhanced` function:

```
HENHMETAFILE          m_hmf;
m_hmf = dcMetaFile.CloseEnhanced();
```

The handle to the metafile is returned when an enhanced metafile is closed. This handle can be played on any DC, using the `CDC::PlayMetaFile` function:

```
pDC->PlayMetaFile( m_hmf, rc );
```

A Metafile Example

As an example of how an enhanced metafile is created and used, this book's CD-ROM includes a sample project named Meta. Meta is a standard AppWizard SDI application with a few simple modifications.

Advanced Graphical Device Interface Programming

CHAPTER 11

375

11

ADVANCED GRAPHICAL
DEVICE INTERFACE
PROGRAMMING

When the Meta application starts, a metafile is created, and the handle is stored by the view class. When a left-click is detected in the Meta client area, a metafile is played in the location of the mouse click. In addition, the location of the mouse click is stored so that the client area is updated correctly when it's repainted.

CMetaView **Class Declaration Changes**

The CMetaView class handles creating and playing the enhanced metafile, as well as storing the collection of points that have received mouse clicks. The CMetaView class needs two new member variables:

- m_rgPoints is a CArray object that stores an array of CPoint objects. The location of left-clicks is stored in this array.

- m_hmfTarget is a handle to an enhanced metafile.

Listing 11.12 shows the changes to the CMetaView class in boldface type. Because this class is created by AppWizard, most of the unchanged parts of the declaration are omitted from the listing.

LISTING 11.12   CHANGES TO THE CMetaView CLASS DECLARATION

```
class CMetaView : public CView
{
...
// Implementation
protected:
    CArray<CPoint,CPoint> m_rgPoints;
    HENHMETAFILE          m_hmfTarget;
...
}
```

Because the CArray class is defined in a separate part of the MFC class library, its definition must be manually added to the project by including the afxtempl.h file in stdafx.h. If you look in the stdafx.h file that's part of the Meta project, you'll see the following #include directive, just before the final #endif:

```
#include <afxtempl.h>
```

CMetaView **Destructor Changes**

The only cleanup required for the CMetaView class is to delete the metafile handle when the view is destroyed. Listing 11.13 contains the source code for the CMetaView destructor.

LISTING 11.13 THE CMetaView DESTRUCTOR

```
CMetaView::~CMetaView()
{
    DeleteEnhMetaFile( m_hmfTarget );
}
```

CMetaView::OnInitialUpdate Changes

When a view is initially displayed, the OnInitialUpdate function is called. The CMetaView class creates an enhanced metafile during OnInitialUpdate and stores the metafile handle for later use. The OnInitialUpdate function must be added to CMetaView using ClassWizard. Listing 11.14 contains the source code for CMetaView::OnInitialUpdate.

LISTING 11.14 CREATING AN ENHANCED METAFILE DURING OnInitialUpdate

```
void CMetaView::OnInitialUpdate()
{
    CMetaFileDC dcMetaFile;

    CDC* pDC = GetDC();
    dcMetaFile.CreateEnhanced( pDC , NULL, NULL, NULL );

    CRect rcCircle(0,0,50,50);
    CRect rcDot(20,20,30,30);

    CBrush brRed( RGB(255,0,0) );
    CBrush brBlue( RGB(0,0,255) );

    CBrush* pOldBrush = dcMetaFile.SelectObject( &brBlue );
    ASSERT( pOldBrush );
    CPen*   pOldPen = (CPen*)(dcMetaFile.SelectStockObject( BLACK_PEN ));

    dcMetaFile.Ellipse( rcCircle );
    dcMetaFile.SelectObject( &brRed );
    dcMetaFile.Ellipse( rcDot );

    dcMetaFile.MoveTo( rcDot.TopLeft() );
    dcMetaFile.LineTo( rcDot.BottomRight() );
    dcMetaFile.MoveTo( rcDot.left, rcDot.bottom );
    dcMetaFile.LineTo( rcDot.right, rcDot.top );

    dcMetaFile.SelectObject( pOldBrush );
    dcMetaFile.SelectObject( pOldPen );

    m_hmfTarget = dcMetaFile.CloseEnhanced();
}
```

Advanced Graphical Device Interface Programming

CHAPTER 11

377

11

ADVANCED GRAPHICAL
DEVICE INTERFACE
PROGRAMMING

The source code in Listing 11.14 creates an enhanced metafile that contains two circles arranged like a target, with a smaller red circle located inside a larger blue circle. An X is drawn to mark the center of the circles.

Note that the source code used to draw the metafile is almost exactly like the source code used to draw on a normal DC. In fact, it's easy to use a generic routine that draws to either a metafile DC or a normal DC, like this:

```
DrawImage( CDC* pDC )
{
    CRect rcCircle(0,0,50,50);
    CBrush brBlue( RGB(0,0,255) );
    CBrush* pOldBrush = pDC->SelectObject( &brBlue );
    pDC->Ellipse( rcCircle );
    // Remaining drawing functions...
}
```

Left-Button Mouse Clicks

When a user clicks the Meta client area using the left mouse button, the metafile is played using the CDC::PlayMetaFile function. Windows 2000 sends a WM_LBUTTONDOWN message to a window when a user clicks the left mouse button. To handle the left mouse button, use ClassWizard to add a message-handling function for WM_LBUTTONDOWN to the CMetaView class. The source code that the Meta application uses for OnLButtonDown is provided in Listing 11.15.

LISTING 11.15 PLAYING A METAFILE AT THE POINT OF A MOUSE CLICK

```
void CMetaView::OnLButtonDown(UINT nFlags, CPoint point)
{
    CDC* pDC = GetDC();
    ASSERT( pDC );
    if( pDC )
    {
        CRect rcTarget( point.x-25,
                        point.y-25,
                        point.x+25,
                        point.y+25 );
        pDC->PlayMetaFile( m_hmfTarget, rcTarget );
    }
    m_rgPoints.Add( point );
}
```

The source code in Listing 11.15 creates a rectangle, rcTarget, 50 units square around the point that's clicked. The metafile is then played in that rectangle. To make larger or smaller images, you can vary the size of rcTarget.

In addition, the location of the mouse click is added to the m_rgPoints collection. In the next section, the OnDraw function will use m_rgPoints to redraw the client area.

CMetaView::OnDraw Changes

The OnDraw function must be provided in case the client area is redrawn. For example, if the client area is hidden by another window or if the Meta application is minimized and restored, the client area must be redrawn. The source code for CMetaView::OnDraw is provided in Listing 11.16.

LISTING 11.16   REDRAWING THE META CLIENT AREA USING METAFILES

```
void CMetaView::OnDraw(CDC* pDC)
{
    int limPoints = m_rgPoints.GetSize();
    if( limPoints > 0 )
    {
        CPoint pt = m_rgPoints[0];
        for( int n = 1; n < limPoints; n++ )
        {
            pt = m_rgPoints[n];
            CRect rc( pt.x-25,
                      pt.y-25,
                      pt.x+25,
                      pt.y+25 );
            pDC->PlayMetaFile( m_hmfTarget, rc );
        }
    }
}
```

The source code in Listing 11.16 is similar to the source code provided in Listing 11.15 for the OnLButtonDown function. However, instead of playing a single metafile at one point, OnDraw plays the metafile for every point stored in m_rgPoints.

Compile and run the Meta application. Figure 11.11 shows the Meta application after several mouse clicks have been registered.

FIGURE 11.11

The Meta sample program after the metafile has been played several times.

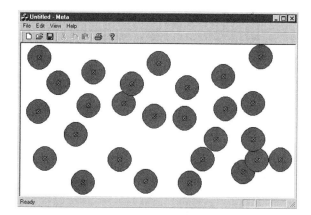

Summary

This chapter discussed the Windows 2000 GDI. The GDI objects used when programming for Windows 2000 were also discussed, and several sample programs were presented.

Owner Draw and Custom Draw

CHAPTER 12

This chapter covers owner-drawn and custom-drawn controls. *Owner Draw* and *Custom Draw* are two ways you can add specialized visual effects to your controls. The steps required to implement Owner Draw and Custom Draw are discussed in this chapter, as is the support offered by MFC and Visual C++ for customizing your controls using these methods. This chapter also includes two sample programs:

- The OwnDraw project creates an owner-drawn list box, where each item appears to be a Windows pushbutton control.
- The CustDraw project creates a listview control that displays each item in a different color, with a mixture of fonts.

These sample programs can be found on the CD-ROM or can be created from scratch using the code in this chapter.

Using Owner-drawn Controls

Owner-drawn controls are controls that are drawn by the control's parent, rather than by the operating system. Owner-drawn controls often add bitmaps, figures, or other special effects in addition to their normal appearance. Owner-drawn controls can also be used to offer extra functionality not included in the standard control.

Here are the five types of controls that can be owner drawn:

- Buttons
- List boxes
- Combo boxes
- Menus
- Listviews

A self-drawn control is similar to an owner-drawn control, but the control-drawing functionality is included in a C++ wrapper class that handles drawing the control. The responsibility for drawing the control rests with the C++ class rather than with the control's owner. From the operating system's point of view, the control is owner drawn. However, any programmer who uses the control does not need to perform any drawing— hence the name *self-drawn*.

Owner-drawn controls give you a chance to add functionality to standard controls without the need to completely rewrite the control from scratch.

Both subclassing and using owner-drawn controls enable you to leverage an existing control so that you can concentrate on adding functionality with your code, rather than duplicating code that has already been written. For example, many early versions of tree controls were actually owner-drawn list boxes.

Your owner-drawn controls probably won't be as complex as the tree control found in the Windows 3.1 File Manager, especially because the standard tree common control is available. However, understanding how an owner-drawn control works can easily help you add extra features to your programs.

Implementing an Owner-drawn Control

In order for an owner-drawn control to work, the owner of the control receives four messages from Windows containing information about the control:

- WM_DRAWITEM
- WM_MEASUREITEM
- WM_COMPAREITEM
- WM_DELETEITEM

It's not necessary for every type of owner-drawn control to handle every message. Table 12.1 lists the Owner Draw messages that must be handled for each type of owner-drawn control.

TABLE 12.1 MESSAGES THAT MUST BE HANDLED FOR OWNER-DRAWN CONTROLS

Message	Button	Menu	Combo Box	List Box	Listview
WM_DRAWITEM	Yes	Yes	Yes	Yes	Yes
WM_MEASUREITEM	No	Yes	Yes	Yes	Yes
WM_COMPAREITEM	No	No	Yes	Yes	Yes
WM_DELETEITEM	No	No	Yes	Yes	Yes

Each of these messages includes a pointer to a structure that contains information used to identify the object to be drawn. In some cases, the structure contains elements that must be updated by the application. For example, WM_COMPAREITEM passes a pointer to a COMPAREITEMSTRUCT structure that's updated with the results of a comparison between two list items.

Handling the WM_DRAWITEM Message

When an owner-drawn control must be painted, Windows sends a WM_DRAWITEM message to the control's owner. If you're using MFC, this message is translated into an OnDrawItem function call. When processing OnDrawItem, your program is expected to draw all aspects of the control, including its selection state and focus rectangle, if needed.

The WM_DRAWITEM message contains two parameters:

- WPARAM. Contains the control ID.
- LPARAM. Contains a pointer to a DRAWITEMSTRUCT.

If you're using MFC, the pointer to the DRAWITEMSTRUCT structure and the resource ID for the list box control are passed as function parameters directly.

The DRAWITEMSTRUCT structure contains everything you need to draw the control. Here are the most commonly used members of a DRAWITEMSTRUCT:

- itemID. Contains an identifier for the item to be drawn. For a menu item, this member contains the resource ID. For a list box or combo box, this member contains the zero-based index of the item to be drawn. List boxes and combo boxes will send -1 for empty controls when the focus rectangle should be drawn for the entire control.
- hDC. Identifies the device context that you should draw into. If you're using MFC, you'll attach an instance of the CDC class to this member variable.
- rcItem. Defines the boundaries of the area to be drawn.
- itemData. Contains a 32-bit value associated with the item.
- itemAction. Indicates the type of drawing to be done. The possible values for this member are shown in Table 12.2.
- itemState. Indicates the new state of the item to be drawn. Possible values for this member are shown in Table 12.3.

TABLE 12.2   POSSIBLE VALUES FOR itemAction

Value	Description
ODA_DRAWENTIRE	The entire item must be drawn
ODA_FOCUS	The item's focus state must be updated
ODA_SELECT	The item's selection state must be updated

TABLE 12.3 POSSIBLE VALUES FOR `itemState`

Value	Description
ODS_DEFAULT	Draw as the default item
ODS_DISABLED	Draw as disabled
ODS_FOCUS	Draw with the input focus
ODS_COMBOBOXEDIT	Draw in the edit window of a combo box
ODS_CHECKED	The menu item is checked
ODS_GRAYED	The menu item is grayed
ODS_SELECTED	The menu item is selected

If the owner-drawn control is a list box or combo box, the WM_DRAWITEM message will be sent once for every item that must be drawn. For example, if eight items are visible in an owner-drawn list box, WM_DRAWITEM will be sent at least eight times when the list box is initially displayed.

Handling the WM_MEASUREITEM Message

Before asking for an item to be drawn, Windows will send the control a WM_MEASUREITEM message to determine the size of the item (owner-drawn buttons will not receive this message). If you're using MFC, this message will be translated by the framework into an OnMeasureItem function call. If the control is a variable-size list box, the WM_MEASUREITEM message is sent for each item in the control. For fixed-size list boxes, the message is sent only once.

The WM_MEASUREITEM message has one parameter: a pointer to a MEASUREITEMSTRUCT structure. This structure must be updated so that Windows will provide enough room for the owner-drawn item to be drawn. Here are the most commonly used members of MEASUREITEMSTRUCT:

- itemID. Contains an identifier for the item to be drawn. For a menu item, this member contains the resource ID. For a list box or combo box, this member contains the zero-based index of the item to be drawn. List boxes and combo boxes will send -1 for empty controls when the focus rectangle should be drawn for the entire control.

- itemWidth. Must be set to the width of the item, in pixels.

- itemHeight. Must be set to the height of the item, in pixels.

- itemData. Contains a 32-bit value previously associated with the item by the application.

Handling the WM_COMPAREITEM Message

The list box and combo box controls provide lists of items that can (optionally) be sorted. For owner-drawn list boxes and combo boxes, the owner of the control must be prepared to sort items contained in the controls, if the LBS_SORT (for list boxes) or CBS_SORT (for combo boxes) style bits are set. Windows will send the control's owner a WM_COMPAREITEM message to request that two items contained in the control be compared. If you're using MFC, this message will be translated into an OnCompareItem function call by the framework.

The WM_COMPAREITEM message has one parameter: a pointer to a COMPAREITEMSTRUCT structure. This structure must be updated so that Windows can determine the relative positions of items located inside the owner-drawn control. Here are the most commonly used members of COMPAREITEMSTRUCT:

- itemID1. Contains the item identifier of the first item to be compared.
- itemData1. Contains a 32-bit value previously associated with the first item by the application.
- itemID2. Contains the item identifier of the second item to be compared.
- itemData2. Contains a 32-bit value previously associated with the second item by the application.

The owner of the control must compare the relative order of the two items and return one of these values:

- -1 (if the first item should be placed before the second item)
- 0 (if both items are equivalent)
- 1 (if the second item should be placed before the first item)

If the relative order of items in the control is not important, the control should not be given a sorted attribute.

Handling the WM_DELETEITEM Message

Owner-drawn list boxes and combo boxes normally contain pointers to dynamically allocated objects. When an item that uses a block of dynamic memory is deleted, Windows sends a WM_DELETEITEM message to the control's owner. If multiple items are removed from the control (if the control is destroyed, for example), a WM_DELETEITEM message will be sent for every item that is deleted. If you're using MFC, the framework will translate this message into an OnDeleteItem function call.

The WM_DELETEITEM message has one parameter: a pointer to a DELETEITEM structure.

This structure is used to identify the item that is being deleted from the control. The most commonly used member of this structure is the `itemData` member, which contains a 32-bit value previously associated with the control item. This 32-bit value is typically a pointer to a dynamically created object.

OwnDraw: An Owner Draw Example

As an example of using owner-drawn controls, the CD-ROM accompanying this book includes a dialog-based MFC project named OwnDraw. The OwnDraw project includes an owner-drawn list box that displays its items as though each item were a pushbutton control.

Figure 12.1 shows the main dialog box for the OwnDraw project.

FIGURE 12.1

The dialog box used by the OwnDraw project.

Three new controls were added to the project, as listed in Table 12.4.

TABLE 12.4   CONTROLS USED IN THE OWNDRAW DIALOG BOX

Control	Resource ID	Attributes
List box	IDC_LIST	Owner draw fixed, unsorted
Edit	IDC_EDIT	
Add pushbutton	IDC_ADD	

ClassWizard was used to associate member variables with the list box and edit controls, as shown in Table 12.5.

TABLE 12.5   MEMBER VARIABLES ASSOCIATED WITH CONTROLS IN OWNDRAW

Control ID	Class	Variable	Category	Type
IDC_LIST	COwnDrawDlg	m_list	Control	CListBox
IDC_EDIT	COwnDrawDlg	m_strEdit	Value	CString

Creating the `CListItem` Structure

A simple list box drawn by Windows normally stores a string for each item it contains. Almost all owner-drawn list boxes and combo boxes store pointers to objects that represent the items they contain. These pointers are passed back to the controls' owners as part of the structure parameter in the Owner Draw message discussed earlier.

The OwnDraw project uses a simple structure named `CListItem` to represent each item in the list box. `CListItem` is just a wrapper around a `CString` member variable, as shown in Listing 12.1. The structure definition for `CListItem` can be found at the top of the `OwnDrawDlg.h` source file.

LISTING 12.1   THE *CListItem* STRUCTURE

```
struct CListItem
{
    CString  m_str;
    CListItem(const CString strItem): m_str(strItem)
    {}
};
```

Handling the Owner Draw Messages

For the OwnDraw project, ClassWizard was used to add three message-handling functions for the Owner Draw messages shown in Table 12.6.

TABLE 12.6   OWNER DRAW MESSAGES SENT TO THE COwnDrawDlg CLASS

Message	Class	Function
WM_DELETEITEM	COwnDrawDlg	OnDeleteItem
WM_DRAWITEM	COwnDrawDlg	OnDrawItem
WM_MEASUREITEM	COwnDrawDlg	OnMeasureItem

Adding Items to the List Box

For the OwnDraw example, items are added to the Owner Draw list box when a user clicks the Add button. ClassWizard was used to add a message-handler function to the COwnDrawDlg class for handling the BN_CLICKED message from the IDC_ADD control. The OnAdd message handler for the Add button is provided in Listing 12.2.

LISTING 12.2   THE MESSAGE HANDLER FOR OWNDRAW'S ADD BUTTON

```
void COwnDrawDlg::OnAdd()
{
    UpdateData();
    if(m_strEdit.IsEmpty() == FALSE)
    {
        CListItem* pItem = new CListItem(m_strEdit);
        ASSERT(pItem);
        m_list.AddString((LPCTSTR)pItem);
    }
}
```

12

OWNER DRAW
AND CUSTOM
DRAW

Handling the WM_MEASUREITEM Message

As discussed earlier, the WM_MEASUREITEM message is sent by Windows to determine the
size of items in a list box. For the OwnDraw project, the list box will draw its items as if
they were buttons; therefore, each item needs to be larger than the default size. As shown
in Listing 12.3, the OnMeasureItem function calls the base class implementation of
OnMeasureItem and then doubles the height of the list box item. This will provide the
drawing routine with enough room to properly draw a button.

LISTING 12.3   PROVIDING MEASUREMENT INFORMATION TO THE OWNER-DRAWN LIST BOX

```
void COwnDrawDlg::OnMeasureItem(int nIDCtl,
                         LPMEASUREITEMSTRUCT lpMeasureItemStruct)
{
    CDialog::OnMeasureItem(nIDCtl, lpMeasureItemStruct);
    lpMeasureItemStruct->itemHeight *= 2;
}
```

In this project, there's only one owner-drawn item in the dialog box; if there were more,
the nIDCtl parameter would contain the resource ID of the item to be measured. You
would need to check nIDCtl to determine which control was requesting measurement
information.

Handling the WM_DRAWITEM Message

The OnDrawItem function is called whenever an item in the list box in OwnDraw needs
to be repainted. The source code for OnDrawItem is provided in Listing 12.4.

LISTING 12.4   DRAWING THE ITEMS CONTAINED IN THE OWNER-DRAWN LIST BOX

```
void COwnDrawDlg::OnDrawItem(int nIDCtl,
                             LPDRAWITEMSTRUCT lpDrawItemStruct)
{
    LPDRAWITEMSTRUCT pdis = lpDrawItemStruct;
    CRect rc = pdis->rcItem;
    CDC* pdcTemp = CDC::FromHandle(pdis->hDC);
    if(nIDCtl != -1)
    {
        CListItem* pItem = (CListItem*)pdis->itemData;
        pdcTemp->SetBkMode(TRANSPARENT);

        if(pdis->itemState & ODS_SELECTED)
        {
            pdcTemp->DrawFrameControl(rc,
                                      DFC_BUTTON,
                                      DFCS_BUTTONPUSH¦DFCS_PUSHED);
            // Move text down and left one pixel to simulate
            // button press.
            rc.OffsetRect(1,1);
        }
        else
        {
            pdcTemp->DrawFrameControl(rc,
                                      DFC_BUTTON,
                                      DFCS_BUTTONPUSH);
        }
        rc.left += 5;
        pdcTemp->DrawText(pItem->m_str,
                          rc,
                          DT_VCENTER¦DT_SINGLELINE¦DT_LEFT);
    }
    if(lpDrawItemStruct->itemAction & ODA_FOCUS)
    {
        CRect rcFocus(pdis->rcItem);
        rcFocus.DeflateRect(3,3);
        pdcTemp->DrawFocusRect(rcFocus);
    }
}
```

COwnDrawDlg::OnDrawItem begins by testing the current item's index. If the index is -1, the WM_DRAWITEM message was not sent for a particular item, but rather for the entire control. In this case, the only action taken is that a focus rectangle will be drawn around the control.

If the WM_DRAWITEM message was sent for a particular item, the DrawFrameControl function is used to draw a button in either the normal or the pressed state. If the button is drawn as if it is pressed, the text label must be shifted down and to the left one pixel in order to match the behavior of normal Windows pushbutton controls.

The focus rectangle is drawn by calling the DrawFocusRect function. This function is also used to remove the current focus rectangle, because the rectangle is drawn using an XOR drawing mode. For this reason, you don't need to check to see if the focus is being set or removed. If the focus rectangle is changing, just call SetFocusRect, and the function will do the right thing.

Handling the WM_DELETEITEM Message

The OnDeleteItem function is called whenever an item in the list box is deleted. The source code for OnDeleteItem is provided in Listing 12.5.

LISTING 12.5 FREEING DYNAMIC RESOURCES ALLOCATED FOR THE OWNER-DRAWN LIST BOX

```
void COwnDrawDlg::OnDeleteItem(int nIDCtl,
                    LPDELETEITEMSTRUCT lpDeleteItemStruct)
{
    CListItem* pItem = (CListItem*)lpDeleteItemStruct->itemData;
    delete pItem;
    CDialog::OnDeleteItem(nIDCtl, lpDeleteItemStruct);
}
```

The OnDeleteItem function casts the itemData member to a pointer to CListItem and then deletes that pointer. If you skip this step, memory leaks will result because the memory allocated to objects placed into the list box won't be deleted.

Compile and run the OwnDraw project. An example of OwnDraw after several items have been added to the list box is shown in Figure 12.2.

FIGURE 12.2

The OwnDraw project with several items in the pushbutton list box.

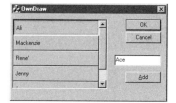

Using Custom Draw

Using the Owner Draw mechanism can be a lot of work, particularly when you're only interested in changing a small detail in the way a control is drawn. For example, if you just want to change the background color for individual items in a list box, you must take over the responsibility for drawing the entire list box.

Fortunately, Windows 2000 includes a facility known as Custom Draw, which allows you to have control over some parts of the control's drawing process while still requiring the operating system to draw other parts of the control. For example, you may be interested in changing just the font for a particular item in a listview control, or you may want each item in a control to be drawn using a different color. In these cases, you should take advantage of Custom Draw and select new fonts or colors for individual items in your control.

Here are the seven controls that can take advantage of Custom Draw:

- Listview
- Treeview
- Toolbar
- Rebar
- Tooltip
- Trackbar
- Header

The Data Structures Used by Custom Draw

There are several structures passed by the operating system to custom-drawn controls. The basic structure is NMCUSTOMDRAW, and it's used for header, trackbar, and rebar controls. The NMCUSTOMDRAW structure is defined like this:

```
typedef struct tagNMCUSTOMDRAWINFO
{
    NMHDR   hdr;
    DWORD   dwDrawStage;
    HDC     hdc;
    RECT    rc;
    DWORD   dwItemSpec;
    UINT    uItemState;
    LPARAM  lItemlParam;
} NMCUSTOMDRAW, FAR * LPNMCUSTOMDRAW;
```

NMCUSTOMDRAW has seven members:

- hdr. An NMHDR structure that's the first member of all common-control notification messages. The NMHDR structure contains the HWND of the control, the control's ID, and the notification code.

- dwDrawStage. Indicates the current drawing operation in progress. (Possible values for this member are detailed in the next list.)

- hdc. A device context for any drawing operations that you perform on the control in response to this message.

- rc. A Windows RECT structure that specifies the rectangle affected by the Custom Draw notification.

- dwItemSpec. Contains the item number for the control. (This information does not apply for all controls.)

- uItemState. Indicates the current state for the item to be drawn. (Possible values for this member are listed later in this section.)

- lItemParam. Contains the 32-bit value passed as an LPARAM to the control as application-specific data. Later in the chapter, a pointer to dynamically created data is stored in this member variable.

Here are the possible values for the dwDrawStage member variable:

- CDDS_PREERASE. Sent before items are erased in preparation for drawing. This is a global notification; it doesn't apply to a specific item in the control.

- CDDS_POSTERASE. Sent after the items have been erased before drawing. This is a global notification; it doesn't apply to a specific item in the control.

- CDDS_PREPAINT. Sent before items are painted. This is a global notification; it doesn't apply to a specific item in the control.

- CDDS_POSTPAINT. Sent after items have been painted. This is a global notification; it doesn't apply to a specific item in the control.

- CDDS_ITEM. A flag combined with the messages listed earlier to create messages that apply to a particular item. The messages in the following list are combinations of the previous messages combined with this flag.

- CDDS_ITEMPREERASE. Sent before a particular item is erased in preparation for drawing.

- CDDS_ITEMPOSTERASE. Sent after a particular item has been erased in preparation for drawing.

- CDDS_ITEMPREPAINT. Sent before a particular item is drawn.

12

OWNER DRAW
AND CUSTOM
DRAW

- CDDS_ITEMPOSTPAINT. Sent after a particular item is drawn.
- CDDS_SUBITEM. A flag that may be combined with CDDS_ITEMPREPAINT and CDDS_ITEMPOSTPAINT when listview and treeview subitems are drawn. This flag is only set when CDRF_NOTIFYSUBITEMDRAW is returned from CDDS_PREPAINT.

More information about drawing stages is provided in the section titled "Understanding Drawing Stages."

Here are the possible values for the uItemState member variable:

- CDIS_CHECKED. Set if the item is checked.
- CDIS_DEFAULT. Set if the item is in a default state.
- CDIS_DISABLED. Set if the item is disabled.
- CDIS_FOCUS. Set if the item has input focus.
- CDIS_GRAYED. Set if the item is grayed.
- CDIS_HOT. Set if the item is currently under the mouse cursor.
- CDIS_INDETERMINATE. Set if the item is in an unknown state.
- CDIS_MARKED. Set if the item is marked.
- CDIS_SELECTED. Set if the item is selected.

Specialized Versions of the Custom Draw Structure

Four specialized, expanded versions of the basic NMCUSTDRAW structure are used for common controls that require more detailed information in order to provide custom drawing support:

- NMLVCUSTDRAW is used for the listview control.
- NMTBCUSTDRAW is used for the toolbar control.
- NMTTCUSTDRAW is used for the tooltip control.
- NMTVCUSTDRAW is used for the treeview control.

Each of these structures contains an NMCUSTOMDRAW structure as its first member. Additional members are added after the initial NMCUSTOMDRAW structure.

NMLVCUSTDRAW contains extra information for the listview control and is defined like this:

```
typedef struct tagNMLVCUSTOMDRAW
{
    NMCUSTOMDRAW nmcd;
    COLORREF     clrText;
    COLORREF     clrTextBk;
    int          iSubItem;
} NMLVCUSTOMDRAW, *LPNMLVCUSTOMDRAW;
```

In addition to the NMCUSTOMDRAW structure, NMLVCUSTOMDRAW contains three other members:

- clrText. The application can store the item's text color in this member variable.

- clrTextBk. The application can store the item's background color in this member variable.

- iSubItem. The member variable that will contain the subitem index for the member to be drawn. This member variable is only valid if the CDDS_SUBITEM flag is set in dwDrawStage.

NMTBCUSTOMDRAW contains extra information for the toolbar control and is defined like this:

```
typedef struct _NMTBCUSTOMDRAW
{
    NMCUSTOMDRAW  nmcd;
    HBRUSH        hbrMonoDither;
    HBRUSH        hbrLines;
    HPEN          hpenLines;
    COLORREF      clrText;
    COLORREF      clrMark;
    COLORREF      clrTextHighlight;
    COLORREF      clrBtnFace;
    COLORREF      clrBtnHighlight;
    COLORREF      clrHighlightHotTrack;
    RECT          rcText;
    int           nStringBkMode;
    int           nHLStringBkMode;
} NMTBCUSTOMDRAW, *LPNMTBCUSTOMDRAW;
```

In addition to the NMCUSTOMDRAW structure, NMTBCUSTOMDRAW contains 12 other members:

- hbrMonoDither. The application can use this member variable to store a handle to a brush that will be used to draw dithered and marked items in the toolbar. If TBCDRF_NOMARK was returned in the prepaint notification message, this member is ignored.

- hbrLines. The application can use this member variable to store a handle to a brush used to draw lines for the toolbar item.

- hpenLines. The application can use this member variable to store a handle to a pen used to draw lines for the toolbar item.

- clrText. The application can store the item's text color in this member variable.

- clrMark. The application can store the color used to draw the background for marked items in this member variable.

- clrTextHighlight. The application can store the color used to draw text on high-lighted toolbar items in this member variable.

- clrBtnFace. The application can store the color used to draw toolbar buttons in this member variable.

- clrBtnHighlight. The application can store the color used to draw highlighted items in this member variable.

- clrHighlightHotTrack. The application can store the color used to draw hot-tracked items in this member variable.

- rcText. When received by the application, this rectangle contains the text rectangle for an item label. The application can adjust the right and bottom coordinates of the rectangle in order to affect the placement of the item's text.

- nStringBkMode. The application can use this member variable to store the background mode used when drawing text on nonhighlighted items.

- nHLStringBkMode. The application can use this member variable to store the background mode used when drawing text on highlighted items.

NMTTCUSTOMDRAW contains extra information for tooltip controls and is defined like this:

```
typedef struct tagNMTTCUSTOMDRAW
{
    NMCUSTOMDRAW nmcd;
    UINT         uDrawFlags;
} NMTTCUSTOMDRAW, FAR *LPNMTTCUSTOMDRAW;
```

In addition to the NMCUSTOMDRAW structure, NMTTCUSTDRAW contains just one other member:

- uDrawFlags. Contains information about how the item should be drawn, using the same flags as the DrawText API function's uFormat flags.

NMTVCUSTOMDRAW contains extra information for the treeview control and is defined like this:

```
typedef struct tagNMTVCUSTOMDRAW
{
    NMCUSTOMDRAW nmcd;
    COLORREF     clrText;
    COLORREF     clrTextBk;
    int          iLevel;
} NMTVCUSTOMDRAW, *LPNMTVCUSTOMDRAW;
```

In addition to the NMCUSTOMDRAW structure, NMTVCUSTOMDRAW contains three other members:

- clrText. If you want to change the color of the item, you must set this member to the color of the item's text. Don't try to change the color through the NMCUSTOMDRAW's device context member—it won't work.

- clrTextBk. If you want to change the background color of the item, you must set this member to the desired color. As is the case with the text color, don't try to change the color through the NMCUSTOMDRAW's device context member.

- iLevel. Indicates the indentation level of the item.

Understanding Drawing Stages

Every control is drawn in several passes (or *drawing stages*). The current drawing stage is provided in the NMCUSTOMCONTROL structure's dwDrawingStage member variable. You should not write your code so that it depends on messages coming in a particular order; however, there is a logical progression to the Custom Draw messages that will be sent to your control:

- The first Custom Draw notification message will have a CDDS_PREPAINT draw stage. Every control type that supports Custom Draw receives this notification message. The default processing for Custom Draw returns CDRF_DODEFAULT, which causes the control to perform default processing. Your Custom Draw notification handler must return a different return value (possible return values are discussed later in this section).

- The last Custom Draw notification message typically has a CDDS_POSTPAINT draw stage.

- Between these two messages, individual items may receive messages that they are being erased and painted, with CDDS_PRE*xxx* messages always appearing prior to CDDS_POST*xxx* messages. There's no guarantee as to the order in which multiple items may receive Custom Draw notification messages.

If you're using Custom Draw with a treeview or listview control, do not attempt to use the iSubItem member if the CDDS_SUBITEM flag is not set. The iSubItem member is invalid without this flag.

In response to the Custom Draw notification message, you must provide a return value to the operating system. Windows will use this value to determine which, if any, Custom

Draw notification messages should be sent to your control for this drawing cycle. The return value must be a combination of one or more of the following flags:

- CDRF_DODEFAULT. The control should continue to perform default processing. No further Custom Draw notifications will be sent for this item.
- CDRF_NOTIFYITEMDRAW. The control should notify the parent when an item is drawn.
- CDRF_NOTIFYPOSTPAINT. The control should send a notification message after the entire control has been painted.
- CDRF_SKIPDEFAULT. The control should not do any further processing at all.
- CDRF_NEWFONT. The parent's Custom Draw function has selected a new font into the device context.
- CDRF_NOTIFYSUBITEMDRAW. The control should notify the parent when a subitem is drawn. This flag has the same value as the CDRF_NOTIFYITEMDRAW flag; therefore, it's not necessary to combine them together.

CustDraw: A Custom Draw Example Using MFC

As an example of how you can use Custom Draw to modify the appearance of common controls, the CD-ROM accompanying this book includes CustDraw, a dialog box-based MFC project. The dialog box used by CustDraw is shown in Figure 12.3.

FIGURE 12.3

The dialog box used by the CustDraw project.

The dialog box used by CustDraw contains the controls listed in Table 12.7 (in tab order).

TABLE 12.7   CONTROLS USED IN THE CUSTDRAW DIALOG BOX

Control	Resource ID	Attributes
Listview	IDC_LIST	Report view
Red radio button	IDC_COLOR_OPT	Group
Green radio button	IDC_COLOR_OPT2	
Blue radio button	IDC_COLOR_OPT3	
Name edit	IDC_NAME	Group
City edit	IDC_CITY	
Cost edit	IDC_COST	
Add pushbutton	IDC_ADD	

ClassWizard was used to associate member variables with the controls in the CustDraw dialog box, as shown in Table 12.8.

TABLE 12.8   MEMBER VARIABLES ASSOCIATED WITH CONTROLS IN CUSTDRAW

Control ID	Class	Member Variable	Type
IDC_LIST	CCustDrawDlg	m_list	CListCtrl
IDC_NAME	CCustDrawDlg	m_strItemLabel	CString
IDC_CITY	CCustDrawDlg	m_strCity	CString
IDC_COST	CCustDrawDlg	m_strCost	CString
IDC_COLOR_OPT	CCustDrawDlg	m_colorOption	int

ClassWizard was also used to add message handlers for the three messages listed in Table 12.9.

TABLE 12.9   ADDITIONAL CUSTDRAW CONTROLS WITH MESSAGE HANDLERS

Class	Object ID	Message	Function
CCustDrawDlg	IDC_ADD	BN_CLICKED	OnAdd
CCustDrawDlg	IDC_LIST	LVN_DELETEITEM	OnDeleteitemList
CCustDrawDlg	IDC_LIST	LVN_GETDISPINFO	OnGetdispinfoList

The CustDraw project uses a structure named CHotel to represent each item in the listview control. CHotel has member variables that track the name, city, and cost for a hotel, as shown in Listing 12.6. The structure definition for CHotel can be found at the top of the CustDrawDlg.h source file.

LISTING 12.6 THE CHotel STRUCTURE CONTAINS SIMPLE HOTEL INFORMATION

```
struct CHotel
{
    int     m_nColorOpt;
    CString m_strName;
    CString m_strCost;
    CString m_strCity;
    CHotel(CString strName, CString strCity, CString strCost, int nColor):
        m_strName(strName),
        m_strCost(strCost),
        m_strCity(strCity),
        m_nColorOpt(nColor)
    {}
};
```

Three manual additions were made to the CCustDrawDlg class declaration:

- A CFont member variable used for drawing normal text was added.
- A CFont member variable used for drawing italic text was added.
- A message handler for the Custom Draw notification message was added.

Listing 12.7 contains the modified CustDrawDlg.h header file (about half of the file has been removed for clarity). Lines that have been added are shown in bold type.

LISTING 12.7 THE CCustDrawDlg.h FILE WITH CHANGES IN BOLD

```
class CCustDrawDlg : public CDialog
{
// Construction
public:
    CCustDrawDlg(CWnd* pParent = NULL);    // standard constructor

// Dialog Data
    .
    .
    .

// Implementation
protected:
    HICON m_hIcon;
    CFont m_hStdFont;
    CFont m_hItalicFont;
```

```
    // Generated message map functions
    //{{AFX_MSG(CCustDrawDlg)
    virtual BOOL OnInitDialog();
    afx_msg void OnSysCommand(UINT nID, LPARAM lParam);
    afx_msg void OnPaint();
    afx_msg HCURSOR OnQueryDragIcon();
    afx_msg void OnAdd();
    afx_msg void OnGetdispinfoList(NMHDR* pNMHDR, LRESULT* pResult);
    afx_msg void OnDeleteitemList(NMHDR* pNMHDR, LRESULT* pResult);
    //}}AFX_MSG
    afx_msg void OnCustDrawList(NMHDR* pNMHDR, LRESULT* pResult);
    DECLARE_MESSAGE_MAP()
};
```

The CustDraw dialog box is initialized in the CCustDrawDlg::OnInitDialog member
function. As shown in Listing 12.8, the listview control is initialized and the CFont member
variables are created in this function. Some parts of CCustDrawDlg::OnInitDialog
have been omitted for clarity. The complete listing can be found on the CD-ROM accompanying this book.

LISTING 12.8   INITIALIZING DIALOG BOX MEMBER VARIABLES IN OnInitDialog

```
BOOL CCustDrawDlg::OnInitDialog()
{
    CDialog::OnInitDialog();
    .
    .
    .
    // TODO: Add extra initialization here
    LV_COLUMN listColumn;
    TCHAR*    rgszColumns[] = { _T("Name"),
                                _T("City"),
                                _T("Cost")};
    listColumn.mask = LVCF_FMT¦LVCF_WIDTH¦LVCF_TEXT¦LVCF_SUBITEM;
    listColumn.fmt = LVCFMT_LEFT;
    listColumn.cx = 60;
    for(int nColumn = 0; nColumn < 3; nColumn++)
    {
        listColumn.iSubItem = nColumn;
        listColumn.pszText = rgszColumns[nColumn];
        m_list.InsertColumn(nColumn, &listColumn);
    }

    CDC* pDC = GetDC();
    int cyFont = -MulDiv(8, pDC->GetDeviceCaps(LOGPIXELSY), 72);
    m_hItalicFont.CreateFont(cyFont, 0, 0, 0, FW_THIN, TRUE,
                             FALSE, FALSE, 0, 0, 0, 0, 0,
                             _T("Arial"));
```

continues

LISTING 12.8   CONTINUED

```
    m_hStdFont.CreateFont(cyFont, 0, 0, 0, FW_THIN, FALSE,
                          FALSE, FALSE, 0, 0, 0, 0, 0,
                          _T("Arial"));
    return TRUE;
}
```

The implementations of the message-handling functions for CustDraw added earlier in the chapter are provided in Listing 12.9. In the OnAdd function, CHotel items are created dynamically and added to the listview control. Text items are not immediately added to the listview control; instead, they are assigned a value of LPSTR_TEXTCALLBACK, which will cause the control to request the text information only as needed. In the OnGetdispinfoList function, text strings are provided to the listview. The OnDeleteitemList function casts the lParam member to a pointer to CHotel and then deletes that pointer to prevent memory leaks.

LISTING 12.9   MESSAGE-HANDLING FUNCTIONS USED BY CUSTDRAW

```
void CCustDrawDlg::OnAdd()
{
    UpdateData();
    CHotel* pHotel = new CHotel(m_strItemLabel,
                                m_strCity,
                                m_strCost,
                                m_colorOption);

    LV_ITEM listItem;
    listItem.mask = LVIF_TEXT|LVIF_PARAM;
    listItem.iSubItem = 0;
    listItem.iItem = m_list.GetItemCount();
    listItem.pszText = LPSTR_TEXTCALLBACK;
    listItem.cchTextMax = 80;
    listItem.lParam = (LPARAM)pHotel;

    m_list.InsertItem(&listItem);
    m_list.SetItemText(listItem.iItem,1, LPSTR_TEXTCALLBACK);
    m_list.SetItemText(listItem.iItem, 2, LPSTR_TEXTCALLBACK);
}

void CCustDrawDlg::OnGetdispinfoList(NMHDR* pNMHDR,
                                     LRESULT* pResult)
{
    LV_DISPINFO* pDispInfo = (LV_DISPINFO*)pNMHDR;
    CHotel* pHotel = (CHotel*)pDispInfo->item.lParam;
    if(pDispInfo->item.mask & LVIF_TEXT)
    {
        LPTSTR& pszText = pDispInfo->item.pszText;
```

```
        switch(pDispInfo->item.iSubItem)
        {
        case 0:
            pszText = (LPTSTR)(LPCTSTR)pHotel->m_strName;
            break;
        case 1:
            pszText = (LPTSTR)(LPCTSTR)pHotel->m_strCity;
            break;
        case 2:
            pszText = (LPTSTR)(LPCTSTR)pHotel->m_strCost;
            break;
        default:
            ASSERT(0);
        }
    }
    *pResult = 0;
}

void CCustDrawDlg::OnDeleteitemList(NMHDR* pNMHDR,
                                    LRESULT* pResult)
{
    NM_LISTVIEW* pNMListView = (NM_LISTVIEW*)pNMHDR;
    CHotel* pHotel = (CHotel*)pNMListView->lParam;
    delete pHotel;
    *pResult = 0;
}
```

The CustDraw project's message handler for the NM_CUSTOMDRAW message is provided in
Listing 12.10. The OnCustomDrawList function requests notifications for all drawing
stages. If the drawing stage applies to a particular item, the foreground and background
colors are changed to the colors specified by the item's CHotel color option. When the
first item in each row is drawn, the italic font is selected into the device context. For
other subitems, the nonitalic font is selected into the device context.

LISTING 12.10   THE MESSAGE HANDLER FOR THE NM_CUSTOMDRAW MESSAGE

```
void CCustDrawDlg::OnCustDrawList(NMHDR* pNMHDR, LRESULT* pResult)
{
    LPNMLVCUSTOMDRAW pDraw = (LPNMLVCUSTOMDRAW)pNMHDR;
    // Ask for everything, just for tracing purposes.
    *pResult = CDRF_NOTIFYITEMDRAW|
               CDRF_NOTIFYPOSTPAINT|
               CDRF_NOTIFYPOSTERASE;

    // Determine the drawing stage.
    DWORD dwDrawStage = pDraw->nmcd.dwDrawStage;
    if(dwDrawStage & CDDS_ITEM)
    {
```

continues

LISTING 12.10 CONTINUED

```
        CHotel* pHotel = (CHotel*)pDraw->nmcd.lItemlParam;

        switch(pHotel->m_nColorOpt)
        {
            case 0: // Red
            pDraw->clrTextBk = RGB(255,0,0);
            pDraw->clrText = RGB(0,0,0);
            break;

            case 1: // Green
            pDraw->clrTextBk = RGB(0,255,0);
            pDraw->clrText = RGB(0,0,0);
            break;

            case 2: // Blue
            pDraw->clrTextBk = RGB(0,0,255);
            pDraw->clrText = RGB(255,255,255);
            break;
        }
        // Change font, depending on item level.
        if((dwDrawStage & CDDS_SUBITEM)&&(pDraw->iSubItem == 0))
        {
            SelectObject(pDraw->nmcd.hdc,
                        (HFONT)m_hItalicFont.m_hObject);
            *pResult |= CDRF_NEWFONT;
        }
        else if((dwDrawStage & CDDS_SUBITEM)&&
                (pDraw->iSubItem == 1 || pDraw->iSubItem == 2))
        {
            SelectObject(pDraw->nmcd.hdc,
                        (HFONT)m_hStdFont.m_hObject);
            *pResult |= CDRF_NEWFONT;
        }
    }
}
```

Build and run the CustDraw project. Figure 12.4 shows the CustDraw project with several items in the listview control.

FIGURE 12.4

The CustDraw project after several items have been added.

Summary

This chapter discussed two methods that you can use to add extra functionality to your controls. Owner draw enables you to customize menus, buttons, list boxes, and other types of controls. Custom draw is offered for some of the newer Windows common controls, and it enables you to modify a small part of how the control is drawn without requiring you to take responsibility for drawing the complete control.

COM and ActiveX

PART

III

IN THIS PART

COM and OLE Concepts

COM (component object model) is the interprocess communication method of choice when building applications for Windows. OLE is the Microsoft technology that enables GUI-centric applications to work together seamlessly. This chapter focuses on the concepts behind these communications methods and presents sample programs that demonstrate how they are used.

Looking at an Overview of COM and OLE

COM is a specification for communication between software components. It was originally introduced by Microsoft in 1993 as the communication mechanism that laid the foundation for OLE 2.0. The previous version of OLE, OLE 1.0, was a much simpler method of interprocess communication that wasn't based on COM. The current version of COM is known simply as *COM*, with no version numbers (although some recently added technologies are known collectively as *COM+*).

As mentioned earlier, COM is the foundation on which OLE rests. COM is a binary specification for a number of technologies that define how objects and systems can interact with each other in an open and scalable manner.

Examining Commonly Used COM and OLE Technologies

COM and OLE define several technologies that can be used to create component-based software. Here's a list of the most commonly used COM and OLE technologies:

- Data transfer
- Drag and drop
- Compound documents
- Visual editing, also known as *in-place activation*
- Automation
- Integration with other applications

Each of these technologies is discussed in the following sections.

Compound Documents

One of the original big-ticket items that came with OLE 2.0 was *compound documents*. A compound document can be used to integrate content from multiple component servers—including text, graphics, audio, and any other data that might be generated. Each document stores unique identifiers known as *Class Identifiers*, or *CLSIDs* that identify the servers used to create and manage individual portions of the document. A CLSID is just one example of a *Globally Unique Identifier*, or *GUID*, a unique 128-bit identifier used to identify different types of COM components. More information about GUIDs, CLSIDs, and other COM identifiers is provided later in the section, "Identifying COM Interfaces and Objects."

Storing information in a compound document enables a user to focus on the document rather than on each application used to create the content stored in the document. Because a component object in the compound document requires editing, the server for that object can be activated automatically using the CLSID for the object's server. Of course, this happens without the user needing to understand the underlying mechanism involved.

A component object can be stored in a compound document in two ways: by linking and by embedding.

A *linked* component resides outside the compound document, and the compound document keeps a reference known as a *moniker* that points to the linked component's location. This reduces the size of the compound document and is very useful when a single item is "owned" by another user, or when a single item is shared among multiple documents, as shown in Figure 13.1.

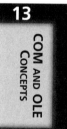

FIGURE 13.1

A linked object is physically located outside the compound document.

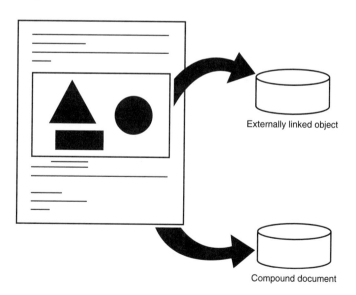

Externally linked object

Compound document

An *embedded* component object is stored inside the compound document, as shown in Figure 13.2. Using embedding is useful when a document must be transferred or relocated, because all the information is stored inside the compound document. In addition, embedded objects can take advantage of visual editing, which is discussed in the next section.

FIGURE 13.2

An embedded object is physically stored inside the compound document.

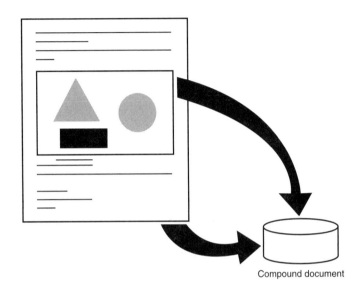

Compound document

Visual Editing

Visual editing, also known as *in-place activation*, allows an OLE container to activate a server for an embedded component object "in place." The container and the server share the user interface, thus enabling a user to interact with a component object without switching applications. This greatly simplifies the user's view of how a document is managed. From the user's perspective, the entire document seems to be edited within a single application.

As an example, consider a spreadsheet object embedded in a word processing compound document, as shown in Figure 13.3.

If the spreadsheet object is edited, the server for the spreadsheet object, Microsoft Excel, activates in place, as shown in Figure 13.4.

As you can see in Figure 13.4, the container and server have merged various elements of their user interfaces. Although the container has not changed, it now hosts many of the menus and toolbar items that belong to the Excel spreadsheet.

After editing is complete, the container resumes control of the user interface, as shown in Figure 13.3.

FIGURE 13.3

An Excel spread-sheet embedded in a Word document.

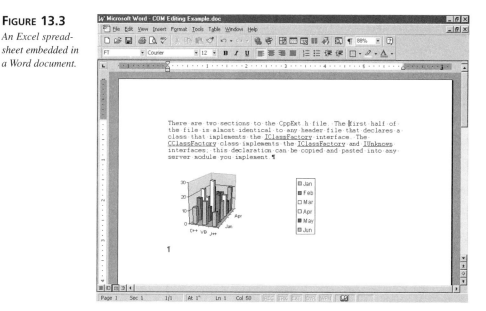

FIGURE 13.4

Microsoft Excel activated inside the Word container.

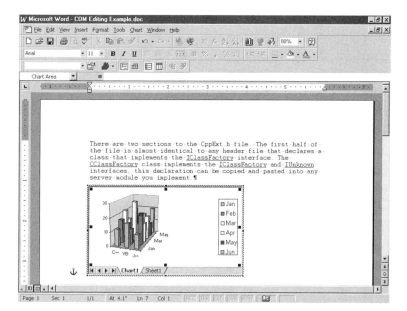

Automation

Automation, formerly known as *OLE Automation*, enables programs and components to expose programmable interfaces that can be controlled by other processes. Automation always involves an Automation controller—usually a programming environment such as Visual Basic or a scripting host such as the Windows Scripting Host (WSH)—and an Automation server that exposes a set of programmable interfaces.

Automation is a large topic—in fact, Chapter 14, "Automation," is devoted entirely to this topic.

OLE Data Transfer

OLE includes an extendable data transfer technology that provides a flexible and efficient method for transferring data from a data source to a consumer. Instead of depending on a single representation of a data object transferred through the Clipboard using a global memory handle, COM and OLE data objects that are aware of the OLE data transfer mechanism can negotiate the most appropriate method for transferring data, depending on the needs and capabilities of the consumer.

When the Clipboard is used, data must be transferred via a global memory handle, which is extremely inefficient for large items such as bitmaps or multimedia clips. The COM data transfer mechanism, sometimes called *Uniform Data Transfer*, or *UDT*, allows data to be transferred as a reference to a file or other storage object, thus speeding up the transfer operation.

Uniform data transfer also supports the idea of notifications when a data source changes its representation of a data object.

Drag and Drop

Drag and drop is built on top of the uniform data transfer mechanism discussed in the preceding section. OLE provides a large set of functions and interfaces that can be used to manage the transfer of data from one object to another visually, instead of through the Clipboard. Chapter 15, "OLE Drag and Drop," discusses this in detail.

Integration with Other Applications

In addition to the capabilities discussed earlier, the component object model implies even greater possibilities yet to come. COM defines a model that can extend the services offered by Windows in a general, flexible way. In fact, many of the new technologies released in recent years for various versions of Windows, such as DirectX and TAPI 3.0, use COM interfaces.

Programming with COM and OLE

Before you look at an example that uses COM and OLE, you should know some of the basics involved with programming using COM and OLE. The following basic topics are discussed in the following sections:

- Understanding and using COM interfaces
- Identifying COM objects and interfaces
- Using IUnknown and the QueryInterface function
- Creating COM objects

After looking at these basic topics, you'll learn about using COM and OLE to create shell extensions for the Windows 2000 shell.

Using COM Interfaces

Under COM, direct access to an object is never permitted. Communication with an object takes place through well-defined interfaces. Restricting access to objects allows COM to be an environment and language-neutral model—nothing in the COM specification restricts you to using C++. In fact, Visual Basic, Delphi, and C all are used to program OLE and COM applications.

All interfaces in the component object model begin with *I* as a standard naming convention (*I* stands for *interface*). A COM interface usually is drawn as shown in Figure 13.5.

FIGURE 13.5

Diagramming the interfaces supported by an object.

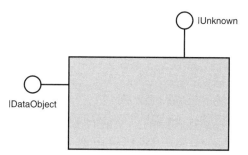

The object is shown as a square box, with one or more open circles, representing jacks, extended from it. These jacks symbolize interfaces supported by the object. Because every object implements the IUnknown interface, it usually is shown alone at the top of the box. The names of individual functions on an interface are not shown.

Identifying COM Interfaces and Objects

As discussed earlier, the component object model specifies that interfaces and objects are identified by 128-bit numbers, known as *globally unique identifiers* (*GUIDs*). A GUID can be used to identify two types of items:

- A GUID used to identify an interface is known as an *interface identifier* (*IID*).
- A GUID used to identify a type of object is known as a *class identifier* (ClassID, or *CLSID*).

Due to the sheer size of a GUID, it's very unlikely that two randomly chosen GUIDs will ever be identical. Even given large numbers of randomly chosen GUIDs, the possibility of a name collision is extremely small.

> **NOTE**
>
> *Never* attempt to reuse GUIDs published in books, magazines, or elsewhere. This is much worse than sharing a toothbrush with someone and has the potential of causing you (and others) endless and difficult-to-resolve pain and suffering. The Windows 2000 Registry and COM are not built to handle the possibility of GUID collisions, which never happen as long as everyone plays by the rules.

To generate your own set of GUIDs, run UUIDGEN from a console window. If you have a network interface card installed on your machine, you'll receive a unique GUID of your very own, similar to the following:

```
d3d834c1-9a3b-11cf-82a0-00608cca2a2a
```

You can display a complete list of UUIDGEN options by using the -? switch. You also can ask for a GUID preformatted into an interface structure as used in the DEFINE_GUID macro by using the -s switch, as shown in Listing 13.1.

Alternatively, the Visual C++ compiler includes GUIDGEN.EXE, a graphical version of UUIDGEN. GUIDGEN enables you to copy GUIDs to the clipboard, where they can easily be pasted into your source code.

LISTING 13.1   A PREFORMATTED GUID GENERATED BY UUIDGEN

```
INTERFACENAME = { /* d3d834c1-9a3b-11cf-82a0-00608cca2a2a */
    0xd3d834c1,
    0x9a3b,
    0x11cf,
    {0x82, 0xa0, 0x00, 0x60, 0x8c, 0xca, 0x2a, 0x2a}
};
```

The `DEFINE_GUID` macro is used to initialize a class ID or interface ID to be equal to a particular GUID. To define a GUID representing an OLE class named `Foo`, a `CLSID_Foo` symbol is initialized using the `DEFINE_GUID` macro:

```
DEFINE_GUID( CLSID_Foo, 0xd3d834c0, 0x9a3b, 0x11cf, 0x82,
             0xa0, 0x00, 0x60, 0x8c, 0xca, 0x2a, 0x2a );
```

If your machine does not have a network interface card, a pseudo-random GUID is synthesized for you. There's a slight chance that this GUID may collide with other GUIDs assigned at random to other COM and OLE programmers. If you're writing an application for distribution, you must install a network interface card for maximum safety. If installing a network card for a few GUIDs is too painful for some reason, drop me an email message at

`mickey.williams@codevtech.com`

I'll be happy to create some safe GUIDs for you.

Handling GUIDs

Due to the length of a GUID, handling GUIDs tends to be more difficult than passing around 32-bit handles. Listing 13.2 shows the structure of a GUID.

LISTING 13.2   THE GUID struct DECLARATION

```
typedef struct _GUID
{
    unsigned long  Data1;
    unsigned short Data2;
    unsigned short Data3;
    unsigned char  Data4[8];
}GUID;
```

13

COM AND OLE CONCEPTS

In the Win32 Registry, a GUID is stored with curly braces at each end, like this:

```
{d3d834c0-9a3b-11cf-82a0-00608cca2a2a}
```

The Win32 SDK also provides several functions used to handle GUIDs, which are listed in Table 13.1.

TABLE 13.1   WIN32 GUID-HANDLING FUNCTIONS

Function	*Description*
CLSIDFromString	Converts a string into a CLSID
CoCreateGuid	Generates a new GUID
IIDFromString	Converts a string into an IID
IsEqualCLSID	Compares two class IDs
IsEqualGUID	Compares two GUIDs
IsEqualIID	Compares two interface IDs
StringFromCLSID	Converts a CLSID into a string
StringFromGUID2	Formats a GUID into a supplied buffer
StringFromIID	Converts an IID into a string

Handling the Versioning Problem

The notion of interfaces in COM is meant to solve two common problems that occur when trying to develop component-based software: tracking versions and maintaining backward compatibility.

After a traditional software component is released, its interfaces must be frozen. Any changes to the component's interface risk breaking existing programs that depend on the current interface. Any change to an existing interface may make the new interface unusable to existing clients of the component. Additionally, any new interfaces remain undiscovered until the client program is rebuilt.

COM removes these issues by defining *interfaces* as groups of one or more related functions that can be applied to an object. Once defined, an interface is never changed. Modifying an interface does not create a new version of an existing interface; instead, it creates a brand new interface, with a new identity and responsibilities.

Using the `IUnknown` Interface

Every COM object supports the `IUnknown` interface. Every COM interface also includes the `IUnknown` interface, which is used as a starting point for all communication in COM. The `IUnknown` interface has three simple but very important functions:

- `AddRef`. Increments an internal reference counter and is called once for every pointer created to a COM interface. Reference counting is discussed in the next section.

- `Release`. Decrements an internal reference counter and is called when pointers to COM interfaces are released. When the counter reaches 0, the object destroys itself.

- `QueryInterface`. Returns a pointer to other COM interfaces supported by the same object. This is the mechanism used to move on past the `IUnknown` interface; it's discussed later in the section titled "Querying for Another Interface."

Reference Counting

The lifetime of a COM object is strictly controlled by an internal reference count maintained by the object that represents the number of pointers clients have created to its interfaces. Several general rules apply to reference counting:

- When an object is created, its constructor sets the reference count to 0.

- Whenever a pointer to an interface is provided to a client of the object, the reference count is incremented by the function that creates the pointer (usually by calling the `AddRef` function).

- When a pointer no longer is used, the internal reference count is decremented by calling `Release`. This enables each object to know how many external clients currently are connected to it. When the internal counter transitions to 0, the object is no longer used, and it usually destroys itself.

These steps can be optimized for objects that aren't created on the heap. For statically created objects, the reference-counting operations are essentially empty operations. However, this is an implementation decision that's made by the server—the client must still follow the rules for reference counting.

As an example, look at the COM interfaces involved in ringing a simulated telephone. In Figure 13.6, a `TelephoneCall` object is created by calling the `CoCreateInstance` function (this function is discussed later in the section titled "Creating an Object"). Because this function returns a pointer to the `IUnknown` interface for the `TelephoneCall` object, the reference count for the object is already incremented when the pointer is returned. At this point, the reference count is 1, because there's one pointer to the `TelephoneCall` object.

13

COM AND OLE
CONCEPTS

FIGURE 13.6

A `TelephoneCall`
*object is created
with one interface
pointer, and the
reference count is
set to 1.*

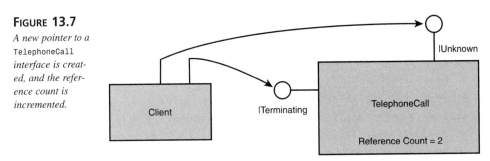

You now have a pointer to an interface for the `TelephoneCall` object, but it's a pointer to its `IUnknown` interface. Note that the pointer does not point to the `TelephoneCall` object; rather, it points to an interface.

In order to get a pointer to the `ITerminating` interface, you must ask your current interface for a pointer to `ITerminating`. When this pointer is passed back to you, the interface count on the `TelephoneCall` object is incremented, as shown in Figure 13.7.

FIGURE 13.7

A new pointer to a
`TelephoneCall`
*interface is creat-
ed, and the refer-
ence count is
incremented.*

After you have the pointer to the `ITerminating` interface, you can start performing useful work, such as ringing the telephone. You don't need the original `IUnknown` interface pointer, however. Before discarding or overwriting this pointer, you must call the `IUnknown::Release` function, which decrements the `TelephoneCall` object's reference count back to 1, as shown in Figure 13.8.

For the purposes of this simple example, assume that the telephone remains unanswered. After you decide to stop ringing the telephone, you call `Release` through the `ITerminating` interface pointer, thus decrementing the `TelephoneCall` object's reference count to 0 and destroying the object, as shown in Figure 13.9.

In practice, there's no way to reliably determine whether you have the last interface pointer to an object. Although `Release` returns the current reference count, in a multi-threaded environment, this information is useful only if you're looking for the last call to

`Release`, which always returns 0. For that reason, it's considered a poor practice to use an interface pointer after calling `Release`.

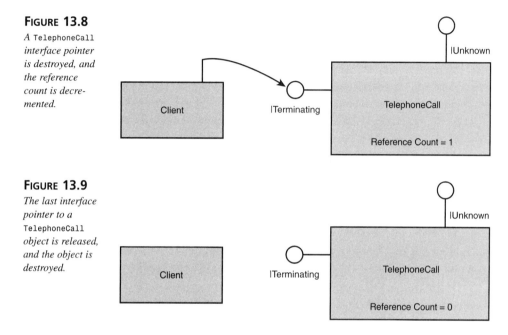

FIGURE 13.8

A `TelephoneCall` *interface pointer is destroyed, and the reference count is decremented.*

FIGURE 13.9

The last interface pointer to a `TelephoneCall` *object is released, and the object is destroyed.*

Querying for Another Interface

A pointer to any interface supported by an object can be retrieved by calling `QueryInterface`. Along with `AddRef` and `Release`, `QueryInterface` is part of the `IUnknown` interface, so it's safe to call `QueryInterface` through any interface pointer. `QueryInterface` accepts two parameters and returns a handle to a result code, as shown in Listing 13.3.

LISTING 13.3   USING `QueryInterface` TO GET A POINTER TO `IFoo`

```
IFoo    *pFoo;
HRESULT hr;
hr=pIUnknown->QueryInterface( IID_IFoo, &pFoo );
if( FAILED(hr) )
{
    // Interface not obtainable, report error or work
    // with other interfaces.
}
else
{
    // Use the IFoo interface, and release it when finished.
    pFoo->Release();
}
```

Several rules define how an object must behave with respect to its implementation of
QueryInterface:

- For successful calls, the interface reference count must be incremented before the
  new interface pointer is returned to the caller.
- For one instance of an object, the same pointer value must be consistently returned
  for a given interface. If you ask for the IFoo interface and get a certain pointer
  value, any future QueryInterface calls for IFoo on the same object's interface
  must return the same value.
- Objects are not allowed to grow new interfaces. If QueryObject fails once, it's
  expected to fail consistently. Likewise, if QueryInterface is successful, it must
  consistently return a pointer to the requested interface.
- There must not be a "maze" in the interface hierarchy. If a QueryInterface call
  returns a pointer to a new interface, it must be possible to call QueryInterface to
  return to the previous interface. Similarly, it must be possible to traverse interfaces
  by obtaining a pointer to interface A, interface B, interface C, and then back to
  interface A.

Handling Return Values

The return value from QueryInterface, like most COM interfaces and functions, returns
an HRESULT. This is a structured 32-bit value that includes more than just the usual
pass/fail information returned from a return code. An HRESULT is structured very much
like a Win32 error code, as shown in Figure 13.10.

FIGURE 13.10

The format for an
HRESULT *return*
code.

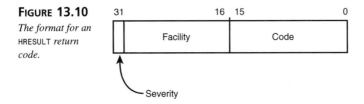

It's possible for a function to return several different flavors of success and failure. In
order to determine whether a function has succeeded, you must use the SUCCEEDED and
FAILED macros, as shown in Listing 13.4.

LISTING 13.4   USING THE SUCCEEDED AND FAILED MACROS

```
HRESULT hr = pObj->GetData(&fetc, &stg);
if(FAILED(hr))
{
```

```
    // Handle failed condition
}
hr = pObj->DoSomethingElse();
if(SUCCEEDED(hr))
{
    // Handle successful return
}
```

Creating an Object

A client creates an instance of a COM object by calling CoCreateInstance and passing a CLSID for the object to be created, as shown in Listing 13.5.

LISTING 13.5   CREATING AN OBJECT USING CoCreateInstance

```
IFoo* pFoo = 0;
HRESULT hr = CoCreateInstance(CLSID_FooBar,
                              NULL,
                              CLSCTX_INPROC_SERVER,
                              IID_IFoo,
                              &pFoo );
if(FAILED(hr))
{
    // Handle error
}
// Use pFoo
.
.
.
pFoo->Release();
```

In Listing 13.5, a FooBar object is created (identified by CLSID_FooBar) via a call to CoCreateInstance. If the object is created successfully, a pointer to the IFoo interface is returned.

Several steps are involved in creating a COM object. All COM objects are created by one of three types of servers:

- In-process servers are implemented in a DLL and run in the client's address space.
- Local servers are EXEs and, like all EXEs, run in their own address space on the same machine as the client.
- Remote servers are EXEs that run on a machine out on the network.

Working with Class Objects

Every COM object is associated with a special object known as a *class object*. The class object, also known as a *class factory*, is responsible for creating instances of the COM object. Every class object is responsible for creating a single CLSID; if you're creating servers for several CLSIDs, you must have a separate class object for each one.

All COM objects are implemented via class objects associated with the COM object's CLSID. This allows COM objects to be created in a standard way by clients, who only need to learn to deal with a single interface. Class objects are required to implement the `IClassFactory` interface, as shown in Figure 13.11.

FIGURE 13.11

A class object implements the `IClassFactory` *interface.*

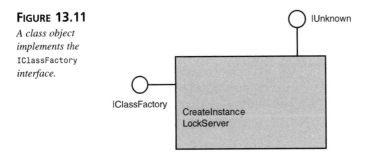

The `IClassFactory` interface adds two functions to the standard `IUnknown` interface:

- `CreateInstance` returns an interface pointer to a logically new instance of the COM object referred to by the CLSID.

- `LockServer` requests that the class object stay resident in memory and not unload itself.

An example of a class object's `CreateInstance` function is provided in Listing 13.6.

LISTING 13.6 AN EXAMPLE OF A CLASS FACTORY `CreateInstance` FUNCTION

```
STDMETHODIMP CClassFactory::CreateInstance(LPUNKNOWN punk,
                                           REFIID riid,
                                           LPVOID* ppv )
{
    *ppv = NULL;
    // Aggregation not supported by this object.
    if(punk != NULL)
        return ResultFromScode(CLASS_E_NOAGGREGATION);

    CCFoo* pFoo = new CFoo;
    if(pFoo == NULL)
        return ResultFromScode( E_OUTOFMEMORY );

    return pFoo->QueryInterface(riid, ppv);
}
```

In Listing 13.6, the `CreateInstance` function for this particular class factory creates a `CFoo` object and performs an initial `QueryInterface` on the new object prior to returning the interface pointer back to the caller.

Each time it's called, the Windows 2000 `CoCreateInstance` function creates an instance of the class object for the CLSID internally. You can perform the same steps yourself by first calling the `CoGetClassObject` API function to retrieve a pointer to the class object. After you have a pointer to the `IClassFactory` interface on the class object, you can easily create one or more COM object instances by calling the `CreateInstance` function, as shown in Listing 13.7.

LISTING 13.7   CREATING INSTANCES OF COM OBJECTS BY USING A CLASS OBJECT

```
HRESULT MyCoCreateInstance(REFCLSID  rclsid,
                           LPUNKNOWN pUnkOuter,
                           DWORD     dwClsContext,
                           REFIID    riid,
                           LPVOID*   ppv)
{
    IClassFactory *pcf = NULL;
    HRESULT hr = CoGetClassObject(rclsid,
                                  dwClsContext,
                                  NULL,
                                  IID_IClassFactory,
                                  (void **)&pcf);
    if(FAILED(hr))
        return hr;
    // Create an instance of rclsid, and return the
    // riid interface in ppvObj
    hr = pcf->CreateInstance(pUnkOuter, riid, ppvObj);
    pcf->Release();
    return hr;
}
```

If you're creating more than a single instance of a COM object, it's more efficient to create the multiple instances using a class object than to call `CoCreateInstance` for each instance.

Finding the Class Object in the Registry

The module containing the COM component's class object is found through the system Registry. If this CLSID is an in-process server, the path to the server's DLL is stored in the `InProcServer32` key:

`HKEY_CLASSES_ROOT\CLSID\<GUID>\InProcServer32 = Foo.dll`

In this example, `<GUID>` is replaced by the full CLSID identifying the object. The name of the requested COM object's server is `Foo.dll`. You can speed loading by specifying a complete path to the server, or you can just place all your server modules in the Windows 2000 System directory.

Looking at In-process Server Requirements

An in-process server must implement three functions, in addition to the functions required by the class object:

- DllMain. The module's entry point. The only work done in this function is to stash the instance handle in case it's needed later.
- DllGetClassObject. Must be exported from the module and is called by Windows 2000 when a new COM class object is created.
- DllCanUnloadNow. Called by Windows 2000 to test whether the DLL can be unloaded. Every object created in the module must increment a global reference counter during construction and decrement this counter when destroyed.

Figure 13.12 shows the typical layout for an in-process server. An in-process server contains DLL-specific functions, at least one IClassFactory interface, and interfaces supporting at least one OLE custom component.

FIGURE 13.12

Contents of a typical COM custom component server.

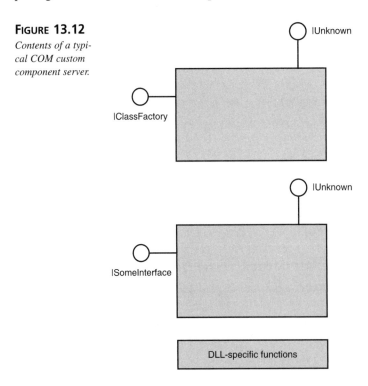

Looking at an Example of a COM Component

The CD-ROM that accompanies this book includes an example of a simple COM component. The CppExt project is a Windows 2000 shell extension that creates a custom context menu after you right-click a C++ file in the shell.

Using the Shell Extension Mechanism

The shell user interface for Windows 2000 uses COM to support user extensions to the shell. By creating and registering in-process servers supporting the shell extension interfaces, you can create several types of shell extensions, as shown in Table 13.2.

TABLE 13.2   WINDOWS 2000 SHELL EXTENSION TYPES

Shell Extension	Function
Icon handlers	Change the appearance of a file's icon on a per-file object basis. By implementing this interface, for example, you can change the icon displayed for a file object based on its internal state, its age, or any other criteria.
Copy hook handlers	Invoked when a file object is copied, moved, or deleted. By implementing this interface, you can supplement or prevent the operation.
Context menu extensions	Add items to the context menu displayed after a file object is right-clicked.
Property sheet extensions	Add pages to the property sheet displayed by the shell for a particular type of file object.
Drag-and-drop handlers	Called after a drag-and-drop operation. They're almost identical to context menu extensions.
Drop target handlers	Control the activity that occurs when a file object is dropped after a drag-and-drop operation.
Data object handlers	Supply the file object during drag-and-drop operations.

All shell extensions implement the IShellExtInit or the IPersistFile interface. They also support additional interfaces used to implement their particular service.

13

COM AND OLE CONCEPTS

Understanding Context Menu Extensions

A context menu extension supports two interfaces:

- IShellExtInit. An interface implemented by several types of shell extensions. IShellExtInit defines one function, Initialize, that provides information a shell extension can use to initialize itself.

- IContextMenu. Implemented exclusively by context menu extensions. IContextMenu defines three functions. QueryContextMenu requests that the shell extension add items to the context menu. GetCommandString is used by the shell to collect string descriptions of the added menu items. InvokeCommand signals to the shell extension that a new menu item has been selected. Each of these interfaces is discussed later in this chapter.

When a user right-clicks a file object that's handled by a context menu extension, the Windows 2000 shell creates an instance of the shell extension, using the mechanism discussed earlier for in-process servers.

Next, the shell uses QueryInterface for the IShellExtInit interface and calls the Initialize function, thus allowing the context menu to store initialization information. A context menu extension must collect information about the file object in this function.

The shell then queries for the IContextMenu interface and calls the QueryContextMenu function. The shell extension must add all its menu items to the context menu during this function call. The extension is not allowed to remove items or to make any assumptions about the final configuration of the menu. It's possible for several shell extensions to be registered for a single file type, and there's no way to ensure that your extension is called last (or first, for that matter). The shell also calls the GetCommandString function in order to collect strings used as canonical verbs and status bar text.

If a menu item added by a context menu extension is selected by the user, IContextMenu::InvokeCommand is called by the shell. This is the function that carries out whatever activity is represented by the menu item.

That's all there is to context menu extensions. In addition to the general-purpose code that must be written for all in-process servers, you really need to implement only four functions for your server.

Creating the Example

CppExt is a Win32 DLL project that contains three files:

- CppExt.def is the project's module definition file.

- CppExt.cpp implements the interfaces required for the shell extension.
- CppExt.h is a header file that contains the declarations needed for CppExt.cpp.

Many of the projects built in prior chapters used the tchar.h string compatibility macros to allow the projects to be built using Unicode or non-Unicode strings. COM is almost entirely Unicode, and all COM examples in the next few chapters are Unicode only. However, there are a few non-Unicode system interfaces that involve the shell API, such as the IContextMenu interface used by CppExt.

> **CAUTION**
>
> If you modify this project, you must not reuse my GUID—use UUIDGEN to create your own CLSID.

Exporting the Required DLL Functions

The module-definition file for the CppExt project is provided in Listing 13.8. The DLL exports two functions: DllCanUnloadNow and DLLGetClassObject. These exports are listed as PRIVATE because they'll only be used by the COM library.

LISTING 13.8 THE MODULE DEFINITION FILE FOR CPPEXT

```
LIBRARY      CppExt
DESCRIPTION "Shell extension for CPP files"

EXPORTS
    DllCanUnloadNow PRIVATE
    DllGetClassObject PRIVATE
```

Creating the Class Declarations

Two classes are declared in the CppExt.h header file. The CCppShellExt class is the actual context menu extension class. The CClassFactory class implements the class object and is used to create instances of CCppShellExt.

Save the contents of Listing 13.9 as CppExt.h. There's no need to add it to the CppExt project, because it's included by the CppExp.cpp file.

LISTING 13.9   THE CppExt.h HEADER FILE

```cpp
// The class ID for the CPP file extension
/* d3d834c0-9a3b-11cf-82a0-00608cca2a2a */
DEFINE_GUID( CLSID_CppExtension, 0xd3d834c0, 0x9a3b, 0x11cf, 0x82,
             0xa0, 0x00, 0x60, 0x8c, 0xca, 0x2a, 0x2a );


#define      OFFSET_COUNTLINES    0


//
// A typical class factory, nothing out of the ordinary. Includes
// the IClassFactory and IUnknown interfaces
class CClassFactory : public IClassFactory
{
public:
    CClassFactory();
    ~CClassFactory();

    // IUnknown
    STDMETHODIMP QueryInterface(REFIID riid, LPVOID* ppv);
    STDMETHODIMP_(ULONG) AddRef();
    STDMETHODIMP_(ULONG) Release();

    // IClassFactory
    STDMETHODIMP CreateInstance(LPUNKNOWN punk,
                                REFIID riid,
                                LPVOID* ppv);
    STDMETHODIMP LockServer(BOOL f);

protected:
    ULONG    m_cRef;
};


//
// The CCppShellExt class
// As a context menu handler, the CCppShellExt class implements the
// IContextMenu and IShellExtInit interfaces.
class CCppShellExt: public IContextMenu, IShellExtInit
{
    ULONG    m_cRef;
    wchar_t m_szFile[MAX_PATH];
public:
    CCppShellExt();
    ~CCppShellExt();
    //
    // IUnknown
    STDMETHODIMP QueryInterface(REFIID riid, LPVOID* ppv);
    STDMETHODIMP_(ULONG) AddRef();
```

```
    STDMETHODIMP_(ULONG) Release();
    //
    // IContextMenu
    STDMETHODIMP QueryContextMenu(HMENU hMenu,
                                  UINT  nMenuIndex,
                                  UINT  nFirstID,
                                  UINT  nLastID,
                                  UINT  nFlags);
    STDMETHODIMP InvokeCommand(LPCMINVOKECOMMANDINFO pInfo);
    STDMETHODIMP GetCommandString(UINT  nItemID,
                                  UINT  nFlags,
                                  UINT* pReserved,
                                  LPSTR pszName,
                                  UINT  cchMax);
    //
    // IShellExtInit
    STDMETHODIMP Initialize(LPCITEMIDLIST pidl,
                            LPDATAOBJECT  pObj,
                            HKEY          hKeyProgID);
private:
    //
    // Operations
    void DoCountCppFile(LPCMINVOKECOMMANDINFO pInfo);
};
```

There are two sections to the CppExt.h file. The first half of the file is almost identical to any header file that declares a class that implements the IClassFactory interface. The CClassFactory class implements the IClassFactory and IUnknown interfaces; this declaration can be copied and pasted into any server module you implement.

The second half of the file declares the CCppShellExt class. This class implements three interfaces: IUnknown, IShellExt, and IShellExtInit. With the exception of the DoCountCppFile function, this code can be reused for any server that implements a context menu extension.

Implementing the In-process Server Module

The actual implementation of the in-process server is spread out over the next few pages. All this code is physically located in the CppExt.cpp source file. Separating it into three separate listings, however, helps simplify the explanation.

Listing 13.10 presents the first part of the CppExt.cpp source file and deals with the basic DLL functions performed by all in-process servers.

13

COM AND OLE
CONCEPTS

LISTING 13.10 BASIC IN-PROCESS SERVER FUNCTIONS IN CppExt.cpp

```cpp
#include <windows.h>
#include <windowsx.h>
#include <shlobj.h>
#include <mbstring.h>

#pragma data_seg(".text")
#define INITGUID
#include <initguid.h>
#include <shlguid.h>
#pragma data_seg()

#include "CppExt.h"

LONG    g_cRef = 0;
HANDLE  g_hInst = NULL;

// --------------------------------------------------------------
// General DLL functions
// --------------------------------------------------------------
// Main DLL entry point - stash the module instance handle for use
// later, return TRUE in all cases.

extern "C" int APIENTRY

DllMain(HANDLE hInst, ULONG uReason, LPVOID pRes)
{
    if(uReason == DLL_PROCESS_ATTACH)
        g_hInst = hInst;
    return TRUE;
}

//
// Every InProc server must support DllGetClassObject. The only
// object supported by this server is CLSID_CppExtension, all
// other requests are rejected. For our extension, a ClassFactory
// object is created, and a QIF is performed for the requested
// interface through the ClassFactory.
STDAPI DllGetClassObject(REFCLSID rcid, REFIID riid, LPVOID *ppv)
{
    HRESULT hr;
    *ppv = NULL; // Always clear the "out" parameter

    if(rcid != CLSID_CppExtension)
        hr = CLASS_E_CLASSNOTAVAILABLE;
    else
    {
        CClassFactory* pFactory = new CClassFactory;
        if(pFactory == NULL)
            hr = E_OUTOFMEMORY;
```

```
        else
        {
            hr = pFactory->QueryInterface(riid, ppv);
        }
    }
    return hr;
}
//
// DllCanUnloadNow is called by the OS to determine if the inproc
// server can be unloaded. If the global reference count is greater
// than zero, S_FALSE is returned to prevent unloading.
STDAPI DllCanUnloadNow()
{
    HRESULT hr = S_FALSE;
    if(g_cRef == 0)
        hr = S_OK;
    return hr;
}
```

The DllGetClassObject function is very similar to a class factory. This function checks that the requesting CLSID matches CLSID_CppExtension and creates an instance of the class factory. The class factory then is queried for the requested interface, and the result is returned to the COM library.

Listing 13.11 contains the next set of functions implemented in CppExt.cpp. This listing contains CClassFactory, which implements the IClassFactory interface.

LISTING 13.11 THE CLASS FACTORY IMPLEMENTATION FROM CppExt.cpp

```
// -------------------------------------------------------------
// IClassFactory implementation
// -------------------------------------------------------------
// The IClassFactory interface is responsible for creating an
// instance of the shell extension. The ctor and dtor increment
// and decrement the DLL's global reference count.
CClassFactory::CClassFactory()
{
    m_cRef = 0;
    g_cRef++;
}

CClassFactory::~CClassFactory()
{
    g_cRef--;
}
```

continues

13

COM AND OLE
CONCEPTS

LISTING 13.11   CONTINUED

```
// IUnknown interfaces for CClassFactory
STDMETHODIMP CClassFactory::QueryInterface(REFIID riid, LPVOID* ppv)
{
    *ppv = NULL;
    if(riid == IID_IUnknown)
    {
        *ppv = (LPUNKNOWN)this;
        m_cRef++;
        return NOERROR;
    }
    else if(riid == IID_IClassFactory)
    {
        *ppv = (LPCLASSFACTORY)this;
        m_cRef++;
        return NOERROR;
    }
    else
    {
        return E_NOINTERFACE;
    }
}

STDMETHODIMP_(ULONG) CClassFactory::AddRef()
{
    return ++m_cRef;
}

STDMETHODIMP_(ULONG) CClassFactory::Release()
{
    if(--m_cRef)
        return m_cRef;
    delete this;
    return 0L;
}

// IClassFactory interfaces - CreateInstance and LockServer.
//
// CreateInstance creates a CCppShellExt object, and returns
// the result of QIF on the requested interface.
STDMETHODIMP CClassFactory::CreateInstance(LPUNKNOWN punk,
                                           REFIID riid,
                                           LPVOID* ppv)
{
    *ppv = NULL;
    if(punk != NULL)
        return CLASS_E_NOAGGREGATION;
```

```
        CCppShellExt* pShellExt = new CCppShellExt;
        if(pShellExt == NULL)
            return E_OUTOFMEMORY;

        return pShellExt->QueryInterface(riid, ppv);
}

// Simple implementation of LockServer, this just increments and
// decrements the global reference count.
STDMETHODIMP CClassFactory::LockServer(BOOL f)
{
        if(f)
            g_cRef++;
        else
            g_cRef--;
        return NOERROR;
}
```

The constructor for CClassFactory sets its internal reference count to and increments the module's global reference count, which represents the number of objects created in the entire module. The destructor decrements this same value.

Note that there are no Win32 synchronization primitives used in these functions. The CppExt shell extension, like most shell extensions, is created in a *single-threaded apartment*, or *STA*. This is a type of COM threading model that guarantees only one thread will access the COM object, even on computers that have multiple CPUs.

In addition to the IUnknown interfaces, CClassFactory implements the two IClassFactory functions: CreateInstance and LockServer. CreateInstance uses the new operator to create a new instance of CppShellExt and returns the result of QueryInterface to the client—in this case, the Windows 2000 shell.

LockServer is used by the shell to ensure that the DLL stays loaded, even if all its objects are destroyed. For an in-process server, a simple solution is to increment and decrement the global object reference count, depending on the value of the flag passed to LockServer. There's a great deal of sample code in other books, and even sample programs available from Microsoft, that imply that this function need not be implemented. This is not correct; all class factories must implement LockServer.

Listing 13.12 contains the last group of functions contained in CppExt.cpp. These are the CCppShellExt functions, which implement the IShellExtInit and IContextMenu interfaces.

13

COM AND OLE
CONCEPTS

LISTING 13.12 THE SHELL EXTENSION IMPLEMENTATION FROM CppExt.cpp

```
// ------------------------------------------------------------
// Shell extension implementation
// ------------------------------------------------------------
// There are three interfaces supported by a context menu extension
// - ICcontextMenu, IShellExtInit, and IUnknown. Additionally, there
// is one private member function, DoCppCount.
//
// The ctor and dtor for the CppShellExt class increment and decre-
// ment the global reference count for the DLL. The ctor also
// handles initialization of member variables.
CCppShellExt::CCppShellExt()
{
    m_cRef = 0L;
    m_szFile[0] = '\0';
    g_cRef++;
}


CCppShellExt::~CCppShellExt()
{
    g_cRef--;
}


// IUnknown interfaces for the Shell Interfaces
STDMETHODIMP CCppShellExt::QueryInterface(REFIID riid, LPVOID* ppv)
{
    if(riid == IID_IUnknown)
    {
        *ppv = (LPUNKNOWN)(LPCONTEXTMENU)this;
        m_cRef++;
        return NOERROR;
    }
    else if(riid == IID_IContextMenu)
    {
        *ppv = (LPCONTEXTMENU)this;
        m_cRef++;
        return NOERROR;
    }
    else if(riid == IID_IShellExtInit)
    {
        *ppv = (LPSHELLEXTINIT)this;
        m_cRef++;
        return NOERROR;
    }
    else
    {
        *ppv = NULL;
        return E_NOINTERFACE;
    }
}
```

```
STDMETHODIMP_(ULONG) CCppShellExt::AddRef()
{
    return ++m_cRef;
}

STDMETHODIMP_(ULONG) CCppShellExt::Release()
{
    if (--m_cRef)
        return m_cRef;
    delete this;
    return 0L;
}


// --------------------------------------------------------------
// IShellExtInit interface
// --------------------------------------------------------------
// IShellExtInit only has one function - Initialize is called to
// prepare your shell extension for calls that will be made on
// other interfaces - in this case, through IContextMenu. The main
// point of interest for a context menu is the name of the file
// object receiving the mouse-click, which is collected using
// DragQueryFile.
STDMETHODIMP CCppShellExt::Initialize(LPCITEMIDLIST pidl,
                                      LPDATAOBJECT  pObj,
                                      HKEY          hKeyProgID)
{
    STGMEDIUM   stg;
    FORMATETC   fetc = {CF_HDROP,
                        NULL,
                        DVASPECT_CONTENT,
                        -1,
                        TYMED_HGLOBAL};
    if(pObj == NULL)
        return E_FAIL;

    HRESULT hr = pObj->GetData(&fetc, &stg);
    if(FAILED(hr))
        return E_FAIL;

    UINT cFiles = DragQueryFile((HDROP)stg.hGlobal,
                                0xFFFFFFFF,
                                NULL,
                                0);
    if(cFiles == 1)
    {
        DragQueryFile((HDROP)stg.hGlobal,
                      0,
                      m_szFile,
                      sizeof(m_szFile));
```

13

COM AND OLE
CONCEPTS

continues

LISTING 13.12 CONTINUED

```
            hr = NOERROR;
    }
    else
        hr = E_FAIL;

    ReleaseStgMedium(&stg);
    return hr;
}
// ------------------------------------------------------------
// IContextMenu interfaces
// ------------------------------------------------------------
//
// QueryContextMenu is called when the shell requests the extension
// to add its menu items to the context menu. It's possible to get
// a NULL menu handle here. Also note that the current (As of this
// writing) Win32 SDK documentation is wrong regarding the nFlags
// parameter. This function should always return the number of new
// items added to the menu.
STDMETHODIMP CCppShellExt::QueryContextMenu(HMENU hMenu,
                                            UINT  nMenuIndex,
                                            UINT  nFirstID,
                                            UINT  nLastID,
                                            UINT  nFlags)
{
    wchar_t szMenu[] = L"Count Lines and Statements";
    BOOL fAppend = FALSE;
    if((nFlags & 0x000F) == CMF_NORMAL)
    {
        fAppend = TRUE;
    }
    else if(nFlags & CMF_VERBSONLY)
    {
        fAppend = TRUE;
    }
    else if(nFlags & CMF_EXPLORE)
    {
        fAppend = TRUE;
    }
    if(fAppend && hMenu)
    {
        BOOL f = InsertMenu(hMenu,
                            nMenuIndex,
                            MF_STRING | MF_BYPOSITION,
                            nFirstID,
                            szMenu);

        return MAKE_HRESULT(SEVERITY_SUCCESS,
                            0,
                            USHORT(1));
```

```
    }
    return NOERROR;

}
//
// InvokeCommand is the "Money Shot". This is a notification that
// the user has clicked on one of the selected items in the context
// menu. The name of the file is not passed to you in this function
// since it was passed in the IShellExtInit::Initialize  function.
STDMETHODIMP
CCppShellExt::InvokeCommand(LPCMINVOKECOMMANDINFO pInfo)
{
    if(HIWORD(pInfo->lpVerb) != 0)
        return E_FAIL;

    if(LOWORD(pInfo->lpVerb) > OFFSET_COUNTLINES)
        return E_INVALIDARG;

    if(LOWORD(pInfo->lpVerb) == OFFSET_COUNTLINES)
        DoCountCppFile(pInfo);
    return NOERROR;
}
//
// GetCommandString is called by the shell to retrieve a string
// associated with a new menu item. Note that pszName is not a
// wide char.
STDMETHODIMP CCppShellExt::GetCommandString(UINT   nItemID,
                                            UINT   nFlags,
                                            UINT*  pReserved,
                                            LPSTR  pszName,
                                            UINT   cchMax)
{
    if(nItemID == OFFSET_COUNTLINES)
    {
        switch(nFlags)
        {
        case GCS_HELPTEXT:
            lstrcpyA(pszName,
                    "Counts lines and semi-colons in a file");
            return NOERROR;

        case GCS_VALIDATE:
            return NOERROR;

        case GCS_VERB:
            lstrcpyA(pszName, "Count");
            break;
        }
    }
    return E_INVALIDARG;
```

continues

LISTING 13.12   CONTINUED

```
}
//
// DoCountCppFile opens the file which is located under the mouse
// click. The name of this file was passed to us in the Initialize
// member function that is part of the IShellExtInit interface. The
// file name was stored in m_szFile. This function opens the file
// and counts the number of newlines and semicolons in the file.
void CCppShellExt::DoCountCppFile( LPCMINVOKECOMMANDINFO pInfo )
{
    HANDLE  hFile = CreateFile(m_szFile,
                               GENERIC_READ,
                               FILE_SHARE_READ,
                               NULL,
                               OPEN_EXISTING,
                               FILE_ATTRIBUTE_COMPRESSED,
                               NULL);
    if(hFile == INVALID_HANDLE_VALUE)
    {
        MessageBox(pInfo->hwnd,
                   m_szFile,
                   L"Can't open file",
                   MB_ICONHAND);
        return;
    }
    BOOL  fRead;
    DWORD dwRead;
    DWORD cSemi = 0;
    DWORD cLines = 0;
    while(1)
    {
        BYTE rgBuffer[1024];
        fRead = ReadFile(hFile,
                         rgBuffer,
                         sizeof(rgBuffer),
                         &dwRead,
                         NULL);
        if(fRead == FALSE || dwRead == 0)
            break;

        for(DWORD dw = 0; dw < dwRead; dw++)
        {
            if(rgBuffer[dw] == _mbctombb(';'))
                cSemi++;
            else if(rgBuffer[dw] == _mbctombb('\n'))
                cLines++;
        }
    }
    wchar_t szMsg[80];
    wchar_t szSemi[] = L"Total Semicolons = ";
```

```
        wchar_t szLines[] = L"Total Lines = ";
        wsprintf(szMsg,
                 L"%s%ld\n%s%ld",
                 (LPCWSTR)szSemi,
                 (DWORD)cSemi,
                 (LPCWSTR)szLines,
                 (DWORD)cLines);
        MessageBox(pInfo->hwnd, szMsg, L"C++ File", MB_ICONINFORMATION);
        CloseHandle(hFile);
}
```

Save the contents from Listings 13.10, 13.11, and 13.12 as `CppExt.cpp` and add this file to the CppExt project. After compiling the CppExt project, you're ready to register the extension and copy the DLL into the Windows 2000 system directory, which is covered in the next section.

Registering the Shell Extension

Like all in-process servers, a shell extension must be registered before it is used. All in-process servers must be registered in the `HKEY_CLASSES_ROOT\CLSID` key. The simplest way to implement these changes is to create a Registry file that will be merged into the system Registry.

Create a new key for the CLSID used by the shell extension and give it a string value with an easy-to-read name—in this case, `C++ Line Counter`. Under this key, add an `InProcServer32` key that marks this class as an in-process server. The value associated with this key is the name of the DLL that implements the server—in this case, `CppExt.dll`. You must also add a `ThreadingModel` key, which is always set to `Apartment` for shell extensions, as shown in Listing 13.13.

LISTING 13.13 REGISTRY FILE ENTRIES REQUIRED FOR A THREAD-SAFE IN-PROCESS SERVER

```
[HKEY_CLASSES_ROOT\CLSID\<GUID>]
   @="C++ Line Counter"
[HKEY_CLASSES_ROOT\CLSID\<GUID>\InProcServer32]
   @="CppExt.dll"
     "ThreadingModel"="Apartment"
```

As in earlier examples, substitute the proper GUID for `<GUID>` in this Registry file fragment.

It's possible to register a context menu handler for all files or for a single file extension. For CppExt, the `.cpp` file extension was used, as shown in Listing 13.14.

LISTING 13.14 REGISTRY FILE ENTRIES REQUIRED FOR A CONTEXT MENU HANDLER

```
[HKEY_CLASSES_ROOT\.cpp]
  @="cpp_auto_file"
[HKEY_CLASSES_ROOT\cpp_auto_file]
  @="C++ File"
[HKEY_CLASSES_ROOT\cpp_auto_file\shellex\ContextMenuHandlers]
  @="CppLineCounter"
[HKEY_CLASSES_ROOT\cpp_auto_file\shellex\ContextMenuHandlers
➥\CppLineCounter]    @="{d3d834c0-9a3b-11cf-82a0-00608cca2a2a}"
```

In addition, when registering a shell extension for Windows 2000, you must add the CLSID for the shell extension under the following key:

```
HKEY_LOCAL_MACHINE\SOFTWARE\Microsoft\Windows\CurrentVersion\
➥\Shell Extensions\Approved
```

The CppExt.reg Registry file provided on the accompanying CD-ROM contains all the entries required to register a context menu shell extension on Windows 2000. To merge this file with your current Registry, right-click the file in Explorer and choose Merge from the context menu.

Debugging a Shell Extension

Debugging an extension to the Windows 2000 shell requires a few steps you might not be accustomed to using. You restart your machine, close the shell, and reload the shell into the Visual C++ debugger. The steps involved are similar to the steps used to debug any DLL:

1. Close all running applications and folders.

2. Restart Windows 2000.

3. Open Visual C++ and ensure that it's the only open application.

4. Close the shell by following the usual steps to shut down Windows 2000. This time, however, click the OK button in the confirmation dialog box while pressing Ctrl+Alt+Shift.

5. After the shell shuts down, open the Project Settings dialog box.

6. Click the Debug tab and enter the path to the Windows 2000 Explorer in the Executable for Debug Session edit control. The path normally is something like C:\WINNT\EXPLORER.EXE.

7. Close the dialog box.

After completing these steps, start a debug session. The shell restarts and runs inside the Developer Studio debugger. You'll be able to set breakpoints and step through the code in your shell extension.

Summary

This chapter presented an overview of basic COM and OLE concepts and provided examples showing how you can use COM and OLE to interact with the Windows 2000 shell.

The next chapter, "Automation," discusses how you can easily create interactive components that can be controlled from programming languages and scripts. You'll also see some examples of the COM support that's built into Microsoft tools such as Visual C++, Visual Basic, and Visual J++.

13

COM AND OLE
CONCEPTS

Automation

CHAPTER

14

Automation is probably the most commonly used COM technology. By exposing portions of their applications that use Automation interfaces, the developers of Visio and Microsoft Word, for example, have made their programs much more flexible and open to extension by end users.

In this chapter, you'll see an example of an application that supports Automation developed using MFC. You'll also see how you can use Visual Basic and VBScript to control applications that allow themselves to be controlled through automation.

This chapter focuses on using Automation to control full applications. Later, in Chapter 17, "Custom COM Objects," you'll use Automation to control simple components.

Creating Programmable Applications Using Automation

Automation (formerly known as *OLE Automation*) allows applications to expose to the outside world selected parts of their functionality. An Automation server exposes properties and methods through the IDispatch interface. Tools such as the Windows Scripting Host (WSH), Visual Basic, Visual Basic for Applications (VBA), and other programs that are clients of an Automation server are known as Automation controllers. The relationship between Automation servers and controllers is shown in Figure 14.1.

FIGURE 14.1
Automation controllers and servers communicate through the IDispatch *interface.*

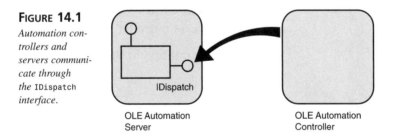

OLE Automation
Server

OLE Automation
Controller

IDispatch

Automation methods are functions exposed to the outside world. For example, Microsoft Word enables you to create and print documents through its Automation methods. A property corresponds to an attribute of an object exposed through Automation. Examples of properties include the size of a document or the font and color used by a particular object.

The `IDispatch` Interface

The interface used for Automation is `IDispatch`, which must be implemented by any object that supports Automation as a server. To determine whether a particular COM object supports Automation, a client can simply call `QueryInterface` for `IDispatch`. If an interface pointer is returned, the COM object is an Automation server, and the controller can access the server's properties and methods.

Data Types Used with `IDispatch`

Automation is a language-independent interface primarily used by scripting languages such as VBScript. Automation is also very useful when it's convenient for the client to discover new properties and methods from a server at runtime, as can be done with Visual Basic and VBA. Microsoft has also built client-side Automation support into Visual J++ and into Visual C++ through MFC.

This flexibility in clients comes at a cost, however. Data passed through this interface must be represented in such a way that all programming languages can understand it. COM defines a set of language-neutral strings, characters, arrays, and other data types that can be exchanged by Automation controllers and servers.

Two data types are associated with Automation:

- `BSTR` is a basic string type that's language independent. The string is similar to strings used in C, with extensions to make it usable in other languages.

- `VARIANT` is a tagged union type used to transfer portably various types across a single interface.

These types are discussed in the following sections.

The Basic String Type

The C and C++ languages define a simple string type as an array of characters terminated by a zero. Unfortunately, most other languages use different representations for their string types. For this reason, COM defines its own "basic string" type, or `BSTR`.

A `BSTR` consists of a Unicode C-style string, prefixed by a four-byte value containing the length of the string, as shown in Figure 14.2. When using a `BSTR` in a C or C++ program, you can treat the `BSTR` much like an ordinary string.

14

AUTOMATION

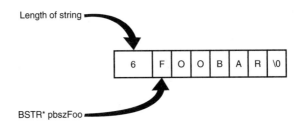

FIGURE 14.2

A BSTR includes the length of the string.

Length of string

6 | F | O | O | B | A | R | \0

BSTR* pbszFoo

Although a BSTR may look very much like a C-style string when you're reading it, take care when modifying a BSTR. In particular, never free a BSTR using free or delete. Also, you should never change the length of a BSTR using the C string library, because these routines will not change the prefixed length of the BSTR.

Windows 2000 provides alternate functions that must be used to manipulate BSTR types. The most commonly used functions include the following:

- SysAllocString creates a BSTR containing the contents of a string passed as a parameter.
- SysFreeString frees a previously allocated BSTR.
- SysReAllocString changes the contents of a BSTR to contain the contents of a string passed as a parameter.
- SysAllocStringLen creates a BSTR and copies a string to it.
- SysReAllocStringLen changes the contents of a BSTR to contain a substring of a string passed as a parameter.
- SysStringLen returns the length of a BSTR.

A problem that many C and C++ programmers encounter is that a BSTR may have embedded '\0' characters inside the string. If you use the C string library functions to determine the length of a BSTR, the value will be truncated at the first zero value contained in the string. You should always use the SysStringLen function to determine the length of a BSTR.

Using the _bstr_t Data Type

The BSTR type can be difficult to manage, especially if you're new to COM programming using C or C++. Because the C and C++ languages don't define the BSTR type, the compiler can't enforce safe programming practices—it will very happily compile code that creates memory leaks or access violations, like this:

```
#include <windows.h>
#include <wchar.h>
```

```
void BadIdea(BSTR& bstr)
{
    // Allocate a BSTR that is never released.
    BSTR bstrLocal = SysAllocString(L"This string will leak.");
    // Overwrite a BSTR using a CRT function.
    wcscpy(bstr, L"This may cause an access violation.");
}

int wmain()
{
    BSTR bstr = SysAllocString(L"Foo");
    BadIdea(bstr);
    wprintf(L"%s\n", (wchar_t*)bstr);
    SysFreeString(bstr);

    return 0;
}
```

Beginning with Visual C++ 5.0, the _bstr_t class is available to help simplify working with BSTR types. The _bstr_t class is defined in comutil.h, along with other useful goodies that can make your COM programming life simpler (such as the _variant_t type, which will be discussed in the section titled "Using the _variant_t Data Type").

The _bstr_t class is just a C++ class wrapper around a BSTR. The big advantage to using _bstr_t is that it has built-in constructors and destructors that will properly issue the correct incantations to allocate and free the underlying BSTR. This allows you to use an instance of _bstr_t as if it were a built-in C++ type. Here's an example:

```
#include <windows.h>
#include <wchar.h>
#include <comdef.h>

void GoodIdea(_bstr_t& bstr)
{
    _bstr_t bstrLocal = L"This string will not leak.";
    bstr = L"This will not cause an access violation.";
}

int wmain()
{
    _bstr_t bstr = L"Foo";
    GoodIdea(bstr);
    wprintf(L"%s\n", (wchar_t*)bstr);

    return 0;
}
```

The _bstr_t type will be covered in detail in Chapter 17.

14

AUTOMATION

The Variant Type

The VARIANT type is a tagged union that contains practically any type of object. The IDispatch interface uses VARIANT objects to pass data to and from Automation servers. The VARIANTARG structure is a typedef of the VARIANT structure—it can be used in place of a VARIANT. The VARIANT structure is defined like this:

```
struct tagVARIANT
{
    union
    {
        struct  __tagVARIANT
        {
            VARTYPE vt;
            WORD wReserved1;
            WORD wReserved2;
            WORD wReserved3;
            union
            {
                LONG            lVal;
                BYTE            bVal;
                SHORT           iVal;
                FLOAT           fltVal;
                DOUBLE          dblVal;
                VARIANT_BOOL    boolVal;
                _VARIANT_BOOL   bool;
                SCODE           scode;
                CY              cyVal;
                DATE            date;
                BSTR            bstrVal;
                IUnknown        __RPC_FAR *punkVal;
                IDispatch       __RPC_FAR *pdispVal;
                SAFEARRAY       __RPC_FAR *parray;
                BYTE            __RPC_FAR *pbVal;
                SHORT           __RPC_FAR *piVal;
                LONG            __RPC_FAR *plVal;
                FLOAT           __RPC_FAR *pfltVal;
                DOUBLE          __RPC_FAR *pdblVal;
                VARIANT_BOOL    __RPC_FAR *pboolVal;
                _VARIANT_BOOL   __RPC_FAR *pbool;
                SCODE           __RPC_FAR *pscode;
                CY              __RPC_FAR *pcyVal;
                DATE            __RPC_FAR *pdate;
                BSTR            __RPC_FAR *pbstrVal;
                IUnknown        __RPC_FAR * __RPC_FAR *ppunkVal;
                IDispatch       __RPC_FAR * __RPC_FAR *ppdispVal;
                SAFEARRAY       __RPC_FAR * __RPC_FAR *pparray;
                VARIANT         __RPC_FAR *pvarVal;
                PVOID           byref;
                CHAR            cVal;
```

```
        USHORT          uiVal;
        ULONG           ulVal;
        INT             intVal;
        UINT            uintVal;
        DECIMAL         __RPC_FAR *pdecVal;
        CHAR            __RPC_FAR *pcVal;
        USHORT          __RPC_FAR *puiVal;
        ULONG           __RPC_FAR *pulVal;
        INT             __RPC_FAR *pintVal;
        UINT            __RPC_FAR *puintVal;

        struct          __tagBRECORD
        {
            PVOID           pvRecord;
            IRecordInfo     __RPC_FAR *pRecInfo;
            }__VARIANT_NAME_4;
        }__VARIANT_NAME_3;

    }__VARIANT_NAME_2;
    DECIMAL decVal;
    }__VARIANT_NAME_1;
};
typedef VARIANT __RPC_FAR *LPVARIANT;
```

The discriminator for the actual data type in the union is contained in the vt member.
Possible values for vt are listed in Table 14.1.

TABLE 14.1 POSSIBLE VALUES FOR THE vt MEMBER OF THE VARIANT STRUCTURE

Value	Meaning
VT_EMPTY	No value was specified.
VT_UI1	Unsigned one-byte character stored in bVal.
VT_UI1 ¦ VT_BYREF	A pointer to an unsigned one-byte character is stored in pbVal.
VT_I2	A two-byte integer value is stored in iVal.
VT_I2 ¦ VT_BYREF	A pointer to a two-byte integer is stored in piVal.
VT_I4	A four-byte integer value is stored in lVal.
VT_I4 ¦ VT_BYREF	A pointer to a four-byte integer is stored in plVal.
VT_R4	An IEEE four-byte real value is stored in fltVal.
VT_R4 ¦ VT_BYREF	A pointer to an IEEE four-byte real is stored in pfltVal.
VT_R8	An eight-byte IEEE real value is stored in dblVal.
VT_R8 ¦ VT_BYREF	A pointer to an eight-byte IEEE real is stored in pdblVal.
VT_CY	A currency value is stored in cyVal.

14

AUTOMATION

continues

TABLE 14.1   CONTINUED

Value	Meaning
VT_CY ¦ VT_BYREF	A pointer to a currency value is stored in pcyVal.
VT_BSTR	A BSTR is stored in bstrVal.
VT_BSTR ¦ VT_BYREF	A pointer to a BSTR is stored in pbstrVal.
VT_NULL	A SQL NULL value was specified.
VT_ERROR	An HRESULT (also known as an SCODE) is stored in scode.
VT_ERROR ¦ VT_BYREF	A pointer to an HRESULT is stored in pscode.
VT_BOOL	A Boolean (true/false) value is stored in bool.
VT_BOOL ¦ VT_BYREF	A pointer to a Boolean value is stored in pbool.
VT_DATE	A value representing a date and time is stored in date.
VT_DATE ¦ VT_BYREF	A pointer to a date is stored in pdate.
VT_DISPATCH	A pointer to an object supporting IDispatch is stored in pdispVal.
VT_DISPATCH ¦ VT_BYREF	A pointer to a pointer to an object supporting IDispatch is stored in the location referred to by ppdispVal.
VT_VARIANT ¦ VT_BYREF	A pointer to another VARIANTARG is stored in pvarVal.
VT_UNKNOWN	A pointer to an object that implements IUnknown is stored in punkVal.
VT_UNKNOWN ¦ VT_BYREF	A pointer to a pointer to IUnknown is stored in ppunkVal.
VT_ARRAY ¦ *<anything>*	An array of data type *<anything>* is passed, with information stored in an array descriptor pointed to by pByrefVal.

When handling a VARIANT object, you have two ways you can simplify your life:

- You can use the built-in Visual C++ compiler support for COM and the _variant_t data type.
- You can use the Variant*xxx* API functions. (These functions are discussed in detail in the next section.)

Using the Win32 SDK Variant Functions

Managing a large discriminated union is always difficult. When the union is as large as VARIANT, it is nearly impossible. Luckily, the Win32 SDK includes functions that are used to properly manage VARIANT structures. These functions understand the maze of rules required to handle VARIANT structures correctly.

For example, if you're clearing a VARIANT, you must call IUnknown::Release if the stored element is a pointer to IUnknown or IDispatch. The most commonly used VARIANT-handling functions follow:

- VariantClear properly frees the contents of a VARIANT. BSTR and OLE interface types are freed properly, and the vt member is set to VT_EMPTY.
- VariantCopy copies one VARIANT to another, adjusting reference counts if needed.
- VariantInit initializes a VARIANT structure.
- VariantChangeType safely converts a VARIANT from one type to another, performing initialization and release operations as required.

Using the _variant_t Data Type

If you're using Visual C++ 5.0 or later, you can take advantage of the _variant_t data type. Like the _bstr_t data type, the _variant_t class is defined in comutil.h and is part of the compiler's built-in COM support.

The _variant_t class is a very thin wrapper around the VARIANT type. The constructor automatically initializes the VARIANT, and the destructor will automatically destroy it. However, as of this writing, _variant_t doesn't support all the types available for VARIANT in Windows 2000. The comutil.h header file includes documentation about exactly which types are supported.

Functions Included in IDispatch

The IDispatch interface includes four functions and is implemented by any COM object that supports Automation. Here's a somewhat simplified version of the IDispatch interface:

```
interface IDispatch : public IUnknown
{
public:
    HRESULT GetTypeInfoCount(UINT *pctinfo);
    HRESULT GetTypeInfo(UINT itinfo,
                        LCID lcid,
                        ITypeInfo **pptinfo);
    HRESULT GetIDsOfNames(REFIID riid,
                        LPOLESTR *rgszNames,
                        UINT cNames,
                        LCID lcid,
                        DISPID *rgdispid );
    HRESULT Invoke(DISPID dispidMember,
                    REFIID riid,
                    LCID lcid,
                    WORD wFlags,
```

14

AUTOMATION

```
                    DISPPARAMS *pdispparams,
                    VARIANT *pvarResult,
                    EXCEPINFO *pexcepinfo,
                    UINT *puArgErr);
};
```

Depending on how you use the `IDispatch` interface, you may implement some or all of these functions:

- `GetTypeInfo` is used to get a pointer to an `ITypeInfo` interface, which is used to determine the Automation support provided by an Automation server.

- `GetTypeInfoCount` is used to get the number of `ITypeInfo` interfaces (either zero or one) supported by an Automation server.

- `GetIDsOfNames` converts method, property, and parameter names into dispatch IDs (or `DISPIDs`). A `DISPID` is an index to a name that's used in calls to `IDispatch`.

- `Invoke` is used to gain access to the properties and methods exposed by the Automation server.

The heart of the `IDispatch` interface is the `Invoke` function. `Invoke` is called by an Automation controller in order to call the programmable interfaces exposed by the Automation server. As I demonstrate later, the MFC library hides much of the complexity of `IDispatch` from you (although this ease of use comes at a price).

IDispatch Interfaces Versus Function Tables

The COM interface is based on C++ virtual function tables. A *virtual function table* is an array of pointers to actual functions, as shown in Figure 14.3.

FIGURE 14.3

COM interfaces use the same in-memory layout as C++ virtual function tables.

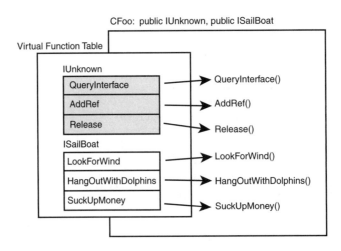

In this figure, the CFoo object derives from the ISailBoat interface. When a client asks for the ISailBoat interface via the QueryInterface function, the base address of the ISailBoat function table array is returned, allowing the client to calculate the address of any function supported by ISailBoat.

In the previous chapter, you implemented the IShellExtInit and IContextMenu interfaces for the CppExt project. By deriving the CCppShellExt class from the IContextMenu and IShellExtInit interfaces, you guaranteed that the function tables for CppExt COM objects were arranged as the client expected.

> **NOTE**
>
> From this discussion, it should be clear that you cannot rearrange the order of functions in an interface. If the order, signature, or semantics of an interface change, you must change the IID for the interface.

When you create interfaces that are accessed through virtual function tables, you're using *vtable binding* (sometimes called *early binding*). This sort of binding to required functions has very little overhead, because each function call has just one level of indirection between the client and server in the optimum case.

If you're using C or C++, vtable binding is the preferred way for your clients to connect to servers because it's very simple to write the required code. However, some types of programming environments don't support passing around function addresses. Early versions of Visual Basic, as well as most scripting languages, fit into this category. For these clients, there's a requirement for a different way for clients to bind to functions supplied by COM servers.

IDispatch and Automation allow scripting languages to work with a single interface towards a server. Instead of using pointers to functions and querying for multiple interfaces, an Automation client works with just one interface: IDispatch.

As discussed in the previous section, the IDispatch interface includes a function, GetIDsOfNames, that enables a client to retrieve an index known as a DISPID that is based on the name of the function. The client can then request the function to be invoked by passing its DISPID to the Invoke function. By tying these two functions together, the client can call functions by name rather than determining addresses. Although this is a lot of work, the scripting engine can hide the required mechanics as an implementation detail. All of this is done to allow users of script languages to use COM objects without worrying about the details of AddRef, Release, and interface pointers.

14

AUTOMATION

Creating an Automation Server Using MFC

As an example of an Automation server, the CD-ROM that accompanies this book includes an MFC-based project named AutoBub. AutoBub can be run as a standalone application or driven by an Automation controller. AutoBub is an SDI application that displays bubbles in its main view, as shown in Figure 14.4.

FIGURE 14.4

AutoBub running as a standalone application.

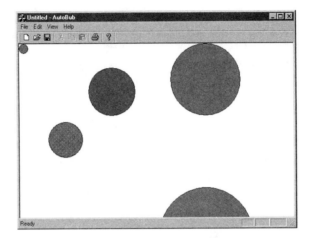

The AutoBub project was created in two steps. First, the AutoBub project was created as a standalone application; then Automation was added.

You can compile and run the project "as is" from the CD-ROM, or you can follow along as the steps are described in the following sections. To get started, use AppWizard to create an SDI application named AutoBub. As you step through the AppWizard pages, select the Automation Support check box on page 3, as shown in Figure 14.5. This step is necessary for any MFC AppWizard project that will expose an Automation interface.

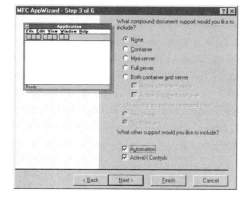

FIGURE **14.5**

Selecting Automation Support using AppWizard.

Modifying the Automation Options

The AutoBub project has some slight modifications to the default Automation settings offered by AppWizard. On AppWizard page 4, click the Advanced button. This displays the Advanced Options dialog box shown in Figure 14.6. Notice that some of the fields have been truncated by AppWizard—instead of "AutoBub," "AutoBu" is displayed. Change the File New Name value to AutoBub and the File Type Name value to AutoBub.Document, as shown in Figure 14.6.

FIGURE **14.6**

Changing the advanced options for AutoBub.

14

AUTOMATION

Modifications to the Document Class

A `CBubble` structure is used to model each bubble displayed by the AutoBub application. In addition to this structure, the `CAutoBubDoc` class must be modified to provide functions to add, count, and retrieve bubble objects. Modifications to the `AutoBubDoc.h` file are shown in Listing 14.1. Changed lines are shown in bold type, and most lines created by AppWizard are not shown.

LISTING 14.1   MODIFICATIONS TO THE CAutoBubDoc CLASS DECLARATION

```
struct CBubble
{
    COLORREF    m_clr;
    int         m_nRadius;
    CPoint      m_ptCenter;
};

class CAutoBubDoc : public CDocument
{
.
.
.
// Operations
public:
    void AddBubble(const CBubble& bub);
    BOOL GetBubble(int nBubble, CBubble* pBub);
    int  GetCount() const;
.
.
.
// Implementation
protected:
    CArray<CBubble,CBubble> m_rgBubble;
.
.
.
};
```

Because the CArray class is used, you must add the following line to the stfafx.h header file:

```
#include <afxtempl.h>
```

This includes the declarations for the MFC template-based collection classes.

Listing 14.2 contains the implementations of three new member functions for the CAutoBubDoc class. These functions handle adding and retrieving CBubble objects into the CArray structure maintained by the document.

LISTING 14.2   NEW AND MODIFIED FUNCTIONS FOR THE CAutoBubDoc CLASS

```
void CAutoBubDoc::AddBubble(const CBubble& bub)
{
    m_rgBubble.Add(bub);
}

BOOL CAutoBubDoc::GetBubble(int nIndex, CBubble* pBub)
```

```
{
    BOOL fReturn = FALSE;
    if(nIndex < GetCount())
    {
        *pBub = m_rgBubble.GetAt(nIndex);
        fReturn = TRUE;
    }
    return fReturn;
}

int CAutoBubDoc::GetCount() const
{
    return m_rgBubble.GetSize();
}
```

Creating a Dialog Box for AutoBub

The AutoBub project includes a dialog box used to add bubbles to its document.
Figure 14.7 shows the Add Bubble dialog box.

FIGURE 14.7

The Add Bubble dialog box used by AutoBub.

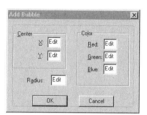

The resource ID for the dialog box is IDD_ADD_BUBBLE. Properties for the controls added
to the dialog box are listed in Table 14.2 (in tab order).

TABLE 14.2 PROPERTY VALUES FOR CONTROLS IN THE ADD BUBBLE DIALOG BOX

Control	Resource ID
Center Group	IDC_STATIC
X Edit control	IDC_EDIT_X
Y Edit control	IDC_EDIT_Y
Color Group	IDC_STATIC
Red Edit control	IDC_EDIT_RED
Green Edit control	IDC_EDIT_GREEN
Blue Edit control	IDC_EDIT_BLUE
Radius Edit control	IDC_EDIT_RADIUS

The CAddBubDlg class is derived from CDialog and manages the IDD_ADD_BUBBLE dialog box. ClassWizard was used to add the CAddBubDlg class to the AutoBub project, using the values from Table 14.3.

TABLE 14.3   VALUES USED FOR THE CAddBubDlg CLASS

Control	Value
Name	CAddBubDlg
Base Class	CDialog
File name	AddBubDlg.cpp
Dialog ID	IDD_ADD_BUBBLE
Automation	None

The CAddBubDlg class includes member variables that are associated with dialog box controls, as shown in Table 14.4.

TABLE 14.4   VALUES FOR NEW MEMBER VARIABLES IN CAddBubDlg

Control ID	Variable Name	Category	Type	Min	Max
IDC_EDIT_X	m_nX	Value	int		
IDC_EDIT_Y	m_nY	Value	int		
IDC_EDIT_RED	m_nRed	Value	int	0	255
IDC_EDIT_GREEN	m_nGreen	Value	int	0	255
IDC_EDIT_BLUE	m_nBlue	Value	int	0	255
IDC_EDIT_RADIUS	m_nRadius	Value	int	0	32000

In order to select the Add Bubble dialog box, the AutoBub menu resource contains a new menu item. The resource ID for the menu item is ID_EDIT_ADD_BUBBLE, and its caption is "&Add Bubble…". The new menu item is shown inside the Visual C++ menu editor in Figure 14.8.

A new message-handling function was added to the CAutoBubView view class to handle the new Add Bubble menu item. The new function has the properties shown in Table 14.5.

FIGURE **14.8**

The new Add Bubble menu selection added to IDR_MAINFRAME.

TABLE **14.5**   HANDLING THE ADD BUBBLE MENU ITEM

Class Name	Object ID	Message	Function
CAutoBubView	ID_EDIT_ADD_BUBBLE	COMMAND	OnEditAddBubble

The source code for CAutoBubView::OnEditAddBubble is provided in Listing 14.3.

LISTING **14.3**   HANDLING THE ADD BUBBLE MENU ITEM

```
void CAutoBubView::OnEditAddBubble()
{
    CAddBubDlg    dlg;
    if(dlg.DoModal() == IDOK)
    {
        CBubble bub;
        bub.m_clr = RGB(dlg.m_nRed, dlg.m_nGreen, dlg.m_nBlue);
        bub.m_ptCenter = CPoint(dlg.m_nX, dlg.m_nY);
        bub.m_nRadius = dlg.m_nRadius;

        CAutoBubDoc* pDoc = GetDocument();
        ASSERT_VALID(pDoc);

        pDoc->AddBubble( bub );
        Invalidate();
    }
}
```

Remember to add an #include directive at the top of the AutoBubView.cpp source file, just after the existing #include directives:

```
#include "AddBubDlg.h"
```

Drawing Bubble Objects for AutoBub

Bubbles are drawn in the CAutoBubView::OnDraw member function, which is called when the view is redrawn. The source code for OnDraw is provided in Listing 14.4.

14

AUTOMATION

LISTING 14.4   DRAWING A COLLECTION OF BUBBLES

```
void CAutoBubView::OnDraw(CDC* pDC)
{
    CAutoBubDoc* pDoc = GetDocument();
    ASSERT_VALID(pDoc);

    for(int n = 0; n < pDoc->GetCount(); n++)
    {
        CBubble aBubble;
        BOOL fResult = pDoc->GetBubble(n, &aBubble);
        if(fResult == FALSE)
            break;

        CBrush br(aBubble.m_clr);
        CBrush* pbrOld = pDC->SelectObject(&br);
        ASSERT(pbrOld);

        CSize offset(aBubble.m_nRadius, aBubble.m_nRadius);
        CRect rcBoundary(aBubble.m_ptCenter - offset,
                         aBubble.m_ptCenter + offset);
        pDC->Ellipse(rcBoundary);
        pDC->SelectObject(pbrOld);
    }
}
```

At this point, the AutoBub project can be compiled and run as a standalone application. Try it out now—before adding the Automation support—so that you can get a feel for adding bubbles using the Add Bubble dialog box.

Adding Automation Support to AutoBub

In this section, you'll see how easy it is to add Automation to an existing MFC project, using AutoBub as an example. Open ClassWizard and click the Automation tab. A Count property is added to the CAutoBubDoc class by clicking the Add Property button and using the values from Table 14.6.

TABLE 14.6   AUTOBUB Count AUTOMATION PROPERTIES

Control	*Value*
External name	Count
Type	long
Get function	CountIs
Set function	(none)
Implementation	Get/Set methods

Two methods—Clear and Add—were added to the CAutoBubDoc class using the values from Tables 14.7 and 14.8, respectively.

TABLE 14.7   VALUES USED TO ADD THE Clear METHOD TO THE CAutoBubDoc CLASS

Control	*Value*
External name	Clear
Internal name	Clear
Return type	void
Parameter list	(none)

TABLE 14.8   VALUES USED TO ADD THE Add METHOD TO THE CAutoBubDoc CLASS

Control	*Value*	*Type*
External name	Add	
Internal name	Add	
Return type	void	
Parameter list	clr	short
	nYPos	short
	nXPos	short
	nRadius	short

After these changes have been made and ClassWizard is closed, the necessary Automation skeleton functions are added to your project. ClassWizard also adds dispatch maps to the CAutoBubDoc class and modifies the AutoBub.odl file.

The complete implementation for the new Automation functions is provided in Listing 14.5.

LISTING 14.5   AUTOMATION METHODS ADDED TO THE CAutoBubDoc CLASS

```
void CAutoBubDoc::Clear()
{
    m_rgBubble.RemoveAll();
    UpdateAllViews(NULL);
}

void CAutoBubDoc::Add(long clr, short nYPos, short nXPos, short nRadius)
{
    CBubble     bub;
```

continues

LISTING 14.5   CONTINUED

```
    bub.m_nRadius = nRadius;
    bub.m_ptCenter.x = nXPos;
    bub.m_ptCenter.y = nYPos;
    bub.m_clr = clr;

    AddBubble(bub);

    UpdateAllViews(NULL);
}

long CAutoBubDoc::CountIs()
{
    return GetCount();
}
```

Note that the Automation functions make use of the existing functions whenever possible.

The ODL file created by ClassWizard is provided in Listing 14.6. Some of the comments have been removed for clarity. You don't have to enter this code yourself—it's provided here so that you can see how the Automation methods and properties are declared using the Microsoft ODL syntax.

ODL (or *Object Definition Language*) is similar to the more modern IDL (or *Interface Definition Language*), which is used to define COM interfaces. Using IDL is discussed in Chapter 16, "COM Threading Models."

LISTING 14.6   THE AUTOBUB ODL FILE

```
[ uuid(06A6EDEB-A2FD-11CF-9C7D-000000000000), version(1.0) ]
library AutoBub
{
    importlib("stdole32.tlb");

    //  Primary dispatch interface for CAutoBubDoc

    [ uuid(06A6EDEC-A2FD-11CF-9C7D-000000000000) ]
    dispinterface IAutoBu
    {
        properties:
            //{{AFX_ODL_PROP(CAutoBubDoc)
            [id(1)] long Count;
            //}}AFX_ODL_PROP

        methods:
            //{{AFX_ODL_METHOD(CAutoBubDoc)
```

```
            [id(2)] void Clear();
            [id(3)] void Add(long clr, short x, short y, short r);
            //}}AFX_ODL_METHOD
    };

    //  Class information for CAutoBubDoc
    [ uuid(06A6EDEA-A2FD-11CF-9C7D-000000000000) ]
    coclass CAutoBubDoc
    {
        [default] dispinterface IAutoBu;
    };
    //{{AFX_APPEND_ODL}}
};
```

One final change must be made for the AutoBub project. By default, Automation servers are not displayed when launched by an Automation controller. This behavior is useful for many Automation servers; however, it defeats the purpose of the AutoBub application. The CAutoBubApp::InitInstance function must be modified as shown in Listing 14.7. InitInstance is a fairly large function, so I've highlighted the changed lines and omitted most of the unchanged lines.

LISTING 14.7   MODIFICATIONS TO THE CAutoBubApp::InitInstance FUNCTION

```
BOOL CAutoBubApp::InitInstance()
{
    .
    .
    .
    // Check to see if launched as OLE server
    if (cmdInfo.m_bRunEmbedded || cmdInfo.m_bRunAutomated)
    {
        // Register all OLE server (factories) as running.  This
        // enables the OLE libraries to create objects from other
        // applications.
        COleTemplateServer::RegisterAll();

        // Application was run with /Automation.  Okay to show the
        // main window in this case.
        if (!ProcessShellCommand(cmdInfo))
            return FALSE;
        return TRUE;
    }
    .
    .
    .
}
```

14

AUTOMATION

After making these changes, compile and run the AutoBub project. AutoBub is now ready to be used as a Automation server. In the next two sections, you'll create Automation controllers using Visual Basic and VBScript.

Using Visual Basic to Create an Automation Controller

The classic Automation controller is Visual Basic. Although Visual Basic now supports early binding via the virtual function table, it's still a very popular Automation controller. In this section, you'll create a 32-bit application that drives AutoBub through its Automation interface. This application, named AutoBasic, displays a dialog box that can be used to add bubbles to an instance of AutoBub. The main form used in the AutoBasic project is shown in Figure 14.9.

FIGURE 14.9

The main form used by the AutoBasic project.

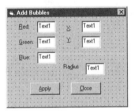

The control name properties are listed in Table 14.9. Properties not listed should be set to their default values. The Apply and Close pushbuttons are elements in a control array named cmd.

TABLE 14.9   NAME PROPERTIES FOR CONTROLS IN THE MAIN AUTOBASIC FORM

Control	Resource ID
X Edit control	txtXPos
Y Edit control	txtYPos
Apply pushbutton	cmd(0)
Close pushbutton	cmd(1)
Red Edit control	txtRed
Green Edit control	txtGreen
Blue Edit control	txtBlue
Radius Edit control	txtRadius

Code in a Visual Basic project is placed into procedures and functions, depending on the object and event affected by the code. Declarations that are used for the entire project belong in the (General) object section. Add a declaration under (General) for the Automation object. It should look like this:

```
Dim BubbleMachine As Object
```

Before the Automation object can be used, it must be initialized by calling the `CreateObject` function. `CreateObject` locates the AutoBub server, creates an instance of it, finds its `IDispatch` interface, and initializes the `BubbleMachine` object. Add the code provided in Listing 14.8 as the `Load` procedure for the `Form` object.

LISTING 14.8 INITIALIZING THE AUTOMATION OBJECT

```
Private Sub Form_Load()
    Set BubbleMachine = CreateObject("AutoBub.Document")
End Sub
```

After the Automation object has been used, it must be released by assigning the `BubbleMachine` object the special value of `Nothing`. Add the code provided in Listing 14.9 as the `Unload` procedure for the `Form` object.

LISTING 14.9 RELEASING AN AUTOMATION OBJECT

```
Private Sub Form_Unload(Cancel As Integer)
    Set BubbleMachine = Nothing
End Sub
```

In order to close the AutoBasic application, `End` must be called. In the AutoBasic project, the `Click` procedure for the `cmd` control array handles the Apply and Close buttons. If an index of zero is passed, the Apply button is pressed. If an index of one is passed, the Close button is clicked. The source code for `cmd_Click` is provided in Listing 14.10.

LISTING 14.10 CREATING A NEW BUBBLE VIA AUTOMATION

```
Private Sub cmd_Click(Index As Integer)
    Static ColorRef As Long, R As Integer, G As Integer, B As Integer
    Static nX As Integer, nY As Integer, nRadius As Integer

    If Index = 0 Then
        ' Make the COLORREF from the RGB components
        R = Val(txtRed) And &HFF&
        G = Val(txtGreen) And &HFF&
        B = Val(txtBlue) And &HFF&
        ColorRef = RGB(R, G, B)
```

continues

14

AUTOMATION

LISTING 14.10   CONTINUED

```
        ' Save the position coords as ints
        nX = Val(txtXPos)
        nY = Val(txtYPos)
        nRadius = Val(txtRadius)
        ' Create a new bubble
        BubbleMachine.Add ColorRef, nX, nY, nRadius

    Else
        End
    End If

End Sub
```

An instance of the AutoBub application is displayed when you run the AutoBasic project. Remember that this isn't the default behavior—usually an MFC-based Automation server remains hidden. Use the AutoBasic dialog box to add bubbles to AutoBub. Figure 14.10 shows both applications running after a few bubbles have been added.

FIGURE 14.10

The AutoBasic and AutoBub applications after a few bubbles have been added.

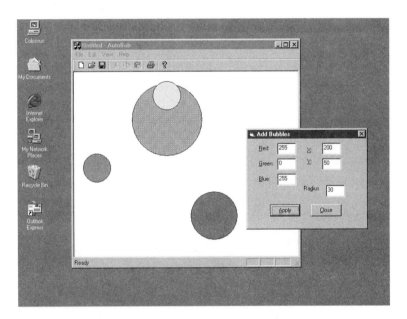

Using Automation in VBScript

The `IDispatch` interface was originally created for use by clients that relied on scripting languages. A commonly used scripting language is VBScript, which is commonly used on Web pages and can also be used to script the Windows 2000 shell via the Windows Scripting Host (WSH).

The Windows Scripting Host and VBScript enable you to write scripts that use any Automation server. These scripts are executed inside the Windows shell using the Windows Scripting Host. The Windows Scripting Host is an extendable scripting engine that has access to the Windows shell and COM interfaces. Today, WSH ships with support for VBScript. Third-party vendors are working on support for Perl and other scripting languages.

An example of using VBScript inside WSH is provided in Listing 14.11. This script creates an instance of the AutoBub server and adds a number of bubbles.

LISTING 14.11 A VBSCRIPT AUTOMATION EXAMPLE THAT RUNS IN THE WINDOWS SCRIPTING HOST

```
'''''''''''''''''''''''''''''''''''''''''''''''''''''''''''''''''
'     BubbleScript.vbs
'
'     VBScript that runs inside the Windows Scripting Host and
'     controls the AutoBub Automation controller. The controller
'     is launched, several bubbles are displayed, then the script
'     displays a message box.
'
'     This example is from "Programming Windows 2000 Unleashed",
'     by Mickey Williams.
'''''''''''''''''''''''''''''''''''''''''''''''''''''''''''''''''
Option Explicit
On Error Resume Next


Dim bubbleMachine
Set bubbleMachine = CreateObject("AutoBub.Document")
if(err <> 0) then
    errmsgtrace "CreateObject"
    Quit
end if


'''''''''''''''''''''''''''''''''''''''''''''''''''''''''''''''''
' Make some bubbles
'''''''''''''''''''''''''''''''''''''''''''''''''''''''''''''''''
```

14

AUTOMATION

continues

LISTING 14.11   CONTINUED

```
bubbleMachine.Add vbRed,     50,   50, 10
bubbleMachine.Add vbGreen,   60,  200, 40
bubbleMachine.Add vbBlue,    80,  350, 20
bubbleMachine.Add vbMagenta, 120, 100, 20
bubbleMachine.Add vbCyan,    100, 300, 10
bubbleMachine.Add vbYellow,  200,  50, 20
bubbleMachine.Add vbBlack,   220, 500, 40
bubbleMachine.Add vbRed,     250, 300, 20
bubbleMachine.Add vbGreen,   280, 400, 100
bubbleMachine.Add vbBlue,    300, 200, 20
bubbleMachine.Add vbMagenta, 320, 300, 10
bubbleMachine.Add vbCyan,    350, 100, 70
bubbleMachine.Add vbYellow,  380, 200, 10
bubbleMachine.Add vbBlack,   400, 400, 100
bubbleMachine.Add vbRed,     420,  50, 20
bubbleMachine.Add vbGreen,   440, 120, 10
bubbleMachine.Add vbBlue,    450, 300, 20


'''''''''''''''''''''''''''''''''''''''''''''''''''''''''''''''''''''
' Display completion message - this also keeps the controller up
' so the bubbles are visible.
'''''''''''''''''''''''''''''''''''''''''''''''''''''''''''''''''''''
msgtrace "done"
'''''''''''''''''''''''''''''''''''''''''''''''''''''''''''''''''''''
' End of the script's main flow.
'''''''''''''''''''''''''''''''''''''''''''''''''''''''''''''''''''''
Quit


'''''''''''''''''''''''''''''''''''''''''''''''''''''''''''''''''''''
' Subroutines:
'
' msgTrace - displays the current time and a message in a message
'            box.
'''''''''''''''''''''''''''''''''''''''''''''''''''''''''''''''''''''
Sub msgTrace(msg)
    WScript.Echo Now & " - " & msg
End Sub


'''''''''''''''''''''''''''''''''''''''''''''''''''''''''''''''''''''
' errMsgTrace - displays the current time,  an error message and a
'               message string in a message box.
'''''''''''''''''''''''''''''''''''''''''''''''''''''''''''''''''''''
Sub errMsgTrace(msg)
    WScript.Echo Now & ". Error Code: " & Hex(Err) & " - " & msg
End Sub
```

If you save this script as `AutoScript.vbs`, the Windows Scripting Host will run the script when it's double-clicked.

Summary

This chapter discussed Automation and the `IDispatch` interface. Automation is the most widely used COM technology, because it allows you to easily expose parts of your applications to the outside world. Automation servers such as Excel, Word, and Visio can easily be controlled by Automation controllers, such as Visual Basic and VBScript. In this chapter, examples of an Automation server and Automation controllers were created.

OLE Drag and Drop

As discussed in Chapter 13, "COM and OLE Concepts," *OLE* is a technology that's built on top of COM. This chapter covers two of the most commonly used OLE technologies: drag and drop and data transfer using the OLE extensions to the Windows Clipboard.

OLE applications use a mechanism known as *uniform data transfer* to exchange information. Uniform data transfer is a much more extendable way of exchanging data than using the traditional Windows 2000 Clipboard operations. Although the basic Windows 2000 Clipboard works fine for transferring small amounts of text, it's not very useful when transferring large objects.

This chapter discusses uniform data transfer, the OLE Clipboard, and OLE drag and drop. You'll also add OLE drag and drop to an MFC application as an example.

Understanding the OLE Clipboard

As you may know, the Clipboard functions offered by Windows 2000—`OpenClipboard`, `SetClipboardData`, `GetClipboardData`, and so on—work with a handle to global data. When transferring large objects such as bitmaps or multimedia clips, these objects must be loaded from disk, created in global memory, and transferred to another program. All this work consumes a large amount of your system's resources and slows down performance. A mechanism that works fine for small text strings really bogs down when transferring large video clips.

The OLE Clipboard uses uniform data transfer as its underlying transport. The OLE Clipboard enables you to describe the data to be transferred as well as its current storage medium. This enables you to avoid transferring megabytes of data unnecessarily, which would have consumed all the global memory available on your machine just to paste a large bitmap.

OLE objects that are the source of a data-transfer operation expose the `IDataObject` interface and are known as *data objects*. The `IDataObject` interface works primarily with two structures:

- `FORMATETC`. Describes the data to be transferred
- `STGMEDIUM`. Describes the current location of the data

Using the `FORMATETC` and `STGMEDIUM` Structures

The `FORMATETC` structure describes the contents involved in an OLE data transfer. When using the Windows 2000 Clipboard, you're limited to describing the data to be transferred as a `DWORD` variable. When using OLE uniform data transfer, an entire structure is used to describe the data, as Listing 15.1 shows.

LISTING 15.1 THE FORMATETC STRUCTURE

```
typedef struct tagFORMATETC
{
    CLIPFORMAT      cfFormat;
    DVTARGETDEVICE  *ptd;
    DWORD           dwAspect;
    LONG            lindex;
    DWORD           tymed;
}FORMATETC;
typedef FORMATETC* LPFORMATETC;
```

The five member variables of the FORMATETC structure specify much more than the format of the data to be transferred. As shown in the following list, descriptions of the target device, the storage medium, and the amount of detail in the data are also supplied:

- cfFormat. Specifies the format of the data represented by this structure. This value can be any of the traditional Windows Clipboard formats, such as CF_TEXT or CF_BITMAP. This value also can refer to formats registered privately by applications using RegisterClipboardFormat. Although Clipboard formats can be used as values, remember that this structure is used for OLE data transfer and has nothing to do with the traditional Windows 2000 Clipboard.

- ptd. Points to a DVTARGETDEVICE structure containing information about the target device for which the data is being composed. This value can be NULL, as when the data is created independently of any particular device—in this case the screen device will be used. If a specific target device is required, such as a printer, an appropriate default device must be selected. The DVTARGETDEVICE structure is discussed immediately after this list.

- dwAspect. Specifies the amount of detail present in the format. This allows multiple views to be supported for a single object on the Clipboard. A bitmap may be present as a metafile, as a thumbnail, as an icon, and in a native 20MB BITMAP structure, for example. Possible aspect values are presented after this list.

- lindex. Identifies a portion of the aspect when data is split across page boundaries. If data is not split across a page boundary, this value is set to –1, which refers to the entire data.

- tymed. Specifies how the data is stored and is taken from one of the TYMED constants, which is discussed later in "The STGMEDIUM Structure" section.

15

OLE DRAG
AND DROP

Handling FORMATETC Structures

Filling in a FORMATETC structure every time you transfer or query the OLE Clipboard can be a real pain. So much so that examples in this chapter use a C++ wrapper class to make using the structure less painful. Listing 15.2 provides the source code for the CFormatEtc class. This class is used in the sample program presented later in this chapter and can be found on the CD-ROM in the OleTree project directory as fmtetc.h.

LISTING 15.2   A C++ WRAPPER FOR THE FORMATETC STRUCTURE

```
// CFormatEtc - a C++ class that wraps the FORMATETC structure.
// All ctor arguments have default values - no arguments are
// required for transferring text.
struct CFormatEtc : public FORMATETC
{
    CFormatEtc(CLIPFORMAT cf = CF_TEXT,
               DWORD dwTymed = TYMED_HGLOBAL,
               DWORD aspect = DVASPECT_CONTENT,
               DVTARGETDEVICE* ptd = NULL,
               LONG lindex = -1);
};

CFormatEtc::CFormatEtc(CLIPFORMAT cf,
                       DWORD dwTymed,
                       DWORD aspect,
                       DVTARGETDEVICE* pTargDevice,
                       LONG lDataIndex)
{
    cfFormat = cf;
    tymed = dwTymed;
    dwAspect = aspect;
    ptd = pTargDevice;
    lindex = lDataIndex;
}
```

The CFormatEtc class initializes itself according to default arguments declared for its constructor. To construct a CFormatEtc object suitable for text data transfer, you can just declare an object, like this:

```
CFormatEtc fe; // Text format transfer
```

To create more elaborate format descriptions, pass parameters to the constructor when initializing the object, like this:

```
CFormatEtc  fe(CF_HBITMAP, TYMED_HGLOBAL, DVASPECT_CONTENT);
```

Because CFormatEtc is derived from FORMATETC, any function that accepts a pointer to a FORMATETC structure will accept a pointer to CFormatEtc.

Using the DVTARGETDEVICE Structure

The DVTARGETDEVICE structure is used to describe a device that data is rendered for, and it's defined as shown in Listing 15.3.

LISTING 15.3   THE DVTARGETDEVICE STRUCTURE

```
typedef struct tagDVTARGETDEVICE
{
    DWORD tdSize;
    WORD  tdDriverNameOffset;
    WORD  tdDeviceNameOffset;
    WORD  tdPortNameOffset;
    WORD  tdExtDevmodeOffset;
    BYTE  tdData[1];
}DVTARGETDEVICE;
```

Think of the DVTARGETDEVICE structure as a header for a block of data. Immediately following the structure is a series of Unicode strings that contain information that can be used to create a device context. Each entry in the DVTARGETDEVICE structure contains an offset into the block of data. For example, tdDriverNameOffset contains the number of bytes from the beginning of the structure to the beginning of the string that holds the driver name string, as shown in Figure 15.1.

FIGURE 15.1

The offsets stored in DVTARGETDEVICE *are offsets into a Unicode data block.*

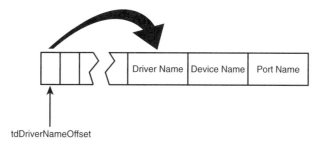

tdDriverNameOffset

The DVASPECT enumerated type specifies the amount of detail present in a particular rendering of the data. If you're dealing with text, this value almost certainly will be DVASPECT_CONTENT, meaning that the rendering should represent the full content of the data. When dealing with graphical data or more complex items, however, other values often are used. Here are the possible values for DVASPECT:

- DVASPECT_CONTENT. Specifies full content. This value requests a representation of an object so that it can be displayed as an embedded object inside a container.
- DVASPECT_DOCPRINT. Specifies a representation of the data content as though it were printed to a printer using the Print command from the File menu. The data may span several pages.
- DVASPECT_ICON. Specifies an icon that represents the object.
- DVASPECT_THUMBNAIL. Specifies a small thumbnail sketch of the data content from the object. A thumbnail is typically a 120×120 pixel Device Independent Bitmap, which is sometimes stored inside a metafile.

Only one of the listed values can be used at any given time—no bitwise ORing is allowed.

Using the STGMEDIUM Structure

The STGMEDIUM structure represents a general-purpose storage object. It basically replaces the global memory handle used to transfer data with the Windows 2000 Clipboard. Listing 15.4 shows the definition of STGMEDIUM.

LISTING 15.4   THE STGMEDIUM STRUCTURE

```
typedef struct tagSTGMEDIUM
{
    DWORD tymed;
    union
    {
        HBITMAP hBitmap;
        HMETAFILEPICT hMetafilePict;
        HENHMETAFILE hEnhMetaFile;
        HGLOBAL hGlobal;
        LPWSTR lpszFileName;
        IStream *pstm;
        IStorage *pstg;
    } u;
    IUnknown *pUnkForRelease;
}STGMEDIUM;
typedef STGMEDIUM *LPSTGMEDIUM;
```

Here are the members of the STGMEDIUM structure:

- tymed. Specifies the type of storage used to represent the data object. A list of possible values is provided later in this section.

- A union of several variables used to refer to the data object's storage. The union's currently valid member can be determined by examining the tymed variable.

- pUnkForRelease. A pointer to an IUnknown method that can be called to release storage for IStorage and IStream objects. This value may be NULL.

The possible values for tymed and the corresponding union variable used to refer to the data object are provided in Table 15.1.

TABLE 15.1   POSSIBLE VALUES FOR tymed AND RELEVANT UNION MEMBERS

Value of tymed	*Corresponding Union Member*
TYMED_NULL	No data
TYMED_HGLOBAL	hGlobal
TYMED_FILE	lpszFileName
TYMED_ISTREAM	pstm
TYMED_ISTORAGE	pstg
TYMED_GDI	hBitmap
TYMED_MFPICT	hMetaFilePict
TYMED_ENHMF	hEnhMetaFile

As you'll see later in this chapter, during a drag-and-drop operation, you often need to free storage that's represented by a STGMEDIUM structure. There's no need for you to try to determine which particular type of object needs to be released from the structure. If you find yourself in a position where you must release the storage contained in a STGMEDIUM structure, call ReleaseStgMedium, passing the address of the STGMEDIUM structure as a parameter. Here's an example:

```
ReleaseStgMedium(&stg);
```

ReleaseStgMedium takes care of determining the proper release method for any STGMEDIUM object.

15

OLE DRAG AND DROP

Using the `IDataObject` Interface

All data objects must expose the `IDataObject` interface. Through `IDataObject`, a data object provides access to all the information required for implementing all sorts of data transfer. The OLE Clipboard, ActiveX controls, and OLE drag and drop all make use of this interface.

A simplified version of the `IDataObject` interface definition is shown in Listing 15.5.

LISTING 15.5 THE `IDataObject` INTERFACE DECLARATION

```
interface IDataObject : public IUnknown
{
public:
    HRESULT GetData(FORMATETC* pformatetcIn, STGMEDIUM* pmedium);
    HRESULT GetDataHere(FORMATETC* pformatetc, STGMEDIUM* pmedium);
    HRESULT QueryGetData(FORMATETC* pformatetc);
    HRESULT GetCanonicalFormatEtc(FORMATETC* pformatectIn,
                                  FORMATETC  *pformatetcOut);
    HRESULT SetData(FORMATETC* pformatetc,
                    STGMEDIUM* pmedium,
                    BOOL fRelease);
    HRESULT EnumFormatEtc(DWORD dwDirection,
                          IEnumFORMATETC** ppenumFormatEtc);
    HRESULT DAdvise(FORMATETC* pformatetc,
                    DWORD advf,
                    IAdviseSink* pAdvSink,
                    DWORD* pdwConnection);
    HRESULT DUnadvise(DWORD dwConnection);
    HRESULT EnumDAdvise(IEnumSTATDATA** ppenumAdvise);
};
```

Nine functions are defined as part of the `IDataObject` interface. Most data objects will provide meaningful implementations of many of these interfaces, although in most cases at least a few of the functions will return `not implemented`. Table 15.2 lists the purpose of each of these functions.

TABLE 15.2 MEMBER FUNCTIONS INCLUDED IN THE `IDataObject` INTERFACE

Function	Purpose
DAdvise	Used when a client needs to be notified when the contents of a data object are changed. The client passes a pointer to an `IAdviseSink` interface to the data object, which uses the `IAdviseSink` interface to notify the client of changes. This type of interaction is similar to the DDE `XTP_ADVISE` protocol and is used primarily when embedding an object into a container.

Function	Purpose
DUnadvise	Breaks a connection previously set up with DAdvise.
EnumDAdvise	Enumerates the advisory connections established by a data object.
EnumFormatEtc	Enables you to enumerate the formats supported by a data object using the IEnumFORMATETC interface.
GetCanonicalFormatEtc	Returns the most general rendering information for a specific data object.
GetData	Returns data in an STGMEDIUM structure, depending on the format described in the FORMATETC structure. Data returned by this function must be freed by the caller. If the data cannot be rendered as requested, an error HRESULT value is returned.
GetDataHere	A rarely used function that enables the caller to specify where to store the contents of data copied by the data object.
QueryGetData	Asks the data object whether data can be transferred in a specific format. This function is one of those rare cases in which you cannot use the SUCCEEDED or FAILED macro. If the data can be transferred in the requested format, S_OK is returned. If the requested format function fails, S_FALSE is returned if the requested format is not supported.
SetData	A rarely used function that allows a client (normally, a consumer) to change the contents stored by a data object.

When you're using MFC, the IDataObject interface is wrapped by the COleDataSource class.

Using OLE Drag and Drop

As discussed earlier, OLE drag and drop uses the OLE Clipboard and uniform data transfer to transfer data from a source and a consumer. Figure 15.2 shows the OLE objects involved in a typical drag-and-drop operation.

15

OLE DRAG
AND DROP

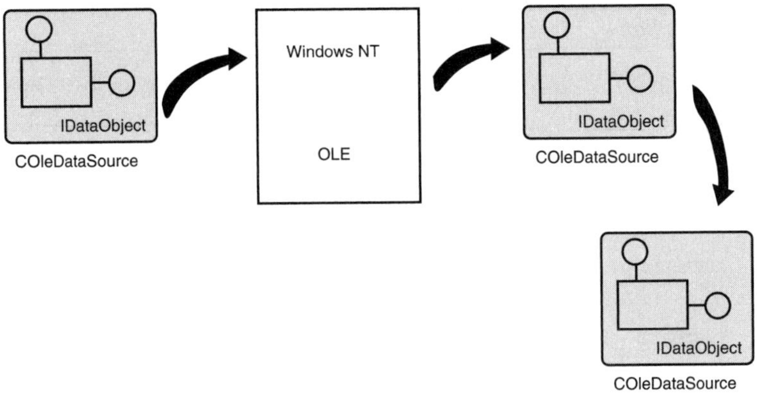

FIGURE 15.2
The various component objects involved in a typical OLE drag-and-drop operation.

As shown in Figure 15.2, three MFC classes are involved in a drag-and-drop operation:

- COleDataSource. Handles collecting the data to be transferred and implements an IDataObject interface. This class handles the source-side interaction with OLE. Unless you need specialized behavior, you can use this class "as is," without deriving from it.

- COleDropTarget. Handles the consumer or destination side of a drag-and-drop operation. You'll always derive a new class from COleDropTarget in order to perform specific behavior required when an object is dropped on a particular window.

- COleDataObject. A wrapper for the IDataObject interface, as discussed earlier. A COleDataObject is passed as a parameter in many of the functions called during the drag-and-drop operation.

An OLE Drag-and-Drop Source

With a small amount of work, any window can be an OLE drag-and-drop source. If you're using MFC, your CWnd-derived class must implement a COleDataSource member variable.

When a drag is detected, you store the data to be transferred in the drag and drop in the COleDataSource member variable. This step is very much like placing an item on the Windows Clipboard. After storing data in COleDataSource, call the COleDataSource::DoDragDrop member function to start the drag-and-drop operation.

DoDragDrop does not return until the drag and drop completes. If DoDragDrop returns DROPEFFECT_MOVE, the drag and drop has been completed successfully, and you should perform whatever tasks are necessary to make the object appear to move. In many cases, this means that the object should be deleted.

An OLE Drag-and-Drop Destination

Implementing a drop target involves a bit more code than implementing a drop source, but it's fairly simple code, especially if you're using MFC. The modifications discussed in this section can be made to any CWnd-derived class, including any control or view.

The key component of an OLE drop target is the IDropTarget interface. MFC wraps the IDropTarget interface in the COleDropTarget class. The first step in implementing a drop target is to derive a class from COleDropTarget and to override three functions:

- OnDragEnter. Called during a drag and drop when the cursor initially passes over the window associated with the COleDropTarget object. In almost all cases, this function does nothing except call OnDragOver.

- OnDragOver. Called during a drag and drop as the cursor moves over the window associated with the COleDropTarget object. This function sets the current drop effect for the cursor.

- OnDrop. Called when the user actually "drops" an object on the window associated with the COleDragTarget object. This function must fetch the data from the OLE Clipboard and paste it into the target window.

The class derived from COleDropTarget must be added to the CWnd-derived class as a member variable. The window class must be registered as a drop target via the COleDropTarget::Register function.

Looking at a Drag-and-Drop Example

As an illustration of how you can use OLE drag and drop in any Windows 2000 application, an example is included on the accompanying CD-ROM. The OleTree example adds OLE drag-and-drop capability to a pair of tree controls. Items can be exchanged between these controls by dragging them from one tree to the other. Items also can be transferred to or from any other applications that support OLE drag and drop, such as Microsoft Word.

OleTree is a dialog-box–based project created with AppWizard. The main dialog box for OleTree is shown in Figure 15.3. Note the new edit control, the new pushbutton control, and the two new tree controls.

15

OLE DRAG AND DROP

FIGURE 15.3

The main dialog box for OleTree.

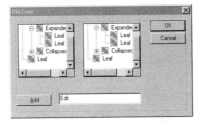

Use the values from Table 15.3 for the new controls added to the main dialog box resource.

TABLE 15.3   RESOURCE AND CONTROL INFORMATION FOR THE MAIN DIALOG BOX

Control	Resource ID	Caption
Edit control	IDC_EDIT	
Add pushbutton	IDC_ADD	&Add
Left tree control	IDC_LEFT	
Right tree control	IDC_RIGHT	

Using the control property sheets, enable the following properties for the two tree controls:

- Has buttons
- Has lines
- Border
- Lines at root

ClassWizard is used to add a new class derived from CTreeCtrl to manage the tree controls to the OleTree project. The new class, CDragTree, includes OLE drag-and-drop functionality. If you're not familiar with adding classes to an existing project using ClassWizard, just click the ClassWizard Add Class button and choose New from the pop-up menu. Table 15.4 contains the properties for the new class.

TABLE 15.4   ATTRIBUTES FOR THE CDragTree CLASS

Attribute	Value
Name	CDragTree
Base Class	CTreeCtrl
File	DragTree.cpp
Automation	None

ClassWizard is used to associate controls in the main dialog box with member variables in the COleTreeDlg class. The controls and their associated member variables are shown in Table 15.5.

TABLE 15.5   CONTROL MEMBER VARIABLES ADDED TO THE OleTreeDlg CLASS

Control ID	Category	Variable Type	Variable Name
IDC_EDIT	Value	CString	m_strEdit
IDC_LEFT	Control	CDragTree	m_treeLeft
IDC_RIGHT	Control	CDragTree	m_treeRight

ClassWizard is used to add message-handling functions to the OleTree project in order to handle messages from the new controls, using the values provided in Table 15.6. Note that messages reflected from the tree view control are prefixed by = inside the ClassWizard Message list box.

TABLE 15.6   MESSAGE-HANDLING INFORMATION FOR THE OLETREE PROJECT

Class Name	Object ID	Message	Member Function
COleTreeDlg	IDC_ADD	BN_CLICKED	OnAdd
CDragTree	CDragTree	=TVN_BEGINDRAG	OnBegindrag

As discussed earlier, COleDropTarget is the MFC base class that wraps the IDropTarget interface. In order to perform OLE drag-and-drop-operations, you must derive a class from COleDropTarget that is specialized for your data—for the OleTree project, this class is named CTreeDropTarget. The declaration for the CTreeDropTarget class is provided in Listing 15.6. This listing is saved as DropTarg.h in the project directory.

LISTING 15.6 THE `CTreeDropTarget` CLASS DECLARATION

```
#pragma once

class CTreeDropTarget:public COleDropTarget
{
// Constructor
public:
    CTreeDropTarget();

// Interfaces
public:
    virtual DROPEFFECT OnDragEnter(CWnd*           pWnd,
                                   COleDataObject* pObj,
                                   DWORD           dwKeyState,
                                   CPoint          pt);
    virtual DROPEFFECT OnDragOver(CWnd*           pWnd,
                                  COleDataObject* pObj,
                                  DWORD           dwKeyState,
                                  CPoint          pt);
    virtual BOOL OnDrop(CWnd*           pWnd,
                        COleDataObject* pObj,
                        DROPEFFECT      de,
                        CPoint          pt);
// Operations
public:
    void SetDragItem(HTREEITEM hItem);
    void SetParent(CTreeCtrl* pTree);

// Implementation
private:
    CTreeCtrl* m_pTree;
    BOOL       m_fIsDragging;
    HTREEITEM  m_hDragItem;

};
```

Listing 15.7 contains the implementation of the `CTreeDropTarget` class. This file is saved as `DropTarg.cpp` and is part of the OleTree project.

LISTING 15.7 THE IMPLEMENTATION OF THE `CTreeDropTarget` CLASS

```
#include "stdafx.h"
#include "DropTarg.h"
#include "fmtetc.h"

//
// CTreeDropTarget constructor
CTreeDropTarget::CTreeDropTarget()
{
```

```
        m_pTree = NULL;
        m_fIsDragging = FALSE;
        m_hDragItem = NULL;
    }


    //
    // OnDragEnter - called when a drag item initially passes over
    // the window associated with this object. In most cases, this call
    // is delegated to OnDragOver.
    DROPEFFECT CTreeDropTarget::OnDragEnter(CWnd*          pWnd,
                                            COleDataObject* pObj,
                                            DWORD           dwKeyState,
                                            CPoint          pt)
    {
        return OnDragOver(pWnd, pObj, dwKeyState, pt);
    }


    //
    // OnDragOver - called as a drag item passes over the window
    // associated with this object. Two things happen in this
    // function. First, the tree control item under the mouse is
    // highlighted to provide feedback to the user. Second, the
    // mouse cursor is set to the move cursor if the OLE Clipboard
    // has text data available, or the copy cursor if the text is
    // available and the Control key is pressed.
    DROPEFFECT CTreeDropTarget::OnDragOver(CWnd*           pWnd,
                                           COleDataObject* pObj,
                                           DWORD           dwKeyState,
                                           CPoint          pt)
    {
        UINT uHitTest = TVHT_ONITEM;
        HTREEITEM hTarget = m_pTree->HitTest(pt, &uHitTest);
        m_pTree->SelectDropTarget(hTarget);

        DROPEFFECT deResult = DROPEFFECT_NONE;
        if(pObj->IsDataAvailable(CF_TEXT))
        {
            if(dwKeyState & MK_CONTROL)
                deResult = DROPEFFECT_COPY;
            else
                deResult = DROPEFFECT_MOVE;
        }
        return deResult;
    }


    //
    // OnDrop - called when the user drops the drag item on our window
    // The text string is collected from the OLE Clipboard, and a new
    // item is created for the tree control.
```

continues

15

OLE DRAG AND DROP

LISTING **15.7**   CONTINUED

```cpp
BOOL CTreeDropTarget::OnDrop(CWnd*            pWnd,
                             COleDataObject*  pObj,
                             DROPEFFECT       de,
                             CPoint           pt)
{
    CFormatEtc  fe;
    STGMEDIUM   stg;
    // Test to see if the dropper can give us text
    BOOL fHasText = pObj->GetData(CF_TEXT, &stg, &fe);
    if(fHasText == FALSE)
        return FALSE;
    LPSTR pszObj = (LPSTR)GlobalLock(stg.hGlobal);
    if(pszObj)
    {
        HTREEITEM hNewItem;
        UINT uHitTest = TVHT_ONITEM;
        HTREEITEM hTarget = m_pTree->HitTest(pt, &uHitTest);
        // Drop to self is not allowed.
        if(m_fIsDragging && (hTarget == m_hDragItem))
            return FALSE;

        if(hTarget != NULL)
        {
            hNewItem = m_pTree->InsertItem(pszObj,
                                           hTarget,
                                           TVI_FIRST);
        }
        else // Add at root
        {
            hNewItem = m_pTree->InsertItem(pszObj,
                                           TVI_ROOT,
                                           TVI_LAST);
        }
        m_pTree->SelectDropTarget(NULL);
        m_pTree->SelectItem(hNewItem);
        GlobalUnlock(stg.hGlobal);
        GlobalFree(stg.hGlobal);
        return TRUE;
    }
    return FALSE;
}

//
// SetParent - called by the CTreeCtrl object associated with this
// drop target. The pointer to the CTreeCtrl object is used to add
// items to the tree, and highlight the drop target.
void CTreeDropTarget::SetParent(CTreeCtrl* pCtrl)
{
    m_pTree = pCtrl;
```

```
}

//
// SetDragItem - called by the CTreeCtrl object when a drag begins
// or ends. The drag item is used to prevent dropping an object on
// itself, which is a meaningless operation.
void CTreeDropTarget::SetDragItem(HTREEITEM hItem)
{
    m_hDragItem = hItem;
    if(hItem)
        m_fIsDragging = TRUE;
    else
        m_fIsDragging = FALSE;
}
```

DropTarg.cpp includes the fmtetc.h file, which is the CFormatEtc class provided earlier in Listing 15.2. DropTarg.cpp defines six functions:

- CTreeDropTarget. The constructor for the CTreeDropTarget class.

- SetParent. Sets a pointer to the CTreeCtrl object that owns this particular instance of CTreeDropTarget. This pointer is used to add items to the tree control after a successful drop.

- SetDragItem. Caches the current item involved in a drag and drop. Unless steps are taken to prevent it, the user can drag an item and drop it on itself. This operation has no purpose and is usually the result of an error. This function is called by the CTreeCtrl object associated with this drop target when a drag is started. If a drop is attempted over the item that started a drag and drop, it is ignored.

- OnDragEnter. Calls the OnDragOver function.

- OnDragOver. Determines the type of feedback returned to the user. In this case, DROPEFFECT_MOVE is returned when the cursor is over a valid target, unless the Ctrl key is pressed, in which case DROPEFFECT_COPY is returned.

- OnDrop. Manages the actual drop event. If a "drop to self" is attempted, the drop attempt is ignored. If a valid drop is attempted, the data is fetched from the OLE Clipboard and inserted into the tree control associated with this drop target.

The CDragTree class needs a few minor modifications, as shown in bold type in Listing 15.8. First, the DropTarg.h header file must be included. Next, two member variables must be added: a CTreeDropTarget member variable and a COleDataSource member variable. In addition, a new member function named Register is added to the class.

LISTING **15.8**   MODIFICATIONS (IN BOLD) TO THE CDragTree CLASS DECLARATION

```
#include "DropTarg.h"
class CDragTree : public CTreeCtrl
{
.
.
.
// Operations
public:
    void Register();

// Implementation
protected:
    CTreeDropTarget m_dropTarget;
    COleDataSource  m_dragSource;
.
.
.
};
```

Listing 15.9 provides the implementation of the CDragTree class. This listing includes only new functions or functions that require modifications. The constructor provided by ClassWizard is not included, for example, because it is not changed.

LISTING **15.9**   MEMBER FUNCTIONS ADDED TO THE CDragTree CLASS

```
// Handle the start of a drag. Since the tree control detects that
// the drag has actually begun, it isn't necessary to detect the
// mouse drag. The text of the drag item is placed onto the OLE
// Clipboard, and DoDragDrop is called. The handle of the item that
// is dragged is passed to m_dropTarget to prevent tree items being
// dropped on themselves.
void CDragTree::OnBegindrag(NMHDR* pNMHDR, LRESULT* pResult)
{
    NM_TREEVIEW* pNMTreeView = (NM_TREEVIEW*)pNMHDR;
    // Only nodes without children are eligible for dragging
    HTREEITEM hDragItem = pNMTreeView->itemNew.hItem;
    if(ItemHasChildren(hDragItem) == FALSE)
    {
        CString strItem = GetItemText(hDragItem);
        if(strItem.IsEmpty() == FALSE)
        {
            HGLOBAL hGlobal = GlobalAlloc(GMEM_SHARE,
                              strItem.GetLength() + 1);
            LPSTR    pszGlobal = (LPSTR)GlobalLock(hGlobal);
            ASSERT(pszGlobal);
            lstrcpy(pszGlobal, strItem);
            GlobalUnlock(hGlobal);
```

```
                m_dragSource.CacheGlobalData(CF_TEXT, hGlobal);

                m_dropTarget.SetDragItem(hDragItem);
                DROPEFFECT  de;
                de = m_dragSource.DoDragDrop(DROPEFFECT_COPY¦
                                             DROPEFFECT_MOVE);
                // The drop is over - delete the drag item if
                // necessary, and reset the drop target.
                if(de == DROPEFFECT_MOVE)
                    DeleteItem(hDragItem);
                m_dropTarget.SetDragItem(NULL);
                SelectDropTarget(NULL);
            }
        }
        *pResult = 0;
}

//
// Register the tree control window as a drop target, and
// pass a pointer to this window, so that the drop target
// can pass messages back to us.
void CDragTree::Register()
{
    m_dropTarget.Register(this);
    m_dropTarget.SetParent(this);
}
```

Two functions are added to `DragTree.cpp`:

- `OnBegindrag`. Handles the notification message sent after a user begins a drag in the tree control. If the drag item has no children, the text label associated with that item is placed on the OLE Clipboard through `m_dragSource` and the `COleSource` object, and a drag and drop is started.

- `Register`. Called by the window that contains the `CDragTree` object—for example, a dialog box or view. Calling this function registers the tree control as an OLE drop target.

Listing 15.10 contains modifications to the `COleTreeDlg` class, with the changed lines shown in bold. Two lines must be added to the `COleTreeDlg::OnInitDialog` function. The `Register` function is called for each tree view control. In addition, the function body must be supplied for the `OnAdd` function. This function is called after the user clicks the Add button in the main dialog box. The function checks to make sure that a string has been entered by the user and then inserts the item at the root level.

15

OLE DRAG AND DROP

LISTING 15.10   MESSAGE-HANDLING FUNCTIONS ADDED TO THE COleTreeDlg CLASS

```
BOOL COleTreeDlg::OnInitDialog()
{
    CDialog::OnInitDialog();
     .
     .
     .
    // TODO: Add extra initialization here
    AfxOleInit();
    m_treeLeft.Register();
    m_treeRight.Register();

    return TRUE;   // return TRUE  unless you set the focus to a control
}

void COleTreeDlg::OnAdd()
{
    UpdateData();
    if(m_strEdit.IsEmpty() == FALSE)
    {
        HTREEITEM hItem = m_treeRight.InsertItem(m_strEdit);
        ASSERT(hItem);
        m_treeRight.SelectItem(hItem);
    }
}
```

An #include directive must be added at the top of the OleTreeDlg.h file, just before the declaration of the COleTreeDlg class:

```
#include "DragTree.h"
```

Before compiling the OleTree project, include the MFC OLE support by adding afxole.h to the stdafx.h header file, just after the existing #include directives:

```
#include <afxole.h>
```

Compile and run the OleTree project. Add a few items to the tree control and then experiment by dragging items between the tree controls. Note that only leaf nodes can be moved. Figure 15.4 shows the OleTree main dialog box after several items have been added to the tree controls.

FIGURE 15.4

The OleTree main dialog box after several drag-and-drop operations.

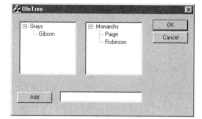

You also can experiment with drag and drops to and from other applications that support OLE drag and drop, such as Microsoft Word.

Summary

This chapter discusses data transfer using OLE uniform data transfer, the OLE Clipboard, and OLE drag and drop. You learned about the MFC classes used to implement OLE drag and drop, and you also looked at a sample project that adds drag-and-drop capability to a pair of tree controls.

15

OLE DRAG AND DROP

COM Threading Models

When developing COM components and applications that use those components, you need to understand COM's threading models. This chapter discusses how multithreading was added to the Component Object Model by introducing the idea of *apartments*.

In this chapter, you'll learn how your application can take advantage of the COM apartment model. You'll also learn the costs and benefits associated with using different types of apartments as well as the rules imposed by COM on using apartments.

COM Threading Alternatives

Before discussing the different threading models available for COM objects today under Windows 2000, let's review how the original COM release partitioned COM objects.

When the Component Object Model was released in 1993, it was strictly single threaded. You had two alternatives to choose from when implementing your COM objects:

- As an in-process server, using a DLL to host your COM object
- As an out-of-process server, using an EXE to host your COM object

These options are discussed in the next few sections.

In-process COM Servers Prior to Apartments

Today, as in previous releases of COM, in-process objects are located in DLLs that are loaded by clients and mapped into the clients' processes by the operating system. Back in the old single-threaded days, there was no overhead imposed by COM—method calls from the client to the COM object incur only one level of indirection through the object's interface. As you'll see later in this chapter, in-process calls can still be this efficient.

When a client requests the operating system to create an instance of a COM object, a series of steps are performed by the operating system and the COM server. Figure 16.1 shows how a client interacted with an in-process server prior to the introduction of apartments.

As shown in Figure 16.1, the steps performed to create and use an instance of an in-process COM object are as follows:

1. The client asks the operating system for an instance of a COM object by calling CoCreateInstance.

2. The operating system searches the Registry for a CLSID and loads the in-process server DLL.

3. The operating system calls DllGetClassObject to retrieve the class factory for the COM server.

4. The operating system uses the class factory to create an instance of the COM object.

5. The operating system returns an interface pointer for the COM object to the client.

6. The client calls through the interface pointer to a function in the DLL.

A major drawback with in-process servers is that they're not as robust as out-of-process servers. Just like any other DLL, an in-process server is located in the client's address space, and if it's poorly written, it can easily cause the client process to crash.

FIGURE 16.1

A client interacts directly with a COM in-process server.

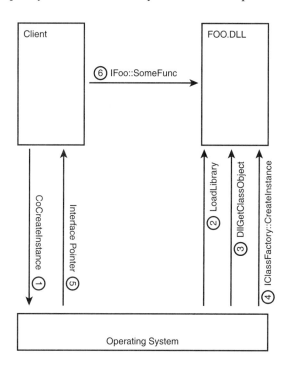

Out-of-Process Servers Prior to Apartments

Out-of-process servers are located in EXE files that are located and launched by the Windows 2000 operating system in a process that's separate from the client's process. This causes a bit of a problem, because all Win32 processes have separate and distinct address spaces. This means that the address of an interface pointer in one process is meaningless if provided directly to a client process.

When COM sees that two processes need to communicate, it creates the necessary plumbing to allow this to happen, as shown in Figure 16.2. The client process communicates through an in-process object known as a *proxy*, and the COM object communicates through an in-process object known as a *stub*.

FIGURE 16.2

*COM uses proxy
and stub objects to
communicate
across process
boundaries.*

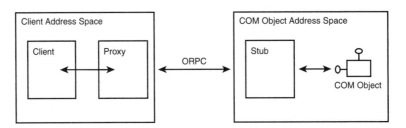

The communication between the proxy and stub objects is performed using the Microsoft *Object Remote Procedure Call (ORPC)* protocol. The process of moving data and addresses across the RPC boundary is known as *marshaling*. Marshaling between apartments is covered later in this chapter. More advanced details about marshaling are discussed in Chapter 17, "Custom COM Objects."

There are several advantages to using the proxy and stub architecture for communicating with out-of-process COM objects:

- The architecture is similar to standard DCE RPC, so it's based on a body of work that's well understood within the computing industry.
- The architecture could be easily extended to distributed cases for DCOM, as you'll see in Chapter 20, "DCOM."
- For the most part, clients and servers can work transparently with other parties via interface pointers without requiring conditional code to deal with in-process servers versus out-of-process servers.

In almost all cases, the only way a client can detect that a COM object is located "out of process" is that function calls to the COM object take longer to complete.

Managing Memory Across Processes

When clients and servers are located in separate address spaces, and memory is allocated and shared between these clients and servers, you know that life is going to become complicated. In COM, straightforward rules have been developed to help simplify the process of allocating and sharing memory between COM components:

- Top-level pointers passed as parameters refer to storage allocated by the caller.
- If memory is passed as an input parameter, it belongs to the client (the *caller*) of the function. The server (the *callee*) must make a local copy of the memory if it's going to use the memory the function returns.
- If dynamically allocated memory is passed as an output parameter, it's allocated by the callee and becomes the caller's responsibility after the function returns.

- If a parameter is used as input and output, the callee must properly release the memory before allocating storage to contain the output.

The *COM task allocator* is responsible for managing memory used by COM objects. When memory is marshaled, COM can only help you marshal storage if it has been allocated with the task allocator.

The COM task allocator exposes functions that work very much like the standard C runtime `malloc`, `free`, and `realloc` functions. You can use the COM task allocator in two ways:

- Directly, by using `IMalloc` interface member functions
- Indirectly, by using `CoTaskMemXXX` API helper functions

Using the `IMalloc` Interface

Here's a simplified definition of the `IMalloc` interface:

```
interface IMalloc : public IUnknown
{
public:
    virtual void* STDMETHODCALLTYPE Alloc(ULONG cb) = 0;
    virtual void* STDMETHODCALLTYPE Realloc(void* pv, ULONG cb) = 0;
    virtual void  STDMETHODCALLTYPE Free(void* pv) = 0;
    virtual ULONG STDMETHODCALLTYPE GetSize(void* pv) = 0;
    virtual int   STDMETHODCALLTYPE DidAlloc(void* pv) = 0;
    virtual void  STDMETHODCALLTYPE HeapMinimize(void) = 0;
};
```

In addition to the three standard `IUnknown` functions, the `IMalloc` interface has six member functions:

- `Alloc`. Allocates a block of memory (similar to the CRT `malloc` function).
- `Realloc`. Requests that a previously allocated block of memory be resized (similar to the CRT `realloc` function).
- `Free`. Releases a block of memory (similar to the CRT `free` function).
- `GetSize`. Returns the size of a block of allocated memory. This value may be larger than the originally requested size if the task allocator has added extra bytes for optimization or alignment purposes.
- `DidAlloc`. Can be used to determine whether this `IMalloc` interface was used to allocate a particular memory block.
- `HeapMinimize`. Requests that the COM task allocator reduce the size of the heap, if possible.

Note that the CRT `calloc` function has no equivalent. All memory retrieved from the COM task allocator may be uninitialized.

A pointer to `IMalloc` is retrieved by calling the `CoGetMalloc` function, as shown in Listing 16.1.

LISTING 16.1 ALLOCATING MEMORY USING THE `IMalloc` INTERFACE

```
STDMETHODIMP CSailInfo::GetSailInfo(SailInfo* psi)
{
    IMalloc* pMalloc = NULL;
    HRESULT hr = CoGetMalloc(1, &pMalloc);
    if(SUCCEEDED(hr))
    {
        psi = (SailInfo*)pMalloc->Alloc(sizeof(SailInfo));
        if(!psi)
            return E_OUTOFMEMORY;
        // Fill in SailInfo here...
        // ...
    }
    return S_OK;
}
```

Using the COM Task Allocator API Functions

As an alternative to using the `IMalloc` interface to the task allocator, you can also use API functions that provide convenient wrappers around `IMalloc`. There are three task allocator API functions:

- `CoTaskMemAlloc` allocates a block of memory from the COM task allocator, just like the `IMalloc::Alloc` function.
- `CoTaskMemFree` frees a block of memory, just like the `IMalloc::Free` function.
- `CoTaskMemRealloc` changes the size of a block of memory, just like the `IMalloc::Realloc` function.

In most cases, using the API functions is more convenient than using `IMalloc` directly. Listing 16.2 provides an example of using `CoTaskMemAlloc`.

LISTING 16.2 ALLOCATING MEMORY USING THE `CoTaskMemAlloc` API FUNCTION

```
STDMETHODIMP CSailInfo::GetSailInfo(SailInfo* psi)
{
    psi = (SailInfo*)CoTaskMemAlloc(sizeof(SailInfo));
    if(!psi)
        return E_OUTOFMEMORY;
    // Fill in SailInfo here...
    // ...
    return S_OK;
}
```

> **NOTE**
>
> Don't be tempted to bypass the COM task allocator. If the COM task allocator is
> bypassed, data will not be marshaled correctly in the out-of-process or cross-
> network cases.

Using COM with Apartments

With the release of COM for 32-bit Windows, there was a need to integrate multithreading into COM. Introducing the possibility of multithreaded COM objects and clients
added a new dimension to the ways that clients and objects interacted with each other.

Because there was already a large body of existing COM programming code, the multithreading solution had to meet the following requirements:

- Existing COM components that are unaware of the multithreading architecture
  must continue to work as expected.

- Only clients and servers that elect to use the multithreading architecture should pay
  any performance penalty—existing applications should not be affected.

- The fact that a particular client or COM server is multithreaded must be an implementation detail that can be changed without affecting the interface contract.

- A COM client must be able to use components that elect to be multithreaded,
  single-threaded, and legacy COM components simultaneously.

In order to meet these requirements, the idea of COM *apartments* was introduced. The
apartment is one of the basic building blocks in COM. Apartments are neither processes
nor threads; rather, they're logical compartments that contain COM objects.

Every COM object lives in exactly one apartment. Once a COM object has been instantiated inside an apartment, it can never change apartments—the relationship between a
COM object and its apartment is static for the life of the COM object. In fact, as you'll
see in Chapter 20, the DCOM wire protocol uses an apartment identifier to determine the
location of a COM object.

There are two types of COM apartments:

- A *single-threaded apartment*, or *STA*, which is only accessed by a single thread

- A *multithreaded apartment*, or *MTA*, which is accessed by multiple threads

In addition, there's a special STA, known as the *main STA*, that's the first STA created
for a process.

Understanding Single-threaded Apartments

Single-threaded apartments are only used by one thread. Any objects that exist in an STA live a simple life—assured that they will only ever be accessed by one thread for their entire lifetime. Objects that live in an STA can rely on this thread affinity and can use thread-local storage to cache information.

When a proxy is involved, the operating system serializes calls to an STA via a message queue running through a hidden window, as shown in Figure 16.3.

FIGURE 16.3

STA method requests are serialized via a message queue.

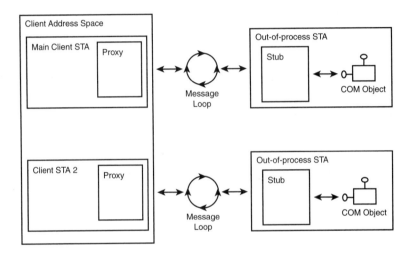

As shown in Figure 16.3, each process can have multiple STAs, and each STA can contain multiple COM objects.

As discussed earlier, the first STA created for a process is known as the *main STA*. This STA contains COM objects that do not indicate any preference for a threading model. The operating system assumes that these COM objects are not aware of the COM threading models and places them into the main STA. Life in this apartment will most closely simulate the happy-go-lucky environment experienced by COM objects before the dawn of multithreaded COM.

Understanding Multithreaded Apartments

Multithreaded apartments are used by multiple threads. When a proxy is involved, the operating system uses a thread pool to service the COM objects in the MTA. Unlike an STA, an MTA does not make any attempt to guarantee thread affinity or serialization between the thread pool and the COM objects in the apartment. On a multiprocessor machine, multiple threads may call a COM object simultaneously.

An MTA does not implement a hidden window in order to synchronize method calls—each method call can be immediately directed to the COM object that it targets (subject to marshaling). There's a maximum of one MTA per process—all MTA resident COM objects are located inside this single apartment.

If your COM component or application makes use of multiple threads and implements synchronization on shared data, you may improve performance by using the MTA.

Choosing Between the STA and MTA

COM is all about choices, particularly when it comes to selecting apartments. Both clients and COM objects get to select apartments for their threads—COM will give everyone what they ask for, and it always works. However, if you want to obtain the maximum performance from your components, it helps to have an understanding of how COM creates apartments and manages communication between these apartments.

Selecting an Apartment for Each Thread

Each client selects a threading model for every thread used to access a COM object. Every thread must call `CoInitialize` or `CoInitializeEx` before touching COM objects or making calls to the COM library. Here's a call to `CoInitialize`:

```
HRESULT hr = CoInitialize(NULL);
```

This is equivalent to requesting that the thread run in an STA:

```
HRESULT hr = CoInitializeEx(NULL, COINIT_APARTMENTTHREADED);
```

Every thread that calls `CoInitialize` or `CoInitializeEx` with the `COINIT_APARTMENTTHREADED` flag will cause a new STA to be created.

To request that a thread run in the MTA that belongs to the process, call `CoInitializeEx` with the `COINIT_MULTITHREADED` flag:

```
HRESULT hr = CoInitializeEx(NULL, COINIT_MULTITHREADED);
```

Any threads that call `CoInitializeEx` run in the same MTA for the process.

If a thread attempts to access a COM object or call a COM function before calling `CoInitialize` or `CoInitializeEx`, the function will be rejected by the operating system, in most cases. Some parts of COM can be used before calling `CoInitialize` or `CoInitializeEx`. For example, the task allocator API functions and the `IMalloc` interface can be used prior to initializing the COM library.

16

COM THREADING
MODELS

Which Apartment Is Best for Your Thread?

STA is fine for many applications, especially if the application is single threaded or if the COM objects are single threaded. As discussed later, it's always more efficient to match the apartment type of your components. For example, the Windows 2000 shell lives in STA; therefore, from a COM perspective, it's much more efficient for code that interacts with the shell to run in an STA than in an MTA.

MTA is great when you have multiple threads that need access to COM objects, especially when those objects can run in an MTA. Unlike in an STA, threads in the MTA can share access to COM objects. In an STA, the COM object can only be accessed by the thread that created it, unless you explicitly take steps to allow access from another thread.

Selecting an Apartment for Each COM Object

Every COM server specifies the type of apartment that its COM objects must live in. Although only two different types of apartments exist, four different types of apartment declarations are available for COM objects:

- `Apartment`. The object must live in an STA. Objects of this type are aware of the COM threading model and know that multiple instances of the object may exist in different STAs within the same process. This may require the class to synchronize access to common data structures.

- `Free`. The object must live in the MTA. The object is aware of the threading model and can be called by multiple threads safely.

- `Both`. The object can live in either the MTA or STA.

- `No entry`. The object is probably not thread aware and must live in the main STA. This type of object can ignore threading issues.

A COM server specifies a threading model in one of two ways:

- Out-of-process servers indicate their threading model by calling `CoInitialize` or `CoInitializeEx` when the server is launched.

- In-process servers are loaded into the calling process and never get a chance to call `CoInitializeEx`. Therefore, they must indicate their threading model in the Registry.

In-process servers indicate the threading model in the Registry as a named value under the `InProcServer32` key for the `CLSID`, as shown in Figure 16.4.

FIGURE 16.4

In-process servers specify their threading model with a Registry value.

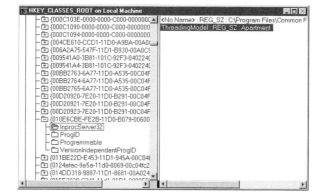

When an in-process server is launched, the operating system determines the appropriate apartment type for the object. If the apartment already exists, the server's class object is placed into the apartment; if necessary, a new apartment is created for the class object. Any instances of COM objects created by the class object will also be placed into this apartment.

As discussed earlier, each threading model has its own set of advantages and disadvantages. Using a threading model of Apartment allows a COM object to avoid many types of multithreading issues by guaranteeing that the object will live in an STA, whereas setting the threading model to Free enables a COM object to take advantage of Win32 multithreading and live in an MTA. Objects that decline to state a threading model are refusing to take part in any sort of multithreading.

But what about objects that specify Both as a threading model? Why choose Both rather than Free? There's a subtle difference between specifying Both or Free as a threading model:

- Choosing a threading model of Free indicates that the COM class absolutely requires an MTA. For example, the class may require worker threads that will cause performance problems inside an STA.

- Choosing a threading model of Both indicates that the COM class is equipped to handle multithreaded apartments. However, because the COM object may be instantiated inside an STA, this option should not be used if the class creates worker threads.

Mismatched Apartments Between Client and COM Object

So, what happens when a client and COM object each select different types of apartments? The good news is that COM will automatically create the exact type of apartment requested—regardless of whether it's a client or a COM class making the request. The bad news is that performance may suffer as a result.

For example, consider the case where a client calls `CoInitializeEx` with `COINIT_APARTMENTTHREADED`, marking the thread as living in an STA. The thread then creates an instance of a COM object that lives in an STA. As shown in Figure 16.5, COM creates an STA, and the COM object and client can communicate directly.

FIGURE 16.5

Communicating "in process" between compatible apartments does not require a proxy.

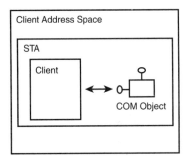

The interaction shown in Figure 16.5 is very efficient and does not require the operating system to establish any sort of proxy for communication between the client and COM object.

Now, consider the case where a client thread calls `CoInitializeEx` with `COINIT_MULTITHREADED`, marking the thread as living in an MTA, and creates an instance of a COM object that lives in an STA. As shown in Figure 16.6, the operating system creates an STA for the COM object and an MTA for the client's thread. The operating system then establishes a proxy/stub to manage communication between the COM object and client. This mechanism for cross-apartment communication is created even if the COM object is in process.

In Figure 16.6, method calls from the client to the COM object are serialized by the operating system through a window procedure. Obviously, this mechanism is going to be much less efficient than the STA-to-STA communication shown in Figure 16.5.

FIGURE **16.6**

Communicating between incompatible apartments requires a proxy.

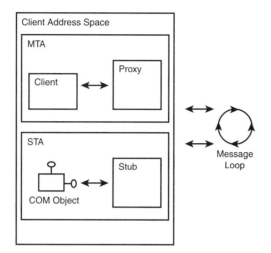

An Example of Cross-apartment Communication

The InProcSta project included on the CD-ROM accompanying this book creates instances of the TestFunc in-process COM object. These COM objects expose a dual interface named ITestFunc. ITestFunc includes one function, MakeRoundTrip, in addition to the IUnknown interfaces. The interface definition for ITestFunc is provided in Listing 16.3.

LISTING **16.3**   INTERFACE DEFINITION FOR THE ITestFunc INTERFACE

```
[
    object,
    uuid(EF13866E-7FFB-11D2-B868-00104B36573E),
    dual,
    helpstring("ITestFunc Interface"),
    pointer_default(unique)
]
interface ITestFunc : IDispatch
{
    [id(1), helpstring("Test func")] HRESULT MakeRoundTrip();
};
```

NOTE

The examples in this chapter use ATL, the Active Template Library. If you're not familiar with ATL or IDL, don't worry—you don't need to be an ATL expert to understand these examples. Building custom COM objects using ATL is discussed in detail in Chapter 17.

16

COM THREADING MODELS

The implementation of the ITestFunc interface is very simple. As shown in Listing 16.4, the MakeRoundTrip function simply returns S_OK to the caller. All this example does is help calculate the overhead for a simple function from the client to the COM object.

LISTING 16.4   THE IMPLEMENTATION OF THE MakeRoundTrip METHOD CALL

```
STDMETHODIMP CTestFunc::MakeRoundTrip()
{
    return S_OK;
}
```

As part of the building procedure for InProcSta, the ATL project will automatically register the projects, class, and interfaces. Before continuing to the next step, build the InProcSta project on your machine so that the TestFunc component is properly registered.

In order to test the efficiency of calling the TestFunc COM object from STA and MTA threads, the CD-ROM includes two versions of the ComTest project. The first version is provided in Listing 16.5 and can be found in the StaClient subdirectory. This version of ComTest initializes the main thread as an STA thread. A similar version of ComTest that creates an MTA can be found in the MtaClient subdirectory. The only difference between the two projects is the thread model passed as a parameter in CoInitializeEx.

LISTING 16.5   A SIMPLE CONSOLE MODE CLIENT THAT MAKES AN STA-TO-STA CALL TO
MakeRoundTrip

```
/*
 * COMTest.cpp
 *
 * A simple console-mode client used to perform some
 * measurements comparing the relative costs of calling
 * COM objects in different types of apartments.
 *
 */

#define _WIN32_WINNT 0x0500
#include <windows.h>
#include <wchar.h>
#include <objbase.h>

#include "inprocsta.h"

double GetElapsedTime();
void   StartTimer();
void   StopTimer();
void   HandleError(LPCWSTR strTitle, HRESULT hr);
```

```
int wmain()
{
    /* Initialize COM library */
    HRESULT hr = CoInitializeEx(NULL, COINIT_APARTMENTTHREADED);
    if(FAILED(hr))
    {
        HandleError(L"CoInitFailed", hr);
        return 0;
    }
    /*
     * Create an instance of the test object, and get a pointer
     * to its ITestFunc interface.
     */
    ITestFunc* pTestFunc = NULL;
    hr = CoCreateInstance(CLSID_TestFunc,
                          NULL,
                          CLSCTX_ALL,
                          IID_ITestFunc,
                          (void**)&pTestFunc);
    if(FAILED(hr))
    {
        HandleError(L"CoCreateFailed", hr);
        return 0;
    }
    /*
     * Call the interface a few times to get the function-call
     * cost for this type of Apartment/Apartment interaction.
     */
    StartTimer();
    for(int i = 0; i < 1000000; i++)
    {
        pTestFunc->MakeRoundTrip();
    }
    StopTimer();
    double elapsed = GetElapsedTime();
    wprintf(L"Elapsed time = %6.3f seconds", elapsed);
    /* Release the interface and the COM library. */
    pTestFunc->Release();
    CoUninitialize();
    return 0;
}

/*
 * Timer routines
 */
#include <time.h>
#include <sys/timeb.h>

_timeb startTime, endTime;
void StartTimer()
```

continues

LISTING 16.5   CONTINUED

```
{
    _ftime(&startTime);
}

void StopTimer()
{
    _ftime(&endTime);
}

double GetElapsedTime()
{
    double msecs = endTime.millitm - startTime.millitm;
    double secs = difftime(endTime.time, startTime.time);
    return secs + (msecs/1000);
}

/*
 * Error handling routine
 */
void HandleError(LPCWSTR strTitle, HRESULT hr)
{
    LPVOID lpMsgBuf;

    FormatMessageW(FORMAT_MESSAGE_ALLOCATE_BUFFER |
                   FORMAT_MESSAGE_FROM_SYSTEM,
                   NULL,
                   hr,
                   MAKELANGID(LANG_NEUTRAL, SUBLANG_DEFAULT),
                   (LPWSTR)&lpMsgBuf,
                   0,
                   NULL);
    MessageBoxW(NULL,
                (LPCWSTR)lpMsgBuf,
                strTitle,
                MB_OK | MB_ICONINFORMATION);
    LocalFree(lpMsgBuf);
}
```

Both versions of ComTest create an instance of the TestFunc class and retrieve a pointer to its ITestFunc interface. The MakeRoundTrip method is called one million times.

Build all three projects in release mode and then run them on your machine. On one of my machines, an IBM 704 server with dual Pentium Pro processors, I get the average execution times shown in Table 16.1.

TABLE 16.1   AVERAGE EXECUTION TIMES FOR COMTEST

Client	COM Class	Time (Seconds)
MTA	In-process STA	142.23
STA	In-process STA	0.047

In order to generate this table, the tests were run three times and averaged. The tests were run with Windows 2000 Beta 2; the times for your configuration will probably be different. No matter what type of machine you have, you'll get results that show a great difference in the overhead for function calls across apartments.

These results show that your application will potentially take a large performance hit if you make method calls across apartments. Of course, most applications don't spend all their time calling across apartments, but it's a good idea to be aware of the fact that you'll incur some extra overhead when calling between STA and MTA apartments.

Other Types of Client/Server Calls

A look at times for other types of inter-apartment calls shows that the biggest change in performance comes when an in-process COM object is moved from a compatible apartment to one that requires a proxy. On my machine, the performance cost is about 50 percent of the cost of moving the component out of process. Keep in mind that these times will vary on your hardware. For example, on a 533MHz Alpha workstation, the times are slightly greater, but the relative times are very close. Table 16.2 contains some timing results for inter-apartment COM method calls. Your results will vary slightly, but the relative performance should be fairly close to the results listed in the table.

TABLE 16.2   TIMING RESULTS FOR DIFFERENT TYPES OF INTER-APARTMENT CALLS TO COM OBJECTS

Client	COM Class	Time (Seconds)
MTA	In-proc STA	142.23
STA	In-proc STA	0.047
MTA	STA executable	260.92
STA	STA executable	289.484
MTA	In-proc MTA	0.047
STA	In-proc MTA	138.49
MTA	MTA executable	261.59
STA	MTA executable	282.54

Marshalling Between COM Apartments

The examples in the previous section discussed the case where the operating system automatically handled communication between apartments for you. This section discusses the case where you must share an interface pointer between apartments.

Consider the case of a client that creates several threads, each of which calls `CoInitializeEx` with `COINIT_APARTMENTTHREADED`. As discussed earlier, each of these threads lives in a separate STA.

In order to preserve thread-affinity rules, keep general order in the universe, and expand the number of examples in books about COM programming, COM interfaces may only be used inside the apartment that created the COM object. If the operating system catches you attempting to use an interface from a foreign thread, the method call will be rejected with an `HRESULT` of `RPC_E_WRONG_THREAD`.

> **NOTE**
>
> Don't try to bend this rule. The operating system cannot catch every possible violation of the wrong-thread rule. For example, a thread that creates an in-process STA can actually pass its interface pointers to other threads and won't be caught by the operating system. However, if that component uses thread-local storage or isn't thread safe, the component will not work correctly.

If you need to pass an interface pointer between apartments, you must first write the state of the interface pointer into a COM stream. The COM stream can then be passed between apartments and reconstituted into an interface pointer as needed.

Windows 2000 provides a function, `CoMarshalInterThreadInterfaceInStream`, that enables you to save the state of an interface pointer in a stream, and it returns an `IStream` interface pointer to that stream:

```
HRESULT hr = CoMarshalInterThreadInterfaceInStream(IID_ITestFunc,
                                                   pTestFunc,
                                                   &g_pStream);
```

`CoMarshalInterThreadInterfaceInStream` has three parameters:

- The IID of the interface to be serialized.

- The interface pointer to be serialized.

- The address of an IStream interface pointer that can be used to access the stream containing the serialized interface pointer. The IStream interface pointer can safely be passed between apartments in the same process.

Windows 2000 also offers CoGetInterfaceAndReleaseStream, which is used to rebuild an interface pointer, given an interface pointer to a stream:

```
ITestFunc* pTestFunc = NULL;
HRESULT hr = CoGetInterfaceAndReleaseStream(g_pStream,
                                            IID_ITestFunc,
                                            (void**)&pTestFunc);
```

CoGetInterfaceAndReleaseStream has three parameters:

- The interface pointer to a stream that contains the serialized interface pointer.

- The IID of the interface pointer to be retrieved.

- The address of the variable that will be filled with the retrieved interface pointer.

The steps required to marshal the interface pointer into a stream across the apartments are shown in Figure 16.7 and detailed in the following list:

FIGURE 16.7

Marshaling an interface pointer between apart-ments.

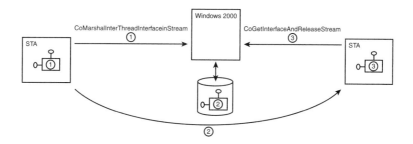

1. The thread that owns the interface pointer must write the interface pointer's state into a COM stream by using the CoMarshalInterThreadInterfaceInStream function.

2. After the state of the interface pointer has been written to the stream, the stream's interface pointer can be safely handed to any apartment in the process.

3. The receiving thread calls CoGetInterfaceAndReleaseStream to rebuild a copy of the interface pointer, based on information serialized to the COM stream.

As a somewhat contrived example of how interface pointers are passed between threads, the CD-ROM includes three projects:

- ExeSta, an EXE COM server that exports a version of the ITestFunc interface used earlier in the chapter.
- AptClient, a client of ExeSta that incorrectly attempts to share an interface pointer between two apartments; the attempt is blocked by the interprocess proxy for ITestFunc.
- AptMarshal, a client of ExeSta that correctly shares an ITestFunc interface pointer between two apartments.

The source code for ExeSta isn't shown here—it's an ATL project very similar to the InProcSta project presented earlier in the chapter (except that it's an EXE server instead of a DLL). The COM objects created by ExeSta live in an STA that's always located out of process from any of its clients.

The Wrong Way to Share Interface Pointers

First, let's look at the wrong way to share interface pointers between apartments. The AptClient.cpp source file is provided in Listing 16.6. The AptClient project also contains the ExeSta_i.c source file from the ATL component.

LISTING 16.6 SHARING RAW INTERFACE POINTERS IN AptClient.cpp

```
/*
 * AptClient.cpp
 * Demonstrates the wrong way to share interface pointers between
 * apartments.
 */
#define _WIN32_WINNT 0x0500
#include <windows.h>
#include <wchar.h>
#include <objbase.h>

#include "exesta.h"

DWORD WINAPI ThreadFunc(LPVOID lpv);
void HandleError(LPCWSTR strTitle, HRESULT hr);

ITestFunc* g_pTestFunc = NULL;

int wmain()
{
    /* Initialize the main STA */
    HRESULT hr = CoInitializeEx(NULL, COINIT_APARTMENTTHREADED);
    if(FAILED(hr))
```

```
    {
        HandleError(L"CoInitFailed", hr);
        return 0;
    }

    /* Get a pointer to the ITestFunc interface */
    hr = CoCreateInstance(CLSID_TestFunc,
                          NULL,
                          CLSCTX_ALL,
                          IID_ITestFunc,
                          (void**)&g_pTestFunc);
    if(FAILED(hr))
    {
        HandleError(L"CoCreateFailed", hr);
        return 0;
    }

    hr = g_pTestFunc->MakeRoundTrip();
    if(FAILED(hr))
    {
        HandleError(L"Method call failed in main STA", hr);
        return 0;
    }

    /* Spin up a second thread to party with our interface ptr. */
    DWORD threadID;
    HANDLE hThread = CreateThread(NULL,
                                  0,
                                  ThreadFunc,
                                  NULL,
                                  0,
                                  &threadID);

    /* Wait for the second thread to complete */
    WaitForSingleObject(hThread, INFINITE);
    g_pTestFunc->Release();
    CoUninitialize();
    return 0;
}

/*
 * The thread function initializes the second STA, and tries to
 * use the raw interface pointer from the first STA. The call
 * is rejected by the proxy.
 */
DWORD WINAPI ThreadFunc(LPVOID lpv)
{
    HRESULT hr = CoInitializeEx(NULL, COINIT_APARTMENTTHREADED);
    if(FAILED(hr))
    {
```

continues

LISTING 16.6 CONTINUED

```
        HandleError(L"CoInit for 2nd STA failed", hr);
        return 0;
    }
    /* This line fails. */
    hr = g_pTestFunc->MakeRoundTrip();
    if(FAILED(hr))
    {
        HandleError(L"Method call in 2nd STA failed", hr);
        return 0;
    }
    CoUninitialize();
    return 0;
}
/*
 * Display an error message using the system error string.
 */
void HandleError(LPCWSTR strTitle, HRESULT hr)
{
    LPVOID lpMsgBuf;

    FormatMessage(FORMAT_MESSAGE_ALLOCATE_BUFFER|
                  FORMAT_MESSAGE_FROM_SYSTEM,
                  NULL,
                  hr,
                  MAKELANGID(LANG_NEUTRAL, SUBLANG_DEFAULT),
                  (LPWSTR)&lpMsgBuf,
                  0,
                  NULL);
    MessageBox(NULL,
               (LPCWSTR)lpMsgBuf,
               strTitle,
               MB_OK | MB_ICONINFORMATION);
    LocalFree(lpMsgBuf);
}
```

The AptClient program creates two threads, each of which joins an STA by calling CoInitializeEx. The program then tries to use an interface pointer created in the first STA in the second STA. In this case, the component is out of process, so the interface pointer actually belongs to a proxy.

Proxies are the hall monitors of COM—and they will check to make sure your thread is allowed to enter the COM object's STA. In this case, the second thread is not allowed to access the interface, and the call will be rejected. The next section shows the correct way to avoid this problem.

The Correct Way to Share Interface Pointers

Now let's look at the correct way to share interface pointers between apartments. The
AptMarshal.cpp source file is provided in Listing 16.7.

LISTING 16.7   SHARING MARSHALED INTERFACE POINTERS IN AptMarshal.cpp

```
/*
 * AptMarshal.cpp
 * Demonstrates the right way to share interface pointers between
 * apartments.
 */
#define _WIN32_WINNT 0x0500
#include <windows.h>
#include <wchar.h>
#include <objbase.h>

#include "exesta.h"

DWORD WINAPI ThreadFunc(LPVOID lpv);
void HandleError(LPCWSTR strTitle, HRESULT hr);

IStream* g_pStream = NULL;

int wmain()
{
    /* Initialize the main STA */
    HRESULT hr = CoInitializeEx(NULL, COINIT_APARTMENTTHREADED);
    if(FAILED(hr))
    {
        MessageBox(NULL, L"CoInitFailed", L"main", MB_ICONHAND);
        return 0;
    }

    /* Get a pointer to the ITestFunc interface */
    ITestFunc* pTestFunc = NULL;
    hr = CoCreateInstance(CLSID_TestFunc,
                          NULL,
                          CLSCTX_ALL,
                          IID_ITestFunc,
                          (void**)&pTestFunc);
    if(FAILED(hr))
    {
        HandleError(L"CoCreateFailed", hr);
        return 0;
    }

    hr = pTestFunc->MakeRoundTrip();
    if(FAILED(hr))
```

continues

LISTING 16.7 CONTINUED

```
    {
        HandleError(L"Method call failed in main STA", hr);
        return 0;
    }

    /* Serialize the interface pointer into a stream */
    hr = CoMarshalInterThreadInterfaceInStream(IID_ITestFunc,
                                               pTestFunc,
                                               &g_pStream);
    if(SUCCEEDED(hr))
    {
        /* Spin up a second thread. */
        DWORD threadID;
        HANDLE hThread = CreateThread(NULL,
                                      0,
                                      ThreadFunc,
                                      NULL,
                                      0,
                                      &threadID);

        /* Wait for the second thread to complete */
        WaitForSingleObject(hThread, INFINITE);
        CloseHandle(hThread);
    }
    else
    {
        HandleError(L"Marshaling failed", hr);
    }

    pTestFunc->Release();
    CoUninitialize();
    return 0;
}

/*
 * The thread function initializes the second STA, and uses the
 * serialized interface pointer from the first STA. The call is
 * accepted by the proxy.
 */
DWORD WINAPI ThreadFunc(LPVOID lpv)
{
    HRESULT hr = CoInitializeEx(NULL, COINIT_APARTMENTTHREADED);
    if(FAILED(hr))
    {
        HandleError(L"CoInit for 2nd STA failed", hr);
        return 0;
    }

    /* Pull the interface pointer out of the stream */
```

```
    ITestFunc* pTestFunc = NULL;
    hr = CoGetInterfaceAndReleaseStream(g_pStream,
                                        IID_ITestFunc,
                                        (void**)&pTestFunc);
    if(FAILED(hr))
    {
        HandleError(L"Unmarshal failed", hr);
        return 0;
    }

    hr = pTestFunc->MakeRoundTrip();
    if(FAILED(hr))
    {
        HandleError(L"Method call in 2nd STA failed", hr);
        return 0;
    }

    pTestFunc->Release();
    CoUninitialize();
    return 0;
}
/*
 * Display an error message using the system error string.
 */
void HandleError(LPCWSTR strTitle, HRESULT hr)
{
    LPVOID lpMsgBuf;

    FormatMessage(FORMAT_MESSAGE_ALLOCATE_BUFFER¦
                  FORMAT_MESSAGE_FROM_SYSTEM,
                  NULL,
                  hr,
                  MAKELANGID(LANG_NEUTRAL, SUBLANG_DEFAULT),
                  (LPWSTR)&lpMsgBuf,
                  0,
                  NULL);
    MessageBox(NULL,
               (LPCWSTR)lpMsgBuf,
               strTitle,
               MB_OK ¦ MB_ICONINFORMATION);
    LocalFree(lpMsgBuf);
}
```

16
COM THREADING MODELS

The source code for `AptMarshal.cpp` in Listing 16.7 looks a great deal like the source code for `AptClient.cpp` in Listing 16.6. The only difference between the two projects is the way the interface pointer is passed between threads.

Instead of using a global `ITestFunc` interface pointer, Listing 16.7 uses a global `IStream` interface pointer. The `IStream` interface pointer is set when the first thread calls the `CoMarshalInterThreadInterfaceInStream` function. The second thread then uses `CoGetInterfaceAndReleaseStream` to pull the interface pointer from the `IStream`.

Summary

This chapter discussed the COM threading model and how multithreaded apartments (MTAs) and single-threaded apartments (STAs) function. Every thread and component must select an apartment to live in; this selection can impact performance and robustness. There are also rules defining how threads running in different apartments may share interface pointers—the pointer must be marshaled by writing it out to a stream, which can then be shared between apartments.

Custom COM Objects

This chapter discusses creating custom COM objects using the ActiveX class library. Many of the issues involved with creating custom components are covered in this chapter—for example, creating custom interfaces using the Interface Definition Language, using monikers, using connection points, and implementing custom marshaling. This chapter includes several examples that demonstrate how the Active Template Library can be used to easily create custom COM objects.

Using IDL

As discussed in earlier chapters, COM is a binary standard that generally tries to remain language neutral. Some languages are more "COM friendly" than others, but COM doesn't make many restrictions on languages, other than:

- The language must be capable of calling a function indirectly, through an interface function table. This function table is commonly called a vtable, because it has the same format commonly employed by C++ compilers to implement virtual functions.

- The language must have a way of tracking reference counting, at least internally. All clients of COM objects must be capable of properly managing reference counting on any COM objects that they use. Some languages, such as Visual Basic, hide the complexity of reference counting from the programmer and manage the reference counting in the language runtime library.

Given these relatively small restrictions, almost all procedural languages can be made to work with COM.

This causes a problem when you're deciding how interfaces for COM objects should be defined. There are nearly as many methods for defining interfaces as there are languages. How should two computing languages that have different philosophies—such as VB and C++, for example—share information about interfaces?

One industry-standard method for defining interactions between clients and servers is *IDL* or *Interface Definition Language*, developed by the Open Software Foundation. If you've developed distributed applications using Remote Procedure Call (RPC) interfaces, you've used IDL to define your interfaces. If you have no experience with RPC, don't worry—IDL has a syntax that's similar to C or C++, with extra extensions that contain necessary information for defining interfaces.

Microsoft uses a version of IDL known as *MIDL*, which stands for *Microsoft Interface Definition Language*. MIDL is very much like IDL, with a few extra syntax features used to help define COM classes and interfaces. A typical MIDL source file is shown in Listing 17.1.

LISTING 17.1 A TYPICAL MIDL SOURCE FILE

```
import "oaidl.idl";
import "ocidl.idl";
    [
        object,
        uuid(84697126-9A17-11D2-B883-00104B36573E),
        dual,
        helpstring("ISailBoat Interface"),
        pointer_default(unique)
    ]
    interface ISailBoat : IDispatch
    {
        [id(1)] HRESULT Tack([in] short newHeading);
        [id(2)] HRESULT Jibe([in] short newHeading);
        [id(3)] HRESULT LeakCash([in] long cashToLeak);
        [id(4)] HRESULT LeakWater([in] long gallonsToLeak);
        [id(5)] HRESULT GetPassengerWeight([out] short* pSize,
                        [out, size_is(,*pSize)] short** rgWeight);
    };

[
    uuid(8469711A-9A17-11D2-B883-00104B36573E),
    version(1.0),
    helpstring("Boat 1.0 Type Library")
]

library CodevBoatLib
{
    importlib("stdole32.tlb");
    importlib("stdole2.tlb");

    [
        uuid(84697129-9A17-11D2-B883-00104B36573E),
        helpstring("SailBoat Class")
    ]
    coclass SailBoat
    {
        [default] interface ISailBoat;
    };
};
```

The MIDL source provided in Listing 17.1 has three main sections (the first line of each section is highlighted in bold):

- The declaration of the ISailBoat interface. This describes the attributes of the interface and specifies the signature for each function in the interface.

- The declaration of CodevBoatLib, which is used to generate a type library. Type libraries are a binary representation of the IDL declaration and are discussed in the section, "Using Type Libraries," later in this chapter.

- The declaration of the `SailBoat` coclass. The component object class, or *coclass*, is declared inside the type library, and it lists the interfaces (and other objects) that are part of the `SailBoat` COM class.

Each of these objects begins with a list of descriptive attributes enclosed in brackets, like this:

```
[object]
```

Attributes are discussed in the next section.

In addition to interfaces and coclasses, here are some other objects you may commonly see in a MIDL file:

- `dispinterface`. Marks an Automation-compatible interface as being derived from `IDispatch`.
- `enum`. Used to create an enumerated type, just as in C and C++.
- `struct`. Used to create an aggregated type, just as in C and C++.
- `union`. Used to create an aggregated type that contains one of several possible types, just as in C and C++.

This is only a partial list. The MIDL documentation in the Platform SDK contains a complete IDL language reference.

Understanding MIDL Attributes

Elements in an IDL source file can be tagged with attributes enclosed in braces. Some of these attributes are optional—you may see the attributes on one interface, but not another. Other attributes are required for all interfaces. For example, a COM interface requires the following two attributes:

- `object`. Specifies to the MIDL compiler that this is a COM interface rather than an RPC interface.
- `uuid`. Contains the COM IID for the interface.

Every COM interface will have these two attributes. The `ISailBoat` interface provided in Listing 17.1 has three additional commonly used attributes:

- `dual`. Specifies that the interface can be called as an Automation interface or through its function table.
- `helpstring`. Contains a description of the interface. This description is embedded into the type library, and some development tools will display this string as an aid to developers using the interface.

- `pointer_default`. Defines the default behavior for pointers in the interface. More information about IDL pointer notation is provided in the section, "Pointers and IDL," later in this chapter.

Here are some other common MIDL attributes:

- `hidden`. Prevents the interface, coclass, or library from being displayed in a browser.

- `size_is`. Specifies the size of a dynamic array using another parameter as an argument, as in `size_is(nSize)`.

- `max_is`. Specifies the maximum index for a dynamic array using another parameter as an argument, as in `max_is(nSize)`.

- `iid_is`. Specifies the COM interface ID for an interface pointer passed as a parameter using another parameter as an argument, as in `iid_is(riid)`.

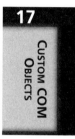

Methods in the `ISailBoat` interface are prefixed with a dispatch ID, an index that's required for Automation interfaces (such as `dual` and `dispinterface`), or any interface derived from `IDispatch`. The dispatch ID is used by Automation to identify each function. Here's the syntax for a method using a dispatch ID:

```
[id(1)] HRESULT SomeFunc();
```

Here are two other common MIDL attributes used with methods:

- `propput`. Specifies a function that's used to set the value of a property exposed by the interface. The last parameter passed to the method must be an `[in]` parameter that will be used to set the property's value. The property must have the same name as the method.

- `propget`. Specifies a method that's used to retrieve a value from a property exposed by the interface. The last parameter passed to the method must be an `[out,retval]` parameter that will be used as the property's value. The property must have the same name as the method.

Each property can have an maximum of one method that contains `propput` and one method that contains `propget`.

Compiling a MIDL Source File

MIDL source files are compiled by invoking the MIDL compiler on the command line:

```
MIDL Sail.idl
```

If you're using Visual C++ to create a custom COM object using the ATL COM Wizard, the MIDL compiler will be invoked automatically for you.

Given an input IDL file named `Sail.idl`, the MIDL compiler generates five files:

- `dlldata.c`. Contains the functions required for the proxy/stub DLL.
- `sail.h`. Contains C and C++ versions of the interface definitions.
- `sail_i.c`. Contains definitions of the CLSIDs and IIDs used by the interfaces, type libraries, and coclasses found in `Sail.idl`.
- `sail_p.c`. Contains proxy/stub marshaling code.
- `sail.tlb`. Contains the type library for `Sail.idl`. The type library is a binary version of the IDL file and is used by programming languages such as Visual Basic that cannot read IDL files. Type libraries are also used by Automation controllers written in other languages in order to discover properties and methods exposed by a COM object.

The `sail_i.c` file is usually included in one of the files used by C or C++ clients of the `ISail` interface, or it's linked into the client executable separately. This file contains the GUIDs used by all the objects found in the source IDL file.

The files `sail_i.c`, `sail_p.c`, `sail.h`, and `dlldata.c` can be compiled together to create a proxy/stub DLL. This DLL is required if you're marshaling non[nd]Automation-compatible interfaces across apartments. More information about creating a proxy/stub DLL is provided in the section, "Compiling and Registering the Standard Proxy/Stub DLL," later in this chapter.

If you're targeting Windows NT 4.0 or later, consider using the `/Oicf` compiler switch when invoking the MIDL compiler. This notifies the MIDL compiler to generate code that uses interpretive marshaling features found only in Windows NT 4.0 and Windows 2000. Interpretive marshaling can greatly reduce the size of the marshaling code used for an interface, and is used for all standard COM interfaces in Windows 2000. If you are building a COM object using the Visual C++ 6.0 ATL COM Wizard, the `/Oicf` compiler switch is defined automatically.

Using Type Libraries

IDL files were originally created with the C and C++ programmer in mind. Many languages cannot use IDL source files or the C and C++ source files generated by the MIDL compiler. For this reason, the MIDL compiler also generates a *type library*, which is a binary representation of the IDL source file.

Languages such as Java and Visual Basic extract information from type libraries instead of using the IDL source. This allows these tools to provide a simple user interface that displays type library information.

If you are programming with C or C++, you can use the LoadTypeLib or LoadRegTypeLib function to load the type library; these functions return a pointer to the ITypeLib interface. A related interface, ITypeLib2, is derived from ITypeLib, and also returns type library attributes. The ITypeInfo and ITypeInfo2 interfaces are used to describe objects in the type library, and are returned by ITypeLib methods.

Using Structures in IDL

Custom structures are defined in IDL much as they are in C and C++. Typically, the structure is defined as a typedef. For example, the following code fragment defines a structure type named MyRect:

```
typedef struct tagMyRect
{
    int left;
    int right;
    int top;
    int bottom;
}MyRect;
```

After the MyRect structure is defined in the IDL file, it can be used just like any other parameter:

```
HRESULT GetOurRect([out]MyRect* pRect);
HRESULT DrawOurRect([in]MyRect* pRect);
```

Structures are not Automation compatible. If you define and use a structure in your IDL, you must use custom interfaces, and you must build and register a proxy/stub DLL for your COM object. This isn't difficult, but it does require an extra step when building your COM objects. The steps required to build and register proxy/stub DLLs are discussed in the section, "Compiling and Registering the Standard Proxy/Stub DLL," later in this chapter.

Using Enumerations in IDL

Like structures, enumerations are defined in IDL just as they are in C and C++. The following fragment defines an enumeration type named BaseballClubs that contains a few major league baseball teams:

```
typedef enum tagBaseballClubs
{
    Padres = 0,
    Braves,
    Yankees,
    Astros,
    Indians,
    Dodgers
}BaseballClubs;
```

17

CUSTOM COM OBJECTS

After the enumeration is defined, it can be used just like any other type:

```
HRESULT PlayBall([in]BaseballClubs* pClub);
HRESULT GetWorldChamps([out]BaseballClubs* pClub);
```

Later in this chapter, the custom COM object defines an enumeration containing different processor types that are capable of running Windows 2000.

Pointers and IDL

If you're one of those people who thought pointers were a difficult topic when learning C or C++, consider what happens when pointers are transmitted between distributed components. If you're writing the IDL for interfaces supported by COM objects, your clients may be in the same process, or they may "out of process," or they may be running on a different machine, as shown in Figure 17.1.

FIGURE 17.1

An interface defines the contract, not the locations of the client or server.

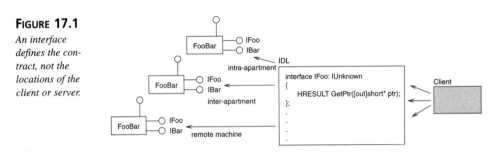

As discussed in the previous chapter, COM objects are placed into apartments that define their threading model. COM objects may be placed in a Multi-Threaded Apartment (MTA) or a Single-Threaded Apartment (STA). There is only one MTA per process, but there may be multiple STAs. The first STA created in a process is known as the main STA. Once a COM object is created inside an apartment, it never moves to another apartment.

When a client is in the same apartment as the server, pointers can be passed directly between the client and server, as shown in Figure 17.2.

When a client and server are located in different processes, a pointer to an address in the client's process is meaningless in the address space of the server. In order for the interface to be useful in both processes, it must be marshaled. As shown in Figure 17.3, an address in the address space of the current process is provided to the client or server.

FIGURE 17.2

No marshaling is needed inside an apartment.

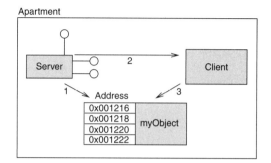

FIGURE 17.3

When data is being marshaled between processes, the pointers are managed by the COM runtime library.

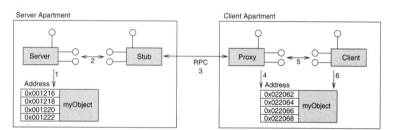

A similar issue occurs when the client and server are located on separate machines. Marshaling of interface pointers between apartments was covered in Chapter 16, "COM Threading Models." Later in this chapter, custom marshaling will be discussed. For now, it's enough to understand that the proxy/stub DLL and the COM library must conspire together to make it possible for pointers to be exchanged across apartment boundaries.

Potentially, a great deal of work may be required when a pointer is shared between processes or machines. You specify the effort required for your pointers by using MIDL attributes.

Three different types of pointers are supported by COM:

- *Full*. This is the most expensive pointer type, and it's indicated with the `ptr` attribute.

- *Unique*. This pointer requires less work from the COM runtime library than a full pointer, because it does not support pointer aliasing. This pointer type uses the `unique` attribute.

- *Reference*. This is the least expensive pointer type, and it does not support aliasing or `NULL` values. This pointer type uses the `ref` attribute.

You can define a different pointer type attribute for each pointer by using the pointer type attribute immediately before the parameter:

```
HRESULT Snore([in, ref] short* pDecibels);
```

Typically, you'll use a single pointer type for most of your pointers. You can define a default pointer type that will be used for all pointers in an interface with the `pointer_default` attribute:

```
[
    object,
    uuid(12345678-1234-1234-1234-000000000099),
    pointer_default(unique)
]
interface ICat : ISleepyAnimal
{
}
```

The default pointer type will be set to `ref` if you don't specify a default pointer type.

The full pointer type allows pointer *aliasing*, where multiple pointers in the function call may refer to the same address. In return for this capability, you incur the cost required when the interface is marshaled—each pointer must be stored in a dictionary that's consulted in order to properly handle aliased pointers.

The full and unique pointer types also allow NULL values, so the marshaling code must test to ensure that values aren't written to a NULL address. This gives you some flexibility when using your interface, but it increases the work required at runtime.

Using Direction Attributes in IDL

Every parameter in an IDL source file has an attribute that includes its direction. This enables the MIDL compiler to create the proper marshaling code for the interface. There are three options:

- [in]. Specifies a parameter that's sent from the client to the server. If the server has a use for the data after the function call completes, it must make a local copy of the data, because it actually belongs to the caller.
- [out]. Specifies a parameter that carries data from the server to the client. This parameter must be a pointer. The client allocates the top-level pointer, but any allocations other than to the top-level pointer are made by the server and become the client's responsibility.
- [in,out]. Specifies that data is allocated by the client and passed to the server, which may optionally free the data and allocate new data for the client. This parameter must be a pointer. The new data, if any, becomes the client's responsibility.

Creating Custom Components Using ATL

The ActiveX Template Library, or *ATL*, is a template-based library that simplifies the building of very efficient COM objects and ActiveX controls. COM objects built with ATL are much smaller than COM objects built using MFC. In fact, COM objects built using ATL approach the size of objects built from scratch without a class library.

The latest version of ATL, version 3.0, is included with the Visual C++ 6.0 compiler. ATL 3.0 includes support for a wide variety of COM objects, such as small COM objects that do not present a user interface, ActiveX controls derived from standard Windows controls, controls optimized for Internet Explorer, and many more.

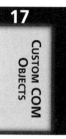

Commonly Used ATL Classes

No matter what type of COM object you plan on building with ATL, there are a few classes you'll use for every project:

- CComObject. Implements IUnknown for your COM object. ATL also includes specialized versions of this class, such as CComObjectStack, if your COM object lives on the stack, and CComAggObject for aggregated COM objects. The CComObject class defined for your project uses multiple inheritance to derive from all interfaces supported by the COM object it represents.

- CComObjectRootEx. A template class that includes the basic IUnknown functionality used by CComObject. This is a template that's instantiated using a threading model class as a parameter. The threading model class contains functions that are threading-model dependent, such as AddRef and Release.

- CComObjectRoot. A typedef made for each project that consists of CComObjectRootEx parameterized with the appropriate threading model class.

- CComModule. Provides the implementation for a COM server suitable for an EXE or DLL. CComModule manages the class factory, class objects, and component registration.

Using the ATL COM Interface Map

ATL uses macros to implement support for QueryInterface through an interface map. These macros are similar to the macros used by MFC to implement message maps.

Conceptually, the ATL interface map macros create a map collection, with each map entry containing an interface ID and information used to find the appropriate interface in the COM object, as shown in Figure 17.4.

FIGURE 17.4

The ATL interface map simplifies support for multiple interfaces.

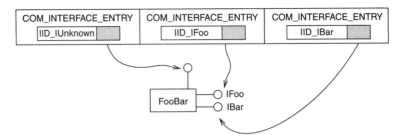

There are several interface map macros. Here are the three most commonly used macros:

- `BEGIN_COM_MAP`
- `END_COM_MAP`
- `COM_INTERFACE_ENTRY`

The interface map begins with the `BEGIN_COM_MAP` macro and ends with the `END_COM_MAP` macro. Between these two macros, more macros can be used to specify the interfaces supported by the COM object:

```
BEGIN_COM_MAP(CMonkey)
    COM_INTERFACE_ENTRY(IEatBananas)
END_COM_MAP()
```

The `BEGIN_COM_MAP` macro is called with the COM object's ATL class as a parameter. All entries inside the interface map are treated as members of this class.

The `COM_INTERFACE_ENTRY` macro is called with the name for the supported interface. The ATL framework uses the Visual C++ `__uuidof()` operator to determine the IID of the interface and adds the interface to the COM object's interface map.

Using ATL Wizards

Two wizards are supplied by Visual C++ to simplify the building of custom COM objects with the ActiveX Template Library:

- *ATL COM AppWizard* is used to create a project that build a module—either a DLL, EXE, or service—that hosts COM objects.
- *ATL Object Wizard* allows you to add a COM object to your project.

These wizards are discussed in the next two sections.

Using the ATL COM AppWizard

The easiest way to create an ATL project is to use the ATL COM AppWizard. This wizard creates a skeleton project for you, based on the type of project you select (see Figure 17.5).

FIGURE 17.5

The ATL COM AppWizard.

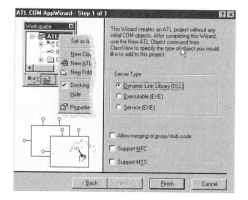

You can build three types of projects using the ATL COM AppWizard:

- *DLL.* The module will be built as an in-process DLL. As discussed in previous chapters, this is the most efficient type of COM object.
- *EXE.* The module will be built as an out-of-process server. As discussed in earlier chapters, this type of COM object is more robust than a DLL object.
- *Service.* The module will be built as a Windows 2000 service.

If you choose to build your project as a DLL, you have three additional options that are enabled in the lower half of the wizard page:

- *Allow merging of proxy/stub code.* This option enables you to include the proxy/stub marshaling code in your DLL, thus reducing the work required to deploy the DLL on other machines. If you do not check this box, you'll need to distribute a separate proxy/stub DLL with the DLL that contains your COM object.
- *Support MFC.* This option enables MFC support in your ATL project. If you absolutely cannot live without MFC in your project, select this check box.
- *Support MTS.* This option adds the MTS libraries to your project.

Given a project named *Espresso*, the ATL COM AppWizard will create the following files for your ATL project:

- stdafx.h. Just as in an MFC project, stdafx.h has all of the standard #include directives that will be built into a precompiled header.
- stdafx.cpp. Just as in an MFC project, stdafx.cpp is used to create the precompiled header file.
- espresso.dsp. The Visual C++ project file.
- espresso.dsw. The Visual C++ workspace file.
- espresso.opt. The Visual C++ workspace options file.
- espresso.ncb. A binary file used by the Visual C++ ClassWizard.
- espresso.rc. The project resource file, which initially contains version information for the project.
- resource.h. The project resource header file.
- espresso.idl. Contains the IDL definitions for the project.
- espresso.cpp. Contains basic functions necessary for the module to interact with COM. DLL projects have a variety of Dll*Xxx* functions. EXE projects have CExeModule member functions; service projects have CServiceModule functions.
- espresso.h. This file is initially empty, but is replaced by a more meaningful version after the MIDL compiler is run against the project's IDL file.
- espressops.mk. The makefile used to build the proxy/stub DLL if required for custom marshaling support.
- espressops.def. The module definition file for the proxy/stub DLL.

If you create a DLL project that allows the proxy/stub code to be merged, the following files will be created:

- dlldatax.c. A source file that must be added to the project in order to merge proxy/stub code into the DLL.
- dlldatax.h. The header file for dlldata.c.

These two files are not automatically added to your project—you must follow the steps outlined later in the section titled "Merging the Proxy/Stub Code with Your DLL."

The following file will be created for all DLL-based projects:

- espresso.def. The module-definition file for the project.

Finally, the following file will be created for all EXE and service projects:

- espresso.rgs. The script file used to insert information into the System Registry.

Using ATL Object Wizard

As discussed earlier, the ATL Object Wizard is used to add an ATL COM object to your project. The ATL Object Wizard is launched by selecting Insert, New ATL Object from the Visual C++ menu. The ATL Object Wizard is shown in Figure 17.6.

FIGURE 17.6

The ATL Object Wizard.

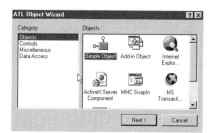

There are four categories of objects that can be inserted into your project:

- *Objects*. Contains ASP components, MMC snap-ins, MTS components, and other basic COM objects.

- *Controls*. Contains controls that are suitable for embedding in ActiveX containers. These objects are discussed in Chapter 18, "Developing ActiveX Controls."

- *Miscellaneous*. Contains a dialog box object that can be added to your project.

- *Data Access*. Contains data provider and consumer objects.

Seven types of COM objects are offered by the ATL Object Wizard:

- *Simple Object*. Generates a simple COM object for the project.

- *Add-in Object*. Creates a COM object that can extend Visual Studio IDE.

- *Internet Explorer Object*. Creates a nonvisual COM object that can be hosted inside Internet Explorer.

- *ActiveX Server Component*. Generates a COM object that can be used with Active Server Pages in IIS.

- *MMC SnapIn*. Creates a COM object that can be used with Microsoft Management Console.

- *MS Transaction Server Component*. Creates a COM object that can be used with MTS.

- *Component Registrar Object*. Creates a COM object that enables you to register individual components in a DLL rather than registering all components at once.

After a COM object has been selected, a property sheet is displayed that enables you to define attributes for the object. Some COM objects display specialized property pages that are specific to their object type. For example, the MTS component includes an MTS page that's used only for that particular object type. All the COM objects will present a Names property page, as shown in Figure 17.7.

FIGURE 17.7

The Names property page contains naming attributes for the COM object.

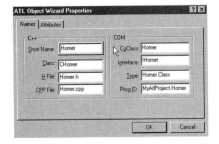

Eight items are displayed on the Names property page:

- *Short Name*. The name of the COM object.
- *Class*. The name of the C++ class that implements the COM object. By default, this is the name of the object prefixed with C.
- *.H File*. The name of the header file for the COM object. By default, this is the name of the COM object with an .H extension.
- *.CPP File*. The name of the implementation file for the COM object. By default, this is the name of the COM object with a .CPP extension.
- *CoClass*. The name of the COM object's coclass. By default, this is the name of the COM object.
- *Interface*. The name of the interface exposed by the COM object. By default, this is the name of the COM object prefixed with I.
- *Type*. A description string that's stored in the Registry under the COM object's prog ID. By default, this is the name of the COM object followed by "Class".
- *Prog ID*. The prog ID for the COM object. By default, this is <project name>.<COM object name>. For example, a project named *Latte* that has a COM object named *Foam* would have a default prog ID of Latte.Foam.

The second tab for most COM objects is the Attributes property page, which is used to collect information about the object, such as its threading model (see Figure 17.8).

FIGURE 17.8

*The Attributes
property page
contains charac-
teristics for the
COM object.*

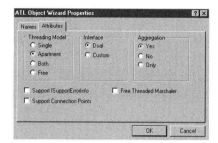

The Attributes property page allows you to define the following properties for the COM object:

- *Threading Model*. The threading model for the COM object. The options for this property are discussed in the next list.

- *Interface*. Select Dual for an Automation-compatible interface or Custom for a COM vtable interface.

- *Aggregation*. The type of aggregation supported by the COM object. The options for this property are discussed in a later list.

- *Support ISupportErrorInfo*. Adds support for the `ISupportErrorInfo` interface to your COM object.

- *Support Connection Points*. Adds support for connection points to your COM object. Using connection points is discussed in the section titled, "Connection Points," later in this chapter.

- *Free Threaded Marshaler*. Adds support for simplified marshaling of interface pointers between apartments, under some circumstances.

The threading model for the COM object can be set to one of the following options:

- *Single*. The COM object is created in the main STA for the process.

- *Apartment*. The COM object is created in an STA.

- *Free*. The COM object is created in an MTA.

- *Both*. The COM object is created in either an STA or MTA, depending on the apartment type of the caller.

Here are the aggregation options for the COM object:

- *Yes*. The COM object may be aggregated by another COM object.

- *No*. Aggregation of the COM object is not allowed.

- *Only*. The COM object must be aggregated by another COM object.

17

**CUSTOM COM
OBJECTS**

Given an object named *Latte*, the ATL Object Wizard will create the following files:

- `Latte.cpp`. Contains the implementation of the `CLatte` class. This file is initially empty.
- `Latte.h`. Contains the header file for the `CLatte` class.
- `Latte.rgs`. The script file used to insert information about `CLatte` into the Registry.

The ATL Object Wizard will also modify the following files:

- `Espresso.cpp`. Modified to add `CLSID_Latte` to the module's object map.
- `Espresso.idl`. Modified to add the new `ILatte` interface.

Merging the Proxy/Stub Code with Your DLL

If your COM component uses custom interfaces, you must supply a DLL that contains marshaling proxy and stub code. Normally, you compile a separate proxy/stub DLL that must be distributed with your COM component.

As discussed earlier in this chapter, the ATL COM Wizard provides an option to allow the proxy/stub DLL to be merged in the server. If you select this option, the `dlldatax.c` and `dlldatax.h` files are added to your project. However, they will not be included in the build—if you want to merge the proxy/stub into your DLL, you must follow these steps:

1. Go to the File tab in the project window and right-click the `dlldatax.c` file. Select Settings from the pop-up menu. The Project Settings dialog box will be displayed.
2. In the General tab in the Project Settings dialog box, clear the check box labeled Exclude File from Build. Keep the dialog box open.
3. Repeat this procedure for the `dlldatax.h` header file.
4. Keep the dialog box open and click on the C++ tab.
5. Choose the Precompiled Headers category from the drop-down list and select the Not Using Precompiled Headers radio button.
6. Choose the Preprocessor category and add `_MERGE_PROXYSTUB` as a preprocessor definition. Make sure that this new symbol is separated from the previous symbol by a comma.
7. Click the OK button to close the dialog box.

When the project is built, the DLL that contains the COM object will also contain the code required for proxy/stub marshaling.

A Custom COM Object Example

As an example of how custom COM objects are created with ATL, the CD-ROM that accompanies the book includes SysInfo, a custom COM object that is a wrapper around the Win32 `GetSystemInfo` function.

The SysInfo project creates an EXE module that includes a simple object named `SystemInfo`. The values used in the Names property sheet for the `SystemInfo` object are listed in Table 17.1.

TABLE 17.1 NAMES PROPERTY SHEET VALUES FOR THE SystemInfo OBJECT

Field	*Name*
Short Name	`SystemInfo`
Class	`CSystemInfo`
.H File	`SystemInfo.h`
.CPP File	`SystemInfo.cpp`
CoClass	`SystemInfo`
Interface	`ISystemInfo`
Type	`SystemInfo Class`
Prog ID	`SysInfo.SystemInfo`

The values used in the Attributes property sheet for the `SystemInfo` object are listed in Table 17.2.

TABLE 17.2 NAMES PROPERTY SHEET VALUES FOR THE SystemInfo OBJECT

Field	*Name*
Threading Model	Both
Interface	Custom
Aggregation	Yes
ISupportErrorInfo	Unchecked
Connection Points	Unchecked
Free Threaded Marshaler	Unchecked

Defining the `ISystemInfo` Interface

The `ISystemInfo` interface has a number of methods, as shown in the IDL provided in Listing 17.2. Lines that were added to the wizard-generated code are shown in bold.

LISTING 17.2   THE ISystemInfo INTERFACE DEFINITION

```
import "oaidl.idl";
import "ocidl.idl";

typedef enum tagProcessorType
{
    Intel386 = 0,
    Intel486,
    IntelPentium,
    IntelPentiumPro,
    MipsR4000,
    Alpha21064,
    Alpha21066,
    Alpha21164,
    PPC601,
    PPC603,
    PPC604,
    PPC603plus,
    PPC604plus,
    PPC620,
}ProcessorType;

[
    object,
    uuid(96848BCE-A68F-11D2-B886-00104B36573E),

    helpstring("ISystemInfo Interface"),
    pointer_default(unique)
]
interface ISystemInfo : IUnknown
{
    HRESULT GetPageSize([out]unsigned long* pdwPageSize);
    HRESULT GetProcessorType([out]ProcessorType* pType);
    HRESULT GetAddressSpaceBounds([out]unsigned long* pdwLowAddr,
                                  [out]unsigned long* pdwHighAddr);
    HRESULT GetProcessorCount([out]short* pCount);
    HRESULT GetProcessorMask([out]long* pMask);
    HRESULT GetProcessorRevisionString([out]BSTR* strRevision);
    HRESULT GetVmAllocationGranularity([out]unsigned long* pdwSize);
};

[
    uuid(96848BC2-A68F-11D2-B886-00104B36573E),
    version(1.0),
    helpstring("SysInfo 1.0 Type Library")
]
library SYSINFOLib
{
    importlib("stdole32.tlb");
    importlib("stdole2.tlb");
```

```
    [
        uuid(96848BCF-A68F-11D2-B886-00104B36573E),
        helpstring("SystemInfo Class")
    ]
    coclass SystemInfo
    {
        [default] interface ISystemInfo;
    };
};
```

The `ProcessorType` enumeration defined above the interface definition is used to specify the type of processor used by the system.

Modifications to the `SystemInfo` Definition

The definition for the `SystemInfo` object is found in the `SystemInfo.h` header file (see Listing 17.3). Modifications to this file are shown in bold.

LISTING 17.3 THE `SystemInfo` COM OBJECT DEFINITION

```
class ATL_NO_VTABLE CSystemInfo :
    public CComObjectRootEx<CComMultiThreadModel>,
    public CComCoClass<CSystemInfo, &CLSID_SystemInfo>,
    public ISystemInfo
{
public:
    CSystemInfo()
    {
    }

DECLARE_REGISTRY_RESOURCEID(IDR_SYSTEMINFO)

DECLARE_PROTECT_FINAL_CONSTRUCT()

BEGIN_COM_MAP(CSystemInfo)
    COM_INTERFACE_ENTRY(ISystemInfo)
END_COM_MAP()

    HRESULT FinalConstruct();

// ISystemInfo
public:
    STDMETHOD(GetVmAllocationGranularity)(unsigned long* pdwSize);
    STDMETHOD(GetProcessorRevisionString)(BSTR* strRevision);
    STDMETHOD(GetProcessorMask)(long* pMask);
    STDMETHOD(GetProcessorCount)(short* pCount);
    STDMETHOD(GetAddressSpaceBounds)(unsigned long* pdwLowAddr,
                                     unsigned long* pdwHighAddr);
```

continues

LISTING 17.3 CONTINUED

```
    STDMETHOD(GetProcessorType)(ProcessorType* pType);
    STDMETHOD(GetPageSize)(unsigned long* pdwPageSize);
protected:
    SYSTEM_INFO m_info;
};
```

The `FinalConstruct` method declared in Listing 17.3 is called by the framework after the COM object has been completed constructed. This enables you to perform initialization work, such as calling virtual functions, that isn't safe in a constructor.

Implementing the `SystemInfo` Object

The implementation of the `SystemInfo` object is found in the `SystemInfo.cpp` source file. A partial listing of the contents of this file is provided in Listing 17.4. The accompanying CD-ROM includes the complete source code for this file.

LISTING 17.4 THE IMPLEMENTATION OF THE SystemInfo COM OBJECT

```
HRESULT CSystemInfo::FinalConstruct()
{
    GetSystemInfo(&m_info);
    return S_OK;
}


STDMETHODIMP CSystemInfo::GetPageSize(unsigned long *pdwPageSize)
{
    *pdwPageSize = (DWORD)m_info.dwPageSize;
    return S_OK;
}


STDMETHODIMP CSystemInfo::GetProcessorType(ProcessorType *pType)
{
    switch(m_info.wProcessorArchitecture)
    {
        case PROCESSOR_ARCHITECTURE_INTEL:
            {
                if(m_info.wProcessorLevel == 3)
                    *pType = Intel386;
                else if(m_info.wProcessorLevel == 4)
                    *pType = Intel486;
                else if(m_info.wProcessorLevel == 5)
                    *pType = IntelPentium;
                else if(m_info.wProcessorLevel == 6)
                    *pType = IntelPentiumPro;
                else
                    return E_FAIL;
```

```
            }
            break;

        case PROCESSOR_ARCHITECTURE_MIPS:
            {
                if(m_info.wProcessorLevel == 4)
                    *pType = MipsR4000;
                else
                    return E_FAIL;
            }
            break;

        case PROCESSOR_ARCHITECTURE_ALPHA:
            {
                if(m_info.wProcessorLevel == 21064)
                    *pType = Alpha21064;
                else if(m_info.wProcessorLevel == 21066)
                    *pType = Alpha21066;
                else if(m_info.wProcessorLevel == 21164)
                    *pType = Alpha21164;
                else
                    return E_FAIL;
            }
            break;

        case PROCESSOR_ARCHITECTURE_PPC:
            {
                if(m_info.wProcessorLevel == 1)
                    *pType = PPC601;
                else if(m_info.wProcessorLevel == 3)
                    *pType = PPC603;
                else if(m_info.wProcessorLevel == 4)
                    *pType = PPC604;
                else if(m_info.wProcessorLevel == 6)
                    *pType = PPC603plus;
                else if(m_info.wProcessorLevel == 9)
                    *pType = PPC604plus;
                else if(m_info.wProcessorLevel == 20)
                    *pType = PPC620;
                else
                    return E_FAIL;
            }
            break;

        case PROCESSOR_ARCHITECTURE_UNKNOWN: // fall through
        default:
            return E_FAIL;
    }
    return S_OK;
}
```

When the COM object is constructed, the ATL framework will call the `FinalConstruct` method. Inside `FinalConstruct`, the `GetSystemInfo` API function is called to collect system processor information from the operating system and store it in the `m_info` member variable. Other method calls pick apart `m_info` and return interesting data to the client process.

Build the SysInfo project. After the `SysInfo` module is successfully compiled, the ATL project will take steps to register the COM object in the system. You won't be able to use the COM object from a client until you build and register the proxy/stub DLL, as described in the next section.

Compiling and Registering the Standard Proxy/Stub DLL

ATL projects include a command-line makefile that's used to build the proxy/stub DLL for each ATL project. This makefile is the only file in the project directory with an `.MK` filename extension. For the SysInfo project, the name of the makefile is `SysInfoPs.MK`. To build the DLL, use the NMAKE utility, like this:

```
nmake SysInfoPs.MK
```

After the proxy/stub DLL has been successfully built, you can register the DLL using the RegSvr32 utility:

```
regsvr32 SysInfoPs
```

If the DLL is successfully registered, a message box will be displayed, as shown in Figure 17.9.

FIGURE 17.9

The RegSvr32 utility is used to register the proxy/stub DLL.

Creating Test Clients for `SystemInfo`

To facilitate testing of the `SystemInfo` COM object, the CD-ROM that accompanies this book includes two console-mode test driver programs:

- *InfoClient* calls each interface and displays the results to the console window using `wprintf`.
- *InfoTimer* reports the time required to call one of the interface methods one million times and is used to collect timing information that will be used to compare performance using standard and custom marshaling.

The InfoClient project was built as a Win32 console application, with the _UNICODE and UNICODE preprocessor symbols defined. The sysinfo_i.c and sysinfo.h files were copied from the SysInfo project directory into the InfoClient project directory. These two files are generated by MIDL when the IDL file is compiled; they contain information about the GUIDs and interface declarations used by the SystemInfo COM object.

The InfoClient project contains one other source file, main.cpp, part of which is provided in Listing 17.5. The accompanying CD-ROM includes the complete source code for this project.

LISTING 17.5 THE INFOCLIENT TEST DRIVER

```
#define _WIN32_WINNT 0x0500
#include <windows.h>
#include <wchar.h>

#include "sysinfo_i.c"
#include "sysinfo.h"

void ProcTypeEnumToString(ProcessorType procType,
                          WCHAR szProcessorType[40]);
void HandleError(LPCWSTR strTitle, HRESULT hr);

// Macro that tests for an error - if an error occurs, a message
// box is displayed, and the program returns.
#define TESTHR(hr,str)if(FAILED(hr)){HandleError(str,hr);return 0;}

int wmain()
{
    ISystemInfo* pInfo = NULL;
    HRESULT hr = CoInitializeEx(NULL, COINIT_MULTITHREADED);
    TESTHR(hr, L"CoInitialize Failed");
    __try{

        hr = CoCreateInstance(CLSID_SystemInfo,
                              NULL,
                              CLSCTX_ALL,
                              IID_ISystemInfo,
                              (void**)&pInfo);
        TESTHR(hr, L"CoCreate Failed");
        short processors;

        hr = pInfo->GetProcessorCount(&processors);
        TESTHR(hr, L"GetProcessorCount Failed");

        long processorMask;
        hr = pInfo->GetProcessorMask(&processorMask);
        TESTHR(hr, L"GetProcessorMask Failed");
```

continues

LISTING 17.5   CONTINUED

```
        ProcessorType procType;
        hr = pInfo->GetProcessorType(&procType);
        TESTHR(hr, L"GetProcessorType Failed");

        WCHAR szProcessorType[40];
        ProcTypeEnumToString(procType, szProcessorType);

        BSTR bstrRevision;
        hr = pInfo->GetProcessorRevisionString(&bstrRevision);
        TESTHR(hr, L"GetProcessorRevisionString Failed");

        unsigned long dwPageSize;
        hr = pInfo->GetPageSize(&dwPageSize);
        TESTHR(hr, L"GetPageSize Failed");

        unsigned long dwMinAddr;
        unsigned long dwMaxAddr;
        hr = pInfo->GetAddressSpaceBounds(&dwMinAddr, &dwMaxAddr);
        TESTHR(hr, L"GetAddressSpaceBounds Failed");

        unsigned long dwVmChunk;
        hr = pInfo->GetVmAllocationGranularity(&dwVmChunk);
        TESTHR(hr, L"GetVmAllocationGranularity Failed");

        wprintf(L"Processors: %d\n"
                L"Processor mask: %#08.8X\n"
                L"Processor type: %s\n"
                L"Revision: %s\n"
                L"Page size: %d\n"
                L"Minimum address: %#08.8X\n"
                L"Maximum address: %#08.8X\n"
                L"Virtual Alloc Granularity: %#04.4X\n",
                (short)processors,
                (long)processorMask,
                (OLECHAR*)szProcessorType,
                (OLECHAR*)bstrRevision,
                (unsigned long)dwPageSize,
                (unsigned long)dwMinAddr,
                (unsigned long)dwMaxAddr,
                (unsigned long)dwVmChunk);

        SysFreeString(bstrRevision);
    }
    __finally
    {
        if(pInfo)pInfo->Release();
        CoUninitialize();
    }
    return 0;
}
```

Build the InfoClient project. When InfoClient is run from the command line, it displays
information about the system, as shown in Figure 17.10.

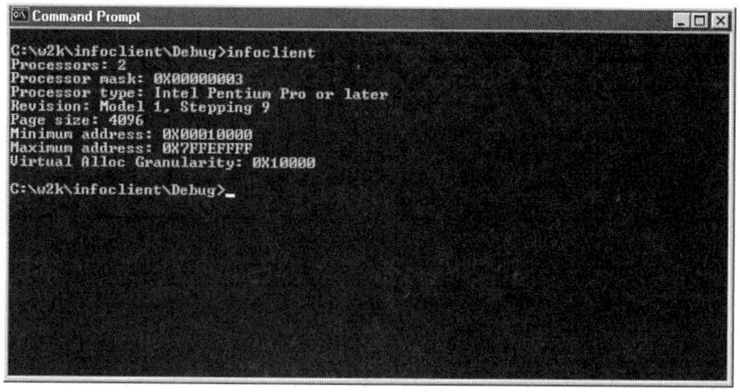

FIGURE 17.10

*The InfoClient
project uses*
SystemInfo *to col-
lect system infor-
mation.*

The InfoTimer project was also built as a Unicode Win32 console application. The sys-
info_i.c and sysinfo.h files for InfoTimer were copied from the SysInfo project directory into the InfoTimer project directory.

In addition to the two include files, the InfoTimer project contains one source file,
main.cpp, which is provided in Listing 17.6.

LISTING 17.6   A TIMING CLIENT FOR SystemInfo

```
#define _WIN32_WINNT 0x0500
#include <windows.h>
#include <wchar.h>

#include "sysinfo_i.c"
#include "sysinfo.h"

void HandleError(LPCWSTR strTitle, HRESULT hr);

// Macro that tests for an error - if an error occurs, a message
// box is displayed, and the program returns.
#define TESTHR(hr,str)if(FAILED(hr)){HandleError(str,hr);return 0;}

double GetElapsedTime();
void    StartTimer();
void    StopTimer();
void    HandleError(LPCWSTR strTitle, HRESULT hr);

int wmain()
{
    ISystemInfo* pInfo = NULL;
    HRESULT hr = CoInitializeEx(NULL, COINIT_MULTITHREADED);
```

continues

LISTING 17.6   CONTINUED

```
    TESTHR(hr, L"CoInitialize Failed");
    __try{

        hr = CoCreateInstance(CLSID_SystemInfo,
                              NULL,
                              CLSCTX_ALL,
                              IID_ISystemInfo,
                              (void**)&pInfo);
        TESTHR(hr, L"CoCreate Failed");

        short processors;
        StartTimer();
        for(int i = 0; i < 1000000; i++)
        {
            hr = pInfo->GetProcessorCount(&processors);
            TESTHR(hr, L"GetProcessorCount Failed");
        }
        StopTimer();
        double elapsed = GetElapsedTime();
        wprintf(L"Elapsed time = %6.3f seconds", elapsed);
    }
    __finally
    {
        if(pInfo)pInfo->Release();
        CoUninitialize();
    }
    return 0;
}

/*
 * Error handling routine
 */
void HandleError(LPCWSTR strTitle, HRESULT hr)
{
    LPVOID lpMsgBuf;

    FormatMessageW(FORMAT_MESSAGE_ALLOCATE_BUFFER¦
                   FORMAT_MESSAGE_FROM_SYSTEM,
                   NULL,
                   hr,
                   MAKELANGID(LANG_NEUTRAL, SUBLANG_DEFAULT),
                   (LPWSTR)&lpMsgBuf,
                   0,
                   NULL);
    MessageBoxW(NULL,
                (LPCWSTR)lpMsgBuf,
                strTitle,
                MB_OK ¦ MB_ICONINFORMATION);
    LocalFree(lpMsgBuf);
```

```
}

/*
 * Timer routines
 */
#include <time.h>
#include <sys/timeb.h>

_timeb startTime, endTime;
void StartTimer()
{
    _ftime(&startTime);
}

void StopTimer()
{
    _ftime(&endTime);
}

double GetElapsedTime()
{
    double msecs = endTime.millitm - startTime.millitm;
    double secs = difftime(endTime.time, startTime.time);
    return secs + (msecs/1000);
}
```

Build the InfoTimer project. When InfoTimer is run from the command line, it calls the GetProcessorCount method for SystemInfo for one million iterations. When InfoTimer is run on one of my machines, it takes an average of about 266 seconds to complete. Later, in the section titled, "Custom Marshaling," you'll see how custom marshaling can be used to reduce this time dramatically.

Using Monikers

A *moniker* is a special type of COM object that's used to locate another COM object. All monikers support the IMoniker interface, which includes functions that are used to manage the moniker and retrieve a pointer to the COM object that the moniker refers to. Monikers are useful when details about how a COM object is located and initiated should be hidden from the client. Here are some examples:

- When a moniker refers to a specific instance of a COM object.
- When a moniker refers to an object that's difficult to locate, such as an item embedded deeply inside another COM object.
- When a COM object is referenced by a display name. This is discussed in the section titled "Creating a Moniker from a Display Name" later in this chapter.

The process of asking a moniker for an interface pointer on the object that it refers to is known as *binding*. The IMoniker interface includes a member function called BindToObject that's used to retrieve an interface pointer from the object that the moniker refers to. The steps required for creating a moniker and binding to the underlying object are as follows:

1. Create an instance of a moniker using one of the techniques discussed later in this chapter, in the section titled, "Creating Moniker Instances."
2. Call BindToObject through the moniker's IMoniker interface.
3. The moniker locates an instance of the desired COM object using whatever means necessary. The actual details of how the COM instance is located or created are implementation details of the moniker.
4. A pointer to the requested interface is returned to the client.
5. The client releases the moniker.
6. The requested COM object is called by the client.

Examples of System Monikers

Windows 2000 includes a number of built-in monikers known as *system monikers*, because they're implemented by the operating system:

- *Class monikers* provide access to a particular COM class.
- *File monikers* provide access to a COM object via a filename that contains persistent data for the COM object.
- *Composite monikers* consist of multiple monikers that are joined together to refer to a single COM object.
- *Item monikers* provide access to an item stored in another COM object, such as a cell in an Excel spreadsheet or a page in a Word document.
- *Pointer monikers* provide a moniker wrapper around an interface pointer.
- *Anti-monikers* are never used by moniker clients—they're used by monikers to re-create a composite moniker.
- *URL monikers* provide a moniker wrapper around a URL address.

Creating Moniker Instances

There are two basic methods used to get an interface pointer to a moniker:

- Create a moniker yourself using one of the Windows 2000 API functions that returns a specific type of moniker.

- Have one created for you by calling an interface function on a COM object that supplies monikers to clients.

As discussed earlier, monikers are themselves COM objects, so you must handle the usual issues of interface lifetime—remember to call `Release` through moniker interfaces when you're finished using them.

Translating Monikers into Text Strings

A moniker can be translated into a text string that represents the moniker. This text string is known as a *display name*, and it provides a very useful way to store a reference to a COM object. For example, the display name for a class moniker has the following format:

```
clsid:1861FFDA-8002-11D2-B868-00104B36573E:
```

This class ID is for the `TestFunc` COM class, which was used in Chapter 16.

The class moniker for a COM class can be used to create an instance of that class and return a pointer to any interface supported by the COM object. To create a class moniker, you must use the `CreateClassMoniker` function:

```
IMoniker* pMk = NULL;
hr = CreateClassMoniker(CLSID_MyComClass, &pMk);
if(FAILED(hr))
{
    // Handle error
}
else
{
    // Use moniker
}
```

The `CreateClassMoniker` function has two parameters:

- The CLSID for the class the moniker will refer to
- The address of an `IMoniker` pointer that will refer to the moniker if the call is successful

`CreateClassMoniker` returns an `HRESULT`, which should be tested using the `SUCCEEDED` or `FAILED` macros. Remember to release the `IMoniker` pointer when you're finished with the moniker.

The source code provided in Listing 17.7 creates and prints a display name for the `TestFunc` COM class from Chapter 16.

LISTING 17.7 CREATING A DISPLAY NAME FROM A MONIKER

```c
#define _WIN32_WINNT 0x0500
#include <windows.h>
#include <wchar.h>

#include "exesta_i.c"
#include "exesta.h"

void    HandleError(LPCWSTR strTitle, HRESULT hr);

int wmain()
{
    HRESULT hr = CoInitializeEx(NULL, COINIT_MULTITHREADED);
    if(FAILED(hr))
    {
        HandleError(L"CoInit Failed", hr);
        return 0;
    }

    // Create moniker for the TestFunc COM class.
    IMoniker* pMk = NULL;
    hr = CreateClassMoniker(CLSID_TestFunc, &pMk);
    if(FAILED(hr))
    {
        HandleError(L"CreateMoniker Failed", hr);
        return 0;
    }

    // Generate a display name for the class moniker, and
    // print it to the console.
    LPOLESTR pszDisplayName;
    hr = pMk->GetDisplayName(NULL, NULL, &pszDisplayName);
    if(SUCCEEDED(hr))
    {
        wprintf(L"%s\n", pszDisplayName);
        CoTaskMemFree(pszDisplayName);
    }
    pMk->Release();

    CoUninitialize();
    return 0;
}


/*
 * Error handling routine
 */
void HandleError(LPCWSTR strTitle, HRESULT hr)
```

```
{
    LPVOID lpMsgBuf;

    FormatMessageW(FORMAT_MESSAGE_ALLOCATE_BUFFER|
                   FORMAT_MESSAGE_FROM_SYSTEM,
                   NULL,
                   hr,
                   MAKELANGID(LANG_NEUTRAL, SUBLANG_DEFAULT),
                   (LPWSTR)&lpMsgBuf,
                   0,
                   NULL);
    MessageBoxW(NULL,
                (LPCWSTR)lpMsgBuf,
                strTitle,
                MB_OK | MB_ICONINFORMATION);
    LocalFree(lpMsgBuf);
}
```

Creating a Moniker from a Display Name

To retrieve a pointer to a COM object from a display name, the `MkParseDisplayName` API function is used:

```
HRESULT hr = MkParseDisplayName(pBindContext,
                                pszDisplayName,
                                &cbEaten,
                                &pMoniker);
```

The `MkParseDisplayName` function has four parameters:

- A pointer to an `IBindContext` interface, which is used to store information about how the moniker should be processed. Using binding context is described later.

- A string that contains the display name for the moniker.

- A pointer to a `ULONG` that will be filled with the number of characters removed from the display name. As a client of the moniker, you don't need to use this information.

- The address of a pointer to the `IMoniker` interface, which will be set if the function succeeds.

`MkParseDisplayName` works with all types of monikers, even custom monikers not provided by Windows 2000.

Connection Points

Connection points are used by *connectable objects* to establish bi-directional communication. Connectable objects communicate with their clients through connection-point interfaces. These are back-channel interfaces that allow a COM server to notify its clients of events. There are two interfaces implemented by a connectable object:

- IConnectionPoint is implemented by a control or other COM object and allows a container or client of the COM object to request event notifications.

- IConnectionPointContainer is used by a client to query the COM object about IConnectionPoint interfaces supported by the object. This interface includes functions that return a pointer to a known IConnectionPoint interface or enumerate IConnectionPoint interfaces supported by a control.

Most ActiveX controls are connectable objects. However, other types of COM objects can implement the IConnectionPointContainer and IConnectionPoint interfaces and thus become connectable objects. The coupling between a connectable client and server is shown in Figure 17.11.

FIGURE 17.11

The interfaces used to implement connectable objects.

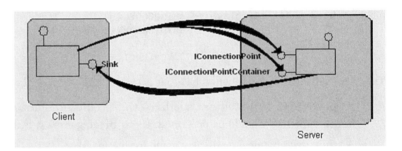

A client interested in a specific IConnectionPoint interface first invokes QueryInterface, requesting the IConnectionPointContainer interface. If an interface pointer is returned, the particular IConnectionPoint interface is requested through IConnectionPointContainer. If the request is successful, the client passes a pointer to its notification sink to the server through the IConnectionPoint interface. The server transmits event notifications to the client using the pointer to the notification sink.

To support connection points in an ATL object, you must select the Support Connection Points option when creating the object using the ATL Object Wizard. A definition of an outgoing interface will be added to the project IDL file. Listing 17.8 is a fragment of an IDL file with an example of an outgoing interface for a COM object named Bothway:

LISTING 17.8 DEFINING AN OUTGOING INTERFACE FOR A CONNECTABLE OBJECT

```
library ConnectExampleLib
{
    importlib("stdole32.tlb");
    importlib("stdole2.tlb");

    [
        uuid(9E0F306C-AA28-11D2-B887-00104B36573E),
        helpstring("_IBothwayEvents Interface")
    ]
    dispinterface _IBothwayEvents
    {
        properties:
        methods:
    };

    [
        uuid(9E0F306B-AA28-11D2-B887-00104B36573E),
        helpstring("Bothway Class")
    ]
    coclass Bothway
    {
        [default] interface IBothway;
        [default, source] dispinterface _ _IBothwayEvents;
    };
};
```

Note that the outgoing interface is named _IBothwayEvents. The outgoing interface is prefixed with _I and has Events added to the name of the COM object.

In order to implement connection-point methods, you must follow these steps:

1. Add methods and properties to the IDL definition for the outgoing interface.

2. Compile the IDL using the MIDL compiler to create a type library containing the connection-point information—the easiest way to do this is to build the project.

3. Right-click the ATL object's icon in the ClassView window and select Implement Connection Points from the pop-up menu. A dialog box will be displayed, as shown in Figure 17.12.

4. As shown in Figure 17.12, the dialog box contains a list of interfaces that can be used to implement connection points. In most cases, this dialog box will contain only one entry—check the outgoing interface and click OK.

FIGURE **17.12**

Implementing connection points for an ATL object.

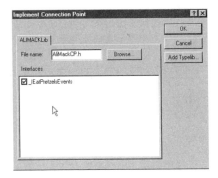

The connection-point class is created with a name generated by prefixing CProxy to the interface name. For the _IBothwayEvents example, the generated class is named CProxy_IBothwayEvents. The connection-point class contains member functions that can be used to generate events that are sent to the container. These functions are named by prefixing Fire_ to the name of the outgoing interface method defined in IDL. For an outgoing method named SayHey, the connection-point class will contain a function with the following name:

```
Fire_SayHey()
```

The new connection-point class is added to the multiple inheritance list for the control. This allows you to fire any event directly. Here's an example:

```
if(eyesShut && snoringLoudly)
    Fire_DadIsSleeping();
```

Connection points are used in Chapter 18 when building controls with ATL. A connection-point interface is used to notify the control's container about events that occur inside the control.

NOTE

You don't need to implement IConnectionPoint or IConnectionPointContainer to exchange interface pointers between COM objects. The connection-point mechanism allows a client and server to negotiate available outgoing interfaces.

If you're specifying a fixed set of interfaces for bi-directional communication, you have no need for connection points.

Custom Marshaling

When interfaces are accessed across apartment boundaries, the method calls must be marshaled. Most of the time, this is a very painless process for you as a developer:

- If your interfaces are derived from IDispatch, you can take advantage of type-library marshaling. If you build your project using ATL, the type library is automatically created and registered for you as part of the build process. Automation interfaces use type-library marshaling by default.

- If you're implementing custom interfaces, you must build and register a proxy/stub DLL, following the steps discussed earlier in this chapter. The proxy/stub DLL uses standard marshaling interfaces exposed by Windows 2000 to marshal data between apartments.

The advantages of standard marshaling are that it's easy to implement, requiring almost no work on your part, and it's very predictable in terms of behavior and performance cost. The proxy and stub are placed into the apartments of the client and server automatically when COM connects the client and server.

Every time the client calls a function on the server, the proxy and stub conspire together to make sure that data is properly marshaled between the apartments. There are times, however, when the standard marshaling offered by COM and Windows 2000 is not the most efficient way to marshal your interface.

Understanding Custom Marshaling

Another marshaling option is to implement *custom marshaling*. Objects that support custom marshaling expose the IMarshal interface, which is used for moving data across apartments. When COM creates an instance of a COM object, it queries the object for IMarshal. If the interface is not supported, COM and Windows 2000 implement standard marshaling. If the COM object supports the IMarshal interface, COM will not create a stub for the COM object—rather, it asks the object, through the IMarshal interface, how data should be marshaled back to the client. The COM object writes a packet of data to a custom proxy that's used to establish communication between the COM object and its proxy in the other apartment.

A simplified version of the IMarshal definition is provided in Listing 17.9.

LISTING 17.9   A SIMPLIFIED VERSION OF IMarshal

```
interface IMarshal : public IUnknown
{
public:
    HRESULT GetUnmarshalClass(REFIID riid,
                              void *pv,
                              DWORD dwDestContext,
                              void *pvDestContext,
                              DWORD mshlflags,
                              CLSID *pCid);
    HRESULT GetMarshalSizeMax(REFIID riid,
                              void *pv,
                              DWORD dwDestContext,
                              void *pvDestContext,
                              DWORD mshlflags,
                              DWORD *pSize);
    HRESULT MarshalInterface(IStream *pStm,
                             REFIID riid,
                             void *pv,
                             DWORD dwDestContext,
                             void *pvDestContext,
                             DWORD mshlflags);
    HRESULT UnmarshalInterface(IStream *pStm,
                               REFIID riid,
                               void **ppv);
    HRESULT ReleaseMarshalData(IStream *pStm);
    HRESULT DisconnectObject(DWORD dwReserved);
};
```

As shown in Listing 17.9, the IMarshal interface has six methods:

- GetUnmarshalClass. Implemented by the server, this method requests the CLSID for the proxy that must be used to unmarshal the stream of bytes that represent the marshaled data for the COM object.

- GetMarshalSizeMax. Implemented by the server, this method requests the largest possible size for the data that will be sent as the initial marshaling packet to the far-end proxy.

- MarshalInterface. Implemented by the server, this function requests the server to write data into an IStream that will be transmitted to the far-end proxy.

- UnmarshalInterface. Implemented by the proxy.

- ReleaseMarshalData. Implemented by the server and proxy, this method is called by the operating system when the marshaling packet must be destroyed before it has been unmarshaled.

- DisconnectObject. Implemented by the server, this function is called to allow servers and custom proxies a chance to shut down.

As you can see from this list, some functions in `IMarshal` are implemented by the COM server object, and some are implemented by a custom proxy, which must be created as part of the custom marshaling process. Here are the steps involved in custom marshaling:

1. A client launches a COM object in another apartment.

2. The COM object is queried for `IMarshal`.

3. The COM object returns a pointer to its `IMarshal` interface.

4. The COM object is asked for the size of its marshaling packet when called through `IMarshal::GetMarshalSizeMax`.

5. The COM object is asked for information about its custom proxy when called through `IMarshal::GetUnmarshalClass`.

6. The COM object is asked to write a marshaling packet into an `IStream` when called through `IMarshal::MarshalInterface`.

7. COM creates a marshaling stream that includes the CLSID of the custom proxy and the marshaling packet supplied by the COM object.

8. COM uses the marshaling stream to create an instance of the custom proxy for the client's apartment.

9. The custom proxy is requested to initialize itself when called through `IMarshal::UnmarshalInterface`.

10. COM returns a pointer to the custom proxy to the client.

Understanding Marshal by Value

The most commonly implemented type of custom marshaling is known as *marshal by value*, or *MBV*. This type of marshaling is implemented to reduce the cost of communicating with a COM object whose internal state rarely changes. With MBV, the state of the COM object is passed to the custom proxy, which handles calls to the object completely within the apartment of the client.

MBV can greatly reduce the amount of overhead required to communicate with a COM object that lies outside the client's apartment. From the client's point of view, all calls are made to a DLL that's inside the client's apartment. The client has no reliable way of knowing that it's talking to a proxy instead of the actual COM object.

Implementing a Custom Proxy

The first step in implementing MBV is to implement the custom proxy that will be loaded into the client's address space. In general, a custom proxy has two responsibilities:

- Unmarshal the data sent from the COM object and use it to initialize the proxy.

- Mimic the COM object's interfaces so that the client believes it's talking to the COM object.

When implementing MBV, the COM object will serialize its state and pass it (by value) to the custom proxy. The custom proxy reads the state and creates a facsimile of the COM object that's reasonable enough to fool a client.

The custom proxy will look very much like the `SystemInfo` COM object. Unlike the `SystemInfo` COM object, where `GetSystemInfo` is called in `FinalConstruct`, the proxy will set the value of `m_info` by reading it directly from the marshaling packet provided by the `IStream` in `UnmarshalInterface`.

The custom marshaling proxy is implemented in an ATL DLL project named SysInfoMbv, which can be found on the CD-ROM accompanying this book. The project was created with the same parameters used for the SysInfo project, except that the SysInfoMbv project creates a DLL server instead of an EXE.

After the SysInfoMbv project was created, a new ATL object named `SystemInfo` was added to the project with the same parameters used earlier in this chapter to add the `SystemInfo` object to the SysInfo project.

NOTE

When implementing MBV, it's a good idea to use the threading model "Both" for your custom proxy. This allows your proxy to be created inside the apartment of the client. Otherwise, your custom proxy might need to be marshaled into the client's apartment, thus erasing any potential performance gains you might have achieved.

It's very important that the proxy support exactly the same interfaces implemented by the `SystemInfo` COM object. Edit the IDL for the SysInfoMbv project so that it looks like the source code provided in Listing 17.10. Modified lines are shown in bold.

LISTING 17.10   IDL FOR THE SYSINFOMBV ATL PROJECT

```
// SysInfoMbv.idl : IDL source for SysInfoMbv.dll
//

// This file will be processed by the MIDL tool to
// produce the type library (SysInfoMbv.tlb) and marshaling code.
```

```idl
import "oaidl.idl";
import "ocidl.idl";

typedef enum tagPprocessorType
{
    Intel386 = 0,
    Intel486,
    IntelPentium,
    IntelPentiumPro,
    MipsR4000,
    Alpha21064,
    Alpha21066,
    Alpha21164,
    PPC601,
    PPC603,
    PPC604,
    PPC603plus,
    PPC604plus,
    PPC620,
}ProcessorType;

[
    object,
    uuid(96848BCE-A68F-11D2-B886-00104B36573E),

    helpstring("ISystemInfo Interface"),
    pointer_default(unique)
]
interface ISystemInfo : IUnknown
{
    [helpstring("method GetPageSize")]
    HRESULT GetPageSize([out] unsigned long* pdwPageSize);

    [helpstring("method GetProcessorType")]
    HRESULT GetProcessorType([out]ProcessorType* pType);

    [helpstring("method GetAddressSpaceBounds")]
    HRESULT GetAddressSpaceBounds([out]unsigned long* pdwLowAddr,
                                  [out]unsigned long* pdwHighAddr);

    [helpstring("method GetProcessorCount")]
    HRESULT GetProcessorCount([out]short* pCount);

    [helpstring("method GetProcessorMask")]
    HRESULT GetProcessorMask([out]long* pMask);

    [helpstring("method GetProcessorRevisionString")]
    HRESULT GetProcessorRevisionString([out]BSTR* strRevision);
```

continues

LISTING 17.10   CONTINUED

```
    [helpstring("method GetVmAllocationGranularity")]
    HRESULT GetVmAllocationGranularity([out]unsigned long* pdwSize);
};

[
    uuid(A1B192CF-A8BE-11D2-B887-00104B36573E),
    version(1.0),
    helpstring("SysInfoMbv 1.0 Type Library")
]
library SYSINFOMBVLib
{
    importlib("stdole32.tlb");
    importlib("stdole2.tlb");

    [
        uuid(A1B192DC-A8BE-11D2-B887-00104B36573E),
        helpstring("SystemInfo Proxy Class")
    ]
    coclass SystemInfo
    {
        [default] interface ISystemInfo;
    };
};
```

The header file for the SystemInfo COM object is found in SystemInfo.h and is provided in Listing 17.11. In addition to the ISystemInfo interface, the SystemInfo COM
object will also implement IMarshal. Modified and added lines are shown in bold.

LISTING 17.11   THE HEADER FILE FOR THE SYSTEMINFO COM OBJECT IN THE CUSTOM
PROXY

```
// SystemInfo.h : Declaration of the CSystemInfo

#ifndef __SYSTEMINFO_H_
#define __SYSTEMINFO_H_

#include "resource.h"        // main symbols

/////////////////////////////////////////////////////////
// CSystemInfo
class ATL_NO_VTABLE CSystemInfo :
    public CComObjectRootEx<CComMultiThreadModel>,
    public CComCoClass<CSystemInfo, &CLSID_SystemInfo>,
    public ISystemInfo, // add a comma on this line
    public IMarshal
{
```

```
public:
    CSystemInfo()
    {
    }

DECLARE_REGISTRY_RESOURCEID(IDR_SYSTEMINFO)

DECLARE_PROTECT_FINAL_CONSTRUCT()

BEGIN_COM_MAP(CSystemInfo)
    COM_INTERFACE_ENTRY(ISystemInfo)
    COM_INTERFACE_ENTRY(IMarshal)
END_COM_MAP()

// ISystemInfo
public:
    STDMETHOD(GetVmAllocationGranularity)(unsigned long* pdwSize);
    STDMETHOD(GetProcessorRevisionString)(BSTR* strRevision);
    STDMETHOD(GetProcessorMask)(long* pMask);
    STDMETHOD(GetProcessorCount)(short* pCount);
    STDMETHOD(GetAddressSpaceBounds)(unsigned long* pdwLowAddr,
                                     unsigned long* pdwHighAddr);
    STDMETHOD(GetProcessorType)(ProcessorType* pType);
    STDMETHOD(GetPageSize)(unsigned long* pdwPageSize);

// IMarshal
public:
    STDMETHOD(GetUnmarshalClass)(REFIID riid, void *pv,
                                 DWORD dwDestContext,
                                 void *pvDestContext,
                                 DWORD mshlflags, CLSID *pCid);
    STDMETHOD(GetMarshalSizeMax)(REFIID riid, void *pv,
                                 DWORD dwDestContext,
                                 void *pvDestContext,
                                 DWORD mshlflags, DWORD *pSize);
    STDMETHOD(MarshalInterface)(IStream* pStm, REFIID riid,
                                void *pv, DWORD dwDestContext,
                                void *pvDestContext,
                                DWORD mshlflags);
    STDMETHOD(UnmarshalInterface)(IStream *pStm, REFIID riid,
                                  void **ppv);
    STDMETHOD(ReleaseMarshalData)(IStream *pStm);
    STDMETHOD(DisconnectObject)(DWORD dwReserved);
protected:
    SYSTEM_INFO m_info;
};

#endif //__SYSTEMINFO_H_
```

17

CUSTOM COM
OBJECTS

The implementation file for the `SystemInfo` COM object is found in `SystemInfo.cpp`. Most of this file is identical to the file provided earlier in Listing 17.4. The new portion of the file that deals with the `IMarshal` interface in the proxy is provided in Listing 17.12. The complete source file for `SystemInfo.cpp` can be found on the CD-ROM.

LISTING 17.12   MARSHALING CODE FOR THE CUSTOM PROXY FROM `SystemInfo.cpp` IN THE SYSINFOMBV PROJECT

```
STDMETHODIMP CSystemInfo::GetUnmarshalClass(REFIID riid,
                                            void *pv,
                                            DWORD dwDestContext,
                                            void *pvDestContext,
                                            DWORD mshlflags,
                                            CLSID *pCid)
{
    return S_OK;
}

STDMETHODIMP CSystemInfo::GetMarshalSizeMax(REFIID riid,
                                            void *pv,
                                            DWORD dwDestContext,
                                            void *pvDestContext,
                                            DWORD mshlflags,
                                            DWORD *pSize)
{
    return S_OK;
}

STDMETHODIMP CSystemInfo::MarshalInterface(IStream* pStm,
                                           REFIID riid,
                                           void *pv,
                                           DWORD dwDestContext,
                                           void *pvDestContext,
                                           DWORD mshlflags)
{
    return S_OK;
}

STDMETHODIMP CSystemInfo::UnmarshalInterface(IStream *pStm,
                                             REFIID riid,
                                             void **ppv)
{
    pStm->Read((void*)&m_info, sizeof(SYSTEM_INFO), NULL);
    return QueryInterface(riid, ppv);
}

STDMETHODIMP CSystemInfo::ReleaseMarshalData(IStream *pStm)
{
```

```
    return S_OK;
}

STDMETHODIMP CSystemInfo::DisconnectObject(DWORD dwReserved)
{
    return S_OK;
}
```

In Listing 17.12, only one function does any real work: UnmarshalInterface. When this function is called on the proxy, the proxy fills the contents of the local m_info structure from an IStream that's provided by COM. In the next section, you'll see how the COM server serializes the contents of its m_info structure into the stream.

Build the SysInfoMbv project. It should compile with no errors and automatically register the custom proxy in the System Registry. There's no need to build or register the proxy/stub DLL located in the project's directory.

Implementing IMarshal on the Server

The next step in implementing MBV is to implement the IMarshal interface on the COM object. In general, a COM object that supports custom marshaling has three responsibilities:

- Provide the CLSID of the custom proxy to the operating system.
- Provide the size of the custom marshaling packet to the operating system.
- Create a marshaling packet and serialize the packet into an IStream that will be provided by COM and the operating system. When you're implementing MBV, the marshaling packet contains the current state of the COM object.

The CD-ROM includes a second version of the SysInfo project in a directory cleverly named *SysInfo2*. This version of SysInfo implements the IMarshal interface and works in tandem with the SysInfoMbv custom proxy.

The modifications made to the SystemInfo.h header file are provided in Listing 17.13. The SystemInfo object has been modified to support the IMarshal interface. Modified and changed lines are shown in bold.

LISTING 17.13 THE CSystemInfo CLASS DEFINITION AFTER IMarshal SUPPORT IS ADDED

```
// SystemInfo.h : Declaration of the CSystemInfo

#ifndef __SYSTEMINFO_H_
#define __SYSTEMINFO_H_
```

continues

LISTING 17.13   CONTINUED

```
#include "resource.h"        // main symbols

/////////////////////////////////////////////////////////////
// CSystemInfo
class ATL_NO_VTABLE CSystemInfo :
    public CComObjectRootEx<CComMultiThreadModel>,
    public CComCoClass<CSystemInfo, &CLSID_SystemInfo>,
    public ISystemInfo, // add a comma on this line
    public IMarshal
{
public:
    CSystemInfo()
    {
    }

DECLARE_REGISTRY_RESOURCEID(IDR_SYSTEMINFO)

DECLARE_PROTECT_FINAL_CONSTRUCT()

BEGIN_COM_MAP(CSystemInfo)
    COM_INTERFACE_ENTRY(ISystemInfo)
    COM_INTERFACE_ENTRY(IMarshal)
END_COM_MAP()

    HRESULT FinalConstruct();

// ISystemInfo
public:
    STDMETHOD(GetVmAllocationGranularity)(unsigned long* pdwSize);
    STDMETHOD(GetProcessorRevisionString)(BSTR* strRevision);
    STDMETHOD(GetProcessorMask)(long* pMask);
    STDMETHOD(GetProcessorCount)(short* pCount);
    STDMETHOD(GetAddressSpaceBounds)(unsigned long* pdwLowAddr,
                                     unsigned long* pdwHighAddr);
    STDMETHOD(GetProcessorType)(ProcessorType* pType);
    STDMETHOD(GetPageSize)(unsigned long* pdwPageSize);

// IMarshal
public:
    STDMETHOD(GetUnmarshalClass)(REFIID riid, void *pv,
                                 DWORD dwDestContext,
                                 void *pvDestContext,
                                 DWORD mshlflags, CLSID *pCid);
    STDMETHOD(GetMarshalSizeMax)(REFIID riid, void *pv,
                                 DWORD dwDestContext,
                                 void *pvDestContext,
                                 DWORD mshlflags, DWORD *pSize);
```

```
        STDMETHOD(MarshalInterface)(IStream* pStm, REFIID riid,
                                    void *pv, DWORD dwDestContext,
                                    void *pvDestContext,
                                    DWORD mshlflags);
        STDMETHOD(UnmarshalInterface)(IStream *pStm, REFIID riid,
                                      void **ppv);
        STDMETHOD(ReleaseMarshalData)(IStream *pStm);
        STDMETHOD(DisconnectObject)(DWORD dwReserved);

protected:
    SYSTEM_INFO m_info;
};
#endif //__SYSTEMINFO_H_
```

The implementation file for the SystemInfo COM object is found in SystemInfo.cpp. Most of this file is identical to the file provided earlier in Listing 17.4. The new portion of the file that deals with the IMarshal interface in the server is provided in Listing 17.14. The complete source file for SystemInfo.cpp can be found on the CD-ROM. Note that the server needs to know the CLSID for the custom proxy. You can either add the include file or simply copy the definition, as done in Listing 17.14.

LISTING **17.14** THE IMPLEMENTATION OF THE SystemInfo COM OBJECT AFTER SUPPORT FOR IMarshal IS ADDED

```
// SystemInfo.cpp : Implementation of CSystemInfo
#include "stdafx.h"
#include "SysInfo.h"
#include "SystemInfo.h"

const CLSID CLSID_SystemInfoMbv = {0xA1B192DC,0xA8BE,0x11D2,
                      {0xB8,0x87,0x00,0x10,0x4B,0x36,0x57,0x3E}};


    .
    .// Existing code omitted for clarity
    .
STDMETHODIMP CSystemInfo::GetMarshalSizeMax(REFIID riid,
                                            void *pv,
                                            DWORD dwDestContext,
                                            void *pvDestContext,
                                            DWORD mshlflags,
                                            DWORD *pSize)
{
    AtlTrace(L"GetMarshalSizeMax\n");
    *pSize = sizeof(SYSTEM_INFO);
    return S_OK;
}
```

continues

LISTING 17.14   CONTINUED

```
STDMETHODIMP CSystemInfo::MarshalInterface(IStream* pStm,
                                           REFIID riid,
                                           void *pv,
                                           DWORD dwDestContext,
                                           void *pvDestContext,
                                           DWORD mshlflags)
{
    AtlTrace(L"MarshalInterface\n");
    return pStm->Write((void*)&m_info, sizeof(SYSTEM_INFO), NULL);
}

STDMETHODIMP CSystemInfo::UnmarshalInterface(IStream *pStm,
                                             REFIID riid,
                                             void **ppv)
{
    AtlTrace(L"Empty - UnmarshalInterface\n");
    return S_OK;
}

STDMETHODIMP CSystemInfo::ReleaseMarshalData(IStream *pStm)
{
    AtlTrace(L"Empty - ReleaseMarshalData\n");
    return S_OK;
}

STDMETHODIMP CSystemInfo::DisconnectObject(DWORD dwReserved)
{
    AtlTrace(L"Empty - DisconnectObject\n");
    return S_OK;
}
```

Build the new version of the SysInfo project. It should compile successfully and register itself in the System Registry. Rerun InfoClient and InfoTimer, the two client test programs created earlier in the chapter. They should both run unmodified against the new MBV version of SysInfo—the only difference being that InfoTimer will run much, much faster. The next section examines performance issues with custom marshaling.

Comparing Custom and Standard Proxy Performance

A custom MBV marshaling implementation greatly reduces the cost of making method calls to a COM server. If you're frequently calling out-of-process COM objects, and the time required for method calls is a bottleneck, you can take advantage of MBV to increase your object's performance.

Table 17.3 compares the time reported by InfoTimer when calling SysInfo with standard marshaling versus custom marshaling. You'll recall that InfoTimer calls an ISystemInfo interface method for one million iterations.

TABLE 17.3 TIMING RESULTS OF STANDARD AND CUSTOM MARSHALING FOR SYSINFO

Marshaling	Time (Seconds)
Standard	266.23
Custom MBV	.109

As you can see in Table 17.3, the difference in the timing results is dramatic. The time could be improved by reducing the amount of work required by the proxy. The current implementation of SysInfo and SysInfoMbv marshal a SYSTEM_INFO structure. This requires the proxy to calculate a number of the responses, such as the processor enumeration and revision string. Slightly better performance could be obtained by marshaling a structure that contained data in its final form, thus reducing the work required by the proxy.

All these performance gains come at a price, however. There are some situations where MBV is not appropriate. MBV has these limitations:

- MBV breaks the COM identity rule. If you have two IUnknown interface pointers, you can compare those two pointers for equality to determine whether they refer to the same object. MBV will provide you with a new proxy (and a new IUnknown pointer) for each apartment in your process. This is usually not a problem when you're using MBV, but you should be aware of this limitation.

- MBV does not provide any way for the client's copy of the COM object to be updated. MBV is useful only when the state of the COM object doesn't change. If you need custom marshaling for objects that are updated, you'll need to implement RPC or some other communication method between the custom proxy and its stub in the remote process.

- MBV does not provide any way for the client to update the COM server object. Again, if you need this facility, you'll need to implement a communication channel back to the COM server object.

- Finally, MBV reduces only a small part of the total performance cost of your application. Unless you're making large amounts of method calls, you're unlikely to see a large performance gain.

17

CUSTOM COM OBJECTS

Summary

This chapter discussed some of the issues involved in creating custom COM objects using the ActiveX Template Library. Examples of creating custom COM objects using ATL were presented, as was an example of implementing MBV.

CHAPTER 18

Developing ActiveX Controls

An *ActiveX control* is a functional piece of code that's packaged into a reusable component, and it offers some guarantees about how it interacts with its clients. Although many ActiveX controls are user interface components, just like the built-in Windows 2000 controls, it's not required that an ActiveX control be visible at runtime.

This chapter discusses ActiveX controls and how they're implemented using MFC and ATL. ActiveX controls are built and then tested inside the ActiveX control test container that's shipped with Visual C++ and the Win32 Platform SDK. The chapter also includes a Visual Basic project that tests the control built using ATL.

What Is an ActiveX Control?

At a minimum, an ActiveX control must be a COM object that supports programming in a visual environment such as Visual Basic, FrontPage, and Visual C++. This means that an ActiveX control must support the IUnknown interface, as well as a few additional interfaces, such as IOleControl and IViewObject2, that allow a visually oriented development environment to interact with the control. This allows for a great deal of latitude when you're deciding how a control is to be implemented—previously, the OLE custom control architecture required support of at least fourteen interfaces, as will be discussed later.

Reducing the number of interfaces required for ActiveX controls makes it possible to create much smaller controls as well as makes it feasible to use ActiveX controls to implement functionality where the size of the control is an important factor. Web pages can be more intelligent when a control is downloaded and activated to your browser. For example, Internet Explorer has support for downloading ActiveX controls from a Web page. Although this opens up a lot of exciting functionality, the size of the control to be downloaded must be kept as small as possible.

ActiveX controls are almost always in-process servers. This is due to several factors:

- ActiveX controls present a user interface through the IViewObject2 interface, and this interface is not marshaled across a process boundary.
- A control loaded "in process" has much faster response time than a local EXE server.
- Historical reasons. Although you could probably whip up some sort of EXE server that supported another in-process COM object that served as the actual control, you wouldn't really have an ActiveX control.

ActiveX Control Interfaces

An ActiveX control typically implements a large number of interfaces. Although the number of mandatory interfaces has been greatly reduced from the number required by the original OLE controls specification, there's still a great deal of work required to implement a control or container from scratch. In the original OLE control specification, an OLE control was expected to support the interfaces listed in Table 18.1. For comparison, the requirements for ActiveX controls are also listed.

TABLE 18.1 INTERFACES REQUIRED FOR ACTIVEX AND OLE CUSTOM CONTROLS

Interface	OLE Control	ActiveX Control
IUnknown	Yes	Yes
IClassFactory or IClassFactory2	Yes	Usually
IConnectionPointContainer	Yes	Usually
IDataObject	Yes	Usually
IDispatch	Yes	Optional
IOleCache2	Optional	Optional
IOleControl	Yes	Yes
IOleInPlaceActiveObject	Yes	Usually
IOleInPlaceObject	Yes	Usually
IOleObject	Yes	Usually
IPersistStorage	See note	See note
IPersistStream	See note	See note
IPersistStreamInit	See note	See note
IProvideClassInfo	Yes	Usually
IRunnableObject	Yes	Usually
ISpecifyPropertyPages	Yes	Usually
IViewObject2	Yes	Yes

An OLE control or ActiveX control is required to implement one of the IPersist*XXX* interfaces—IPersistStorage, IPersistStream, or IPersistStreamInit. An ActiveX control is not required to support any of these interfaces unless the control is persistent. Because a control usually saves only its internal properties, the control usually implements the simplest of these interfaces—IPersistStream.

Although an ActiveX control need not support all the interfaces supported by an OLE control, most ActiveX controls will continue to be very "control-like." That is, they will still appear to be connectable objects, will be embeddable, and will draw themselves through `IViewObject2`. Connection points and connectable objects are discussed in Chapter 17, "Custom COM Objects."

ActiveX Control Properties, Events, and Methods

Interaction with an ActiveX component takes place via properties, events, and methods:

- A *property* is an attribute associated with the control.
- An *event* is a notification message passed to the container by the control.
- A *method* is an exposed function that can be applied to the control via `IDispatch`.

I'll discuss each of these interaction methods in the next few sections.

Properties

Properties are exposed by ActiveX controls as well as by the client site where the control is located. There are four basic types of properties:

- *Ambient properties* are provided to the control by the container. The control uses these properties in order to "fit in" properly. Commonly used ambient properties include the container's background color, default font, and foreground color.
- *Extended properties* are implemented by the container but appear to be generated by the control. For example, the tab order of various controls in a container are extended properties.
- *Stock properties* are control properties implemented by the ActiveX control development kit. Examples of stock properties are the control's font, the caption text, and the foreground and background colors.
- *Custom properties* are control properties you implement.

Events

An *event* is used to send a notification message to the control's container. Typically, events are used to notify the container when mouse clicks or other events take place. There are two basic types of events:

- *Stock events* are implemented by the ActiveX control development kit and are invoked just like a function call, such as `FireError`.

- *Custom events* are implemented by you, although the MFC and ATL class libraries and Visual C++ handle much of the work for you.

Methods

Methods implemented by ActiveX controls are exactly like the methods implemented for Automation, as discussed in Chapter 14, "Automation." In fact, methods are generally implemented through Automation using the `IDispatch` interface.

ActiveX controls built with MFC always expose their methods via `IDispatch`. Controls built with ATL can use either a dual interface, as discussed in Chapter 17, or a custom interface.

An ActiveX Control Example

As an example of creating an ActiveX control, the CD-ROM accompanying this book includes an ActiveX control that subclasses the existing Windows edit control. You can either use the completed project from the CD-ROM or follow along as the control is created from scratch.

The AxEdit control is similar to the basic Windows edit control, except it exposes properties that allow it to accept only numbers, letters, or a combination of both. When `WM_CHAR` is received by the control, it's processed as shown in Figure 18.1.

FIGURE 18.1

Handling `WM_CHAR` *in AxEdit.*

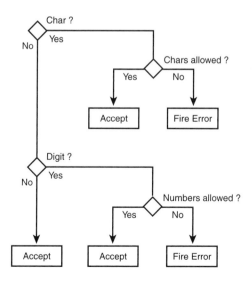

The property flags `m_fTextAllowed` and `m_fNumbersAllowed` are exposed as properties that can be changed by the AxEdit control's container.

Creating the Project

To get started creating the AxEdit control, use MFC ActiveX ControlWizard to create an MFC ActiveX control project. The initial page from the MFC ActiveX ControlWizard is shown in Figure 18.2. This page allows you to specify the basic characteristics of the project, such as the number of controls handled by this server, whether help files should be generated, and so on. Accept all the default options presented on this page by clicking the Next button.

FIGURE 18.2

The first page of the MFC ActiveX ControlWizard.

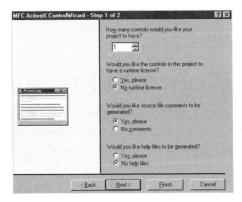

The second ControlWizard page is shown in Figure 18.3. This page allows you to change the names associated with the control and its interfaces as well as to define properties for the control. There's also a drop-down list that allows a base class to be specified for the control. Select EDIT from the drop-down list to make the AxEdit control subclass the standard edit control.

FIGURE 18.3

The second page of the MFC ActiveX ControlWizard.

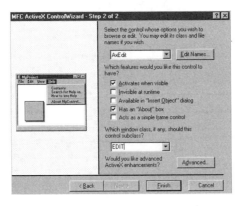

Click the button labeled Finish. A list of the files to be created is displayed. Click the OK button, and the skeleton project is created.

Drawing the Control

All visible ActiveX controls must be capable of drawing themselves. Even controls that aren't visible when active should draw something as an aid during program development. The AxEdit control is visible at runtime, and it should appear to be a standard edit control.

You might think that because AxEdit subclasses the standard edit control, it can draw itself. Unfortunately, the only control I've found that can draw itself correctly is the pushbutton control. For most controls, you must be prepared to handle the drawing yourself.

When an ActiveX control project is initially created, the control's OnDraw function draws an ellipse inside the bounding rectangle. The changes to OnDraw required for the AxEdit control are provided in Listing 18.1.

LISTING 18.1 USING THE OnDraw FUNCTION TO DRAW AN EDIT CONTROL

```
void CAxEditCtrl::OnDraw(
        CDC* pdc, const CRect& rcBounds, const CRect& rcInvalid)
{
    COLORREF    clrBackground = TranslateColor(GetBackColor());
    CBrush*     pOldBrush;
    CBrush      brBackground(clrBackground);

    pdc->FillRect(rcBounds, &brBackground);
    pOldBrush = pdc->SelectObject(&brBackground);
    pdc->SelectObject(pOldBrush);
    DoSuperclassPaint(pdc, rcBounds);
    CRect rc(rcBounds);
    pdc->DrawEdge(rc, EDGE_SUNKEN, BF_RECT);
}
```

The code provided in Listing 18.1 does three things. First, it fills the control's bounding rectangle with the ambient background color. Next, it calls DoSuperclassPaint to allow the edit control a chance to not draw itself properly. Finally, it draws a three-dimensional edge along the control's bounding rectangle.

Defining Properties for AxEdit

There are four properties used by AxEdit: the Font and Text stock properties and the fTextAllowed and fNumbersAllowed custom properties.

Using ClassWizard, add the stock properties for the AxEdit control. Select the Automation tab and then click the Add Property button. Fill in the dialog box using the values provided in Table 18.2.

TABLE 18.2 STOCK PROPERTIES FOR THE AxEDIT CONTROL

External name	Implementation
Font	Stock
Text	Stock

Use ClassWizard to add a custom property named `fNumbersAllowed` to the AxEdit project. Click the Add Property button and use the values provided in Table 18.3.

TABLE 18.3 THE `fNumbersAllowed` CUSTOM PROPERTY FOR THE AxEDIT CONTROL

Control	Value
External name	fNumbersAllowed
Type	BOOL
Variable name	m_fNumbersAllowed
Notification function	OnFNumbersAllowedChanged
Implementation	Member variable

Use ClassWizard to add the `fTextAllowed` property by following the steps used to add the previous properties. Use the values provided in Table 18.4.

TABLE 18.4 THE `fTextAllowed` CUSTOM PROPERTY FOR THE AxEDIT CONTROL

Control	Value
External name	fTextAllowed
Type	BOOL
Variable name	m_fTextAllowed
Notification function	OnFTextAllowedChanged
Implementation	Member variable

Modify the `CAxEditCtrl` class constructor to contain code that initializes the custom properties added in the previous steps. The modified constructor is shown in Listing 18.2 with changed lines shown in bold type.

LISTING 18.2 MODIFICATIONS (IN BOLD) TO THE `CAxEditCtrl` CONSTRUCTOR

```
CAxEditCtrl::CAxEditCtrl()
{
    InitializeIIDs(&IID_DOleEdit, &IID_DOleEditEvents);
```

```
    m_fTextAllowed = TRUE;
    m_fNumbersAllowed = TRUE;
}
```

Every control created using AppWizard includes a default property page. The AxEdit
property page is modified by adding two checkboxes that control the states of the
m_fTextAllowed and m_fNumbersAllowed flags. Open the IDD_PROPAGE_AXEDIT dialog
box resource and add two checkbox controls, as shown in Figure 18.4.

FIGURE 18.4

*The property page
used by AxEdit.*

Table 18.5 lists the properties for the checkbox controls. All properties that aren't listed
should be set to the default values.

TABLE 18.5   PROPERTY VALUES FOR CHECKBOX CONTROLS IN THE AXEDIT PROPERTY PAGE

Control	Resource ID	Caption
Numbers checkbox	IDC_CHECK_NUMBERS	&Numbers Allowed
Text checkbox	IDC_CHECK_TEXT	&Text Allowed

Use ClassWizard to associate CAxEditPropPage member variables with the controls,
using the values shown in Table 18.6.

TABLE 18.6   VALUES FOR NEW MEMBER VARIABLES IN CAxEditPropPage

Control ID	Variable Name	Category	Type	Property Name
IDC_CHECK_NUMBERS	m_fNumbersAllowed	Value	BOOL	fNumbersAllowed
IDC_CHECK_TEXT	m_fTextAllowed	Value	BOOL	fTextAllowed

The optional property name field is used by ClassWizard to generate source code that
exchanges the values from the property sheet to the control class. The DDP_ and DDX_
macros are used to transfer and validate property page data. The code used to transfer the
value of the IDC_CHECK_TEXT control looks like this:

```
//{{AFX_DATA_MAP(CAxEditPropPage)
DDP_Check(pDX,IDC_CHECK_TEXT, m_fTextAllowed, _T("fTextAllowed"));
DDX_Check(pDX, IDC_CHECK_TEXT, m_fTextAllowed);
//}}AFX_DATA_MAP
DDP_PostProcessing(pDX);
```

Inside the control class, you must collect the values from the property page during DoPropExchange, as shown in Listing 18.3.

LISTING 18.3   COLLECTING PROPERTIES FROM THE PROPERTY PAGE

```
void CAxEditCtrl::DoPropExchange(CPropExchange* pPX)
{
    ExchangeVersion(pPX, MAKELONG(_wVerMinor, _wVerMajor));
    COleControl::DoPropExchange(pPX);

    PX_Bool(pPX, _T("fNumbersAllowed"), m_fNumbersAllowed);
    PX_Bool(pPX, _T("fTextAllowed"), m_fTextAllowed);
}
```

The AxEdit control supports the stock font property. An easy way to give the control access to all the available fonts is to add the standard font property page to the control. The property pages associated with an ActiveX control are grouped together between the BEGIN_PROPPAGEIDS and END_PROPPAGEIDS macros. Listing 18.4 shows how the standard font property page is added to the control using the PROPPAGEID macro. Remember to change the second parameter passed to the BEGIN_PROPPAGEIDS macro, which is the number of property pages used by the control object.

LISTING 18.4   ADDING THE STANDARD FONT PROPERTY PAGE TO AXEDIT

```
BEGIN_PROPPAGEIDS(COleEditCtrl, 2)
    PROPPAGEID(COleEditPropPage::guid)
    PROPPAGEID(CLSID_CFontPropPage)
END_PROPPAGEIDS(COleEditCtrl)
```

As will be demonstrated when we test the control later in this chapter, adding the font property page, along with exposing the stock font property, allows a user to easily change the control font. The only code that's written is shown in Listing 18.4.

Handling Character Input

As discussed earlier, AxEdit uses exposed properties to determine whether characters entered on the keyboard are to be stored in the edit control. If an invalid character is entered, an Error event is fired to the control's container.

The message sent to the control as characters are input to the control is WM_CHAR. Using ClassWizard, add a message-handling function to the CAxEditCtrl class, using the values from Table 18.7.

TABLE 18.7 HANDLING THE WM_CHAR MESSAGE IN CAxEditCtrl

Class Name	Object ID	Message	Function
CAxEditCtrl	CAxEditCtrl	WM_CHAR	OnChar

The source code for the CAxEditCtrl::OnChar function is provided in Listing 18.5.

LISTING 18.5 HANDLING THE WM_CHAR MESSAGE IN CAxEditCtrl::OnChar

```
void CAxEditCtrl::OnChar(UINT nChar, UINT nRepCnt, UINT nFlags)
{
    if( _istdigit(nChar) )
    {
        if( m_fNumbersAllowed == FALSE )
        {
            FireError( CTL_E_INVALIDPROPERTYVALUE,
                        _T("Numbers not allowed") );
        }
        else
        {
            COleControl::OnChar(nChar, nRepCnt, nFlags);
        }
    }
    else if( _istalpha(nChar) )
    {
        if( m_fTextAllowed == FALSE )
        {
            FireError( CTL_E_INVALIDPROPERTYVALUE,
                        _T("Characters not allowed") );
        }
        else
        {
            COleControl::OnChar(nChar, nRepCnt, nFlags);
        }
    }
    else
        COleControl::OnChar(nChar, nRepCnt, nFlags);
}
```

18

DEVELOPING
ACTIVEX
CONTROLS

The OnChar handler tests for valid characters based on the property flags
m_fTextAllowed and m_fNumbersAllowed. Valid characters are passed to
COleControl::OnChar, the base class handler for WM_CHAR. If an invalid character is
detected, an Error event is fired to the control's container.

Modifying the Control's Bitmap

When an ActiveX control is used in a tool such as Developer Studio, Visual Basic, or the ActiveX control test container, a bitmap associated with the control is displayed to the user. In Visual Basic, the bitmap is added to the control palette used to design dialog box resources. In the test container, a toolbar button displaying the bitmap is added to the container's toolbar.

Open the IDB_AXEDIT bitmap resource and edit the bitmap image, as shown in Figure 18.5. Save the bitmap and compile the AxEdit project.

FIGURE 18.5

The IDB_AXEDIT bitmap resource.

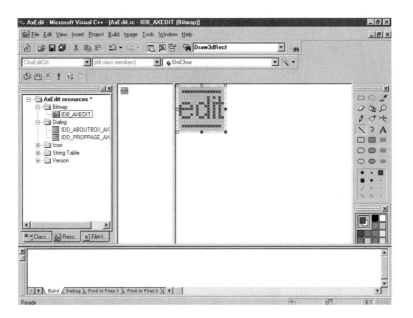

Testing an ActiveX Control

After following the steps in the previous sections, you're in possession of an AxEdit ActiveX control. However, because the control is an in-process server located in a DLL, it can't be run as an EXE. Testing an ActiveX control requires a few extra steps, which are discussed in this section.

Choosing a Test Container for Your Control

Every ActiveX control requires a control container. The simplest control container is the ActiveX control test container included with Visual C++ and the Win32 Platform SDK. Other ActiveX control containers include Microsoft Access and Visual Basic.

You should test an ActiveX control using as many test containers as possible. In this chapter, AxEdit is tested with `TSTCON32.EXE`, the ActiveX control test container.

Using the TSTCON32 Test Container

In order to launch the AxEdit control in the Developer Studio debugger, you must specify the application used to load the control. You can do this by following these steps:

1. Select Settings from the Project menu in Developer Studio. The Project Settings dialog box is displayed.
2. Click the tab labeled Debug.
3. Click the arrow located next to the edit control labeled Executable for Debug Session; then select ActiveX control Test Container from the pop-up menu. The edit control will be filled with the proper path.
4. Click the OK button to dismiss the dialog box and save your changes.

After you've made these changes, the Developer Studio debugger can be used to launch the test container. Clicking the Go icon in the toolbar or otherwise starting a debug session causes the test container to be displayed, as shown in Figure 18.6.

FIGURE 18.6

The ActiveX control test container.

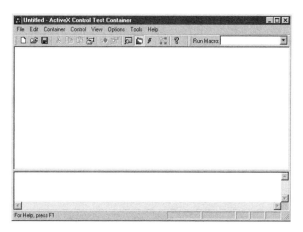

When an ActiveX control created by ControlWizard is compiled, the control is automatically registered. To display a list of all registered controls, select Insert New Control from the Edit menu. A dialog box containing all available ActiveX controls is displayed. Select the AxEdit control and then click the OK button. The AxEdit control is inserted into the test container, as shown in Figure 18.7.

FIGURE 18.7

The ActiveX control test container and the AxEdit control.

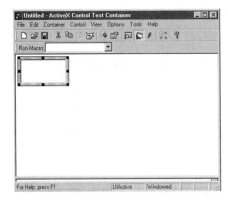

FIGURE 18.7

The ActiveX control test container and the AxEdit control.

Testing Properties

The test container can be used to test your control's properties in two ways:

- Through an Automation interface that lists all exposed properties and methods
- Through your control's property sheet

To access all the methods, including properties, implemented by an ActiveX control, select Invoke Methods from the Control menu. An Invoke Methods dialog box is displayed, as shown in Figure 18.8.

FIGURE 18.8

Accessing the methods exposed by AxEdit.

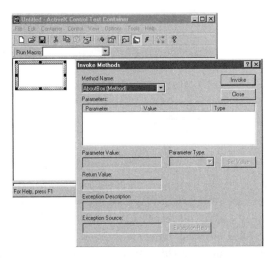

To display the list of methods exposed by the control, click the drop-down list. Every method and property can be accessed and changed through this dialog box, even if the property isn't accessible through the control's property sheet. To invoke a particular method, select the method name from the drop-down list, set any required parameter values, and then click the Invoke button.

A slightly easier way to access properties is provided through the control's property sheet. The test container can be used to invoke the control's property sheet by selecting Properties|AxEdit Control Object from the Edit menu. The property sheet for AxEdit is shown in Figure 18.9.

FIGURE 18.9

The property sheet used by AxEdit.

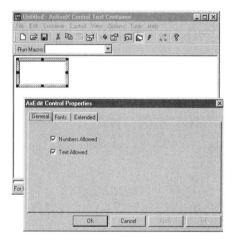

In addition to the ActiveX control test container, you should test your control in other containers, such as Visual Basic. Using Visual Basic to test ActiveX controls is discussed later, at the end of this chapter.

Creating ActiveX Controls with ATL

In addition to MFC, you can use the ActiveX Template Library to build your ActiveX controls. This is the same ATL library used in Chapter 17 to create custom COM objects.

Here are the ATL classes that are specific to ActiveX controls:

- CWindow. Similar to the MFC CWnd class but much lighter weight; this class provides easy access to a number of commonly used functions.

- CWindowImpl. Derived from CWindow and used by the control class to subclass and superclass an existing window class; it implements the ATL message map.
- CDialogImpl. Derived from CWindow and used to implement dialog boxes.
- CContainedWindow. Derived from CWindow and used to model a window contained in another object. If you superclass or subclass an existing window, an instance of CContainedWindow will represent the original window.

In addition to these classes, ATL provides support for adding properties, events, and connection points to your ActiveX control. These features are discussed in the following sections.

Implementing Stock Properties Using ATL

The easiest way to add a stock property to an ATL control is with the ATL Object Wizard. The Stock Properties tab enables you to add stock properties by moving the property name between two list boxes, as shown in Figure 18.10.

FIGURE 18.10
The ATL Object Wizard's Stock Properties tab.

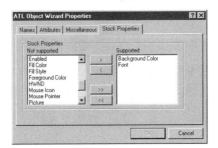

The class header for the ATL control object contains a property map that tracks all properties exposed by the control.

The property map begins with the BEGIN_PROP_MAP macro and ends with the END_PROP_MAP macro. Inside the property map are a series of macros that specify properties supported by the ATL object, as shown in Listing 18.6.

LISTING 18.6   AN EXAMPLE OF AN ATL PROPERTY MAP

```
BEGIN_PROP_MAP(CTestButton)
    PROP_DATA_ENTRY("_cx", m_sizeExtent.cx, VT_UI4)
    PROP_DATA_ENTRY("_cy", m_sizeExtent.cy, VT_UI4)
    PROP_ENTRY("BackColor", DISPID_BACKCOLOR, CLSID_StockColorPage)
    PROP_ENTRY("ForeColor", DISPID_FORECOLOR, CLSID_StockColorPage)
END_PROP_MAP()
```

Stock properties are implemented using the PROP_ENTRY macro. PROP_ENTRY has three
parameters:

- The description of the stock property
- The DISPID for the stock property
- The CLSID of the property page used for entering the property (or CLSID_NULL if no
  property page is used)

Each stock property has a specific DISPID that refers to the property. For example,
DISPID_BACKCOLOR is the dispatch ID for the control's background color. The ATL
Object Wizard knows all about these names—if you're adding a stock property by hand,
you have two choices:

- Create a dummy project and then add the stock property. You can add the stock
  property by hand using the DISPID that the ATL Object Wizard used.
- Look in the Platform SDK's OleCtl.h header file for standard DISPIDs. This file
  contains all the standard Automation DISPIDs. Search for DISPID_AUTOSIZE, which
  is at the start of the list.

In addition to adding an entry to the property map, the ATL Object Wizard also adds a
member variable to your class declaration for every property. However, the ATL Object
Wizard doesn't add any code that attaches the member variable to the property map
entry—it's not needed.

The mapping between stock properties and member variables is done in the ATL class
library. Every stock property is mapped to a particular member of an anonymous union
declared in the ATL CComControlBase class. When implementing a stock property by
hand, you again have two choices:

- Create a dummy project, as described earlier, and use the variable name selected
  by the ATL Object Wizard
- Look in the anonymous union declared in the CComControlBase class and select
  the proper variable yourself

Whichever method you choose, make sure you name the variable correctly. If you define
a different name for the variable, your project will compile, but your property variable
won't be updated correctly.

Implementing Custom Properties Using ATL

Implementing custom properties is similar to implementing stock properties. One obvious difference between stock and custom properties is that you must name the custom

18

DEVELOPING
ACTIVEX
CONTROLS

properties yourself. Custom properties are added by right-clicking the IDL icon in the ClassView window and selecting the Add Properties item from the pop-up menu. A dialog box will be displayed, as shown in Figure 18.11.

FIGURE 18.11

Adding a property to an ATL object.

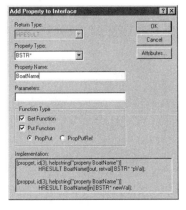

The dialog box shown in Figure 18.11 is used to add the named property, the necessary IDL statements, and the necessary glue code in your class so that the property can be exposed to the outside world.

You must provide the following values:

- *Property Type*. The Automation-compatible type that contains the property.
- *Property Name*. The name of the property as it will be exposed to the outside world. This is the name that VB will display in its property page for your control.
- *Parameters*. Any additional parameters you would like to have applied to the property.
- *Get Function*. If checked, this option causes a function to be generated to retrieve the property from the control. If this option is cleared, the property cannot be read.
- *Put Function*. If checked, this option causes a function to be generated to set the control's property. If this option is cleared, the property is read-only.
- *PropPut/PropPutRef*. If the PropPutRef radio button is selected, the property is set by reference, which is more efficient for large objects.

The Attributes button allows you to set IDL attributes, such as hidden or call_as, for the property.

As an example, consider a project named TestBtn that exposes a ThreadID property. To enable this property, you would fill in the Add Property to Interface dialog box with the values from Table 18.8.

TABLE 18.8 SAMPLE VALUES FOR THE ADD PROPERTY TO INTERFACE DIALOG BOX

Control	Value
Property Type	long
Property Name	ThreadID
Parameters	(none)
Get Function	Checked
Put Function	Checked
PropPut	Selected

Given these values, Visual C++ would create the following IDL for the new property:

```
interface ITestButton : IDispatch
{
    // Existing interfaces omitted
    [propget, id(1), helpstring("property ThreadID")]
    HRESULT ThreadID([out, retval] long *pVal);
    [propput, id(1), helpstring("property ThreadID")]
    HRESULT ThreadID([in] long newVal);
};
```

Visual C++ would also create class member functions to implement the necessary interface declared by this IDL fragment. What Visual C++ will *not* do is declare a member variable for you. You must add a member variable (if needed) and fill in the skeleton member functions provided by Visual C++, as shown in Listing 18.7.

LISTING 18.7 AN EXAMPLE OF MEMBER FUNCTIONS USED TO PROVIDE ACCESS TO CUSTOM PROPERTIES

```
STDMETHODIMP CTestButton::get_ThreadID(long *pVal)
{
    *pVal = m_threadID;
    return S_OK;
}

STDMETHODIMP CTestButton::put_ThreadID(long newVal)
{
    m_threadID = newVal;
    return S_OK;
}
```

Visual C++ will not automatically add the custom property to the property map, so it will not be persisted automatically. If you want the property to be persistent, you must add an entry to the property map using the PROP_DATA_ENTRY macro, as shown in Listing 18.8.

LISTING 18.8 ADDING A CUSTOM PROPERTY TO THE PROPERTY MAP

```
BEGIN_PROP_MAP(CTestButton)
    PROP_DATA_ENTRY("_cx", m_sizeExtent.cx, VT_UI4)
    PROP_DATA_ENTRY("_cy", m_sizeExtent.cy, VT_UI4)
    PROP_DATA_ENTRY("ThreadID", m_threadID, VT_I4)
    PROP_ENTRY("Caption", DISPID_CAPTION, CLSID_NULL)
END_PROP_MAP()
```

The PROP_DATA_ENTRY macro has three parameters:

- The description of the property
- The member variable that contains the property's value
- The Automation tag that suits the variable type

A complete list of valid Automation tags can be found in the Visual C++ online documentation in the COM and ActiveX folder. One good source can be found if you search for a document titled "VARIANT and VARIANTARG."

Using Ambient Properties with ATL

Ambient properties can be retrieved by calling functions implemented in the CComControlBase class. Three of the most commonly used ambient properties and the functions used to access them are provided in Table 18.9.

TABLE 18.9 COMMONLY USED AMBIENT PROPERTIES AND ACCESS FUNCTIONS

Property	*Function*
Background Color	GetAmbientBackColor
Foreground Color	GetAmbientForeColor
Font	GetAmbientFont

The online documentation for Visual C++ has more examples of ambient property functions. Go to the index and search for topics that begin with GetAmbient. CComControlBase also has a catch-all member function named GetAmbientProperty that will return the value of any ambient property given its DISPID.

Implementing Events in an ATL Project

Events are implemented in an ATL project by adding outgoing events to the project's `IDispatch` interface for events. This interface is declared in the project's IDL file inside the library block, as shown in bold in the following code fragment:

```
[
    uuid(7AFFD2D2-8701-11D2-B875-00104B36573E),
    version(1.0),
    helpstring("Foo 1.0 Type Library")
]
library FOOLib
{
    importlib("stdole32.tlb");
    importlib("stdole2.tlb");
    [
        uuid(7AFFD2E2-8701-11D2-B875-00104B36573E),
        helpstring("_IFooExampleEvents Interface")
    ]
    dispinterface _IFooExampleEvents
    {
        properties:
        methods:
        [id(1), helpstring("method OnMyEvent")] HRESULT OnMyEvent();
        [id(2), helpstring("method OnTheRoad")] HRESULT OnTheRoad();
    };
    [
        uuid(7AFFD2E1-8701-11D2-B875-00104B36573E),
        helpstring("FooExample Class")
    ]
    coclass FooExample
    {
        [default] interface IFooExample;
        [default, source] dispinterface _IFooExampleEvents;
    };
};
```

The name of the event interface is based on the name of the ATL object. In this IDL fragment, the event interface for the `FooExample` ATL object is `_IFooExampleEvents`.

As discussed in Chapter 17, you must compile the project's type library before using the built-in Visual C++ support for generating connection points. After you've compiled the type library, connection points are added by right-clicking the ATL object's icon in the ClassView window and then selecting the Implement Connection Point menu item from the pop-up menu. A dialog box will be displayed, as shown in Figure 18.12.

18

DEVELOPING ACTIVEX CONTROLS

FIGURE **18.12**

*Implementing
connection points
for an ATL object.*

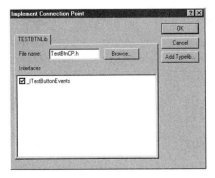

As shown in Figure 18.12, the dialog box will contain any interfaces suitable for generating connection points. Check the appropriate entry in the list box and click OK. The connection point class will be created with a name generated by prefixing CProxy to the interface name. For example, given an event interface named _ITestButtonEvents, the generated class will be named CProxy_ITestButtonEvents.

The connection point class will contain member functions that can be used to generate events that will be sent to the container. Every event will have a function of the form

```
Fire_OnMyEvent()
```

where OnMyEvent is actually the name of the event to be fired. For example, the IDL fragment earlier in this section had the following event:

```
[id(1), helpstring("method OnMyEvent")] HRESULT OnMyEvent();
[id(2), helpstring("method OnTheRoad")] HRESULT OnTheRoad();
```

These events would result in these two functions:

```
class CProxy_ITestButtonEvents
{
public:
    HRESULT Fire_OnMyEvent()
    HRESULT Fire_OnTheRoad()
};
```

The new connection point class is added to the multiple inheritance list for the control. This allows you to fire any event directly:

```
if(waterLevelRising && pumpRunning)
    Fire_SailboatSinking();
```

Adding Message and Event Handlers

There are two ways to add handlers for messages and events to an ATL project. The graphical way is to right-click the ATL object's C++ class icon in ClassView and select

Add Windows Message Handler from the pop-up menu. A dialog box will be displayed, as shown in Figure 18.13.

FIGURE 18.13

The New Windows Message and Event Handlers dialog box.

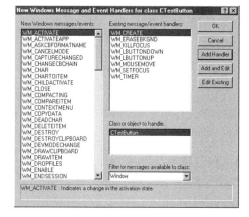

You can easily add handlers for Windows messages by selecting a message from the left column and clicking the Add Handler button.

Another option is to manually add the handlers to the class message map using the `MESSAGE_HANDLER` macro:

```
MESSAGE_HANDLER(WM_ERASEBKGND,OnEraseBkgnd)
```

The `MESSAGE_HANDLER` macro has two parameters:

- The Windows message to be handled
- The name of the member function that will handle the message

If you're handling notification events from a `WM_COMMAND` message, you must use the `COMMAND_CODE_HANDLER` macro:

```
COMMAND_CODE_HANDLER(LBN_DBLCLICK, OnLbDblClicked)
```

The `COMMAND_CODE_HANDLER` macro also has two parameters;

- The notification message sent in `WM_COMMAND`
- The name of the member function that will handle the message

Either of these macros can be used inside the message map, which begins with the `BEGIN_MSG_MAP` macro and ends with the `END_MSG_MAP` macro, as shown in Listing 18.9.

LISTING 18.9   A TYPICAL ATL MESSAGE MAP

```
BEGIN_MSG_MAP(CMyButton)
    MESSAGE_HANDLER(WM_CREATE, OnCreate)
    COMMAND_CODE_HANDLER(BN_CLICKED, OnClicked)
    CHAIN_MSG_MAP(CComControl<CTestButton>)
ALT_MSG_MAP(1)
    // Alternate window message handling
END_MSG_MAP()
```

Note that the message map in Listing 18.9 also contains an ALT_MAP macro. This marks the beginning of an alternate message map that can be used to handle messages from another window within a single message map.

An ActiveX Control Built with ATL

This book's CD-ROM includes PopButton, an ATL-based ActiveX control that super-classes the standard Windows pushbutton. When an instance of PopButton is placed on a dialog box or Visual Basic form, it looks like a label. Figure 18.14 shows several PopButtons on a Visual Basic form.

FIGURE 18.14

The PopButton initially looks like a label.

When the mouse passes over a PopButton, the control's edges are redrawn so that it looks like a pushbutton, as shown in Figure 18.15.

FIGURE 18.15

The PopButton control looks like a button when the mouse hovers over it.

The Basic Design of PopButton

PopButton is based on a standard Windows pushbutton, with one major difference: The button is flat until the mouse moves over it. In order for the control to be drawn properly, PopButton must be able to perform the following tasks:

- Detect when the mouse is clicked over the control.
- Track the current state of the button (flat, up, or down).
- Track the current focus state of the control so that the focus rectangle can be drawn correctly.

In addition, PopButton must use a set of stock properties that a user of the button might want to adjust:

- Background Color
- Foreground Color
- Tab Stop
- Caption

Two events are sent from the PopButton control to its container:

- OnClicked is sent when the PopButton control is clicked. This event is sent if the user clicks the button using the mouse or selects the button using the keyboard.
- OnHover is sent when the PopButton control enters a raised, or "hover," state. This event notifies the container that the mouse is hovering over the control and allows the container to update a status bar or provide some other type of feedback.

Messages Handled by PopButton

PopButton handles messages sent by the operating system, as well as one message sent by the underlying button control. The button control must handle the following Windows messages:

- WM_MOUSEMOVE. Sent as the mouse passes over the control
- WM_SETFOCUS. Sent just before the control receives input focus
- WM_KILLFOCUS. Sent just before the control loses input focus
- WM_LBUTTONDOWN. Sent when the user presses down on the primary mouse button over the control
- WM_LBUTTONUP. Sent when the user releases the primary mouse button over the control
- WM_ERASEBKGND. Sent just before the control is painted by Windows
- WM_MOUSELEAVE. Sent as the mouse moves away from the control's window

18

DEVELOPING
ACTIVEX
CONTROLS

In addition, the control handles one notification message sent by the pushbutton control:

- BN_CLICKED. Sent when the user successfully clicks the button control

As you might expect, the BN_CLICKED message is sent when the user clicks the button with a mouse. The message is also sent if the user selects the button using the keyboard.

Handling the Raised and Flat Button States

The WM_MOUSEMOVE and WM_MOUSELEAVE messages are used together in order to control the raised appearance of the PopButton. As discussed earlier, the button is initially drawn flat, as shown previously in Figure 18.14.

When a WM_MOUSEMOVE message is received by the control, the control redraws itself in the raised state, as shown previously in Figure 18.15.

After the control has been drawn in the raised state, the control must handle two cases:

- When the user clicks the control
- When the user moves the mouse away from the control

The first case is easily handled and is discussed in the next section. However, if the mouse is moved away from the control, no event is sent to the control's window! In order to detect the departure of the mouse, the Win32 TrackMouseEvent function is called when the mouse initially moves over the control's window. When the mouse is moved away from the control, a WM_MOUSELEAVE message is received by the control, and the button is returned to its flat state.

Handling Button Clicks

Three messages are used to draw the control and report events when the user clicks the PopButton control. WM_LBUTTONUP and WM_LBUTTONDOWN messages are sent from the operating system as the user presses and releases the primary mouse button over the control. In response to these messages, the control is drawn in either the down state (for WM_LBUTTONDOWN) or the raised state (for WM_LBUTTONUP).

When the user clicks the PopButton control, the underlying button will generate a BN_CLICKED notification message. This message is used to create an OnClicked event that's sent to the control's container.

Handling the Focus Rectangle

One important visual indicator supplied by any user interface component is the focus rectangle. If the focus rectangle isn't drawn correctly, the user may be confused about the input state of the control.

Two messages are used to draw the focus rectangle. The WM_SETFOCUS message is sent just before the control receives input focus and causes the familiar dotted focus rectangle to be drawn around the control. The WM_KILLFOCUS message is sent just before focus is lost by the control and causes the focus rectangle to be removed.

It's so important that the focus rectangle be drawn correctly that Windows offers an API function that handles it all for you:

```
DrawFocusRect(hdc, lprc);
```

You call DrawFocusRect with two parameters: the device context that you're drawing into and the rectangle that describes the focus rectangle's boundaries. This function is also called to remove the focus rectangle—if you call it a second time with the same rectangle, the focus rectangle is removed.

Creating the PopBtn Project

The PopBtn project is used to create the PopButton control; it was created using the Visual C++ ATL Control Wizard. The control is a DLL project, as shown in its ATL COM Wizard page in Figure 18.16.

18

DEVELOPING
ACTIVEX
CONTROLS

FIGURE 18.16

The ATL COM Wizard, as used to create the PopBtn project.

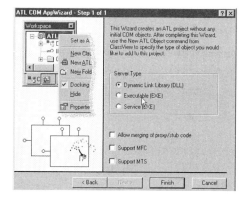

The PopBtn ActiveX control project does not use any of the optional features offered by ATL Control Wizard. None of these options is suitable for this ActiveX control:

• *Allow merging of proxy/stub code.* This option doesn't apply to ActiveX controls because they're always used in process. Selecting this option doesn't cause any real harm, but it does increase the size of your control.

- *Support MFC*. The entire purpose of ATL is to enable the creation of small, fast controls. In keeping with that theme, the PopBtn project does not use MFC. If you must use MFC, be aware that you're adding a large amount of mainly unnecessary code to your control project. If you can't live without MFC, consider using the MFC Library for your control.

- *Support MTS*. This option adds support for the Microsoft Transaction Server threading model. This option isn't selected for the PopBtn project because it's not an MTS component.

Click Finish to generate the PopBtn project files.

Adding the PopButton Control Class to the PopBtn Project

The ActiveX component in the PopBtn project is implemented by adding an ATL object into the project with the ATL Object Wizard. Start by selecting New ATL Object from the Insert menu.

There are several different categories of ATL objects available from the ATL Object Wizard:

- *Objects*. As discussed in Chapter 17, this category contains different types of custom COM objects.

- *Controls*. Contains different types of ActiveX controls that can be added to your project, as discussed later.

- *Miscellaneous*. Contains a dialog box object that can be added to your project.

- *Data Access*. Contains data provider and consumer objects.

There are seven different types of control objects:

- *Full Control*. Generates an object that implements a full ActiveX control that can be hosted in all containers

- *Property Page*. Generates an object that provides a property page

- *Composite Control*. Generates an object that can contain multiple windows

- *HTML Control*. Generates an object that uses a Web page as its user interface

- *Lite Control*. Similar to a full control but supports only the minimum interfaces required for Internet Explorer

- *Lite Composite Control*. Similar to a composite control but supports only the minimum interfaces required for Internet Explorer

- *Lite HTML Control*. Similar to an HTML control but supports only the minimum interfaces required for Internet Explorer

The PopBtn project will implement a full control. Select Controls from the list box on the left side of the wizard and then select Full Control as the control type, as shown in Figure 18.17.

FIGURE 18.17

The ATL Object Wizard.

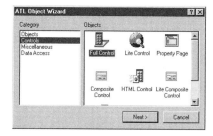

After you've selected the type of control to be built, you must define the control's attributes using the ATL Object Wizard dialog box. This dialog box has four tabs, with each tab used to define a different set of properties for the control.

The number of tabs available for an ATL object varies depending on the object type. A full control has four tabs, as shown in Figure 18.18.

FIGURE 18.18

The ATL Object Wizard Properties dialog box.

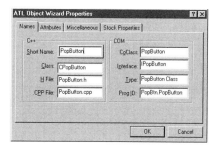

The Names tab for a full control is just like the Names tab used in custom COM objects in Chapter 17. The name of the ATL object added to the PopBtn project is PopButton. The properties in the Names tab for the PopButton object are provided in Table 18.10. You'll only need to fill in the short name for the ATL Object—the other fields will be filled in automatically.

TABLE 18.10   CONTENTS OF THE NAMES TAB FOR THE POPBUTTON CONTROL

Property	Value
Short Name	PopButton
Class	CPopButton

continues

TABLE 18.10   CONTINUED

Property	Value
.H File	PopButton.h
.CPP File	PopButton.cpp
CoClass	PopButton
Interface	IPopButton
Type	PopButton Class
Prog ID	PopBtn.PopButton

The second tab is labeled Attributes and, again, is identical to the Attributes tab discussed in Chapter 17. This tab is used to collect information about the threading model and other object attributes, as shown in Figure 18.19.

FIGURE 18.19

The ATL object attributes used for PopButton.

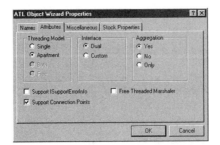

The values used for PopButton are provided in Table 18.11. Keep the default values for all these options, except for the checkbox labeled Support Connection Points. Connection points are used to supply events to the control's container, so make sure the checkbox is selected.

TABLE 18.11   CONTENTS OF THE ATTRIBUTES TAB FOR THE POPBUTTON CONTROL

Property	Value
Threading Model	Apartment
Interface	Dual
Aggregation	Yes
Support ISupportErrorInfo	Unchecked
Support Connection Points	**Checked**
Free Threaded Marshaler	Unchecked

The third tab is labeled Miscellaneous and contains attributes that apply specifically to ActiveX controls. The Miscellaneous tab is shown in Figure 18.20.

FIGURE 18.20

The contents of the Miscellaneous tab for the PopButton ATL object.

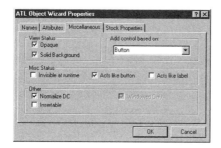

Here are the properties contained in the Miscellaneous tab:

- *Opaque.* Specifies that the control is completely opaque, with none of the container allowed to show through the control. Selecting this option causes the control to be drawn slightly faster.

- *Solid Background.* Specifies that the control has a solid background rather than a pattern-filled background.

- *Add control based on.* Specifies a standard Windows control that is subclassed or superclassed by the ActiveX control. PopButton superclasses the standard Windows pushbutton control.

- *Invisible at runtime.* Indicates that the button will never be visible at runtime.

- *Acts like a button.* Specifies that the control is a button and can draw a default button rectangle around the control. (This option is selected for PopButton.)

- *Acts like a label.* Specifies that the control can replace the container's label.

- *Normalize DC.* Specifies that the device context (DC) should be normalized before it's passed to the control class's OnDraw function. (This option is usually selected.)

- *Insertable.* Specifies that the ActiveX control should be listed as an insertable object in general-purpose OLE containers such as Word.

- *Windowed Only.* Specifies that the control should never be created as a windowless control. Containers that support the OC 96 specification, such as Internet Explorer, will create windowless controls as an optimization whenever possible.

Values used by the PopButton object in the Miscellaneous tab are provided in Table 18.12, with nondefault values shown in bold type.

18

DEVELOPING ACTIVEX CONTROLS

TABLE 18.12 CONTENTS OF THE MISCELLANEOUS TAB FOR THE POPBUTTON CONTROL

Property	Value
Opaque	Checked
Solid Background	Checked
Add control based on	**Button**
Invisible at runtime	Unchecked
Acts like a button	**Checked**
Acts like a label	Unchecked
Normalize DC	Checked
Windowed Only	**Checked**
Insertable	Unchecked

The final tab in the dialog box is labeled Stock Properties; it contains a list of all stock properties that can be implemented by an ActiveX control, as shown in Figure 18.21.

FIGURE 18.21

The contents of the Stock Properties tab for the PopButton ATL object.

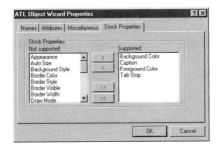

The following stock properties are used by the PopButton control:

- Background Color
- Foreground Color
- Tab Stop
- Caption

After you've selected the stock properties listed here, close the dialog box. The ATL New Object Wizard will generate the necessary code and add it to the project.

Handling the `BevelSize` Custom Property

The PopButton object will expose a custom property that contains the size, in pixels, of the button's beveled edge. Add a custom property to the PopButton object by right-clicking the `IPopButton` icon in ClassView and selecting Add Property from the pop-up menu. Use the values from Table 18.13 to add the `BevelSize` property.

TABLE 18.13   VALUES USED TO ADD THE `BevelSize` PROPERTY

Control	Value
Property Type	short
Property Name	BevelSize
Parameters	(none)
Get Function	Checked
Put Function	Checked
PropPut	Selected

Click OK to generate the IDL and skeleton C++ code for the property. As part of adding the property to the project, `get_` and `put_` access functions are added to the project. The access functions for the `BevelSize` property are shown in Listing 18.10, with new lines shown in bold. The new lines store the property in the `m_cBevelSize` member variable.

LISTING 18.10   THE `get_` AND `put_` ACCESS FUNCTIONS FOR THE `BevelSize` PROPERTY

```
STDMETHODIMP CPopButton::get_BevelSize(short *pVal)
{
    *pVal = m_cBevelSize;
    return S_OK;
}

STDMETHODIMP CPopButton::put_BevelSize(short newVal)
{
    m_cBevelSize = newVal;
    return S_OK;
}
```

Add a declaration for the `m_cBevelSize` member variable at the end of the `CPopButton` class declaration, after the other public member variables:

```
short  m_cBevelSize; // Stores size of beveled edge
```

18

DEVELOPING ACTIVEX CONTROLS

Adding Outgoing Events

As discussed earlier, the PopButton control will provide two events to its containers:

- OnClick will be sent when the button is clicked.
- OnHover will be sent when the button is raised.

Open the PopBtn.IDL file and add the two lines shown in bold in Listing 18.11 to the _IPopButtonEvents interface. Alternatively, you could also add the events by right-clicking the _IPopButtonEvents icon in ClassView and selecting Add Method from the pop-up menu.

LISTING 18.11   CHANGES TO THE PopButton.IDL FILE TO ADD OUTGOING EVENTS (IN BOLD)

```
library POPBTNLib
{
    importlib("stdole32.tlb");
    importlib("stdole2.tlb");

    [
        uuid(220DB0C9-89BD-11D2-B877-00104B36573E),
        helpstring("_IPopButtonEvents Interface")
    ]
    dispinterface _IPopButtonEvents
    {
        properties:
        methods:
        [id(1), helpstring("OnClick event")] HRESULT OnClick();
        [id(2), helpstring("OnHover event")] HRESULT OnHover();
    };

    [
        uuid(220DB0C8-89BD-11D2-B877-00104B36573E),
        helpstring("PopButton Class")
    ]
    coclass PopButton
    {
        [default] interface IPopButton;
        [default, source] dispinterface _IPopButtonEvents;
    };
};
```

Before proceeding, compile the skeleton project. This will compile the type library and make it possible to add the event connection points for the control.

After the project has been compiled, add the connection points to the PopButton project by right-clicking the CPopButton icon and selecting Implement Connection Point from the pop-up menu. Select the checkbox next to _IPopButtonEvents and click the OK button. The CProxy_IPopButtonEvents class will be automatically generated and added to the project.

Modifications to the Message Map

Seven messages must be added to the CPopButton message map. Six of the messages are generated by the operating system, and one message, BN_CLICKED, is generated by the superclassed pushbutton control.

As discussed earlier, you can open the dialog box that adds message-handling functions by right-clicking the CPopButton icon in ClassView and selecting Add Windows Message Handler from the pop-up menu. Add handlers for these messages:

- WM_ERASEBKGND
- WM_KILLFOCUS
- WM_LBUTTONDOWN
- WM_LBUTTONUP
- WM_MOUSEMOVE

You must also manually add COMMAND_CODE_HANDLER macros for the BN_CLICKED and WM_MOUSELEAVE messages to the message map. The finished message map is shown in Listing 18.12, with the manually added macros shown in bold. Note that all the message handlers are in the main part of the message map. Make sure your message map doesn't have any message-handling macros in the alternate message map.

LISTING 18.12 THE MESSAGE MAP FOR THE POPBUTTON PROJECT

```
BEGIN_MSG_MAP(CPopButton)
    MESSAGE_HANDLER(WM_CREATE, OnCreate)
    MESSAGE_HANDLER(WM_SETFOCUS, OnSetFocus)
    MESSAGE_HANDLER(WM_ERASEBKGND, OnEraseBkgnd)
    MESSAGE_HANDLER(WM_KILLFOCUS, OnKillFocus)
    MESSAGE_HANDLER(WM_LBUTTONDOWN, OnLButtonDown)
    MESSAGE_HANDLER(WM_LBUTTONUP, OnLButtonUP)
    MESSAGE_HANDLER(WM_MOUSEMOVE, OnMouseMove)
    MESSAGE_HANDLER(WM_MOUSELEAVE, OnMouseLeave)
    COMMAND_CODE_HANDLER(BN_CLICKED, OnClicked)
    CHAIN_MSG_MAP(CComControl<CPopButton>)
ALT_MSG_MAP(1)
    // Replace this with message map entries for superclassed Button
END_MSG_MAP()
```

18

DEVELOPING
ACTIVEX
CONTROLS

Initializing the `CPopButton` Object

Before adding the code needed to initialize the `CPopButton` class, add an enumeration used to track button states to the `PopButton.cpp` source file. Insert the contents of Listing 18.13 just above the declaration of the `CPopButton` class.

LISTING 18.13 THE `BtnState` ENUMERATION

```
enum BtnState { bsFlat, bsDown, bsHover };
```

Earlier in this chapter, when the stock properties were added to the PopButton ATL object, the ATL Object Wizard inserted member variables to hold these stock values into the `CPopButton` class. Those values are shown in Listing 18.14. Add the member variables shown in bold to the class declaration.

LISTING 18.14 ADDITIONAL MEMBER VARIABLES USED BY `CPopButton` (IN BOLD)

```
OLE_COLOR          m_clrBackColor;
CComBSTR           m_bstrCaption;
OLE_COLOR          m_clrForeColor;
BOOL               m_bTabStop;
CComPtr<IFontDisp> m_pFont;      // Contains ambient font
BtnState           m_btnState;   // Tracks button state
bool               m_fHasFocus;  // TRUE is button has focus
short              m_cBevelSize; // Stores size of beveled edge
```

The `m_cBevelSize` member variable is used to store the `BevelSize` property. As noted in the comments, the other variables track the current button, the input focus state for the control, and the ambient font.

Add the lines shown in bold in Listing 18.15 to the `CPopButton` constructor.

LISTING 18.15 THE CONSTRUCTOR FOR THE `CPopButton` CLASS, WITH CHANGES IN BOLD

```
CPopButton() :
    m_ctlButton(_T("Button"), this, 1),
    m_btnState(bsFlat),
    m_fHasFocus(false),
    m_cBevelSize(2)
{
    m_bWindowOnly = TRUE;
}
```

The default handler for `OnCreate` will superclass a default instance of the Windows `BUTTON` class. The PopButton control must superclass a `BUTTON` with pushbutton attributes, so modify the `OnCreate` member function as shown in Listing 18.16 by changing the lines in bold.

LISTING 18.16 CHANGES MADE TO THE `OnCreate` MEMBER FUNCTION (IN BOLD)

```
LRESULT OnCreate(UINT , WPARAM , LPARAM , BOOL& )
{
    RECT rc;
    GetWindowRect(&rc);
    rc.right -= rc.left;
    rc.bottom -= rc.top;
    rc.top = rc.left = 0;
    m_ctlButton.Create(m_hWnd,
                       rc,
                       _T("BUTTON"),
                       WS_CHILD|BS_PUSHBUTTON);
    return 0;
}
```

Retrieving Ambient Properties

When the control is initially loaded, it will collect the current foreground color, background color, and font from its container. A good time to collect ambient properties is when the control and its container negotiate the client site. Add the source code in Listing 18.17 to the `PopButton.cpp` source file. This function will override the base class implementation of `SetClientSite` and will store the ambient values of these three properties.

LISTING 18.17 A NEW VERSION OF `SetClientSite` THAT COLLECTS AMBIENT PROPERTIES FROM THE CONTAINER

```
STDMETHODIMP CPopButton::SetClientSite(LPOLECLIENTSITE pSite)
{
    HRESULT hr = CComControlBase::IOleObject_SetClientSite(pSite);
    if(!m_pFont && pSite)
    {
        hr = GetAmbientFontDisp(&m_pFont);
    }
    GetAmbientBackColor(m_clrBackColor);
    GetAmbientForeColor(m_clrForeColor);
    return hr;
}
```

18

DEVELOPING ACTIVEX CONTROLS

Add the following member function declaration to the CPopButton class. A good place to locate it is just after all the member variables used to track properties:

```
STDMETHOD(SetClientSite)(LPOLECLIENTSITE pSite);
```

Handling Focus Events for the Control

When a focus event is received by the control, the focus member variable is set with the new input focus state, and the control's window is invalidated. The control's container is also notified that the control is changing its view.

Listing 18.18 contains the OnSetFocus and OnKillFocus member functions, which handle the WM_SETFOCUS and WM_KILLFOCUS events, respectively. Add the lines shown in bold.

LISTING 18.18   THE OnSetFocus MEMBER FUNCTION FOR THE CPopButton CLASS, WITH CHANGES IN BOLD

```
LRESULT OnSetFocus(UINT uMsg, WPARAM wParam, LPARAM lParam,
                                            BOOL& bHandled)
{
    LRESULT lRes = CComControl<CPopButton>::OnSetFocus(uMsg,
                                                        wParam,
                                                        lParam,
                                                        bHandled);

    if (m_bInPlaceActive)
    {
        DoVerbUIActivate(&m_rcPos,  NULL);
        if(!IsChild(::GetFocus()))
            m_ctlButton.SetFocus();
    }
    m_fHasFocus = true;
    Invalidate();
    FireViewChange();
    return lRes;
}


LRESULT OnKillFocus(UINT uMsg, WPARAM wParam, LPARAM lParam,
                                            BOOL& bHandled)
{
    m_fHasFocus = false;
    Invalidate();
    FireViewChange();
    return 0;
}
```

Handling Mouse Events for the Control

The following four message handlers control mouse and click events for the CPopButton class:

- OnLButtonDown updates the button state variable and invalidates the control's rectangle so that it will be redrawn.

- OnLButtonUp updates the button state variable and invalidates the control's rectangle so that it will be redrawn. If the mouse is currently over the control, the new button state is bsHover; if the mouse is not over the control, the new button state is bsFlat.

- OnMouseMove updates the button state if the current button state is bsFlat. If the button is moving from bsFlat to bsHover, the control's rectangle is updated so that it will be redrawn. In addition, the OnHover event is fired to the control's container. A timer is started that will be used to redraw the button as flat if the mouse moves away from the control.

- OnClick is sent to the CPopButton class when the underlying button control generates a click event. In response, the OnClick member function will fire an OnClick event to the container.

Add the lines shown in bold in Listing 18.19 to the mouse-handling functions in the CPopButton class.

LISTING 18.19   MOUSE-HANDLING EVENTS FOR THE CPopButton CLASS

```
LRESULT OnLButtonDown(UINT uMsg, WPARAM wParam, LPARAM lParam,
                                              BOOL& bHandled)
{
    // Change the state to bsDown, and redraw the control
    m_btnState = bsDown;
    Invalidate();
    FireViewChange();
    m_ctlButton.DefWindowProc(uMsg, wParam, lParam);
    return 0;
}

LRESULT OnLButtonUP(UINT uMsg, WPARAM wParam, LPARAM lParam,
                                              BOOL& bHandled)
{
    if(MouseOverCtl())
        m_btnState = bsHover;
    else
        m_btnState = bsFlat;
    Invalidate();
```

continues

18

DEVELOPING
ACTIVEX
CONTROLS

LISTING 18.19   CONTINUED

```
        FireViewChange();
        m_ctlButton.DefWindowProc(uMsg, wParam, lParam);
        return 0;
}

LRESULT OnMouseMove(UINT uMsg, WPARAM wParam, LPARAM lParam,
                                                BOOL& bHandled)
{
        if(m_btnState == bsFlat)
        {
            // Moving from flat to hover...
            Fire_OnHover();
            m_btnState = bsHover;
            Invalidate();
            FireViewChange();

            TRACKMOUSEEVENT tme;
            ZeroMemory(&tme,  sizeof(tme));
            tme.cbSize = sizeof(tme);
            tme.dwFlags = TME_LEAVE;
            tme.hwndTrack = m_hWnd;
            TrackMouseEvent(&tme);
        }
        m_ctlButton.DefWindowProc(uMsg, wParam, lParam);
        return 0;
}

// BN_CLICKED
LRESULT OnClicked(WORD wNotifyCode, WORD wID, HWND hWndCtl, BOOL&
bHandled)
{
        Fire_OnClick();
        m_btnState = bsFlat;
        Invalidate();
        FireViewChange();
        bHandled = TRUE;
        return 0;
}
```

When the mouse leaves the control window, the operating system will send the control a
WM_MOUSELEAVE message. When this message is received, the button state is updated, and
the control's rectangle is invalidated. Add the source code in Listing 18.20 to the
PopButton.h header file.

LISTING 18.20   THE WM_MOUSELEAVE MESSAGE HANDLER FOR THE CPopButton CLASS

```
LRESULT OnTimer(UINT uMsg, WPARAM wParam, LPARAM lParam,
                                     BOOL& bHandled)
{
    m_btnState = bsFlat;
    Invalidate();
    FireViewChange();
    bHandled = TRUE;
    return 0;
}
```

Several functions in CPopButton need to determine if the mouse cursor is over the control. The function provided in Listing 18.21 returns TRUE if the mouse is over the control; otherwise, it returns FALSE. Add this function to the CPopButton class.

LISTING 18.21   THE MouseOverCtl MEMBER FUNCTION

```
BOOL MouseOverCtl()
{
    RECT  rc;
    POINT pt;

    GetWindowRect(&rc);
    GetCursorPos(&pt);

    return PtInRect(&rc, pt);
}
```

Drawing the Control

The most complex part of the PopButton control involves drawing the control. Before getting into the actual drawing code, there are two helper functions that make it easy to determine which state the button is in. Listing 18.22 contains the IsSelected and IsRaised member functions, which are used by the CPopButton class when drawing the control.

LISTING 18.22   THE IsSelected AND IsRaised MEMBER FUNCTIONS

```
BOOL IsSelected()
{
    return m_btnState == bsDown;
}

BOOL IsRaised()
{
    return m_btnState == bsHover;
}
```

The source code provided in Listing 18.23 handles the work of drawing the pop-up button control. Add the entire listing to the `CPopButton` class.

LISTING 18.23   DRAWING FUNCTIONS USED BY THE CPopButton CLASS

```
//
// Draw the flat button, including focus rectangle if the control
// currently has the focus.
HRESULT OnDraw(ATL_DRAWINFO& di)
{
    RECT& rc  = *(RECT*)di.prcBounds;
    HDC    hdc = di.hdcDraw;

    COLORREF clrFore, clrBack;
    OleTranslateColor(m_clrForeColor, NULL, &clrFore);
    OleTranslateColor(m_clrBackColor, NULL, &clrBack);
    SetTextColor(hdc, m_clrForeColor);
    HBRUSH hbrBtn = CreateSolidBrush(m_clrBackColor);

    FillRect(hdc, &rc, hbrBtn);
    DrawEdges(hdc, &rc);
    DrawButtonText(hdc, &rc, m_bstrCaption);

    if(m_fHasFocus)
    {
        InflateRect(&rc, -2, -2);
        DrawFocusRect(hdc, &rc);
    }

    DeleteObject(hbrBtn);
    return 0;
}


//
// Draw the button's edges, based on the current control state.
// The button can either be flat, raised, or pushed down, depending
// on the button's state.
void DrawEdges(HDC hdc, LPRECT pRect)
{
    if(IsSelected())
    {
        // If the button is selected, draw it in the down state.
        Draw3dRectEdges(hdc,
                    pRect,
                    GetSysColor(COLOR_3DSHADOW),
                    GetSysColor(COLOR_3DHIGHLIGHT),
                    m_cBevelSize);
        InflateRect(pRect, -m_cBevelSize, -m_cBevelSize);
        // Move the button contents to the right to simulate the
        // button being pushed down.
```

```
            OffsetRect(pRect, m_cBevelSize, m_cBevelSize);
    }
    else if(IsRaised())
    {
        // If the button is in hover mode, draw it in the up state.
        Draw3dRectEdges(hdc,
                        pRect,
                        GetSysColor(COLOR_3DHIGHLIGHT),
                        GetSysColor(COLOR_3DSHADOW),
                        m_cBevelSize);
        InflateRect(pRect, -m_cBevelSize, -m_cBevelSize);
    }
    else
    {
        // We're drawing a flat button, but we'll still deflate the
        // rectangle so the button contents don't move around.
        InflateRect(pRect, -m_cBevelSize, -m_cBevelSize);
    }
}

// Draw the caption for the button, using the ambient font.
void DrawButtonText(HDC hdc, LPRECT prc, LPWSTR wstrLabel)
{
    COLORREF clrText = GetSysColor(COLOR_BTNTEXT);
    int nOldBkMode = SetBkMode(hdc, TRANSPARENT);
    COLORREF clrTextOld = SetTextColor(hdc, clrText);

    HFONT hCtlFont=NULL;
    HFONT hOldFont=NULL;

    CComQIPtr<IFont,&IID_IFont> pFont(m_pFont);
    if(pFont)
        pFont->get_hFont(&hCtlFont);
    if(hCtlFont)
        hOldFont = (HFONT)SelectObject(hdc, hCtlFont);

    DrawTextEx(hdc,
               wstrLabel,
               lstrlen(wstrLabel),
               prc,
               DT_CENTER¦DT_VCENTER¦DT_SINGLELINE,
               NULL);

    SelectObject(hdc, hOldFont);
    SetTextColor(hdc, clrTextOld);
    SetBkMode(hdc, nOldBkMode);
}

//
// Draws the edges for a 3D rectangle. Actually just breaks the
```

continues

LISTING 18.23   CONTINUED

```
// rectangle down into its coordinates, which are passed to the
// Draw3dCoordsEdges function.
void Draw3dRectEdges(HDC      hdc,
                     LPCRECT  pRect,
                     COLORREF clrTopLeft,
                     COLORREF clrBottomRight,
                     int      cBevel)
{
    if(!hdc || !pRect) return;

    Draw3dCoordsEdges(hdc,
                      pRect->left,
                      pRect->top,
                      pRect->right - pRect->left,
                      pRect->bottom - pRect->top,
                      clrTopLeft,
                      clrBottomRight,
                      cBevel);
}


//
// Draws the edges for a 3D rectangle.
// Accepts parameters for:
//     The device context
//     The coordinates for the rectangle to be drawn in 3-D
//     The color for the left and top edges
//     The color for the right and bottom edges
//     The size of the bevel
// Note that this function doesn't fill the center of the rect.
void Draw3dCoordsEdges(HDC      hdc,
                       int      x,
                       int      y,
                       int      cx,
                       int      cy,
                       COLORREF clrTopLeft,
                       COLORREF clrBottomRight,
                       int      cBevel)
{
    FastFillCoords(hdc, x, y, cBevel, cy - cBevel, clrTopLeft);
    FastFillCoords(hdc, x, y, cx - cBevel, cBevel, clrTopLeft);
    FastFillCoords(hdc, (x + cx) - cBevel, y, cBevel, cy,
                                                clrBottomRight);
    FastFillCoords(hdc, x, (y + cy) - cBevel, cx, cBevel,
                                                clrBottomRight);
}


//
// Given a set of coordinates for a rectangle, quickly fill the
```

```
// area with a color, using ExtTextOut. ETO is the fastest way to
// fill a small area with color.
void FastFillCoords(HDC hdc, int x, int y, int cx, int cy,
                                              COLORREF clr)
{
    if(!hdc) return;

    COLORREF clrOld = SetBkColor(hdc, clr);
    RECT rc;
    rc.left = x;
    rc.top = y;
    rc.right = x + cx;
    rc.bottom = y + cy;
    ExtTextOut(hdc, 0, 0, ETO_OPAQUE, &rc, NULL, 0, NULL);
    SetBkColor(hdc, clrOld);
}
```

Listing 18.23 contains six functions:

- `OnDraw` determines the proper colors for the control and calls the `DrawEdges` and `DrawButtonText` functions to perform most of the drawing work.

- `DrawEdges` draws the edges of the control rectangle based on the control's current state. This function calls `Draw3dRectEdges` to draw the beveled edges.

- `DrawButtonText` fills the center of the button with the caption text.

- `Draw3dRectEdges` draws a rectangle in 3-D based on a `RECT` passed as a parameter. This function breaks the rectangle into coordinates and calls `Draw3dCoordEdges`.

- `Draw3dCoordsEdges` draws a rectangle in 3-D based on coordinates passed as a parameter. This function makes four calls to `FastFillCoords` to draw the beveled edges of the rectangle.

- `FastFillCoords` is a function that uses `ExtTextOut` to fill a rectangle with a specified color.

Compile the PopBtn project. You can test the control using the ActiveX control container by following the steps outlined earlier in this chapter. In the next section, a Visual Basic project will be created that uses the PopButton control.

Testing PopButton with Visual Basic

This section creates a Visual Basic project named PopTest that uses the PopButton control. The project can be found on this book's CD-ROM, or you can build the project yourself using the steps presented here.

Adding the PopButton Control to the VB Toolbox

To add the PopButton component to the VB component palette, follow these steps:

1. Right-click on the component palette and select Components from the pop-up menu. The Components dialog box will be displayed.

2. Select PopBtn 1.0 Type Library from the list of registered components. Make sure the checkbox is checked.

3. Click the OK button to add the control to the palette.

Creating the PopTest Project

PopTest is a Visual Basic project consisting of one form that contains three PopButtons, one label, and one command button, as shown in Figure 18.22. Each of the controls uses its default name provided by Visual Basic.

FIGURE 18.22

The main form in PopTest.

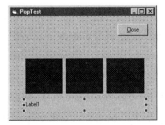

The source code for the PopTest project is provided in Listing 18.24.

LISTING 18.24 SOURCE CODE FOR THE POPTEST VB PROJECT

```
Private Sub Command1_Click()
    Unload Me
End Sub

Private Sub PopButton1_OnClick(Index As Integer)

    Select Case Index
        Case 0
            MsgBox "Hello from Huey"
        Case 1
            MsgBox "Hello from Dewey"
        Case 2
            MsgBox "Hello from Louie"
    End Select

End Sub
```

```
Private Sub PopButton1_OnHover(Index As Integer)

    Select Case Index
        Case 0
            Label1 = "Hovering over Huey"
        Case 1
            Label1 = "Hovering over Dewey"
        Case 2
            Label1 = "Hovering over Louie"
    End Select

End Sub
```

Run the PopTest project. The text label is updated for hover events, and clicking on any of the PopButton controls will cause a message box to be displayed. Figure 18.23 shows an example of the PopTest project running.

FIGURE 18.23

The PopTest project running with several PopButton controls on one form.

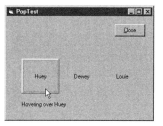

Summary

This chapter discussed creating and testing ActiveX controls. ActiveX controls are smaller and simpler versions of OLE custom controls. Although an ActiveX control is required to support fewer interfaces than the older OLE custom controls, it's believed that most ActiveX controls will continue to be very similar to OLE custom controls, although you now have the flexibility to omit an interface if your control doesn't require it.

Visual C++ simplifies the task of creating an ActiveX control through the MFC and ATL class libraries and their associated wizards. For example, the MFC ActiveX ControlWizard is very similar to AppWizard, and it guides you through the steps required to create a skeleton version of your control.

Asynchronous
COM

This chapter discusses one of the most exciting developments in COM offered by Windows 2000: asynchronous method calls towards COM components. This new feature allows COM to be used in situations where it's not feasible to allow a client to block indefinitely until a server completes processing a request. This chapter discusses the new interfaces introduced to COM to support asynchronous methods calls and includes examples of using asynchronous COM method calls.

Synchronous and Asynchronous Methods in COM

Prior to Windows 2000, COM interfaces consisted primarily of synchronous method calls. The few asynchronous calls that existed in COM were used in the IAdviseSink interface to implement DDE-like notification services. COM places restrictions on how these asynchronous functions are implemented—you're not allowed to make a synchronous COM call from within any of the IAdviseSink asynchronous methods.

In a synchronous world, clients are not in control of their own destinies. A client is forced to wait while a server does its work. The client cannot perform other work once the method call has started, and the client has no way to cancel the method call. The client has no option but to wait for the method call the complete. Problems with server workload or network latency can seriously impact client performance.

The primitive asynchronous support offered in IAdviseSink did allow the client to invoke a method call and continue without work while the method completed, but there was no way for you to implement a custom interface that had these characteristics. IAdvise gained its synchronous behavior through the sort of sleight of hand that's possible for operating system components.

It was possible to implement asynchronous communication prior to Windows 2000 by using custom marshaling. As shown in Figure 19.1, this solution uses a thread pool in the marshaling proxy stub to give the appearance of asynchronous behavior.

FIGURE 19.1

Roll-your-own asynchronous method calls using custom marshaling and a thread pool.

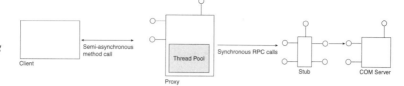

Here's a list of the problems with implementing asynchronous method calls in this manner:

- It's really difficult. Implementing custom marshaling and maintaining the thread pool requires a great deal of skill.

- It doesn't work in cases where the client and server are in the same apartment. To support a full range of deployment options, you need a separate asynchronous calling scheme for intra-apartment cases.

- It's not even really asynchronous. It appears to be asynchronous, but this behavior really depends on custom functions implemented in the proxy.

- Custom marshaling increases your maintenance costs. If you add a new interface to a COM object that supports custom marshaling, you must rework your proxy and stub code.

What's needed is support for asynchronous method calls built into the operating system.

Asynchronous Method Support in Windows 2000

Asynchronous COM in Windows 2000 has some impressive characteristics:

- It works side by side with existing COM components.

- Windows 2000 clients can make asynchronous calls to existing COM components by recompiling the proxy—there's no need to recompile the component.

- COM clients built for Windows NT 4.0 and earlier can still achieve the expected synchronous behavior when calling a Windows 2000 component.

- No changes have been made to the DCOM wire protocol, so low-level tools will continue to work as expected with asynchronous COM.

19

ASYNCHRONOUS COM

You may be surprised that you can obtain asynchronous behavior without recompiling the COM server. As you'll see a later in this chapter, adding asynchronous capabilities to your COM objects may be as simple as making small changes to your IDL file and recompiling your proxy/stub DLL. Adding asynchronous capabilities to components used within the client's apartment requires changes in the COM object.

Asynchronous COM introduces the *call object*, which is the focus point for all asynchronous method calls. The call object is created through ICallFactory, a new interface exposed by objects that support asynchronous COM. As shown in Figure 19.2, the call object acts as an asynchronous intermediary to a COM object.

FIGURE 19.2

The call object enables asynchronous behavior for a COM object.

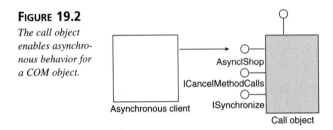

As will be described in detail later in this chapter, the call object exposes asynchronous interfaces to the client. When the client uses the asynchronous interface, the call object makes a synchronous call to the COM object. While the call object is managing the asynchronous call, it cannot be used for any other method calls.

The synchronous interfaces still exist, and they can be called directly without involving the call object. Legacy clients that are not aware of the ICallFactory interface will only use the synchronous interfaces.

Asynchronous Support in IDL

In order for an interface to be used asynchronously, it must be marked as asynchronous in the interface's IDL definition using the new Windows 2000 attribute named async_uuid. Using async_uuid as an attribute alerts the MIDL compiler that it should create asynchronous proxy/stub marshaling code for the interface. Listing 19.1 shows this new attribute highlighted in bold.

LISTING 19.1   USING THE async_uuid INTERFACE ATTRIBUTE TO DEFINE AN
ASYNCHRONOUS INTERFACE

```
[
    object,
    uuid(00700700-7007-11D2-B889-00104B36573E),
    async_uuid(00800800-8008-11D2-B88A-00104B36573E),

    helpstring("ITakeTime Interface"),
    pointer_default(unique)
]
interface ITakeTime : IUnknown
{
    [helpstring("This method takes a while to execute")]
    HRESULT TakeSomeTime([out]BSTR* pbstr);
};
```

The async_uuid attribute specifies the interface ID that will be used for the asynchronous version of the interface. The synchronous version still exists, and it can be called by a client. The MIDL compiler generates a friendly symbolic name for the asynchronous interface that prefixes Async to the existing interface name. Using the ITakeTime definition from Listing 19.1, the MIDL compiler will create a new asynchronous interface named AsyncITakeTime, similar to the definition shown in Listing 19.2.

LISTING 19.2   A SIMPLIFIED VERSION OF THE MIDL-GENERATED ASYNCHRONOUS
INTERFACE DEFINITION

```
interface AsyncITakeTime : public IUnknown
{
public:
    HRESULT Begin_TakeSomeTime(void);
    HRESULT Finish_TakeSomeTime(BSTR *pbstrClerk);
};
```

The asynchronous interface defines two new methods for each method in the synchronous interface:

- A method used to initiate processing of the asynchronous call. This method is prefixed with Begin_ and contains parameters with the [in] attribute, if any.
- A method used to complete processing of the asynchronous call. This method is prefixed with Finish_ and contains parameters with the [out] attribute, if any.

These asynchronous methods will exist in the proxy DLL after it's compiled. Clients that use a proxy DLL to communicate with a client in another apartment can use the rebuilt proxy/stub DLL to make asynchronous calls without rebuilding the COM server.

19

ASYNCHRONOUS COM

Other New Asynchronous Components in Windows 2000

Several new interfaces and COM objects are used to implement asynchronous COM methods in Windows 2000:

- The ICallFactory interface is used to create call objects. Any COM object that supports asynchronous behavior must expose this interface. It's possible, even desirable, to create a proxy that supports this interface, even though the underlying COM object may not.

- The call object is used to provide a synchronization point for all asynchronous communication. All asynchronous interfaces and methods are exposed through call objects.

- AsyncIXxx interfaces are asynchronous versions of synchronous interfaces. As discussed in the previous section, the MIDL compiler automatically generates AsyncIXxx interfaces in the header file that it generates from the IDL file.

- ISynchronize is an interface exposed by the call object that's used to determine whether an asynchronous method call has been completed.

- ICancelMethodCalls is an interface exposed by the call object that allows a client to cancel an asynchronous method call.

Each of these interfaces and COM objects is discussed in the following sections.

Using the Call Object

All asynchronous COM activities rotate in an orbit around call objects. The call object is new in Windows 2000—it's used by a client to begin, track, and complete an asynchronous method call. Each call object can handle one asynchronous method call at any given time. A single client thread may have several instances of call objects in various states, but each call object may only have a single asynchronous method call outstanding at any given time.

A client retrieves a call object through the ICallFactory interface, which is exposed by the server. Proxies that have been compiled with asynchronous attributes also expose this interface. The call object is responsible for managing asynchronous communication with the server—the DCOM wire protocol has not been changed to manage asynchronous communication.

For example, consider the most common case where asynchronous COM provides the most benefit—communication with a COM object that's out of process or even located on a remote computer. As shown in Figure 19.3, communication between a proxy that implements asynchronous versions of the server's COM interfaces and the actual COM object is still synchronous.

FIGURE 19.3

Communication between a call object and a COM server is still synchronous.

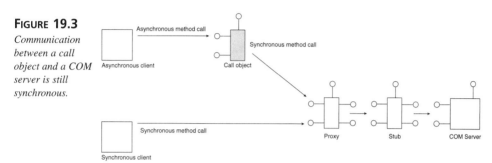

The asynchronous method call shown in Figure 19.3 follows these steps:

1. The client creates an instance of the COM server. Because the COM server is an EXE, the operating system creates a proxy and stub for the client to communicate with the server.

2. The client queries the COM object for `ICallFactory`. In this case, the COM object does not support `ICallFactory`, but the proxy has been rebuilt from an IDL definition that includes the `async_uuid` attribute. The proxy returns an interface to its `ICallFactory` interface.

3. The client creates a call object for the asynchronous version of `IShop` from the call factory, asking for the `AsyncIShop` interface as its initial interface pointer.

4. The client calls `AsynchIShop::Begin_TakeSomeTime` to begin the asynchronous method call. This method contains all the `[in]` parameters passed to the COM object.

5. The call object creates a thread that makes a synchronous method call to the COM object's `ITakeTime::TakeSomeTime` method.

6. The COM object processes the method call synchronously and returns the result to the proxy.

19

ASYNCHRONOUS COM

7. Meanwhile, the client thread has been free to perform other work. At some point, the client calls the proxy's `ISynchronize::Wait` method. This method is similar to the Win32 `WaitForSingleObject` API function, and it typically blocks until the asynchronous method call can be completed.

8. When the proxy completes the synchronous call to `ITakeTime::TakeSomeTime`, it signals to the machinery handling the `ISynchronize` interface that the asynchronous method call can be completed.

9. The client calls `AsynchIShop::Finish_TakeSomeTime` to complete the asynchronous method call. This method contains all the `[out]` parameters received from the COM object.

10. The client can either release the call object or reuse it in another asynchronous call.

It may seem as though this list contains a lot of steps for just one method call, but many of these steps involve creating the call object and acquiring pointers to the interfaces required to implement asynchronous method calls. You would typically perform these steps to create a series of call objects and then reuse the call objects as needed. As shown in Figure 19.4, each client thread may have several asynchronous call objects available for use at any given time.

FIGURE 19.4

Each client may have multiple call objects for each interface.

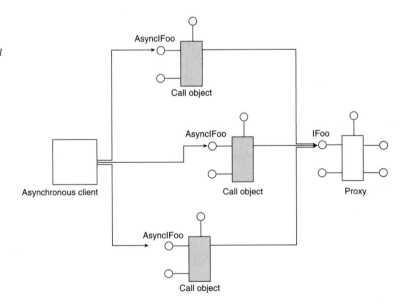

Using the `ICallFactory` Interface to Create Call Objects

The `ICallFactory` interface is used to create an instance of a call object. Every COM object that supports asynchronous interfaces must support `ICallFactory`—this is the only way to create the call objects that are required to make asynchronous method calls. Each COM object has a unique call object that's used to access its unique set of interfaces.

Asynchronous behavior for an interface is always implemented in the proxy, if one exists. The only time the underlying COM object must support `ICallFactory` is when the COM object is used in the same apartment as the client. As discussed earlier in the chapter, it's possible for a proxy to support `ICallFactory`, even if the underlying COM object does not support asynchronous method calls, simply by modifying the IDL and rebuilding the proxy/stub DLL.

The client obtains a pointer to `ICallFactory` via `QueryInterface`. The proxy will return the pointer to the `ICallFactory` interface implemented by the proxy, which can then be used to create multiple call objects.

A simplified definition of the `ICallFactory` interface is provided in Listing 19.3.

LISTING 19.3 THE `ICallFactory` INTERFACE

```
interface ICallFactory : public IUnknown
{
public:
    HRESULT CreateCall(REFIID riid,
                       IUnknown *pCtrlUnk,
                       REFIID riid2,
                       IUnknown** ppv);
};
```

The `ICallFactory` interface has one method: `CreateCall`. The `CreateCall` method has four parameters:

- The interface ID for the asynchronous interface.
- A pointer to a controlling `IUnknown` interface if aggregation is used or `NULL` if no aggregation is performed.
- The interface ID of the initial interface pointer to be returned from the call object. This may be the same value as the first parameter.
- The address of a pointer to a COM interface that will receive the initial interface pointer from the call object.

19

ASYNCHRONOUS COM

A client may use the call factory to create several call objects that can be used over the lifetime of the client, as shown in Listing 19.4.

LISTING 19.4   USING ICallFactory TO CREATE SEVERAL CALL OBJECTS

```
struct ASYNC_OBJS
{
    AsyncIPark* pPark;
    AsyncIShop* pShop;
    AsyncICharge* pCharge;
     };


HRESULT LoadCallObjects(IUnknown* punk, ASYNC_OBJS& obs)
{
    HRESULT hr;
    ICallFactory* pcf = NULL;

    ZeroMemory(&obs, sizeof(ASYNC_OBJS));

    try
    {
        hr = punk->QueryInterface(&pCallFactory);
        if(FAILED(hr)) throw hr;

        hr = pCallFactory->CreateCall(IID_AsyncIPark,
                               NULL,
                               IID_AsyncIPark,
                               (IUnknown**)&obs.pPark);

        if(FAILED(hr)) throw hr;
        hr = pCallFactory->CreateCall(IID_AsyncIShop,
                               NULL,
                               IID_AsyncIShop,
                               (IUnknown**)&obs.pShop);

        hr = pCallFactory->CreateCall(IID_AsyncICharge,
                               NULL,
                               IID_AsyncICharge,
                               (IUnknown**)&obs.pCharge);
        if(FAILED(hr)) throw hr;
    }
    catch(HRESULT hr)
    {
        if(pcf) pcf->Release();
        if(obs.pPark) obs.pPark->Release();
        if(obs.pShop) obs.pShop->Release();
        if(obs.pCharge) obs.pCharge->Release();
    }
    return hr;
}
```

Using `ISynchronize` to Wait for Asynchronous Completion

The `ISynchronize` interface is used to provide a client with information about the current state of an asynchronous method call. The call object usually exposes `ISynchronize` by aggregating a system-provided synchronization object. The `ISynchronize` interface is used by the client to determine whether the asynchronous method has been completed.

A simplified definition of the `ISynchronize` interface is provided in Listing 19.5.

LISTING 19.5   THE `ISynchronize` INTERFACE

```
interface ISynchronize : public IUnknown
{
public:
    HRESULT Wait(DWORD dwFlags, DWORD dwMilliseconds);
    HRESULT Signal();
    HRESULT Reset();
};
```

`ISynchronize` contains three methods:

- `Wait`
- `Signal`
- `Reset`

The `Wait` method has two parameters:

- `dwFlags` is normally set to `COWAIT_ALL`, although you can use any value from the `COWAIT_FLAGS` enumeration. The only other member of this enumeration is `COWAIT_ALERTABLE`, which is signaled after an Asynchronous Procedure Call is queued.

- `dwMilliseconds` is the amount of time the calling thread is prepared to wait for the method to complete. You can pass `INFINITE` to wait forever, or you can pass a value of zero to test the current condition of the method without waiting.

The `Wait` method returns `S_OK` if the asynchronous method has completed. It returns `RPC_S_CALLPENDING` if the method has not completed before the timeout period expires. Note that `RPC_S_CALLPENDING` is a successful return code, so the `FAILED` and `SUCCEEDED` macros can't be used to differentiate between it and `S_OK`.

The `Signal` method is used by the call object to indicate that the asynchronous method call has completed.

The `Reset` method is used by the call object to restore the `ISynchronize` interface to a new "unsignaled" state.

Using `ICancelMethodCalls` to Cancel an Asynchronous Method Call

The `ICancelMethodCalls` interface is exposed by a call object and is used to cancel an outstanding asynchronous method call. You can also use `ICancelMethodCalls` to determine whether a method call has already been cancelled.

A simplified definition of the `ICancelMethodCalls` interface is provided in Listing 19.6.

LISTING 19.6   THE `ICancelMethodCalls` INTERFACE

```
interface ICancelMethodCalls: public IUnknown
{
public:
    HRESULT Cancel(ULONG ulSeconds);
    HRESULT TestCancel(void);

};
```

`ICancelMethodCalls` contains two methods:

- `Cancel`
- `TestCancel`

The `Cancel` method has one parameter that's used to indicate how long the client is prepared to wait for the server to acknowledge the cancellation request. You can pass a value of `RPC_C_CANCEL_INFINITE_TIMEOUT` to specify that the client will wait forever, or you can pass a value of zero to force an immediate return to the client.

The `Cancel` method is only a cancellation request. It does not mean that the server will actually stop processing work. It many cases, the asynchronous behavior may be implemented in a proxy that's working with an EXE server that does not natively support asynchronous method calls.

The `TestCancel` method is used to determine whether an asynchronous call has been canceled. You can use this method to poll the call object to determine whether a cancellation request has been completed. If the method has been canceled, `TestCancel` will return `RPC_E_CALL_CANCELED`. If the method is still executing, `TestCancel` will return `RPC_S_CALL_PENDING`.

Making Fire-and-Forget Method Calls

A commonly used programming pattern that employs asynchronous COM is known as Fire and Forget. This pattern allows you to make numerous asynchronous method calls without waiting for the method to complete. In fact, you don't even call the completion half of the asynchronous method.

To use Fire and Forget, follow these steps:

1. Create an instance of the call object and retrieve a pointer to your desired interface.
2. Call a `Begin_xxxx` method to start an asynchronous method call.
3. Immediately release the call object instance.

This pattern is useful when a server needs to communicate with a large number of clients and doesn't need to retrieve the results of the operation. The limitation is that there's no way for you to know whether your function call was successful.

An Asynchronous COM Example

The CD-ROM that accompanies the book contains several examples that demonstrate asynchronous method calls. There are four project subdirectories used in this chapter:

- *AsyncTest* contains an ATL project named AsyncTest. This project builds a COM server that's used for the examples in this chapter.
- *SyncClient* contains a console-mode project that uses the synchronous interface exposed by AsyncTest.
- *AsyncProxy* contains a modified proxy/stub DLL that implements asynchronous method calls for the AsyncTest COM server.
- *AsyncClient* uses the asynchronous proxy to make asynchronous method calls to the AsyncTest COM server.

The `IShop` Interface

The examples in this chapter use the `IShop` interface, which is provided in Listing 19.7 in IDL.

LISTING 19.7 THE IShop INTERFACE DEFINITION

```
import "oaidl.idl";
import "ocidl.idl";
    [
        object,
        uuid(C57B11E4-AF61-11D2-9935-00104B36573E),

        helpstring("IShop Interface"),
        pointer_default(unique)
    ]
    interface IShop : IUnknown
    {
        [helpstring("method FindSalesClerk")]
        HRESULT FindSalesClerk([out] BSTR* bstrClerkName);
    };

[
    uuid(C57B11D6-AF61-11D2-9935-00104B36573E),
    version(1.0),
    helpstring("AsyncTest 1.0 Type Library")
]
library ASYNCTESTLib
{
    importlib("stdole32.tlb");
    importlib("stdole2.tlb");

    [
        uuid(C57B11E5-AF61-11D2-9935-00104B36573E),
        helpstring("Shop Class")
    ]
    coclass Shop
    {
        [default] interface IShop;
    };
};
```

The IShop interface contains one method: FindSalesClerk. FindSalesClerk takes a nontrivial amount of time to execute due to a call to the Win32 Sleep function, which simulates the time required to actually find a sales clerk. FindSalesClerk also has an [out] parameter, which will be filled with the name of the sales clerk when the function returns.

The AsyncTest Project

The AsyncTest project is an ATL-based EXE server. AsyncTest contains one simple COM object named Shop. The values used in the Names property sheet for the Shop object are listed in Table 19.1.

TABLE 19.1   NAMES PROPERTY SHEET VALUES FOR THE Shop COM OBJECT

Field	*Name*
Short Name	Shop
Class	CShop
.H File	Shop.h
.CPP File	Shop.cpp
CoClass	Shop
Interface	IShop
Type	Shop Class
Prog ID	AsyncTest.Shop

The values used in the Attributes property sheet for the Shop object are listed in Table 19.2.

TABLE 19.2   NAMES PROPERTY SHEET VALUES FOR THE Shop COM OBJECT

Field	*Name*
Threading Model	Free
Interface	Custom
Aggregation	Yes
ISupportErrorInfo	Unchecked
Connection Points	Unchecked
Free Threaded Marshaler	Unchecked

As discussed earlier, the IShop interface has one method: FindSalesClerk. The implementation of FindSalesClerk is provided in Listing 19.8.

LISTING 19.8   THE CShop::FindSalesClerk FUNCTION

```
STDMETHODIMP CShop::FindSalesClerk(BSTR *bstrClerkName)
{
    // Hide from customer for a while
    Sleep(5000);
    *bstrClerkName = SysAllocString(L"Zaphod");
    if(*bstrClerkName)
        return S_OK;
    else
        return E_OUTOFMEMORY;
}
```

19

ASYNCHRONOUS COM

The `FindSalesClerk` function sleeps for five seconds and then fills `bstrClerkName` with the name of a helpful sales clerk.

After building the AsyncTest project, you must also build and register the proxy/stub DLL. Build the proxy/stub from the command line in the project directory with this command:

```
nmake AsyncTestps.mk
```

Register the proxy/stub DLL with this command:

```
RegSvr32 AsyncTestps
```

The proxy/stub DLL must be rebuilt and re-registered whenever the project's IDL changes.

A Synchronous Test Client

The SyncClient subdirectory contains the SyncClient project, a Win32 console-mode project that makes synchronous calls to the AsyncTest COM server. The source code used for SyncClient is provided in Listing 19.9.

LISTING 19.9   A SYNCHRONOUS TEST DRIVER FOR THE IShop INTERFACE

```cpp
/*
 * SyncClient - main.cpp
 *
 * Tests synchronous version of the IShop interface.
 */

#define _WIN32_WINNT 0x0500
#include <windows.h>
#include <wchar.h>

#include "asynctest.h"
#include "asynctest_i.c"

void    HandleError(LPCWSTR strTitle, HRESULT hr);

int wmain()
{
    IUnknown*   punk = NULL;
    IShop*      pShop = NULL;
    BSTR        bstr;

    // Initialize COM library
    HRESULT hr = CoInitializeEx(NULL, COINIT_MULTITHREADED);
    if(FAILED(hr))
```

```
    {
        HandleError(L"CoInitFailed", hr);
        return 0;
    }

    // Use SEH to ensure that interface reference are cleaned up.
    __try
    {
        // Create an instance of the COM object.
        hr = CoCreateInstance(CLSID_Shop,
                              NULL,
                              CLSCTX_ALL,
                              IID_IUnknown,
                              (void**)&punk);
        if(FAILED(hr))
        {
            HandleError(L"CoCreate Failed", hr);
            __leave;
        }

        // Query for IShop.
        hr = punk->QueryInterface(&pShop);
        if(FAILED(hr))
        {
            HandleError(L"QIF for IShop Failed", hr);
            __leave;
        }

        // Make the function call.
        hr = pShop->FindSalesClerk(&bstr);
        if(FAILED(hr))
        {
            HandleError(L"Method call Failed", hr);
            __leave;
        }
        wprintf(L"The sales clerk's name is %s\n", bstr);
    }
    __finally
    {
        SysFreeString(bstr);
        if(punk) punk->Release();
        if(pShop) pShop->Release();
        CoUninitialize();
    }
    return 0;
}

/*
 * Error handling routine
 */
```

continues

LISTING 19.9   CONTINUED

```
void HandleError(LPCWSTR strTitle, HRESULT hr)
{
    LPVOID lpMsgBuf;

    FormatMessageW(FORMAT_MESSAGE_ALLOCATE_BUFFER|
                   FORMAT_MESSAGE_FROM_SYSTEM,
                   NULL,
                   hr,
                   MAKELANGID(LANG_NEUTRAL, SUBLANG_DEFAULT),
                   (LPWSTR)&lpMsgBuf,
                   0,
                   NULL);
    MessageBoxW(NULL,
                (LPCWSTR)lpMsgBuf,
                strTitle,
                MB_OK | MB_ICONINFORMATION);
    LocalFree(lpMsgBuf);
}
```

The SyncClient directory also includes copies of the `AsyncTest_i.c` and `AsyncTest.h` files from the AsyncTest project directory. These files were generated by the MIDL compiler when the AsyncTest project was built.

Build and run the SyncClient project. If you use a debugger to step through the source code, you'll see that the client blocks for approximately five seconds after calling `FindSalesClerk`. In the next two sections, we'll convert the `IShop` interface into an asynchronous version so that the client won't be forced to wait for the server.

The Second Version of the `IShop` Interface

The AsyncProxy subdirectory contains the asynchronous version of the AsyncTest proxy/stub DLL. Three files are copied into the AsyncProxy subdirectory from the AsyncTest directory. These three files will be used to build the proxy/stub DLL that supports asynchronous method calls:

- `AysncTest.idl`
- `AsyncTestps.mk`
- `AsyncTestps.def`

The `AsyncTest.idl` file was modified by adding the `async_uuid` attribute to the `IShop` interface. The new version of the `AsyncTest.idl` file is provided in Listing 19.10, with the modified line shown in bold.

LISTING 19.10   THE ASYNCHRONOUS VERSION OF THE AsyncTest IDL FILE

```
// AsyncTest.idl : IDL source for AsyncTest.dll
//

// This file will be processed by the MIDL tool to
// produce the type library (AsyncTest.tlb) and marshalling code.

import "oaidl.idl";
import "ocidl.idl";
    [
        object,
        uuid(C57B11E4-AF61-11D2-9935-00104B36573E),
        async_uuid(127B59FE-AF70-11D2-9935-00104B36573E),

        helpstring("IShop Interface"),
        pointer_default(unique)
    ]
    interface IShop : IUnknown
    {
        [helpstring("method FindSalesClerk")]
        HRESULT FindSalesClerk([out] BSTR* bstrClerkName);
    };

[
    uuid(C57B11D6-AF61-11D2-9935-00104B36573E),
    version(1.0),
    helpstring("AsyncTest 1.0 Type Library")
]
library ASYNCTESTLib
{
    importlib("stdole32.tlb");
    importlib("stdole2.tlb");

    [
        uuid(C57B11E5-AF61-11D2-9935-00104B36573E),
        helpstring("Shop Class")
    ]
    coclass Shop
    {
        [default] interface IShop;
    };
};
```

19

ASYNCHRONOUS COM

Asynchronous behavior is only supported beginning with Windows 2000. Depending on the version of your C++ compiler, you may need to modify the AsyncTestps makefile to define the _WIN32_WINNT symbol as 0x500 or later. Listing 19.11 shows the modified portion of the AsyncTestps makefile, with the changed portion shown in bold.

LISTING 19.11   CHANGES TO THE AsyncTestps.mk MAKEFILE (IN BOLD)

```
.c.obj:
    cl /c /Ox /DWIN32 /D_WIN32_WINNT=0x0500 /DREGISTER_PROXY_DLL \
        $<
```

Build the new version of the proxy/stub by running nmake from the command line:

```
nmake AsyncTestps.mk
```

After building the new proxy/stub DLL, register it from the command line using RegSvr32:

```
RegSvr32 AsyncTestps.dll
```

You're now ready to make asynchronous method calls towards the AsyncTest server.

The Asynchronous Test Client

The AsyncClient subdirectory contains the AsyncClient project, a Win32 console-mode project that makes asynchronous calls to the AsyncTest COM server. The source code used for AsyncClient is provided in Listing 19.12.

LISTING 19.12   AN ASYNCHRONOUS TEST DRIVER FOR THE IShop INTERFACE

```
/*
 * AsyncClient - main.cpp
 *
 * Tests asynchronous versions of the IShop interface.
 */

#define _WIN32_WINNT 0x0500
#include <windows.h>
#include <wchar.h>

#include "asynctest.h"
#include "asynctest_i.c"

void HandleError(LPCWSTR strTitle, HRESULT hr);

int wmain()
{
    IUnknown* punk = NULL;
    ICallFactory* pCallFactory = NULL;
    AsyncIShop* pShopAsync = NULL;
    ISynchronize* pSynchro = NULL;
    BSTR bstr;

    // Initialize COM library
```

```
HRESULT hr = CoInitializeEx(NULL, COINIT_MULTITHREADED);
if(FAILED(hr))
{
    HandleError(L"CoInitFailed", hr);
    return 0;
}

// Use SEH to ensure that interface reference are cleaned up.
__try
{
    // Create an instance of the COM object.
    hr = CoCreateInstance(CLSID_Shop,
                          NULL,
                          CLSCTX_ALL,
                          IID_IUnknown,
                          (void**)&punk);
    if(FAILED(hr))
    {
        HandleError(L"CoCreate Failed", hr);
        __leave;
    }

    // Get a pointer to the proxy's call factory.
    hr = punk->QueryInterface(&pCallFactory);
    if(FAILED(hr))
    {
        HandleError(L"QIF for call factory failed", hr);
        __leave;
    }

    // Create a call object.
    hr = pCallFactory->CreateCall(IID_AsyncIShop,
                                  NULL,
                                  IID_AsyncIShop,
                                  (IUnknown**)&pShopAsync);
    if(FAILED(hr))
    {
        HandleError(L"CreateCall Failed", hr);
        __leave;
    }

    // Query the call object for ISynchronize.
    hr = pShopAsync->QueryInterface(&pSynchro);
    if(FAILED(hr))
    {
        HandleError(L"QIF for ISynchronize Failed", hr);
        __leave;
    }
```

continues

LISTING 19.12 CONTINUED

```
        // Start the asynchronous function call.
        hr = pShopAsync->Begin_FindSalesClerk();
        if(FAILED(hr))
        {
            HandleError(L"Async Begin Failed", hr);
            __leave;
        }
        wprintf(L"Call to sales clerk started asynchronously\n");

        //
        // Simulate doing other work by sleeping for
        // few seconds.
        //
        Sleep(2000);

        // Wait for method call to complete.
        hr = pSynchro->Wait(COWAIT_WAITALL, INFINITE);
        if(FAILED(hr))
        {
            HandleError(L"ISynchronize::Wait Failed", hr);
            __leave;
        }

        // Complete the function call, and recover parameters.
        hr = pShopAsync->Finish_FindSalesClerk(&bstr);
        if(FAILED(hr))
        {
            HandleError(L"Completion Failed", hr);
            return 0;
        }
        wprintf(L"The sales clerk's name is %s\n", bstr);
    }
    __finally
    {
        SysFreeString(bstr);
        punk->Release();
        pCallFactory->Release();
        pShopAsync->Release();
        pSynchro->Release();
        CoUninitialize();
    }
    return 0;
}

/*
 * Error handling routine
 */
void HandleError(LPCWSTR strTitle, HRESULT hr)
{
```

```
    LPVOID lpMsgBuf;

    FormatMessageW(FORMAT_MESSAGE_ALLOCATE_BUFFER|
                   FORMAT_MESSAGE_FROM_SYSTEM,
                   NULL,
                   hr,
                   MAKELANGID(LANG_NEUTRAL, SUBLANG_DEFAULT),
                   (LPWSTR)&lpMsgBuf,
                   0,
                   NULL);
    MessageBoxW(NULL,
                (LPCWSTR)lpMsgBuf,
                strTitle,
                MB_OK | MB_ICONINFORMATION);
    LocalFree(lpMsgBuf);
}
```

The SyncClient directory also includes copies of the `AsyncTest_i.c` and `AsyncTest.h` files from the AsyncProxy project directory. You must use the files that were created after the `async_uuid` attribute was added to the `IShop` interface.

Build and run the AsyncClient project. Now if you use a debugger to step through the client code, you'll see that the call to `Begin_FindSalesClerk` immediately returns to the caller. After the call to `ISynchronize::Wait` returns, the `[out]` parameters from the interface are collected using `Finish_FindSalesClerk`.

Summary

This chapter has discussed the new support for asynchronous COM method calls introduced in Windows 2000. The new interfaces and components associated with asynchronous COM, such as call objects and the `ICallFactory` interface, were discussed. An example that demonstrated using asynchronous method calls was also presented.

19

ASYNCHRONOUS COM

DCOM

CHAPTER

20

Distributed COM makes it possible for you to use COM components across machine boundaries. This chapter covers topics that are related to Distributed COM, such as location transparency, security, and controlling where COM components are activated in the network.

Location Transparency

Distributed COM, or DCOM, takes advantage of a COM property known as *location transparency*. Location transparency is one of the key concepts in COM; it allows a client to use a COM object without needing to know where the actual COM object exists. Because clients connect to COM objects through interface pointers, there's no need for a client to use a different communication method for remote clients.

With COM, interfaces don't change as they are moved into a different process or even to a remote machine. For example, if you were to create an IEspresso interface, the IEspresso interface would appear to be IEspresso, no matter where the COM object was located. If a COM object is located in another apartment, COM and the operating system will create proxies to marshal interfaces and data between the client and server, as shown in Figure 20.1.

FIGURE 20.1

A proxy moves an object's interfaces into the client's apartment.

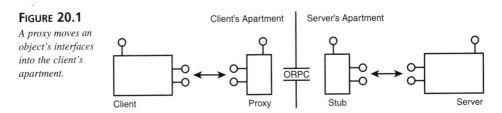

DCOM takes the notion of location transparency to an extreme and enables a client to use a COM object located in another computer, as shown in Figure 20.2.

FIGURE 20.2

DCOM enables communication between clients and COM objects over a network.

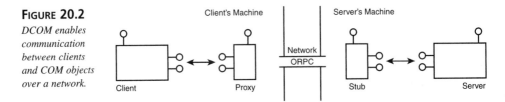

Before we dive into the specifics of DCOM, the next section describes a high-level view of how a COM object is instantiated on a remote machine.

Creating an Instance of a Remote Object

This section describes some of the basic ways a client can create an instance of a COM object on a remote computer. In order to simplify the discussion, security issues are largely postponed in this section. Security is discussed later in the section "Security in DCOM."

Naming a Remote Computer Implicitly

In keeping with the idea of location transparency, a client can create an instance of a COM object on a remote machine implicitly (that is, without specifying the location of the COM object). Creating an instance in this way begins in the System Registry.

As discussed in previous chapters, every creatable COM class has a key in the Registry under `HKEY_CLASSES_ROOT`. One named value under this key specifies the application ID, or AppID, for the module used to create the class:

```
[HKEY_CLASSES_ROOT\CLSID\<class ID GUID>]
    AppId = <app ID GUID>
```

An AppID is a GUID that identifies the process used to create one or more COM classes. Information about remote activation and security is stored under the AppID. Each AppID has a separate entry in the Registry under the following key:

```
[HKEY_CLASSES_ROOT\AppID\<app ID GUID>]
```

There may be more than one CLSID in the Registry that refer to each AppID key, as shown in Figure 20.3, because the same module may house multiple COM classes—the AppID contains information about the module rather than the class.

FIGURE 20.3

Each AppID may be referred to by several CLSID Registry entries.

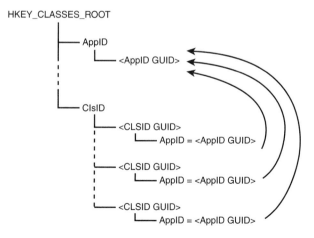

20

DCOM

The AppID key has several named values that are interesting when you're working with DCOM; there's a great deal of security information stored under this key that will be discussed later in this chapter. One key is used specifically for locating a DCOM server—the RemoteServerName named value. If the operating system discovers a computer name in this value, it will attempt to activate the component on the remote machine.

> **NOTE**
>
> The RemoteServerName value provides a convenient way for you to enable clients to use components in remote computers without hard-coding the location of the remote machines in code. However, if a client explicitly asks for a component to be activated on a specific machine, this Registry value will be ignored.

Active Directory can be used to store information about the location of COM servers. Information kept in the Registry can be placed into a General Policy Object, or GPO, which is used to update a user's Registry configuration.

Explicitly Creating a COM Object Remotely

In addition to using the RemoteServerName value found in the System Registry, you can also specify the location of a COM component programmatically. Here are the two Win32 function calls that are most often used to create remote instances of components:

- CoGetClassObject
- CoCreateInstanceEx

These two functions take the COSERVERINFO structure as a parameter that describes the location of the remote component:

```
typedef struct  _COSERVERINFO
{
    DWORD        dwReserved1;
    LPWSTR       pwszName;
    COAUTHINFO*  pAuthInfo;
    DWORD        dwReserved2;
}COSERVERINFO;
```

The COSERVERINFO structure has four members:

- dwReserved1 is reserved and must be set to zero.

- pwszName is the name of the remote computer used to instantiate the component. The name can be in any form that can be resolved on the network. This includes dotted quad IP addresses, UNC names, and domain format names. For example, L"ali.codevtech.com" is a valid name, as is L"\\BoatHouse" and L"10.1.1.24".

- pAuthInfo is a pointer to a COAUTHINFO structure that contains security information used for this activation request. To use default security, pass NULL as this parameter.

- dwReserved2 is reserved and must be set to zero.

The CoGetClassObject function returns a pointer to the class object's IClassFactory interface, as shown in the code fragment in Listing 20.1.

LISTING 20.1   CREATING A REMOTE INSTANCE OF IClassFactory USING CoGetClassObject

```
COSERVERINFO csi;
ZeroMemory(&csi, sizeof(csi));
csi.pwszName = L"slartibartfast.codevtech.com";

IClassFactory* pcf = NULL;
HRESULT hr = CoGetClassObject(CLSID_MyClass,
                              CLSCTX_ALL,
                              &csi,
                              IID_IClassFactory,
                              (LPVOID*)&pcf);
```

The CoGetClassObject function has five parameters:

- The CLSID of the class object to be created.

- The creation context that the class object must adhere to. CLSCTX_ALL allows the class object to be created anywhere. Other, more restrictive values can be found in the CLSCTX enumeration.

- The address of a COSERVERINFO structure that specifies how a remote activation of the class object is to be handled. If this value is NULL, the class object will be created using information from the Registry.

- The interface ID of the initial interface to be returned from the class object. This value is usually IID_ClassFactory.

- The address of an interface pointer that's compatible with the IID passed in the previous parameter. If the call to CoGetClassObject is successful, this parameter can be used to access an interface on the class object.

As with most COM functions, CoGetClassInfo returns an HRESULT that's used to determine whether the call succeeded or failed.

20

DCOM

CoCreateInstanceEx is an updated version of CoCreateInstance that offers two improvements:

- A COSERVERINFO structure may be passed as a parameter, thus allowing a client to specify a remote computer to handle the activation request.

- The client can request an array of initial interface pointers using an array of MULTI_QI structures, thus reducing the number of network roundtrips required when working with the interface.

CoCreateInstanceEx works very much like CoCreateInstance, although it has extra parameters that are used mostly for creating remote instances, as shown in Listing 20.2.

LISTING 20.2 CREATING A REMOTE INSTANCE OF A COM OBJECT USING CoCreateInstanceEx

```
MULTI_QI[2]  mqi;
ZeroMemory(&mqi, sizeof(mqi));
mqi[0].pIID = &IID_IEspresso;
mqi[1].pIID = &IID_ILatte;

COSERVERINFO csi;
ZeroMemory(&csi, sizeof(csi));
csi.pwszName = L"slartibartfast.codevtech.com";

HRESULT hr = CoCreateInstanceEx(CLSID_MyClass,
                                NULL,
                                CLSCTX_ALL,
                                &csi,
                                2,
                                &mqi);
```

The CoCreateInstanceEx function has six parameters:

- The CLSID of the class object to be created.

- If the new instance is to be aggregated, a pointer is needed to the IUnknown interface of the controlling outer object. Otherwise, pass NULL as this parameter.

- The creation context that the class object must adhere to. CLSCTX_ALL allows the class object to be created anywhere. Other, more restrictive values can be found in the CLSCTX enumeration.

- The address of a COSERVERINFO structure that specifies how a remote activation of the class object is to be handled. If this value is NULL, the class object will be created using information from the Registry.

- The number of MULTI_QI structures in the array passed as the last parameter.
- An array of one or more MULTI_QI structures, with each element used to specify a separate interface.

CoCreateInstanceEx returns an HRESULT that's used to determine whether the call succeeded or failed. As discussed later, each element in the MULTI_QI array also has an HRESULT that provides a return code specific to that interface.

The MULTI_QI structure is used by CoCreateInstanceEx to enable a client to request an array of interface pointers for the created instance. The MULTI_QI structure is defined as this:

```
typedef struct _MULTI_QI
{
    const IID*  pIID;
    IUnknown *  pItf;
    HRESULT     hr;
}MULTI_QI;
```

The MULTI_QI structure has three members:

- pIID is a pointer to an interface ID. This is the only parameter that must be a nonzero value when the CoCreateInstanceEx function is called.
- pItf is an interface pointer that will be filled if the call is successful.
- hr is an HRESULT that's associated with this MULTI_QI element.

Other Functions Used to Create Remote Instances

COM has two other, less commonly used functions that can be used to create and initialize instances of COM objects on remote computers:

- CoGetInstanceFromFile creates an instance of a COM object and initializes it using a filename passed as a parameter.
- CoGetInstanceFromStorage creates an instance of a COM object and initializes it using an IStorage pointer passed as a parameter.

These functions accept a pointer to an optional COSERVERINFO structure that can be used to specify the remote computer that should instantiate the COM object.

Using the IMultiQI Interface

Earlier, in Listing 20.2, CoCreateInstanceEx is used to create an instance of the CLSID_MyClass COM object and return pointers to the IEspresso and ILatte interfaces.

The ability to return multiple interfaces when you're creating the COM object helps reduce unnecessary network traffic. DCOM also introduces the `IMultiQI` interface, a synthesized interface that enables a client to request multiple interfaces in a single roundtrip. A simplified version of `IMultiQI` is provided in Listing 20.3.

LISTING 20.3   A SIMPLIFIED VERSION OF THE `IMultiQI` INTERFACE DEFINITION

```
interface IMultiQI : IUnknown
{
    HRESULT QueryMultipleInterfaces([in]ULONG cMQIs,
                                    [in,out] MULTI_QI *pMQIs);
};
```

The `IMultiQI` interface includes one method: `QueryMultipleInterfaces`. This method has two parameters:

- The number of interfaces requested
- An array of `MULTI_QI` structures (one element for each requested interface pointer)

As with `CoCreateInstanceEx`, the return value from `QueryMultipleInterfaces` is `S_OK` if all requested interfaces were returned. If the return value is `CO_S_NOTALLINTERFACES`, you must test each `MULTI_QI` element's `hr` member value to determine the status of each requested interface.

Your distributed COM object does not need to actually implement the `IMultiQI` interface—the standard proxy implements this interface and passes multiple `IUnknown::QueryInterface` method calls to your COM object.

Determining Whether an External Reference Is Valid

Like all distributed systems, DCOM must be concerned with clients and servers that fail or disappear due to network problems. When clients and servers are located in separate machines, connected via networks that are never 100% reliable, there must be a method to detect machines or connections that have disappeared or stopped responding. DCOM uses a sophisticated protocol based on pinging to test the state of connections between clients and servers.

A simplified version of this operation is that every connection between distributed clients and servers is tested by sending a ping message from the client machine to the server. If the server fails to answer a series of pings, the client will receive an `HRESULT` with a value such as `RPC_S_SERVER_UNAVAILABLE` or `RPC_E_DISCONNECTED` when making method calls using the interface pointer. If a server detects that a client has stopped ping-ing, the interface reference count will be decremented, resulting in the server instance possibly being released.

A detailed explanation is slightly more complex. If each client object communicated directly with each server object, a great deal of network bandwidth, as well as server pro-cessing capacity, would be dedicated to handling garbage collection for COM connec-tions. Consider a large network with thousands of clients, with each client maintaining a dozen or so references to different servers in the network. DCOM would quickly over-whelm such a network if it used a simplistic ping protocol.

When resolving DCOM messages, the client and server machines use a service known as the *OXID Resolver*. The OXID Resolver supports an RPC (not COM) interface called IOXIDResolver. The client creates a *ping set* on the server machine, with each connec-tion between client and server represented in the ping set. The client, therefore, needs to send only one ping message, known as a *simple ping*, to represent all of the connections in a ping set. When the membership of the ping set changes because a connection has been added or dropped, the ping set is updated by sending a *complex ping* message to the server. The complex ping message contains information only about connections that have been added or dropped. This process is known as *delta pinging*.

Currently, pinging is performed in two-minute intervals. If a client fails three consecutive ping intervals, its connection is released on the server. This means that it can take up to six minutes for a server to detect that a client has disappeared.

Security in DCOM

Security is not just a DCOM issue; many of the security issues discussed in this chapter apply to COM in general. However, once you venture out of a single machine into the network, you must deal with COM security issues. Most problems with DCOM applica-tions are really security problems.

COM security is based on Windows 2000 security, but it uses COM-specific APIs and interfaces. One reason for this is that COM is available on platforms other than Windows, such as some versions of UNIX.

COM allows you to specify security attributes at the following levels:

- *Per machine.* Each computer can have a set of security attributes that are used unless overridden by a process or user. These setting are located in the Registry.
- *Per process.* Each process can have security attributes that are used unless overrid-den. These settings can be located in the Registry or set programmatically.

20

DCOM

- *Per interface.* Each interface can have a set of security attributes that may differ from other interfaces in the same process. These settings are set programmatically.

You can also specify default security attributes that may be used or overridden, as desired, by applications and clients.

Types of Security

COM uses two basic types of security:

- *Activation security* determines whether a particular user is allowed to create an instance of a COM object. Activation security is applied only when a client attempts to create an instance of a COM object. The Service Control Manager will look into the Registry to determine whether the calling process is allowed access to the desired COM object. If not, the call is rejected. Activation security attributes are set using the DCOM Config tool or through an installation program that sets the Registry values. The specific keys and named values involved in this process are discussed later in the chapter. DCOM Config is a COM configuration utility that is included on every Windows 2000 machine.

- *Call security* determines whether a particular user is allowed to *access* an existing COM object. Call security is potentially applied for every call made to a COM interface method. Call security can be used to guarantee that each method call is made by an authenticated user, and it can optionally be used to ensure that payload data has not been corrupted. The different levels of call security are discussed in the next section.

In addition, there are Registry keys and functions that control the context in which a COM object is launched. They also specify the type of impersonation and cloaking that can be performed by the server on behalf of a client.

Understanding Call Security

The strength of the call security applied for a COM object is defined by specifying an authentication level. Here are the seven authentication levels:

- `RPC_C_AUTHN_LEVEL_NONE`. No call-level authentication is performed.
- `RPC_C_AUTHN_LEVEL_CONNECT`. The credentials of the client will be authenticated when it first establishes a connection with the server. If a connectionless transport is used for DCOM, this option is the same as `RPC_C_AUTHN_LEVEL_PKT`.
- `RPC_C_AUTHN_LEVEL_CALL`. Authentication is performed once, when the server receives the underlying RPC call.

- `RPC_C_AUTHN_LEVEL_PKT`. Authenticates that the contents of the DCOM packet came from the authenticated client but does not attempt to verify the integrity of the data.
- `RPC_C_AUTHN_LEVEL_PKT_INTEGRITY`. Authenticates the client's identity and verifies that no data has been modified in the method call.
- `RPC_C_AUTHN_LEVEL_PKT_PRIVACY`. Authenticates the client's identity, verifies that the data has not been modified, and encrypts the message packet.

In addition, here's another authentication level that's set aside to represent a default value:

- `RPC_C_AUTHN_LEVEL_DEFAULT`. Indicates that the normal security blanket negotiation algorithm is used. Security blankets are discussed later in the section "Understanding Security Blankets."

Understanding Cloaking and Impersonation

COM clients and servers use two methods that enable a COM server to assume the role of a client:

- Impersonation
- Cloaking

Impersonation has always been available in DCOM, and it works exactly like the impersonation method discussed in Chapter 7, "Distributed Security." A server assumes the security level and identity of the client in order to determine whether a client is allowed to perform a specific task. The problem with impersonation is that it does not work across multiple machine boundaries; a COM server that calls another COM server on a client's behalf cannot project the original client's identity to the next server.

Cloaking allows a COM server to control the identity that's sent to another COM server on a client's behalf. If a client allows delegation, the COM server can use cloaking to assume the client's identity and project that identity across machine boundaries to other COM servers.

Setting Security Levels for a Computer

Default security permissions for a computer are located in the Registry under the `HKEY_LOCAL_MACHINE` Registry key. A number of values must be set properly to manage DCOM. By default, DCOM is permitted for administrators and other power users. If you decide to actively manage DCOM, it's a good idea to learn which parts of the Registry are used by the operating system for DCOM.

20

DCOM

Enabling or Disabling DCOM for a Computer

The first value, EnableDCOM, can be used to enable or disable DCOM for the entire machine:

```
[HKEY_LOCAL_MACHINE\Software\Microsoft\OLE]
    EnableDCOM=Y
```

If the EnableDCOM named value is set to Y or y, remote machines are allowed to launch remote instances of COM objects on this machine, subject to further security permissions. If the value is N or n, remote access is not allowed. This is the first checkpoint for determining whether a DCOM connection can be established.

If you're using DCOM Config, this value is set in the Default Properties tab.

Setting Default Launch Permissions for a Computer

The DefaultLaunchPermission value is used to specify an ACL for principals that are allowed to launch COM servers. The DefaultLaunchPermission named value has the REG_BINARY type and is located under HKEY_LOCAL_MACHINE:

```
[HKEY_LOCAL_MACHINE\Software\Microsoft\OLE]
    DefaultLaunchPermission=<acl>
```

This value is not used if the COM server has a LaunchPermission value set under its AppID key. By default, administrators, the interactive user, and the system account are allowed launch permissions through this Registry key.

Setting Default Access Permissions for a Computer

The DefaultAccessPermission value is used to specify an ACL for principals that are allowed to access a running COM server. The DefaultAccessPermission value has the REG_BINARY type and is located under HKEY_LOCAL_MACHINE:

```
[HKEY_LOCAL_MACHINE\Software\Microsoft\OLE]
    DefaultAccessPermission=<acl>
```

This value is not used if the COM server has called CoInitializeSecurity or if the COM server has an AccessPermission value set under its AppID key. By default, this ACL is empty.

Setting Legacy Security Permissions for a Computer

To be sure, COM is a moving target. Security and distributed features have evolved into COM over the last few releases of Windows NT and various service packs. Windows

2000 allows you to define default values for COM servers that are unaware of DCOM security options. These options are as follows:

- The authentication level
- The impersonation level
- Mutual authentication availability
- Security on AddRef and Release method calls

The LegacyAuthenticationLevel value is used to specify the default authentication level used by a COM server when interacting with a remote client. The LegacyAuthenticationLevel value has the REG_WORD type and is located under HKEY_LOCAL_MACHINE:

```
[HKEY_LOCAL_MACHINE\Software\Microsoft\OLE]
    LegacyAuthenticationLevel=<Authentication level>
```

The authentication level must be a value between 1 and 6, as shown in Table 20.1.

TABLE 20.1 LEGACY AUTHENTICATION LEVELS

Value	Authentication Level
1	RPC_C_AUTHN_LEVEL_NONE
2	RPC_C_AUTHN_LEVEL_CONNECT
3	RPC_C_AUTHN_LEVEL_CALL
4	RPC_C_AUTHN_LEVEL_PKT
5	RPC_C_AUTHN_LEVEL_PKT_INTEGRITY
6	RPC_C_AUTHN_LEVEL_PKT_PRIVACY

The legacy authentication level is not used if the COM server has called CoInitializeSecurity. If the legacy authentication level is not set and the COM server has not called CoInitializeSecurity, the system will use a value of RPC_C_AUTHN_LEVEL_CONNECT.

The LegacyImpersonationLevel value is used to specify the default impersonation level used by a COM server when acting on behalf of a remote client. The LegacyImpersonationLevel value has the REG_WORD type and is located under HKEY_LOCAL_MACHINE:

```
[HKEY_LOCAL_MACHINE\Software\Microsoft\OLE]
    LegacyImpersonationLevel=<Impersonation level>
```

The impersonation level must be a value between 1 and 4, as shown in Table 20.2.

TABLE 20.2   LEGACY IMPERSONATION LEVELS

Value	Impersonation Level
1	RPC_C_IMP_LEVEL_ANONYMOUS
2	RPC_C_IMP_LEVEL_IDENTIFY
3	RPC_C_IMP_LEVEL_IMPERSONATE
4	RPC_C_IMP_LEVEL_DELEGATE

The impersonation levels are defined as follows:

- RPC_C_IMP_LEVEL_ANONYMOUS. Not available in the initial release of Windows 2000. This value allows a client to connect to a server anonymously.

- RPC_C_IMP_LEVEL_IDENTIFY. Allows a server to impersonate the user for the purposes of checking the client's ACL. However, the server cannot access system objects while impersonating the client.

- RPC_C_IMP_LEVEL_IMPERSONATE. Allows the server to impersonate the client when acting on its behalf. Unlike earlier versions of Windows NT, Windows 2000 allows impersonation across multiple computers if cloaking is used.

- RPC_C_IMP_LEVEL_DELEGATE. New to Windows 2000. This impersonation level allows the server to impersonate the client on this and other machines on the network.

The value stored as the LegacyImpersonationLevel is not used if the COM server has called CoInitializeSecurity. If this value is not set, and the server fails to call CoInitializeSecurity, the operating system will use a value of RPC_C_IMP_LEVEL_IDENTIFY.

Mutual authentication enables both the client and server to authenticate the other party, instead of the more typical client-only authentication. This allows a client to ensure that the server is really who it says it is. By default, mutual authentication is turned off in Windows 2000. Mutual authentication was not available for Windows NT 4.0, and it's available in Windows 2000 only when Kerberos is used as the security provider. The LegacyMutualAuthentication value is used to specify whether mutual authentication is in use. The LegacyMutualAuthentication value has the REG_SZ type and is located under HKEY_LOCAL_MACHINE:

```
[HKEY_LOCAL_MACHINE\Software\Microsoft\OLE]
    LegacyMutualAuthentication=<Y or N>
```

The value is either Y, to enable mutual authentication, or N, to disable it. If the value is not found, mutual authentication is disabled.

In a distributed environment, it's possible for a poorly written, or even malicious, program to call AddRef or Release on interfaces that it doesn't control. Enabling secure references forces the operating system to authenticate calls to AddRef and Release to ensure that these methods are called only by appropriate clients. The LegacySecureReferences value is used to specify whether secure references are enabled. The LegacySecureReferences value has the REG_SZ type and is located under HKEY_LOCAL_MACHINE:

```
[HKEY_LOCAL_MACHINE\Software\Microsoft\OLE]
    LegacySecureReferences=<Y or N>
```

The value is either Y, to enable secure references, or N, to disable them. If the value is not found, secure references are disabled.

Setting Security Attributes for a Process

Security attributes for a process can be set in two ways:

- Through the Registry AppID associated with a process
- Programmatically by calling CoInitializeSecurity

These approaches are discussed in the following sections.

Controlling Security Through the AppID Key

As discussed earlier in this chapter, every process that uses COM can be associated with an AppID. COM objects that are built using modern tools, such as Visual Basic or the ATL wizards in Visual C++, will automatically generate AppIDs that are registered when the component is registered. Client applications do not automatically register themselves, so AppIDs must be added to the Registry through some other means, such as a Registry script or Registry API functions.

Each AppID key may use four named values to specify process-wide security attributes:

- RunAs is a REG_SZ value that specifies the account to be used to execute the component. If the value is set to Interactive User, the process will run with the credentials of the current interactive user. Running as the interactive user is very helpful during debugging, but it will not allow the component to run if no user is currently logged on to the machine. If the process is meant to run under a specific user account, you must use the DCOM Config utility to define a password.

- LaunchPermission is a REG_BINARY value that stores an ACL defining the security principals allowed to launch COM objects grouped in this AppID. This value overrides the LegacyLaunchPermission value discussed earlier. A process can override this value by calling CoInitializeSecurity.

- AccessPermission is a REG_BINARY value that stores an ACL defining the security principals allowed to access COM objects grouped in this AppID. This value overrides the LegacyAccessPermission value discussed earlier. A process can override this value by calling CoInitializeSecurity.

- AuthenticationLevel is a REG_DWORD value that specifies the authentication level for calls made to COM objects grouped under this AppID key. This named value has the same range of values as the LegacyAuthenticationLevel value discussed earlier. If present, this value will override LegacyAuthenticationLevel. A process can override this value by calling CoInitializeSecurity.

Manipulating the Registry to provide security information is usually done with the DCOM configuration utility, which is discussed later in this chapter. Configuring the security attributes for clients and COM objects in this manner is sometimes called *declarative security*, as opposed to *programmatic security*, which is discussed in the next section.

Using CoInitializeSecurity to Define Security Attributes

Using the Registry is useful in some cases, but finer control can be obtained by using programmatic security, such as calling specific COM functions and using COM interfaces to control security attributes. The primary function used to control COM security is CoInitializeSecurity:

```
IAccessControl* pAccessCtrl = NULL;
// Initialization of pAccessCtrl omitted...
HRESULT hrSec = CoInitializeSecurity(pAccessCtrl,
                                     -1,
                                     NULL,
                                     NULL,
                                     RPC_C_AUTHN_LEVEL_CONNECT,
                                     RPC_C_IMP_LEVEL_IDENTIFY,
                                     NULL,
                                     EOAC_ACCESS_CONTROL,
                                     0);
```

`CoInitializeSecurity` has nine parameters:

- A pointer to an object that the operating system can use to determine security attributes for the process. This can be a pointer to the `IAccessControl` interface, a pointer to a `SECURITY_DESCRIPTOR` structure, or a GUID for an AppID. You can also pass a `NULL` value if you're turning off security for this interface. Each of these options is discussed later in this chapter.

- The number of elements in the array of `SOLE_AUTHENTICATION_SERVICE` structures passed as the next parameter. Normally, you pass -1 for this parameter, and COM will determine the correct authentication service for you.

- An array of `SOLE_AUTHENTICATION_SERVICE` structures, each of which defines an authentication service that will be used for incoming method calls. Normally, you'll pass -1 as the previous parameter and `NULL` as this parameter; this enables COM to select a reasonable authentication service.

- The fourth parameter is reserved and must be set to `NULL`.

- A minimum authentication level for this process. If a client attempts to call this process with a lower authentication level, the method call will be rejected.

- The impersonation level that's granted to servers when this process is placing an outgoing COM method call. This value has no effect on incoming method calls.

- A pointer to a `SOLE_AUTHENTICATION_LIST` structure. If and when this process acts as a client, this parameter is used to negotiate the authentication level. Usually, you set this parameter to `NULL`.

- One or more flags that indicate the security capabilities of the process. These values are taken from the `EOLE_AUTHENTICATION_CAPABILITIES` enumeration and are discussed next.

- The last parameter is reserved and must be `NULL`.

The `EOLE_AUTHENTICATION_CAPABILITIES` enumeration contains a number of flags that are used to define security attributes for the process. The values from this enumeration are defined as follows:

- `EOAC_NONE`. Specifies that no capability flags are set.

- `EOAC_DEFAULT`. Capabilities should be determined using the security blanket negotiation algorithm.

- `EOAC_MUTUAL_AUTH`. Not used.

- `EOAC_STATIC_CLOAKING`. The thread's token, if any, will be used to determine the client's identity. The client's identity is checked on the first method call to each proxy, as well as each time `CoSetProxyBlanket` is called.

- EOAC_DYNAMIC_CLOAKING. The thread's token, if any, will be used to determine the client's identity. The client's identity is checked on each method call to a proxy, thus making this option more expensive than static cloaking

- EOAC_ANY_AUTHORITY. Any SSL server certificate will be trusted, even if the top-level certificate isn't trusted. This is useful when the top-level certificate authority isn't installed on the computer.

- EOAC_SECURE_REFS. Reference counting will be authenticated to prevent processes from interfering with reference counts for object instances to which they do not have access. This can prevent malicious or poorly written applications from releasing objects that belong to you. The authentication level must not be set to none if this flag is used. This feature adds a small performance cost.

- EOAC_ACCESS_CONTROL. Specifies that the first parameter passed to CoInitializeSecurity is a pointer to an IAccessControl interface. COM uses the IAccessControl interface to determine the security attributes for the process.

- EOAC_APPID. Specifies that the first parameter passed to CoInitializeSecurity is a pointer to an AppID's GUID. COM uses the values stored for this AppID to determine the security attributes for the process.

- EOAC_MAKE_FULLSIC. Specifies that DCOM should generate SSL principal names in the *Full Subject Issuer Chain*, or fullsic, format described in RFC 1779.

- EOAC_REQUIRE_FULLSIC. Specifies that COM must fail CoUnmarshalInterface for any interface that contains SSL principal names that are not in a fullsic-compliant format.

- EOAC_AUTO_IMPERSONATE. Every method call will automatically impersonate the identity of the calling party. The authentication level must not be set to none.

- EOAC_DISABLE_AAA. Prevents any processes from being launched with the caller's identity (a feature known as *Activate-As-Activator*). This flag is useful only when dealing with a process that makes outbound COM method calls.

Any process that wants to control its security attributes must call CoInitializeSecurity fairly quickly. If a process does not call CoInitializeSecurity, COM will call it with default parameters. The best approach is to call CoInitializeSecurity immediately after calling CoInitializeEx. Once COM determines the security needs for a process for the first time, it will not allow CoInitializeSecurity to be called. A typical reason for COM to determine the security attributes for a process is when marshaling or unmarshaling an interface. After marshaling has taken place in a process, or if CoInitializeSecurity has already been set, calls to CoInitializeSecurity will fail with an HRESULT of 0x80010119, RPC_E_TOO_LATE.

Applications and components written in C or C++ usually have no problem meeting this requirement. If you write applications in Visual Basic, you'll find it impossible to call `CoInitializeSecurity`, because the runtime environment makes certain COM method calls before your code gets a chance to run.

Using `IAccessControl` to Define Security Attributes

The `IAccessControl` interface is used to manage security via a COM interface. `IAccessControl` uses Unicode versions of the `ACTRL_ACCESS` structures discussed in Chapter 7. The `IAccessControl` interface isn't terribly well documented in early releases of Windows 2000, and it requires you to build up an `ACTRL_ACCESS` structure that's used to define security information.

At the time this book was written, the IID for `IAccessControl` was not included in any of the standard Win32 header files. The example presented later in Listing 20.5 inserts this value manually. If you receive errors for this line of code, you can safely comment it out.

Listing 20.4 is a simplified version of the `IAccessControl` interface.

LISTING 20.4   THE `IAccessControl` INTERFACE

```
interface IAccessControl : public IUnknown
{
public:
    HRESULT GrantAccessRights(PACTRL_ACCESSW pAccessList);

    HRESULT SetAccessRights(PACTRL_ACCESSW pAccessList);

    HRESULT SetOwner(PTRUSTEEW pOwner, PTRUSTEEW pGroup);

    HRESULT RevokeAccessRights(LPWSTR lpProperty,
                               ULONG cTrustees,
                               TRUSTEEW prgTrustees[]);

    HRESULT GetAllAccessRights(LPWSTR lpProperty,
                PACTRL_ACCESSW_ALLOCATE_ALL_NODES* ppAccessList,
                PTRUSTEEW* ppOwner,
                PTRUSTEEW* ppGroup);

    HRESULT IsAccessAllowed(PTRUSTEEW pTrustee,
                            LPWSTR lpProperty,
                            ACCESS_RIGHTS AccessRights,
                            BOOL* pfAccessAllowed);
};
```

The IAccessControl interface has six methods:

- GrantAccessRights. Merges a new ACTRL_ACCESS list with the existing access rights on the object. ACTRL_ACCESS lists were discussed in Chapter 7.
- SetAccessRights. Defines a new set of access rights using a new ACTRL_ACCESS list.
- SetOwner. Sets an item's owner or group.
- RevokeAccessRights. Removes any explicit entries for the list of trustees.
- GetAllAccessRights. Gets the entire list of access rights, the owner, the group, or a combination of the three for the object.
- IsAccessAllowed. Determines whether the trustee has allowed access to a named property.

An example of using IAccessControl to control security for a process is shown in Listing 20.5.

LISTING 20.5   USING IAccessControl TO PROVIDE SECURITY ATTRIBUTES TO CoInitializeSecurity

```
const IID IID_IAccessControl = {0xEEDD23E0,0x8410,0x11CE,
                          {0xA1,0xC3,0x08,0x00,0x2B,0x2B,0x8D,0x8F}};

IAccessControl* pAccessCtrl = NULL;
HRESULT hrSec = CoCreateInstance(CLSID_DCOMAccessControl,
                          NULL,
                          CLSCTX_INPROC_SERVER,
                          IID_IAccessControl,
                          (void**)&pAccessCtrl);

if(SUCCEEDED(hrSec))
{
    // Define two access entries - one for the system account,
    // and one for codevtech\\mickeyw.
    ACTRL_ACCESS_ENTRY ae[2];
    ZeroMemory(&ae, sizeof(ae));

    ae[0].fAccessFlags = ACTRL_ACCESS_ALLOWED;
    ae[0].Access = COM_RIGHTS_EXECUTE;
    ae[0].Inheritance = NO_INHERITANCE;

    ae[0].Trustee.MultipleTrusteeOperation = NO_MULTIPLE_TRUSTEE;
    ae[0].Trustee.TrusteeForm = TRUSTEE_IS_NAME;

    ae[0].Trustee.TrusteeType = TRUSTEE_IS_USER;
    ae[0].Trustee.ptstrName = L"CODEVTECH\\mickeyw";
```

```
        ae[1].fAccessFlags = ACTRL_ACCESS_ALLOWED;
        ae[1].Access = COM_RIGHTS_EXECUTE;
        ae[1].Inheritance = NO_INHERITANCE;

        ae[1].Trustee.MultipleTrusteeOperation = NO_MULTIPLE_TRUSTEE;
        ae[1].Trustee.TrusteeForm = TRUSTEE_IS_NAME;

        ae[1].Trustee.TrusteeType = TRUSTEE_IS_USER;
        ae[1].Trustee.ptstrName = L"NT Authority\\System";


        ACTRL_ACCESS_ENTRY_LIST accessEntryList;
        accessEntryList.cEntries = 2;
        accessEntryList.pAccessList = ae;

        ACTRL_PROPERTY_ENTRY propEntry;
        propEntry.fListFlags = 0;//ACTRL_ACCESS_PROTECTED;
        propEntry.lpProperty = NULL;
        propEntry.pAccessEntryList = &accessEntryList;

        ACTRL_ACCESS access;
        access.cEntries = 1;
        access.pPropertyAccessList = &propEntry;

        hrSec = pAccessCtrl->SetAccessRights(&access);

        if(SUCCEEDED(hrSec))
        {
            hrSec = CoInitializeSecurity(pAccessCtrl,
                                    -1,
                                    0,
                                    NULL,
                                    RPC_C_AUTHN_LEVEL_CONNECT,
                                    RPC_C_IMP_LEVEL_IDENTIFY,
                                    NULL,
                                    EOAC_ACCESS_CONTROL,
                                    0);
        }
        pAccessCtrl->Release();
}
```

Listing 20.5 begins by creating an instance of the system-supplied
`CLSID_DCOMAccessControl` class. This COM class is supplied by the operating system
and provides a default implementation of `IAccessSecurity` that's sufficient for most
needs. Most of the remaining code creates an `ACCESS_ENTRY` structure that grants access
to two principals—the author and the built-in System account—and then uses the structure to initialize the security instance.

20

DCOM

The call to `CoInitializeSecurity` passes the pointer to `IAccessControl` as the first parameter. To indicate that the first parameter is an `IAccessControl` parameter, you need to set the eighth parameter to `EOAC_ACCESS_CONTROL`. If other capability flags are needed, they must be `OR`'ed with `EOAC_ACCESS_CONTROL`.

Using `SECURITY_DESCRIPTOR` to Define Security Attributes

As discussed in Chapter 7, securable objects in Windows 2000 are associated with a `SECURITY_DESCRIPTOR` structure. This structure contains security attributes such as the object's owner, and two access-control lists, or `ACL`s, that describe how users and groups interact with the object. One `ACL`, known as the Discretionary Access Control List, or `DACL`, contains entries that allow or deny access to the object. An `ACCESS_ALLOWED_ACE` is an entry that grants access to a particular user or group, and an `ACCESS_DENIED_ACE` is an entry that denies access to a particular user or group. Another type of `ACL` is the System Access Control List, or `SACL`, which identifies users and groups that cause a security event to be generated.

If you're comfortable using Win32 security descriptors, you may prefer to use `CoInitializeSecurity` with a `SECURITY_DESCRIPTOR` structure. There are two ways to use a Win32 security descriptor with `CoInitializeSecurity`:

- Use the Win32 structures directly.
- Use the ATL `CSecurityDescriptor` class.

This section provides examples of both methods.

Even if you're accustomed to using Win32 security, two idiosyncrasies of COM security might trip you up:

- The system account must be given access to the COM object. If the system account doesn't have access to your object, you may see all sorts of odd problems, such as out-of-memory errors.
- The `SECURITY_DESCRIPTOR` structure must have process-owner and process-group SIDs defined. You generally don't need to do this for most Win32 security functions, but COM requires it.

Listing 20.6 provides an example of using `CoInitializeSecurity` with a Win32 `SECURITY_DESCRIPTOR` structure.

LISTING 20.6   USING SECURITY_DESCRIPTOR TO PROVIDE SECURITY ATTRIBUTES TO `CoInitializeSecurity`

```
SECURITY_DESCRIPTOR* pSecurityDescriptor;
PACL                 pAccessControlList;
```

```
DWORD                  cbSecurityDescriptor;
DWORD                  cbAccessControlList;

// Set the size of the security descriptor, assuming that we
// will only have one entry in the DACL.
cbSecurityDescriptor = sizeof(SECURITY_DESCRIPTOR)+
                       (2 * sizeof(ACCESS_ALLOWED_ACE))+
                       sizeof(ACL)+
                       GetSidLengthRequired(8);

// Allocate a chunk o' RAM for the security descriptor
pSecurityDescriptor = (SECURITY_DESCRIPTOR*)calloc(1,
                                      cbSecurityDescriptor);
if(!pSecurityDescriptor)
{
    // Handle error - not enough memory
}

InitializeSecurityDescriptor(pSecurityDescriptor,
                    SECURITY_DESCRIPTOR_REVISION);

// The DACL is located immediately after the security descriptor,
// find it and initialize it.
pAccessControlList = (PACL)((PUCHAR)pSecurityDescriptor +
                              sizeof(SECURITY_DESCRIPTOR));
cbAccessControlList = cbSecurityDescriptor -
                              sizeof(SECURITY_DESCRIPTOR);
InitializeAcl(pAccessControlList,
              cbAccessControlList,
              ACL_REVISION);

// Look up user mickeyw, and use his SID to make an entry
// in the DACL, along with System.
DWORD      cbDomain = MAX_PATH;
DWORD      cbSid = MAX_PATH;
PSID       pSid = calloc(1, cbSid);
WCHAR      szDomain[MAX_PATH];
SID_NAME_USE sidUse;

BOOL fLookup = LookupAccountName(NULL,
                                 L"mickeyw",
                                 pSid,
                                 &cbSid,
                                 szDomain,
                                 &cbDomain,
                                 &sidUse);
if(fLookup == FALSE)
{
    // Handle error - could not find user mickeyw
    // (This is likely to happen on non-codev
    // domains :)
```

20

DCOM

continues

LISTING 20.6   CONTINUED

```
}

PSID pSidSystem = GetSystemSid();
PSID pSidProcessOwner = GetProcessOwnerSid();
PSID pSidProcessGroup = GetProcessGroupSid();

AddAccessAllowedAce(pAccessControlList,
                    ACL_REVISION,
                    COM_RIGHTS_EXECUTE,
                    pSid);

AddAccessAllowedAce(pAccessControlList,
                    ACL_REVISION,
                    COM_RIGHTS_EXECUTE,
                    pSidSystem);

SetSecurityDescriptorDacl(pSecurityDescriptor,
                          TRUE,
                          pAccessControlList,
                          FALSE);
SetSecurityDescriptorGroup(pSecurityDescriptor,
                           pSidProcessGroup,
                           FALSE);
SetSecurityDescriptorOwner(pSecurityDescriptor,
                           pSidProcessOwner,
                           FALSE);

HRESULT hrSec = CoInitializeSecurity(pSecurityDescriptor,
                          -1,
                          0,
                          NULL,   // Reserved
                          RPC_C_AUTHN_LEVEL_CONNECT,
                          RPC_C_IMP_LEVEL_IDENTIFY,
                          NULL,
                          0,
                          0);

FreeSid(pSidSystem);
free(pSecurityDescriptor);
free(pSid);
free(pSidProcessOwner);
free(pSidProcessGroup);
```

Listing 20.6 starts off by creating a security descriptor that contains a DACL with
two ACEs—one for the author and another for the system account. When
CoInitializeSecurity is called with a pointer to a SECURITY_DESCRIPTOR structure,
you don't need to pass any specific capability flags in the eighth parameter.

Listing 20.6 makes use of some helper functions that retrieve the group and owner for
the current process, as well as the SID for the built-in System account. These functions
are provided in Listing 20.7.

LISTING 20.7   HELPER FUNCTIONS USED TO CREATE COMMONLY USED SIDS

```
/*
 * Returns a SID for the system account.
 * The SID must be freed using the Win32 FreeSid() function.
 */
PSID GetSystemSid()
{
    PSID pSidRet = NULL;
    SID_IDENTIFIER_AUTHORITY sidAuth = SECURITY_NT_AUTHORITY;
    AllocateAndInitializeSid(&sidAuth,
                             1,
                             SECURITY_LOCAL_SYSTEM_RID,
                             0, 0, 0, 0, 0, 0, 0,
                             &pSidRet);
    return pSidRet;
}


/*
 * Returns the SID for the current process owner. The SID
 * must be freed using the c runtime free() function.
 */
PSID GetProcessOwnerSid()
{
    PSID pSidRet = NULL;
    HANDLE hToken;
    HANDLE hProcess = GetCurrentProcess();
    BOOL fOpened = OpenProcessToken(hProcess,
                                    TOKEN_QUERY,
                                    &hToken);
    if(fOpened != FALSE)
    {
        TOKEN_USER* pUserToken = NULL;
        DWORD        cbUserToken;
        // Get the size required for the user token
        GetTokenInformation(hToken, TokenUser,NULL,0,&cbUserToken);
        if(ERROR_INSUFFICIENT_BUFFER != GetLastError())
            return NULL;

        pUserToken = (TOKEN_USER*)malloc(cbUserToken);
        if(!pUserToken)
            return NULL;

        BOOL fToken = GetTokenInformation(hToken,
                                          TokenUser,
```

20

DCOM

continues

LISTING 20.7   CONTINUED

```
                                               pUserToken,
                                               cbUserToken,
                                               &cbUserToken);
        if(fToken)
        {
            DWORD cbSid = GetLengthSid(pUserToken->User.Sid);
            pSidRet = (PSID)malloc(cbSid);
            if(pSidRet)
            {
                CopySid(cbSid, pSidRet, pUserToken->User.Sid);
            }
        }
        free(pUserToken);
    }
    return pSidRet;
}

/*
 * Returns the SID for the primary group of the current process.
 * The SID must be freed using the c runtime free() function.
 */
PSID GetProcessGroupSid()
{
    PSID pSidRet = NULL;
    HANDLE hToken;
    HANDLE hProcess = GetCurrentProcess();
    BOOL fOpened = OpenProcessToken(hProcess,
                                    TOKEN_QUERY,
                                    &hToken);
    if(fOpened != FALSE)
    {
        TOKEN_PRIMARY_GROUP* pGroupToken = NULL;
        DWORD        cbGroupToken;

        // Get the size required for the primary group token
        GetTokenInformation(hToken,
                            TokenPrimaryGroup,
                            NULL,
                            0,
                            &cbGroupToken);
        if(ERROR_INSUFFICIENT_BUFFER != GetLastError())
            return NULL;

        pGroupToken = (TOKEN_PRIMARY_GROUP*)malloc(cbGroupToken);
        if(!pGroupToken)
            return NULL;

        BOOL fToken = GetTokenInformation(hToken,
                                          TokenPrimaryGroup,
```

```
                                   pGroupToken,
                                   cbGroupToken,
                                   &cbGroupToken);
        if(fToken)
        {
            DWORD cbSid = GetLengthSid(pGroupToken->PrimaryGroup);
            pSidRet = (PSID)malloc(cbSid);
            if(pSidRet)
            {
                CopySid(cbSid, pSidRet, pGroupToken->PrimaryGroup);
            }
        }
        free(pGroupToken);
    }
    return pSidRet;
}
```

The `CSecurityDescriptor` class is part of the ATL class library, and it greatly simplifies the task of managing security descriptors. If your COM object is written with ATL, it's a good idea to use this class—it can really cut down on the amount of security code that you need to create yourself. Unfortunately, this class is not well documented in the Visual C++ documentation.

`CSecurityDescriptor` is basically a C++ class wrapped around a Win32 `SECURITY_DESCRIPTOR` structure. Here are some of the more helpful methods offered by `CSecurityDescriptor`:

- `Initialize`. Initializes the security descriptor so that access is granted to everyone
- `InitializeFromProcessToken`. Grants access to everyone and also sets the security descriptor's owner and group SIDs using the current process token
- `InitializeFromThreadToken`. Grants access to everyone and also sets the security descriptor's owner and group SIDs using the current thread token
- `Allow`. Adds an `ACCESS_ALLOWED_ACE` representing a specified security principal to the security descriptor's DACL, properly merging the new ACE into the DACL if required
- `Deny`. Adds an `ACCESS_DENIED_ACE` representing a specified security principal to the security descriptor's DACL, properly merging the new ACE into the DACL if required
- `Revoke`. Removes a specified security principal from the security descriptor's DACL

Listing 20.8 is an example of the same security code presented in Listing 20.6 but rewritten to take advantage of `CSecurityDescriptor`.

20

DCOM

LISTING 20.8 USING THE ATL CSecurityDescriptor CLASS TO DEFINE SECURITY ATTRIBUTES

```
CSecurityDescriptor sd;
sd.InitializeFromProcessToken();
sd.Allow(L"codevtech\\mickeyw",COM_RIGHTS_EXECUTE);
sd.Allow(L"NT Authority\\System",COM_RIGHTS_EXECUTE);
HRESULT hrSec = CoInitializeSecurity(sd,
                                     -1,
                                     0,
                                     NULL,  // Reserved
                                     RPC_C_AUTHN_LEVEL_CONNECT,
                                     RPC_C_IMP_LEVEL_IDENTIFY,
                                     NULL,
                                     0,
                                     0);
```

In Listing 20.8, note that sd is passed directly to CoInitializeSecurity. The CSecurityDescriptor class includes a conversion operator that converts an instance of CSecurityDescriptor into a pointer to its contained SECURITY_DESCRIPTOR structure.

Using an AppID to Define Security Attributes

Another way to use CoInitializeSecurity is to pass an AppID that contains the desired security attributes. This is a useful option in cases where you want to have multiple security profiles stored in the Registry. Each profile can be stored as an AppID, and when the COM object is initialized, one of the AppIDs is selected to be used as the security profile. Listing 20.9 provides an example of using an AppID with CoInitializeSecurity.

LISTING 20.9 USING AN APPID TO PROVIDE SECURITY ATTRIBUTES TO CoInitializeSecurity

```
// A GUID that is used as an AppID
static const GUID AppIDPo = {0x4FB6BB00, 0x3347, 0x11D0,
                {0xB4, 0x0A, 0x0, 0xAA, 0x0, 0x5F,0xF5, 0x86}};

// ... Code to initialize AppID in registry omitted ...

HRESULT hrSec = CoInitializeSecurity((void*)&AppIDPo,
                                     -1,
                                     0,
                                     NULL,  // Reserved, must be NULL
                                     RPC_C_AUTHN_LEVEL_CONNECT,
                                     RPC_C_IMP_LEVEL_IDENTIFY,
                                     NULL,
                                     EOAC_APPID,
                                     0);
```

Disabling Security with `CoInitializeSecurity`

Finally, you can use `CoInitializeSecurity` to completely turn off security for a process. This is useful if you're debugging a problem and you want to make sure that it isn't security related, or if you're working in a controlled environment and you don't really need security checking.

To turn off server-side security checking, pass `NULL` as the security descriptor and `RPC_C_AUTHN_LEVEL_NONE` as the authentication level, as shown in Listing 20.10.

LISTING 20.10 TURNING OFF SECURITY FOR A SERVER PROCESS USING `CoInitializeSecurity`

```
HRESULT hrSec = CoInitializeSecurity(NULL,
                                     -1,
                                     0,
                                     NULL,  // Reserved, must be NULL
                                     RPC_C_AUTHN_LEVEL_NONE,
                                     RPC_C_IMP_LEVEL_IDENTIFY,
                                     NULL,
                                     0,
                                     0);
```

Understanding Security Blankets

A *security blanket* is a collection of security attributes that represents the settings used for interface proxies within a process. Normally, all interface proxies within a client process will use the same security attributes, but COM provides interfaces and functions that enable a client to assign different security settings for each interface. The server security blanket cannot be changed once it has been defined.

After client and server processes specify their security settings with `CoInitializeSecurity` (you'll recall that this function is called by COM automatically for processes that do not call it explicitly), COM negotiates the proper default security blanket for the two processes. Some parameters passed to `CoInitializeSecurity` are useful only on the server side; the following attributes are copied to the security blanket:

- An ACL
- Server-side `EOAC` capability flags

Likewise, some parameters passed to `CoInitializeSecurity` are useful only on the client side; the following attributes are copied to the security blanket:

- The impersonation level

20

DCOM

- The client side `EOAC` capability flags, such as secure references and auto-impersonate
- The authentication identity

Here are the negotiated parts of the security blanket:

- The authentication service is selected based on the services passed by client and server. If both client and server elect to use the default authentication service, COM will select Kerberos for Windows 2000 machines, followed by NTLMSSP if Kerberos is inappropriate. It will select SSL as a third choice.
- The authorization service is selected based on the negotiated authentication service.
- The principal name is selected based on the negotiated authentication service.
- The authentication level is set to the highest level selected by client or server.

Setting Client-side Security Attributes for an Interface

The client can manipulate its security blanket through the `IClientSecurity` interface. The standard Windows 2000 COM proxy manager implements `IClientSecurity`—it's rarely implemented directly by a COM object. This means that any time you, as a client, have a standard proxy, you can manage your security blanket for this proxy through `IClientSecurity`. If your proxy uses custom marshaling, it's possible that the custom proxy will not support the `IClientSecurity` interface. Also, COM objects that live in the same apartment as the client will not support manipulating the client-side security blanket unless the object provides direct support for the `IClientSecurity` interface.

A simplified version of the `IClientSecurity` interface is provided in Listing 20.11.

LISTING 20.11 THE `IClientSecurity` INTERFACE

```
interface IClientSecurity : public IUnknown
{
public:
    HRESULT QueryBlanket(IUnknown* pProxy,
                         DWORD* pAuthnSvc,
                         DWORD* pAuthzSvc,
                         OLECHAR** pServerPrincName,
                         DWORD* pAuthnLevel,
                         DWORD* pImpLevel,
                         void** pAuthInfo,
                         DWORD* pCapabilites);
```

```
HRESULT SetBlanket(IUnknown* pProxy,
                   DWORD dwAuthnSvc,
                   DWORD dwAuthzSvc,
                   OLECHAR* pServerPrincName,
                   DWORD dwAuthnLevel,
                   DWORD dwImpLevel,
                   void* pAuthInfo,
                   DWORD dwCapabilities);

HRESULT CopyProxy(IUnknown* pProxy,
                  IUnknown** ppCopy);
};
```

The `IClientSecurity` interface has three member functions:

- `QueryBlanket`. Returns the current security blanket settings for a proxy.
- `SetBlanket`. Defines attributes used for the proxy's security blanket. This method is typically used to raise the authentication level for an interface.
- `CopyProxy`. Creates a copy of an interface pointer on the proxy.

Listing 20.12 shows how `IClientSecurity` can be used to change the security blanket for a proxy. In this case, the authentication level is set to its highest level, `RPC_C_AUTHN_LEVEL_PKT_PRIVACY`.

LISTING 20.12   USING `IClientSecurity` TO CHANGE A PROXY'S AUTHENTICATION LEVEL

```
HRESULT SwitchInterfaceToEncryptedPackets(IUnknown* punk)
{
    IClientSecurity* pClientSecurity = NULL;
    HRESULT hr = punk->QueryInterface(IID_IClientSecurity,
                                      (void**)&pClientSecurity);
    if(FAILED(hr))
        return hr;

    DWORD    dwAuthentication;
    DWORD    dwAuthorization;
    OLECHAR* pszPrincipal;
    DWORD    dwImpersonation;
    DWORD    dwCapabilities;

    // Call QueryBlanket to determine current settings.
    hr = pClientSecurity->QueryBlanket(punk,
                                       &dwAuthentication,
                                       &dwAuthorization,
                                       &pszPrincipal,
                                       0,
```

continues

20

DCOM

LISTING 20.12 CONTINUED

```
                                          &dwImpersonation,
                                          0,
                                          &dwCapabilities);

    if(SUCCEEDED(hr))
    {
        // Set proxy blanket to identical values, except for the
        // authentication level.
        hr = pClientSecurity->SetBlanket(punk,
                                          dwAuthentication,
                                          dwAuthorization,
                                          pszPrincipal,
                                          RPC_C_AUTHN_LEVEL_PKT_PRIVACY,
                                          dwImpersonation,
                                          0,
                                          dwCapabilities);
    }
    pClientSecurity->Release();
    CoTaskMemFree(pszPrincipal);
    return hr;
}
```

In the function shown in Listing 20.12, the current settings for the proxy's security blanket are retrieved before new values are set. You must always retrieve the existing values for the security blanket unless you intend to set each parameter to a specific and possibly new value.

COM also includes three helper functions that enable you to manipulate the client side of the security blanket without dealing with the IClientSecurity interface pointer:

- CoSetProxyBlanket, which can be used instead of IClientSecurity::SetBlanket
- CoQueryProxyBlanket, which can be used instead of IClientSecurity::QueryBlanket
- CoCopyProxy, which can be used instead of IClientSecurity::CopyProxy

Managing Server-side Security

COM also includes IServerSecurity, an interface that can be used by a COM server to manage security on the server side. This interface is useful when a COM process needs to manage security more interactively than what's possible using the programmatic methods discussed earlier.

A simplified version of the IServerSecurity interface is provided in Listing 20.13.

LISTING 20.13 THE ISServerSecurity INTERFACE

```
interface IServerSecurity : public IUnknown
{
public:
    HRESULT QueryBlanket(DWORD*      pAuthnSvc,
                         DWORD*      pAuthzSvc,
                         OLECHAR**   pServerPrincName,
                         DWORD*      pAuthnLevel,
                         DWORD*      pImpLevel,
                         void**      pPrivs,
                         DWORD*      pCapabilities);
    HRESULT ImpersonateClient(void);
    HRESULT RevertToSelf(void);
    BOOL    IsImpersonating(void);
};
```

The ISServerSecurity interface has four member functions:

- QueryBlanket. Enables the server to retrieve security blanket information about the client.

- ImpersonateClient. Called by the server to impersonate the client. This only works if the client allows itself to be impersonated by the server.

- RevertToSelf. Called by the server while impersonating a client. This function causes the server to revert back to its normal security settings.

- IsImpersonating. Returns TRUE if the current thread is impersonating the client. Returns FALSE otherwise. This is one of the few COM methods that does not return an HRESULT.

To retrieve a pointer to the ISServerSecurity interface, the server must call the CoGetCallContext function.

COM also includes three helper functions that enable you to manage security on the server side without dealing with the ISServerSecurity interface pointer:

- CoQueryClientBlanket, which can be used instead of ISServerSecurity::QueryBlanket

- CoImpersonateClient, which can be used instead of ISServerSecurity::ImpersonateClient

- CoRevertToSelf, which can be used instead of ISServerSecurity::RevertToSelf

20

DCOM

Using the DCOM Configuration Utility

The DCOM configuration utility, known as *DCOM Config*, is shipped with every Windows 2000 system and is used to declaratively configure DCOM Registry entries that control security and other attributes used by DCOM. DCOM Config allows you access to security and protocol defaults for the following items:

- The entire computer
- A particular process

DCOM Config is launched from a DOS prompt by typing the following:

```
DcomCnfg
```

If you use DCOM, you'll be launching DCOM Config quite a bit, so you should consider adding a shortcut to C:\Winnt\DcomCnfg.exe to your Visual C++ tools menu.

Keep in mind that any system-wide settings configured with DCOM Config will be overridden by settings made for a specific AppID with DCOM Config. Also, any attributes set programmatically with CoInitializeSecurity will override systemwide and AppID-specific configuration settings.

Using DCOM Config to Set Systemwide Attributes

When initially launched, DCOM Config presents a list of registered AppIDs, as shown in Figure 20.4. The Applications tab is used to select individual AppIDs to be configured.

FIGURE 20.4

The Applications tab from the DCOM configuration utility.

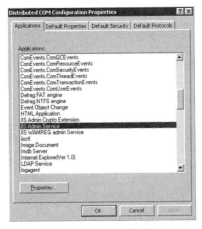

DCOM Config has three additional tabs that are used to control different types of systemwide settings:

- *Default Properties.* From here, you can enable or disable DCOM for the entire machine and set default authentication and impersonation levels. Items on this page control Registry settings found under the `HKEY_LOCAL_MACHINE\SOFTWARE\Microsoft\Ole` Registry key.

- *Default Security.* From here, you can set default launch, access, and configuration permissions for processes that do not call `CoInitializeSecurity` or provide their own AppID-specific setting.

- *Default Protocols.* From here, you can define allowed network protocols and their relative priorities.

Using DCOM Config to Set Attributes for a Specific AppID

Applications that have specific configuration needs can be managed by double-clicking on the process name in the Applications tab or by clicking the Properties pushbutton. DCOM Config will display a property sheet that's used to configure AppID-specific attributes for the process. The General tab is initially displayed, as shown in Figure 20.5.

FIGURE 20.5

The General tab from the DCOM configuration utility.

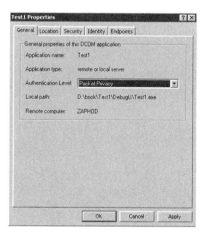

Here are the five categories of settings that can be configured for each AppID by DCOM Config:

- *General.* From here, you can display information about the location of the application and change the authentication level.

20

DCOM

- *Location.* From here, you can define the location where the COM process should execute.
- *Security.* From here, you can override the systemwide default security settings.
- *Identity.* From here, you can define the account that the application will run under.
- *Endpoints.* From here, you can define the network protocol and endpoints that the application will use.

Each of the AppID-specific settings made using DCOM Config will override settings made on a systemwide basis. In a similar way, any programmatic settings made by the application will override AppID-specific settings.

Summary

This chapter discussed DCOM and many of the issues that must be addressed when using COM in a distributed environment. This chapter covered location transparency as well as the enhancements made to COM to make it possible to use COM components transparently across machine boundaries. This chapter also discussed security and how security attributes can be set in a declarative way in the Registry or programmatically through `CoInitializeSecurity` and other functions and interfaces. The chapter also discussed the DCOM configuration utility, DCOM Config, which can be used to modify DCOM settings in the System Registry.

COM+

IV

In This Part

An Introduction to COM+ Services

This is the first chapter of the COM+ services section. This chapter is an introduction to the transaction aspect of COM+ services. To start the chapter, an introduction into transactions and their workings is given. You need to understand how transactions function; otherwise, you won't understand why the COM+ components are written the way they are. Then a simple component is shown using Visual Basic. This simple component expands on how to write code that interacts with its resource. Also, notice the terminology used—the word *MTS* is absent. The reason is because COM+ services are an evolution of MTS.

Introducing Transactions

Source: Webster's Revised Unabridged Dictionary (1913) [web1913]

transaction \Trans*ac'tion\, n. [L. transactio, fr. transigere, transactum, to drive through, carry through, accomplish, transact; trans across, over + agere to drive; cf. F. transaction.

1. The doing or performing of any business; management of any affair; performance.
2. That which is done; an affair; as, the transactions on the exchange.
3. (Civil Law) An adjustment of a dispute between parties by mutual agreement.

The dictionary states that a transaction means *to carry through*. It's the act of completing something 100 percent. This is absolutely important, because a transaction ensures completeness.

Consider, for example, a bank. You go to the nearest ATM machine and decide to get some money. Here are the steps you follow:

1. Insert your card into the ATM.
2. Punch in your PIN number.
3. Decide the amount of money to withdraw.
4. Press Validate to process the transaction.
5. The account is debited by the requested amount.
6. Remove your card from the machine.
7. Remove the money from the machine.

All these steps are one transaction. Imagine a case in which the ATM delays the debiting of your account, and it fails. When the ATM has given you your money, it cannot run after you and ask for it back to retry the transaction. This is a very important fact about transactions. Once a transaction has been carried through, it cannot be rolled back. Although you may think the worst part of this failure is that the bank loses money, it is, in fact, worse. What happens is that money is produced. Money is produced because the transaction has debited from its ledgers a specific sum of money. And yet you hold

An Introduction to COM+ Services

CHAPTER 21

683

21

AN INTRODUCTION
TO COM+
SERVICES

money in your hand. Therefore, if you take that money and deposit it in your account, those money bills are considered new. This is illegal, since only governments can produce money.

As a reference for later sections, consider the following diagram shown in Figure 21.1.

FIGURE 21.1

Sample transactions involving two people and two accounts.

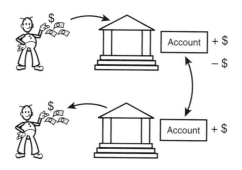

This sample transaction is an example of three different transactions. The first is the taking of money and then crediting an account. The second transaction is when an account is debited and then another account is credited a certain amount of money. The last transaction is the debiting of an account of a sum and then the paying of that sum in cash. Through all these transactions, money is never created or lost. This is important, because even if the money is electronic, it must be accounted for.

ACID: The Four Commandments of Transaction Processing

ACID is an acronym for the four commandments of a transaction system. These commandments are atomicity, consistency, isolation, and durability. Unlike other systems, where certain parts of the system are exempt from certain rules, in a transaction-based system, everything must play by the rules—this includes the transaction system, the server components, and the client components. Shortcuts and hacks are not tolerated and will cause problems in the long term of the development. A transaction system is like a chain, which is only as strong as its weakest link.

Atomicity

In the first example of representing a transaction, the requirement was for the account to be successfully debited a certain amount of money. If that transaction were to be interrupted or a crash were to occur, the transaction must fail. If the transaction fails, the person doing the withdrawal expects the account to remain at the same level. *Atomicity* requires that either the transaction commits or aborts. With either a success or failure, it's absolutely imperative that the state be maintained. It's a winner-take-all situation.

Sidestepping the main topic for a moment, in a static building design class exam, the following statement was made: Getting 85 percent of the question right does not mean you get 85 percent of the marks. A bridge that's 85 percent correct will still fall. Therefore, you must either get 100 percent correct or nothing. This is a hard way to grade exams, but it's the truth. Transaction code must be written to the same harsh reality.

Consistency

Consistency doesn't mean a correct program. Consistency is the application of a consistent methodology. When money is loaned from a bank or deposited, interest is calculated. The interest is either for you or against you. A problem with interest is that half cents cannot be paid or collected. Therefore, the amount must be to the nearest cent. The value must be rounded off. Rounding off is not a simple issue, because there are two ways of doing it—rounding up or rounding down. In most cases, the banks round either up only or down only. It makes it simple and consistent. What would be incorrect for the bank is to round down when paying interest and round up when collecting interest. That would be inconsistent.

Consistency is a much-desired aspect of writing transaction code, because, with a consistent state, it's predictable to say, when an account is credited a sum of money, it always gets the same amount. When interest is calculated, it's always calculated the same way. This way, when a transaction is finalized, the end result will always be the same. Consistency cannot be enforced by the transaction system. Good testing and good programming techniques can only enforce consistency. A good way of enforcing consistency is to document your rules and business processes.

Isolation

During a running transaction, data is altered and can be considered to be in a state of limbo. Consider the situation of the bank transferring money from one account to another. When money is debited from one account and placed in another, there's a state of limbo between when the original account is debited and the other account is credited. This limbo state requires a certain amount of time. If during this limbo state, another transaction needs to credit the account, which amount does it see? Does it see the old level or the new level? There's no conclusive answer, but transaction systems take the point of view that the data has not been altered. This means that if the other transaction wants to see the data, it sees the *old* data.

The job of the transaction system is not yet complete. If the other transaction system wants to modify the data, the transactions must be kept isolated. The two updates must be kept isolated; otherwise, a potential update could occur on data that was supposed to be written.

An Introduction to COM+ Services

CHAPTER 21

685

21

AN INTRODUCTION
TO COM+
SERVICES

The other problem that may occur involves *stale* data. Transaction A reads some data. Transaction B reads and updates the data. Transaction B updates the data. The data held by Transaction B is considered stale. To get around this, you'll either need to write relative code or version-checking code. Relative code is used when the value in the record does not matter, because the other value is incremented or decremented. Version checking is used when the version of the data is checked before it's updated. This type of work is not done by the transaction system—it must be done by the programmer.

Durability

The concept of durability specifies that if anything goes wrong, the transacted data will still be there. This concept is very important because the scope of it involves more than just the software. Go back to the example of the money being withdrawn from the account. If the transaction goes through and the monies are given out, then a crash in the system will not influence the outcome of that transaction. When the system reboots from the crash, the transaction will still be there. If the system crash is from the result of the hard disk corruption and it requires a new hard disk and installation, then the transaction has been lost if the transaction is only stored on the one hard disk. Therefore, it's absolutely imperative that a certain amount of redundancy be used—in other words, the transaction needs to be stored on some other media. The concept of durability ensures that no matter what the cause of the problem is, a completed transaction is a completed transaction. There's no way of undoing it, changing it, or deleting it.

> **TIP**
>
> Durability within a transaction is not just a software issue. It's a hardware *and* software issue. MTS/COM+ only supports the software aspect of durability. Once a transaction is written to hard disk, it's assumed to be durable. To ensure further durability, a cluster server with RAID needs to be implemented.

Types of Transactions

A transaction occurs when a series of business process steps is completed to get some result.

When the actions are combined into a series of steps, they can be called transactions. To make a transaction system complete, transaction coordinators are required. They make it possible to roll back information or commit information. The simplest transaction type is known as a *flat transaction*.

Flat Transactions

The flat transaction occurs when the series of business processes is in a sequential order—in other words, there's a start point and an end point. If anything goes wrong in between, all the work is undone and removed from the various resources.

Back in Figure 21.1, the first transaction occurs when the money is added to the account and then added to the database. This is the resource. To add this money, two steps are involved: the teller accepts the money and then adds it to the database. The teller manipulates some program that performs the necessary business logic to add the amount of money to the resource.

The business logic is as follows:

- A BEGIN transaction command is issued to the resource from the logic. It tells the resource that some work will commence and that a transaction context needs to be associated with the system user. If there are any other currently running transactions, they are not associated with the new transaction. In other words, it's a brand new context.

- The client ID is retrieved from the resource. This information is stored within the logic. The transaction context manages any references to the resource. From this query, the client ID is used to modify the client's account.

- The last step is for the logic to issue the COMMIT WORK transaction command. Any work that has been done will be made durable if the two-phase commit is successful. The two-phase commit will be discussed shortly, but for now, consider it as a way of stating that the data will be made durable. If anything fails, a ROLLBACK WORK is issued, which causes all work to be removed from the resource since the BEGIN transaction command.

A flat transaction is considered *flat* because it can only contain one BEGIN transaction command and one COMMIT transaction command to make the data durable. Once a BEGIN has been started, another BEGIN would start another independent transaction.

Flat transactions need to be timed properly, because, depending on the amount of time between a BEGIN and a COMMIT or ROLLBACK, the system will be either scalable or slow. A large amount of time will cause resources to be locked, and any ROLLBACK operations will require many steps to be replaced. A too-small amount of time will cause complicated resource states. The best flat transaction scheme is discussed in the next chapter in the section "Activities."

Other Types of Transactions

Other types of transactions exist; however, COM+ services do not support any of them. Therefore, if you know anything regarding save points, long transactions, and nested transactions, you should forget it for now.

Two-Phase Commit

When a transaction needs to make the data durable, it calls a two-phase commit. Using a two-phase commit, a sort of communication occurs among the resources, the component, and the transaction coordinator. It is similar to getting married. In the marriage ceremony, the two people come together and hold hands. The priest asks the groom whether he wants to marry the bride. The groom replies yes. Then the priest asks the bride whether she wants to marry the groom. The bride says yes. Then the priest considers both parties to be married. The bride and groom are the resources and the priest is the transaction monitor.

In reality, the priest is the transaction coordinator. The bride and groom are the resources, which in most cases will be databases as shown in the following diagram.

FIGURE 21.2
Various pieces involved in a two-phase commit.

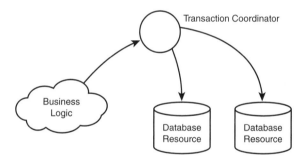

Unlike a marriage, the resources do not initiate the two-phase commit. In Figure 21.2 there is some business logic that has performed some action on the resource. It communicates with the transaction coordinator and initiates the two-phase commit. Here are the components involved in a two-phase commit:

- *Local prepare*. Each local resource prepares for the commit.

- *Distributed prepare*. A prepare request is sent to each transaction's outgoing session.

- *Decide*. If all vote yes and all outgoing sessions vote yes, then a durable transaction commit record is written that states the transaction managers and the resource managers.

- *Commit*. Each resource is invoked and informed of the voting commit outcome; then the message is sent on the outgoing transaction session.

- *Complete*. When all resources have acknowledged the commit message, a complete commit log record is written. When the message is durable, the resources needed for the transaction are freed.

Understanding Transactions Within COM+

Now let's consider the bigger picture of COM+ services—the middle tier of three-tiered systems (see Figure 21.3).

FIGURE 21.3

Three-tiered COM+ application system.

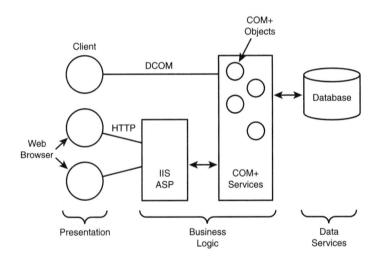

In this diagram, you see three main functional layers. (I use the word *functional* because it does not imply that each layer is assigned to a physical computer.) N-tier computing is many client/server systems put together. For example, when the client communicates to the business logic, it will use COM. And when the COM components talk to the database, it will be using the resource protocol. There are two client/server systems in this N-tier system. The glue between is called *middleware*, which can be COM, HTTP, or anything that moves data from one physical location to another. In this book, there's not much of a discussion of middleware because it's assumed to exist.

An Introduction to COM+ Services

CHAPTER 21

689

21

AN INTRODUCTION
TO COM+
SERVICES

The three layers are defined as follows:

- *Presentation*. The presentation layer is the layer that interacts with the user. At this layer, the user interface is presented. The user interface is neither thin nor dumb. It contains the necessary logic to perform its task. Also, the user interface may be physically big. For example, a graph control that maps the prices of competitors for the past year is not a lightweight control in terms of bytes. In terms of function, it is lightweight, because it does not modify the prices and does not attempt to comprehend the business process. An optimization for saving network communication costs involves adding some simple data-validation rules at this layer.

- *Business logic*. This layer is "GUI-less" and processes the information passed to it from the presentation layer. It contains the business rules required to manage the application. It provides a usable interface to the data services layer. At this layer, the business process is responsible for consolidating the various data sources. This layer does not contain data; rather, it processes data.

- *Data services*. This layer is a statement management layer. It provides the persistence of the data that's processed at the business logic layer. This layer is called *data services* because the data can be stored within a spreadsheet, email system, database, or even persistent business objects.

The middle tier implements the transactions using the architecture shown in Figure 21.4.

FIGURE 21.4

The architecture of the middle tier.

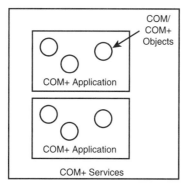

In this chapter, we'll write COM objects that exist as COM+ applications. You should understand that a COM object is an individual object that has been exposed to the COM layer. A COM component is one or more COM objects bundled as a binary package, called a dynamic link library (DLL).

COM+ Application

In Windows 2000, MTS and COM+ have been integrated; they're now one and the same. The integration goes beyond a simple transaction context; it extends into an infrastructure concept. When various COM objects are combined using a logical business process concept, it's called a COM+ application. The COM+ application isn't dependent on any COM component. It's a grouping that can be done at the administrative level.

Why the grouping? When a COM+ application is created, a context is also created. Whenever any COM object is instantiated, it's shielded with a context. This architecture is called *interception* and is illustrated in Figure 21.5.

FIGURE 21.5

Interception architecture.

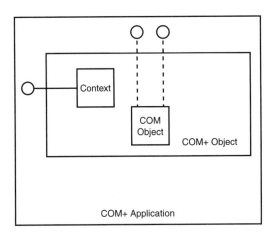

The purpose of interception is to act as a middle entity between the consumer and the COM object itself. The middle entity is a context. Having a context makes it possible to control all aspects of the COM object and for the COM object to know how it's being manipulated, all without code being added. For example, because the middle entity understands that the COM object is transaction based, it can start a transaction. On the other hand, if the COM object were to crash, the context can abort the transaction automatically. This is helpful because any consumer of the COM object will not crash. The consumer will only get the message that the COM object has crashed. This promotes stability.

The Distributed Transaction Coordinator

The context is not responsible for managing the transaction, and it isn't responsible for managing the two-phase commit. This is the responsibility of the Distributed Transaction Coordinator (DTC), as shown in Figure 21.6.

FIGURE 21.6
Architecture of DTC and COM+ objects.

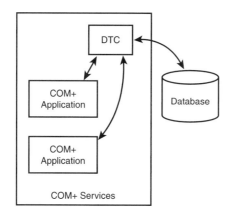

When a context is started and transaction support is desired, the context will connect to a transaction. This transaction may be new, or it may already exist from the consumer COM object. This transaction is connected to the DTC. It provides the wiring between the various COM objects and the resources. For example, if the new COM object were to access another resource or modify an existing resource, those actions will be part of the overall transaction. Of course, the DTC does not do this in isolation. It gets help from the individual resource managers and resource dispensers.

Resource Dispensers

Consider the situation of sitting in a restaurant and ordering a meal. A waiter will typically take your order and relay that order to the kitchen. The kitchen will make the meal, and the waiter will give you the meal once it's ready from the kitchen. In effect, the waiter is acting as a way of accessing the kitchen resource. The waiter is a *resource dispenser*. The COM object is the person being waited on. The COM object, when it connects to the resource, has no idea where the resource comes from—it just gets the information. The waiter does the same thing. The food, for that matter, could be shipped in from several time zones away. The COM object can do with the data what it wants. Likewise, a waiter does not care whether you eat the food or dance the dance of two-thousand scarves on it. The resource dispenser just manages the various connections and tries to optimize access to the resource. Examples are the Shared Memory and ODBC resource dispensers.

Resource Manager

Consider a situation in which the waiter serves all the meals. When the client who's eating the meal is finished, he must pay for it. At this point, the waiter comes back with a tab of all the food items eaten. Now comes an important point: When the original order was submitted, where was that state information kept? It's typically kept on a piece of paper or in a computer, but not the waiter's mind, because the waiter has other things to consider. This separation of who keeps the state is what the resource manager does. A resource manager manages the state of the data. It's not involved in dispensing its own state, because the resource dispenser does that. A typical resource manager is SQL Server. Writing a resource manager is much more complicated than writing a resource dispenser because of the state issue. Managing state efficiently is not a simple task.

A quick side note on the management of state needs to be made: The Shared Memory Manager resource dispenser seems to take on the job of a resource manager. However, this is not the case, because the Shared Memory Manager, when it crashes, will not retain the state. The resource manager, however, will retain memory. Going back to the waiter example, the waiter might remember things such as how many people are at the table and the number of soupspoons needed. However, the waiter will not remember how many potatoes have been consumed from the storage area. The resource manager does that.

Building a Transactionable COM+ Component

A plain-vanilla COM object that wants to participate in a transaction must do the following things:

- It must be COM compatible. This is an absolute must because it's the only way to build reusable components on the Windows platform.

- The COM component must be "in process" and implement items such as `IClassFactory`, `DllGetClassObject`, and so on.

- It must use standard COM marshaling. A rule of thumb is that if something can be expressed in MIDL, then most likely, it can be marshaled. Under no circumstance can `IMarshal` be used, because it will be called by MTS.

- The component must support self-registration through its CLSID using the `DLLRegisterRoutine`.

- It must follow the ACID commandments. This means that no shortcuts can be taken, even though they may result in a slightly smaller or faster object.

Building a COM Object Using Visual Basic

In this section, we'll write a simple COM component that supports transactions. This COM object represents some client. It will contain the following properties:

- Name of company
- Street address
- City

This COM object will have only one method: add. For this example, you'll need to create a VB ActiveX DLL project called VBBookstore and then add a class called clsClient, like this:

```
Option Explicit

'local variable(s) to hold property value(s)
Private mvarcompanyName As String 'local copy
Private mvarstreet As String 'local copy
Private mvarcity As String 'local copy

Public Property Let city(ByVal vData As String)
'used when assigning a value to the property, on the left side of
➡ an assignment.
'Syntax: X.city = 5
    mvarcity = vData
End Property

Public Property Get city() As String
'used when retrieving value of a property, on the right side of
➡ an assignment.
'Syntax: Debug.Print X.city
    city = mvarcity
End Property

Public Property Let street(ByVal vData As String)
'Syntax: X.street = 5
    mvarstreet = vData
End Property

Public Property Get street() As String
'Syntax: Debug.Print X.street
    street = mvarstreet
End Property

Public Property Let companyName(ByVal vData As String)
'Syntax: X.companyName = 5
    mvarcompanyName = vData
End Property
```

```
Public Property Get companyName() As String
'Syntax: Debug.Print X.companyName
    companyName = mvarcompanyName
End Property

Public Function add() As Boolean
    On Error GoTo addError

    Dim objCtxt As ObjectContext
    Dim objCon As New Connection
    Dim strSQL As String

    Set objCtxt = GetObjectContext()

    objCon.Provider = "MSDASQL"
    objCon.ConnectionString = _
        "driver={SQL Server};uid=sa;server=cronos;database=windows2000"
    objCon.ConnectionTimeout = 10
    objCon.CursorLocation = adUseNone
    objCon.Open

    strSQL = "INSERT INTO clients (company_name, street, city) " _
        & " VALUES (" _
        & "'" & mvarcompanyName & "'," _
        & "'" & mvarstreet & "'," _
        & "'" & mvarcity & "')"
    objCon.Execute strSQL
    objCtxt.SetComplete
    add = True
    Exit Function

addError:
    objCtxt.SetAbort
    add = False
End Function
```

In this class, notice that properties (`companyName`, `street`, and `city`) were used to define the object. The properties were built using the VB Class Builder utility. In the past, for performance reasons, properties were not used. The problem was that DCOM and properties caused network bottlenecks. With COM+, this has changed, because the COM object can be queued. This makes it possible to set some properties and send the object on its way.

The add method combines all the properties into a SQL statement that inserts the data into the resource. In the `add` method, the first step is to set the error handler. You'll want to set it so that whenever anything goes wrong, it will automatically undo the work. The next step is to retrieve the transaction context using the method call `GetObjectContext()`. A connection using ADO is established to the resource.

ADO (or Active Data Objects) is the data access technology promoted by Microsoft. The variable strSQL contains the SQL INSERT statement, which is executed using objCon.Execute. If everything works correctly, the call objCtxt.SetComplete tells the context that all is OK and that the work can be made durable. In the error handler, if anything goes wrong, the method objCtxt.SetAbort is called to erase any work done on the resource.

Adding Transaction Support

The second step in adding transaction support is to indicate it using the Visual Basic property sheet. Note though, because I'm using Visual Basic 6.0, old terminology will be used. This means the term MTS and not COM+ will be used. Open the class and view the property sheet, as shown in Figure 21.7.

FIGURE 21.7

An attribute used to set COM+ transaction capabilities.

This attribute needs to be set so that it's "transaction capable." The value you'll want is RequiresTransaction. This means that for the component to execute properly, it requires an active transaction in the context. If there is no active transaction, one will be created.

If, at this point, you attempt to run the component by pressing F5, you'll get the error message shown in Figure 21.8.

This error indicates that the component is not entirely capable yet of running within the COM+ application. To solve this problem, you first need to compile the component using the File, Make VBBookStore.dll menu. Next, open the Project, VBBookstore Properties menu and set the project to "binary compatibility" in the Component tab. The last step is to register the component within the COM+ application.

FIGURE 21.8

*Visual Basic bina-
ry compatibility
problem.*

Using Stored Procedures and Views

In the simple component, the database is accessed using Active Data Objects (ADO). ADO is the preferred data-access technology within the Visual Basic development environment.

In the past, ODBC has been used to access relational databases. Although it has worked well, it does have some problems. The biggest problem is that it only works well with relational databases. A spreadsheet or document does not fit the model well, even though there are ODBC drivers available for them. OLE DB is an extension of the ODBC architecture in that it's used for accessing any kind of data. The data can be object oriented, relational, in spreadsheet format, and so on.

However, you can only use the OLE DB COM interfaces within the Visual C++ environment. Within Visual Basic, a simplification layer called *ADO* is used. In the sample component, a simple ADO command is shown. In a production development environment, this will not do. The reason is that ADO solves a problem generically, yet specific to a vertical application domain. The solution that will be proposed is for enterprise application developers.

Stored Procedure and View Architecture

In our production development situations, we developed a stored procedure and view architecture. For the adding, deleting, and manipulating of data, stored procedures are used. For the reading and retrieving of data, views are used. The reasons for this type of architecture are Abstraction, Security, Let the database folks do their work, and Performance.

Reason #1: Abstraction

COM works well because it creates usable interfaces. The interface is an intention of how the implementation works. The details of the implementation are of no concern to the consumer of the interface. The same logic applies to the resource, except that the

interface is a stored procedure or a view. Using either of these techniques, you can update or change the database schema without adversely affecting the application. In the age of data warehousing, this ability will become invaluable. Coding to the underlying resource schema is like using global variables.

Reason #2: Security

The problem with implementing security in a SQL-based database is that it's only implemented on a per-user basis, regardless of the application calling it. Consider the diagram shown in Figure 21.9.

FIGURE 21.9

An example of using ISQL to bypass application database security.

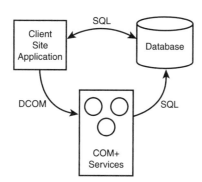

In Figure 21.9, a traditional fat client is used to access the database. As a side note, a fat client is not necessarily bad. Even with the multitiered architecture proposed, a fat client can still access the business objects. The key, really, is in designing to the proper layers. Now, back to the security issue. The client communicates to the database through the database layer and asks for information. Suppose that this information is the salary income for all employees. If the person who logged in has a ranking of x and the SELECT returns a record of employee $x + 1$, then this other employee has a lower rank and therefore should not have direct access to that record. This sort of security is called *need to know*. All SQL databases, with one exception, do not support this (Oracle is that exception). Another problem is that the database can be viewed and manipulated using any application. To the client application, it does not matter whether it's the client program or the fat client that connects and queries the database. Using a stored procedure approach makes it possible to implement a need-to-know security framework—one that restricts anyone to simply browse the database.

Reason #3: Let the Database Folks Do Their Work

A view and stored procedure architecture makes it simpler to build a complex architecture. Let's be honest; very often program developers have no idea of what a good database design is. It's not that they cannot program, they simply aren't database developers. Administrators, on the other hand, work with databases everyday and need to be able to manage large amounts of data. They will know what makes a good database design and how to optimally extract the data.

Reason #4: Performance

If some of the logic is placed into the stored procedure, the performance is enhanced because the statement is already precompiled. With SQL 6.5, the stored procedure is compiled the first time it's loaded. However, you can preload a stored procedure so that it has a higher performance factor. With performance, there's an added benefit—database-specific SQL. However, this may make it more difficult to port the SQL code to another database.

ADO and Helper Objects

To make it easier to use the ADO objects, you should create a few helper objects. This way, the code is centralized and easier to change if needed. To use ADO, you need to reference the ADO library, as shown in Figure 21.10. This can be a very interesting situation because there are various ADO libraries. This is because the versions have been incremented, and programs often install older editions.

FIGURE 21.10

An ADO library reference needed in a Visual Basic project.

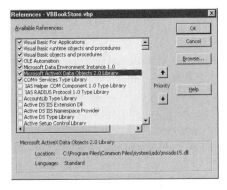

ADO Architecture

The ADO architecture is very simple.

Figure 21.11 shows the hierarchy, but with ADO, this hierarchy is not necessary. For example, to run a simple query, you can execute it directly on the Recordset object without explicitly creating the Connection object. This does not mean a Connection object is not created. Instead, the creation of the Connection object is managed within the Recordset object.

FIGURE 21.11
ADO architecture.

ADO Object Model

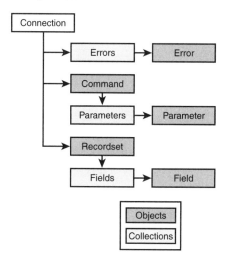

There are three main objects: Connection, Command, and Recordset. The root object is the Connection object. It manages the connection to the resource. From the Connection object, a Command object can be executed or a Recordset object can be retrieved.

Accessing a View

Starting with the simpler task first, let's access a client view. We could issue the command SELECT * FROM viewFullClient. This would be like the ADO code in the simple component. What's not optimal with this solution is that the connection programming code is in the method code. This makes it very difficult to update the code if the driver changes.

Connecting to the Database

The solution is to write a generic connection class. This class would contain all the operations or information necessary to make a connection the database:

```
Option Explicit

Public objConnection As adodb.Connection

Public Database As String
Public SQLTimeOut As Long
```

```
Public IsoLevel As Long
Public AccessMode As Long

Private Sub Class_Initialize()
    Set objConnection = New Connection
End Sub

Private Sub Class_Terminate()
    If objConnection.State = adStateOpen Then
        Dim retCode As Boolean
        retCode = Disconnect()
    End If
    Set objConnection = Nothing
End Sub

Public Property Get isConnected() As Boolean
    If objConnection.State = adStateOpen Then
        isConnected = True
    Else
        isConnected = False
    End If

End Property

Public Function Connect() As Boolean
    Dim tmpDriver As String

    With objConnection
        If .State = adStateOpen Then
            Dim returnVal As Long
            returnVal = Disconnect
            If returnVal = False Then
                GoTo ExitConnect
            End If
        End If

        .ConnectionTimeout = 10
        .ConnectionString = "driver={SQL Server};uid=sa;server=cronos;
➥database=windows2000"
        .Provider = "MSDASQL"
        .CursorLocation = adUseNone

        .Open

        If Err.Number <> 0 Then
            GoTo ExitConnect
        End If

        Database = CStr(.DefaultDatabase)
        SQLTimeOut = CLng(.CommandTimeout)
        IsoLevel = CLng(.IsolationLevel)
```

21

AN INTRODUCTION
TO COM+
SERVICES

```
        AccessMode = CLng(.Mode)
    End With

    Connect = True
    Exit Function

ExitConnect:
    Connect = False
End Function

Public Function Disconnect() As Boolean
    With objConnection
        .Close
        Disconnect = True
    End With
End Function
```

In the above helper object, there are two methods, `Connect` and `Disconnect`, which connect to the resource and disconnect from the resource, respectively. Connecting to a resource can be either extremely easy or extremely difficult.

In OLE DB, when a resource exposes itself, it needs a physical component. This can be a native OLE DB driver or an ODBC driver. The ODBC driver is exposed to the OLE DB using an OLE DB[nd]to-ODBC bridge driver. For ODBC, the native OLE DB provider is MSDASQL. SQLOLEDB is used to connect to Microsoft SQL Server. MSDAORA is used to connect to Oracle. When one of these providers is used, a connection string is required.

Here's where things can become complicated. When you're using a native OLE DB driver, you'll most likely specify the database you want to work with. In the ODBC case, you'll specify which ODBC DSN you want to work with. For the case where there is no DSN, you'll need to specify more items. In the preceding example, a "DSN-less" connection is used because the driver and database are specified. For a DSN-based ODBC connection, you would simply specify `DSN=`*`ODBC source name`*.

If you were to use the native OLE DB provider for SQL Server, you would need to use the following string:

```
Provider=SQLOLEDB;Data Source=cronos;Initial Catalog=windows2000;
➥User Id=sa;Password=
```

Once your connection string has been built, before you open the resource, you should specify `ConnectionTimeout` and where the cursor should be located. The timeout defines how long the client will wait before a connection to the server is established. By default, it's set to 15 seconds, but in the sample code, it's set to 10 seconds. `cursorLocation` is more important because it can determine the performance. In the code, it's set to none.

The other possible value is `adUseClient`, which is for a client cursor. This type of cursor is more flexible, because the local cursor library manages it. However, there may be a performance and data synchronization hit. The other value is `adUseServer`, which specifies the use of a resource-specified cursor. This cursor may have less functionality, but it may offer more performance. Which to use depends on the resource and in which context it's being used. You should experiment and look at the documentation for possible advantages of each.

Generating a View Result

Now you'll want to access the view. Without adding extra overhead to ADO (it's already a simplification), you can perform two operations within a view. The first is a criterion selection and then an iteration through the resultset.

The simplest way to query the view is by creating a SQL `SELECT` statement, but you name the view instead of the table. A helper within the class will build the `SELECT` statement, and the consumer of the class only needs to pass the name of the view. The criterion will be passed using a `PARAM` and `VALUE` combination, which will be converted into a set of SQL statements. Here's the statement:

```
Option Explicit

Public Enum sqlCommandTypeEnum
    sqlStatement = 1
    sqlView = 2
End Enum

Public objConnection As clsDBConnect
Public objRecordset As Recordset
Public strSQL As String
Public sqlCommandType As sqlCommandTypeEnum

Private mvarViewName As String
Private existCriterion As Boolean

Private Sub Class_Initialize()
    sqlCommandType = sqlStatement
    Set objRecordset = New Recordset
End Sub

Private Sub Class_Terminate()
    Set objConnection = Nothing
    Set objRecordset = Nothing
End Sub

Public Property Let view(inpVal As String)
    mvarViewName = inpVal
```

```vb
        strSQL = "SELECT * FROM " & mvarViewName
        sqlCommandType = sqlView
        existCriterion = False
    End Property

    Public Property Get view() As String
        view = sqlStatement
    End Property

    Public Sub AddLongCriterion(param As String, value As Long)
        Dim strValue As String

        strValue = CStr(value)
        Call AddStringCriterion(param, strValue, False)
    End Sub

    Public Sub AddStringCriterion(param As String, value As String,
    ➥ isString As Boolean)

        If existCriterion = False Then
            strSQL = strSQL & " WHERE "
            existCriterion = True
        Else
            strSQL = strSQL & " and "
        End If
        If isString = True Then
            strSQL = strSQL & param & " = '" & value & "'"
        Else
            strSQL = strSQL & param & " = " & value
        End If
    End Sub

    Public Function Execute() As Boolean
        Select Case sqlCommandType
            Case sqlStatement
                If objConnection.objConnection.CommandTimeout < 20 Then
                    objConnection.objConnection.CommandTimeout = 20
                End If
                objConnection.objConnection.Execute sqlStatement
            Case sqlView
                objRecordset.Open strSQL, objConnection.objConnection,
                ➥ adOpenForwardOnly, adLockReadOnly, adCmdText
                If objRecordset.EOF And objRecordset.BOF Then
                    Execute = False
                Else
                    Execute = True
                    objRecordset.MoveFirst
                End If
            Case Else
                ' Not supported, raise an error
        End Select

    End Function
```

To use this class, you must follow these steps:

1. Associate an active connection with the view by setting `objConnection` with an active `clsDBConnect` object.

2. The property view, when it's set, builds a simple `SELECT * from [view]` statement.

3. If any criterion needs to be added, you need to call the `AddLongCriterion` or `AddStringCriterion` method, which adds the following to the SQL select statement:

   `WHERE param1=value1 AND … paramx=valuex`

   The difference between the string and the long criteria is that the string requires extra quotes.

4. Finally, the method execute is called. It creates the recordset by calling `objRecordset.Open` with the built-in SQL statement and active DB connection. It's assumed that you'll want a forward-only cursor (`adOpenForwardOnly`) and that it will be a read-only operation.

When execute is called, how does ADO know whether there are any records? The old way used to be to ask for the record count. If it was zero, there were no records. However, in ADO and OLE DB, this is not possible. The reason is simple—current databases have millions and millions of records. Asking for a record count would require unnecessary processing time. Therefore, to figure out whether there are any records available, you need to see whether the recordset cursor has set the beginning of file (BOF) and end of file (EOF) to `True`. This means that the cursor is at the beginning and end of the recordset at the same time. This can only occur when there are no records. In the example, if the recordset exists, the cursor is set to the first record using `MoveFirst`.

> **TIP**
>
> Even if you try to use a record count, most times it will not even work or will give an incorrect answer.

Consuming the Class

The last step is to consume the class with a new method in the client object called `GetClient`, which is based on the client ID. This method retrieves a client from the resource and sets its appropriate properties:

```
Public Function GetClient(inpId As Long) As Boolean
    Dim objCon As New clsDBConnect
```

An Introduction to COM+ Services

CHAPTER 21

705

21

AN INTRODUCTION
TO COM+
SERVICES

```
    Dim objSQL As New clsDBSQLExecute

    If objCon.Connect() = False Then
        GoTo EXIT_GetClient
    End If

    Set objSQL.objConnection = objCon
    objSQL.view = "viewClients"
    objSQL.AddLongCriterion "id", inpId
    If objSQL.Execute() = False Then
        GoTo EXIT_GetClient
    End If

    mvarcompanyName = objSQL.objRecordset.Fields("company_name")
    mvarstreet = objSQL.objRecordset.Fields("street")
    mvarcity = objSQL.objRecordset.Fields("city")

    GetClient = True
    Exit Function

EXIT_GetClient:
    GetClient = False
End Function
```

This method follows the consumer steps. The only additional requirement is that you
need to call `clsDBConnect.Connect` before you call `clsDBSQLExecute.Execute`.
Otherwise, an error will occur. If no errors occur, the resultset is correct. To retrieve the
values from the recordset object, call the `Recordset.Fields` collection directly. The
`Fields` collection accepts as an index a numeric or field name value.

TIP

Although it's tempting to use a numeric index in the `Fields` collection, you
should avoid doing so. The problem is that, in most cases, people call a SELECT
using SELECT *. This is easier, but if the view is altered, the index may be incorrect. A solution would be to name the fields directly. However, sometimes views
have about 50 fields. Maintaining this number of fields in a SELECT statement
becomes cumbersome. What's more, using indexes to reference the fields
becomes cryptic—what is 1 in field terms? Therefore, you should take the performance hit and use the field names directly.

Accessing a Stored Procedure

This process involves the use of stored procedures to add, delete, or update a record or records. In this case, the simple ADO command will be rewritten to use the following stored procedure:

```
CREATE PROCEDURE addSimpleClient
    @companyName varchar(255),
    @street varchar(255),
    @city varchar( 255)
AS
    insert into clients (company_name, street, city)
       VALUES (@companyName, @street, @city)
    return -100
```

The previously defined SQL stored procedure is simple in that it only calls the SQL INSERT statement. An argument could be made to convert this into an INSERT statement. However, this stored procedure does not do any error handling. Since this is an add procedure, very often the add stored procedure will do an update when the client exits. The advantage of doing this is that when adding or updating a record it is only one roundtrip.

Defining the Stored Procedure Class

A new class to simplify stored procedures would be very similar in design to the view class. The objective is to automate the calling of stored procedures. The following assumptions are made:

- No resultsets are returned on a general basis. (A very large database vendor makes returning recordsets very complicated and therefore this assumption is ideal.)

- The first parameter is always a return code and specifies the error code of the stored procedure. This value is dependent on the database and needs to be established appropriately.

- By default, the character parameters have a predetermined length if not specified.

The class is defined as follows:

```
Option Explicit
Public objConnection As clsDBConnect
Public objRS As Recordset
Public spParameters As adodb.Parameters

Private mObjCommand As adodb.Command
Private mStoredName As String

Private Sub Class_Initialize()
    Set objRS = New Recordset
    Set mObjCommand = New Command
    Set spParameters = mObjCommand.Parameters
End Sub
```

```
Private Sub Class_Terminate()
    On Error Resume Next

    If objRS.State = adStateOpen Then
        objRS.Close
    End If

    Set spParameters = Nothing
    Set mObjCommand = Nothing
    Set objRS = Nothing
    Set objConnection = Nothing

End Sub

Public Sub inputParameter(paramName As String, paramvalue As Variant,
➥ Optional paramType As DataTypeEnum, Optional length As Long)

    If paramType = 0 Then
        paramType = adVarChar
    End If
    If length = 0 Then
        Select Case paramType
            Case adVarChar
                length = 255
            Case Else
                ' Leave it as 0
        End Select
    End If
    mObjCommand.Parameters.Append _
        mObjCommand.CreateParameter(paramName, paramType, adParamInput,
        ➥ length, paramvalue)

End Sub

Public Sub outputParameter(paramName As String, Optional paramType As
➥ DataTypeEnum, Optional length As Long)

    If paramType = 0 Then
        paramType = adVarChar
    End If
    If length = 0 Then
        Select Case paramType
            Case adVarChar
                length = 255
            Case Else
                ' Leave it as 0
        End Select
    End If

    mObjCommand.Parameters.Append _
        mObjCommand.CreateParameter(paramName, paramType, adParamOutput,
        ➥ length, 0)

End Sub
```

```
Private Sub returnValue()
    Dim prm As Parameter

    Set prm = mObjCommand.CreateParameter("Return", adInteger,
    ➡adParamReturnValue, , 0)
'    ORACLE HACK
'     Set prm = mObjCommand.CreateParameter("RETURN_VALUE", adNumeric,
'     ➡ adParamReturnValue, , 0)
'      Set prm = mObjCommand.CreateParameter("RETURN_VALUE", adInteger,
'      ➡ adParamReturnValue, , 0)
    mObjCommand.Parameters.Append prm

End Sub

Public Sub Execute()
    mObjCommand.Execute
End Sub

' NOTE: Not available for Oracle
' Execute the stored procedure, a resultset is
' expected as a result of it
' All input and output parameters for this stored procedure have to be
➡set beforehand
Public Sub ExecuteRecordset()
    Set objRS = mObjCommand.Execute
End Sub

Public Function GetParamValue(paramName As String)
    GetParamValue = mObjCommand.Parameters(paramName)
End Function

Public Property Get spName() As String
    spName = mStoredName
End Property

Public Property Let spName(ByVal vData As String)
    mStoredName = vData
    Set mObjCommand.ActiveConnection = objConnection.objConnection
    mObjCommand.CommandText = vData
    mObjCommand.CommandType = adCmdStoredProc
    Call returnValue
End Property

Public Property Get spReturnValue() As Long
    spReturnValue = mObjCommand(0)
End Property
```

In a stored procedure, there are input parameters and output parameters. The difference is that if a stored procedure parameter returns a value, it is considered an output parameter. In this class, there are explicit methods for each. In ADO, the Command object is used to call a stored procedure or a procedure with multiple parameters. For example, the following would require a Command object:

```
SELECT * FROM viewClients WHERE clientId=?
```

The question mark represents a value that's not defined. To specify this value in a stored procedure or SQL, command parameters need to be created. When the Command object is instantiated, a Command.Parameters collection is created. Initially, it will be empty; to add a parameter, you call Parameters.Append. However, it requires an object of the type parameter. This can be done by calling

```
Command.CreateParameter( Name, Type, Direction, Size, Value)
```

where

- Name is a string representing the name of the parameter.
- Type is a value specifying the type of parameter (for example, adVarChar).
- Direction specifies whether this parameter is an input (adParamInput), output (adParamOutput), input and output (adParamInputOutput), or return value (adParamReturnValue).
- Size specifies the maximum size of the data type.
- Value specifies the value for the parameter.

Creating the various parameters can happen in any order. However, appending them to the Parameters collection must, in most cases, happen in a specific order. For example, there are versions of the SQL Server ODBC driver where the name of the parameter is irrelevant but the order is relevant. Or, for the Oracle driver, both the name and order are relevant. Check your documentation. The number of parameters must match the number required. If these do not match, an error will occur.

Once the method Command.Execute has been called, you can inspect the Parameters collection to see any of the return values. In this implementation, the first parameter is a return value. It's recommended only as a way to return errors. Return parameters are only allowed in a certain range, which is dependent on the implementation of the database. Returning something out of this range will result in unpredictable behavior. If you want to return the value of the added client ID, you should add an output parameter.

Consuming the Class

To consume the class, a specific order again must be followed:

1. Associate an active connection with the view by setting objConnection with an active clsDBConnect object.

2. Set the property `spName`, which represents the name of the stored procedure. The `Commnds.CommandType` property should be set to `adCmdStoredProcedure`. This way, you don't need to create a SQL statement that executes the stored procedure.

3. If any parameters exist, you must add them individually, specifying their direction.

4. Call the `execute` method. It executes the stored procedure.

5. Retrieve the result code using the property `spReturnValue`. It can be checked for correctness.

A consumption of this class would look like this:

```
Public Function AddNew() As Boolean
    On Error GoTo ERROR_AddNew

    Dim objCtxt As ObjectContext
    Dim objCon As New clsDBConnect
    Dim objSP As New clsDBsp

    Set objCtxt = GetObjectContext()
    If objCon.Connect() = False Then
        GoTo ERROR_AddNew
    End If

    Set objSP.objConnection = objCon
    objSP.spName = "addSimpleClient"
    objSP.inputParameter "companyName", mvarcompanyName
    objSP.inputParameter "street", mvarstreet
    objSP.inputParameter "city", mvarstreet
    objSP.Execute

    If objSP.spReturnValue <> -100 Then
        GoTo ERROR_AddNew
    End If

    objCtxt.SetComplete
    AddNew = True
    Exit Function

ERROR_AddNew:
    objCtxt.SetAbort
    AddNew = False

End Function
```

What Has Been Shown?

The preceding component uses good MTS programming style. Here are some reasons why:

- In general, values are not passed in using methods. Instead, they're set and retrieved using properties. As a result, they're more flexible and allow for simpler programming because you don't need to remember mile-long method calls. Using queued components incurs no performance hit when executing over a network.

- The database connection and transaction context are created and retrieved on a per-method basis. This means that resources are acquired late and released quickly. For MTS, this ensures scalability, because the component is stateless.

- The general ADO libraries are adapted to solving the problem in the domain. As a result, writing application code is quicker and requires less testing.

The first and last reasons are self explanatory, but the second one requires some more explanation, which is given in the next chapters.

Adding Components to a COM+ Application

Now that the component has been compiled, it's ready to be added to a COM+ application. A COM+ application provides a way of grouping COM objects to form an application.

> **Note**
>
> Note that at the time of this writing, the build of Windows 2000 was 1946. Therefore, the released edition may have features not available at the time of writing.

Creating an Application

Start the Component Services Explorer. The dialog box shown in Figure 21.12 will appear.

In the Explorer view under the node COM+ applications, you'll find all the applications that use some of the services COM+ offers. The individual nodes represent applications.

In previous versions of MTS, they were called *packages*. It's not recommended that you create applications that contain all the COM objects. The application concept does support *nesting*. This means that an application could theoretically contain thousands of COM objects. You should package an application according to a domain.

FIGURE 21.12

Component Services Explorer.

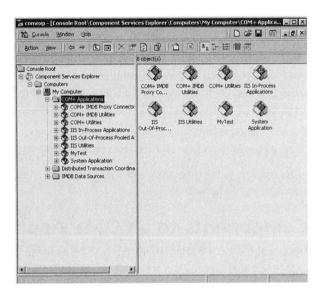

To create a new package, select the node COM+ applications and right-click. From the pop-up menu, select New, Application. This starts the COM Application Install Wizard. Click the Next button. The dialog box shown in Figure 21.13 will appear.

FIGURE 21.13

Starting a COM+ application.

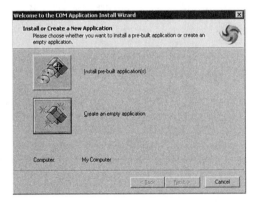

You have two options for creating a new package:

- *Prebuilt application.* This installs an application that has been built using the application `export` command.
- *Empty application.* This installs an empty application that does not contain any COM objects.

Press the Empty Application button. The next dialog box specifies the name of the application (see Figure 21.14).

FIGURE 21.14

Identifying a COM+ application name.

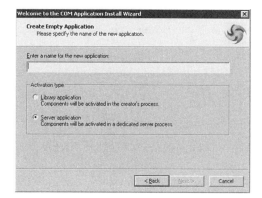

In the text box labeled Enter a Name for the New Application, enter **BookStore**. There are two option buttons used to specify whether the application will run within Server Application process space or within the Library process space. The default is Server Application process space, which means that COM+ services will manage the process. You can specify the library process space, but doing so limits the functionality. Click the Next button and the security settings will appear. You need to specify which user security attributes will be used to execute the application. Currently, this is set to Interactive User. In a debugging situation, this setting is okay. It's recommended, though, that the user be given local administrative authority. This helps avoid problems in the future. However, do not use this in a production setting; you'll then need to carefully consider the various options. Click the Next button. The dialog box presents a thank-you message. Click Finish to create the application.

Inspecting the Application Properties

The next step is to inspect the various settings of the application. Right-click the BookStore node and select Properties from the pop-up menu. This causes the BookStore Properties dialog box to appear. This dialog box has several tabs, which are discussed in the following sections.

General Tab

The first tab on the Bookstore Properties dialog box is the General tab. Under this tab, you have the following features (see Figure 21.15):

- *Bookstore* defines the name of the package. This can be edited.

- *Description* is a description of the package.

- *Application ID* is the GUID used to identify the application. You can use this to debug Visual C++ components.

FIGURE 21.15

General COM+ application properties.

Security Tab

The next tab on the Bookstore Properties dialog box is the Security tab. Under this tab, you have the following features (see Figure 21.16):

- *Authentication level.* This identifies the amount of security used when packets of information are exchanged among the various COM+ applications, clients, and so on. The combo box is sorted from lowest level to highest level.

- *Impersonation level.* When a client makes a connection to the COM+ application, it has an associated security token. When the COM+ application accesses resources, it can impersonate the user. How it does this depends on the setting.

Here are the available options:

> *Default.* The machine-wide impersonation level is used.

> *Anonymous.* The server security token is anonymous and does not contain any information regarding the client.

> *Identity.* The server security token is identical to the client making the access to the COM+ application.

> *Impersonate.* This is identical to Identity, with some restrictions.

> *Delegate.* The server can pass around the client credentials to any other machine.

- *Security level.* When a client accesses a COM+ application, the security can be enforced at the application level or at the application and component levels.

- *Enforce application-level access checks.* COM+ authenticates the user according to the role assigned to the user when accessing the COM object. Roles offer the advantage of specifying various users in groups.

- *Use process access permissions.* The Windows NT ACL is used to perform security checks when the COM objects are accessed. COM+ library applications cannot use this type of security. It's recommended that you set up a role-based security mechanism.

FIGURE 21.16

COM+ application security properties.

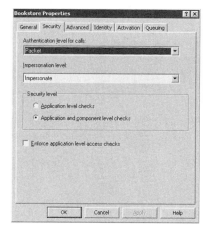

Advanced Tab

The third tab on the Bookstore Properties dialog box is the Advanced tab. Under this tab, you have the following features (see Figure 21.17):

- *Server Process Shutdown.* When a COM object is accessed, the application is hosted by a process. You can define when the process shuts down and releases all its resources. When the radio button Leave Running when Idle is selected, the process will remain. This has the advantage of quicker response time initially. By selecting the Minutes Until Idle Shutdown radio button, you can define a shutdown to occur after a specific amount of time. The advantage to this option is that resources can be conserved. The timeout has the advantage of saving the initialization performance loss if there's a lull in traffic. A timeout value of zero tells the component to never shut down.

- *Permission.* Checking the boxes in this area specifies that scripts and other applications cannot delete and change the COM+ application.

- *Debugging.* Makes it possible to launch the application directly into a debugger.

- *Enable Compensating Resource Managers.* When resources that do not support transactions are used, a CRM makes it possible for a resource to participate within the two-phase commit.

- *Enable 3GB support.* Makes it possible for the COM object developer to access 3GB of memory when using the Windows 2000 Enterprise edition.

FIGURE 21.17
COM+ application advanced properties.

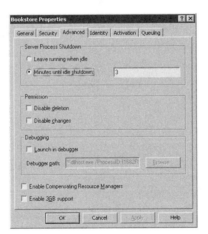

Identity Tab

The Identity tab was already discussed when the package was created.

Activation Tab

The fifth tab on the Bookstore Properties is the Activation tab. Under this tab, you have the following features:

- *Activation Type.* Specifies how the component is activated. A library activation will put the component within the process space of the library process. The only catch with this is that the process must be running on the same machine as the COM object. The components also have less functionality. When Server Activation is specified, the COM+ environment provides the hosting process. This is the preferred technique, because it provides access to all the COM+ services.

- *Remote Server.* At the time of this writing, the purpose was not fully documented. In the release version it should be documented in the COM+ administration help file.

Queuing Tab

The final tab on the Bookstore Properties dialog box is the Queuing tab. Under this tab, you have the following feature (see Figure 21.18):

- *Queuing properties.* This works only for COM objects that support the queuing concept. When a package is specified as "queued," the COM objects marked queuable within the application can receive messages. To mark a package as queuable, check the Queued check box. To set up a listener, check the Listen check box. This will start up the process and wait for requests.

FIGURE 21.18

COM+ application queuing properties.

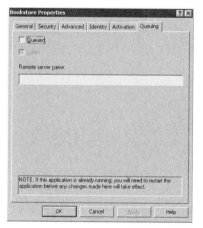

Adding a Component

The next step is the addition of the component within the application. You can do this by double-clicking the newly created application node, BookStore. Two subnodes appear: Components and Roles. Select the Components node and then right-click it. From the pop-up menu, select New, Component. Again, a wizard appears. This time, the wizard helps you register a component within the application. Press the Next button and the dialog box shown in Figure 21.19 will appear.

FIGURE 21.19

Starting the COM+ Component Install Wizard.

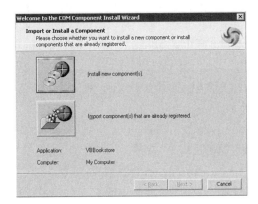

This dialog box has two options:

- *Install new components.* This option allows you to install COM objects resident within a COM component. The COM component will be added to the COM+ application by searching and loading the DLL.

- *Import components that are already registered.* This option allows you to install COM objects based on their ProgID within the Registry. It assumes the COM object is already registered.

Select the Install New Components button.

The File Finder dialog will appear first. Select a file and click OK. A File common dialog box appears. Find the VBBookStore DLL and click OK. The following dialog box will appear (see Figure 21.20).

Click the Next button and then the Finish button. The COM Explorer is shown in Figure 21.21.

FIGURE 21.20

COM+ objects.

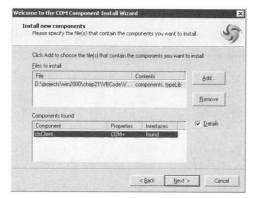

TIP

Figure 21.20 does not show this problem, but if classes are appearing that shouldn't, it's because the `Instancing` property is set incorrectly. To solve this problem, set the `Instancing` to `Private`. This makes sure the class will not be generated within the type library. This is not defined to be external because it may do things that are not COM friendly. An example would be not setting the transaction attributes properly.

FIGURE 21.21

The newly registered COM+ object.

Inspecting the COM Object

The next step is to inspect the various settings of the COM object. Right-click the object and select Properties from the pop-up menu.

Transaction/Concurrency Tab

Under the Transaction/Concurrency tab, you'll find the following features (see Figure 21.22):

- *Threading model.* This indicates the threading model that the COM object executes in.

- *Transaction support.* A check box that defines whether a transaction context will be defined. This attribute can be set manually or, as in our example, retrieved from the COM object itself and preset. The following options are possible:

    Ignored. Any active transactions are ignored and not used.

    Not Supported. The component does support transactions.

    Required. A transaction context is required. If it exists, as from a call originating within another transaction, it will be used. Otherwise, a new transaction is started.

    Requires New. A new transaction is started regardless if one already exists. Do not confuse this with nesting, because the new transaction outcome does not impact any other currently running transaction.

    Supported. If there's a transaction from another object call, it is used; otherwise, the component runs without a transaction context.

- *Synchronization.* This concept has not yet been discussed, but it will be discussed in detail in the next chapter. When a COM object is used within a COM+ context, the object needs to be stateless. It will use JIT activation and ASAP deactivation. This means that the component can be reused prematurely. Synchronization makes it possible to define how JIT activation is defined. The terms JIT and ASAP relate to how a COM object is referenced, which is explained in Chapter 22, "Building Components for COM+ Services." In cases where transactions are involved, options that aren't possible are disabled.

FIGURE 21.22

COM+ object transaction/ synchronization/ concurrency properties.

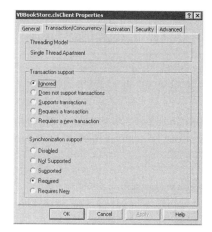

21

AN INTRODUCTION TO COM+ SERVICES

Activation Tab

The next tab is the Activation tab. Figure 21.23 shows the following features:

- *Object Pooling*. Object pooling can be enabled only for COM objects that are stateless. An optimization would be to implement the IObjectControl interface. This is shown in next chapter. If object pooling can be used, you can specify the minimum pool size. This determines that whenever the application starts, that number of COM objects will be instantiated. The maximum size defines the maximum number of objects that will be created. The text box Creation Timeout specifies how much time the COM object waits before it instantiates another COM object.

- *Object Construction*. When a COM object is instantiated within the COM+ application, you can specify a string that's passed to the construction method. Using this string, dynamic database connections or any other dynamic administration features can be implemented.

- *Enable Just In Time Activation*. This enables the object only when the client needs it.

- *Component supports dynamic load balancing*. Checking this box allows the component to be dynamically load-balanced across various machines. Dynamic load balancing reads the response time and, if necessary, references a component in another location.

- *Component supports events and statistics*. This option makes it possible for the COM object to accept events and COM+ application statistics.

- *Must be activated in caller's context*. At the time of this writing, this feature was not fully documented. It will be documented in the COM+ SDK when Windows 2000 is released.

Security Tab

The next tab you see is the Security tab. Its features are shown in Figure 21.24:

- *Enforce component-level access checks.* Enables role-based security for the component. Role-based security can be implemented within the COM object, or it can be specified in this tab.

- *Roles explicitly set for selected items.* You can specify specific roles from the available roles in the COM+ application. To select a role, you need to check it from the list box.

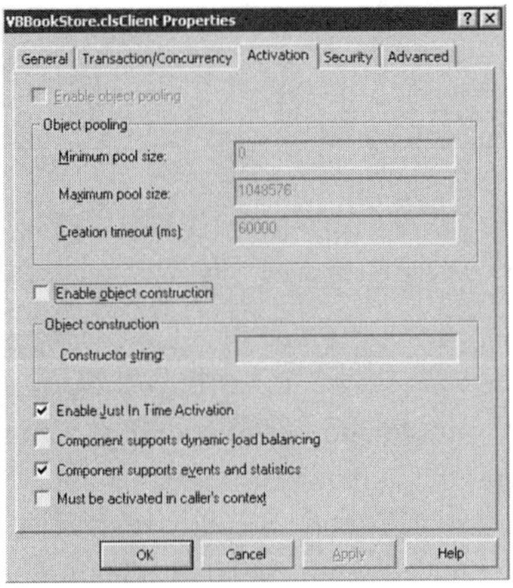

FIGURE 21.23

COM+ object activation properties.

FIGURE 21.24

COM+ object security properties.

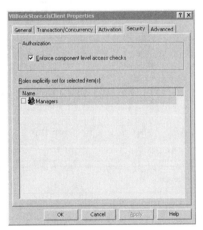

Advanced Tab

The last tab is the Advanced tab. This tab, as shown in Figure 21.25, has one feature:

- *Queuing exception class.* At the time of this writing, this feature was not fully documented. In the release version of Windows 2000, it is documented in the COM+ SDK.

FIGURE 21.25

COM+ object advanced properties.

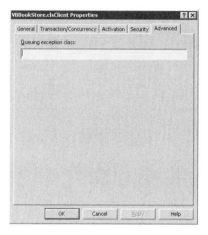

Implementing a Test Client

Developing COM components is one part of the development process. The other part is the actual testing. The testing of a component needs to occur in isolation, which means that only specific situations are tested. This does not mean including the component in the project and then testing it. The problem with testing a component within a project is that the coverage will not be adequate.

Visual Studio supports debugging across environments and layers. For example, client to browser to Web server to component and to database. To test the client properly and in an easy manner requires quite a bit of work. A better way to test and implement the client is to use the scripting interface. In Windows 2000, scripting is integrated into the operating system. Using a language such as JScript, you can call various COM objects. This is the preferred solution. For the sample COM components, the following script was used:

```
function tstClient() {
    var tmpObject;

    tmpObject = WScript.CreateObject("VBBookstore.clsClient");
```

```
        tmpObject.companyName = "euSOFT";
        tmpObject.street = "Muehlweg 1";
        tmpObject.city = "Freudenberg";
        if( tmpObject.add() == true) {
            WScript.Echo( "Add worked ok");
        } else {
            WScript.Echo( "Add did not work");
        }
    }

function tstGetClient() {
    var tmpObject;

    tmpObject = WScript.CreateObject("VBBookstore.clsClient");
    if( tmpObject.GetClient( 1) != false) {
        WScript.Echo("Client info is " + tmpObject.companyName);
    } else {
        WScript.Echo("Could not get the client");
    }

}

function tstSPClient() {
    var tmpObject;

    tmpObject = WScript.CreateObject("VBBookstore.clsClient");

    tmpObject.companyName = "euSOFT 2";
    tmpObject.street = "Muehlweg 1";
    tmpObject.city = "Freudenberg";
    if( tmpObject.AddNew() == true) {
        WScript.Echo( "Add worked ok");
    } else {
        WScript.Echo( "Add did not work");
    }
}


//tstGetClient();
//tstClient();
tstSPClient();
```

Three tests are used in this script:

- `tstGetClient`. Retrieves the client and outputs it to the console
- `tstClient`. Adds a client using the `INSERT` SQL statement
- `tstSPClient`. Adds a client using the stored procedure

Using this script as a basis, you can build a testing scenario that can be used in regression tests for correctness. Scripting also requires less programming expertise than using Visual Basic or Visual C++.

Summary

The purpose of this chapter is to provide you with a basic understanding of how transactions and COM+ transactions function. You learned about transactions and how they function. You built a simple component and accessed a database using a stored procedure and view architecture. You also learned how to write a stateless component. When you went through the simple component example, a stateless component was written by default. Finally, you learned how to register a component.

Building Components for COM+ Services

In this chapter, the topic of building Component Service components is expanded. This chapter starts out with a description of what a good component is. The various options of how to build good components are explored. Then, a more sophisticated transaction component is built using Visual C++. The focus of the example is to outline the interaction of the component with the transaction context and show how to influence the transaction context. Then, the interaction of various transaction combinations and how they affect the ongoing transaction will be explored.

A Good Component Service Component

In the preceding chapter, the COM+ component was written to get the database connection at the method call level and then release it at the end of the method call. This operation in a traditional environment will cost processing time, because retrieving a database connection requires time. With COM+, it's done on purpose, because COM+ supports the concept of stateless objects.

Lifetimes/Statelessness

When I first used MTS, before COM+, I learned the concept of *lifetimes*. I considered what they're trying to achieve. There's a reason why lifetimes are so critical. To fully understand the concept of a lifetime, you need to take a step back and consider how things are done traditionally.

A Bit of Legacy

Let's imagine that there are no COM+ services. The tools we'll use are traditional tools, and some parts are from other vendors. Consider the following system shown in Figure 22.1.

In this example is an object called Client. User represents some data used when the client logs onto the Web site. In its simplest form, User only contains information such as name, email, and password. However, Client can be more complicated and contain other data such as address, conferences attended, and so on. The question now is when the client logs on, how is the User object instantiated? In a pure object-oriented (OO) context, the answer is that the data is transferred from an object-oriented database to memory and then kept there while it's being used.

This seems correct, because using a SQL approach, the data would have to be converted from SQL database format into a native format. With an OO database, this is not necessary, and it makes our lives simpler. However, there are some big flaws.

FIGURE 22.1
*Sample Web
architecture.*

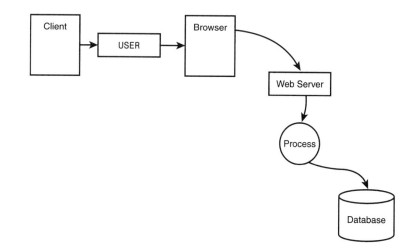

First, the data is loaded into memory. When another client logs in and retrieves the same data as the first client, what does the other client get? Is it a handle to instance in memory or does it create a new object instantiation? Another question: What happens in the situation of concurrency? Let's walk through both cases.

In the case of getting a handle to the existing object in memory, there are concurrency issues that the programmer of the object must handle. What happens if client 1 modifies an address and then client 2 modifies the address again? Who writes the correct address?

In the case of creating a new copy, there are no concurrency problems, because each client has a copy of the data. However, the extra copy of data requires extra resources. Instantiating the object requires extra processing cycles. What's more, if either client changes the object, the other client will not see the changes, because each client will instantiate the object for the lifetime of the application.

For either situation, the object is kept in memory. Now imagine that the object is changed and the machine crashes. During this long period of time, the data may or may not have been written to the resource. However, a crash will erase all the data, so all the steps must be redone.

For all these problems, code can be written to solve them. However, this type of code is not simple to write, nor is it simple to debug. The extra programming is not good because the developer is forced to write system code. *System code* is code that has nothing to do with the solution but provides a framework for the application code. System code might involve writing a transaction monitor or a directory service on top of a transaction monitor. Software vendors usually do this type of programming.

The type of programming that you'll want to do is application programming. *Application programming* is when you solve a specific business problem. It's also called *vertical application programming*.

State of the System

Before I show how COM+ solves these problems, let's look at the problem of maintaining state and handling errors on our own. The following source code contains an error:

```cpp
class TestState {
public:
    TestState() { }
    ~TestState() { }

    int someMethod( int param) {
        try {
            m_value = param + 1;

            return anotherMethod( param);
        } catch( ...) {
            return 0;
        }
    }
    void anotherMethod( int param) {
        //...
    }
private:
    int m_value;
};
```

Did you find it? The error is the assignment of m_value. This is incorrect because the method anotherMethod could throw an exception. If this happens, the value m_value has already been set. The exception would then have to set the value of m_value to the old value. This is difficult because the old value has not been kept. Very often, keeping the old value is not possible because the new value is required to perform the calculation.

Stateless Objects

The problem we have is managing data and keeping it consistent. A transaction system will do this, but a certain programming style is associated with it—stateless programming.

A stateless architecture works very well if the resources are able to understand caching. The theoretical problem with stateless programming is that the data must always be fetched from the hard disk, which costs time. Also, a stateless object must instantiate the resources, which again costs time.

> **NOTE**
>
> Stateless programming is when the object being called does not have a previous state from which to reference the next action. The caller provides this information. It's as if the called object were called for the first time.

However, these arguments are moot if the resource understands caching properly. For example, if a call is made 20 times to the same record, a good resource will cache the data. This makes the lookup much faster. A smart cache acts like an on-demand resource loader. It decides when data needs to be loaded, discarded, or saved for later reuse. A good cache mechanism follows the ACID method and ensures that the data is correct.

What about the cache coherence problem? This is solved by the resource, not by the application programmer. This forces a separation of the application programmer and the system programmer. This separation results in better code.

Just-in-Time Activation

If the database connections can be reused, is there some way the User object can be reused? There is, because the object is considered "stateless." Also, keep in mind that 1,000 active users do not always equal 1,000 concurrent users. Maybe only 100 of the users are actually doing work. The rest are drinking coffee, discussing last night's game, or chatting. Therefore, instead of instantiating 1,000 objects, you should instantiate 100 objects and share them among the 1,000 users.

The recycling is possible because it already has been defined that all the objects are stateless and do not contain data. This means that creating an object would be just as quick as getting a database connection, because the cache contains an available object. This magic is handled by COM+ services and is known as *Just-in-time activation*.

Just-in-time activation is like RAM on any modern operating system. In a typical case, a machine might have 128MB of RAM, but to allow it to handle bigger tasks, the administrator can tell the machine that it has 256MB of virtual RAM. This is a trick in that pages of memory are being swapped in and out of memory from the hard disk. When this swapping occurs, of course, it's slower than using the available RAM. However, the trick with virtual RAM is that it assumes the programs running will not reference all the memory at once.

This is the same trick just-in-time activation uses. It knows when to associate a connection and when to take away that connection. All this is done without the owner objects knowing what's going on, just like the RAM that's being referenced from the hard disk. The program, in this case, thinks it's RAM.

Lifetimes

If objects are stateless and are considered business processes with virtual references, how is a system developed? The answer is *lifetimes*. However, there are two types of lifetimes—a physical lifetime and an activated lifetime (also called an *activity*). This is illustrated in Figure 22.2.

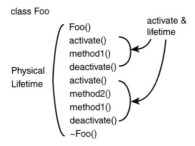

FIGURE 22.2

The different lifetimes of an object.

In this diagram, the *physical lifetime* involves the object from the time it's instantiated to when it's deleted. The *activity* is the lifetime while the object is referenced. The activity lifetime is needed so that the object can be cached to provide the best trade-off between resources and access time.

Activities

The lifetime you're likely to use most often is the activity lifetime. Activities are needed because reality dictates that it's impossible to write a purely stateless object. The state must be kept somewhere. If it isn't kept in the COM object, it must be kept somewhere else.

In human terms, an activity is a conversation. Each sentence is a reference to the previous statement. If the statements have no references, the conversation would go nowhere. You would be constantly asking, "What did you just say?" However, a conversation does not last forever. A conversation covers a few points, and then that part of it is done. Activities do the same thing. It is possible to maintain state outside the COM object and pass it in—through library programming.

An activity should be short and can be measured in terms of minutes or seconds. It contains a series of steps that perform some type of function that represents a business process. An activity contains a series of sequential steps. However, activities can be called in any order.

Imagine attending a conference. To do this, you would identify yourself and then register to attend the conference. Converting this into a computer system, you would have two activities. The first activity is becoming a user. You will want to do this because you will want to download the slides or demo source code. The second activity is the registration process. In an activity approach, the objects that are part of the user activity are not the same as the registration activity. The reason is that in each activity you are interested in similar, but different, information. Hence, what happens is you sometimes get object redundancy using an activity approach. An OO purist will become very nervous with that comment. However, it is a valid point, because the activities are different domains and should not be shared. The problem with sharing is not the sharing itself, but the bugs. If a shared object has a bug in one activity, it must be tested in all activities. This can take more time and money.

Designing for Activities

This is perhaps the most important section in the entire chapter, so you should read it carefully.

The key concept of an activity is that it accomplishes a task. Activities never need to use threads or semaphores. They are considered single `User` objects. The only exception to this rule may be the singleton. A *singleton* is used when only one instance of the object is allowed. You should avoid them, because they force sequential access and can limit scalability.

An activity encompasses one action that can be translated into a transaction. The point of an activity is to ensure that it's granular enough so that it's not specific to any underlying data. This is important, because an activity must be able to be executed on different underlying data abstractions (see Figure 22.3).

FIGURE 22.3
Activities and domains.

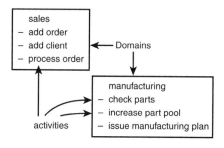

The abstraction must be met because the activity of a process is a well-known entity and tends to live in very long cycles. What changes is the way that the activity interacts with its data to create new data or pieces of information. The processing of the newly constructed data is yet another form of activity, and the activity has a direct correlation to the state of the system.

An activity does not cross domains. A domain boundary is a series of activities that are grouped into a single object or series of objects that make up a physical entity. If the activity were to cross domains, a dependency would be created between the two domains. This cross-dependency hampers maintainability and scalability and results in lean resources. A domain may be compromised of other domains and some objects.

It is correct to build up a hierarchy of domains, where a new domain allows the cross-referencing of two domains. However, the proper way of implementing this is to use a helper object that cross-references the two objects dynamically. This way, the two cross-referenced objects use interfaces of each other but do not depend on quizzing the correctness of each other.

Writing Transactional Components

Now let's go over a few rules for writing transactional COM+ objects:

- All COM+ objects must be stateless. This means that when objects are activated, they always appear as fresh objects.
- COM+ objects do not use the programming constructor to initialize any COM+ features, because when a constructor is being called, the COM+ layer is not totally initialized.
- All COM+ objects get resources late and release them early to promote scalability. Because of the COM+ caching and optimization, it's okay to retrieve a database connection at the method call level.
- All COM+ objects use activities to do work. The activities are directly related to a business operation.

Creating a General Transaction Component

The simplest COM object to create is one that supports transactions but does not explicitly call the transaction context. This way of creating objects is okay, but it allows for less tuning (see Figure 22.4).

FIGURE 22.4

Single COM+ object being called.

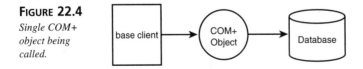

A client creates a single object. This object is added to the COM+ application with the attribute -Requires a transaction. Here's some JavaScript code that could be used to call this client:

```
var objClient;
objClient = WScript.CreateObject("Sample.Object.1");
objClient.method1();
objClient.method2();
objClient = null;
```

When the object is instantiated in the script, a transaction is started. When method1 and method2 are called, the transaction context is not manipulated. In these situations, COM+ services will consider the methods as part of an activity and not deactivate the object. The object is deactivated when the reference to the object is destroyed, as is done in the last JavaScript line. At this point, COM+ services will instantiate a two-phase commit and attempt to make the data durable.

What did that code show? It is not necessary to call the transaction context. This means it is not necessary to convert old business objects. There is a problem with this approach. The old business objects assume that the transaction or activity is limited to the calling of method1 and method2. Now suppose a new script writer who does not understand the business objects or transactions properly decides to call method3 in the same script. COM+ transaction says, great, the transaction includes method3. The bug is that at an abstraction level the activity is only method1 and method2. method3 belongs to another activity.

So you see that although it is easy to run and execute a transaction, sometimes it may have undesirable side effects. And the side effects are what will add bugs to your system. Therefore when using old business objects, make sure that they are activity based.

This approach is best used for simple situations. It's also appropriate for legacy situations where rewriting the COM object may be too much work.

Creating a Transaction COM+ Object Using Visual C++

The most effective way to create a COM+ services object is to create it using ATL. To create a COM object, start the Visual C++ environment. From the menu bar, select File, New. The resulting dialog box is shown in Figure 22.5.

From the Project tab, select ATL COM AppWizard and enter the Project name VCBookStore. Then click the OK button.

FIGURE 22.5

Creating a Visual C++ COM component project.

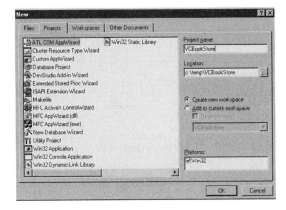

In the first AppWizard screen, make sure the Support MTS box is checked (see Figure 22.6). This will include all the MTS headers that you'll need. This brings up a bit of an issue. Windows 2000 does not require you to include `mts.h`. Instead, you can include `autosvcs.h`. However, there's no support from the wizard; therefore, anything you add will have to be done manually. Click the Finish button and let the wizard generate the project.

FIGURE 22.6

Defining the type of project.

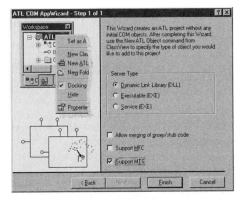

TIP

Do not combine MFC and ATL haphazardly. Although it's possible, MFC is a great user interface library. Its role as a server framework is limited. ATL is much better for business objects that do not have a GUI.

The next step is to create a component. From the class view, right-click and select New ATL Object from the pop-up menu.

By default, the dialog box selects the category "Objects" and the object type "SimpleObject," as shown in Figure 22.7. This is correct. Click on the Next button.

FIGURE 22.7

Adding a COM+ object.

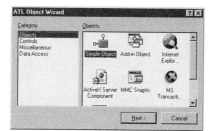

In the short name type NIOrder, as shown in Figure 22.8. Then, click on the Attributes tab to get the dialog box shown in Figure 22.9.

FIGURE 22.8

Identifying the name of the COM+ object.

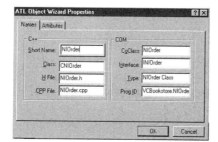

FIGURE 22.9

Defining the COM+ object properties.

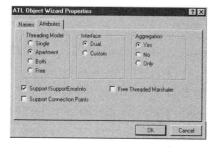

Keep all the default settings, but check the Support ISupportErrorInfo check box.

One option is to select Both as the Threading Model setting. Only select this if you want your component to be able to run as a free threaded object. Finally, click the OK button. Now you have a COM+ services component. The next step is to add some plumbing.

Specifying the Transaction Attribute

With COM+, the transactional attribute is specified at the IDL level. Here's an example:

```
[
    object,
    uuid(AD8A2F1F-9D18-11D2-86DF-0000B45FCBCB),
    dual,
    helpstring("IICaller Interface"),
    pointer_default(unique),
    TRANSACTION_REQUIRED
]
interface IICaller : IDispatch
{
    [id(1), helpstring("method callChild")] HRESULT callChild();
};
```

The attribute TRANSACTION_REQUIRED is added to the property list of the interface. COM+ services will pick up this information and set the default transaction characteristic. Here are the various options:

- TRANSACTION_REQUIRED

- TRANSACTION_SUPPORTED

- TRANSACTION_NOT_SUPPORTED

- TRANSACTION_REQUIRES_NEW

Retrieving the Transaction Context Interface

In our development, whenever a method or property is called, the transaction context must be retrieved. It's retrieved using the following function:

```
HRESULT GetObjectContext (
    IObjectContext** ppInstanceContext );              [out]
```

This function returns an IObjectContext interface pointer. You can't use this function from within the C++ class constructor, destructor, or any method within the IUnknown interface. This is because at that point, the transaction context might not be valid. However, because we're using ATL, IUnknown will not be a topic of discussion.

For every method or property, the prototype implementation would be as follows:

```
STDMETHODIMP CIntroUser::add(BSTR firstName, BSTR lastName,
BSTR email, BSTR password)
{
    CdbouserAdd2001 var;
    IObjectContext *pCtxt;

    GetObjectContext( &pCtxt );
```

```
    // Some work
    pCtxt->Release();
    return S_OK;
}
```

The `IObjectContext` interface pointer is a raw interface and therefore must be released using `IUnknown::Release`.

When this function is called, it returns an `S_OK` if the interface has been retrieved and is valid. However, consider the case where the component has not yet been imported into the MTS catalog. Calling this function will result in `CONTEXT_E_NOCONTEXT` being returned. The returned interface pointer in `ppInstanceContext` will not be valid and should not be used. Otherwise, a GPF could result. For other circumstances, either `E_INVALIDARG` or `E_UNEXPECTED` may be returned. If either of these return codes are returned, the interface is not valid and should not be used. Once all operations on the context are complete, the `Release` method must be called.

Simplifying the Interface Count

Working with raw COM interface pointers is not all that fun. The reason is that calling `QueryInterface` and decrementing the reference count must be done manually.

A simpler way to use the interface is to use the included COM compiler support. The COM compiler support classes were introduced in Visual C++ 5.0. Using these classes, it's much easier to write code that uses COM interface pointers. The technique is called *smart pointers*. Smart pointers are template-based classes that embed the reference counting and type conversion within the class. In the case of the COM compiler classes, they also throw exceptions. Here's an example:

```
try {
    IObjectContextPtr ptrCtxt;

    _com_util::CheckError( GetObjectContext( ptrCtxt));

    // Some operations
} catch( _com_error err) {
    return err.Error();
}
```

All the methods are embedded within an exception block. Any COM error will be caught in the exception handler. The object `_com_error` is a wrapper class for the `HRESULT`. To retrieve the `HRESULT`, call the method `_com_error::Error()`. The advantage of using exception handling is that any problems will automatically be caught. It's not necessary to write explicit `if` blocks. Also, it's not possible to bypass writing `if` blocks with COM, because COM or the COM objects will not always do what you want.

22

BUILDING
COMPONENTS FOR
COM+ SERVICES

The newest versions of the Platform SDK have already defined smart pointer typecasts for IObjectContext (IObjectContextPtr). The method _com_util::CheckError checks to see whether any errors are generated when a COM method or function call is made. If an error occurs, an exception is generated.

Working with the Transaction Context

Let's look more closely at the transaction context interface IObjectContext. This interface allows you to control the transaction outcome within the COM+ object. It represents a wrapper to the transaction context. It's also specific to the object that retrieves it. This means that this interface pointer cannot be passed to another object, because it doesn't represent the right context. The full interface is defined as follows:

```
struct __declspec(uuid("51372ae0-cae7-11cf-be81-00aa00a2fa25"))
IObjectContext : IUnknown
{
    //
    // Raw methods provided by interface
    //

    virtual HRESULT __stdcall CreateInstance (
        REFGUID rclsid,
        REFGUID riid,
        void * * ppv ) = 0;
    virtual HRESULT __stdcall SetComplete ( ) = 0;
    virtual HRESULT __stdcall SetAbort ( ) = 0;
    virtual HRESULT __stdcall EnableCommit ( ) = 0;
    virtual HRESULT __stdcall DisableCommit ( ) = 0;
    virtual BOOL __stdcall IsInTransaction ( ) = 0;
    virtual BOOL __stdcall IsSecurityEnabled ( ) = 0;
    virtual HRESULT __stdcall IsCallerInRole (
        BSTR bstrRole,
        BOOL * pfIsInRole ) = 0;
};
```

The interface can be broken down into three categories:

- *Transaction outcome.* This category includes DisableCommit, EnableCommit, SetAbort, and SetComplete. The transaction outcome methods influence how the transaction will end when the component is deactivated. The object can specify that the transaction is ready for writing or that everything went wrong and needs to stop. Also, the object can say, "Wait one minute and let me do a couple more things until I'm ready to decide whether everything is okay." Yet another possibility is that the object can say, "I'm not yet finished, but what I've done is okay whether the transaction is aborted or committed."

22

BUILDING COMPONENTS FOR COM+ SERVICES

- *Querying*. This category includes `IsCallerInRole`, `IsInTransaction`, and `IsSecurityEnabled`. The querying methods allow the object to ask whether it's in the correct security role. Most of the time, for example, you won't want to let people withdraw thousands of dollars. An even better question is whether security is even enabled. The object can ask, "Am I even running within a transaction context?" This is critical, because if the object is not within a transaction context, aborting a transaction might not have any influence on the database it's working with.

- *COM+ object instantiation*. This category includes `CreateInstance`. The COM component creation method is used to create objects that will participate in the same transaction as what's currently running. This is absolutely important, because if a method call invokes an object that's not running, the same transaction context may make data durable that should not be durable.

Transaction Outcome Methods

Because you'll use the next set of functions many, many times, you should understand how they work. The easiest way to understand these functions is to think of them as light switches, as shown in Figure 22.10.

FIGURE 22.10
The transactional switches.

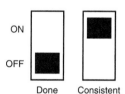

ON

OFF

Done   Consistent

The two switches are set using the four transaction outcome functions. The lookup table is defined as follows:

Method	Switch: Done	Switch: Consistent
DisableCommit	Off	Off
EnableCommit	Off	On
SetAbort	On	Off
SetComplete	On	On

These functions are compared to switches because during the method call, the functions can be set and reset as often as needed. They are evaluated only when the method returns control to the caller. Therefore, calling `SetAbort` and then calling `SetComplete` means that the last call, `SetComplete`, will be acted upon.

Wait, I'm Not Done: `DisableCommit`

When `DisableCommit` is called, the Done switch is off and the Consistent switch is off. The ramifications are that the COM object will not be deactivated for reuse. However, if a two-phase commit were to be started, it would be aborted. Also, any work that has been accomplished would be erased. The definition of this method is as follows:

```
HRESULT IObjectContext::DisableCommit ( );
```

There are no parameters, but the return codes must be obeyed. An S_OK return code indicates that the switches have been successfully set. On the other hand, a CONTEXT_E_NOCONTEXT return code indicates that although the interface where the method has been called is valid, the object is not participating in a transaction.

Okay, Some Work Is Done: `EnableCommit`

The difference for `EnableCommit` is that the Consistent switch is on. As with the `DisableCommit` method, the object is not yet done and cannot be deactivated. However, unlike `DisableCommit`, if a two-phase commit is started, it will commit the data. If this happens, the object will be deactivated regardless of the outcome of the transaction. The definition of this method is as follows:

```
HRESULT IObjectContext::EnableCommit ( );
```

Again, as is the case with `DisableCommit`, S_OK indicates that the method call was successful. However, a return code of CONTEXT_E_NOCONTEXT means that the object is not participating in a transaction but is running within the MTS environment.

Oops, Everything Went Wrong: `SetAbort`

When everything goes wrong and any work performed on the transaction needs to be aborted, `SetAbort` must be called. It will abort everything and force all objects to be deactivated when the control returns to the caller. This method is defined as follows:

```
HRESULT IObjectContext::SetAbort ( );
```

Again, as is the case with `DisableCommit`, S_OK indicates that the method call was successful, and a return code of CONTEXT_E_NOCONTEXT means that the object is not participating in a transaction but is running within the COM+ services.

Everything Is Okay: `SetComplete`

This method is an indication that the transactional work committed thus far can be committed. The key word here is *indication*, because whether or not the transaction survives is up to the two-phase commit. If the two-phase commit is successful, the transactional work will be committed. Regardless of the result of the two-phase commit, the object is deactivated when it returns control to the caller. This method is defined as follows:

```
HRESULT IObjectContext::SetComplete ( );
```

Again, as is the case with `DisableCommit`, `S_OK` indicates that the method call was successful, and a return code of `CONTEXT_E_NOCONTEXT` means that the object is not participating in a transaction but is running within the COM+ services environment.

What to Do When Jumping Out of a Method

Telling the COM+ services what you're doing is important because only then can COM+ services recover resources. If you do not tell COM+ services everything, then partially telling your resources what you are doing may result in unpredictable behavior, because when a COM object executes within a COM+ application, it uses just-in-time activation and deactivation. A COM+ object that does not implement this properly will create unreliable results.

An Activity Example

Let's go through an example of creating an invoice. The purpose is to define the activities and which transaction outcome method to call. Here's the business process:

1. Get an order number.
2. Set the client name and address.
3. Add an ordered part to the order.
4. Keep adding parts until the order is complete.
5. Close the order.

What's the activity in this example? Is the activity step 1 only? Is it a combination of steps 1, 2, 3, and 4? The answer is that there are two activities. The first activity is the generation of the order number, and the second is the creation of the order.

It would be optimal to make the activity all the steps. However, the problem is that the order entry could take many hours in the worst case. In this situation, the shared resource is the generation of the order number, because most order numbers are incremental. A long transaction would lock the record or records and not allow anyone else to generate any orders. A question then arises: What if the order does not get generated? The answer is that it's canceled and marked as canceled in the database. Although this is wasteful of order numbers, it's a determined result. In real life, if an order is filled out using paper and then stopped half-way through, the order is not re-created. It's considered canceled. Also, adding the programming resources to manage this using canceled order number reuse is not worth the programming effort.

The second part of the transaction can be long because it's a personal transaction. This means no two people are creating the same order simultaneously—or at least the chances of it are very small. Therefore, there's no resource lockup, because the records are locked to a specific person.

When step 2 returns, the method calls `EnableCommit`. This is correct because the order has an associated client. A forced commit would create an order that has no ordered items. Although this is not good financially, it's okay at the business level. An empty order does not induce any business processes. The advantage of calling `EnableCommit` is that if the order is forced to be saved, the order creator does not need to go through all the steps of creating the order. Instead, he or she can simply search for the client and continue adding ordered items. Also, by no means is a `SetComplete` or `SetAbort` correct, because that would mean the activity is finished, which is not the case.

Steps 3 and 4 involve the process of adding ordered parts to the order. Each time an order is added, `DisableCommit` is called. The reason why this is correct is that half an order is not a valid state. Consider the situation where the data-entry person partially adds an order, goes for coffee, and then the data is written to the database. He or she may forget about the order and therefore send out half an order to the client. The client, in turn, will receive only half an order, which is frustrating for the client.

Finally, if all goes okay, the order is closed in step 5. This method calls `SetComplete`, which starts the two-phase commit. Now the object is deactivated and can be potentially reused or pooled, depending on the configuration.

It's possible throughout any of these steps to call `SetAbort` to cancel any part of the transaction. This causes an automatic erasing of the data from the resource and keeps the database clean.

Querying

The querying methods are in place so that it's possible to decide which action to take. For example, there are situations when the component doesn't run within a transaction but rather within COM+ services. Should the component return an error stating that it must run within a transaction? That's a question for the application programmer. The next section discusses what type of transactional information can be discovered.

Is There a Transaction? `IsInTransaction`

This entire long-winded discussion of transactions is not worth the paper it's printed on if the object is not participating in a transaction. Therefore, a check has to be available that tells the object whether it's in a transaction. This is the purpose of the method `IsInTransaction`, which is defined as follows:

```
BOOL IObjectContext::IsInTransaction ( );
```

If the method returns a TRUE value, the object is executing within a transaction. A FALSE value indicates that the object is not executing within the context of a transaction. This method can also be partially used to check whether the object is configured properly in the COM+ services catalog. For example, if a check proves that the object is not in a transaction and yet the object is registered in a package, the transaction property is set to "Does not support transactions." If this is unacceptable, the object can stop processing and send an error back to the caller.

Who Are You? IsCallerInRole

Not everyone can add to or delete generated invoices. You can use regular security, but using roles is a simpler solution. The role in use can be checked using the following functions:

```
HRESULT IObjectContext::IsCallerInRole (
    BSTR bstrRole,              [in]
    BOOL* pfIsInRole);          [out]
```

The first parameter defines the role to be checked for, and the second return parameter indicates whether the first parameter is part of that role. You can't perform a security check to see which roles the component is running under. This method only allows a query—test-and-react-type programming. If the pfIsInRole parameter is TRUE, the user is in that role. However, keep in mind that the parameter will return TRUE if security is not enabled on the component. Otherwise, if the component is not running within the role, it will return FALSE.

The return parameter indicates whether the return value in pfIsInRole is correct. A correct value is indicated by S_OK. Now consider the case where the input role is not found in the catalog. In this case, the TRUE or FALSE value is not enough to indicate what has happened. In this situation, the return code is CONTEXT_E_ROLENOTFOUND. A sample implementation would be as follows:

```
// check for security
if (lAmount > 500 || lAmount < -500) {
        BOOL bInRole;
        BSTR bstrRole;
        bstrRole = SysAllocString(L"Managers");
        hr = pObjectContext->IsCallerInRole(bstrRole, &bInRole);
        SysFreeString(bstrRole);
        if (!SUCCEEDED(hr)) goto Error;
        if (!bInRole) {
            wcscpy(*pbstrResult,
                L"Need 'Managers' role for amounts over $500");
            hr = S_FALSE;
            goto Error;
        }
}
```

This method is a very powerful security method because it allows the programmer to determine whether the caller is in a correct role to be able to execute certain functionality. In this sample source code, the security check involves making sure that the caller is

22

BUILDING
COMPONENTS FOR
COM+ SERVICES

a manager if the transfer amount is greater than 500 dollars. The role is something specific to COM+ services, and it's a custom group that's based on all components within a package. Users are put into roles through the COM+ services. You should use roles and not Windows 2000 security directly, because not all transaction functions use the Windows 2000 security functions directly. One catch is that if security is not enabled, the function returns TRUE. This will not be correct in many instances. The way around this problem is to check whether security is enabled with the function IsSecurityEnabled.

Is This Safe? `IsSecurityEnabled`

This function is important because if the previously defined function is used, you must know whether security has been enabled. The definition of this method is as follows:

```
BOOL IObjectContext::IsSecurityEnabled ( );
```

A TRUE value indicates that the object does have security enabled, whereas a FALSE value indicates that security is not enabled. The security is enabled or disabled at the administrative level.

In the preceding example, the method would return TRUE because the check box Enable Authorization Checking is checked. An exception to the security check working properly occurs if the server is configured to run the base client's process space.

The last function provides the ability to create objects. Although a new or COM create would be okay, the problem is that those methods do not support transactions. Using those methods, the COM object would be created, but it may not necessarily execute within the same transaction.

`CreateInstance`

Up to this point, all the transaction examples have dealt with a single COM object. Most transactions will be multiobject based. To tie all the COM objects into one transaction, the transaction context interface provides a COM object creation method. It's defined as follows:

```
HRESULT IObjectContext::CreateInstance (
    REFCLSID rclsid,            [in]
        REFIID riid,            [in]
        LPVOID FAR* ppvObj );         [out]
```

This method is similar to a normal COM creation method. The first parameter is a reference to a coclass ID of the COM object. The second parameter is an interface ID that the COM object has implemented. The last parameter represents the returned interface of the instantiated COM object. That's all you need to know for now.

Creating a Transaction COM+ Object Using Visual Basic

Let's look at some Visual Basic transaction source code from the preceding chapter:

```
Public Function add() As Boolean
    On Error GoTo addError

    Dim objCtxt As ObjectContext
    Dim objCon As New Connection
    Dim strSQL As String

    Set objCtxt = GetObjectContext()

    objCtxt.SetComplete
    add = True
    Exit Function

addError:
    objCtxt.SetAbort
    add = False
End Function
```

In this sample source code, the same pattern is used as that of the Visual C++ program. The first step is to retrieve the object `ObjectContext`. This is a Visual Basic wrapper. Note that you don't need to call `Release`. Unlike the Visual C++ environment, Visual Basic uses the object `ObjectContext`. `ObjectContext` is almost identical to `IObjectContext`, with a few differences:

```
[
    odl,
    uuid(74C08646-CEDB-11CF-8B49-00AA00B8A790),
    helpstring("ObjectContext"),
    helpcontext(0x00205ad9),
    dual,
oleautomation
]
interface ObjectContext : IDispatch {
HRESULT CreateInstance(
            [in] BSTR bstrProgID,
            [out, retval] VARIANT* pObject);
HRESULT SetComplete();
HRESULT SetAbort();
HRESULT EnableCommit();
HRESULT DisableCommit();
HRESULT IsInTransaction([out, retval] VARIANT_BOOL* pbIsInTx);
HRESULT IsSecurityEnabled([out, retval] VARIANT_BOOL* pbIsEnabled);
HRESULT IsCallerInRole(
                    BSTR bstrRole,
                    [out, retval] VARIANT_BOOL* pbInRole);
```

```
HRESULT Count([out, retval] long* plCount);
HRESULT Item(
                       [in] BSTR name,
                       [out, retval] VARIANT* pItem);
HRESULT _NewEnum([out, retval] IUnknown** ppEnum);
HRESULT Security([out, retval] SecurityProperty** ppSecurityProperty);
HRESULT ContextInfo([out, retval] ContextInfo** ppContextInfo);
   };
```

In general, the interface functions identically to the C++ implementation. However, there are some differences. For instance, the `CreateInstance` method accepts as an input parameter a ProgID as an object. When you create an object, be careful how you convert the object. For example, you should stay away from object declarations. Instead, use interface data types. The following is an example of how not to convert an object:

```
dim myObj as Object
Set myObj = ctxt.CreateInstance("Prog.Id")
```

Here's a better method:

```
dim myObj as SomeObject
set myObj = ctxt.CreateInstance("Prog.Id")
```

The main reason why this is a better method is that it does not use the `IDispatch` to reference the methods of the object.

The other properties—`Item`, `Count`, and `Security`—relate to functionality that will be explained in other chapters in this section of the book.

Specifying the Transaction Attribute

To specify the Visual Basic transaction attribute, open the Visual Basic environment and create a class file. Then, from the Properties dialog box shown in Figure 22.11, look at `MTSTransactionMode`.

FIGURE 22.11

Visual Basic transactional properties.

You can specify the following standard properties:

- `NotAnMTSObject` is not a transactional property within the COM+ services.
- `RequiresTransaction` is `TRANSACTION_REQUIRED`.
- `UsesTransaction` is `TRANSACTION_SUPPORTED`.
- `NoTransactions` is `TRANSACTION_NOT_SUPPORTED`.
- `RequiresNewTransaction` is `TRANSACTION_REQUIRES_NEW`.

Using COM Compiler Support

The COM compiler support classes make it a breeze to work with COM interfaces. Basically, the COM compiler support classes perform the following functions:

- When used in conjunction with the `#import` tag, they generate an easy-to-use interface for methods and properties.
- They define a simpler variant and `BSTR` class.
- They include an automatic reference-counting scheme.
- They use assignment overloading with `QueryInterface` to make it simple to assign variables to interface.

The notation for using COM compiler support is as follows:

```
#import "file" attributes
```

Or you can use this:

```
#import <file> attributes
```

Here are the file types involved:

- A type library (such as TLB or ODL)
- An executable file (EXE)
- A library file (such as DLL or OCX)
- A compound document that contains a type library definition
- Anything that can be understood by the `LoadTypeLib` WINAPI

What is generated is a series of classes that make it possible to use COM objects as if they were regular C++ objects. The output includes TLI (type library implementation) and TLH (type library header) files. These files can be used without calling `#import`. They're straight C++. This process is illustrated in Figure 22.12.

FIGURE 22.12

The TLH and TLI generation process.

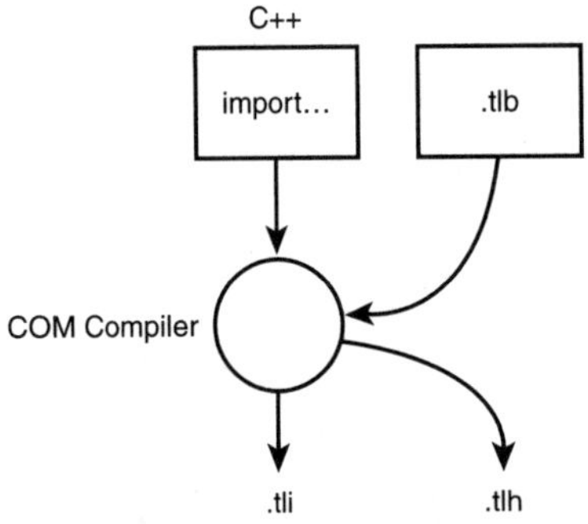

TLH and TLI: Examining the Output

Consider the following actual IDL definition:

```
[
    object,
    uuid(AD8A2F1F-9D18-11D2-86DF-0000B45FCBCB),
    dual,
    helpstring("IICaller Interface"),
    pointer_default(unique)
]
interface IICaller : IDispatch
{
    [id(1), helpstring("method callChild")] HRESULT callChild();
};
```

When this IDL is compiled as part of a library, the COM compiler will generate the following code:

COMCompiler.TLH

```
// Created by Microsoft (R) C/C++ Compiler Version 11.00.0000 (c9163f02).
//
// Debug/COMCompiler.tlh
//
// C++ source equivalent of Win32 type library C:\docs\COMCompiler\
// Debug\COMCompiler.dll
// compiler-generated file created 11/05/97 at 02:09:19 - DO NOT EDIT!

#pragma once
#pragma pack(push, 8)
#include <comdef.h>
namespace COMCOMPILERLib {
//
// Forward references and typedefs
//
struct /* coclass */ Caller;
```

```
struct __declspec(uuid("421a0bce-5574-11d1-a503-0080c886ec30"))
/* dual interface */ ICaller;
//
// Smart pointer typedef declarations
//
_COM_SMARTPTR_TYPEDEF(ICaller, __uuidof(ICaller));
//
// Type library items
//
struct __declspec(uuid("421a0bcf-5574-11d1-a503-0080c886ec30"))
Caller;
// [ default ] interface ICaller
struct __declspec(uuid("421a0bce-5574-11d1-a503-0080c886ec30"))
ICaller : IDispatch
{
    //
    // Wrapper methods for error-handling
    //
    HRESULT callChild ( );
    //
    // Raw methods provided by interface
    //
    virtual HRESULT __stdcall raw_callChild ( ) = 0;
};
//
// Wrapper method implementations
//
#include "Debug/COMCompiler.tli"
} // namespace COMCOMPILERLib
#pragma pack(pop)
```

COMCompiler.TLI

```
// Created by Microsoft (R) C/C++ Compiler Version 11.00.0000 (c9163f02).
//
// Debug/COMCompiler.tli
//
// Wrapper implementations for Win32 type library C:\docs\ProMTS\08chap\
// COMCompiler\Debug\COMCompiler.dll
// compiler-generated file created 11/05/97 at 02:09:19 - DO NOT EDIT!

#pragma once

//
// interface ICaller wrapper method implementations
//

inline HRESULT ICaller::callChild ( ) {
    HRESULT _hr = raw_callChild();
    if (FAILED(_hr)) _com_issue_errorex(_hr, this, __uuidof(this));
    return _hr;
}
```

Without any attributes, all the generate COM classes are encapsulated within a namespace. In this example, it's COMCOMPILERLib. I recommend that you leave it "as is," because in the future there will be class naming conflicts. Without a namespace, interfaces require a longer, more-complex naming convention.

COM uses a vtable (virtual table) as a method signature. Now, look at how the COM compiler generates the vtable. It creates two methods: callChild and raw_callChild. The method callChild is what you would use in your implementation. The method raw_callChild is part of the vtable and represents the COM object. Here are the reasons for the two methods:

- The COM compiler can generate an exception if the method returns an incorrect answer.
- The exposed method uses the simpler wrapper classes for BSTRs and variants.
- Properties are implemented like properties and not like method calls using "out" pointers.

The smart pointer is defined in _COM_SMARTPTR_TYPEDEF, which is a macro that creates a type that adds Ptr to the interface. Therefore, in our example

ICaller

becomes

ICallerPtr

This makes it possible for any interface to be converted into a smart pointer. Just use the macro definition and the interface you want as a smart pointer. The only difference is that the wrapper methods will not be visible, because the COM compiler generates them.

Tip

When passing a COM compiler–generated class back to the original caller using an [out] parameter, you need to use the notation ptrRet = smrtPtr.Detach(), because when a smart pointer class is assigned, an AddRef is not called. This could cause the object to be released too early.

COM Compiler Command Attributes

You can specify a variety of attributes in the file that will help you in importing your typelib information. The most common attribute that you may use is the `no_namespace` tag. It allows you to add your typelib information without a namespace definition. Although this makes it easier to define and implement objects, it's really a trade-off, because you open yourself to the possibility that two suppliers might name their objects identically. For example, an object named `String` is very generic and could be a part of many libraries. Therefore, you should leave the namespace extension.

While we're on the topic of namespaces, keep in mind that the COM compiler creates a namespace based on the library name defined in the component IDL file. Very often, this name is obtuse and not fun to reference. In fact, the namespace being used by the component could conflict with the namespace of another component.

When you're creating a typelib that needs to be used in an MTS context, such as the `IObjectContext::CreateInstance` function, the method expects to see GUID definitions such as `IID_xxx` and `CLSID_xxx`. By default, the COM compiler does not generate this information. Instead, the interface pointer and the method `__uuidof` is used to retrieve the GUID. Here's an example:

```
__uuidof( IMySampleInterface)
```

Here's the same example represented in old GUID terms:

```
IID_MySampleInterface
```

Both are okay, but to make the COM compiler generate the old GUIDs, the attribute `named_guids` has to be added to the `#import` line.

Very often in COM components, some elements are defined that have already been defined elsewhere. And, very often in these cases, a conflict will happen and an error will be reported. This error makes it impossible to compile the application or component. The simplest solution to this problem is to *not* add the conflicting component, but very often this means that it's impossible to use both components at the same time. This is another unpleasant occurrence. The way that the COM compiler solves this is by adding the attribute `exclude`:

```
exclude("item1", "item2", ...)
```

Here, `itemx` can be anything defined within the component being imported.

Generating and Catching Errors with `com_error`

All COM compiler classes like to generate exceptions. This approach reduces the number of `if` statements that you need to write. It makes code much easier to read and understand. Whenever any COM operation goes awry, a _com_error is generated.

Raising _com_error Objects

To be able to issue a _com_error object, the object has to be thrown. Although it might seem logical to use

```
throw _com_error(..)
```

this is not the proper way to throw the exception. The correct way is to use the method _com_raise_error. However, the problem with this is that the definition is not given in the `comdef.h` file—it's undefined. However, it is defined in the newest version of Visual C++ 6; therefore, you should upgrade to this version. If, however, you cannot upgrade, you should add the following definition to your source code or to your `comdef.h` file:

```
void __stdcall _com_raise_error(
HRESULT hr, IErrorInfo* perrinfo = 0) throw(_com_error);
```

This is the official way to issue an error, per the Visual C++ documentation. The input error code is a valid HRESULT error code. Two other functions are available for issuing errors. They are defined as follows:

```
void __stdcall _com_issue_error(HRESULT) throw(_com_error);
void __stdcall _com_issue_errorex(
HRESULT, IUnknown*, REFIID) throw(_com_error);
```

These functions work similar to how the _com_raise_error method works, except that it's possible to identify the object raising the error and the reference interface. By default, the COM compiler–generated objects use _com_issue_errorex in the methods if anything goes wrong. Here's some sample source code that shows how to raise an _com_error exception:

```
_com_issue_error( E_NOTIMPL);
_com_raise_error( E_NOTIMPL);
```

Here's a sample try/catch block that will catch the preceding example:

```
try {
...
}
catch( _com_error obj) {
printf( "Error is %s\n", obj.ErrorMessage());
}
```

There's nothing complex about this exception block. However, as the code stands in its current form, it will only catch the _com_error exception.

Working with Any Data: `_variant_t`

When COM and OLE were introduced, it was possible to work with variant data types. It's a data type that can represent any other data type. For languages such as BASIC that are based on variant data types, this is appropriate. However, for a typed language such as C++, it becomes a problem. As such, throughout the history of COM and OLE, writing C++ code to handle variants has never been any fun. With the COM compiler support, there's another class that wraps the variant data type into something. This class is simpler and more effective because it uses overloading to convert a data type into a variant. Because of its simplicity, there isn't really much to explain, except to show you some source code that demonstrates how the variant data type can be used:

```
_variant_t var;
_variant_t var2((long)12);

var = (short)12;
var = "Hello";
```

This is very simple, but yet there's a trick. Notice that when var is assigned a value of 12, a type has to be declared. The reason for this is because 12 can be an int, long, or short. Encapsulated within the class is all the legwork to ensure that the variant is properly declared and assigned. If, however, you are passed a VARIANT and want to convert it into a _variant_t type, all you have to do is assign it as shown in the following example:

```
VARIANT vtText;

VariantInit( &vtText );
V_VT( &vtText) = VT_BSTR;
V_BSTR( &vtText) = SysAllocString( L"12" );

testCopy = vtText;
```

Another operation that's needed is the ability to change the variant from one type to another. For example, in the preceding source code, the variant type is VT_BSTR, but because the string represents a number, it could be a short, long, or int. To do this, you need to change the types using the following method:

```
void ChangeType( VARTYPE vartype, const _variant_t* pSrc = NULL )
➥ throw( _com_error );
```

The first parameter, vartype, is the destination variant type. This is directly analogous to the types introduced with OLE Automation, such as VT_BSTR, VT_I4, and so on.

The second parameter is used to define a source used for conversion. This means that if pSrc is not NULL, the contents of pSrc are converted to the type vartype and then copied to the referenced _variant_t object. Anything being referenced in the current object is lost. The default is NULL, which means that reference object is to be converted into the type desired.

The functions for clearing the variant are a bit odd:

```
void Clear( ) throw( _com_error );
```

This method clears the currently referenced variant and sets it to nothing. The other method is one that sets the variant to a string value (SetString). The odd thing about this method is that it does not differ from the overloaded char * operator. Therefore, the exact purpose is unknown. It's simpler to use the overloaded operator.

Working with BSTRs: _bstr_t

The final class discussed is perhaps one of the most needed classes. This class makes it simple to convert strings from BSTRs to wide chars or normal chars. Like the variant, it wraps most of its conversions within a set of overloaded operators. Here's a typical scenario:

```
_bstr_t bstrVar( "Hello");
char *tempHello;

tempHello = bstrVar;
```

This example does nothing but convert a string to a _bstr_t type in the constructor. With the overloaded assignment operator, it's then converted back into a normal char string. However, there's a catch to using this class. Consider the following example:

```
void func( BSTR input) {
    _bstr_t var( input, true);
    char *result;

    result = var;
    return;
}
```

The reason the BSTR input parameter is used as the _bstr_t constructor parameter is that it's easier to convert. However, the problem with the conversion is that the raw bytes are manipulated and the BSTR that's passed in is created by the caller of the class. Therefore, the input BSTR has to be copied into another buffer. If this didn't occur, then when the _bstr_t variable destroys itself, it will attempt to free the BSTR, and because the BSTR was not created by the function, an error will occur. Therefore, it's imperative that the input buffer is copied to before anything is done.

Working with Multiple COM+ Objects

When you're writing COM+ objects, in most cases, there will not be one COM+ object doing all the work. A COM+ object may instantiate another object, which may instantiate another, and so on. In this situation, there are two fundamental issues:

- When a COM object is instantiated, how will the COM+ transaction attribute affect the current transaction context if it exists?
- When multiple COM objects are combined into one transaction, how does the transaction outcome method determine the outcome of the transaction?

Transaction Lifetimes for Combined COM+ Objects

When a COM+ object instantiates a new COM+ object using regular COM calls, such as CoCreateInstance or CreateObject (VB), it does not cross transaction boundaries.

In Figure 22.13, the other COM+ object has been created using CoCreateInstance. As a result, the COM+ object exists in another transaction. Because COM+ services only support flat transactions, the two transactions have no dependency on each other regarding the outcome of the transactions.

FIGURE 22.13
Defining the root object of a transaction.

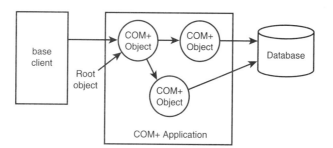

There is a tie between the two COM+ objects. The newly created COM+ object is called a *root object*. A root object has special properties. When it's deactivated, it commits or aborts the transaction. Any non-root object only indicates what it thinks should be the transaction outcome. Root objects also deactivate all other COM+ objects within the transaction. This means that if any non-root objects are referenced, the reference will be invalid.

Using `IObjectContext::CreateInstance`

In order to have the created COM+ object running within the same transaction, you need to use the method `IObjectContext::CreateInstance`. It's not a guarantee that the object will run within the same transaction. That's dependent on how the transaction attributes are set. Here are the attributes of interest to you:

- *Requires a transaction*. If the object creating the child does not have a transaction context, it will be created for the child. If the object has a transaction context, the child will inherit the parent's context.
- *Supports transactions*. If the object creating the child does not have a transaction context, MTS will not create one. If the object has a transaction context, the child will inherit the parent's context.
- *Requires a new transaction*. Regardless of whether the object has a transaction context, MTS will create a new transaction context for the child.
- *Ignored/does not support transactions*. Either way, this COM+ object will not participate in the transaction or any other transaction.

Using these settings, let's create a scenario that involves various objects instantiated with `IObjectContext::CreateInstance` as in the following list:

- Requires a transaction: Object A, Object D, Object F
- Supports transactions: Object B
- Requires a new transaction: Object C
- Does not support transactions: Object E

The root object is Object A, and it creates Objects B and C. Object B creates Object D, and Object C creates Objects E and F. The two transactions are shown in Figure 22.14.

The two transactions are independent of each other. For the second transaction, Object B is the root object. When it's deactivated, the transaction will be committed or aborted.

Getting the Aborted Transaction Error

In the various situations, the root object is the last object to deactivate. The transaction commit starts only if the root object calls `SetComplete`, and it, in turn, returns `S_OK`. At this stage, the two-phase commit starts. Now comes a problem: What happens if the transaction aborts for one reason or another? The answer is that COM+ services will return to the caller `CONTEXT_E_ABORTED` if the transaction aborts.

FIGURE 22.14

The transactions used in this example.

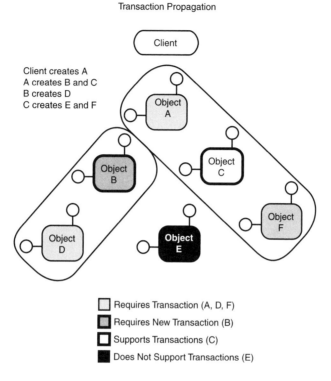

Transaction Propagation

Client

Client creates A
A creates B and C
B creates D
C creates E and F

Object A

Object C

Object B

Object F

Object D

Object E

☐ Requires Transaction (A, D, F)
▨ Requires New Transaction (B)
☐ Supports Transactions (C)
■ Does Not Support Transactions (E)

Which Method Do I Use?

Which method is used? The CoCreateInstance variety or the IObjectContext variety? It depends on where you're creating the object. If you're the base client, your only solution is CoCreateInstance (which you have already learned). However, when you're within the COM+ object, you should use IObjectContext::CreateInstance. This way, the activity can be defined at the administrative level. This gives you the ability with scripting to build activities dynamically based on the situation.

Multi-COM Object Transaction Outcomes

When multiple COM+ objects are executed within one transaction, the transaction outcome methods help determine the outcome. What happens if one calls SetComplete, another calls DisableCommit, and so on? A scenario using Objects A, B, and C is created, as shown in Figure 22.15.

FIGURE 22.15

A scenario of objects being called.

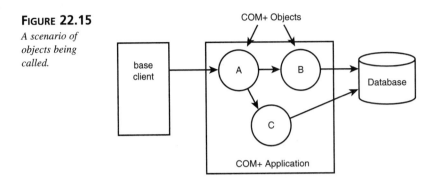

Object A is called the root object of the automatic transaction. The base client instantiates Object A. This causes a COM+ application to start, which causes a transaction to be started. For the scope of this calling sequence, it's assumed that both Objects B and C share the same transaction.

Object B Calling SetAbort

In this scenario, Object B, prior to returning control to Object A, calls SetAbort. If Object A does not pick up this error, it will still call Object C. However, because Object B has aborted the transaction, no work will be saved, regardless what Object C does. If Object C performs a long operation, processor cycles will be wasted. Therefore, it's important to check whether all the methods worked correctly.

Object A Calling SetAbort

In this example, the outcome of the transaction is the same because the root object calls SetAbort. The pattern to this and the last scenario is that if any of the participating objects call SetAbort, the transaction will be aborted, because all the objects involved must call SetComplete in order for the transaction to be a candidate for the two-phase commit.

Object B Calling EnableCommit

In this example, Object B calls EnableCommit. This time, the transaction will commit, because EnableCommit keeps the object activated and signals to the transaction context that the transactional work can be committed.

Object B Calling DisableCommit

In this example, Object B calls DisableCommit. This time, the transaction will abort, even though everything else concerned is ready to commit. The reason is that DisableCommit keeps the object activated and tells the COM+ application that object is not ready to commit and therefore must be aborted.

Object A Calling `EnableCommit/DisableCommit`

In this example, Object A calls either `DisableCommit` or `EnableCommit`. Both Object B and Object C have called `SetComplete` to have their work committed. However, the transaction work will be considered inconsistent. After the control returns to the base client, Object A will remain activated, whereas Objects B and C will be deactivated and available for reuse. If, in a later action, `SetComplete` is called, the work previously done will be a candidate for committal. If, however, `SetAbort` is called, the transactional work will be aborted.

Object B Calling `SetAbort`

In this example, Object A can still call either `DisableCommit` or `EnableCommit`. However, Object B has called `SetAbort` while Object C has called `SetComplete`. Again, Object A will remain activated, whereas Object B and Object C will be deactivated and available for reuse. The only difference now is that the transaction is doomed for aborting. Object B has clearly stated that its work cannot be committed, so all other work cannot be committed either. Therefore, when in the end Object A calls either `SetComplete` or `SetAbort`, all transactional work accomplished will be aborted.

Error Handling

To stop the wasted processor cycles, you need to handle return codes. This is typically known as the `HRESULT` code. The COM layer, to indicate what has happened, uses the `HRESULT` codes. You cannot simply create an error code and then return it. Specific techniques are involved.

In Visual C++, the default error to return is `S_OK`. In Visual Basic, you would do nothing. If something goes wrong, you can return `S_FALSE` or any other COM error in a Visual C++ program. With Visual Basic, you would set the `Err` object. With a tuned component, COM+ services will pass an error directly as long as it's not `S_OK` or `S_FALSE`. With those errors, COM+ services may change the error code to reflect a failed transaction.

Passing Parameters and Interfaces

In a multi-COM+ object situation, data is passed back and forth. The question is how to pass parameters and what are the limitations of passing parameters.

Parameter Limitations

Parameters within COM+ objects must support standard marshaling. In other words, if you try to use anything that requires the interface `IMarshal`, it will not work. COM+ services ignore the `IMarshal` interface.

The other aspect is the consumer of the parameter, which is exposed by the interface. Let's say the consumer is Visual C++. Visual C++ has the ability to understand any data type, which can be expressed using IDL. The only catch is that typelib marshaling cannot be used. You'll need to create a proxy stub.

The problem with using this type of interface is that only Visual C++ or a language like it can understand the interface. If the consumer is JavaScript, the interface must support IDispatch. IDispatch adds the constraint that the interface can only use Automation data types.

For performance purposes, it's recommended that you pass parameters by value.

Passing Objects to Other Objects

You can't pass a raw COM interface using a method, because the raw COM interface bypasses the context. What you need to do is retrieve and pass the context interface pointer. However, in a previous section, you learned that the transaction context interface pointer cannot be used outside the current COM+ object.

The solution to this problem is to use the following method:

```
void* SafeRef (
    REFIID riid              [in]
    UNKNOWN* pUnk )          [in]
```

The first parameter is the interface ID that's being requested. An example could be IID_IUnknown. The second parameter is the COM this pointer or IUnknown. Returned will be either NULL or a valid, safe reference interface pointer. To apply this in an ATL object, consider the following source code:

```
CComPtr< IObjectContext> pCtxt;
CComPtr< IChild> child;
CComPtr< IUnknown> me;

GetObjectContext( &(pCtxt.p));
try {
    _com_util::CheckError( pCtxt->CreateInstance( CLSID_Child,
__uuidof( child.p), (void **)&(child.p)));

        me.p = reinterpret_cast< IUnknown *>(SafeRef( __uuidof( IUnknown),
        GetUnknown()));

        child->callChild( me);

        pCtxt->SetComplete();
} catch( _com_error err) {
    pCtxt->SetAbort();
    return err.Error();
}
return S_OK;
```

This method creates a child COM object called `child`. It's created using `IObjectContext::CreateInstance`. This is not a necessary step. It's only added so that the COM component executes within the same transaction. `CoCreateInstance` could have been used. Getting back to the source and looking at the highlighted section, note that `SafeRef` is used to retrieve the `IUnknown` interface. Again, I tend to always use `IUnknown` because it's the easiest interface to work with and to pass from COM object to COM object. Also, it allows decoupling of the components, which makes version changes less dramatic. The first parameter uses the function `__uuidof` to retrieve the UUID of the interface. This makes it easier because you don't have to search for the `IID_xxx` definition. The second parameter uses the ATL template function `GetUnknown` to retrieve the `IUnknown` interface of the object. You can use the C++ `this` pointer, but the problem with `this` is that it's not reliable. For nonaggregated COM objects, the `this` pointer is indeed the correct `IUnknown` interface pointer. However, that's the only case, which, again, is applicable to the MTS case, because MTS does not allow aggregation. But according to the original ATL developers, `this` should not be used because it might not be supported in the future. Therefore, use `this` at your own risk. Once the method has returned, `reinterpret_cast` is used to convert the pointer to the `IUnknown` interface pointer.

The final interface pointer, `me`, is now a safe COM object reference. It may be used within an MTS context or external to the MTS context. Before the sample usage is shown, we have something to consider. When a safe reference is retrieved from the object, the reference count is incremented; therefore, `Release` must be called. To make this easy, I used `CComPtr` to manage the reference counting. Here's an example:

```
STDMETHODIMP CChild::callChild(IUnknown *parent)
{
    CComPtr<IParent> correctParent;
    long retValue;

    parent->QueryInterface( &(correctParent.p));

    correctParent->callbackAdd( 1, 2, &retValue);

    return S_OK;
}
```

When the method is called, the interface is converted into `IParent`. Again, the reference count is managed by the `CComPtr` class. When the interface has been retrieved, the method `callbackAdd` is called. Because `IObjectContext::CreateInstance` has been called, the child and parent may share the same transaction context. But let's think what this means. When the child is called and it performs some work using the parent as its basis, where does the transaction happen? When the client has the control and it executes within a different transaction (or no transaction), the work done in that scope is specific to the child object. A call back to the parent does not force a transaction context switch, because when the call is made from the child to the parent, the context used is not the original parent but rather the child, if it exists. This also raises another point regarding security. If the child does not have access to the parent object, it cannot perform its work.

An important note. At the time of this writing, the need for SafeRef was documented. However, there was talk of not needing this function. Therefore, this section may or may not apply. If it does not apply, ignore this section. It will not apply if in the Platform SDK documentation the function SafeRef has been deprecated.

Passing Other Objects

If, within an object, other objects have been created using IObjectContext::CreateInstance or CoCreateInstance, they are safe and can be passed as parameters. Another case in which this is okay is when QueryInterface is called on the object. It's safe to call QueryInterface on a SafeRef interface pointer.

Summary

This chapter outlined how to build a full-featured COM+ object. Although you don't need to use the transaction context, doing so makes the component more predictable and controllable. Also shown in this chapter were transaction interactions among various COM+ objects.

CHAPTER 23

Using COM+ with the IIS

In this chapter, the topic of building Web applications using the Microsoft Internet Information Server (IIS 5.0) is explored. The chapter starts out with an explanation of what Active Server Pages (ASP) are. The key concepts are explained and demonstrated. Shown throughout are techniques on how to build practical ASP applications. Finally, the discussion moves into how to integrate COM+ objects with ASP.

Basis of a Web Application

The first step in understanding how to write a Web application is to understand the elements we have in our arsenal. Note that in this chapter, all the techniques are cross-browser capable. This means no ActiveX COM controls are used on the client side. When developing a Web application using the Microsoft server-side technologies, you use the following items:

- *A database*. For some read-only operations, it's simpler to access the database directly.
- *Components*. Most of the business logic is encapsulated within components.
- *Scripting*. Server-side and client-side scripting are available in languages such as JScript; it's also possible to use other languages such as VBScript, PerlScript, PythonScript, RexxScript, and so on.

In a traditional Web architecture, the client requests a Web page such as something.htm or something.html. This file is a static file that the Web server sends to the client. It is a sort of cross-platform file server using the HTTP protocol to send the data to the client.

ASP is different from a traditional Web application architecture. In ASP the server is instructed within the ASP page to execute some commands and send the results of those commands as a stream to the client. The stream can generate either HTML 4.0 or it can be Dynamic HTML. In advanced situations, the ASP can even generate XML data. In all these situations, the key element is that the data is sent as a sequential stream to the client. I point out that this is a sequential stream because when data has been sent, it cannot be called back.

In detail, an ASP file is similar to an HTML page, but it contains extra commands. These commands are in the form of scripting elements. The script can contain loops, decision statements, and reference COM objects that do something to generate more data for the stream. The script or the COM objects can access a database or some external device that is generating data.

An Overview of ASP

The overall steps are detailed in the following list and illustrated in Figure 23.1:

FIGURE 23.1

ASP architecture.

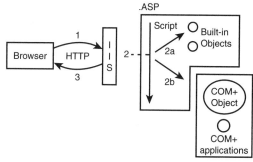

- *Step 1.* The browser makes a request to the server (for example, `http://server/something/default.asp`).

- *Step 2.* The request is converted to an ASP request. The ASP page is loaded into the processor and then parsed. The parsing starts at the top of the page and continues until the bottom of the page is reached. At the start of this process, a stream is opened by default. The stream is a return buffer. This is defined in step 3.

- *Step 2a.* During the request processing, references can be made to the ASP built-in objects. These objects contain information about the client, the server, and the request. The built-in objects are `Application`, `ASPError`, `ObjectContext`, `Request`, `Response`, `Server`, and `Session`.

- *Step 2b.* During the request processing, objects can be referenced that are COM+ applications. These objects usually perform some business processes. Typically, these are custom objects.

- *Step 3.* Whatever stream content has been generated by the script processing is sent to the client. By default, when and in what order the content is to be sent to the client are not defined. You can specify this using the `Response` built-in object.

Remember that ASP works using the stream concept. For example, when a stream has a byte written, you cannot revoke that byte. Also, the information in the stream must be sent in a specific order. It was mentioned previously that the stream is sent using the HTTP protocol. This means that to influence how the HTTP protocol sends the stream, the HTTP methods need to be called before the stream is actually sent. If you attempt to change the HTTP stream characteristics in midstream, you will generate an ASP error.

A Quick Script Example

A script on the ASP page can be defined in several ways. You can use server-side scripts and client-side scripts. Server-side execution happens on the side of the HTTP server, whereas client-side execution happens in the Web browser. Consider the following ASP script:

```
<%
var obj;
obj = 1 + 1;
%>
<script language="jscript">
function clientFunc() {
var obj;
obj= 1 + 1;
}
</script>
<script language="jscript" runat=server>
function serverFunc() {
var obj;
obj= 1 + 1;
}
</script>
```

This script has three sections. The first block of code is a server-side script. The characters <% and %> begin and end this block. Note that you cannot use these tags for client-side scripting. The second block, which appears between the <script> and </script> tags, is a client-side scripting block, because there's no runat attribute within the first <script> tag. The second <script> tag contains a server-side script, because it does contain a runat=server attribute.

ASP Applications

ASP applications are not like traditional compiled applications. In a traditional application, a series of sources is written using a language such as C++. Then a compiler translates these files into object code and the various object code pieces are linked into an executable.

The Web is different because everything is dynamic and processed at the time of request. For example, consider the following URL:

```
http://www.myurl.com/directory/default.asp
```

The http specifies the HTTP protocol. The server is specified by the www.myurl.com. The /directory specifies the virtual directory. And the file is default.asp. In Web server terms, the virtual directory is mapped to a directory on the hard disk. In ASP terms, the virtual directory is still mapped to the hard disk. Additionally, the virtual directory represents an ASP application. All ASP files retrieved from this virtual directory will share the same Session and Application variables. The concepts of Session and Application will be discussed later, but in short they are used to store state.

State and scope form a core functionality of ASP. State can be used to define a series of active objects, variables, or tasks. However, state is dependent on the scope at which the state was declared. The following scopes can be defined:

- *Function*. When a variable is declared at the function level, it exists only within that function. After the function has been exited, the value is lost.

- *Page*. When an ASP page is being retrieved, the processing of the page starts from the top and goes to the bottom. If during this processing a variable is declared, the variable exists for the life of the page.

- *User*. When a specific user accesses an ASP page within the ASP application, a token is associated with that user. The token is a cookie that is returned to the client browser. Then when the client retrieves another page within the ASP application, the token is associated with any state established in a previous ASP request. One caveat with User scope state is that it is subject to timeout. Timeout applies when the delta between two ASP requests exceeds the Application defined time amount. When timeout executes, any state that has been established is released. Note that an ASP application is not the only environment that uses this technique. An example is ODBC, which uses timeout to cancel a database connection. Therefore, if you keep an ODBC database connection and that timeout is less than the ASP timeout, you have invalid calls and errors.

- *Everybody.* In the user scope, the state is associated with a specific client. If it is desired to create a state that can be shared between the various users, everybody scope applies. This scope needs synchronization because it applies to all users.

Page Scope

Page scope may seem simple to handle. However, it's actually more complicated than it appears. Consider the following example:

```
<%
var value1;
value1 = 2;
%>
<script language=javascript runat=server>
var value2;

value2 = value1 + 3;
function valueBefore() {
return value2;
}
```

```
function valueAdd() {
value2 = value2 + value1 + 3;
return value2;
}
function valueAfter() {
return value2;
}
</script>
Output values are
<br>Value 1:(<%=value1%>)
<br>Value 2:(<%=value2%>) direct access before
<br>Value 2:(<%=valueBefore()%>) before adding
<br>Value 2:(<%=valueAdd()%>) adding
<br>Value 2:(<%=valueAfter()%>) after adding
<br>Value 2:(<%=value2%>) direct access after
```

This code segment shows the various situations on how page scope applies. It was previously mentioned that the page is processed starting at the top and then ending at the bottom. This applies only to instructions that reside within the page scope. These instructions are executed in sequential order. Therefore, order is critical. The other code pieces are functions and are called from the page scope. The order in which they are called does not matter, nor does their location on the page.

This code segment is interesting because of the results that it returns:

2, , , -1.#IND,-1.#IND and -1.#IND

However, we expect the results to be

2, 5, 5, 10, 10 and 10

Why the difference? The answer is that lines 6 and 8 are not executed. They are part of a block that is called up when the page execution requires it. This means no declarations or commands will have any effect. The only time that page scope applies is when the objects are declared within <% and %> tags.

The reason the values -1.#IND are output is because of how variables are managed within a scripting environment. Scripting does not understand the concept of data types. Within a scripting environment, all data types are variant. A variant data type is a data type that can be of any type. It can be an integer, string, currency, or object. There are no restrictions, generally. The exceptions in the scripting environment are arrays, which are beyond the scope of this book. Therefore, when attempting to do something with the variable like an addition operator, it does not understand, because the addition could also mean a string concatenation (this is JavaScript specific). And because it does not understand, it will output the error value -1.#IND, which means this is not a number. To check the type, you could use the following code:

```
typeof( value2)
```

This will return one of the following strings: "number", "string", "boolean", "object", "function", or "undefined".

User Scope

When a token is created to build a state between ASP requests, it is stored in a COM object called Session. This COM object is an intrinsic object within the ASP environment. It is not a complicated object, because its sole purpose is to store state. This is done by assigning a value to the Session object while defining a key as an identifier. Here's an example:

```
Session("SomeData") = 3
```

Like the scripting environment, there are no specific data types when the Session object is assigned. Everything is a variant. This means that when you're developing, you won't know what the data type is unless you query for it.

> **TIP**
>
> Even though not necessary, it is good practice to initialize your state values. This does two things—declares a specific value, which makes your code more readable, and type-defines your variable.

Because the session's at the user level, you don't have to deal with concurrency issues. Using variables is straightforward—whenever you need one, you assign it. If you're retrieving the value of an unassigned variable, an empty value is returned. This may seem odd, but it makes sense. In C++, an unassigned variable returns an unknown value. Scripting will initialize an unassigned variable to an empty value. This is not a NULL value. It is a value without value. In most situations this does not matter, but when performing operations where a value is assumed, you will get unpredictable results (as shown in the preceding script). This is another reason to initialize your variables.

It's possible to store objects within the Session object. Here's how to create an object:

```
Session("MyObject") = Server.CreateObject("Simple.Object");
```

If the creation is successful, the object can be used directly, like this:

```
Session("MyObject").someMethod( param1);
```

On the other hand, an unsuccessful creation results in a NULL value, and this must be checked.

Everybody Scope

The Application object is a built-in object that has global ASP application scope. Each client that establishes a unique Session object will be able to see the same Application object. The purpose of the Application object is to share data and information among the individual clients. Because the object has Application scope, the problem of variable corruption exists. The methods Lock and Unlock must be used to solve this problem. Setting a variable to the Application object is the same as setting a variable to the Session object. Here's an example:

```
<%
Application.Lock();
Application("AValue") = "something";
Application.UnLock();
%>
```

The only additions are the Lock and Unlock method calls. A Lock call locks the entire Application object and provides synchronization. This means only one user may access the Application object. If the page is referenced by many concurrent users, scalability will be hampered. This is because the others must wait while the user modifies the value. The key is to use this sparingly and quickly. When Lock is called without an Unlock method call, Unlock will be called after the page has finished processing.

Setting and Resetting the State

Using Session-level and Application-level objects is okay, but you need to know how to set the correct initial values. Each application has a global.asa file. The global.asa file is located in the root of the virtual directory of the ASP application. This file can contain up to four events, as follows:

```
function Session_OnStart() {
}
function Session_OnEnd() {
}

function Application_OnStart() {
}
function Application_OnEnd() {
}
```

The order of the events is as follows:

1. The Web server is started.
2. Client requests an ASP page for the first time.
3. The `Application_OnStart` event is processed.
4. The `Session_OnStart` event is processed for the user.

None of these events is triggered if an HTM or HTML page is referenced. The page referenced must be an .ASP page.

The `Session_OnEnd` event is called when the user is removed from the Web Application. This can occur in two ways. The first is if the Session or User timeout transpires. The second is if an ASP page calls Session.Abandon. This invokes only the `Session_OnEnd` event.

Logically, it would seem that the `Application_OnEnd` event should be invoked when all users have been removed. However, practically this is not the case. The `Application_OnEnd` event is triggered only when the server is shut down (as of the time of this writing).

When you're writing code within the `global.asa` file, you need to be concerned with timeouts, because if the ASP is combined with a SQL query, a timeout conflict can occur. Doing the math, if a script has a timeout value of 90 seconds and the SQL query has a 45-second timeout, then in the 46th second, any access to the SQL query will result in an error.

Built-in ASP Objects

Beyond the built-in `Application` and `Session` objects, there are five other built-in objects. These objects provide the mechanism that can be used to interact with ASP. For example, Figure 23.1 shows that there are a request stream and a response stream. Therefore, there are two built-in ASP objects called `Request` and `Response`. Here are the formal definitions of the other ASP objects:

- `ASPError`. This is a new object introduced with IIS 5.0. It provides the ability to retrieve an error that has been generated within the ASP execution context.
- `ObjectContext`. This object makes it possible to interact with the transaction context when the ASP page is executed.
- `Request`. This object represents the incoming stream and contains information about the request. It also contains information about the incoming parameters, cookies, and client-side certificates.

- `Response`. This object represents the outgoing stream. Here, you can define HTTP headers, create a buffer for delayed sending, and work with other HTTP items.

- `Server`. This is a simple utility object that's used to instantiate other COM objects. These COM objects can be used to enhance the functionality of ASP scripts.

Building a Web Application

Because of the state requirements, building a Web application can seem to be in conflict with building COM+ components, but that's not the case. Therefore, before the aspects of building components are discussed, this section will outline the framework for building Web applications. A framework is needed to keep code maintenance from becoming a nightmare.

Every Web application has a main page. Consider the following main page in Figure 23.2.

FIGURE 23.2

A sample Web application.

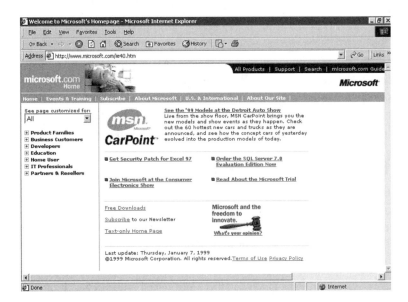

Looking closely on this page, you will see three sections: Banner (along the top of the page), Navigation (along the left side of the page), and Meat (the rest of the page). They are explained as follows:

- *Banner*. This usually appears at the top of the Web page. It can also appear at the bottom of the Web page, but it's more effective at the top. The banner is an application definition section. For example, if you're in the root application, the banner may be blue. If you're in the support section, it may be yellow. General navigation may be available, but it's not needed. The banner may also contain advertisements. In general, the banner is simply a section of a Web page that makes the page look nicer.

- *Navigation*. This is a section of a Web page that traditionally appears on the left. However, it can also be found on the right. This section contains the navigation tools available in the Web page. The navigation method is typically a series of nodes. For example, it could be a text box with a button that executes some action.

- *Meat*. This section appears in the remaining area. It contains the main information the user is actually interested in. This section should not be too long. The less the user has to scroll, the easier the Web page is to read.

The three-section approach is realized using HTML frames for each section. But there is an issue with frames: Many people object to them because they make for a more difficult end-user experience. In fact, this is true only if the end user attempts to print the page. This is because when you print, you need to specifically tell which section to print. And more often than not, you will end up printing the banner or the navigation section.

This to me is not an excuse. The reason is that a non-frame approach makes for more-difficult coding and more maintenance problems. This is because all the code is thrown onto one page. A compromise would be to offer a printing page on your Web site for information that may be printed.

Understanding Web Activities

When building an application, you need to outline a business process. Consider the diagram shown in Figure 23.3.

23

USING COM+ WITH THE IIS

FIGURE 23.3

A sample business decision diagram.

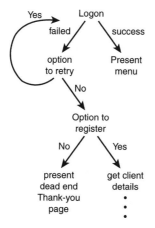

In this process, the user is logged on. The process of logging on involves a series of steps and decisions at various nodes (also called *operations*). These operations must occur sequentially. For example, the node registration of a client can be reached only if the logon attempt fails. This is a task-navigation concept.

Now consider the sample business decision shown in Figure 23.4—in the context of a Web application. It does not work because browsers can bookmark any operation and jump to it directly. This means that there may not be a context based on some previous operation. Without a context, presenting the material becomes increasingly difficult. It could be argued that a Web page does have a starting point—the root directory. However, this really isn't true because a starting point is purely optional and can easily be overridden.

Defining Some Theory

To build a clean Web application, you need to identify the activities. Is this activity the same as an activity from the COM+ services? The answer is yes. However, there's an extra dimension. In the COM+ activity, the state is only kept within it. There's no discussion on how the activity, as defined in the previous COM+ chapters, was started.

Look at Figure 23.4. The logon routines have been encapsulated into two activities: The first is a logon activity, and the second is a registration activity. Once the logon activity has been cleared, the main operations activity can be started.

FIGURE 23.4

An improved business decision diagram.

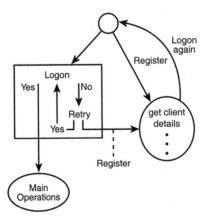

The individual activities make up a transaction. However, to get to the activities, you must define an extra step of dependencies. For example, to get to the main operations activity, you need to pass the logon activity. The registration activity can be accessed from the root action or from a failed logon activity. However, the registration activity cannot be used to access the main operations activity. This is a dependency definition.

Between the various activities, a context must be kept. This context defines which activities have been cleared; it has nothing to do with transaction or COM+ contexts. Some argue that this is not a good thing, because it requires more resources. This is true, but with an efficient context design, it becomes simpler to build Web applications.

Types of Web Activities

Web activity design can be classified in five general categories:

- *Information.* This is the simplest type of activity. It's a read-only operation that can be password protected, database driven, or use static pages. It's *informational* because the global key has no impact on how the data is generated or displayed. When this information is being generated, it can either be used with ASP directly or call a component. This type of task is a one-to-many distribution mechanism. An example would be the display of news or corporate pages.

- *Need to know.* This is a read-only activity, like the information activity, but it's dependent on the global key. When the page content is generated, it considers the global key and then potentially shows unique content for each global key. An example would be the displaying of a paycheck, which is unique for each person.

- *Application.* This is an input/output activity. It's dependent on the global key and displays information that directly correlates with the global key. When data is input, the global key is required to correlate the data being saved to the user. A key characteristic of this task is that it uses components for its input/output operations. An example would be a registration system, which allows the editing of attendee details by the attendee.

- *Anonymous.* This is an input/output activity, but it does not require a global key. The difference between this and the application task is that there's no global key. This does not mean that the `Session` object is not used. The `Session` object may still be used, but only to determine that the current user is the same user. An example would be an attendee who's registering for a conference, but the details are filled out once and never seen again on the Web site.

- *Add-on.* There are activities that do not fall into any of the preceding categories. They may or may not require a global key. These tasks might not even be Web based. The point of these tasks is to perform certain other tasks that are not part of the main business process. Code may have to be written and some parts of other tasks may be reused, but they stand alone. Examples are data backups, database-filling operations, and system maintenance.

23

USING COM+
WITH THE IIS

Why the various activities? By being able to distinguish the various types of activities, you can define dependencies to the task. In the logon example, the registration activity is anonymous. This makes it possible to place the registration almost anywhere in the process flow. The logon activity is anonymous as well. However, the main operations activity can be either need-to-know or application. This means the dependency of the global key needs to be defined. Being able to split the activities makes it possible for you to build modular, reusable Web applications.

Implementing the Theory

The preceding activity technique cannot be enforced and is purely optional. However, by using it, your application development is much simpler. The rest of this chapter focuses on the implementation of activities and some common ASP tasks.

Processing HTML Forms

The most common operation in a Web application is the processing of Web forms. To do this, you use a `Request` object to retrieve the information about the form.

The `QueryString` and `Form` collections perform the same function but are used in different situations. For example, consider the following HTML form:

```
<HTML>
<HEAD>
<META NAME="GENERATOR" Content="Microsoft Visual Studio 6.0">
<TITLE></TITLE>
</HEAD>
<BODY>
<form action=formProc.asp method=post>
<br>Field 1: <INPUT type="text" id=txtField1 name=txtField1>
<br>Field 2: <INPUT type="text" id=txtField2 name=txtField2>
<INPUT type="submit" value="Submit" id=submit1 name=submit1>
</form>
</BODY>
</HTML>
```

In this HTML form, the action involves the ASP page `formProc.asp`. The method is of the type `POST`. In HTTP, it's possible to pass parameters from the client to the server using `POST` or `GET`. The difference between the two is where the parameters are located in the HTTP header. Also, `POST` can handle larger amounts of data (which can even be binary). The `GET` method can handle only regular HTML form parameters. In this sample ASP page, you'll want to read the value of the fields txtField1 and txtField2.

> **TIP**
>
> There's something strange about the INPUT tags. There are two attributes, ID and NAME, and both have the same name. Why? The answer is because of DHTML. In DHTML, to be able to reference an element using a name, you must include an ID attribute. However, for legacy purposes, the NAME attribute has been kept because the form-processing functionality requires it. Therefore, you need to keep both attributes and label them the same.

Here's the formproc.asp page:

```
<%@ Language=Javascript %>
<HTML>
<HEAD>
<META NAME="GENERATOR" Content="Microsoft Visual Studio 6.0">
</HEAD>
<BODY>

<p>Form collection
<br>Field 1: <%=Request.Form("txtField1")%>
<br>Field 2: <%=Request.Form("txtField2")%>
</p>

<p>Querystring collection
<br>Field 1: <%=Request.QueryString("txtField1")%>
<br>Field 2: <%=Request.QueryString("txtField2")%>
</p>

<p>Full collection
<br>Field 1: <%=Request("txtField1")%>
<br>Field 2: <%=Request("txtField2")%>
</p>

</BODY>
</HTML>
```

This ASP page contains three code blocks. The first block retrieves the values using Request.Form. This method retrieves a value as per the passed-in value from the POST collection. The second code block retrieves the values using Request.QueryString. This method retrieves the value as per the parameter from the GET collection. The last code block retrieves the parameter from any of the five collections, including POST and GET.

In the form code segment, the POST method was used; therefore, the output will look like this:

```
Form collection

Field 1: sdf

Field 2: df

Querystring collection

Field 1:

Field 2:

Either collection

Field 1: sdf

Field 2: df
```

If the form method is changed to method=GET, the following output will be generated:

```
Form collection

Field 1:

Field 2:

Querystring collection

Field 1: sdfsdf

Field 2: sdsdfsdf

Either collection

Field 1: sdfsdf

Field 2: sdsdfsdf
```

Managing Cookies

To store persistent information without using a Session or Application object, you need to use cookies. You can access the cookie from the Request collection. For example, the following code iterates through all the available cookies:

```
<%@ Language=Javascript %>
<%Response.Cookies("Something") = "something";%>
<HTML>
```

```
<HEAD>
<META NAME="GENERATOR" Content="Microsoft Visual Studio 6.0">
</HEAD>
<BODY>

<h1>Cookie enumeration</h1>
<%
var cookieCollection = new Enumerator( Request.Cookies);

while( ! cookieCollection.atEnd()) {
    var aCookie = cookieCollection.item();
    cookieCollection.moveNext();
%>
<br>Value is <%=aCookie.toString()%>
<%
}
%>
</BODY>
</HTML>
```

All collections can be iterated through using the JavaScript Enumerator object. This object does not have a Count property. It can iterate through a collection only in a forward direction (moveNext). During this process, it can move back to the beginning (moveFirst). To check whether you're at the end the method, you can use atEnd. Finally, to retrieve the item, the method item is used. The object that's returned is of the type within the collection. If there is no item or an empty collection exists, the JavaScript undefined value is returned.

Creating Cookies

To send a cookie to the client, you use the Response.Cookie collection. The simplest way of sending a cookie is as follows:

```
<%@ Language=JavaScript %>
<%Response.Cookies("someCookie") = "Hello world";%>
<HTML>
```

This creates a cookie that's valid only for the life of the browser. When the browser is closed, the cookie disappears. There's no time limit for the cookie. These attributes are defined using the following notation:

```
<%@ Language=Javascript %>
<%
    Response.Cookies("SomeCookie") = "Some other cookie";
    Response.Cookies("SomeCookie").Expires = "July 7, 1999";
    Response.Cookies("SomeCookie").Path = "/";
%>
<HTML>
```

In this example, the cookie has a set path for which it's valid and an expiration date. The path defines when the cookie is sent from the client to the server. If the cookie is outside the URL, it isn't sent. The expires attribute creates a persistent cookie, even if the browser is closed.

To Keep a Cookie or Not

Cookies are, at times, controversial. Some say they're good and some say they're bad. The reason for cookies is simple. When the original HTTP protocol was developed, it was considered stateless. Although this may seem like a good thing considering our sample transaction-processing system, it really isn't. The real problem is that the statelessness is per request. For example, when a request for a page is made, the page is served and the connection is terminated. Therefore, unless the full transaction runs in one HTTP request, it becomes very tedious. For every request, a context has to be created. ASP uses cookies to identify the user and build a Session object. A *cookie* is a simple token used to identify the user. It's text based and does not execute any code. Therefore, a cookie is not bad, because it does not know anything but the context on a specific server.

A problem that needs to be discussed is what happens if the cookie was not accepted. This can happen if the browser does not accept cookies or the user of the browser simply does not accept the cookie. For example, Microsoft Internet Explorer allows the user to decline acceptance of a cookie. A more critical situation is when a system administrator has turned off the ability to keep Session objects. This presents a problem because it means keeping the state is not possible. In this case, you need an alternate plan and a way of determining whether the browser can support it without causing havoc. The following code shows how to test for cookies.

```
<%@ LANGUAGE="VBSCRIPT" %>
<HTML>
<HEAD>
<META NAME="GENERATOR" Content="Microsoft Visual InterDev 1.0">
<META HTTP-EQUIV="Content-Type" content="text/html; charset=iso-8859-1">
<META HTTP-EQUIV="REFRESH" CONTENT="5; URL=hellotest.asp">
<TITLE>Document Title</TITLE>
</HEAD>
<BODY>
<H1>Hello</H1>
<%
On Error Resume Next
Session("TestBrowser")="Hello"
On Error Goto 0
%>
</BODY>
</HTML>
hello.asp
<%@ LANGUAGE="VBSCRIPT" %>
```

```
<%
On Error Resume Next
if IsEmpty(Session("TestBrowser")) true then
Response.Redirect "helloNoCookie.asp"
Else
Response.Redirect "helloAllowCookie.asp"
End if
On Error Goto 0
%>
<HTML>
<HEAD>
<META NAME="GENERATOR" Content="Microsoft Visual InterDev 1.0">
<META HTTP-EQUIV="Content-Type" content="text/html; charset=iso-8859-1">
<TITLE>Document Title</TITLE>
</HEAD>
<BODY>
<H1>Hello</H1>
</BODY>
</HTML>
```

These code segments represent two valid HTML pages. The `hello.asp` page is the first one called. If your HTTP server uses `default.asp` as its default page, then you should rename `hello.asp`. `Hello.asp` is a sort of splash screen. When the page is loaded, it outputs `Hello`. For your situation, it could be your corporate logo. Below the Hello message is a bit of code that assigns the `Session("TestBrowser")` variable to some value. The value does not really matter. Because we're dealing with the unknown, `On Error Resume Next` is a necessity. Otherwise, a runtime error will be generated and the system will not continue processing the page. The key to this page is the `<META HTTP-EQUIV="REFRESH" CONTENT="5; URL=hellotest.asp">` tag. After the page has finished loading, it waits five seconds and loads the page that will test the value of the `Session("TestBrowser")` variable. If the cookie for the `Session` object is not accepted under any circumstances, the `hellotest.asp` page should be able to determine this right away. Looking at the next code segment that represents `hellotest.asp`, you can see that the magic is in the header. The `if IsEmpty( Session("TestBrowser"))` then statement checks to see whether the variable exists. You cannot perform a direct check here because it would immediately register an error. If the variable is empty, the cookie cannot be set—for example, the browser does not, for one reason or another, have the ability to set the cookie. If the `if` statement proves true, the client is redirected to a page that's intended for a non-`Session` ASP page; otherwise, its business as usual. It's necessary to wrap the `if` statement in another `On Error Resume Next` in case the `IsEmpty` test fails. Even if the test fails, the next statement is within the `if` and the end effect of being directed to a page for non-`Session` capability is achieved. The key to this trick is to make the `hello.asp` page appear as close as possible to a splash screen. Only then will the client not be misled into believing something isn't correct.

ServerVariables **Collection**

The last collection to discuss is the ServerVariables collection. In the early days of Web servers, this collection was used to identify the server and client environment and provide access to the HTTP headers sent by the client. Now there are more settings, because of evolution and the Microsoft framework. There are many different headers. The following code retrieves all HTTP headers sent by the client:

```
<%@ Language=Javascript %>
<HTML>
<HEAD>
<META NAME="GENERATOR" Content="Microsoft Visual Studio 6.0">
</HEAD>
<BODY>

<p><%=Request.ServerVariables("ALL_HTTP")%></p>
</BODY>
</HTML>
```

The preceding code returns this:

```
HTTP_ACCEPT:image/gif, image/x-xbitmap, image/jpeg, image/pjpeg,
application/vnd.ms-excel, application/msword,
application/vnd.ms-powerpoint, */*
HTTP_ACCEPT_LANGUAGE:en-us
HTTP_CONNECTION:Keep-Alive
HTTP_HOST:athena
HTTP_USER_AGENT:Mozilla/4.0 (compatible; MSIE 4.01; Windows NT)
HTTP_COOKIE:Something=something;
SPSESSIONIDGQQGQQAA=DHLDDJGAHGFHLNHMLMNDABOO
HTTP_ACCEPT_ENCODING:gzip, deflate
```

This information is important because it tells you a few things about the client. For example, you can see that the client is using a browser based on the language "en-us." In a multilanguage Web site, this would make it possible to send English content. You can also see that the user is using Internet Explorer version 4.01 on Windows NT.

These headers are not the raw headers. The raw headers do not have the HTTP_ part. This means that if a client sends the HTTP header

```
MyContent: Hey folks
```

you can access it as follows:

```
<%=Request.ServerVariable("HTTP_MyContent")%>
```

There are other headers that can be retrieved. The full list is available in the Microsoft documentation. These values pertain to security certificates, server information, and so on.

Handling ASP Errors

IIS 5.0 introduces the ability to catch ASP errors yourself. In previous versions, you would receive error messages on the Web page showing the error. However, these errors were terse and referenced numbers that nobody understood. This has changed with the ASP error. It makes it possible to figure out what the error is trying to tell using strings, and is retrieved using `Server.ErrorObject`. The following section discusses how you catch an error on a Web page.

Handling the 500-100 Error

With IIS 5.0, you can handle the custom error 500 value 100. This error is an HTTP error that says the server has caught an unhandled exception and therefore cannot continue processing this request. This error is called up whenever compilation faults, preprocessing faults, or runtime errors occur.

Using the IIS snap-in, you can handle this error via another ASP page. When that page is called, the `ASPError` object is activated and can be handled as follows:

```
<%@ Language=JavaScript %>
<HTML>
<HEAD>
<META NAME="GENERATOR" Content="Microsoft Visual Studio 6.0">
</HEAD>
<BODY>
The Error is ( <%=Server.GetLastError().Source()%>)
</BODY>
</HTML>
```

This page is called up using a `Server.Transfer` method; therefore, all the `Session` information will be available.

Using Exception Handling

IIS 5.0 uses JScript 5.0, which introduces exception handling. Using exception handling, you can trap an error and display it. Consider the following example:

```
<%@ Language=JavaScript %>
<HTML>
<HEAD>
<META NAME="GENERATOR" Content="Microsoft Visual Studio 6.0">
</HEAD>
<BODY>
<%
try {
    if( something == nothing) then
} catch( e) {
%>
```

```
    Error is ( <%=Server.GetLastError().ASPDescription()%>)
<%
}
%>
</BODY>
</HTML>
```

This example contains a JScript syntax fault. The keyword `then` exists only in VBScript. This will cause a fault in JScript. You can capture the error using the `try...catch` exception block. Then, using `Server.GetLastError`, you can access the `ASPError` object.

The `ASPError` object has the following properties:

- `ASPCode`. Error code generated by IIS 5.0.
- `Number`. When a COM object generates an error, it contains the COM error number.
- `Source`. Indicates who generated the error—IIS, scripting, or a COM object.
- `FileName`. The name of the ASP file that generated the error.
- `LineNumber`. The line number in the ASP file where the error was generated.
- `Description`. A description of the error.
- `ASPDescription`. The IIS error string.

Defining a Global Key

Moving from activity to activity creates a context, called a *global key*. A global key can be a simple number or a complex COM object. Using a number is fine because it's very small and lightweight. The number could be a key within the database.

If you use a COM object, you should assume that the COM object will live for a long time. It should not support deactivation because that would invalidate the global key. The COM object should have a small memory footprint because thousands of instances of the COM object could potentially be created.

When looking for a global key, you should use the most efficient one. For many online applications, you would typically use the email address. This is usually unique and easy to debug. However, don't think that only *one* global key is necessarily needed. There can be multiple keys, depending on the task being done.

A Global Key Example

Here's an example of defining a global key (in this case, the user ID):

```
function Session_onStart() {
Session("userId") = -1;
}
```

This global key is a numeric value, because within the database, the value is used to identify the user. Notice that ID is set to -1, which indicates that the user is invalid.

Global Keys and Web Farms

When developing Web applications that run on a Web farm, you cannot maintain a global key. When a user accesses a Web site, the Web farm redirects the request to a server that can process it the quickest. The point of a Web farm is to load-balance the Web request. You cannot perform load balancing using a Session object, because the Session object information is specific to a Web server. Therefore, when in a Web farm, the user must always be redirected to the correct Web server.

If, however, load balancing is desired, the solution is to store the key on the client side using cookies. For example, the following solution could be used:

```
function Session_OnStart() {
Response.Cookies("userid") = 111;
}
```

Here, the key is stored in a cookie. It's important that the information stored in the cookie is not critical information, because it's stored as clear text. If it's important that the information not be readable, you can use encryption to store the information. If you want to store binary information within a cookie, the buffer should be UUEncoded. *UUEncoding* is the process of converting a binary buffer into an ASCII buffer. To read this cookie, you would use the following ASP code:

```
<p>Key is (<%=Request.Cookies("userid")%>)</p>
```

Grouping of Activities

The ability to define activities on an abstract level is desirable. The objective is to define them in terms of ASP applications. Within ASP, there are three possible groupings:

- *ASP application.* A complete set of pages will be grouped as an ASP application. Within the application are subfolders (pages that define one activity). A typical activity would be information, because it doesn't need a context.

- *Subfolder.* ASP applications cannot share session variables; therefore, multiple tasks must be placed within one subfolder. Creating a subfolder can do this. It's not advisable that you put all your tasks into the root application folder because this could complicate the maintenance of the various tasks as well as make them harder to understand.

- *Naming.* Two different naming techniques are followed. The first is used when all Web pages have been put into a directory that represents the activity. Typically, in an input/output type activity, there's a form and the processing of that form. Here's an example:

```
form: myForm.asp
processing of the form: processingTheForm.asp
```

This is okay, but it introduces a problem when there are 10 files within the directory. Which form processes which page? Opening the page and checking the form tag could show you the answer, but this is an extra step, which can become tedious. Here's a better solution:

```
form: myForm.asp
processing of the form: myFormProc. asp
```

This situation is easy to understand because of Proc added at the end of the filename. Proc is added because in Project view, the two files will be located next to each other.

When a form can be displayed in multiple ways, this should be added to myForm.asp as a big if statement. If, however, this appears to be messy, then myFormProc has to be labeled as something meaningful. The Proc at the end should remain.

In the second scenario, multiple tasks are placed within one directory. The naming of pages within the same task should carry the same prefix. Again, using this method, the files appear as one group within the Project view of Visual InterDev.

Enforcing Order

The big problem with Web pages is that any Web page can be referenced. This means an activity can be started without a context. The solution to this problem is to enforce order by using application-flow restrictions. Order can be enforced in various ways, as shown in Figure 23.5.

FIGURE 23.5
Various application-order techniques.

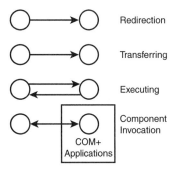

Redirection

Transferring

Executing

Component Invocation

COM+ Applications

These four different redirections make it possible to return to the client-specific content, even though they did not request it formally. This makes it possible to enforce the order.

Automatic Client-side Redirection

The simplest method of redirection is to use client-side redirection, which is started by the server. In the example of the main operations activity, being logged on is a dependency. The sample main operations page (`MainOperationDefault.asp`) would look like this:

```
<%@ Language=JavaScript %>
<%    if( Session("userId") == -1) {
         Response.Redirect( "../Logon/Default.asp");
      }%>
<HTML>
```

If the user ID is `-1`, the user is redirected using `Response.Redirect` to the `../logon/default.asp` page. In this example, the logon activity has been added as a subfolder to the main project. The double dot indicates relative notation, which assumes that all other activities are "subprojects" of the main project. The advantage of doing this is that the activity can be reused.

This may seem like a server-side redirection, but, in fact, it's a client-side redirection. This is illustrated in Figure 23.6.

FIGURE 23.6

A server causing a client-side redirection.

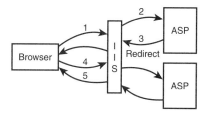

The steps are as follows:

1. An HTTP request is made by the client.
2. The HTTP request is converted into an ASP request.
3. ASP realizes that order is not enforced and sends back a client redirection in the form of a URL, which is propagated to the client.
4. The client browser comprehends this and automatically issues another request using the returned URL.

   Again the request is converted into an ASP request.
5. Content is sent back to the client.

The `Response.Redirect` method sends an HTTP redirect, which causes another client connection to be established. This type of redirection costs more bandwidth because it requires a second connection. The advantage is that the redirection can be to any location.

Automatic Redirection Within a Page

In the script shown by the preceding example, the `Response.Redirect` method call was placed at the top of the page. This is because content is sent as a stream back to the client. And from previous explanations, ASP script processing occurs from the top of the page to the bottom. If the method call were placed within the main script, an error would occur because the client has received some content and cannot in midstream load a new page.

Does this mean you can do redirection only at the top of a script page? No, to use the `Response.Redirect` method anywhere throughout the page, you will need to use the ASP buffering mechanism. Using the buffering mechanism, the stream content is buffered at the server until an explicit command sends the stream. This way it is possible to do a redirection in mid-page processing.

The previous example could be rewritten as this:

```
<%@ Language=JavaScript %>
<%Response.Buffer = true%>
<HTML>
<HEAD>
<META NAME="GENERATOR" Content="Microsoft Visual Studio 6.0">
</HEAD>
<BODY>

<%    if( Session( "userId") == -1) {
        Response.Redirect("../logon/default.asp");
    }%>

</BODY>
</HTML>
<%Response.End()%>
```

The first line sets `Response.Buffer` to `True`. This indicates that the stream should be buffered. Now, a `Response.Redirect` can be issued in midstream.

To send the content to the client, you can use either `Response.End` or `Response.Flush`. `Response.Flush` sends the content built up so far. If `Response.Flush` is called, you cannot call `Response.Redirect`. `Response.End` is similar to `Response.Flush`, except that it ends script processing. If you want to clear the content and then rebuild it, you can use `Response.Clear`. This resets the buffer.

Automatic/Informational

Another way of automatically redirecting a Web page is to use the HTTP `refresh` command, as follows:

```
<head>
<meta http-equiv="Content-Type"
      content="text/html; charset=iso-8859-1">
<meta name="GENERATOR" content="Microsoft FrontPage
      (Visual InterDev Edition) 2.0">
<META HTTP-EQUIV="REFRESH" CONTENT="5" url="nextstep.asp">
<title>Document Title</title>
</head>
```

In this example, the Web page is returned to the user and displayed. The META tag defines a `refresh` value of five seconds. This means that the current page is displayed for five seconds and then the page specified by the URL attribute is retrieved.

This sort of mechanism is ideal for displaying messages before the real page is displayed. Examples include a thank-you message for registering a program and an informational page regarding content.

Manual

The last sort of redirection is also the simplest. It involves using a hyperlink on a Web page that links to the next page. This type of redirection cannot be underestimated. An example would be an informational page that requires a confirmation. The confirmation would indicate that the user understands the process he or she is about to follow.

Automatic Server-side Redirection

With the introduction of Windows 2000, the intrinsic IIS COM objects have been extended to include server-side redirection. Server-side redirection is better than client-side redirection because it doesn't cause another connection to be built. Here's an example:

```
<%@ Language=JavaScript %>
<HTML>
<HEAD>
<META NAME="GENERATOR" Content="Microsoft Visual Studio 6.0">
</HEAD>
<BODY>
Logon process
<%    if( Session("userId") == -1) {
          Server.Transfer( "../logon/default.asp");
      }%>

</BODY>
</HTML>
```

The `Server.Transfer` method performs a redirection on the server side. Here are the advantages to using this method:

- The `Session` and `Application` information is transferred among the various applications. This means it extends beyond the boundaries of the current application.

- This method can occur midstream in the script-processing process; therefore, you don't need to build a buffer.

The big disadvantage to this method is that you cannot transfer the method to a Web server outside the current server.

Embedding an Activity

Sometimes redirection is not the best solution, such as when an activity needs to be embedded within another activity. To do this in IIS 5.0, you use a method called `Server.Execute`. This method has the same effect as making a module call. The advantage to using this method is that you can build a page incrementally. For example, in the previous frames example, you could build frames on the server side. This would involve three different calls to `Server.Execute`. It also provides absolute control regarding the context. Here's an example:

```
<%@ Language=JavaScript %>
<HTML>
<HEAD>
<META NAME="GENERATOR" Content="Microsoft Visual Studio 6.0">
</HEAD>
<BODY>
Logon process
<%    if( Session("userId") == -1) {
        Server.Execute( "../logon/default.asp");
    }%>

</BODY>
</HTML>
```

The output here will be identical to the output in the previous example, except the page is not redirected using Server.Execute.

Making It Simpler with JavaScript

The redirection process can be simplified in two ways. The first way is to write a COM object that manages the state and the step the task is at. The other (more interesting) way is to build a JavaScript object that manages the location and step automatically. Consider the following script:

```
<SCRIPT language=javascript runat=server>
function taskManager() {
```

```
this.isOk = _isOk;
this.writeOut = _writeOut;
this.atDefault = _atDefault;
this.resetState = _resetState;

Response.Buffer = true;
}

function _isOk( currStep) {
if( this.currentTask != getLocalApp()) {
Response.Redirect( Session("defaultPage"));
} else {
if( (Session("currentStep") + 1) == currStep) {
return true;
} else {
return false;
    }
  }
}

function _writeOut() {
Session("currentStep") = Session("currentStep") + 1;
Response.Flush();
}

function _atDefault() {
Session("currentTask") = getLocalApp();
Session("currentStep") = 0;
}

function getLocalApp() {
var location = new String( Request.ServerVariables("URL"));
var c1, first, second;
first = 0;
second = 0;
for( c1 = 0; c1 < location.length; c1 ++) {
if( location.charAt( c1) == "/") {
second = first;
first = c1;
    }
  }
return location.substring( second + 1, first);
}

function resetTask() {
Session("currentStep") = 0;
Session("currentTask") = "";
}

</script>
```

In JavaScript, the object is created using the function `taskManager` and then specifying the data members (`this.isOk`) and data methods (`this.writeOut`). The name of the class is the same as the name of the function—`taskManager`. The `taskManager` class is a wrapper to a series of `Session` variables—`currentTask` and `currentStep`. They keep track of where the user is currently. The `isOk` method retrieves the current local task from the URL and then compares it to the `Session("currentTask")` variable. If they do not match, the current page is redirected to the `Session("defaultPage")` default page. Otherwise, the current step is checked to make sure it's one greater than the last successfully finished page.

Here's how to implement this class in the `Session("defaultPage")` default page:

```
<%@ Language="javascript" %>
<!--#include file="../task.asp" -->
<%
var task = new taskManager;
task.atDefault();
%>
<HTML>
```

The JavaScript object is created using the new `taskManager` command. Because this is the default page, it's assumed that the current task is okay. This is because the `atDefault()` command will make sure the correct page is loaded and that the current task is executing.

Then, in each of the task-associated pages, the following code must be added:

```
<%@ Language="javascript" %>
<!--#include file="../task.asp" -->
<%
var task = new taskManager;
if( task.isOk( 1) == false) {

    }
%>
<HTML>
```

In this case, the method `task.isOk` is called. It checks to make sure the page can be called after the default page. If so, the method returns `True`. If it returns `False`, the page needs to handle the failure. An example would be to redirect to another page so that the task state could be made valid.

The Point of JavaScript Objects

The point of this sample object was not to show a foolproof way of developing a redirection—it lacks the dependency-enforcement steps needed for the solution to be complete. However, what it shows is how development can be object oriented within a scripting environment. Notice also how the files are included using the server-side `include` command `<!--#include ... -->`. The other aspect of the JavaScript object is that it has access to all the ASP server objects, such as `Response` and `Request`.

Is it recommended that you use JavaScript objects in your development processes? The answer is a definite yes. However, you should keep the development of these objects to the length of about what was shown in the redirection or a bit more. Let's put it this way: You do not want to write thousand-line scripts, because they will be slow and hard to maintain. Writing objects based in a scripting language is quicker than invoking the C++ environment and building full-blown objects. JavaScript objects cannot inherit and therefore are ill-suited for complex object-oriented development. They are best-suited for a shallow task simplification. When I use the term shallow, I mean development, which could be solved using macros. Scripting does not support macros, therefore objects are the applicable solution. For example, throughout the DevDays Web site, a series of database connections to retrieve user information was constantly used. This code was moved into an object, which makes it easier to write the code.

This ends our discussion of writing tasks and defining an architecture for Web applications. From here, we'll discuss content, component calling, and creation. Order is an important aspect of Web applications. This is especially true if the Web site will live beyond six months and pieces of it will be reused. Without order, it doesn't matter how clean and simple the components have been written; the Web application will become a nightmare with very obscure bugs.

A Simpler Way of Managing Objects

Creating objects using the `Server.CreateObject` notation can be a bit tedious because of the extra script code required. It's possible to write the following in the `global.asa` file:

```
<OBJECT SCOPE=Session RUNAT=server PROGID=Simple.Object id=MyObject>
</OBJECT>
```

In this example, the object is created when a session starts, as specified by the `SCOPE` attribute. This way of creating the object has an advantage in that it's simpler to reference the object, like this:

```
MyObject.someMethod( param1);
```

The `SCOPE` tag can also be `Application`, which means there will be only one instance of the object created. This is also called a *singleton*. If neither scope is specified and the text is embedded within a page, the object is created using page scope.

Cleaning Up the Objects

After an object has been created, you may want to remove the object from memory. Using the Remove method, you can specify an object and have it removed. Here's an example:

```
Session.Contents.Remove("someitem")
```

This method is not limited to objects—it can include numeric or string values.

If all the items need to be cleared, the method RemoveAll is used:

```
Session.Contents.RemoveAll()
```

Working with Binary Data

Handling large amounts of data requires extra effort within ASP. Using a POST method, you can upload megabytes of data to a server. Handling binary data on the server side cannot be accomplished using standard techniques.

Reading Binary Data

The method Request.BinaryRead needs to be used when you're reading binary data. Here's an example:

```
<%@ LANGUAGE="VBSCRIPT" %>
<%
Server.ScriptTimeout = 36000
PostSize = Request.TotalBytes

BytesRead = 0
For i = 1 to (PostSize/1024)
        ReadSize=1024
PostData = Request.BinaryRead(ReadSize)
BytesRead = BytesRead + ReadSize
Next

ReadSize=TotalBytes - BytesRead
If ReadSize <> 0 Then
PostData = Request.BinaryRead(ReadSize)
        BytesRead = BytesRead + ReadSize
End If

Response.Write BytesRead
Response.Write " bytes were read."
%>
```

Because a large POST can take quite a bit of time to execute, you need to change the timeout script (Server.ScriptTimeout). Otherwise, the script will time out before the information is uploaded. The next step is to determine how many bytes have been uploaded using the method `Request.TotalBytes`. Next, via a loop, you can read the bytes in packet sizes of 1KB (1,024 bytes) using `Request.BinaryRead`. This method asks for just one parameter, which specifies the number of bytes that can be retrieved. Returned is a variant that contains an array of single-byte values.

Writing Binary Data

The other task is writing binary data. This step is not more complicated, but it does require the additional step of defining what the data is. Consider the following example:

```
<%
Response.Buffer = true;
Response.ContentType = "image/gif";

var objBinary = Server.CreateObject("Example.BinaryObject");

Response.BinaryWrite( objBinary.binaryPicture);
Response.End();
%>
```

Keep in mind that if binary data is being sent, no other data can be sent. There's only one output stream, and when a commitment is made to send binary data, any other operations will cause stream corruption. To simplify the sending of the data, the first step is to create a buffer using `Response.Buffer = True`. Then, the binary data type needs to be specified using `Response.ContentType`. This is a MIME data type. If this is not specified, the client browser will assume the data is a text file and process it as such. In this case, the data is an image file.

The data is written to the stream using `Response.BinaryWrite`. It accepts only a single parameter—a variant array of single bytes. Finally, when all the binary data has been written, it can be sent using `Response.End`.

Writing Dynamic Code

You can write Web applications using ASP and Dynamic HTML in two ways. First, you can write the code in a normal programming environment. This means that the variables and modules are predetermined. The other way is to write applications using the dynamic nature of the Web.

Generating Code

One way of writing dynamic code is to separate the client-side and server-side data. Consider the following ASP code:

```
Here is some text (
<%
if( testValue == true) {
```

```
Response.Write( "My Success");
}
%>
)

<BR>
Here is some other text (
<%if( testValue == true) {%>
My success
<%}%>
)
```

Both methods produce the following output:

```
Here is some text (My Success)
```

The difference between the two is that the first output is created by an ASP built-in object. The second uses the inherent script-processing power.

In the first block, if the test is successful, the string is written using `Response.Write`. Using this mechanism, it's difficult for you to update the string with anything that contains HTML text because the passed-in data is a buffer that needs to be assembled. If the data needs to be assembled using a tool such as the Visual InterDev Designer, it's not possible, because the designer will not read the buffer.

The second solution has its advantages. When the page is scanned, the `if` block appears above and below the `My Success` string. On a programming level, the `My Success` HTML would be translated as a sort of super variable that needs to be sent to the client. This is a superior design method because this page can be scanned by the Visual InterDev Designer and modified to be any HTML. It's also easier to read because it makes a clear distinction between client-side code and server-side code. However, this involves many hours of development.

Dynamic Content Sizing

One thing that's very annoying about Web sites is that they're programmed to a certain size. If the Web browser client area is altered, the Web page does not adjust to fit the new screen area. The Web is not static; it is dynamic. The content has the ability to adjust itself to the surrounding environment. So, if dynamic Web pages are so much better, why the static trend? The answer is that it's easier to control the user experience with static pages. This is important because a bad Web site will create a bad experience. Solving this problem involves a multistep solution. The first step is to split the Web page into multiple sections, as per the original design.

The effect that's desired is that when the browser is widened, the text will adjust, but when the browser is narrowed, the text adjusts to a point. What you want to avoid is a situation where the browser is made so narrow that the user must constantly scroll to read your content. Here's the way to avoid this:

```
<table width="100%">
<tr>
    <td>
        <br><img src="images/1ptrans.gif" height="5"><br>
    </td>
</tr>
</table>
```

Here, a table is created at the full width of the screen. However, within one of the cells is a transparent image. The transparent image is the minimum width of the cell. The image could be a 1-pixel–high image. What the image does is force a toolbar to appear when the minimum size has been reached. At that point, the cell does not shrink, and the formatting appears "as is." When the cell is increased, the text automatically resizes itself.

The other desired effect is to be able to place controls and text at certain locations, even if the browser changes width. Consider the example shown in Figure 23.7.

FIGURE 23.7

Centering a control on a page.

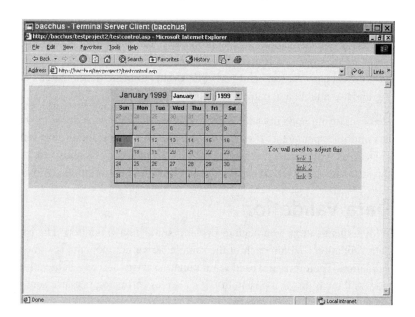

In this example, the calendar control is kept in the center of the Web page. The way to accomplish this is to use the HTML span and table tags, like this:

```
<span style="BACKGROUND: lawngreen; WIDTH: 62%">
<table width="100%" border=0>
```

23

**USING COM+
WITH THE IIS**

```
<tr>
<td align=right >
<OBJECT classid=clsid:B0FD63A1-F41D-11D1-A555-00C04F94E891
height=178 width=210>
</OBJECT>
</td>
</tr>
</table>
</span>
<span style="BACKGROUND: lawngreen; WIDTH: 33%">
<p>
<center>You will need to adjust this</center>
<center><a href="something" class=Item id=link1>link 1</a></center>
<center><a href="something" class=Item id=link2>link 2</a></center>
<center><a href="something" class=Item id=link3>link 3</a></center>
</P>
</span>
```

There are two span areas. One has a width of 62 percent, and the other has a width of 33 percent. If the span areas are followed with a BR tag, then both are placed at the same level. When the browser is resized, the span areas are automatically realigned. The purpose of the span areas is to create regions where content can be placed. In this example, one region contains a table where the calendar control is aligned to the right. In the other region a series of hyperlinks appears. Why use the span areas and not a table—wouldn't both achieve the same thing? The problem is that when elements are placed within a table and then updated dynamically, it causes flicker. The hyperlinks in the other region have the mouse "roll-on" and "roll-off" events to make them switch colors. Color switching updates a table and causes a flicker.

However, using span does have its problems, as well. Consider some other content that has multiple span areas. If one of those span areas does not allow a minimum sizing, the span areas will realign themselves on two separate regions above each other. To avoid this, use the one-pixel, transparent-image trick and a minimum size will be enforced.

Data Validation

With authentication, you need to perform some data validation. The issue is, how much data validation? Within each of the sample server components is some amount of data validation. Therefore, it would seem unnecessary to add any data validation on the client side. Although this is a possibility, it's also less efficient, because sending data from the client to the server uses bandwidth. It makes more sense to add some preliminary data validation. Typically, the checks are empty fields or really simple business process rules. One of the most efficient ways of adding a data validation rule is as follows:

```
<script language=javascript runat=server>
function ProcessUpdate( form) {
```

```
var dispString = "";
if( form.optSex.value == "") {
dispString += "\nHerr oder Frau";
    }
if( form.txtFirstName.value == "") {
dispString += "\nVornamen";
    }
if( form.txtLastName.value == "") {
dispString += "\nNamen";
    }
if( form.txtPostCode.value == "") {
dispString += "\nPLZ";
} else {
var tempString = new String( form.txtPostCode.value);
if( tempString.length > 5 || tempString.length < 4) {
dispString += "\nPLZ ist inkorrect";
        }
    }
if( form.txtCity.value == "") {
dispString += "\nStadt";
    }
if( form.txtStreet.value == "") {
dispString += "\nStrasse";
    }
if( form.txtTelephone.value == "") {
dispString += "\nTelefonnummer";
    }
if( form.optCountry.value == "") {
dispString += "\nLand";
    }
if( dispString != "") {
window.alert( "Die Inhalte der folgenden Felder sind fehlerhaft:"
      + dispString);
} else {
form.submit();
    }

}
</script>
...
<input type="button" value="Continue" name="cmdUpdate"
      onClick="ProcessUpdate( this.form);">
...
```

23

USING COM+
WITH THE IIS

This Web page has a form, and looking at the bottom of the source, you'll see a submit button. The submit button is not of the type Submit but of the type button. This makes the form a bit simpler. When the button is clicked, the method ProcessUpdate is called. Passed in is the form that needs to be validated. This decision was chosen because non-DHTML browsers cannot cope with direct referencing of the form on the Web page. In the `ProcessUpdate` function, the first declaration is a string called `dispString` . This string is the error string. The next set of statements is a series of `if` statements. They check to make sure the various form field elements are not empty. If one of them is empty, the error is added to the `dispString`. Notice the occurrence of \n at the beginning of the string. This puts all the errors on their own lines and makes for a cleaner appearance. Look at the code piece `var tempString = new String` . This is an example of going beyond the simple empty field check. It checks to make sure that the entered `postal code` has a length of four or five characters. This represents a valid German, Austrian, or Swiss postcode. After all the checks have been called, the last test is to see whether `dispString != ""` is true. If it contains something, one of the validations has failed and should be displayed. If `dispString` is still empty, `form.submit` is called, and the data is sent to the server for further processing.

There are other ways of performing data validation, but this technique serves our purpose because it's simple and easy to debug. Another reason for using this script "as is" is that it's compatible with DHTML as well as with HTML 3.2. This reduces the number of scripts that need to be written.

Another question that arises with data validation is how to indicate to the user that certain fields must be filled out and certain others must not. The typical solution is to add an asterisk beside the field name and indicate that it's a required field. This is okay, but two better solutions exist. The first solution is compatible with HTML 3.2 and DHTML:

```
<td width="20%" height="30">
PLZ, Stadt
</td>
<td width="50%" height="30">
<input type="text" name="txtPostCode" value="" size="5">
<img src="images/required.gif" border=0>
</td>
```

In this solution, the name of the field is given in the first field, `<td>`. In the second field is the `<input>` field and than an image, `<img>`. This image is a red arrow that indicates the field must be filled out. This is more attractive than the asterisk because it looks better visually.

If the browser application is destined to be run in a DHTML-compatible browser, then a cleaner solution would be as follows:

```
<td width="20%" height="30">
PLZ, Stadt
</td>
<td width="50%" height="30">
<input type="text" name="txtPostCode" value="" size="5"
style=BACKGROUND_COLOR: yellow>
</td>
```

In this example, instead of using an image, color is used to indicate the required fields. This is accomplished by using the style effect of the input element. In this case, the background color is set to yellow. The color can be anything that you choose, but yellow, light green, and light cobalt blue are the best choices. They do not distract, yet they indicate that something is different. There's one catch though. You need to use a color that creates a contrast, because users who are colorblind need to be able to see the contrast in colors. However, if you want to be on the safe side, you should use the image as an indicator.

Downloading Files

A very common task is the batch creation of a file that, at some later point in time, needs to be downloaded. The only catch is that it must be either hidden or specific to a user and hidden. For example, consider the situation of a registered user accessing a licensed copy of the file. If this file were in the virtual directory, any user who knows this directory could access the file, because the ASP security checks apply only if the file is an ASP file. There are other script tricks to get around this, but it becomes complicated. However, a free component is available that allows for the downloading of files anywhere on the server. Consider the following source code example:

```
<%@  Language=JavaScript %>
<%
var currFile;
currFile = Server.CreateObject("ASPFserv.Download");
currFile.ContentType = "application/x-zip-compressed";
currFile.GetFile("D:\\work\\enterpriseVC\\docs.zip");
%>
<HTML>
```

This source code is placed at the top of the file. The freeware component ASPFserv.Download is instantiated and then assigned to the variable currFile. Because of the way this component works, any HTML on the page does not get processed. The file SimpleDownload.asp is a byte stream that represents the file being downloaded. The name of the file that's downloaded is the name of the file where the script exists, without the extension .asp. The extension that's assigned is the MIME type or the currFile.ContentType. In this example, the MIME type is a zip file. Therefore, the extension .zip is added. The file that's downloaded is whatever currFile.GetFile is retrieving. Because the file can be anywhere on the server, it can be in a place that's not open to the Web server, or it can be generated dynamically on a per-user basis. Because of the way the component works, it can be used only at the page level and not at the Session or Application level.

Sending Email

When a person registers for a conference, a confirmation is often sent via email. This does two things. It validates that the email address given is valid, and it confirms that the user is part of the conference. Another reason for sending mail is to provide the user with his or her password when it's forgotten. Many different email products are available for sending email. Consider the following source code:

```
var objMail, sMessageText;
sMessageText = "Hello world";
sMessageText = sMessageText + "\n\rChristian Gross";
objMail = Server.CreateObject("ABMailer.Mailman");
Application.Lock();
objMail.Clear();
objMail.MailDate = "12/12/1998";
objMail.MailSubject = "Sample Greeting";
objMail.ReplyTo = "me@youremail.com";
objMail.SendTo = request("txtEmail");
objMail.ServerAddr = "mail.amberg.net";
objMail.ServerAddr = "194.2.23.98";
objMail.ServerPort = 25

objMail.MailMessage = sMessageText;
objMail.SendMail();
Application.Unlock();
```

In this example, the email to be sent is a "Hello World" example. The server component is instantiated by calling `Server.CreateObject("ABMailer.Mailman")`. This component is single-threaded and therefore can be accessed only by one client at a time. To synchronize mail access, `Application.Lock` is called. Now the mail message is cleared and a few attributes regarding the server address, port, and email address are specified. After all these things are done, the email is sent by calling `objMail.SendMail`.

Sending mail is simple if only standard text is sent. However, there are other options such as sending file attachments and sending data as HTML. In such cases, the task becomes more complicated. With this added complexity, a better mail component is needed. When mail is sent, it needs a relay server, which is typically the corporate mail server. However, you should make sure the administrator of that server knows you're sending email. With the advent of spamming, many email servers now do not allow for the relaying of large amounts of email.

Browser Capabilities

Consider the scenario of building an international Web site. Before you start, a few questions need to be answered. For example, which languages will this Web site support? Which browsers will it support? The answers to these two questions can make building a

Web site simple or complex. Will the Web site be written to support a basic functionality and therefore have limitations or will there be two Web sites written to support two different browsers/languages? There is no simple solution to these problems. However, in any solution that's implemented, the browser capabilities must be determined. By understanding what the browser is capable of, you can implement specific solutions without having intervention on behalf of the user. There are two capabilities that need to be tested: browser type and languages supported.

Browser Type

When a browser accesses a Web site, it gives its identity to the server. The token is given as an HTTP header. To get it, you could use the following code:

```
Request.ServerVariables( "HTTP_USER_AGENT")
```

This returns the type of browser. Here's an example:

```
Mozilla/4.0 (compatible; MSIE 4.01; Windows NT)
```

The string text starts off by defining which level of compatibility is supported—in this case, Mozilla level 4.0. (*Mozilla* is the nickname given to the Netscape browser.) However, because Internet Explorer supports more features (such as DHTML), more information is needed. For example, the browser type is MSIE 4.01, and it's currently running on the Windows NT platform. Using this information, you can build a specific Web site. Also, you can extrapolate whether the browser supports frames and DHTML.

Using this browser component, you can easily differentiate the major versions of browsers. Sometimes, however, smaller issues arise: Are frames supported? What about background sounds? Does the browser use Windows 16-bit code or is it a beta? Has a custom feature been introduced that changes whenever the browser changes? The point is that the details complicate the entire issue. The solution is to use a component that ships with the ASP framework. It's the browser capability component. Consider the following source code:

```
<%
var bc;
bc = Server.CreateObject("MSWC.BrowserType")
%>
<table border=1>
<tr>
<td>Browser</td>
<td> <%=bc.browser%></td></tr>
<tr>
<td>Version</td>
<td><%=bc.version%></td></TR>
<tr>
```

23

USING COM+
WITH THE IIS

```
<td>Frames</td>
<td><%=bc.Frames%></td></tr>
<tr>
<td>Tables</td>
<td><%=bc.Tables%></td></TR>
<tr>
<td>BackgroundSounds</td>
<td><%=bc.BackgroundSounds%></td></tr>
<tr>
<td>VBScript</td>
<td><%=bc.vbscript%></td></tr>
<tr>
<td>JScript</td>
<td><%=bc.javascript%></td></tr>
</tr>
<tr>
<td>My property</td>
<td><%=bc.myprop%></td>
</tr>
</table>
```

The server object that needs to be instantiated is MSWC.BrowserType. This object is unique in that when it's created, it attempts to cross-reference the HTTP_USER_AGENT value with a value within a file called browscap.ini. For example, the following code appears in this file:

```
[Mozilla/4.0 (compatible; MSIE 4.0; Windows NT)]
parent=IE 4.0
platform=WinNT
beta=False

[Mozilla/4.0 (compatible; MSIE 4.*)]
parent=IE 4.0
```

The format is similar to the format found in an INI file. There is a series of headers that are cross-referenced with the HTTP_USER_AGENT value string. After it has been found, the properties that are part of that heading identify what the browser is capable of. This means that you can build a database of features and associate it with a browser. The component is a bit more sophisticated, because it can combine certain features using an inheritance scheme. Consider the example of IE 4.0 and IE 4.01. They have some minor differences but share the same major feature set. Therefore, instead of adding all of the feature database twice in the browscap.ini file, you can define a parent. Now, take a look at the preceding browscap.ini file. You won't see IE 4.01 listed; instead, you'll see the IE 4.* wildcard. This version has the parent IE 4.0, which contains the following feature set:

```
[IE 4.0]
browser=IE
Version=4.0
```

```
majorver=4
minorver=0
frames=TRUE
myprop=something else
tables=TRUE
cookies=TRUE
backgroundsounds=TRUE
vbscript=TRUE
javascript=TRUE
javaapplets=TRUE
ActiveXControls=TRUE
Win16=False
beta=False
AK=False
SK=False
AOL=False
crawler=False
cdf=True
DHTML=TRUE
```

This feature set is much more complete. It states the version number type, the browser type, whether or not frames are supported, whether or not VBScript is supported, and much more. These features are properties that are directly accessible as COM properties. Now, going back to the first browser cap source code, you see various properties referenced. These properties match values in the above source code. The browser cap object has the ability to cross-reference the various values.

This makes the component very powerful because it can take on any properties as defined in the browscap.ini file. However, it also opens up errors—if this file is improperly defined, the programs that rely on its information may potentially fail.

It is possible now to build content that adjusts itself depending on the browser making the request. To do this properly, you would selectively generate content as shown in the following example:

```
<INPUT id=txtSample name=txtSample
<%if( bc.DHTML == true) { %>
style="BACKGROUND-COLOR: yellow"
<% }%>>
```

This example includes an input field. In the case, when the browser supports Dynamic HTML (DHTML == TRUE), the background color is changed to yellow. For any other browser, this feature is not included. The advantage of this component is readily apparent—it does not require the developer to know which browser is used but rather which features are supported. Here's the other example:

```
<%@ Language=javascript %>
<%
var bc;
```

23

USING COM+
WITH THE IIS

```
bc = Server.CreateObject("MSWC.BrowserType");
if( bc.DHTML == true) {
Response.Redirect( "/DHTMLVersion.asp");
}
%>
<HTML>
```

In this example, when the document is loaded, it checks to see whether the browser supports Dynamic HTML (DHTML == TRUE). If so, the user is redirected to another page that supports Dynamic HTML.

Languages Supported

The other case is to add elements that are language dependent. As the popularity of the Web increases, the number of Web users who do not speak English will increase. Therefore, the Web site must be localized. The traditional approach to multiple-language Web sites is to add flags for the individual languages and then let the user choose which language to use. This is okay, but it's not an optimal solution.

Instead, an optimal solution would be for the language to be chosen based on what the browser tells the server. Here's a way you can do this:

```
Request.ServerVariables("HTTP_ACCEPT_LANGUAGE");
```

The following setting is returned for American English:

```
en-us
```

This setting is returned for standard German:

```
de
```

Both Internet Explorer and Netscape Navigator support this feature. The language setting is not dependent on which browser is installed but rather on the settings for the computer. Therefore, if the regional settings (located in the Control Panel) are German, then de is returned. Content based on each language would be created in the same way as that shown for the browser, using either a piece-by-piece or a page redirection approach.

Building Web sites that support multiple languages, browsers, and/or technologies is not easy. However, it's worth the effort because it gives the Web site a much nicer look and feel. As a side note, when you're developing a site that contains a localized site, make sure you have someone helping who really understands the specific language. Using a translation service will not cut it, because each country uses modern lingo that's often overlooked.

Component Development

It's possible to write almost all your application code in script or to use JavaScript objects. However, sometimes it's more efficient to write using components. Components make it possible to encapsulate logic and simplify the development of ASP pages. Components also make it possible for the Web developers to focus on the user interface and for component developers to focus on business logic. Consider the following source code:

```
<%@ Language=Javascript %>
<HTML>
<HEAD>
<META NAME="GENERATOR" Content="Microsoft Visual Studio 6.0">
</HEAD>
<BODY>

<table border=1>
<%
var counter;
var c1;
counter = 0;
for( c1 = 0; c1 < 10; c1 ++) {
    counter = (counter * 2) + 2;
%>
    <tr><td><%=c1%></td><td><%=counter%></td></tr>
<%
}
%>
</table>
</BODY>
</HTML>
```

This source code generates a table that contains a sequence of numbers. What we'll do in the next section is convert this code into a component that can be used from within ASP.

A Simple ASP Component

A simple ASP component does not need anything other than a COM interface. The implementation code would look like this:

```
class ATL_NO_VTABLE CCounter :
    public CComObjectRootEx<CComSingleThreadModel>,
    public CComCoClass<CCounter, &CLSID_Counter>,
    public IDispatchImpl<ICounter, &IID_ICounter,
            &LIBID_ASPCOMPONENTLib>
{
public:
```

```
    CCounter()
    {
    }

DECLARE_REGISTRY_RESOURCEID(IDR_COUNTER)
DECLARE_NOT_AGGREGATABLE(CCounter)

DECLARE_PROTECT_FINAL_CONSTRUCT()

BEGIN_COM_MAP(CCounter)
    COM_INTERFACE_ENTRY(ICounter)
    COM_INTERFACE_ENTRY(IDispatch)
END_COM_MAP()

// ICounter
public:
    STDMETHOD(getValue)(long *retvalue);
    STDMETHOD(reset)();

private:
    long m_counter;
};

STDMETHODIMP CCounter::reset()
{
    m_counter = 0;
    return S_OK;
}

STDMETHODIMP CCounter::getValue(long *retvalue)
{
    m_counter = (m_counter * 2) + 2;
    *retvalue = m_counter;
    return S_OK;
}
```

Here, two methods are used. The first method resets the counter (CCounter::reset), and
the second method returns a value in the sequence (CCounter::getValue). Here's how
you would use this object in the new ASP page:

```
<%@ Language=Javascript %>
<HTML>
<HEAD>
<META NAME="GENERATOR" Content="Microsoft Visual Studio 6.0">
</HEAD>
<BODY>
<OBJECT RUNAT=server PROGID=ASPComponent.Counter.1
        id=objCounter> </OBJECT>
<table border=1>
<%
// Following code is used if the
// OBJECT tag did not exist
```

```
// var objCounter;
// objCounter = Server.CreateObject("ASPComponent.Counter.1");
objCounter.reset();
var c1;

for( c1 = 0; c1 < 10; c1 ++) {
%>
<tr><td><%=c1%></td><td><%=objCounter.getValue()%></td></tr>
<%
}
%>
</table>
</BODY>
</HTML>
```

In this piece of code, the COM object is instantiated on the ASP page (this needs to be defined). There are two ways to do this. The first is to use the OBJECT tag. To do this, you need to supply three parameters:

- RUNAT=server. This tells the ASP parser that the object will be instantiated on the server side. If this isn't added, the object is instantiated on the client side.
- PROGID. This is the COM PROGID used to instantiate the object. You could use CLSID, but it's more abstract and harder to understand.
- Id. This defines the object identifier used by the scripts to reference the instantiated objects.

The other way to instantiate the object is to use the Server.CreateObject method. This method requires the PROGID of the COM object as a parameter. If the COM object instantiation is successful, the object is returned. In the preceding code piece, this technique has been commented, but added as reference.

After the object has been instantiated, it can be called just like a built-in ASP object. In this example, objCounter.reset is called. Also, in the loop, the method objCounter.getValue() is used to access the value.

You might be wondering why the getValue method is a return value when it's defined as pointer in the implementation. The answer lies in the definition of the IDL:

```
[
    object,
    uuid(BBC090F3-71E4-11D2-9BC8-0010A4F15EA7),
    dual,
    helpstring("ICounter Interface"),
    pointer_default(unique)
]
interface ICounter : IDispatch
{
```

23

USING COM+
WITH THE IIS

```
        [id(1), helpstring("method reset")] HRESULT reset();
        [id(2), helpstring("method getValue")] HRESULT
getValue([out,retval]long *retvalue);
    };
```

In the declaration of getValue, the parameter is defined as out and retval, which means it's a return parameter.

A Richer ASP Component

The current implementation of the component does not use any objects exposed by the ASP object model. The problem with the current HTML implementation is that it doesn't save any programming effort. It still involves quite a bit of coding. To cut down on the amount of HTML coding, you can access the ASP object model. The way to do this is shown in Figure 23.8.

FIGURE 23.8

ASP and COM+ conceptual architecture.

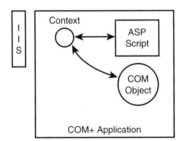

A question that may arise is how ASP, the object model, can be accessed from within the COM object. This can be explained by looking at how IIS is designed. For explanation purposes, the diagram shown in Figure 23.8 is not entirely correct. It is, however, *conceptually* correct, and for the scope of this book, we'll leave it at that.

A COM+ application runs IIS, and when a request for Web page arises, IIS does not process the request directly but hands it off to a COM+ application. The COM+ application then runs the ASP script or retrieves the file. This is done to promote robustness and scalability. If the retrieval process crashes, IIS can continue handling requests. Previously, a crash in one Web application would bring down the entire IIS application, which in turn would disable an entire Web server.

This COM+ application will process an ASP page. If that ASP page references a COM object, the in-process COM object will run within the context of the COM+ application. ASP is *richer* in that it considers itself a service that's part of the COM+ application.

Now, a situation exists in which if the COM+ application context were to be accessed, it would contain a reference to the ASP context. In fact, this is how the COM object works with the ASP object model. Does this mean all COM objects that use the ASP object model must be transactional? No, not at all. Remember that the COM+ application is a concept of applying context. That context can be transactional or it can be ASP.

An ASP Helper Object

Here's a helper object that simplifies the access to the ASP object model:

```
class ASPObjReference
{
public:
    enum {
        get_Server      = 0x0001,
        get_Response    = 0x0002,
        get_Request     = 0x0004,
        get_Session     = 0x0008,
        get_Application = 0x0010,
        get_All         = 0xFFFF
    };

    IRequest*           Request(){ _
            ASSERT(m_piRequest!=NULL);
            return m_piRequest; }
    IResponse*          Response(){ _
            ASSERT(m_piResponse!=NULL);
            return m_piResponse; }
    ISessionObject*     Session(){ _
            ASSERT(m_piSession!=NULL);
            return m_piSession; }
    IServer*            Server(){ _
            ASSERT(m_piServer!=NULL);
            return m_piServer; }
    IApplicationObject* Application(){ _
            ASSERT(m_piApplication!=NULL);
            return m_piApplication; }

    HRESULT Init( DWORD dwFlags) {
        try {
            IObjectContextPtr pObjContext;

            _com_util::CheckError( GetObjectContext( &pObjContext));

            IGetContextPropertiesPtr pProps;

            pProps = pObjContext;

            _bstr_t bstrObj;

            if( dwFlags & get_Request) {
```

```
                      bstrObj = "Request";
                      GetServerObject( pProps, bstrObj,
                              IID_IRequest, (void**)&m_piRequest);
              }
              if( dwFlags & get_Response) {
                      bstrObj = "Response";
                      GetServerObject( pProps, bstrObj,
                              IID_IResponse, (void**)&m_piResponse );
              }
              if( dwFlags & get_Session) {
                      bstrObj = "Session";
                      GetServerObject( pProps, bstrObj,
                              IID_ISessionObject, (void**)&m_piSession );
              }
              if(dwFlags & get_Server) {
                      bstrObj = "Server";
                      GetServerObject( pProps, bstrObj,
                              IID_IServer, (void**)&m_piServer );
              }
              if(dwFlags & get_Application) {
                      bstrObj = "Application";
                      GetServerObject( pProps, bstrObj,
                              IID_IApplicationObject, (void**)&m_piApplication
);
              }
      } catch( _com_error err) {
          return err.Error();
      }
      return S_OK;
  }
  static void GetServerObject( IGetContextProperties*
      pProps, BSTR bstrObjName,
      const IID& iid, void **ppObj) {

      _ASSERT( pProps );
      _ASSERT( bstrObjName );
      _ASSERT( ppObj );
      if ( pProps && bstrObjName && ppObj ) {
          *ppObj = NULL;
          _variant_t vt;
          _com_util::CheckError( pProps->GetProperty(
                  bstrObjName, &vt));
          if( V_VT( &vt) == VT_DISPATCH) {
              IDispatch* pDispatch = V_DISPATCH(&vt);
              if ( pDispatch ) {
                  _com_util::CheckError(
                  pDispatch->QueryInterface( iid, ppObj));
              }
          }
      }
      return;
  }
```

```
private:
    CComPtr<IRequest>      m_piRequest; //Request Object
    CComPtr<IResponse>     m_piResponse; //Response Object
    CComPtr<ISessionObject>   m_piSession; //Session Object
    CComPtr<IServer>      m_piServer; //Server Object
    CComPtr<IApplicationObject> m_piApplication;//Application Object
};
```

Here, the main concept is to first retrieve the IObjectContext interface using the method
GetObjectContext. This interface can then be queried using QueryInterface for the
interface IGetContextProperties. Since I am using smart pointers, this querying is
done automatically. The purpose of this interface is to allow for the access of various
COM+ services available from the context as properties (for example,
IGetContextProperties::GetProperty). It's important that you understand that this
method will not always return an interface, because if the context is not running within
an ASP execution, the property will not exist. It's a purely dynamic situation. Therefore,
error checking is not optional. With respect to the preceding source code, the property
retrieval is performed in the static method GetServerObject.

Using the ASP Object Model

Here's an implementation of this helper object:

```
STDMETHODIMP CASPWrapper::generate(long iterations)
{
    try {
        m_refASP.Init( ASPObjReference::get_Response);

        ASPCOMPONENTLib::ICounterPtr ptr( "ASPComponent.Counter.1");

        long c1;
        char buffer[ 512];

        ptr->reset();
        m_refASP.Response()->Write( _variant_t( "<table>"));
        for( c1 = 0; c1 < iterations; c1 ++) {
            sprintf( buffer, "<tr><td>Iteration
%ld</td><td>%ld</td></tr>",
                    c1, ptr->getValue());
            m_refASP.Response()->Write( _variant_t( buffer));
        }
        m_refASP.Response()->Write( _variant_t( "</table>"));

    } catch( _com_error err) {
        return err.Error();
    }
    return S_OK;
}
```

23

USING COM+
WITH THE IIS

In this example, the method generate has as a parameter the number of iterations that will be generated. Notice that the entire code is encapsulated within an exception. This way, if anything goes wrong, it will be caught. The first step is to retrieve the context using m_refASP.Init. Then, the next step is to instantiate the ICounter object.

> **TIP**
>
> It might seem more effective to embed the ASP code within the original ICounter interface. However, the problem with this is that ICounter may not be used within an ASP context. By adding the ASP code directly to the ICounter interface, the component must be used within an ASP context.

The next step is to call the ICounter::Reset method to reset the sequence. Then, some data is written to the stream using Response.Write. The ASP objects accept only variant data; therefore, all data must be converted to this type. This can easily be done using the COM compiler support class _variant_t. This method is used multiple times to write all the HTML content to the stream.

The last step is to create an ASP page, as follows:

```
<%@ Language=JavaScript %>
<HTML>
<HEAD>
<META NAME="GENERATOR" Content="Microsoft Visual Studio 6.0">
</HEAD>
<BODY>
<OBJECT RUNAT=server PROGID=ASPComponent.ASPWrapper.1
        id=objASPCounter> </OBJECT>
<%objASPCounter.generate(10);%>
</BODY>
</HTML>
```

This time, the ASP code is much simpler, and it generates the table for you automatically. As a designer, you can now focus on building the application and the user interface. The downside is that whatever the COM object generates cannot be easily modified. Therefore, if the table is not to your liking, you may need to recompile the COM object. However, because the ASP COM object is a wrapper to the underlying object, you can use the underlying object directly, bypassing the ASP object.

Legacy and the Wizard

A bigger issue involves a problem with the ATL wizard. If the ATL wizard is used to generate an ASP component, it generates the component using the old method of activating an ASP component. The old method uses the methods `OnStartPage` and `OnEndPage` and retrieves the various ASP objects from the `IScriptingContext` `interface`. This method, although still supported, is considered obsolete and should be avoided.

Transacted ASP Pages

Most of the components are called from a Web page, and this is the first contact with the server, which is a good point to start a transaction. With IIS 5.0, you can start transaction-based Web pages. A transaction is identified as follows:

```
<%@Language=JavaScript transaction=supported%>
```

The `transaction` keyword must be added to the first line of the ASP script. In this example, the Web page supports transactions. There is also requires new, required, and not supported. The values required and requires new ones start new transactions, whereas the others do not.

ASP works with transactions at the page level. This means that at the end of a page script, the transaction will be committed or aborted. A transaction instantiated by ASP can last only for the duration of the page. If this is adequate, it's good to use this type of transaction because multiple components can be used within the same transaction context. This way, whatever action is taken by any of the components can be committed or aborted.

Consider the following source code:

```
<%@ Language=JavaScript transaction=required%>
<HTML>
<HEAD>
<META NAME="GENERATOR" Content="Microsoft Visual Studio 6.0">
</HEAD>
<BODY>
<h1>The transaction example</h1>
<%
try {
var tempObject;
tempObject = Server.CreateObject("Registration4.UserImpl4.1");
tempObject.firstname = "Christian";
tempObject.lastname = "Gross";
tempObject.email = "me@someone.com";
tempObject.password = "cc";
tempObject.writeObject();
Session("tempObject") = tempObject;
} catch( e ) {
%>
```

```
<h2>Error is <%=e%></h2>
<%}%>

<%
function OnTransactionCommit(){
    Response.Write( "Transaction Complete");
}

function OnTransactionAbort(){
    Response.Write( "Transaction Abort");
}
%>
</BODY>
</HTML>
```

In this example, a transaction is started when the page is loaded. Then, the object creation and manipulation routines are carried out within a JavaScript exception block. Therefore, if anything goes wrong with any of the methods, an instantiation failure of the tempObject object would occur. The properties are assigned and then finally tempObject.writeObject is called, which writes the properties to the database. After this last script command, the transaction is committed by the ASP framework.

In the current iteration of the object, the tempObject.writeObject method calls IObjectContext::SetComplete. Therefore, the transaction will complete successfully, and ASP will trigger the event OnTransactionCommit. In this event, you can add whatever code is needed to indicate that the transaction is successful. Consider the situation, though, where tempObject.writeObject calls IObjectContext::DisableCommit like the properties. In this situation, the commit attempted by the ASP page will result in the event OnTransactionAbort, and all the work will be removed. An IObjectContext::EnableCommit would have resulted in OnTransactionCommit.

In any case, when the ASP page is in control of the transaction, the components involved in the transaction are deactivated. This deactivation is important, because the line Session("tempObject") = tempObject will hold an invalid reference, which cannot be accessed.

If the component needs to survive multiple pages, the ASP page cannot be made transactional. The component is then responsible for starting the transaction. You can now store the object in the Session("tempObject") variable and use it on multiple pages. However, the Session object must be cleared, because it will be deactivated when the transaction commits or aborts. You will not get a transaction complete or abort event at the ASP level in this situation.

Summary

In this chapter, the topic of building Web applications using the Microsoft Internet Information Server (IIS) was explained. You also received an explanation of what Active Server Pages are, along with a demonstration of the key concepts. Shown throughout the chapter were techniques on how to build practical ASP applications. The chapter discussed how to integrate COM+ objects with ASP and also showed some of the practical aspects of building a Web application.

23

USING COM+
WITH THE IIS

Using the COM+ In-Memory Database

This chapter focuses on the COM+ in-memory database (IMDB). IMDB is a new technology that has been released for the first time with Windows 2000. This chapter explains why there's a need for IMDB. It also discusses how to use IMDB with either Visual Basic or Visual C++.

In-Memory Database (IMDB)

IMDB is a RAM-based, ISAM-based database. It serves one purpose: It makes it possible to access read-mostly data. You may be wondering what read-mostly data is.

To answer this question, consider the following scenario: Some company has an internal order-processing application. The number of products that this company sells might number a few thousand. When the details of the application are filled out, the most time taken involves retrieving product numbers. A standard database would optimize by caching the product information within RAM. Now consider the situation where another table is loaded into RAM. However, there is not enough room for both the products table and the new table. What does the database do? It will automatically start an optimization algorithm and decide what information to keep in RAM. The problem is that the new table is only referenced five times and it can be part of a slower transaction. So now your optimized system is not so optimized. It will experience a moment of slowness until the new table can be unloaded again.

With IMDB you can force load all the data into memory. It will never be unloaded to the hard disk. This way the application using the data will always be fast. What happens when you run out of RAM? The system becomes incredibly slow because it is constantly swapping data other than the IMDB. However, IMDB is an application that is based on your tuning.

Architecture of IMDB

Tuning is required, and this tuning involves IMDB. With IMDB, you can load a table from a database into memory or keep state information in memory. It's an optimized situation. Therefore, the size of the cache and information stored within it must be calculated; otherwise, IMDB becomes a liability. To understand IMDB, imagine IMDB as a giant piece of RAM cache. And within that RAM cache you store data and tables.

Types of Storage

Tables from other OLE DB providers can load directly into cache. This cache model is called *write through*. Here are its advantages:

- It's a real table that has added performance from being RAM-based.
- The data can be updated. This updates the source of the data, which is transparent from the original client.

The other way of working with IMDB is to create tables directly. These tables are considered standalone tables, because there's no association with any durable data. It's like state management without the costs of the hard disk I/O. However, remember that the data is not durable, and any machine failure will cause the state to be deleted. To avoid this situation, you should use clustering techniques.

The client accesses the data in IMDB using OLE DB. IMDB is a Level 1 OLE DB provider. This means it does not support the ICommand interface. It supports only table-level access. There is no SQL for IMDB. The architecture of IMDB is shown in Figure 24.1.

FIGURE 24.1

IMDB architecture.

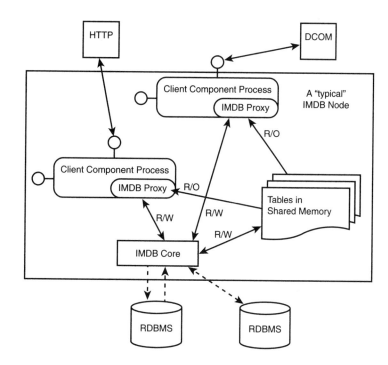

The IMDB cache is a piece of shared memory. When a remote client, such as HTTP, or DCOM accesses the shared memory, it must do so through a local component. The local component and the cache must be on the same machine; otherwise, the performance benefits will be negated. The local component must be a DLL as well as COM+ compatible, because the IMDB core may need to use transactions.

IMDB Proxy

When the component accesses the cache, the IMDB proxy is loaded in the component's process space. The IMDB core does this. The proxy is implemented in `MSIMDBPR.DLL`. This proxy is the interface to the IMDB core and the interface to the shared memory.

The IMDB proxy has the intelligence to know whether data is being read or written. This makes it possible to perform some speedups. When data is read, the proxy will read it directly from the shared memory. That data is mostly read, which makes for a dramatic speed improvement, because the overhead of some DB core or caching algorithm is avoided.

However, when it's necessary to update a table, the proxy hands the request to the IMDB core. The IMDB core will then do all the legwork regarding the locking management. NT's Fast LPC services ensure that the communication between the IMDB proxy and IMDB core stays fast. Of course, because this is an update, it's slower than a read operation. Overall, though, it's still faster than a durable database.

IMDB Core

The IMDB core is implemented in `MSIMDBCR.DLL` and has the following responsibilities:

- Populating cached tables
- Managing indexes
- Coordinating communication between the various IMDB proxies
- Coordinating the various locks for access to the data
- Managing transactions
- Persisting a change (when necessary)
- Managing the connection to the IMDB proxy DLLs

A DLL does not magically load itself. The IMDB service (`IMDBSRV.EXE`) is the server process that loads the core.

Isolation

IMDB supports the following transaction-isolation models:

- *Optimistic*. Rarely blocks for access. Aborts on discovery of isolation violation.
- *Pessimistic*. Isolation violation is prevented by blocking access to data. Aborts only for deadlocks.

The following transaction-isolation levels are possible for IMDB:

- *Read Committed*. No locking is required for reading because of the cache versions of noncommitted data.
- *Repeatable Read*. When data is locked, read, unlocked, and then locked and read again, the same data will be read.

The preferred and default isolation level for the IMDB is Read Committed. In this mode, the client is allowed to read data from the cache without a read lock. Information has to be communicated between the client and the IMDB server process, and the Read-Committed isolation level is, by far, the most efficient method.

64-bit Memory Space

With Windows 2000, it's possible to access 64-bit memory. This is called the *Very Large Memory (VLM) architecture*. To use VLM from a 32-bit operating system requires extra programming effort. With IMDB, that memory space is just a really big cache. This means you can take advantage of the 64-bit memory space without having to write 64-bit code.

For applications that use the 3GB model, a utility must be used to switch the `LARGE_ADDRESS_AWARE_BIT`. The `BOOT.INI` file must be updated to use 3GB of memory.

Security

IMDB uses integrated security and impersonation of MTS package accounts to secure itself and database access. On startup, the IMDB service looks for an IMDB Trusted Users role in the system application in the COM+ catalog. The IMDB Trusted Users role is added to the catalog during COM+ setup.

It's a good idea to create a local Windows NT group (for example, IMDB Users) and add it to the role. If you want system administrators to be able to access IMDB, add the Administrators group as well.

24

USING COM+
IN-MEMORY
DATABASE

The IMDB service reads the catalog only when it starts up. Here are some points to keep in mind:

- If you add a user to the role while IMDB is running, you'll need to stop and restart it before the new user entry will take effect.
- If you add the IMDB Users group before you start IMDB, you can add users to the group (using Computer Management) without shutting down IMDB for the change to be recognized. You'll have to log off that user and then back on, as usual.

For best results, create a Users group and add it to the System role.

> **NOTE**
>
> IMDB does not require this role to be present to run in some configurations. For instance, if you log on using an account that's a member of the Administrators group and then run your COM+ applications as the interactive user, you won't need to set up the IMDB Trusted Users role. However, if you want to run the IMDB service as a non-Administrator user, you will need to add the IMDB Trusted Users role in the system application and populate it with the appropriate groups and users.

How IMDB Calculates Memory Usage

When the IMDB server starts up, the following calculations are used to determine the amount of RAM to use. When the value is specified in the administration utility, use this:

```
Memory = max ( user specified value )
```

When the value is not specified in the administration utility or it's set to 0, use this (for Intel machines only):

```
Memory = max ( 16MB, Min ( Virtual memory - 256MB, Physical memory -
32MB))
```

Here's what to use on Alpha machines:

```
Memory = max ( 16MB, Physical memory - 32MB)
```

A Simple Example

For this example, the purpose is to go through the motions of using IMDB. This example will be used in an ASP page that accesses some data on the server. Consider the following code:

```
<%@ Language=Javascript %>
<HTML>
<HEAD>
<META NAME="GENERATOR" Content="Microsoft Visual Studio 6.0">
</HEAD>
<BODY>
<%
var conn;
var rs;

conn = Server.CreateObject( "ADODB.Connection");

conn.Provider = "MSIMDB";
conn.ConnectionString = "Pubs";
conn.CursorLocation = adUseNone;
conn.Open();
%>
</BODY>
</HTML>
```

This piece of code creates an ADO connection to an IMDB source. Note that conn.Provider is MSIMDB, which is the IMDB. The conn.Connection string is Pubs, which specifies the IMDB data source that will be used as a reference, and conn.CursorLocation is set to None, because the cursor is not an SQL DB–type cursor. Finally, the IMDB database can be opened.

This example shows that programming an IMDB connection is like writing ADO code. The slightly tricky part involves the configuration of IMDB.

Setting Up IMDB

Before IMDB can even be used, it needs to be set up. First, you need to start the Component Services Explorer (see Figure 24.2).

Select the My Computer node and right-click. From the pop-up menu, select Properties and then select the Options tab (see Figure 24.3).

24

USING COM+
IN-MEMORY
DATABASE

FIGURE 24.2

*Component
Services Explorer
showing IMDB
data sources.*

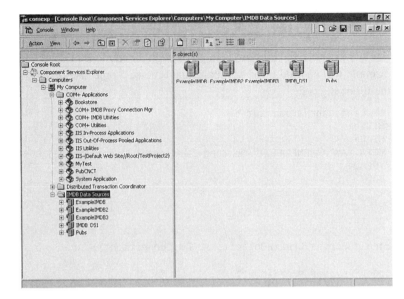

FIGURE 24.3

IMDB options.

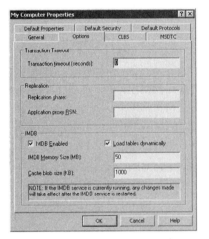

By default, IMDB is not started. Select the IMDB check box to enable it (see Figure 24.3). The IMDB data source connects to a database as specified in the IMDB data source. You can also specify whether or not a table is loaded dynamically. If the check box Load Tables Dynamically is not checked, then when IMDB is started, the tables specified in the Tables folder will be loaded. Why load tables dynamically? Because fewer initial resources are required. However, keep in mind that the first client to reference a table will get a performance hit while the table is being loaded.

The text box IMDB Memory Size specifies the amount of RAM that IMDB will use. You should keep this amount below the actual size of RAM. Otherwise, the performance hit of memory being swapped to disk negates the purpose of IMDB. What's the optimal size? It depends on your hardware and software configuration. Using Performance Monitor, you can see how much memory is being utilized. However, the rule of thumb is that more RAM is better.

The last text box, Cache Blob Size, specifies whether the binary large object (blob) will be cached. If it's larger than the amount specified, the blob is not cached. Blobs in a database are binary fields of undetermined sizes. Although, ideally, all of the blob should be stored, this is not practical. An example would be the caching of a full-feature film. Therefore, only a certain amount of the blob will be cached.

Setting Up an IMDB Data Source

To set up an IMDB data source, select the node IMDB Data Sources under the My Explorer node. To add another node, right-click and then select a new data source (see Figure 24.4).

FIGURE 24.4

Setting the IMDB data source definition.

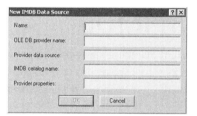

The New IMDB Data Source dialog box has the following five text boxes:

- *Name*. The name that the IMDB data source will be assigned.

- *OLE DB provider name*. This is the provider that will be used as the underlying data source. For an ODBC source, it's MSDASQL. For a SQL Server OLE DB provider, it's SQLOLEDB, and for an Oracle database, it's MSDAORA.

- *Provider data source*. This depends on the OLE DB provider you're using. For ODBC, it's the ODBC data source name. For SQL Server and Oracle, it's the server name.

- *IMDB catalog name*. This specifies the database you want to connect to. This applies only to ODBC and SQL Server. For Oracle, this should be left blank.

- *Provider properties*. This is an optional field where you can specify some other parameters. By far, the most common parameter will be a custom security logon.

24

USING COM+
IN-MEMORY
DATABASE

In the development cycle, this is the simplest method. For SQL Server, you would use "uid=sa;pwd=". This is to log on as System Administrator (sa), and no password is needed. This string is not applicable for Oracle, and it needs to use "userid=xxx;password=xxx".

When these fields have been filled out, click the OK button.

Referencing Resource Tables

To select the IMDB data source, double-click the Tables folder node. Right-click and select New|Table. This pops up a dialog box with one text box. In this text box, type in the name of a table from the reference database and then click the OK button. This specifies the table that will be loaded.

> **CAUTION**
>
> Do not reference an underlying table twice. This will cause coherence problems.

Some Details on IMDB

From the discussion so far, it would seem that there's nothing extraordinary about IMDB. It's just another OLE DB provider. In a sense, this is true. However, there are some other considerations that must be taken into account. These considerations depend on the context and language being used.

What's Supported at the OLE DB Level

There aren't many situations where you would use OLE DB directly. The only exception involves the Visual Studio 6.0 OLE DB consumer templates. The following interfaces are supported:

Object	Interface
DSO	IDBCreateSession
	IDBInitialize
	IDBProperties
	IPersist
	ITableDefinition
Error	IErrorInfo
	IErrorRecords

Object	Interface
Rowset	IAccessor
	IChapteredRowset
	IColumnsInfo
	IConvertType
	IRowset
	IRowsetChange
	IRowsetIdentity
	IRowsetIndex
	IRowsetInfo
	IRowsetLocate
	IRowsetUpdate
Session	IGetDataSource
	IOpenRowset
	ISessionProperties
View	IAccessor
	IViewChapter
	IViewFilter
	IViewSort

How the Specifics Relate to the OLE DB Consumer Templates

The IMDB OLE DB provider is special in nature and does not always work as you might expect.

For example, it does not support OLE DB notifications or the ITransaction interface. What this means is that from the CSession class, the methods StartTransaction, Abort, Commit, and GetTransactionInfo cannot be used. It does not mean that there's no transaction facility, but rather that the transaction cannot be controlled. The IMDB requires that the client accessing it is within a COM+ application that uses that transaction.

Also, there's no support for ICommand because IMDB does not have a command processor—it's an ISAM database. To retrieve the data, you would use the IOpenRowset interface. Through this interface you can browse and filter the cached tables. All tables that will be cached must have indexes associated with them.

With the OLE DB consumer templates, the only possible solution is the static accessor or the manual accessor. Anything else will cause errors.

The easiest method is to use the standard accessor and then let the wizard generate the code. This has the advantage of keeping everything lean and fast, yet simple. Consider the following sample source for OLE DB:

```
class CdboauthorsAccessor
{
public:
    TCHAR m_auid[12];
    TCHAR m_aulname[41];
    TCHAR m_aufname[21];
    TCHAR m_phone[13];
    TCHAR m_address[41];
    TCHAR m_city[21];
    TCHAR m_state[3];
    TCHAR m_zip[6];
    VARIANT_BOOL m_contract;
 BEGIN_COLUMN_MAP(CdboauthorsAccessor)
    COLUMN_ENTRY(1, m_auid)
    COLUMN_ENTRY(2, m_aulname)
    COLUMN_ENTRY(3, m_aufname)
    COLUMN_ENTRY(4, m_phone)
    COLUMN_ENTRY(5, m_address)
    COLUMN_ENTRY(6, m_city)
    COLUMN_ENTRY(7, m_state)
    COLUMN_ENTRY(8, m_zip)
    COLUMN_ENTRY_TYPE(9, DBTYPE_BOOL, m_contract)
END_COLUMN_MAP()
    // You may wish to call this function if you are inserting a record
    ➥ and wish to initialize all the fields, if you are not going to
    ➥ explicitly set all of them.
    void ClearRecord()
    {
        memset(this, 0, sizeof(*this));
    }
};
 class Cdboauthors : public CTable<CAccessor<CdboauthorsAccessor> >
{
public:
    HRESULT Open()
    {
        HRESULT          hr;
         hr = OpenDataSource();
        if (FAILED(hr))
            return hr;
        return OpenRowset();
    }
    HRESULT OpenDataSource()
    {
        HRESULT          hr;
```

```
            CDataSource db;
            CDBPropSet    dbinit(DBPROPSET_DBINIT);
            //dbinit.AddProperty(DBPROP_AUTH_PERSIST_SENSITIVE_AUTHINFO,
            ➥false);
            //dbinit.AddProperty(DBPROP_AUTH_USERID, OLESTR("sa"));
            dbinit.AddProperty(DBPROP_INIT_DATASOURCE, OLESTR("Pubs"));
            dbinit.AddProperty(DBPROP_INIT_PROMPT, (short)4);
            //dbinit.AddProperty(DBPROP_INIT_LCID, (long)1033);
            hr = db.Open(_T("MSDASQL"), &dbinit);
            if (FAILED(hr))
                return hr;
            return m_session.Open(db);
    }
    HRESULT OpenRowset()
    {
            // Set properties for open
            CDBPropSet    propset(DBPROPSET_ROWSET);
            propset.AddProperty(DBPROP_IRowsetChange, true);
            propset.AddProperty(DBPROP_UPDATABILITY, DBPROPVAL_UP_CHANGE ¦
            ➥DBPROPVAL_UP_INSERT ¦ DBPROPVAL_UP_DELETE);
            return CTable<CAccessor<CdboauthorsAccessor> >::Open
            ➥(m_session, _T("dbo.authors"), &propset);
    }
    CSession    m_session;
};
```

When you're connecting to an IMDB data source, some changes have to be made. Therefore, lines 54, 55, and optionally line 58 need to be commented out. There's no need to specify a user name and password because IMDB uses impersonation or explicit user definition for the security.

The static accessor is okay because, as specified in line 72, CCommand (ICommand) is not used. Instead CTable is used, which binds to the IOpenRowset interface. When IOpenRowset::OpenRowset is called, it does not specify an index, as shown by the following source code:

```
hr = session.m_spOpenRowset->OpenRowset(NULL, &dbid, NULL, GetIID(),
    (pPropSet) ? 1 : 0, pPropSet, (IUnknown**)GetInterfacePtr());
```

This is good because IMDB does not support the explicit definition of the indexes. The index used is read from the in-memory table. IMDB cannot index on autoincrement fields or on timestamp fields.

Binding of the Data

When you're using static accessors, the binding is in the space of the client. Consider the diagram shown in Figure 24.5.

FIGURE 24.5

OLE DB segment memory.

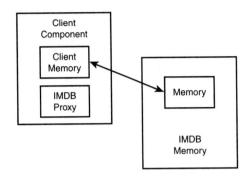

With OLE DB, the data for the recordset is stored in a contiguous memory buffer. Either the client COM object or the IMDB server can provide this memory buffer. IMDB does not provide a memory buffer; instead, the client must provide the buffer. Using either a static accessor or a manual accessor, you must provide the memory. Also, all values must be either *by value* or *by reference*. The data type bindings DBTYPE_VECTOR and DBTYPE_ARRAY are not supported.

Fetching of Data

IMDB does not fetch data when it's being bound. It also does not fetch data on the IRowset::GetNextRows call. This is because the data is already in memory. What happens is that IMDB creates bookmarks for the rows specified. This has the benefit of being very fast. The data is retrieved when IRowset::GetData is called. However, in the implementation of CRowset::MoveNext, both are called in the same method.

Using Bookmarks

To save processing time, you'll often want to pass around a recordset that has been bound to IMDB. An example would be a bound rowset that needs to set another COM object. For instance, you could use Object1::GetAllValues, which allows iteration of the object set, like so:

```
IRowsetPtr rowset = m_accessor.GetInterface();
IUnknownPtr unk = rowset;

op->setCursor( unk, m_accessor.m_hRow);
_com_util::CheckError( ptr->QueryInterface( pVal));
(*pVal)->AddRef();
```

In this piece of code, the rowset interface is retrieved and converted to IUnknown. Then the specific rowset is bound to another COM object using the method call

```
SecondObject::setCursor( IUnknown *ptr, unsigned long hRow):
```

```
CAccessorRowset< CManualAccessor> m_accessor;
```

```
_com_util::CheckError( pUnk->QueryInterface( &(m_accessor.m_spRowset)));
_com_util::CheckError( m_accessor.Bind());
m_accessor.m_hRow = hrow;
_com_util::CheckError( m_accessor.GetData());
```

The accessor used is CManualAccessor, because the static accessor can be bound dynamically. (Do not use CDynamicAccessor.) Then, the rowset interface is retrieved using the QI (A COM IUnknown::QueryInterface call) and bound to the accessor. This establishes the connection between IMDB and the rowset. However, in order to know which record you're looking at, m_hRow needs to be set. You won't know what this value is because it's internal to the database. For example, with SQL Server, this value is an actual record count index. Finally, you call GetData to retrieve the data at the current location. This technique is legal and can be used to pass a rowset around to various COM+ objects.

Support for Blob Data

In most cases, blobs will not be cached in the IMDB database. With IMDB, a blob is cached if requested and if the size of the blob is less than one percent of the entire IMDB cache.

Accessing a blob, in most cases, does not make use of standard field methods. When working with blobs, you should consider them to be file-based COM objects. Look at the following code, for example:

```
class CCategories {
public:
    ISequentialStream*    pPicture;
 BEGIN_COLUMN_MAP(CCategories)
    BLOB_ENTRY(4, IID_ISequentialStream, STGM_READ, pPicture)
END_COLUMN_MAP()
};
    CTable<CAccessor<CCategories> > categories;
    ULONG           cb;
    BYTE          myBuffer[65536];
    categories.Open(session, _T("Categories"));
    while (categories.MoveNext() == S_OK)
    {
        do
        {
            categories.pPicture->Read(myBuffer, 65536, &cb);
        } while (cb > 0);
        categories.pPicture->Release();
    }
}
```

In this example, the field is called BLOB_ENTRY. It's then specified as a read-only STGM_READ field. This is bound using the ISequential stream pPicture variable. When this variable is used, the data is read like a file. When the field is no longer being used, it is released. This is normally necessary with a regular database, because the field is cached in and out of RAM. If it isn't released, the COM object will remain. With IMDB, the situation is a bit different because the data is always kept in RAM and therefore can be considered valid all the time. However, this is not a general rule because the documentation does not specify it.

When using IRowset::GetData or IRowsetChange::SetData, you have several ways to operate on the blob data:

- GetData. The data can be placed in a memory buffer, assuming that the size of the blob is known.
- SetData. You can supply a memory buffer, assuming that the size of the blob can be predetermined. Whether this method can be called depends on whether the data can be stored as one contiguous memory segment.
- GetData. You can use an ISequentialStream interface pointer with STGM_READ or STGM_CREATE.
- SetData. You can supply an ISequentialStream interface pointer and the length of the stream. In other words, you can't pass in an object of any length.

How do these cases influence where the object is cached? In the first three cases, the data is cached in IMDB and written to the underlying data source, whenever possible. If it cannot be stored in IMDB, it's stored in the underlying data source.

In the last method, the data is written directly to the IMDB data cache. This depends on whether the blob is small enough. If the blob is too large, the data is written directly to the underlying data source. In this situation, the blob is considered to be in write-through mode.

This is one big exception, though, in the case of a transaction. When a transaction occurs and a record has just been created, the data is somewhere in RAM (it could be IMDB, swapped pages, and so on). This is not an inconsistency, but it has to do with the concept of ACID, which states that only a successful transaction can have a correct state. A successful transaction will have a cache state as defined in the previous paragraphs.

When you're using IRowsetUpdate, the modified blobs will be cached in client memory. Therefore, you should make sure the blob is small enough to fit into memory. Once IRowsetUpdate::Update has been called, the blob will be made durable.

So what does this mean in a nutshell? It means that the more RAM you have, the better off you are. It also means that caching pictures, small audio clips, and small video clips is okay. However, when you're dealing with blob data that extends into the gigabyte range, IMDB is not the solution. IMDB for smaller blobs is managed whether the blobs cached or not, because there's no explicit mechanism to remove the blobs from cache.

Creating Tables

Up to this point, the discussion has revolved around the fact that the table is defined as a basis in another database. This is the preferable method, because any failure is recoverable. However, because the data is read mostly, it's cached and quickly accessible.

There is the need sometimes to create a table dynamically. Or the data is to be kept temporarily. An example could be a shopping cart where the purchase list is kept in RAM and not on the hard disk. To do this you need to create your table and index in an @IMDBTEMP database.

When you're creating a table, the `ITableDefinition` interface has to be used. This interface has the facility to create a table and then incrementally add, remove, or modify columns. IMDB cannot cope with this. Therefore, these actions should be avoided. To create a table, you must pass in the column definition as data to the `ITableDefinition::CreateTable` method. The `DBPROP_TBL_SMALLTABLE` property (type `VT_BOOL`; read/write) must be specified.

IMDB supports a way to optimize the index creation and storage for memory consumption. All tables in @IMDBTEMP that have this property set to `TRUE` upon creation will use this optimization. `TRUE` is the default setting.

At this point, you must also define an index; otherwise, IMDB will not be able to function. The following properties for `IIndexDefinition::CreateIndex` can be specified:

Property	Type	Default Value	Read/Write
DBPROP_INDEX_ NULLSCOLLATION	VT_I4	DBPROP_NC_LOW	Read/Write
DBPROP_INDEX_NULLS	VT_I4	0	Read/Write
DBPROP_INDEX_UNIQUE	BOOL	FALSE	Read/Write

Supported Data Types

When the wizard generates the static accessor, the data map does not specify the OLE DB data type. This is figured out from the type of variable within the COLUMN_ENTRY macro. Here's a list of supported OLE DB data types:

DBTYPE_I2	DBTYPE_UI4
DBTYPE_I4	DBTYPE_I8
DBTYPE_R4	DBTYPE_UI8
DBTYPE_R8	DBTYPE_GUID
DBTYPE_CY	DBTYPE_BYTES
DBTYPE_DATE	DBTYPE_STR
DBTYPE_BOOL	DBTYPE_WSTR
DBTYPE_DECIMAL	DBTYPE_NUMERIC (up to a limit of 38)
DBTYPE_UI1	DBTYPE_DBDATE
DBTYPE_I1	DBTYPE_DBTIME
DBTYPE_UI2	DBTYPE_DBTIMESTAMP

The data types DBTYPE_VARIANT, DBTYPE_BSTR, and DBTYPE_IUNKNOWN are supported in the accessor map. If the IMDB data type is long and defined as DBTYPE_VARIANT in COLUMN_ENTRY, IMDB will coerce it.

The data types DBTYPE_VARIANT, DBTYPE_BSTR, and DBTYPE_IUNKNOWN are not supported in dynamically created tables that do not reference a data source table.

The Details of Using ADO

When you're using ADO, the situation has been that you're connecting to a relational database or, potentially, an object-oriented database. IMDB is an ISAM OLE DB provider. This is different than a relational model and has some ramifications when you're specifying settings.

ADO Connection Strings

When you're connecting to an IMDB, the following connection string (connection.ConnectionString) can be used:

```
"provider=msimdb;data source=IMDB_DSN"
```

Using this notation, you don't have to specify the connection.provider property.

The notation

```
"data source=IMDB_DSN"
```

or

```
"IMDB_DSN"
```

can be used if the `connection.Provider` property is set to `MSIMDB`. The difference with these notations is that the IMDB data sources are enumerated until the desired one is found.

ADO Data Source Objects

When an IMDB connection has been made, it will connect to your resource. You can't iterate through the IMDB catalog using the `DBPROP_CURRENTCATALOG` property. Any attempt to do so will result in an error.

It's assumed that you know which tables you want to use ahead of time. IMDB is not the general provider. You cannot enumerate the tables in a catalog or look at certain properties of the table. It's assumed that you know what you are accessing. Therefore, if what you're trying to do doesn't work, it's a configuration situation.

ADO Recordset Default Lock Type

Since the data is read-mostly, the default lock type for a recordset is `adLockReadOnly` and `adLockOptimistic`.

ADO `CursorLocation` Property

When you're developing IMDB applications, the client consuming the IMDB data will reside on the same machine. Also, the cursor location should be `adUseNone`. This forces the ADO recordset to communicate directly with the provider. It also moves the responsibility of rowset functionality (find, filter, and so on) to the provider.

Using `adUseNone` has the benefit of ensuring maximum performance. However, because you're dealing with an ISAM provider, less functionality can be used. In general, the ramifications of cursor location is dependent on the consumer of the data. The advice is to keep it simple.

Creating Tables Using a Schema

For ADO DDL, the optional `IDBSchemaRowset` interface for sessions is used to populate the `Tables`, `Procedures`, and `Views` collections as well as subordinate collections, such as `Columns` and `Indexes`. Without support for `IDBSchemaRowset`, these collections will not populate with information regarding the structure of the currently active connection.

However, ADO DDL will work to support the creation of new collections as well as the deletion of existing ones, assuming the caller can identify them uniquely by name alone.

Summary

This chapter focused on learning about IMDB and what it can do. IMDB is just like another OLE DB provider, with a few exceptions. IMDB is a specialized COM+ service that's used to tune applications based on a few conditions. IMDB works very well when it's used for high performance on read-mostly data. Outside this scope, however, IMDB becomes less efficient and should be avoided.

CHAPTER 25

Advanced COM+
Services

The purpose of this chapter is to introduce the rest of the COM+ material. The chapter is split into four main sections. The first section discusses improving scalability using object pooling and load balancing. In the second section, some advanced topics regarding transactions are discussed. Examples include controlling the transaction from the client context. The third section discusses the queued component—a sort of asynchronous communication without the overhead of the full MSMQ implementation. Finally, the topic of event services in COM+ is discussed. One service that's exposed is the publish-and-subscribe mechanism.

Scalability Through Object Pooling and Load Balancing

In previous editions of MTS, object pooling was only a concept. There was no direct implementation of it. With COM+, object pooling has become a reality. What is object pooling and why is it good? To answer these questions, let's go back and consider a typical production situation.

In the diagram shown in Figure 25.1, there are many clients. However, because not all the clients are currently using the objects, just-in-time (JIT) activation connects only those clients that require attention. To use this mechanism, the objects must be stateless. This way, an object can be reused in a pool of objects.

FIGURE 25.1

A sample production system.

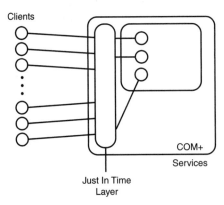

For object pooling to be supported, the only requirement is that the COM object must be stateless. An optimization is to implement IObjectControl.

Implementing `IObjectControl`

The lifetime of a pooled object is different from that of a regular object.

The physical lifetime is when the constructor and destructor of the class are called. The COM+ transaction lifetime is when the methods `IObjectControl::Activate` and `IObjectControl::Deactivate` are called. This is shown in Figure 25.2.

FIGURE 25.2
Lifetimes of a pooled object.

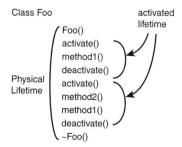

In Chapter 21, "An Introduction to COM+ Services," you learned that the COM object's Activation tab makes it possible to specify whether or not the object can be pooled. A pool minimum and maximum size can also be specified. When the COM+ application is loaded, the minimum number of COM objects are instantiated. In this instance, only the constructors of the classes are loaded.

When a client creates a pool instance object, COM+ services will inspect the pool for an available instance. If one exists, that instance is referenced. If none are available and the number of pooled objects is less than the maximum amount, COM+ services will wait for the time-out specified in the COM object property sheet. If this is exceeded, another instance of the object is created and referenced.

On the reference interface, the method `IObjectControl::Activate` will be called. At this point, any transaction constructor methods can be called. All COM calls are valid at this stage. Then the reference will have been JIT-activated and available to the client. Once the client is done, COM+ services will call `IObjectControl::Deactivate`, which is the transaction destructor. Finally, the object instance is returned to the pool of available objects.

Consider the situation shown in Figure 25.3.

FIGURE 25.3

*Pooled objects
calling other
pooled objects.*

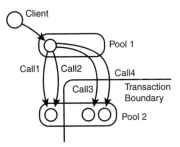

When a pooled object calls another pooled object, it gets a specific reference. After the pooled object is done, it releases the reference. During the life of the transaction, the same type of object is requested. It will then get the same object reference until the transaction ends. If the call is to another transaction, the reference will not be to the original object. Instead, it will be to another object.

The interface IObjectControl, at the time of this writing, could only be implemented by Visual J++ and Visual C++. Visual Basic cannot be pooled because it stores information in the TLS (Thread local storage), which makes it "nonpoolable."

The interface IObjectControl has three methods. The first two have already been discussed. The remaining method is IObjectControl::CanBePooled. This method is used to define whether the object can be pooled. Returning a TRUE indicates that pooling is allowed. A FALSE value indicates that pooling is not allowed.

If you run the Visual C++ ATL Object wizard to create an MTS object, the following code is generated:

```
HRESULT CExample::Activate()
{
    HRESULT hr = GetObjectContext(&m_spObjectContext);
    if (SUCCEEDED(hr))
        return S_OK;
    return hr;
}

BOOL CExample::CanBePooled()
{
    return TRUE;
}

void CExample::Deactivate()
{
    m_spObjectContext.Release();
}
```

This is a full implementation of IObjectControl. The Activate method retrieves the currently active transaction context. This is assigned to a CComPtr< IObjectContext> m_spObjectContext variable. Using m_spObjectContext, you can influence the outcome of the transaction regardless of the method called. If a specific method forces an ASAP deactivation, the transaction context is released in the Deactivate method.

It may seem that this interface is not very complicated. This is true, but there is one ramification that must considered. The object is alive all the time. Therefore, if the object leaks any memory, the leak will be slow but steady. In time, the server will crash or simply function very slowly. It's absolutely imperative that the object, when it's being recycled, is like being newly instantiated. What this means is that the state for a newly created object and a recycled object should be identical. For example, the following code is not good:

```
HRESULT CExample::Activate()
{
    HRESULT hr = GetObjectContext(&m_spObjectContext);
    if (SUCCEEDED(hr))
        return S_OK;

    if( didSet == false) {
        // Do something
        ...
        didSet = true;
    }
    return hr;
}

void CExample::Deactivate()
{
    m_spObjectContext.Release();
}
```

In this example, an instance member variable, didSet, is checked (using if). If it has not been set, then something should occur. This sort of behavior is used so that instantiation only occurs once. The problem with this code is that it isn't undone in Deactivate. In other words, when the object is recycled, it has the same characteristics as a newly created object.

Dynamic Load Balancing

The other way of achieving scalability is with load balancing. Using load balancing, you can consider a group of computers as one communication point. Keep in mind that this isn't clustering, because clustering ensures failover. Load balancing makes it possible to move processing tasks from a heavily utilized machine to an underutilized machine.

Implementing load balancing is an administrative issue, because it does not involve any interfaces. However, several programming issues are involved. Figure 25.4 illustrates accessing the local data and how it balances the load.

FIGURE 25.4

Load balancing and accessing local data.

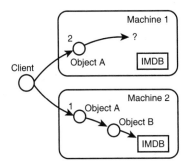

In step 1, the client calls object A, which then calls object B. Object B, for the scope of the transaction, stores some data within IMDB. Now, when another object of type A is referenced, the load-balancing routine determines machine 1 to be less loaded. Therefore, the process is shifted. However, now the reference to object B and the IMDB database becomes invalid. This sort of programming should generally be avoided. For example, IIS cannot be load-balanced when Session state information is kept.

How Load Balancing Functions

There are many different ways to implement load balancing. COM+ services load balancing uses a response time technique. If the calling response to the object is too low, the process is load-balanced. The load balancing granularity happens at the COM+ object level. The GetClassObject and CreateInstance requests are intercepted. After receiving either of these requests, the load balancer locates the best location to instantiate the object. The creation is then moved to the machine and a reference is returned to the object.

Some Advanced Transaction Concepts

This section outlines some of the smaller yet advanced details of transaction programming.

Avoiding Deadlocks and Blocking

In transaction programming, the issue of deadlocks can occur. Deadlocks occur in the following situation:

There are two records: a and b. If component 1 is working with record a, it is blocking access to this record. If component 2 is working with record b, it is blocking access to its record. At the same time, component 2 accesses record a and component 1 accesses record b. Instant deadlock occurs.

This is correct and incorrect. It depends on how the isolation of the transaction system is implemented. This is because ACID says that only one process will see the modified data. Therefore, when a deadlock occurs, it is not a deadlock, but a timeout. One transaction will succeed and the other will fail.

This is the theory. The reality is that a deadlock can occur due to compromises made for performance and efficiency reasons. However, most databases have deadlock detection and will time-out when one occurs. A deadlock will be converted in a block, which reduces scalability.

Stale Data

One of the side effects of deadlock detection is stale data conditions. Stale data occurs when a record reads old data and makes an update on that data. During this process, another record has updated the data. This means that the original reader has stale data. So when the original person updates the data, it may be incorrect.

To stop this, a timestamp column can be added. A timestamp is like a version stamp. Whenever a row is added or updated, the timestamp column updates. It's a sort of version control system. Consider the extending of the client table with an extra field called verStamp. When a selection is made, it goes as follows:

```
select id, username, password verStamp from clients where  id = @id
```

The field verStamp is then used in the update, like this:

```
update clients set ... where id = @id and tsequal( verStamp, @inpVerStamp)
```

This way, if anyone updates the record while another user is working with it, the update will fail. At that point, the business object can take an alternate action.

IObjectConstruct Interfaces

When you're developing transaction components, one of the most annoying problems involves building a database connection. The reason is because you don't know what the name of the DSN is. One solution is to compile the name of the resource into the COM object. However, this solution involves the administrator setting up the correct resource.

Another solution would be to set it dynamically using a reference file. However, with COM+, this isn't necessary anymore. A new interface called IObjectConstruct serves this purpose. The definition of IObjectConstruct is as follows:

```
IObjectConstruct : public IUnknown
    {
    public:
        virtual HRESULT STDMETHODCALLTYPE Construct(
            /* [in] */ IDispatch __RPC_FAR *pCtorObj) = 0;
    };
```

This interface has only one method: the Construct method. When this interface is implemented, the Construct method is called when the COM object is instantiated. The instantiation string is enabled by checking the Enable Object Construction check box. You learned about this in the discussion about the Security tab in Chapter 21. A string can be entered in the text box. This defines some information about how the COM object can be used.

This interface makes it possible to implement a constructor without requiring the use of the physical constructor. The advantage of this constructor is that the COM layer will be initialized and made usable. Here's a sample implementation of the method:

```
STDMETHODIMP CConstTest::Construct(IDispatch * pUnk)
{
    try {
        IObjectConstructString * pString = NULL;
        _com_util::CheckError( pUnk->QueryInterface(IID_
        ➡IObjectConstructString, (void **)&pString));

        if( pString != NULL) {
            BSTR szConstruct;
            pString->get_ConstructString(&szConstruct);

            // do some work

            SysFreeString(szConstruct);
            pString->Release();
        }
    } catch( _com_error err) {
        ;
    }
    return S_OK;
}
```

When this method is passed in, the pUnk variable represents an interface where the object construction interface can be retrieved. The first step is to call QueryInterface and request the IObjectConstructString interface. This interface has a property called ConstructString that contains the construction string. At this point, some dynamic customization can be performed.

This brings up an important point. This method can be used to store some custom information. However, there's no destructor, which means that any data that's kept must be of a type that does not require an explicit destruction. In other words, all types must be autodestructors and cannot be dependent on the COM layer.

Special-Case Transaction Control

Manipulating a transaction is simple if the COM+ object is executed using the JIT and transaction attributes. However, consider the situation in which a COM+ object is not running within the context of a JIT. An example of this would be when the administrator sets the transaction attribute to `Ignored`. The reason for this is specialized—for example, the administrator might not want to let the component be deactivated. For these types of components, performing transactions becomes difficult. Windows 2000 adds many new interfaces to handle the various situations.

Defining `IObjectContextInfo`

The only interface that will be discussed here is `IObjectContextInfo`. This interface is an extension of the `IObjectContext` interface and is defined as follows:

```
IObjectContextInfo : public IUnknown
    {
    public:
        virtual BOOL STDMETHODCALLTYPE IsInTransaction( void) = 0;
        virtual BOOL STDMETHODCALLTYPE IsSecurityEnabled( void) = 0;
        virtual HRESULT STDMETHODCALLTYPE IsCallerInRole(
            /* [in] */ BSTR bstrRole,
            /* [retval][out] */ BOOL __RPC_FAR *pfInRole) = 0;
        virtual HRESULT STDMETHODCALLTYPE GetTransaction(
            IUnknown __RPC_FAR *__RPC_FAR *pptrans) = 0;
        virtual HRESULT STDMETHODCALLTYPE GetTransactionId(
            /* [out] */ GUID __RPC_FAR *pGuid) = 0;
        virtual HRESULT STDMETHODCALLTYPE GetActivityId(
            /* [out] */ GUID __RPC_FAR *pGUID) = 0;
        virtual HRESULT STDMETHODCALLTYPE GetContextId(
            /* [out] */ GUID __RPC_FAR *pGuid) = 0;
};
```

This interface may seem similar because the first three methods are identical to `IObjectContext`. The one that's different is the `GetTransaction` method. Calling this method will return an interface pointer to the `ITransaction` interface, which is defined as follows:

```
ITransaction : public IUnknown
    {
    public:
        virtual HRESULT STDMETHODCALLTYPE Commit(
            /* [in] */ BOOL fRetaining,
```

```
              /* [in] */ DWORD grfTC,
              /* [in] */ DWORD grfRM) = 0;
virtual HRESULT STDMETHODCALLTYPE Abort(
              /* [unique][in] */ BOID __RPC_FAR *pboidReason,
              /* [in] */ BOOL fRetaining,
              /* [in] */ BOOL fAsync) = 0;
virtual HRESULT STDMETHODCALLTYPE GetTransactionInfo(
              /* [out] */ XACTTRANSINFO __RPC_FAR *pinfo) = 0;
};
```

This is not a new interface. Instead, it's an interface used in OLE DB. Using this interface, you can control the transaction without having the JIT effect on the COM+ object. This provides the ability to fine-tune the transaction. Note, though, that the parameters to the methods are a bit more complicated. The Commit method's parameters are defined in the following sections.

Retaining

This flag defines whether you can work on the rowset after a commit or abort. This flag is combined with the OLE DB property DBPROP_COMMITPRESERVE. This property defines whether a rowset is available after a commit or abort. When a commit or abort is called, a DBPROP_COMMITPRESERVE VARIANT_TRUE value allows further operations on the currently selected rowset. A VARIANT_FALSE value indicates that the rowset should be considered invalid. In this situation, any references to a rowset should be released, because they contain no data. Combining the flag and property, you get the following side effects on the data and transaction:

DBPROP_ COMMIT PRESERVE	fRetaining	Rowset State After Commit	Resulting Transaction Mode of Session
FALSE	FALSE	Not available	Autocommit
FALSE	TRUE	Not available	Manual
TRUE	FALSE	Available	Autocommit
TRUE	TRUE	Available	Manual

grfTC

When the grfTC method is called, the two-phase commit is started. You can perform an *asynchronous commit*, meaning that the method returns immediately. You can also wait for the result of the two-phase commit. The following values can be used:

- XACTTC_ASYNC. The method initiates the two-phase commit and returns immediately.

- XACTTC_ASYNC_PHASEONE. The method waits for the first phase of the two-phase commit to complete.

- XACTTC_ASYNC_PHASETWO. The method waits for the second phase of the two-phase commit to complete.

- XACTTC_SYNC. Same value as XACTTC_ASYNC_PHASETWO.

The last parameter must be zero. Depending on which phase the method returns, you can determine whether or not the commit was successful.

Abort

This method is similar in functionality to Commit. Its parameters are defined as follows:

- pBoidReason. A BOID that tells the system why the transaction was aborted. NULL can be passed in as a value.

- fRetaining. Identical to the fRetaining parameter of the Commit method.

- fAsync. If this value is set to TRUE, the Abort method is asynchronous and returns immediately.

GetTransactionInfo

The last method, GetTransactionInfo, retrieves the properties of the currently running context. An example is the isolation level of the transaction.

Retrieving IObjectContextInfo

In order to retrieve the IObjectContextInfo interface, you must call the method GetObjectContext. It returns an interface pointer to IObjectContext. Performing a QI on this interface returns the interface for IObjectContextInfo. Here's a sample implementation:

```
IObjectContext * pObjectContext = NULL;
hr = GetObjectContext(&pObjectContext);
IObjectContextInfo    * pObjTx = NULL;
pObjectContext->QueryInterface(IID_IObjectContextInfo,
➥(void **)&pObjTx);
```

Controlling Transactions from the Client

Instantiating a COM+ object is as simple as creating another COM object. However, there may be times when it's desirable to create multiple COM objects and bind them into one transaction. This cannot be done from the base client, as is. An additional interface needs to be used. The problem is that the base client does not have a transaction context associated with it.

As shown in Figure 25.5, when standard COM object instantiation routines are used, there will be two transactions. Each transaction does not know about the other.

FIGURE 25.5

An example of a base client instantiating two COM+ objects.

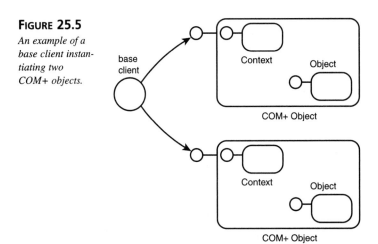

One way to combine various objects within one transaction is to create a helper object that creates the objects.

In Figure 25.6, the first object is also called the *root object* and is responsible for creating the transaction objects. The root object can combine all the objects into one transaction. The advantage of this is that the life of the transaction is well defined. The disadvantage of this technique is that another object might potentially need to be written. (In practice, other objects are created as part of a business process.)

FIGURE 25.6

An example of using the root object to create other objects.

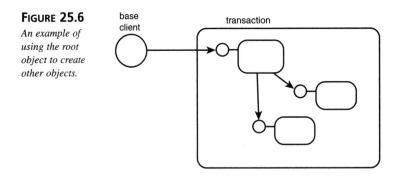

Creating Two COM Objects Running in the Same Transaction

Let's consider a situation in which it's desired to control the transaction from the base client. To do this, you must use the interface ITransactionContextEx, which is defined as follows:

```
ITransactionContextEx : public IUnknown
    {
    public:
        virtual HRESULT STDMETHODCALLTYPE CreateInstance(
            /* [in] */ REFCLSID rclsid,
            /* [in] */ REFIID riid,
            /* [iid_is][retval][out] */ void **pObject) = 0;
        virtual HRESULT STDMETHODCALLTYPE Commit( void) = 0;
        virtual HRESULT STDMETHODCALLTYPE Abort( void) = 0;
    };
```

There are three methods. The first method, CreateInstance, is similar in functionality to IObjectContext::CreateInstance. You need to pass in the coclass (REFCLSID) and interface ID (REFIID), and the resulting interface pointer is returned. Here's a sample implementation:

```
#include <autosvcs.h>

int main() {
    ITransactionContextEx *ptrTransCtxt = NULL;

    CoCreateInstance( CLSID_TransactionContextEx, NULL, 0,
    ➥IID_ITransactionContextEx, (void **)&ptxctx1);

    IClient *pClient1, *pClient2;

    ptrTransCtxt->CreateInstance( CLSID_ImplClient1, IID_IClient,
    ➥ (void**)&pClient1);
    ptrTransCtxt->CreateInstance( CLSID_ImplClient2, IID_IClient,
    ➥ (void**)&pClient1);
    pClient1->Release();
    pClient2->Release();
    ptrTransCtxt->Release();
}
```

The first step is to instantiate the ITransactionContextEx interface object. After the object has been instantiated, you can create two other objects (IClientX pClient1, pClient2) using CreateInstance. These two objects will now be running within one transaction, if the transaction attributes are correct.

To understand this, look at the `CreateInstance` methods a bit closer. The interface `IClient` is not implemented in the same object. It's implemented in two different objects: `CLSID_ImplClient1` and `CLSID_ImplClient2`. If either one of these objects has the transaction attribute `REQUIRES_NEW`, a new transaction is started. On the other hand, if either of these objects has no support for the transaction attribute, a transaction doesn't apply. The advantage to using this technique is that the programmer can assume that there will only be one transaction. The administrator can then decide whether this will actually happen.

Controlling the Transaction

The other two methods of the `ITransactionContextEx` interface allow the base client to control the transaction. The method `Commit` is analogous to `SetComplete`, and `Abort` is analogous to `SetAbort`. However, if a COM object within a transaction calls `SetAbort` and the base client calls `Commit`, the transaction will abort.

> **CAUTION**
>
> Using this interface makes it easy to wire COM+ objects into one transaction. A problem can arise if the base client does not keep the duration of the transaction short. For example, the client could create multiple objects and start calling methods. Because the root object is no longer the first instantiation COM+ object but rather the `ITransactionContextEx` interface, it's no longer in control of the transaction. This means a delayed call to `Commit` will lock resources and cause scalability problems.

Queued Components

When two components want to communicate over a network, the classical solution is to use DCOM. A DCOM call is like a regular COM call, except that it's across a network. It uses the RPC (remote procedure call) architecture. The problem with this architecture is that it tends to flood the network with traffic, because every call, if it's a property or a method call, will be routed on the network.

Another problem with DCOM occurs when things go wrong with the server. DCOM relies on the server being active. If the requested server is not available or is disconnected abruptly, the client will hang. If the server is part of a transaction, it will be aborted. Overall, this solution has its problems.

A preferred solution is to use a messaging architecture. This is preferred because of its ability to deal with failure. Using DCOM within a local area network may be okay, outside of the fact that it requires quite a bit of bandwidth. For noisy or unreliable communications, messaging is better. Using messaging, you can retry sending the data until it has been received.

Figure 25.7 shows the architecture for two machines. The communications between the two machines is accomplished using MSMQ. A base client calls the order object, which, in turn, accesses the order database. During this operation, a message is generated. This entire operation involves one transaction. The message is then sent to the second machine, where it calls a shipping object, which, in turn, updates the shipping database.

FIGURE 25.7

An example of messaging archi-tecture.

Messaging Application

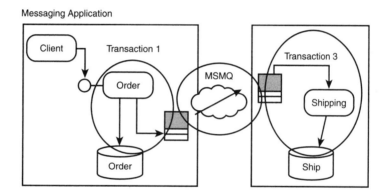

So what's the point of this operation if it can be solved using DCOM? The point is that by using messages, the base client can perform more operations without waiting to see the result of the shipping operation. A message is sent to the destination machine and the action is executed. This is a type of batch processing. More details on MSMQ (Microsoft Message Queue) and messaging will be given later in Chapter 29, "Cluster Server."

What Are Queued Components?

Queued components are a specific type of message. Chapter 21 showed you how to define a COM+ application as "queuable" and a COM+ object as "queued." What this means is that when the object is referenced, it can be referenced as a message.

MSMQ is very powerful and flexible, but it requires the programmer to do the marshaling of the data. Queued components simplify this by doing the marshaling automatically for you (see Figure 25.8).

FIGURE 25.8

Transport proto-col neutrality with queued components.

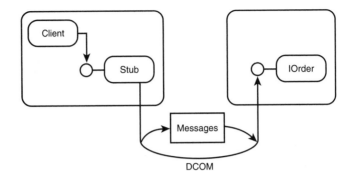

With queued components, there's still a stub that resembles an interface on another machine. The difference lies in which protocol the stub uses to communicate to the serv-er. One option is to use messages, which is the functionality that queued components provides. The other option is to use DCOM. But in either situation the client is just acti-vating a COM object as shown by the following code:

```
Set Ship = GetObject("queue:/new:QCSamp.Ship")
Ship.OrderNumber = 1234
Ship.CustomerID = 789
Ship.LineItem 10, "Widget"
Ship.Process
```

In the preceding source code, the Visual Basic client calls GetObject, but it uses the queue COM moniker. A COM moniker provides a way of referencing a resource using some naming convention. You use the CLISD moniker with COM. Using "queue" is the queued component moniker, which is new to Windows 2000. Next, a series of properties and methods are called (OrderNumber, CustomerID, and LineItem). The last method is Process, which sends the message.

How Queued Components Work

Queued components create messages by intercepting all the properties and method calls and saving them to a buffer. In Figure 25.9, the various properties and methods (num, custid, and Line) are called and a recorder records the steps sequentially. The buffer is sent to the queue when the transaction on the recorder side commits. After the buffer reaches the destination server, the player loads the transmitted message buffer and plays the various methods using sequential methods.

FIGURE 25.9

The queued component recorder.

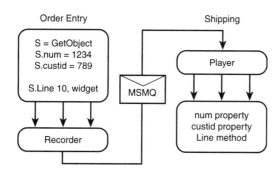

Here are some important points to keep in mind:

- The queued component message must contain by-value parameters. You can't send parameters by reference.

- The communication is one-way, and no response can be sent.

- The recorder will finish recording everything before any messages are played on the server side.

Although it may seem silly to not have messages return to the sender, this is an important feature. Queued components are asynchronous messages and therefore can never expect returned answers. If they did, this would imply a *synchronous* operation, which can be handled better using DCOM.

Specifying Explicit Moniker Attributes

When you're instantiating the queued component, the default moniker would look like this:

```
queue:/new:QCSamp.Ship
```

This specifies that whatever is created is a queued component. The new file moniker provides a way of creating a COM object: It's like using `CoCreateInstance`.

To specify a specific queue, you can use the following notation:

```
queue:ComputerName=bacchus,Priority=3/new:Ship
```

This moniker specifies that a queued component is to be created, and the name of the computer where the queued component is located is "bacchus." When the message for the queued component is sent, a priority of 3 is to be used.

This introduces another side effect. Consider the situation in which two messages are sent to a queued component. The first message has a low priority, and the other has a high priority. However, the low-priority message is sent out first, and the high-priority message is sent out last. Over a long distance, the order in which the messages arrive and are replayed may be in reverse. Therefore, it's vital that the queued components reflect an event-driven architecture that does not rely on a specific order of messages.

Writing Queued Components

Writing a queued component is not so different from writing a normal COM object. The difference lies in the administration and the attributes. Here's an example:

```
[
    helpstring("IShip Interface"),
    uuid(CB34A1A4-28C2-11D2-B5B6-00C04FC340EE),
    object, dual, nonextensible, hidden, pointer_default(unique),
    QUEUEABLE
]
interface IShip : IDispatch
{
    [id(1), propput] HRESULT CustomerId([in] long lCustomerId);
    [id(2), propput] HRESULT OrderId([in] long lOrderId);
    [id(3)]    HRESULT LineItem([in] long lItemId, [in] long lQuantity);
    [id(4)]    HRESULT Process([in] long lFlags);
}
```

In this IDL file, the attribute QUEUEABLE is defined within the interface properties. This specifies that the component can be defined as a queued component. The definition is from the include file mtxattr.h. Otherwise, you would need to write your queued component as if it were a stateless transactional component.

Sending a Return Message Using Queued Components

With queued components, the real problem is how to send return messages. When a message is sent, the receiver of the message does not have a direct connection to the sender. Therefore, in order for the receiver to be able to return a message, a notify architecture must be established (see Figure 25.10).

In this architecture, the client creates an order. The transaction is committed, and the message is sent to start the second transaction. This transaction then formulates a message. Upon success, the message is sent back to the originator in the form of a Notify message. The Notify message starts the third transaction and updates the database. It's that simple.

FIGURE 25.10

Notify callback architecture.

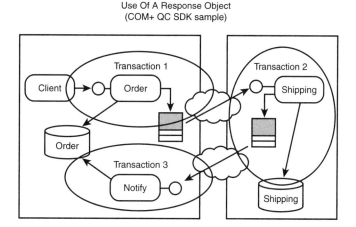

Use Of A Response Object
(COM+ QC SDK sample)

What's important here is that all this must be written using custom COM objects. The Notify COM object is nothing more than a simple object that updates the database and indicates what has happened. How does a transaction know whether the last transaction occurred successfully? It doesn't, and there's no way of tying those two transactions together. The only way of knowing what has happened is to leave a piece of state information. This can be done easily using IMDB. This promotes high-speed access with full transaction capabilities.

There are three transactions in this architecture, and each is independent. Although it may seem logical to tie them together, it's not advisable (in fact, it's not even possible). The reason is because queued components are asynchronous in nature, and they execute long transactions. Long transactions tie up resources and reduce scalability. The solution to using multitransaction situations is to define a log and a series of "undo" operators. The undo operators will be called whenever anything goes wrong.

Distributing Information Asynchronously

The COM programming model is one in which a request is made and then processed. Whether you're using straight COM or DCOM, the request is handled synchronously. Using queued components, however, the request is handled asynchronously. In both of these situations, the client requests something from the server.

Another set of problems involves the server informing the client that changes occurred. Although this may seem to involve asynchronous programming, it's better defined via callback programming, as shown in Figure 25.11.

FIGURE 25.11

An example of using a callback.

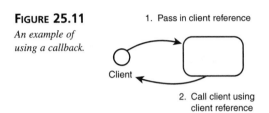

1. Pass in client reference

Client

2. Call client using client reference

The client sends a message to the server. In this message is a reference to the client. In Windows programming, this reference is a Windows message function. In the event services architecture, this is a COM interface. Whenever anything changes, the server informs the client of the changes using this reference.

Introducing Publisher/Subscriber Architecture

The callback architecture can be generalized into what's known as the *publisher/subscriber architecture*. In Figure 25.12, the architecture shows that the client wants some information. However, the information distribution is to be shared among multiple clients. This type of application involves those that have information (publishers) and those that want information (subscribers). Neither knows of the other at development time.

In a publisher/subscriber architecture, the client applies to a subscription that's made available by a publisher. The publisher is informed of this request. When the publisher has new data, it queries to find out who has subscribed. Those subscribers then get the new information via the IXXEvent interface.

You can build a subscription architecture using COM connection points. However, this is not an ideal solution because the publisher and subscriber are tightly coupled. Connection points assume that there's one publisher of information. When a connection point is established, it's not persistent. It's also not possible to intercept the connection point and perform some other work.

FIGURE 25.12

Publisher/subscri-ber architecture.

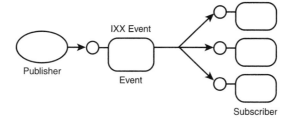

Windows 2000 includes a COM+ event service. This service handles the plumbing of the subscription mechanism and provides the following features:

- Events are fired at the abstract level using COM interface IDs.
- Subscriptions can be persistent.
- There can be many publishers of information.
- The subscriber has to be active while waiting for a message.
- Events can survive failure.
- The event service is component based and therefore supports full security, load balancing, and transactions.

The pieces of the entire process are shown in Figure 25.13.

FIGURE 25.13

COM+ events-based subscription service.

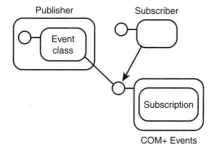

Building a Publisher/Subscriber Project

To build an application using this architecture, the first step is to determine what information the client will subscribe to. An example of information could be a stock ticker.

This is the I*XX*Event object. As an example, consider the following event interface:

```
[
    object,
    uuid(55d81670-6567-11d1-88c8-0080c7d771bf),
    dual,
    oleautomation,
    helpstring("StockEvents Interface"),
    pointer_default(unique)
]
interface IStockEvents : IDispatch
{
    [id(1), helpstring("method StockPriceChange")]
            HRESULT StockPriceChange ( BSTR StockSymbol, double Price );
    [id(2), helpstring("method NewStock")]
            HRESULT NewStock ( BSTR StockSymbol, BSTR CompanyName );
};
```

This interface is used for communication among the various pieces. In a typical development situation, an IDL file is created. Then, a type library is compiled. Depending on the language, the IDL file or type library is referenced throughout the various projects.

In Figure 25.13, the event class is used. The publisher defines the interface as part of the subscription; then the various subscription clients implement the interface to capture the event.

The publisher of a subscription has the responsibility of sending content to the various subscribers. This is done using a COM+ object.

The first step a publisher takes is to register itself with the COM+ event service. In the sample code, the object is the SimplePublisherATL COM object. A sample registration of a publisher follows:

```
HRESULT hr = S_OK;
 LPOLESTR    strGUID;

 CComBSTR bstrPublisherID;
 CComBSTR bstrPublisherName;

 CComPtr<IEventSystem> spIEventSystem;
 CComPtr<IEventPublisher> spIEventPublisher;

 hr = CoCreateInstance(CLSID_CEventSystem,
                        NULL,
```

```
                              CLSCTX_SERVER,
                              IID_IEventSystem,
                              (void**)&spIEventSystem);

    if (FAILED(hr))
    {
        Error("Failed to create IEventClass", IID_IStockPublisher, hr);
        return hr;
    }

    hr = CoCreateInstance(CLSID_CEventPublisher,
                              NULL,
                              CLSCTX_SERVER,
                              IID_IEventPublisher,
                              (void**)&spIEventPublisher);

    if (FAILED(hr))
    {
        Error("Failed to create IEventPublisher", IID_IStockPublisher, hr);
-       return hr;
    }

    hr = StringFromIID(CLSID_StockPublisher, &strGUID );
    if (FAILED(hr))
    {
        Error("Failed to convert GUID to OLESTR", IID_IStockPublisher, hr);
        return hr;
    }

    bstrPublisherID = strGUID;
    CoTaskMemFree(strGUID);

    bstrPublisherName = str_StockPublisherName;

    hr = spIEventPublisher->put_PublisherID(bstrPublisherID);
    if (FAILED(hr))
    {
        Error("Failed to put PublisherID ", IID_IStockPublisher, hr);
        return hr;
    }

    hr = spIEventPublisher->put_PublisherName(bstrPublisherName);
    if (FAILED(hr))
    {
        Error("Failed to put PublisherName ", IID_IStockPublisher, hr);
        return hr;
    }

    hr = spIEventSystem->Store(PROGID_EventPublisher, spIEventPublisher);
    if (FAILED(hr))
    {
```

```
        Error("Failed to Store EventPublisher ", IID_IStockPublisher, hr);
        return hr;
    }
```

The event services will manage all aspects of the subscription. To connect to it, the
IEventSystem interface pointer is instantiated using CoCreateInstance. This interface
has the ability to accept either a publisher or a subscriber of the event. It's defined as a
parameter within the various methods.

The next step is to instantiate a publisher definition COM+ interface. The interface
IEventPublisher is a read/write property that defines the specific publisher. One very
important facet of COM+ events and subscriptions is that there are no specific interface
references. Instead, abstract COM ProgIDs are used to define the attributes. This makes
it possible to easily load balance and scale the components and instantiate them regardless of the situation. In the long term, this makes for more flexible programming and uti-
lization.

For a publisher to be defined, the CLSID of the publisher needs to be extracted using
StringFromIID. Then that string is converted into a BSTR and stored in the
IEventPublisher::PublisherID property. Stored within the
IEventPublisher::PublisherName property is the ProgID of the publishing component.

The last step is to store the publisher within the COM+ event services using the method
IEventSystem::Store. The first parameter defines that the item to be stored is a publisher (PROGID_EventPublisher).

Removing a publisher and event class is simpler, as shown by the following code:

```
STDMETHODIMP CStockPublisher::Uninstall()
{
    LPOLESTR    strGUID;
    HRESULT hr = S_OK;
    int         errorIndex;

    CComPtr<IEventSystem> spIEventSystem;

    hr = CoCreateInstance(CLSID_CEventSystem,
                          NULL,
                          CLSCTX_SERVER,
                          IID_IEventSystem,
                          (void**)&spIEventSystem);

    // ------------------------------------------------
    //      Delete a publisher
    // ------------------------------------------------
    hr = StringFromIID(CLSID_StockPublisher, &strGUID);
    CComBSTR bstrCriteria("PublisherID=");
```

```
        bstrCriteria += strGUID;

        CoTaskMemFree(strGUID);

        hr = spIEventSystem->Remove(PROGID_EventPublisher, bstrCriteria,
        ➥ &errorIndex);

        // ------------------------------------------------
        //      Delete an event
        // ------------------------------------------------
        hr = StringFromIID(CLSID_StockEvents, &strGUID);
        bstrCriteria = "EventClassID=";
        bstrCriteria+= strGUID;

        CoTaskMemFree(strGUID);

        hr = spIEventSystem->Remove(PROGID_EventClass, bstrCriteria,
        ➥&errorIndex);

        return hr;
}
```

Again, a connection to the IEventSystem is established and then a string is built using PublisherID. Finally, the method IEventSystem::Remove is called. The way this method works is that it builds a query that selects a series of subscriptions and then removes them. For the publisher class and the event class, the removal steps are identical.

The next step for the publisher is to define the event it will broadcast to the various subscribers. This is known as *defining the event class*. An example follows:

```
CComPtr<IEventClass> spIEventClass;


hr = CoCreateInstance(CLSID_CEventClass,
                      NULL,
                      CLSCTX_SERVER,
                      IID_IEventClass,
                      (void**)&spIEventClass);
if (FAILED(hr))
{
    Error("Failed to create IEventClass", IID_IStockPublisher, hr);
    return hr;
}

hr = StringFromIID(CLSID_StockEvents, &strGUID);
if (FAILED(hr))
{
    Error("Failed to create String from IID", IID_IStockPublisher, hr);
    return hr;
}
```

```
bstrEventClassID = strGUID;
CoTaskMemFree(strGUID);

bstrEventProgID = str_StockEventsProgID;

hr = StringFromIID(IID_IStockEvents, &strGUID);
if (FAILED(hr))
{
    Error("Failed to create String from IID", IID_IStockPublisher, hr);
    return hr;
}
bstrFiringIID = strGUID;
CoTaskMemFree(strGUID);

// Set The Properties of the EventClass
hr = spIEventClass->put_EventClassID(bstrEventClassID);
if (FAILED(hr))
{
    Error("Failed to set EventClassID", IID_IStockPublisher, hr);
        return hr;
}
hr = spIEventClass->put_EventClassName(bstrEventProgID);
if (FAILED(hr))
{
    Error("Failed to set EventClassName", IID_IStockPublisher, hr);
    return hr;
}

hr = spIEventClass->put_FiringInterfaceID(bstrFiringIID);
if (FAILED(hr))
{
    Error("Failed to FiringInterfaceID", IID_IStockPublisher, hr);
    return hr;
}

// Store into the EventSystem
hr = spIEventSystem->Store(PROGID_EventClass, spIEventClass);
if (FAILED(hr))
{
    Error("Failed to store EventClass from the EventSystem",
    ➡IID_IStockPublisher, hr);
    return hr;
}
```

Like the publisher definition, the event class definition is accomplished through the use of ProgIDs. An event class is defined by instantiating the IEventClass interface. The interface that needs to be associated with this event is IStockEvent. The interface is defined in the property IEventClass::FiringInterfaceID. A CLSID needs to be associated with the interface in the property IEventClass::EventClassID. Also, the accompanying ProgID is associated with the property IEventClass::EventClassName.

The CLSID and ProgID make it possible for the COM+ event services to understand the interface being broadcast. Therefore, in your IDL, a coclass that references the interface being broadcast must be defined. Here's an example:

```
[
    uuid(DD011223-E8EA-11D1-B994-00C04F990088),
    version(1.0),
    helpstring("SimplePublisherATL 1.0 Type Library")
]
library SIMPLEPUBLISHERATLLib
{
    importlib("stdole32.tlb");
    importlib("stdole2.tlb");

    [
        uuid(877E7998-E8EC-11D1-B994-00C04F990088),
        helpstring("StockPublisher Class")
    ]
    coclass StockPublisher
    {
        [default] interface IStockPublisher;
    };

    [
        uuid(f89859d1-6565-11d1-88c8-0080c7d771bf),
        helpstring("StockEvent Class")
    ]
    coclass StockEvents
    {
        [source] interface IStockEvents;
    };

};
```

The event services class is then registered with the COM+ event services. This is done by calling the method `IEventSystem::Store`, The first parameter (`PROGID_EventClass`) indicates that the definition is an event class.

The publisher has performed both its tasks and optionally can fire some events. The firing of events is the result of some method calls on the object. The original `IStockEvent` interface had two methods (`StockPriceChanged` and `NewStock`). A sample implementation of firing `NewStock` follows:

```
CComPtr<IStockEvents> spIStockEvents;
HRESULT hr;

hr = CoCreateInstance(CLSID_StockEvents,
                      NULL,
                      CLSCTX_SERVER,
```

```
                        IID_IStockEvents,
                        (void**)&spIStockEvents);
if (FAILED(hr))
{
    Error("Failed to create IStockEvents from EventSystem",
    ➥IID_IStockPublisher, hr);
    return hr;
}

hr = spIStockEvents->NewStock(bstrNewStockSymbol, bstrCompanyName );
if (FAILED(hr))
{
    Error("Failed to invoke NewStock", IID_IStockPublisher, hr);
    return hr;
}
```

In this example, the coclass `StockEvents` is called. The previous IDL's coclass did not refer to any implementation but yet it's instantiated using `CoCreateInstance`. The way this works is that the COM object being instantiated is part of the COM+ event services. It's like a stub, and it executes on the publisher's machine.

When the method `IStockEvents::NextStock` is called, the stub is called and then the message is broadcast. Stored within the stub is a cache of subscribers. The list of subscribers comes from the COM+ event services event store. The message will instantiate the COM+ objects that implement the `IStockEvents` interface and subscribe to the event. Each subscriber gets the same message, but in a sequential order.

CAUTION

A timeout due to very slow communication lines may confuse COM+ event services and cause a subscriber to miss a message.

Implementing a Subscriber

When a message is broadcast, a client component receives the event. The client must be a COM object.

The subscription is a multistep process, and it needs an identifier (GUID). This identifier could be defined as follows:

```
const GUID guid_StockPriceChangeSub = { 0x6b1046e6, 0xe922, 0x11d1,
➥{ 0xb9, 0x94, 0x0, 0xc0, 0x4f, 0x99, 0x0, 0x88 } };
const GUID guid_NewStockSub = { 0x6b1046e7, 0xe922, 0x11d1,
➥{ 0xb9, 0x94, 0x0, 0xc0, 0x4f, 0x99, 0x0, 0x88 } };
```

With a subscription identifier, multiple event cycles can be defined on the same interface. The subscriber needs to define which event cycle it's interested in.

Now the publisher of the event class needs to be implemented. Here is an example:

```
STDMETHODIMP CStockSubscriber::Install()
{
    CComBSTR bstrSubscriptionID;
    CComBSTR bstrSubscriptionName (str_StockPriceChangeSub);
    CComBSTR bstrPublisherID;
    CComBSTR bstrEventClassID;
    CComBSTR bstrMethodName;
    CComBSTR bstrSubscriberClass;

    HRESULT hr = S_OK;
    LPOLESTR strGUID;

    CComPtr<IEventSubscription> spIEventSubscription;
    CComPtr<IEventSystem> spIEventSystem;

    hr = CoCreateInstance(CLSID_CEventSystem,
                          NULL,
                          CLSCTX_SERVER,
                          IID_IEventSystem,
                          (void**)&spIEventSystem);

    hr = CoCreateInstance(CLSID_CEventSubscription,
                          NULL,
                          CLSCTX_SERVER,
                          IID_IEventSubscription,
                          (void**) &spIEventSubscription);

    hr = StringFromIID(guid_StockPriceChangeSub, &strGUID);

    bstrSubscriptionID = strGUID;
    CoTaskMemFree(strGUID);

    hr = StringFromIID(IID_IStockPublisher, &strGUID);

    bstrPublisherID = strGUID;
    CoTaskMemFree(strGUID);

    hr = StringFromIID(CLSID_StockEvents, &strGUID);

    bstrEventClassID = strGUID;
    CoTaskMemFree(strGUID);

    bstrMethodName = "StockPriceChange";

    hr = StringFromIID(CLSID_StockSubscriber, &strGUID);
```

```
        bstrSubscriberClass = strGUID;
        CoTaskMemFree(strGUID);

        // Set EventSubscription Properties
        hr = spIEventSubscription->put_SubscriptionID (bstrSubscriptionID);
        hr = spIEventSubscription->put_SubscriptionName
        ➥(bstrSubscriptionName);
        hr = spIEventSubscription->put_PublisherID(bstrPublisherID);
        hr = spIEventSubscription->put_EventClassID (bstrEventClassID);
        hr = spIEventSubscription->put_MethodName(bstrMethodName);
        hr = spIEventSubscription->put_SubscriberCLSID(bstrSubscriberClass);

        CComVariant PropertyBagValue("MSFT");
        CComBSTR     PropertyBagName("StockSymbol");
         hr = spIEventSubscription->PutPublisherProperty(PropertyBagName,
        ➥&PropertyBagValue);
         hr = spIEventSystem->Store(PROGID_EventSubscription,
        ➥spIEventSubscription);


        // Add the Event for NewStocks
        hr = StringFromIID(guid_NewStockSub, &strGUID);
        bstrSubscriptionID = strGUID;
        CoTaskMemFree(strGUID);

        bstrMethodName = "NewStock";
        bstrSubscriptionName  = str_NewStockSub;

        // Set EventSubscription Properties
        hr = spIEventSubscription->put_SubscriptionID (bstrSubscriptionID);
        hr = spIEventSubscription->put_SubscriptionName
(bstrSubscriptionName);
        hr = spIEventSubscription->put_PublisherID(bstrPublisherID);
        hr = spIEventSubscription->put_EventClassID (bstrEventClassID);
        hr = spIEventSubscription->put_MethodName(bstrMethodName);
        hr = spIEventSubscription->put_SubscriberCLSID(bstrSubscriberClass);

        // Store into the EventSystem
        hr = spIEventSystem->Store(PROGID_EventSubscription,
        ➥spIEventSubscription);

        return hr;
    }
```

This piece of code is fairly long, and the entire piece does not need explanation. In order for a subscriber to be defined, the COM+ event service interface needs to be instantiated (line 16). Then, the event subscription interface needs to be instantiated (line 22). This interface is responsible for managing the subscription for the COM object.

In a nutshell, the subscription ID defined previously needs to be set to the property `SubscriptionID`. The other important property is `PublisherID`. Generally speaking, this is not an important property, but it becomes important when filtering by the publisher is required. The property `EventClassID` represents the co-class of the interface that's being subscribed to. In this example, it's `StockEvents`, which is the interface `IStockEvents`. To determine which method an event should be fired on, the property `MethodName` is set. Finally, the property `SubscriberCLSID` is set to the object that will be called. This CLSID is also used to perform subscriber-side filtering. After all these properties have been set, the subscription is added to the `IEventSystem` interface using the method store.

Lines 58 to 60 make it possible to define a publisher property. This property is useful when you want to filter for a specific value. In this situation, for the `StockPriceChange` event, the subscriber wants information about the MSFT stock. Of course, this subscription definition applies if the publisher performs some filtering.

Removing a subscription is identical to removing a publisher or event class. The difference involves the query string and the ProgID. Here's a sample implementation:

```
CComBSTR     bstrCriteria;
int errorIndex;
LPOLESTR     strGUID;

hr = StringFromIID(guid_StockPriceChangeSub, &strGUID);

bstrCriteria = "SubscriptionID=";
bstrCriteria += strGUID;
CoTaskMemFree(strGUID);

hr = spIEventSystem->Remove(PROGID_EventSubscription, bstrCriteria,
➥ &errorIndex);
```

When a COM object wants to receive an event, it needs to implement the event being broadcast. This is a requirement, because COM+ event services would otherwise have no idea where to send the message. Here's an example of implementing an event:

```
class ATL_NO_VTABLE CStockSubscriber :
    public CComObjectRootEx<CComSingleThreadModel>,
    public CComCoClass<CStockSubscriber, &CLSID_StockSubscriber>,
    public ISupportErrorInfo,
    public ISubscriberControl,
    public IDispatchImpl<IStockSubscriber, &IID_IStockSubscriber,
    ➥ &LIBID_SIMPLESUBSCRIBERATLLib>,
    public IDispatchImpl<IStockEvents, &IID_IStockEvents, &LIBID_
    ➥SIMPLESUBSCRIBERATLLib>
{
...
}
```

The easiest way to implement the interface is to use the Visual C++ Implement Interface Wizard. Also, you must remember to change your IDL to reflect that you've implemented the `IStockEvents` interface, as shown in the following example:

```
[
    uuid(9922BBAF-E91D-11D1-B994-00C04F990088),
    version(1.0),
    helpstring("SimpleSubscriberATL 1.0 Type Library")
]
library SIMPLESUBSCRIBERATLLib
{
    importlib("stdole32.tlb");
    importlib("stdole2.tlb");

    [
        uuid(9922BBBD-E91D-11D1-B994-00C04F990088),
        helpstring("StockSubscriber Class")
    ]
    coclass StockSubscriber
    {
        [default] interface      IStockSubscriber;
        interface IStockEvents;
        interface ISubscriberControl;
    };
};
```

In this example, `IStockEvents` is part of the co-class `StockSubscriber`.

> **TIP**
>
> To simplify the Implement Interface Wizard's interface, first change the IDL. Compile the IDL and then right-click to implement the interface. This way, the current project type library will have the `IStockEvents` interface available.

Defining Filters

When the events are generated as shown previously, all the subscribers get all the messages. However, it may be preferable for specific subscribers to get specific events. You can accomplish this using one of two different methods: publisher filtering or subscriber filtering.

Subscriber is the simpler of the two filtering techniques. It has the drawback that the message is sent to the destination subscriber. To activate this filter, the subscribing COM object needs to implement the `ISubscriberControl` interface. An example of the header and IDL is given in the previous source code pieces. An example of implementing this interface with a single method is as follows and can be seen in Figure 25.14:

```
STDMETHODIMP CStockSubscriber::PreEventCall(IEventSubscription
➥*spIEventSubscription)
{
        HRESULT hr = S_OK;
        CComBSTR    SubscriptionName;
        _TCHAR  MessageText[150];
hr = spIEventSubscription->get_SubscriptionName(&SubscriptionName);
    if (FAILED(hr))
    {
        Error("Failed to get SubscriptionName", IID_IStockSubscriber, hr);
        return hr;
    }
        wsprintf(MessageText, TEXT("SubscriptionName is [%S]"),
        ➥SubscriptionName);
        return S_OK;
}
```

FIGURE 25.14

Event filtering in Subscriber.

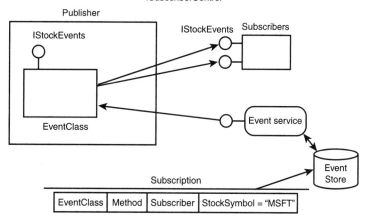

The method is passed in an IEventSubscription interface. Using this passed-in interface, you can retrieve all aspects of the subscription event being triggered. At this point, the COM object can take further action.

Filtering in the Publisher

This filtering is a bit more complicated because it occurs on the publisher side. When a filter is called, another object is called with the method being triggered. This method can filter out the properties and modify them (see Figure 25.15).

FIGURE 25.15

Event filtering in Publisher.

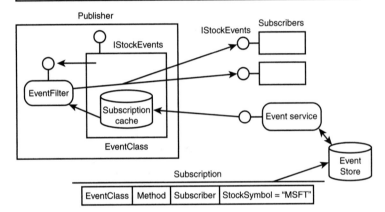

COM Events
Filtering in Publisher

```
interface IStockEvents
(
        HRESULT StockPriceChange (BSTR StockSymbol, double Price);
);
```

Here's an example:

```
CHECK_RESULT( CoCreateInstance(CLSID_PublisherFilter,
        NULL,
        CLSCTX_SERVER,
        IID_IPublisherFilter,
            (void**)&spIPublisherFilter) );
 CComBSTR    bstrMethodName("StockPriceChange");
 CHECK_RESULT(spIStockEvents->QueryInterface(IID_IEventControl,
        (void **)&spIEventControl));
 CComPtr<IEventObjectCollection> spIEventObjectCollection;
CHECK_RESULT(spIEventControl->GetSubscriptions (bstrMethodName, NULL,NULL,
        &spIEventObjectCollection));
 // Give the Collection of Subscriptions to the PublisherFilter
CHECK_RESULT(spIPublisherFilter->Initialize(bstrMethodName,
        spIEventObjectCollection));
 // Set the PublisherFilter
CHECK_RESULT(spIEventControl->SetPublisherFilter(bstrMethodName,
        spIPublisherFilter));
 bstrStockSymbol = L"MSFT";
 Price        = 154.25;
CHECK_RESULT (spIStockEvents->StockPriceChange ( bstrStockSymbol, Price
));
```

COM+ event services need to be informed of the filtering class. In this example, the class is `CLSID_PublisherFilter`. In a previous step, the `IStockEvents` class was instantiated. Remember that when this interface is instantiated, it's a stub to the COM+ event services. This is mentioned because the filtering class needs a reference to the current subscriptions. The interface `IStockEvents` is queried for the `IEventControl` interface. This interface makes it possible to interact with the details of the event and its associated subscriptions. The subscription details are of interest and are therefore retrieved (line 13). The next step is to call the `Initialize` method of the filtering class. This method is used like a constructor to set up the filtering class for any further calls.

The last step is to associate the publisher interface with the `IEventControl` interface (line 21). Now, if any calls to the event are made, the publisher filter class will receive the events first.

The publisher filter class is a COM object that implements the `IPublisherFilter` interface and the event that it's filtering.

The `IPublisherFilter` interface is defined as follows:

```
[
object,
uuid(465e5cc0-7b26-11d1-88fb-0080c7d771bf),
helpstring("IPublisherFilter Interface"),
pointer_default(unique)
]
interface IPublisherFilter : IUnknown
{
    [helpstring("User-called method to initialize the publisher
    ➥filter after it is installed")]
        HRESULT Initialize([in] BSTR methodName, [in,unique] IDispatch*
        ➥dispUserDefined);

    [helpstring("Prepare to fire all subscriptions in your collection")]
        HRESULT PrepareToFire([in] BSTR methodName, [in] IFiringControl*
        ➥firingControl);
};
```

The first method, `Initialize`, has already been discussed. Here's a sample implementation:

```
STDMETHODIMP CPublisherFilter::Initialize( BSTR bstrMethodName,
            IDispatch* pIDispSubColl)
{
    HRESULT                   hr = S_OK;
    IEventObjectCollection*   pISubColl = NULL;
    if (!pIDispSubColl)
        return E_INVALIDARG;
    hr = pIDispSubColl->QueryInterface (IID_IEventObjectCollection,
    ➥ (void **) &pISubColl);
```

```
    m_spStockPriceChange_Collection = NULL;
        if (wcscmp(bstrMethodName, L"StockPriceChange") == 0)
        {
        m_spStockPriceChange_Collection = pISubColl;
        }
    m_spNewStock_Collection = NULL;
    if (wcscmp(bstrMethodName, L"NewStock") == 0)
        {
        m_spNewStock_Collection = pISubColl;
        }
    return hr;
}
```

In this example, the `Initialize` event is used to store the subscription collection. Which one is stored depends on the passed-in method name (`bstrMethodName`).

Once the subscription is about to fire, the method `PrepareToFire` is called. This method can be used to store the `IEventControl` interface, as shown in the following example:

```
STDMETHODIMP CPublisherFilter::PrepareToFire(BSTR bstrMethodName,
➥IFiringControl* pIFiringControl)
{
    if (!pIFiringControl)
        return E_INVALIDARG;

    if (wcscmp(bstrMethodName, L"StockPriceChange") == 0)
    {
        m_spIStockPriceFiringControl = pIFiringControl;
    }

    if (wcscmp(bstrMethodName, L"NewStock") == 0)
    {
        m_spINewStockFiringControl = pIFiringControl;
    }

    return S_OK;
}
```

Finally, all the variable settings are used when the filter captures a method event. In the event interface defined thus far, the `StockPriceChange` or `NewStock` event can be filtered. The filter has the ability to search through the various subscriptions to see who should receive the event. This process can be slow; therefore, you should design it carefully. A filter that takes too long will not be scalable.

Consider the following implementation:

```
STDMETHODIMP CPublisherFilter::StockPriceChange(BSTR bstrStockSymbol,
➡ double dPrice)
{
    long              cPubCacheSubs = 0;
    HRESULT           hr = S_FALSE;
    CComPtr<IEnumEventObject> spIEnumSubs = NULL;
    // Get an Enum of subscriptions from the collection
    hr = m_spStockPriceChange_Collection->get_NewEnum (&spIEnumSubs);
    // See how many Subscriptions there are in the Enum
    hr = m_spStockPriceChange_Collection->get_Count(&cPubCacheSubs);
    CComBSTR bstrPublisherProperty = L"StockSymbol";
    for (USHORT i = 0; i < cPubCacheSubs; i++)
    {
        ULONG     cCount = 1;
        CComBSTR bstrPropertyValue;
        CComVariant varPropertyValue;
         CComPtr<IUnknown> spIUnk = NULL;
        CComQIPtr<IEventSubscription, &IID_IEventSubscription>
        ➡spIEventSubscription;
         // Get a Subscription from the Enum
        hr = spIEnumSubs->Next(cCount, (struct IUnknown **)&spIUnk,
        ➡&cCount);
        spIEventSubscription = spIUnk;
         // Get this Subscription's filter criteria
        hr = spIEventSubscription->GetPublisherProperty
        ➡(bstrPublisherProperty,
                                        &varPropertyValue);
        bstrPropertyValue = varPropertyValue.bstrVal;
    // Compare company names here
  if (wcscmp(bstrStockSymbol, bstrPropertyValue) == 0)
   m_spIStockPriceFiringControl->FireSubscription (spIEventSubscription);
    }
     return S_OK;
}
```

This method retrieves an interface pointer to the collection of subscriptions currently available in the event cache. The next step is to iterate through the subscriptions and check which subscription should be triggered. The event will be triggered if the bstrStockSymbol matches the publisher property. In an earlier subscription definition, the subscription had a filter of "MSFT." Therefore, if both now match, the IEvenControl::FireSubscription event will be triggered.

Summary

This chapter is an introduction to advanced COM+ programming. Although this statement may seem contradictory, it's not. COM+ has the ability to tune all aspects of the COM+ application. This was not possible with COM and the NT Option Pack. However, with all this flexibility comes the responsibility of knowing when to apply what. This chapter also introduced some of the common advanced COM+ topics, including object pooling, load balancing, queued components, and COM+ events.

Distributed Windows 2000 Services

PART
V

IN THIS PART

Pipes

This chapter focuses on the interprocess communication using pipes. A *pipe* is a point-to-point connection used to exchange data between two Windows processes. In this chapter, you'll learn about anonymous and named pipes, and you'll create several sample applications that demonstrate how pipes are used in Windows 2000 applications.

Examining Pipe Types

A *pipe* is a communications channel that Windows applications can use for interprocess communications. Two basic types of pipes exist:

- *Anonymous pipes.* Used primarily for communication between related processes, such as a parent and a child process. Anonymous pipes cannot be used over a network.

- *Named pipes.* Used for communication between any two processes that know the name of the pipe. Unlike anonymous pipes, named pipes can be accessed over a network.

When you're opening, reading, and writing to pipes, the standard Windows 2000 file-handling functions are used: ReadFile, ReadFileEx, WriteFile, WriteFileEx, and CreateFile. In addition, named pipes support overlapped, asynchronous I/O, as discussed in Chapter 4, "Files." Using named pipes for asynchronous I/O is discussed later in this chapter, in the section "Using Named Pipes."

Using Anonymous Pipes

An anonymous pipe is used only for communication on the same machine, and almost always between a parent and a child process. An anonymous pipe is always asymmetrical: one end of the pipe is always used for writing, and one end always is used for reading. For bidirectional communication, you must use two pipes.

When a parent process needs to communicate with a child process, anonymous pipes are used, as shown in Figure 26.1. The parent process substitutes the standard input and output handles of the child process with anonymous pipe handles. From the point of view of the child process, it's communicating with the standard input and output.

Communication using anonymous pipes always involves blocking or polling. *Blocking*, which is discussed in Chapter 3, "Threads and Processes," occurs when a thread is kept waiting for an operation to complete. *Polling*, as it relates to pipes, requires the calling process to continuously check to see if an operation has completed.

FIGURE 26.1
Substituting pipe handles for standard input and output.

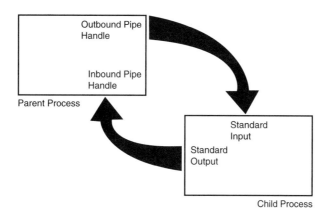

Creating and Closing an Anonymous Pipe

You create an anonymous pipe by calling the CreatePipe function. CreatePipe returns a TRUE or FALSE value, indicating whether the pipe was created. Here's an example:

```
BOOL fCreated = CreatePipe (&hRead, &hWrite, &sec, 0);
```

CreatePipe uses four parameters:

- The address of the variable that will store the pipe's read handle
- The address of the variable that will store the pipe's write handle
- The address of a SECURITY_ATTRIBUTES structure, or NULL to use a default security descriptor
- The buffer size for the pipe, or 0 to use system default sizes

Anonymous pipe handles are usually inherited by a child process, which means that a valid SECURITY_ATTRIBUTES structure must be used with anonymous pipes, because the default security descriptor will not allow a pipe handle to be inherited. The following code initializes a SECURITY_ATTRIBUTES structure and uses it to create an anonymous pipe with inheritable handles:

```
SECURITY ATTRIBUTES sec;
sec.nLength = sizeof(SECURITY ATTRIBUTES);
sec.lpSecurityDescriptor = NULL;
sec.bInheritHandle = TRUE;
CreatePipe(&hRead, &hWrite, &sec, 0);
```

To close an anonymous pipe handle, you use the general-purpose CloseHandle function:

```
CloseHandle (hRead);
```

A pipe is not destroyed until all open handles, including inherited handles, are closed.

Reading and Writing to Anonymous Pipes

You use the ReadFile and WriteFile functions to read and write to anonymous pipes. These functions are blocking; they return only when the specified number of bytes are transferred or an I/O error occurs.

To read from a pipe, you need to pass the pipe's read handle to ReadFile, as in this example:

```
BOOL fRead = ReadFile (hRead,
                       szBuffer,
                       sizeof(szBuffer),
                       &dwRead,
                       NULL);
if(fRead == FALSE ¦¦ dwRead == 0)
{
    // Handle error
}
```

The fifth parameter to ReadFile normally is an OVERLAPPED structure. This parameter is always NULL for anonymous pipes because asynchronous communication is not performed. Feel free to create an OVERLAPPED structure; Windows 2000 will just ignore it.

To write to a pipe, you pass the pipe's write handle to the WriteFile function, as shown in this code:

```
BOOL fWrite = WriteFile (hWrite,
                         szBuffer,
                         sizeof(szBuffer),
                         &dwWritten,
                         NULL);
if(fWritten == FALSE ¦¦ dwWritten == 0)
{
    // Handle error
}
```

As with ReadFile, the fifth parameter passed to WriteFile is the address of an OVER-LAPPED structure that is ignored by Windows 2000 when writing to anonymous pipes.

Communicating with Another Process Using Anonymous Pipes

The parent process typically creates two anonymous pipes and allows the child process to inherit the pipe handles. As shown in Figure 26.1, the child process must have access to at least two of the four pipe handles—the other two handles do not need to be inherited.

In many cases, the child process may not be aware that it is communicating over a pipe. As discussed earlier, a common method for communicating with a child process is to change the standard input and output handles for the child process to use the pipe handles. The child process then can read and write to its standard input and output handles. When started from the command line, the child process acts like any other console mode application; when launched as a child process, it communicates exclusively with the parent process.

To enable a parent process to communicate with a child process using anonymous pipes, follow these steps:

1. Save the standard input and output handles used by the parent process for later use.

2. Create the anonymous pipes used for communication with the child process. This results in the creation of four pipe handles: two pipes, each with two ends.

3. Arbitrarily define how each pipe handle will be used. The parent process uses the write handle for one pipe and the read handle for the other pipe; the child process uses the remaining handles.

4. Create a noninheritable copy of the parent's pipe write handle. This handle must not be inherited by the child process, because the parent will close the pipe to signal that all data has been written to the pipe.

5. Close the parent pipe's original write handle.

6. Set the standard input and write handles to use the child process's read and write handles.

7. Create the child process.

8. Close the child pipe's write handle from within the parent process.

9. Change the standard input and output handles for the parent process back to the original values stored in step 1.

The parent and child processes now can communicate over the anonymous pipes. Each of the pipes can be read from and written to until the pipe is destroyed. In practice, you must create a protocol based on the message length, or you must read and write from the pipe until the pipe is destroyed, as demonstrated in the following section.

Looking at an Example Using Anonymous Pipes

As an example of how anonymous pipes are used, two sample programs have been created and included on this book's CD-ROM. The first program, Hex, reads characters from standard input, converts them into hexadecimal format, and sends the result to standard output. In order to simplify the example, these projects are not Unicode enabled; however, they can easily be converted to use Unicode if needed.

The Hex application believes that it is reading and writing to its standard input and output devices. In fact, when run as a console application, Hex accepts characters from the keyboard and echoes their ASCII hexadecimal equivalents to the display.

First, create a console mode project named Hex and then add the source code from Listing 26.1 to the project as Hex.c.

LISTING 26.1 THE Hex.c SOURCE USED TO FILTER INPUT INTO HEXADECIMAL OUTPUT

```c
#include <windows.h>

#define IN_BUF_SIZE   256
#define OUT_BUF_SIZE (3*IN_BUF_SIZE)

int main()
{
    BYTE    rgBytesInput[IN_BUF_SIZE];
    char    szOutputBuff[OUT_BUF_SIZE];
    HANDLE  hStdInput  = GetStdHandle(STD_INPUT_HANDLE);
    HANDLE  hStdOutput = GetStdHandle(STD_OUTPUT_HANDLE);
    DWORD   dwRead;
    DWORD   dwCharIndex;
    DWORD   dwWritten;
    BOOL    fResult = TRUE;

    do{
        fResult = ReadFile(hStdInput,
                           rgBytesInput,
                           IN_BUF_SIZE,
                           &dwRead,
                           NULL);
        if(fResult == FALSE ¦¦ dwRead == 0) break;

        for(dwCharIndex = 0; dwCharIndex < dwRead; dwCharIndex++)
        {
            int ch = rgBytesInput[dwCharIndex];
            wsprintf(&szOutputBuff[dwCharIndex*3], " %02X", ch);
        }

        fResult = WriteFile(hStdOutput,
                            szOutputBuff,
                            dwRead*3,
                            &dwWritten,
                            NULL);
    }while(fResult == TRUE && dwWritten > 0);
    return 0;
}
```

When built with _MBCS defined, the non-Unicode version of the program will work on the command line. Any input provided to the program is returned in hexadecimal format. Pressing A and then Enter, for example, displays the following:

41 0D 0A

The ASCII value for A is 41, and the ASCII values for the line-feed and carriage return characters are 0D and 0A, respectively.

The second program used in this example is AnonPipe. The AnonPipe project creates a child process using Hex.exe and uses a pair of anonymous pipes to communicate with the child process. First, create a console mode project named AnonPipe and then add the source code provided in Listing 26.2 to the project as AnonPipe.c.

LISTING 26.2 THE AnonPipe.c SOURCE USED TO CREATE TWO ANONYMOUS PIPES

```c
#include <windows.h>

int ErrorHandling(LPTSTR lpszMsg);

int main()
{
    HANDLE hProcess = GetCurrentProcess();
    HANDLE hDuplicateWrite = NULL;
    BOOL   fCreated = FALSE;
    char   szBuff[] = "Fuzzy Wuzzy was a bear";
    char   szTrans[255];
    DWORD  dwRead = 0;
    DWORD  dwWritten = 0;
    // These handles are used to cache the standard input and
    // output handles.
    HANDLE hStdIn  = GetStdHandle(STD_INPUT_HANDLE);
    HANDLE hStdOut = GetStdHandle(STD_OUTPUT_HANDLE);

    HANDLE hChildRead = NULL;
    HANDLE hChildWrite = NULL;
    HANDLE hParentRead = NULL;
    HANDLE hParentWrite = NULL;

    STARTUPINFO         si;
    PROCESS_INFORMATION pi;
    SECURITY_ATTRIBUTES sec;

    sec.nLength = sizeof(SECURITY_ATTRIBUTES);
    sec.lpSecurityDescriptor = NULL;
    sec.bInheritHandle = TRUE;
```

continues

LISTING 26.2   CONTINUED

```
// Create two anonymous pipes, defining child and
// parent ends for each pipe:
// hChildRead   <------  hParentWrite
// hChildWrite  ------>  hParentRead
CreatePipe(&hChildRead, &hParentWrite, &sec, 0);
CreatePipe(&hParentRead, &hChildWrite, &sec, 0);

// Change the standard input and output handles to
// use the "child" ends of the anonymous pipes.
SetStdHandle(STD_INPUT_HANDLE, hChildRead);
SetStdHandle(STD_OUTPUT_HANDLE, hChildWrite);

// Make a non-inheritable duplicate of the pipe handle
// used to communicate between parent and child -- this way
// the child won't increment the usage count on this handle.
DuplicateHandle (hProcess,
                 hParentWrite,
                 hProcess,
                 &hDuplicateWrite,
                 0,
                 FALSE,
                 DUPLICATE_SAME_ACCESS);
CloseHandle(hParentWrite);

// Start the child process
memset(&si, 0, sizeof (STARTUPINFO));
si.cb = sizeof(STARTUPINFO);

fCreated = CreateProcess("hex.exe",
                         NULL,
                         NULL,
                         NULL,
                         TRUE,
                         0,
                         NULL,
                         NULL,
                         &si,
                         &pi);
if(fCreated == FALSE)
    return ErrorHandling("Creating Child Process");

// Restore the original standard input and output handles.
SetStdHandle(STD_INPUT_HANDLE, hStdIn);
SetStdHandle(STD_OUTPUT_HANDLE, hStdOut);

// Send a message to the child process, then close the
// pipe handle, in order to notify the child that the message
// is finished.
WriteFile(hDuplicateWrite,
```

```
                szBuff,
                sizeof(szBuff),
                &dwWritten,
                NULL);
    CloseHandle(hDuplicateWrite);
    //Read the result from the child process, and display it
    //to the standard output.
    ReadFile(hParentRead, szTrans, sizeof(szTrans), &dwRead, NULL);
    WriteFile(hStdOut, szTrans, dwRead, &dwWritten, NULL);
    return 0;
}

//
//Display an error message based on the operating system's
//latest error.
int ErrorHandling(LPTSTR lpszTitle)
{
    char szBuffer[256];
    FormatMessage(FORMAT_MESSAGE_FROM_SYSTEM,
                NULL,
                GetLastError(),
                MAKELANGID(LANG_ENGLISH, SUBLANG_ENGLISH_US),
                szBuffer,
                256,
                NULL),
    MessageBox(NULL, szBuffer, lpszTitle, MB_ICONSTOP);
    return 1;
}
```

Compile the AnonPipe project. Before executing AnonPipe, make sure that the Hex.exe executable created by the previous project is found somewhere in the path. When AnonPipe is launched, it creates a Hex child process and sends the string "Fuzzy Wuzzy was a bear" to the child process for translation. The Hex child process converts the string to hexadecimal and returns it to the AnonPipe process, which appears in hexadecimal format, like this:

```
46 75 7A 7A 79 20 57 75 7A 7A 79 20 77 61 73 20 61 20 62 65 61 72 00
```

You can extend this example to use any sort of child process that expects to read and write from its standard input and output handles.

Using Named Pipes

Named pipes are similar to anonymous pipes, except that they have several features that make them well suited for communication between unrelated processes:

- Named pipes can be referenced by name, instead of just by a handle.
- Named pipes have more flexible connection options than anonymous pipes.
- Unlike anonymous pipes, named pipes can be used over a network.
- Named pipes can use asynchronous, overlapped I/O.

The name of a named pipe always follows this format:

```
\\machine_name\pipe\pipe_name
```

A pipe named "foo" on a machine named "pongo," for example, looks like this:

```
\\pongo\pipe\foo
```

When a pipe is referred to on its own machine, a dot is substituted for the machine name:

```
\\.\pipe\foo
```

Note that pipe names are not case sensitive.

A named pipe instance connects one server with one client. If multiple clients connect to a server using the same named pipe, multiple instances of the named pipe are created; there is no communication directly between the clients.

Examining the Types of Named Pipes

You can create named pipes as blocking or nonblocking. The *nonblocking* type of pipe is not really asynchronous; after you issue a read or write request to the pipe, you must continue to call the read or write request until the pipe finishes the operation. These pipes are often called *polling pipes*. For maximum efficiency, pipes should be opened in *blocking* mode, with asynchronous read and write operations implemented using overlapped structures or completion routines.

You can create pipes as byte-type or message-type pipes. A *byte-type* pipe sends and receives data as a stream of bytes, with no implied division of data sent in separate writes to the pipe. A *message-type* pipe separates the data written to the pipe into a separate packet that can be read from the pipe as a single chunk of data.

After a byte-type pipe is created, it can be opened and read from only as a byte-type pipe. After creating a message-type pipe, however, you can read it as a message-type pipe or a byte-type pipe.

As an option, a pipe can wait to return a result of a write operation until the data is delivered to the other end of the named pipe; this option is called *write-through*. A message-type pipe always has write-through enabled; byte-type pipes must have this option explicitly enabled.

Creating and Closing a Named Pipe

You can create a named pipe by calling the `CreateNamedPipe` function. `CreateNamedPipe` returns a handle to a created pipe instance if successful, or it returns `INVALID_HANDLE_VALUE` if the pipe can't be created. Here's an example:

```
HANDLE hPipe = CreateNamedPipe(_T("\\\\.\\pipe\\Foo"),
                               PIPE_ACCESS_DUPLEX,
                               PIPE_TYPE_MESSAGE¦
                               PIPE_READMODE_MESSAGE¦
                               PIPE_WAIT,
                               PIPE_UNLIMITED_INSTANCES,
                               4096,
                               4096,
                               INFINITE,
                               &sa );
if(hPipe == INVALID_HANDLE_VALUE)
{
    // Handle error
}
```

The parameters used by `CreateNamedPipe` follow:

- The name of the pipe. The pipe always is created initially on the local machine, using a dot in place of the machine name, as shown in the preceding code.

- The read, write, and security attributes for the pipe. In this case, the pipe is opened in *duplex* mode, meaning that the pipe is bidirectional.

- The pipe mode and blocking characteristics of the pipe. In this case, the pipe is created in message mode for both reading and writing, and it's created as a blocking pipe.

- Either the number of instances allowed for the pipe or `UNLIMITED_PIPE_INSTANCES` (to indicate that an unlimited number of instances is permitted).

- The number of bytes reserved for the pipe's output buffer.

- The number of bytes reserved for the pipe's input buffer.

- Either the time-out period for a pipe operation in milliseconds or `INFINITE` for no timeout.

- A pointer to a `SECURITY_ATTRIBUTES` structure. If `NULL` is passed as this parameter, the pipe receives the security descriptor of the current access token.

Table 26.1 lists the read, write, and security attributes for the pipe.

TABLE 26.1 READ, WRITE, AND SECURITY ATTRIBUTES FOR NAMED PIPES

Attribute	Function
ACCESS_SYSTEM_SECURITY	Specifies that the client side of the pipe will have write access to the named pipe's SACL (SACLs were discussed in Chapter 7, "Distributed Security").
FILE_FLAG_OVERLAPPED	Specifies that read, write, and connect operations can be performed asynchronously using an OVERLAPPED structure.
FILE_FLAG_WRITE_THROUGH	Indicates that write-through mode is enabled.
PIPE_ACCESS_DUPLEX	Specifies a bidirectional pipe.
PIPE_ACCESS_INBOUND	Specifies a pipe used for incoming traffic to the server side of the pipe.
PIPE_ACCESS_OUTBOUND	Specifies a pipe used for outgoing traffic from the server side of the pipe.
WRITE_DAC	Indicates that the client side of the pipe will have write access to the named pipe's discretionary access control list.
WRITE_OWNER	Indicates that the client side of the pipe will have write access to the named pipe's owner.

Table 26.2 lists the pipe mode and blocking characteristics of the pipe.

TABLE 26.2 MODE AND BLOCKING ATTRIBUTES FOR NAMED PIPES

Attribute	Function
PIPE_NOWAIT	Indicates that nonblocking mode is enabled. As discussed earlier, this mode should be avoided.
PIPE_WAIT	Indicates that blocking mode is enabled. This mode is the default and is preferred over the nonblocking option.
PIPE_READMODE_BYTE	Indicates that data is read from the pipe as a stream of bytes.
PIPE_READMODE_MESSAGE	Indicates that data is read from the pipe as a stream of messages.
PIPE_TYPE_BYTE	Indicates that data is written to the pipe as a stream of bytes.
PIPE_TYPE_MESSAGE	Indicates that data is written to the pipe as a stream of messages.

You close a named pipe handle by calling the ever-popular CloseHandle function:

```
CloseHandle(hPipe);
```

Connecting and Using a Named Pipe

A pipe must be placed into listening mode by the pipe's server process before a client can use it. A server process places a pipe into listening mode by calling the ConnectNamedPipe function. If the pipe is not using overlapped I/O, the call to ConnectNamedPipe blocks, or waits, until it times out or a client is connected to the pipe. Listing 26.3 shows a typical call to ConnectNamedPipe.

LISTING 26.3   PLACING A NAMED PIPE INTO LISTENING MODE USING ConnectNamedPipe

```
BOOL fConnected = ConnectNamedPipe(hPipe, NULL);
if(fConnected ¦¦ GetLastError() == ERROR_PIPE_CONNECTED)
{
    // Connected to a client
}
else
{
    // Handle error condition
}
```

The ConnectNamedPipe function has two parameters:

- The pipe handle
- The address of an OVERLAPPED structure, which is used for overlapped I/O

The ConnectNamedPipe function returns TRUE if a client connects to the pipe successfully or FALSE if an error occurs. If a client connects to a pipe after the pipe is created but before the server process calls ConnectNamedPipe, the return value is FALSE, and GetLastError returns ERROR_PIPE_CONNECTED.

In most cases, it's perfectly okay to continue processing, as shown in Listing 26.3. Be aware that if you attempt to call ConnectNamedPipe on a pipe handle that's already open, you'll receive the same error message. It's up to you to structure your code so that you can separate these cases.

A client process opens a handle to a named pipe by using the CreateFile function and passing the full name of the pipe as the filename. If a handle to the pipe cannot be opened using the parameters passed to CreateFile, INVALID_HANDLE_VALUE is returned, as shown in Listing 26.4.

LISTING 26.4 OPENING THE CLIENT SIDE OF A NAMED PIPE

```
HANDLE  hPipe = CreateFile(_T("\\\\pongo\\pipe\\lucky"),
                            GENERIC_READ ¦ GENERIC_WRITE,
                            0,
                            NULL,
                            OPEN_EXISTING,
                            0,
                            NULL);
if(m_hPipe == INVALID_HANDLE_VALUE)
{
    // Handle error creating pipe.
}
DWORD dwPipeState = PIPE_READMODE_MESSAGE;
BOOL fChangedState = SetNamedPipeHandleState(hPipe,
                                             &dwPipeState,
                                             NULL,
                                             NULL);
```

By default, `CreateFile` opens a pipe handle as a byte-type pipe. In Listing 26.4, `SetNamedPipeHandleState` specifies a message-type pipe.

When you're opening named pipe handles, the parameters for `CreateFile` are very similar to the ones for opening existing disk files:

- The full pipe name
- The read and write access for the pipe handle
- The share mode (which always is set to 0 for named pipes)
- A pointer to a `SECURITY_ATTRIBUTES` structure, or `NULL` if the pipe handle will use the security descriptor of the current access token
- The handle-creation information (which always is set to `OPEN_EXISTING` for named pipes)
- The file attribute flags (set to 0 for named pipes)
- The address of an `OVERLAPPED` structure if the pipe is opened in `OVERLAPPED` mode, or `NULL` if the pipe will block until the `CreateFile` function is completed

Looking at a Named Pipe Example

Two sample programs that demonstrate the use of named pipes are included on this book's CD-ROM. BardServ provides a series of quotations from Shakespeare via a named pipe "Quote." NPClient is a dialog-based MFC program that connects to the named pipe supplied by BardServ and displays a quotation in its main dialog box.

Although the source code assumes that both programs are located on the same machine, it's easy to modify NPClient to work across a network.

A Named Pipe Server Application

The BardServ application is a fairly simple server application. It spins in a `while` loop, creating and connecting named pipes for client processes, as shown in Figure 26.2.

FIGURE 26.2
The basic architecture of BardServ.

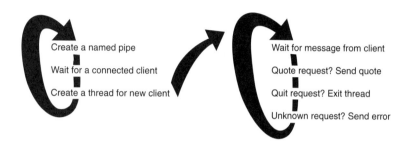

Most of the time, BardServ is blocked on a call to `ConnectNamedPipe`, waiting for a client process to connect to the other side of a pipe. When a client connects to the named pipe, BardServ creates a thread to service that client, creates a new pipe, and then blocks again on a call to `ConnectNamedPipe`.

Listing 26.5 shows the most of the source code for the `BardServ.c` source file. The complete listing can be found on this book's CD-ROM. This is the only source file in the BardServ console mode project.

LISTING 26.5   THE BARDSERV SOURCE CODE

```
#include <windows.h>
#include <tchar.h>
#ifndef UNICODE
    #include <stdio.h>
#endif

#define BUFFERSIZE 256
const int cTimeout = INFINITE;

const TCHAR g_szPipe[] = _T("\\\\.\\pipe\\Quote");
const TCHAR g_szUnknown[] = _T("Unknown request");
const TCHAR g_rgszQuotes[][350] = {
    //Henry V
    {_T("We few, we happy few, we band of brothers;\n")
     _T("For he today that sheds his blood with me\n")
     _T("Shall be my brother; be he ne'er so vile,\n")
```

continues

LISTING **26.5**   CONTINUED

```
            _T("This day shall gentle his condition.\n")
            _T("And gentlemen in England, now abed,\n")
            _T("Shall think themselves accursed they were not here;\n")
            _T("And hold their manhoods cheap whiles any speaks\n")
            _T("That fought with us upon Saint Chrispin's day.\n") },
        //Hamlet
        {_T("There are more things in heaven and earth, Horatio,\n")
         _T("Than are dreamt of in your philosophy.\n") },
        //Richard III
        {_T("Now is the winter of our discontent\n")
         _T("Made glorious summer by this sun of York;\n") }
};

int   ErrorHandling(LPCTSTR lpszTitle);
DWORD PipeFunc(LPARAM lparam);

int _tmain()
{
    // Create a security descriptor that has a NULL ACL
    // that allows unlimited access.
    SECURITY_ATTRIBUTES     sa;
    SECURITY_DESCRIPTOR*    psd;
    psd = (SECURITY_DESCRIPTOR*)LocalAlloc(LPTR,
                            SECURITY_DESCRIPTOR_MIN_LENGTH);
    InitializeSecurityDescriptor(psd,SECURITY_DESCRIPTOR_REVISION);
    SetSecurityDescriptorDacl(psd, TRUE, NULL, FALSE);
    sa.nLength = sizeof(sa);
    sa.lpSecurityDescriptor = psd;
    sa.bInheritHandle = TRUE;

    // Hang in a loop, creating named pipe instances and
    // waiting for a client to connect.  There is a teeny,
    // tiny hole where two clients might try to connect
    // at the same time; however this is an extremely small
    // time gap.
    while(1)
    {
        BOOL fConnected;
        HANDLE hPipe = CreateNamedPipe(g_szPipe,
                                PIPE_ACCESS_DUPLEX,
                                PIPE_TYPE_MESSAGE |
                                PIPE_READMODE_MESSAGE |
                                PIPE_WAIT,
                                PIPE_UNLIMITED_INSTANCES,
                                BUFFERSIZE,
                                BUFFERSIZE,
                                cTimeout,
                                &sa);
        if(hPipe == INVALID_HANDLE_VALUE)
            return ErrorHandling(_T("CreatePipe Failed"));
```

```
            _tprintf(_T("Main thread waiting for a client\n"));
            fConnected = ConnectNamedPipe(hPipe, NULL);
            if(fConnected || GetLastError() == ERROR_PIPE_CONNECTED)
            {
                // Connected - now spin off a thread to manage this
                // pipe. Execution continues in PipeFunc.
                HANDLE hThread;
                DWORD  dwThreadID;
                hThread = CreateThread(NULL,
                                       0,
                                       (LPTHREAD_START_ROUTINE)PipeFunc,
                                       (LPVOID)hPipe,
                                       0,
                                       &dwThreadID);
                _tprintf(_T("Thread 0x%02X connected to a client\n"),
                         dwThreadID);
                if(hThread == INVALID_HANDLE_VALUE)
                    ErrorHandling(_T("CreateThread Failed"));
            }
            else
            {
                CloseHandle(hPipe);
                    return ErrorHandling(_T("Connect Failed"));
            }
        }
    LocalFree(psd);
    return 0;
}


// PipeFunc --
// Manages a thread containing one pipe instance. If the client
// sends "Quit", the thread exits; otherwise, a new quotation is sent
// to the client.
DWORD PipeFunc(LPARAM lparam)
{
    HANDLE hPipe = (HANDLE)lparam;
    static int ndx = 0;
    TCHAR  szBuffer[BUFFERSIZE];
    DWORD  dwRead, dwWritten;
    BOOL   fWrite;
    while(1)
    {
        LPCTSTR pszWrite;
        DWORD   cbWrite;
        BOOL fRead = ReadFile(hPipe,
                              szBuffer,
                              BUFFERSIZE,
                              &dwRead,
                              NULL);
```

continues

LISTING 26.5   CONTINUED

```
        if(fRead == FALSE || dwRead == 0) break;
        if(_tcsicmp(_T("Quit"), szBuffer) == 0)
        {
            DWORD dwThreadID = GetCurrentThreadId();
            _tprintf(_T("Thread 0x%02X closing connection\n"),
                        dwThreadID );
            break;
        }
        else if(_tcsicmp(_T("Quote"), szBuffer) == 0)
        {
            pszWrite = g_rgszQuotes[ndx];
            if(++ndx == 3)
            ndx = 0;
        }
        else
            pszWrite = g_szUnknown;

        cbWrite = (lstrlen(pszWrite)*sizeof(TCHAR))+sizeof(TCHAR);
        fWrite = WriteFile(hPipe,
                            pszWrite,
                            cbWrite,
                            &dwWritten,
                            NULL );
        if(fWrite == FALSE || dwWritten == 0) break;
    }
    FlushFileBuffers(hPipe);
    DisconnectNamedPipe(hPipe);
    CloseHandle(hPipe);

    return NO_ERROR;
}
```

Inside _tmain, BardServ creates a SECURITY_ATTRIBUTES structure that allows any client to connect to the pipe. BardServ then enters a loop, creating and connecting pipes for clients. When a client is connected to a pipe, BardServ spins up a thread for that client and passes the pipe handle to the thread function for handling.

In addition to _tmain, BardServ has two other functions:

- ErrorHandling. Displays a system-supplied text string when an error is detected.
- ThreadFunc. Handles the threads that are spun up for every connected pipe. A client can request a quotation by sending the Unicode string "Quote" to BardServ. If the client sends "Quit", the thread closes the pipe and exits. If the client sends anything else, an error message is returned.

A Named Pipe Client Application

The NPClient project is an example of a dialog-based MFC application that uses named pipes to exchange information with another process. In this case, NPClient connects to BardServ via a named pipe and displays a quotation from Shakespeare in its main dialog box.

The main dialog box for NPClient is shown in Figure 26.3. Note that a new static text control is included that covers most of the dialog box area; a new pushbutton control is also included.

FIGURE 26.3

The main dialog box for NPClient.

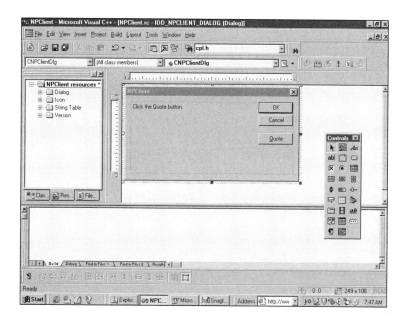

Table 26.3 contains the resource IDs for new controls added to the main dialog box.

TABLE 26.3 RESOURCE AND CONTROL INFORMATION FOR THE MAIN DIALOG BOX

Control	Resource ID	Caption
Static text control	IDC_MSG	Click the Quote button
Quote button	IDC_QUOTE	&Quote

ClassWizard was used to add a message-handling function to the CNPClientDlg class. This function handles BN_CLICKED messages from the Quote button, as shown in Table 26.4.

TABLE 26.4   MESSAGE-HANDLING INFORMATION FOR CNPClientDlg

Class Name Function	Object ID	Message	Member
CNPClientDlg	IDC_QUOTE	BN_CLICKED	OnQuote

The CNPClientDlg class is modified by adding a named pipe handle and extra member functions to take care of the communications through the named pipe. The changes shown in bold in Listing 26.6 have been made to the CNPClientDlg class declaration.

LISTING 26.6   CHANGES (IN BOLD) TO THE CNPClientDlg CLASS DECLARATION

```
class CNPClientDlg : public CDialog
{
.
.
.
// Implementation
protected:
    HICON  m_hIcon;
    HANDLE m_hPipe;

    void SendQuitMsg();
    int  ErrorHandling(LPCTSTR lpszTitle);
    void GetQuote();
.
.
.
};
```

Listing 26.7 contains the source code for the CNPClientDlg::OnQuote member function, which is called when the user clicks the Quote button. The OnQuote function attempts to open the client side of the named pipe, fetches a quotation, and then releases the named pipe.

LISTING 26.7   THE CNPClientDlg::OnQuote MEMBER FUNCTION

```
void CNPClientDlg::OnQuote()
{
    m_hPipe = CreateFile(_T("\\\\.\\pipe\\Quote"),
                         GENERIC_READ | GENERIC_WRITE,
                         0,
                         NULL,
                         OPEN_EXISTING,
                         0,
                         NULL);
```

```
    if(m_hPipe == INVALID_HANDLE_VALUE)
    {
        ErrorHandling(_T("CreateFile Failed"));
        return;
    }
    DWORD dwPipeState = PIPE_READMODE_MESSAGE;
    BOOL fChangedState = SetNamedPipeHandleState(m_hPipe,
                                                 &dwPipeState,
                                                 NULL,
                                                 NULL);
    if(fChangedState == FALSE)
    {
        ErrorHandling(_T("SetNamedPipeHandleState Failed"));
        return;
    }
    //Get a quotation from the BardServ, and quit the connection
    GetQuote();
    SendQuitMsg();
    CloseHandle(m_hPipe);
}
```

Three additional functions exist for CNPClientDlg:

- ErrorHandling. Handles system error messages, same as in BardServ.

- GetQuote. Sends the string "Quote" to BardServ and waits for the quotation to be returned. After reading the quotation from the pipe, GetQuote displays the message in the dialog box.

- SendQuitMessage. Sends the string "Quit" to BardServ in order to shut down the pipe.

Listing 26.8 shows the source code for the remaining CNPClientDlg member functions.

LISTING 26.8 ADDITIONAL MEMBER FUNCTIONS FOR CNPClientDlg

```
void CNPClientDlg::GetQuote()
{
    const int cBuffer = 1024;
    TCHAR szBuffer[cBuffer];
    ASSERT(m_hPipe != INVALID_HANDLE_VALUE);

    TCHAR szMsg[] = _T("Quote");
    DWORD dwWritten, dwRead;

    BOOL fWritten = WriteFile(m_hPipe,
                              szMsg,
                              sizeof(szMsg),
                              &dwWritten,
                              NULL);
```

continues

LISTING 26.8   CONTINUED

```
    if(fWritten == FALSE || dwWritten == 0)
    {
        ErrorHandling(_T("WriteFile failed"));
        return;
    }
    BOOL fRead = ReadFile(m_hPipe,
                          szBuffer,
                          cBuffer,
                          &dwRead,
                          NULL);
    if(fRead == FALSE || dwRead == 0)
    {
        ErrorHandling(_T("ReadFile failed"));
        return;
    }
    szBuffer[dwRead] = '\0';
    SetDlgItemText(IDC_MSG, szBuffer);
}

void CNPClientDlg::SendQuitMsg()
{
    ASSERT(m_hPipe != INVALID_HANDLE_VALUE);
    DWORD dwWritten;
    TCHAR szQuit[] = _T("Quit");
    BOOL fWritten = WriteFile(m_hPipe,
                              szQuit,
                              sizeof(szQuit),
                              &dwWritten,
                              NULL );
}

int CNPClientDlg::ErrorHandling(LPCTSTR lpszTitle)
{
    TCHAR szBuffer[256];
    FormatMessage(FORMAT_MESSAGE_FROM_SYSTEM,
                  NULL,
                  GetLastError(),
                  MAKELANGID(LANG_ENGLISH, SUBLANG_ENGLISH_US),
                  szBuffer,
                  256,
                  NULL);
    MessageBox(szBuffer, lpszTitle, MB_ICONSTOP);
    return 1;
}
```

Compile and run the BardServ and NPClient projects. While debugging or testing named pipes, I find it helpful to run two instances of the Visual C++ Developer Studio at the same time—one for each end of the pipe.

Figure 26.4 shows three copies of NPClient running with one copy of BardServ. Note the status messages displayed in the BardServ console window.

FIGURE 26.4

Three instances of NPClient running with BardServ.

Summary

This chapter explained how you can use pipes for interprocess communications in Windows 2000 applications. You learned about using named and anonymous pipes. You also created two sets of sample applications—two programs that demonstrate how anonymous pipes are used, and two programs that demonstrate named pipes.

Active Directory

This chapter discusses Active Directory programming. Active Directory is the new, enterprisewide directory service for Windows 2000. Active Directory supports both the industry-standard LDAP API and the Microsoft Active Directory Services Interface (ADSI). ADSI can be used by clients of all types, whether they're written in C, C++, Visual Basic, or a scripting language such as VBScript. This chapter's examples use Visual C++ and Visual Basic with ADSI to demonstrate Active Directory client programming.

An Overview of Active Directory

Active Directory is the directory service included with Windows 2000. Active Directory, like all directories, is similar to a database. Items can be added and removed from Active Directory, and items in Active Directory are, in most cases, persistent. Also, as is the case with databases, items stored in the directory have attributes that can be viewed and modified by directory clients. However, unlike a typical database, Active Directory is optimized to provide very fast responses to queries made against the directory. Changes to the directory, especially changes to the directory's structure, are not executed as quickly as queries.

Although a directory is similar to a database, it's not suitable for storing large amounts of arbitrary information. Active Directory is not well-suited for constant updates of frequently changing information or for storing large data items.

Namespace Organization

A directory is often referred to as a *namespace*, which is a storage area that contains objects with unique names. Objects stored in a directory may contain attributes that make each object unique. For example, printers stored in a directory have attributes that specify their name, model, number, and location. A user stored in Active Directory typically has a name, email address, and location, as shown in Figure 27.1.

FIGURE 27.1

A typical user and her attributes as stored in a directory.

Name: Gwen Baldwin

Email: gb@codevtech.com

Location: Engineering

Items stored in the directory may be simply objects, as in the case of a user, or they may be containers. A container is a directory object that can contain other objects. Examples of containers are domains and membership lists. Containers may contain other containers, giving the directory its characteristic tree shape, as shown in Figure 27.2.

FIGURE 27.2

A directory container contains other objects.

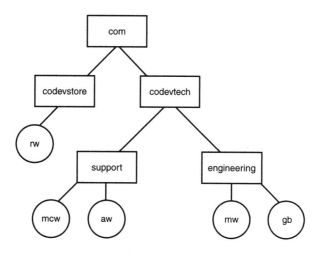

Each item in the tree has a *distinguished name*, or DN, that uniquely specifies the object's location in the directory tree. Here's an example of a DN for a user:

```
CN=Ali Williams/CN=Marketing/CN=Users/DC=CodevTech/DC=COM
```

Every object's distinguished name is made up of a number of components that describe the path taken from the root of the directory namespace to the object. Each DN includes a *relative distinguished name*, or RDN, that differentiates the object from its parent and siblings. Figure 27.3 shows an example of an Active Directory namespace tree.

FIGURE 27.3

Distinguished names and relative distinguished names in a directory.

RDN="cn=Users"

RDN="cn=Marketing"

RDN="cn=Ali Williams"
DN = "/CN=Ali Williams/CN=Marketing/CN=Users/DC=CodevTech/DC=com"

Every RDN is unique within a particular container. This property ensures that DNs are always unique within an Active Directory namespace. In Figure 27.3, the RDN of the leaf object is Ali Williams. The RDN of the parent is Marketing.

The string format for distinguished names was originally specified in RFC 1779. This RFC specifies a set of keywords used to compose DNs. Table 27.1 contains a partial list of these keywords.

TABLE 27.1 COMPONENTS USED TO COMPOSE X.500 DISTINGUISHED NAMES

Keyword	Description
CN	Common name
L	Locality
ST	State or province
O	Organization
OU	Organizational unit
C	Country
STREET	Street address

RFC 1779 serves to define how distinguished names found in X.500 networks are presented. X.500 is an OSI protocol rather than an Internet protocol, so it has no keyword defined to indicate an Internet domain name. Active Directory adds a frequently used IETF extension, DC, which stands for *domain component*.

Each object is also assigned a GUID that uniquely identifies it. An object may be renamed several times during its lifetime in the Active Directory, but its GUID will remain constant. This allows you to return to specific objects in the directory, even if they have been renamed, simply by storing the objects' GUIDs.

Understanding Trees and Forests

As described earlier, a directory tree is a contiguous namespace, where all the objects in the tree can be traced back to a common node. An Active Directory *domain tree* is composed of one or more domains that share a directory, use a common schema, and are configured in the same way. In a large enterprise, it may not be desirable, or even possible, for the directory to be placed into one domain tree. Active Directory allows you to divide your directory namespace into *forests*, which contain one or more domain trees, as shown in Figure 27.4.

FIGURE 27.4

A directory name-space may be divided into forests that contain multiple domain trees.

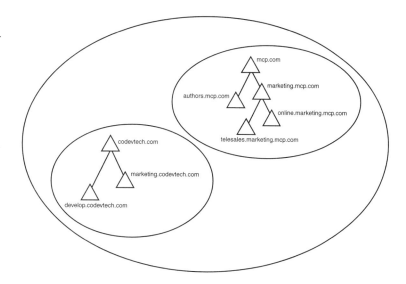

As shown in Figure 27.4, trees in a forest do not share the same namespace. Active Directory uses Kerberos to establish transitive trust relationships among trees in a forest. The name of the directory tree located at the root of a forest is used to identify the forest.

Using ADSI to Manage Active Directory

As discussed earlier in this chapter, Active Directory can be managed through the industry-standard LDAP protocol. Unfortunately for Visual Basic, Java, and scripting language users, the LDAP API is written in C and is very C-oriented. In order to simplify the task of developing directory-enabled applications in any language, Microsoft has introduced the *Active Directory Services Interfaces*, or ADSI. ADSI is a COM-based API that enables applications written in any Automation-compatible programming language to have complete access to directory services.

ADSI is an abstraction layer that enables any Automation-compatible client to have access to directory services. The focus of this chapter is on using ADSI to access Active Directory. However, ADSI can be used to access any directory that's compatible with Novell NDS or LDAP 2.0. Examples of directory services that can be accessed through ADSI include Novell's NDS, Netscape's Directory Server, and SLAPD from the University of Michigan.

An ADSI client communicates with the ADSI provider, which acts as a proxy for the directory service. The client usually does not need to access the directory service directly.

ADSI was originally released as an add-on to Windows NT 4.0 and could be used to manage the Windows NT 4.0 directory service (NTDS), Internet Information Server, and Novell NDS. Most interfaces exposed by ADSI are Automation-compatible and are suitable for use with any programming language that supports Automation, such as Visual Basic and VBScript, in addition to C and C++ clients. If you are using a language that supports vtable binding, such as C or C++, you can also take advantage of ADSI's more efficient non-Automation interfaces.

ADSI also includes an OLE DB provider so that you can use OLE DB and ADO to manipulate directory service information. Although using OLE DB to manage Active Directory is not discussed in this chapter, sample programs are included in the Platform SDK that demonstrate this usage.

Using ADSI in Visual Basic and Visual C++

Before we dive into the examples in this chapter, here are a few tips for working with ADSI in Visual Basic and Visual C++.

When using ADSI in Visual Basic, you must add a reference to the Active DS type library.

If you're using Visual C++ to create an ADSI client, you must perform the following tasks:

- Include the `activeds.h` header file.
- Link to the `activeds.lib` and `adsiid.lib` libraries.
- Use Unicode strings when calling ADSI functions. The examples in this chapter are all compiled using Unicode.

ADSI Binding Strings

The first step in working with directory objects using ADSI is to bind to a directory object. As part of the binding process, ADSI and the directory will locate the directory object that you're interested in, authenticate your security credentials, and create an ADSI COM object to manage your interaction with the directory object.

The act of binding requires you to specify at least three things if you're using C or C++:

- The bind string that identifies the object you're interested in

- The COM interface ID that identifies the COM interface that you'll use initially to interact with the directory
- The address of a COM interface pointer that will contain your requested interface when the binding function returns

These three items are the *minimum* requirement for binding to a directory object using ADSI. You may also specify a user name and password that will be used to generate credentials for the bind operation.

The bind string, also known as the ADsPath, has different formats for different ADSI directory providers. Here are the four providers that ship with Windows 2000:

- Novell NetWare
- Novell NDS
- Windows NT
- LDAP

Only the LDAP provider is used with Active Directory, and this is the provider used for almost all of this chapter's examples. Some examples also use ADs:, which is the top-level ADSI provider namespace. For information about other ADSI providers, consult the Platform SDK documentation.

An LDAP ADsPath always begins like this:

```
LDAP://
```

The provider name is case sensitive and must include a colon, which is considered part of the provider's name. Immediately following the provider name, the ADsPath may contain a server name, IP address, or domain name. Here are examples:

```
LDAP://ace.codevtech.com
LDAP://codevtech.com
```

The ADsPath may also specify a port number if a port other than the well-known LDAP port (389) is used:

```
LDAP://ace.codevtech.com:2555
```

In order to bind to a specific object in the directory, you must specify a directory object using a distinguished name:

```
LDAP://ace.codevtech.com/CN=Jen Smith,CN=Users,DC=codevtech,DC=com
```

If no server or domain name is specified, the Windows 2000 locator service will be used to find the best match for an Active Directory domain controller.

27

ACTIVE
DIRECTORY

ADSI Helper Functions

ADSI includes a set of helper functions that simplify tasks commonly performed in C and C++, such as creating an enumerator object and binding to a specific location in the directory. Here are some of the most commonly used helper functions:

- `ADsGetObject`. Binds to an ADSI object using the thread's current security credentials.
- `ADsOpenObject`. Like `ADsGetObject`, this helper function binds to an ADSI object, except that it accepts specific user credentials to be used for the operation.
- `ADsGetLastError`. Returns the last error code for the calling thread, including a text description or the error.
- `ADsBuildEnumerator`. Builds an enumerator object for an ADSI container passed as a parameter.
- `ADsEnumerateNext`. Returns one or more elements from an enumerated collection.
- `ADsFreeEnumerator`. Releases resources previously allocated in a call to `ADsBuildEnumerator`.

Using `ADsGetObject` and `ADsOpenObject`

`ADsGetObject` and `ADsOpenObject` are used to bind to an element in the directory. Both functions locate the desired element and return an interface pointer on an ADSI object used to manage it. The `AdsOpenObject` function takes a user name and password that are used to establish credentials for accessing the object.

The `ADsGetObject` function is the simpler of the two functions:

```
IADsDomain* pDomain = NULL;
HRESULT hr = ADsGetObject(L"WinNT://codevtech.com",
                          IID_IADsDomain,
                          (void**)&pDomain);
```

The `ADsGetObject` function has three parameters:

- A Unicode string that contains the directory path to the object. Some examples of paths are provided later in this section.
- The interface ID that specifies the COM interface to be returned.
- The address of a COM interface pointer that will contain the requested interface pointer if the function succeeds.

The ADsOpenObject function is similar to ADsGetObject, except that it allows a user name and password to be passed as parameters:

```
HRESULT hr = ADsOpenObject(L"WinNT://codevtech.com",
                           L"Administrator",
                           L"rene",
                           ADS_SECURE_AUTHENTICATION,
                           IID_IADsContainer,
                           (void**)&pUsersContainer);
```

The ADsOpenObject function has six parameters:

- A Unicode string that contains the directory path to the object. Some examples of paths are provided later in this section.

- A username that will be used together with the next parameter to generate credentials.

- A password that will be used together with the previous parameter to generate credentials.

- An authentication option that specifies how the specified user will be authenticated. Values for this parameter are discussed later in this section.

- The interface ID that specifies the COM interface to be returned.

- The address of a COM interface pointer that will contain the requested interface pointer if the function succeeds.

The following values may be passed as the authentication option in a call to ADsOpenObject:

- ADS_SECURE_AUTHENTICATION. Causes the WinNT ADSI provider to use NTLM authentication and the Active Directory provider to use Kerberos (or NTLM if Kerberos is not available). If the username and password parameters are NULL, the credentials of the currently logged-on user will be used.

- ADS_USE_ENCRYPTION. Specifies that ADSI must use encryption; Active Directory requires that Certificate Server be available in the network.

- ADS_READONLY_SERVER. Requires that ADSI connect to the PDC or BDC when connecting to the WinNT ADSI provider. If ADSI is using the Active Directory provider, this flag notifies ADSI that a writable server is not required.

- ADS_PROMPT_CREDENTIALS. The user credentials will be prompted for at the beginning of the authentication process, if the selected SSPI provider supplies the required user interface.

- ADS_NO_AUTHENTICATION. Attempts anonymous binding to the directory provider. The WinNT ADSI provider does not support this flag.

The format for directory paths depends on the ADSI provider. The WinNT provider uses strings in the following format:

```
WinNT://codevtech.com/Users/mickeyw
```

As discussed earlier, the LDAP provider used for Active Directory uses an X.500-style format:

```
LDAP://CN=Users,DC=codevtech,DC=com
```

Examples provided throughout the rest of the chapter use the `ADsGetObject` function to perform serverless binding.

Using the ADSI Enumerator Helper Functions

Although COM enumerators are quite easy to use in Visual Basic, they are somewhat difficult to use in C and C++, particularly when you're using them for the first time. ADSI provides three functions that simplify the enumeration of container objects in the directory.

The `ADsBuildEnumerator` function is used to create an enumerator for a specified container:

```
IEnumVARIANT*  pUserEnum = NULL;
HRESULT hrEnum = ADsBuildEnumerator(pUsersContainer, &pUserEnum);
```

The `ADsBuildEnumerator` function has two parameters:

- An `IADsContainer` interface pointer
- The address of an `IEnumVARIANT` interface pointer that will be set to the enumerator interface if the function succeeds

The `ADsEnumerateNext` function is used to retrieve one or more elements from the enumeration:

```
ULONG   ulFetch = 0;
VARIANT var;
HRESULT hrEnum = ADsEnumerateNext(pUserEnum, 1, &var, &ulFetch);
```

The `ADsEnumerateNext` function has four parameters:

- An `IEnumVARIANT` interface pointer associated with the enumerator object.
- The number of elements requested.
- The address of one or more variant variables that will be filled with the elements requested from the enumerator.
- The address of an unsigned long variable that will contain the number of elements returned from the enumerator. If this value is 0, no elements remain in the enumerator.

The `ADsFreeEnumerator` function is used to free the enumerator object created earlier through a call to `ADsBuildEnumerator`:

```
HRESULT hrEnum = ADsFreeEnumerator(pUserEnum);
```

The `ADsFreeEnumerator` function has one parameter: an `IEnumVARIANT` interface pointer associated with the enumerator object.

Examples of using the enumerator functions are provided in samples presented during the rest of this chapter.

Serverless Binding and ADSI

In the previous sections, the code fragments explicitly used the `codevtech.com` domain when binding to the directory. Although this simplifies the code fragment, it's not a good programming practice, because it needlessly ties your code to a specific domain. Active Directory supports LDAP 3.0 *serverless binding*, a feature that enables you to avoid hard-coding domain or server names when managing the directory of the currently logged-on user.

Active Directory supports the standard `rootDSE` attribute. This attribute is not part of any directory namespace; instead, it's used to collect information about the directory. To bind to `rootDSE`, use this path to bind to your default Active Directory domain controller:

```
LDAP://rootDSE
```

You can use this path to select a specific LDAP server:

```
LDAP://aServerName/rootDSE
```

The `rootDSE` directory object has a number of properties that can be retrieved in order to discover information about the directory server. Here are the most useful attributes for serverless binding:

- `DefaultNamingContext`. The distinguished name for the directory's domain
- `SchemaNamingContext`. The distinguished name for the directory's schema container
- `ConfigurationNamingContext`. The distinguished name for the directory's configuration container
- `RootDomainNamingContext`. The distinguished name for the root domain of the directory's forest
- `DnsHostName`. The DNS address for the directory server
- `ServerName`. The distinguished name for the server object for this directory server in the configuration container

Listing 27.1 contains a code fragment that illustrates serverless binding. Most code examples presented in this chapter use similar methods to avoid hard-coding the domain or server names.

LISTING 27.1   USING SERVERLESS BINDING WITH ADSI

```
int wmain()
{
    WCHAR wszQuery[512] = L"LDAP://CN=Users,";
    CoInitializeEx(NULL, COINIT_APARTMENTTHREADED);

    // Bind to the current domain controller
    IADs*   pRoot = NULL;
    VARIANT var;
    HRESULT hr = ADsGetObject(L"LDAP://rootDSE",
                              IID_IADs,
                              (void**)&pRoot);
    if(FAILED(hr))
    {
        // HandleError
    }
    hr = pRoot->Get(L"DefaultNamingContext",&var);
    if(FAILED(hr))
    {
        // HandleError
    }
    // Append DC naming context to the path.
    wcscat(wszQuery,var.bstrVal);
    VariantClear(&var);
    pRoot->Release();

    // The wszQuery string now contains a DN for the Users
    // node in the directory.

    // Remaining code omitted...
}
```

In Listing 27.1, the wmain function begins by declaring a Unicode string containing a fragment of an LDAP DN. The wszQuery string is initialized as this:

LDAP://CN=Users,

In order to be useful, the string must include domain components, like this:

LDAP://CN=Users,DC=codevtech,DC=com

The purpose of this code fragment is to add the domain components to the wszQuery string.

After initializing the COM runtime library, the `wmain` function in Listing 27.1 calls `ADsGetObject` to bind to the `rootDSE` directory object. The `ADsGetObject` function is asked to return a pointer to the `IADs` interface, a base interface that's supported by all ADSI objects. `IADs` is used to retrieve basic attribute information about an object—in this case, the `IADs::Get` method is used to retrieve `DefaultNamingContext`, which fills a variant type with a string containing the local domain components:

```
CN=codevtech,CN=com
```

The remaining code in Listing 27.1 concatenates the local domain components with the current value of `wszQuery`, resulting in a string that can be used to bind to the Users node of the directory on any system.

Determining the serverless binding string in Visual Basic is much simpler than using the equivalent C++ code. Listing 27.2 is an example of a code fragment that's the Visual Basic version of serverless binding.

LISTING 27.2 SERVERLESS BINDING IN VISUAL BASIC

```
Private Sub ServerlessBind()
    Dim rootDSE As IADs
    Dim strPath As String

    Set rootDSE = GetObject("LDAP://rootDSE")
    strPath = "LDAP://CN=Users," & _
            rootDSE.Get("defaultNamingContext")
    '' The strPath string now contains a DN for the Users node
    '' in the directory.

    '' Remaining code omitted

End Sub
```

In Listing 27.2, the `ServerlessBind` function sets a pointer to the `rootDSE` ADSI object. Next, the default naming context is retrieved and appended to the string `"LDAP://Users,"`, forming a DN for the Users node in the directory.

COM Interfaces Exposed by ADSI

Ten categories of COM interfaces are offered by ADSI:

- *Core*. Interfaces that provide basic management of ADSI objects
- *Non-Automation*. Interfaces that do not use Automation and enable C and C++ clients to have low-overhead access to ADSI objects

- *Persistent object.* Interfaces that manage persistent data in the directory
- *Dynamic object.* Interfaces that work with dynamic data, such as commands, in the directory service
- *Security.* Interfaces that provide authentication and authorization facilities to an ADSI client
- *Property Cache.* Interfaces used to manipulate properties in the property cache
- *Extension.* Interfaces that enable a client to extend the functionality of existing ADSI classes
- *Schema.* Interfaces that enable the directory schema to be managed and extended
- *Data Type.* Interfaces that support access to ADSI data types
- *Utility.* Interfaces that are used to provide helper functions, such as parsing ADSI pathnames

The following sections describe the more commonly used interface categories in more detail.

Using ADSI Core Interfaces

The ADSI core interfaces are used to manage directory objects and include the following dual interfaces:

- IADs. This interface is supported by every directory object and is used to manage basic information about the object, such as its path, name, description, and other basic properties, as well as information about the object's container.
- IADsContainer. This interface is supported by all directory container objects and enables a client to enumerate and manage child objects.
- IADsNamespaces. An interface used to manage the collection of namespaces in the directory.
- IADsOpenDSObject. This interface is used when a client must supply security credentials and obtain a security context before interacting with the underlying directory service.

Listing 27.3 contains a fragment of a C++ program that illustrates how the IADs and IADsNamespaces interfaces can be used to display the name of each namespace in the directory. This program is part of the Namespace project that can be found on the CD-ROM that accompanies this book.

LISTING 27.3 USING IADs AND IADsNamespaces TO ENUMERATE THE DIRECTORY
NAMESPACES

```
int wmain()
{
    CoInitializeEx(NULL, COINIT_APARTMENTTHREADED);
    IADsContainer* pNamespaces = NULL;
    HRESULT hr = ADsGetObject(L"ADs:",
                              IID_IADsContainer,
                              (void**)&pNamespaces);
    if(FAILED(hr))
    {
        ErrorHandling(L"ADsGetObject");
        return 0;
    }
    // Create an ADSI enumerator for the collection.
    IEnumVARIANT*  pEnum = NULL;
    hr = ADsBuildEnumerator(pNamespaces, &pEnum);
    if(FAILED(hr))
    {
        ErrorHandling(L"ADsBuildEnumerator");
        pNamespaces->Release();
        CoUninitialize();
        return 0;
    }
    // While the enumerator continues to fetch new elements...
    wprintf(L"Name\t\tClass\n");
    while(SUCCEEDED(hr))
    {
        BSTR     bstrName, bstrClass;
        ULONG    ulFetch = 0;
        VARIANT var;
        // Retrieve the next element from the collection.
        hr = ADsEnumerateNext(pEnum, 1, &var, &ulFetch);
        if(!ulFetch) break;
        // QI the element for the IADs interface.
        IADs*        pNamespace = NULL;
        IDispatch* pDisp = V_DISPATCH(&var);
        hr = pDisp->QueryInterface(&pNamespace);
        if(SUCCEEDED(hr))
        {
            // Display information about the collection element.
            pNamespace->get_Name(&bstrName);
            pNamespace->get_Class(&bstrClass);

            wprintf(L"%-15s%-15s\n", bstrName,
                                    bstrClass);
            // Free BSTRs and interface.
            SysFreeString(bstrName);
            SysFreeString(bstrClass);
```

27

ACTIVE
DIRECTORY

continues

LISTING 27.3   CONTINUED

```
              pNamespace->Release();
         }
         pDisp->Release();
    }
    // Clean up enumerator.
    ADsFreeEnumerator(pEnum);
    CoUninitialize();
    return 0;
}
```

After initializing the COM runtime library, Listing 27.3 calls `ADsGetObject` to bind to the top-level node of the ADSI namespace and retrieve a pointer to the `IADsContainer` interface on an ADSI object. After some error-handling code, the `ADsBuildEnumerator` function is used to create an enumerator that can be used to iterate over the directory objects stored in the ADSI container object referenced through `IADsContainer`.

ADSI enumerators always work with the variant type. In this case, the enumerator is used to enumerate child objects, so the code follows these steps:

1. Collect the next variant element from the enumerator. If no more elements are available, `ADsEnumerateNext` will return 0 for the number of elements fetched, and you must break out of the loop.

2. Retrieve the `IDispatch` interface pointer from the variant element. This is the default Automation interface for a child object stored in the container.

3. Query for the ADSI interface that you'll work with. In Listing 27.3, the call to `QueryInterface` asks for `IADs`, which is supported by all ADSI objects.

4. Perform whatever work is required using the interface pointer retrieved for the child object.

5. Release the interfaces to the child object. Remember to release the initial `IDispatch` interface pointer to the child object.

6. Loop around to enumerate further, until no more child objects exist in the enumeration.

Continuing with the source code in Listing 27.3, after the enumeration loop is finished, the enumerator is no longer needed, so it's released using `ADsFreeEnumerator`.

Using ADSI Non-Automation Interfaces

Most of the ADSI interfaces are implemented as dual interfaces, meaning that they may be called using Automation interfaces by scripting clients or through vtable interfaces by C and C++ clients.

In order to provide low-overhead access to the directory, two ADSI interfaces are not Automation-compatible and can be called only through the vtable:

- IDirectoryObject. A non-Automation interface that provides low-overhead access to a directory object. This interface provides a subset of the functionality provided by the IADs dual interface.

- IDirectorySearch. A non-Automation interface that's used to perform queries on the directory. All directories do not support this interface; as of Beta 3, only the LDAP ADSI provider exposes it.

The IDirectorySearch interface has a large number of methods. Here are some of the more popular methods:

- SetSearchPreference. Specifies the options to be used to perform a search.

- ExecuteSearch. Executes a search and returns a search handle back to the caller.

- GetFirstRow. Returns the first row of a search result to the caller.

- GetNextRow. Returns the next row of a search result to a caller. If GetFirstRow has not been previously called, this function returns the first row.

- GetColumn. Returns data from a particular column in the search result.

- FreeColumn. Frees resources allocated by an earlier call to GetColumn.

- CloseSearchHandle. Releases a handle to a search result and frees any allocated memory.

Listing 27.4 contains a fragment of the Search project, which can be found on the CD-ROM that accompanies this book. The Search project uses the IDirectorySearch interface to display information about users in the directory.

LISTING 27.4 USING IDirectorySearch TO SEARCH FOR USERS IN ACTIVE DIRECTORY

```
ADS_SEARCHPREF_INFO g_rgSearchPref[3];
DWORD g_dwPrefs = 0;

int  ErrorHandling(LPCTSTR lpszTitle);
void PrintColumnToConsole(PADS_SEARCH_COLUMN pCol);
void SetSearchPrefs();

int wmain()
{
    CoInitializeEx(NULL, COINIT_APARTMENTTHREADED);
    WCHAR wszQuery[512] = L"LDAP://CN=Users,";

    // Bind to the current domain controller
```

continues

27

ACTIVE DIRECTORY

LISTING 27.4   CONTINUED

```
IADs*    pRoot = NULL;
VARIANT var;
HRESULT hr = ADsGetObject(L"LDAP://rootDSE",
                          IID_IADs,
                          (void**)&pRoot);
if(FAILED(hr))
{
    ErrorHandling(L"ADsGetObject - rootDSE");
    CoUninitialize();
    return 0;
}
hr = pRoot->Get(L"DefaultNamingContext",&var);
if(FAILED(hr))
{
    ErrorHandling(L"Get default naming context");
    CoUninitialize();
    return 0;
}
// Append DC naming context to the path.
wcscat(wszQuery,var.bstrVal);
VariantClear(&var);
pRoot->Release();
// Use IDirectorySearch to perform a search for directory
// users, and display some basic information.
IDirectorySearch* pSearch = NULL;
hr = ADsGetObject(wszQuery,
                  IID_IDirectorySearch,
                  (void**)&pSearch);
if(FAILED(hr))
{
    ErrorHandling(L"ADsGetObject");
    CoUninitialize();
    return 0;
}
SetSearchPrefs();
hr = pSearch->SetSearchPreference(g_rgSearchPref, g_dwPrefs);
if(FAILED(hr))
{
    ErrorHandling(L"IDirectorySearch::SetSearchPreference");
    pSearch->Release();
    CoUninitialize();
    return 0;
}
LPWSTR rgszAttributes[] = { L"ADsPath",
                            L"Name",
                            L"samAccountName" };
ADS_SEARCH_HANDLE hSearch = NULL;
```

```
        DWORD dwCount= sizeof(rgszAttributes)/sizeof(LPWSTR);

    hr = pSearch->ExecuteSearch(L"objectClass=user",
                                rgszAttributes,
                                dwCount,
                                &hSearch);
    if(SUCCEEDED(hr))
    {
        hr = pSearch->GetNextRow(hSearch);
        while(SUCCEEDED(hr) && hr != S_ADS_NOMORE_ROWS)
        {
            ADS_SEARCH_COLUMN column;
            for(unsigned int ndx = 0; ndx < dwCount; ndx++)
            {
                hr = pSearch->GetColumn(hSearch,
                                        rgszAttributes[ndx],
                                        &column);
                if(hr == E_ADS_COLUMN_NOT_SET)
                    continue;
                wprintf(L"[%s] = ", rgszAttributes[ndx]);
                PrintColumnToConsole(&column);
                pSearch->FreeColumn(&column);
                wprintf(L"\n");
            }
            wprintf(L"\n");
            hr = pSearch->GetNextRow(hSearch);
        }
    }
    pSearch->CloseSearchHandle(hSearch);
    pSearch->Release();
    CoUninitialize();
    return 0;
}
```

27

ACTIVE
DIRECTORY

Listing 27.4 begins by initializing the COM runtime library and performing serverless binding to the Users node in Active Directory. The ADsGetObject function is used to execute the bind operation and return a pointer to the IDirectorySearch interface.

The SetSearchPrefs function is called to define parameters used for the search operation. SetSearchPrefs fills an array of ADS_SEARCHPREF_INFO with values that define parameters for the search operation, such as the maximum amount of time that can be spent on the search, the maximum size of a result, and the scope of the search operation. SetSearchPrefs isn't shown here, but it can be found on the CD-ROM that accompanies the book. The preferences for the search are associated with the IDirectorySearch interface by calling the SetSearchPreference method and passing the array of ADS_SEARCHPREF_INFO and the number of elements in the array as parameters.

Next, the `IDirectorySearch::ExecuteSearch` method is called. This function takes four parameters:

- An LDAP search filter. In this case, the results are filtered to include only directory users.
- An array of Unicode strings that contain the columns to be returned in the search result.
- The number of columns to be searched.
- The address of an `ADS_SEARCH_HANDLE` structure that's used for further operations on the search result.

The `IDirectorySearch::GetNextRow` method is called to retrieve the first row from the search result. The contents for each column in the row are retrieved using the `GetColumn` method. The data for each column is returned in an `ADS_SEARCH_COLUMN` structure, which is cracked and printed in the `PrintColumnToConsole` function. This function is not shown here due to its size, but it can be found on the accompanying CD-ROM as part of the Search project. Columns and rows are iterated until the search result has been completely parsed.

After all columns and rows have been displayed, the search handle is released by calling the `CloseSearchHandle` function, followed by releasing interface pointers and uninitializing the COM runtime library.

Using ADSI Persistent-Object Interfaces

ADSI persistent-object interfaces are used to manage directory objects that are permanent members of the directory, such as users, computers, and domains. Here are the interfaces in this category:

- `IADsCollection`. An interface that's used to represent a set of data. A client uses this interface to enumerate the elements in the set.
- `IADsComputer`. An interface that represents the attributes of a computer, including its name, description, operation system, and owner.
- `IADsDomain`. An interface that represents information about a network domain, such as the maximum password age and other password attributes.
- `IADsFileService`. An interface that represents a file service.
- `IADsFileShare`. An interface that enables the management of network file share information, such as its description or the number of users permitted to access the share point.
- `IADsGroup`. An interface that facilitates group membership management through the directory service.

- `IADsLocality`. An interface that enables management of locality information in directories that organize membership by region.

- `IADsMembers`. An interface that's used to manage a collection of directory objects that belong to a particular group.

- `IADsO`. An interface that enables management of organization or company information in directories that categorize membership by organization.

- `IADsOU`. An interface that enables management of departmental information in directories that categorize membership by organizational unit.

- `IADsPrintjob`. An interface that's used to manage a print job in a printer queue.

- `IADsPrintQueue`. An interface that enables management of printer information, such as the printer's name and description.

- `IADsService`. An interface that represents a running system service, such as the RAS or fax service. The `IADsFileService` interface is derived from `IADsService`.

- `IADsUser`. An interface that enables management of user account information, such as a user's password, name, description, phone number, and department.

Listing 27.5 contains a Visual Basic subroutine that enumerates the users in a domain using the `IADsUser` interface. This subroutine is part of a small Visual Basic project named VBFuncs, which can be found on this book's accompanying CD-ROM.

LISTING 27.5 USING THE `IADsUser` INTERFACE TO ENUMERATE USERS IN A DOMAIN

```
Private Sub EnumerateUsers(strDomain As String)

    Dim Users As IADsContainer
    Dim User As IADsUser
    Dim obj As IADs
    Dim strPath As String

    'Clear the results listbox
    lst.Clear

    strPath = "LDAP://CN=Users," & strDomain
    Set Users = GetObject(strPath)
    Users.Filter = Array("User")

    For Each User In Users
        Set obj = User
        lst.AddItem User.Name + " - (" + obj.ADsPath + ")"
    Next

End Sub
```

In Listing 27.5, the EnumerateUsers subroutine takes the default naming context as the strDomain string parameter. In the VBFuncs project, the default naming context is cached so that it can be easily used without requiring a function call to ADSI. The EnumerateUsers subroutine uses strDomain to bind to the Users node in the directory. Next, the function sets a filter on the Users container and enumerates each user, adding name and path information about each user to a list box.

Using ADSI Dynamic-Object Interfaces

Some objects in the directory are transient rather than permanent. The following dynamic-object interfaces are used to manage these objects:

- IADsComputerOperations. An interface that can be used to determine the current state of a remote computer or perform a shutdown remotely
- IADsFileServiceOperations. An interface used to return the currently open sessions or resources for a file service
- IADsPrintJobOperations. An interface used to examine, interrupt, or resume a network print job
- IADsPrintQueueOperations. An interface used to manage the current state of a print queue
- IADsResource. An interface used to manage an open file service resource, such as a file opened on a remote network share
- IADsServiceOperations. An interface used to manage installed system services
- IADsSession. An interface used to manage an open network file service session

Using ADSI Security Interfaces

ADSI includes interfaces that support managing security descriptors, ACLs, and ACEs for directory objects. Here's a list of these interfaces:

- IADsSecurityDescriptor. An interface used to manage or copy a security descriptor for an object in the directory
- IADsAccessControlList. An interface used to manage an ACL for an object in the directory
- IADsAccessControlEntry. An interface used to manage an ACE for an object in the directory

Additional Resources

Here's a list of some sources on the Web for information about ADSI and Active Directory:

- Probably the best place to get ADSI information is `www.15seconds.com`. This Web site is primarily focused on Active Server development issues, but its section on ADSI is first-rate, with numerous articles and how-to's as well as useful links to the Microsoft Web site.

- Microsoft has Active Directory and ADSI Web sites; however, the URLs for these sites are incredibly long and likely to change by the time you read this. As of this writing, most Windows 2000 technology sites still have NT5 embedded in their URLs. The easiest way to navigate to the Microsoft site is to visit `msdn.microsoft.com` first and then navigate to the ADSI or Windows 2000 pages.

- A great page for general LDAP information can be found at the University of Michigan at `www.umich.edu/~dirsvcs/LDAP`. The Web site doesn't have any information on ADSI, but it has links to all sorts of LDAP, X.500, and general directory information.

Summary

This chapter discussed using Active Directory and ADSI. The chapter began with an overview of the major features of Active Directory and the LDAP protocol. The major ADSI interfaces and functions were also discussed, and several examples in Visual Basic and Visual C++ were presented.

Using MSMQ

This chapter discusses Microsoft Message Queue, a mechanism used to send information between applications. The most commonly used features of MSMQ are discussed in this chapter. Also, examples are provided that use the Win32 API, and an MSMQ client example that's written in Visual Basic is provided.

An Introduction to the Microsoft Message Queue Server

As its name suggests, Microsoft Message Queue Server, or MSMQ, provides support for message queues. A *message queue* is a communication path between applications located in a distributed environment. Unlike named pipes, sockets, DCOM, and other protocols used for similar purposes, a message queue allows computers that aren't currently connected to communicate through its message store-and-forward capacity. The term *message queue* sometimes leads to confusion, because a message queue is not involved with messaging as the term is commonly used to apply to email and similar systems. Message queues can transport all types of data; they aren't limited to just sending text messages.

Several types of messages queues are supported by MSMQ. In general, a message queue is a reliable, persistent transportation medium that's located between two or more applications, as shown in Figure 28.1.

FIGURE 28.1

Message queues enable reliable communication between applications.

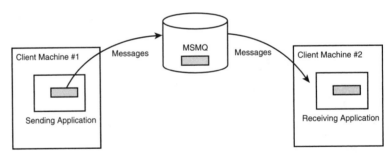

As shown in Figure 28.1, one application, known as the *sending application*, creates messages and places them into the message queue. Another application, known as the *receiving application*, retrieves messages from the queue. A unique quality of message queues is that the two applications can communicate even if they're never connected to the network at the same time. MSMQ will store messages until they can be delivered to their destinations.

MSMQ Versus Named Pipes

From a high-level view, a message queue looks a great deal like a named pipe. Here are a few of the differences between named pipes and message queues:

- Most importantly, message queues can be used to ensure delivery of messages sent between disconnected clients. If a message cannot be delivered, the message can be stored in the message queue until delivery is possible.

- A message queue is maintained by the operating system, not an application. Message queues can accept messages even if the application that's interested in reading the message is unavailable.

- Message queues are maintained in Active Directory, so it's very easy for an application to discover the location of a message queue.

- Message queues support transactions; named pipes do not.

- Message queues are easily used from languages other than C or C++. As you'll see later in this chapter, Visual Basic can easily be used with message queue.

Microsoft Message Queue Server, or MSMQ, was originally introduced as part of the Windows NT 4.0 option pack. As originally delivered, MSMQ used SQL Server to store the current state of message queues in a database known as the Message Queue Information Store, or MQIS. In Windows 2000, MSMQ has better integration with the operating system and uses Active Directory to store this information.

Installing MSMQ

Before you use MSMQ, you must install the MSMQ components on your Windows 2000 machines. There are four different types of MSMQ installations:

- *MSMQ Active Directory Server* must be installed on a Windows 2000 domain controller and is usually the first MSMQ component installed in your network. The MSMQ server contains messages queues and message queue management software.

- *MSMQ Routing Server* is an MSMQ server that provides intermediate store-and-forward capability for messages. This type of server is generally used between remote Windows 2000 sites. Routing servers are also used to route messages between computers running different network transport protocols.

- *MSMQ Independent Client* is the default client installation. An independent client contains message queues and management software. If contact with Active Directory is lost, messages will be stored on a local queue until contact can be regained with Active Directory.

28

USING MSMQ

- *MSMQ Dependent Client* is a lightweight client installation that doesn't include local message queues of management software. This type of client cannot send messages if contact with Active Directory is lost.

If the MSMQ components weren't installed during the initial installation of Windows 2000, you must install them before using any of the examples in this chapter. The easiest way to do this is to run the Add/Remove Programs applet in Control Panel. If you attempt to use message queue services on a machine that doesn't have message queue components installed, you'll receive an HRESULT with an error of MQ_ERROR_SERVICE_NOT_AVAILABLE.

Types of Messages Queues

There are several types of messages queues, and they fall into two basic categories:

- *Application queues*. Used by applications to pass messages.
- *System queues*. Created and maintained by the operating system.

Application queues are created by processes that use MSMQ and include the following queue types:

- *Message queues*. Used to send messages from one application to another.
- *Administration queues*. Used by a sending application to receive notification feedback generated by MSMQ about the status of a message.
- *Response queues*. Used to receive responses sent from a receiving application back to a sending application.
- *Report queues*. Used to track tracing information about the progress of a message through a message queue. Trace report messages are usually generated by MSMQ, but it's also possible for a receiving application to generate a report message.

MSMQ also creates and manages a set of system queues that are used to help support the management of the queuing service. Although you have access to these queues, you don't need to create them yourself—they're created by MSMQ automatically. System queues include the following:

- *Journal queues*. Used to track messages that are successfully removed from a message queue.
- *Dead letter queues*. Used to store messages that cannot be delivered.

Public Queues Versus Private Queues

Message queues can be defined as either *public* or *private*. A public queue can be located by other applications through Active Directory, whereas a private queue cannot. In general, a private queue is used only by applications on the local computer. Private queues tend to be faster than public queues, because they don't require support from Active Directory. They also work when Active Directory is not available—for example, when a client laptop computer is disconnected from the network or connected in a workgroup.

The name of a message queue is known as its *pathname*. Public and private queues are named differently. A public queue has a pathname in this format:

```
ComputerName\QueueName
```

The computer name can be the NetBIOS name or the fully qualified DNS name. Here are examples of public queue pathnames:

```
kenzie.codevtech.com\teletubbyqueue
```

```
KENZIE\teletubbyqueue
```

A private queue pathname includes the `Private$` substring between the computer and queue names, like this:

```
ALI\Private$\pongoqueue
```

When a message queue is on the local computer, the computer name can be replaced by a dot:

```
.\teletubbyqueue
```

The message queue's pathname is specified when the queue is created, and it can't be changed.

MSMQ Object Properties

When working with MSMQ, you use three types of objects: machines, queues, and messages. Each of these objects has properties that can be set, retrieved, and changed using the MSMQ API functions. There are three classes of properties used with MSMQ, one for each type of MSMQ object:

- *Machine properties.* Associated with the queue manager on a particular machine. These properties are stored in Active Directory. Machine properties are accessed through the MQQMPROPS structure.

- *Queue properties*. Associated with a particular message queue. Properties for public queues are stored in Active Directory. Properties for private queues are stored on the computer that hosts the queue. Queue properties are accessed through the MQQUEUEPROPS structure.

- *Message properties*. Associated with individual messages sent through the queue. Some properties are assigned by the application that creates the message, and other properties are assigned by MSMQ as the message is sent through the message queue. Properties for messages are contained in the individual messages. Message properties are accessed through the MQMSGPROPS structure.

As discussed in this list, each type of MSMQ object has its own structure used to contain properties. Each of these structures stores properties as arrays of property IDs, property values, and HRESULT values, as shown in Figure 28.2.

FIGURE 28.2

Properties are arranged into arrays.

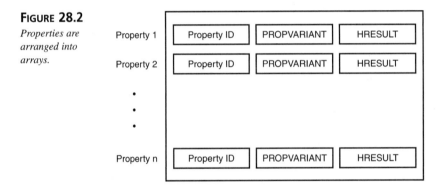

As shown in Figure 28.2, property values are stored as arrays of PROPVARIANT structures. PROPVARIANT is a discriminated union contained in a structure similar to the COM VARIANT structure.

Variables of PROPVARIANT are used just like COM variant variables. You must specify the type of the data stored in the PROPVARIANT union as well as set the proper variable, like this:

```
rgMsgPropVar[ndx].vt = VT_LPWSTR;
rgMsgPropVar[ndx].pwszVal = L"Test Msg Unleashed";
```

A common mistake is to forget to set the vt member variable or to set this variable to the wrong value. This value is used to determine the particular union member used to store the data; if it's incorrect, the results are unpredictable. In the following sections, the description of each property includes the property's type. Type information is also provided in the Platform SDK documentation.

Queue Properties

Every message queue has a collection of properties that determine the behavior of the queue. With the exception of the queue pathname, all properties are optional. As discussed in the preceding section, each property is passed as a PROPVARIANT structure. More information about PROPVARIANT will be provided later in this chapter.

Here are the available properties:

- PROPID_Q_AUTHENTICATE. An unsigned char (VT_UI1) that indicates whether the queue requires authenticated messages. A value of MQ_AUTHENTICATE indicates that the queue will pass only authenticated messages. A value of MQ_AUTHENTICATE_NONE indicates that the queue will support authenticated and nonauthenticated messages. If this property is not explicitly set, a value of MQ_AUTHENTICATE_NONE is used.

- PROPID_Q_BASEPRIORITY. A short int (VT_I2) that specifies the base priority for messages placed in the queue. The property applies only to public queues. The range of values for this property is -32768 through 32767. If this property isn't set, a default value of 0 is assumed.

- PROPID_Q_CREATE_TIME. A long int (VT_I4) that indicates the time the queue was created. The time returned is based on the number of seconds after January 1, 1970. This can be used in functions that expect a time_t variable, such as ctime. This property is read-only because it's set by the operating system.

- PROPID_Q_INSTANCE. A GUID (VT_CLSID) that identifies the queue instance. This property applies only to public queues. This value is set by the operating system when the queue is created and is read-only.

- PROPID_Q_JOURNAL. An unsigned char (VT_UI1) that specifies whether a queue maintains a journal queue. A value of MQ_JOURNAL indicates that an entry is placed into a journal queue for each message successfully removed from the queue. A value of MQ_JOURNAL_NONE indicates that no journal is maintained. If this property isn't set by the application, the default value is MQ_JOURNAL_NONE.

- PROPID_Q_JOURNAL_QUOTA. An unsigned long int (VT_UI4) that specifies the maximum size, in kilobytes, for the journal queue. The default value for this property is INFINITE, which allows for an unlimited journal size.

- PROPID_Q_LABEL. A Unicode string (VT_LPWSTR) that describes the queue. The label can be used as search criteria when you're browsing for queues, and it's also displayed in the MSMQ portion of the Active Directory Computers and Users MMC snap-in. If no label is specified, the queue will have an empty string as a label.

28

USING MSMQ

- PROPID_Q_MODIFY_TIME. A long int (VT_I4) that indicates the most recent time queue properties were modified. The time returned is based on the number of seconds after January 1, 1970. This can be used in functions that expect a time_t variable, such as ctime. This property is read-only because it's set by the operating system.

- PROPID_Q_PATHNAME. A Unicode string (VT_LPWSTR) that's the message queue pathname to the queue. The total length of the pathname cannot exceed 124 characters, but names longer than 64 characters may cause performance problems. This is the only property that's mandatory for a message queue.

- PROPID_Q_PRIV_LEVEL. An unsigned long int (VT_UI4) that specifies the privacy level required by the queue. There are three possible values for this property: MQ_PRIV_LEVEL_NONE indicates that the message queue will accept only nonprivate messages. MQ_PRIV_LEVEL_BODY indicates that the queue will accept only private, encrypted messages. The default value, MQ_PRIV_LEVEL_OPTIONAL, indicates that the queue will accept either type of message.

- PROPID_Q_QUOTA. An unsigned long int (VT_UI4) that specifies the maximum size, in kilobytes, for the message queue. The default value is INFINITE, which allows for an unlimited queue size.

- PROPID_Q_TRANSACTION. An unsigned char (VT_UI1) that specifies how the queue participates in transactions. There are two possible values: A value of MQ_TRANSACTIONAL indicates that the message must be defined as part of a message queue transaction. A value of MQ_TRANSACTIONAL_NONE indicates that the queue cannot participate in transactions. If this property isn't explicitly set by an application, the default value is MQ_TRANSACTIONAL_NONE.

- PROPID_Q_TYPE. A GUID (VT_CLSID) that identifies the queue type. This property is used by applications that need to apply a family type identifier to multiple queues. If no value is set by an application, the default value is NULL_GUID.

Application-specific properties are defined when the message queue is created. Messages can be changed with the MQSetQueueProperties function and retrieved with the MQGetQueueProperties function. An example of defining queue properties when a queue is created is provided later in this chapter.

Message Properties

Each message sent through the message queue includes a number of properties. Some properties are set by the application, and other properties are set by MSMQ as the message proceeds through the message queue. A lot of properties are available for messages.

For a complete list, consult the Platform SDK documentation. Here are the most commonly used properties:

- PROPID_M_BODY. An array of bytes (VT_VECTOR|VTUI1) that contains the body of the message. The maximum size of the message body is 4MB.

- PROPID_M_BODY_SIZE. An unsigned long int (VT_UI4) that indicates the number of bytes in the message body.

- PROPID_M_BODY_TYPE. An unsigned char (VT_U1) that specifies the type of data contained in the message body. The default value is 0, in which case the receiving application should assume that the data is an array of bytes.

- PROPID_M_DELIVERY. An unsigned char (VT_U1) that specifies the message delivery type. There are two possible values for this property: MQMSG_DELIVERY_RECOVER-ABLE specifies that the message is stored in a backup file until it's delivered, and MQMSG_DELIVERY_EXPRESS specifies that the message is not stored in a backup file. Messages marked as MQMSG_DELIVERY_EXPRESS are transmitted more quickly but may be lost in case of computer failure. If no value is specified for this property, the default value is MSMQ_DELIVERY_EXPRESS.

- PROPID_M_LABEL. A Unicode string (VT_LPWSTR) of up to 250 Unicode characters that specifies the message label.

- PROPID_M_LABEL_LEN. An unsigned long int (VT_UI4) that contains the length of the message label.

- PROPID_M_PRIORITY. An unsigned char (VT_U1) that specifies the priority level for the message. Messages with a higher priority will be processed before lower-priority messages. The priority level must be between 0 and 7, with a default value of 3.

- PROPID_M_TIME_TO_BE_RECEIVED. An unsigned long int (VT_UI4) that specifies the number of seconds the message can wait before it must be delivered or removed from the message queue. If no value is specified for this property, the default value is INFINITE, which allows the message to wait indefinitely to be delivered.

Application-defined message properties are set when the message is placed into the message queue. The properties associated with a message are retrieved when the message is read from the message queue. Examples of sending and receiving messages are provided later in this chapter.

28

USING MSMQ

Computer Properties

The third type of MSMQ properties is machine properties. Machine properties aren't used as often as queue and message properties. Here are the most commonly used machine properties:

- PROPID_QM_ENCRYPTION_PK. An array of bytes (VT_VECTOR¦VT_UI1) that contains the public encryption key used by the computer
- PROPID_QM_MACHINE_ID. A GUID (VT_CLSID) that identifies the computer
- PROPID_QM_PATHNAME. A Unicode string (VT_LPWSTR) that specifies the pathname of the computer

All machine properties are read-only. Machine properties are retrieved using the MQGetMachineProperties function.

Memory Allocation

In general, your application allocates memory buffers that are passed to MSMQ, which copies the contents of the buffer. Your application remains responsible for memory that it allocates when setting or retrieving MSMQ properties.

You can also request that MSMQ allocate the buffer for a property by passing VT_NULL as the variant property type. When the property is returned, MSMQ will have filled in the property type and allocated data, if required, for the property.

If MSMQ allocates memory for a property value returned to your application, you must free the memory using the MQFreeMemory function. For example, if you retrieve the PROPID_Q_TYPE property, passing VT_NULL as the variant's type, MSMQ will allocate data for the property, which must be freed in order to avoid a memory leak. Listing 28.1 is an example of a function that retrieves a property and then frees the memory buffer returned by the message queue.

LISTING 28.1   USING THE MQFreeMemory FUNCTION TO AVOID MEMORY LEAKS

```
HRESULT GetQueueTypeGuid(LPWSTR pwszFormatName, GUID* pguid)
{
    // Set up queue property structures.
    MQQUEUEPROPS    queueProps;
    PROPVARIANT     queuePropVar;
    MSGPROPID       queuePropID;

    queuePropID = PROPID_Q_TYPE; //Request queue type guid
    queuePropVar.vt = VT_NULL;   //MSMQ will supply type and buffer

    queueProps.cProp = 1;  // array contains one element
```

```
    queueProps.aPropID = &queuePropID;
    queueProps.aPropVar = &queuePropVar;
    queueProps.aStatus = NULL;

    // Retrieve queue property
    HRESULT hr = MQGetQueueProperties(pwszFormatName,
                                      &queueProps);
    if(SUCCEEDED(hr))
    {
        // Copy guid to buffer passed as parameter
        MoveMemory(pguid, queuePropVar.puuid, sizeof(GUID));
        // Free MSMQ supplied buffer
        MQFreeMemory(queuePropVar.puuid);
    }
    return hr;
}
```

You don't need to use MSFreeMemory for properties that are copied to buffers supplied by your application. For example, if you allocate a buffer for the message body using mal-loc, you must use free to release the buffer.

Using a Message Queue with the Win32 API

The Win32 API includes functions used to create and manage message queues. All MSMQ functions begin with *MQ*, such as MQCreateQueue. All MSMQ functions also return an HRESULT. However, in early Windows 2000 Beta releases, the text translation for the HRESULT codes is not available through the FormatMessage function. A list of error codes returned by MSMQ functions is provided in the mq.h header file.

Here are the most commonly used message queue functions:

- MQCreateQueue. Creates a message queue
- MQOpenQueue. Opens a handle to an existing message queue
- MQCloseQueue. Closes a handle to a message queue
- MQPathNameToFormatName. Translates a message queue pathname into a format name
- MQSendMessage. Sends a message over a message queue
- MQReceiveMessage. Reads a message from a message queue
- MQDeleteQueue. Deletes a message queue

When using the Win32 API to create and manage message queues, you must include the MSMQ header file:

```
#include <mq.h>
```

The `mq.h` header file includes the declaration for PROPVARIANT as well as descriptions for all error and warning HRESULT codes returned from MSMQ functions.

You must also modify your project to link with the MSMQ library, `mqrt.lib`. To modify a Visual C++ 6.0 project, follow these steps:

1. Select Settings from the Project menu. This will cause the Project Settings dialog box to be displayed.

2. Select the Link tab on the Project Settings dialog box.

3. Select the General category from the drop-down list and add `mqrt.lib` to the beginning of the Object/Library Modules edit control.

4. Close the Project Settings dialog box.

> **NOTE**
>
> MSMQ API functions accept Unicode strings only. To simplify this chapter's examples, all the projects are compiled with the _UNICODE and UNICODE preprocessor symbols defined.

Creating a Message Queue

The first step in using any of the message queue functions is to create a message queue. A message queue is created with the MQCreateQueue function:

```
HRESULT hr = MQCreateQueue(pSecDescriptor,
                           &queueProps,
                           wszFormat,
                           &cbFormat);
```

The MQCreateQueue function has four parameters:

- A pointer to a SECURITY_DESCRIPTOR for the queue. You can pass NULL for this value to use the default security settings; these settings allow the process that creates the queue to send messages and allow all other processes the ability to receive them.

- A pointer to an MQQUEUEPROPS structure that specifies the initial properties for the queue.

- The address of a buffer that will receive the format string for the message queue. This must be a Unicode string buffer.

- A pointer to a DWORD that contains the size of the buffer passed in the previous parameter. If the buffer is too small, MQCreateQueue will return an HRESULT with a value of MQ_INFORMATION_FORMATNAME_BUFFER_TOO_SMALL, and it will store the required buffer size in this variable.

Properties Used When Creating a Message Queue

The only property that's required when you're creating a message queue is the pathname. As discussed earlier, the pathname for a public message queue consists of the computer name and the name of the message queue, separated by a backslash:

```
kenzie.codevtech.com\teletubbyqueue
```

In addition to this mandatory property, here are some other commonly used properties:

- PROPID_Q_JOURNAL. Used to specify that messages removed from the queue are placed into a journal queue

- PROPID_Q_LABEL. Used to specify a label for the message queue

An Example of Creating a Message Queue

Listing 28.2 contains a console mode application that creates a message queue. The source code in Listing 28.2 is part of the CreateQueue project, which can be found on the CD-ROM that accompanies this book.

LISTING 28.2   CREATING A MESSAGE QUEUE

```
#define _WIN32_WINNT 0x0500
#include <windows.h>
#include <mq.h>
#include <wchar.h>

void HandleError(LPCWSTR strTitle, HRESULT hr);
void GetQueueNameFromUser();
void InitQueueProps();

#define MAX_PROPS  5
#define MAX_FORMAT 256
#define MAX_BUFFER 512

// Global data used by the example
WCHAR g_szComputerName[MAX_BUFFER];
WCHAR g_szQueueLabel[] = L"Unleashed Msg Queue Example";
WCHAR g_szQueueName[MAX_BUFFER];
WCHAR g_szQueuePath[MAX_BUFFER * 2];
```

continues

28

USING MSMQ

LISTING 28.2   CONTINUED

```
// Data structures used for the message queue.
MQQUEUEPROPS   g_queueProps;
PROPVARIANT    g_rgQueuePropVar[MAX_PROPS];
QUEUEPROPID    g_rgQueuePropID[MAX_PROPS];
HRESULT        g_rgQueueResults[MAX_PROPS];
WCHAR          g_szFormat[MAX_FORMAT];

int wmain()
{
    GetQueueNameFromUser();
    InitQueueProps();

    DWORD cbFormat = MAX_FORMAT;
    HRESULT hr = MQCreateQueue(NULL,
                               &g_queueProps,
                               g_szFormat,
                               &cbFormat);
    if(FAILED(hr))
    {
        HandleError(L"Create Queue Failed", hr);
        return 0;
    }
    else
    {
        MessageBox(NULL,
                   g_szQueuePath,
                   L"Message Queue Created",
                   MB_OK);
    }
    return 0;
}

// Initialize property values for the message queue.
void InitQueueProps()
{
    // Set queue name
    DWORD cbProps = 0;
    g_rgQueuePropID[cbProps] = PROPID_Q_PATHNAME;
    //g_rgQueuePropVar[cbProps].vt = VT_LPWSTR;
    g_rgQueuePropVar[cbProps].vt = VT_UI1;
    g_rgQueuePropVar[cbProps].pwszVal = g_szQueuePath;
    cbProps++;

    // Set journaling on
    g_rgQueuePropID[cbProps] = PROPID_Q_JOURNAL;
    g_rgQueuePropVar[cbProps].vt = VT_UI1;
    g_rgQueuePropVar[cbProps].bVal = MQ_JOURNAL;
    cbProps++;
```

```
        // Set queue label for administration purposes
        g_rgQueuePropID[cbProps] = PROPID_Q_LABEL;
        g_rgQueuePropVar[cbProps].vt = VT_LPWSTR;
        g_rgQueuePropVar[cbProps].pwszVal = g_szQueueLabel;

        g_queueProps.cProp = cbProps;
        g_queueProps.aPropID = g_rgQueuePropID;
        g_queueProps.aPropVar = g_rgQueuePropVar;
        g_queueProps.aStatus = g_rgQueueResults;
}

// Error handling routine, modified to display the
// HRESULT if the error text cannot be found.
void HandleError(LPCWSTR strTitle, HRESULT hr)
{
    LPVOID lpMsgBuf;

    DWORD dwRet = FormatMessageW(FORMAT_MESSAGE_ALLOCATE_BUFFER¦
                        FORMAT_MESSAGE_FROM_SYSTEM,
                        NULL,
                        hr,
                        MAKELANGID(LANG_NEUTRAL, SUBLANG_DEFAULT),
                        (LPWSTR)&lpMsgBuf,
                        0,
                        NULL);
    if(dwRet == 0)
    {
        // Can't find error text, display HRESULT instead.
        lpMsgBuf = LocalAlloc(LPTR, 42);
        if(lpMsgBuf)
        {
            wsprintf((LPWSTR)lpMsgBuf,
                    L"HRESULT = 0x%X",
                    hr);
        }
    }
    MessageBoxW(NULL,
                (LPCWSTR)lpMsgBuf,
                strTitle,
                MB_OK ¦ MB_ICONINFORMATION);
    LocalFree(lpMsgBuf);
}

// Collect computer and queue names from the user.
void GetQueueNameFromUser()
{
    do{
        wprintf(L"Computer name for the message queue:");
        _getws(g_szComputerName);
        wprintf(L"Name of the message queue:");
```

continues

LISTING 28.2   CONTINUED

```
        _getws(g_szQueueName);

    }while(!lstrlen(g_szComputerName) || !lstrlen(g_szQueueName));

    wsprintf(g_szQueuePath,
            L"%s\\%s",
            g_szComputerName,
            g_szQueueName);
}
```

In Listing 28.2, CreateQueue.cpp begins by requesting the message queue path from the user. This code can be found in the GetQueueNameFromUser function, which is straight-forward C code. Next, the initial properties for the message queue are defined in the InitQueueProps function. InitQueueProps defines three properties for the message queue:

- The message queue pathname is set as requested by the user.
- Journaling is turned on.
- The queue label is set to "Unleashed Msg Queue Example".

These properties are defined in arrays of PROPVARIANT and QUEUEPROPID. The addresses of these arrays are placed in an MQQUEUEPROPS structure that's passed as a parameter in a call to MQCreateQueue. If an error occurs, an error message is displayed to the user; otherwise, the queue is successfully created and the program ends.

You can view the current status of MSMQ on a server with the Active Directory Users and Computers MMC snap-in. When this snap-in is initially used, it does not display MSMQ information. You must follow these steps to view the state of message queues on a message queue server machine:

1. Start the Directory Users and Computers snap-in by selecting Directory Management from the Administrative Tools menu (Start, Programs, Administrative Tools, Directory Management).
2. Select Users, Group, and Computers as containers from the MMC View menu.
3. Select Advanced Features from the same menu.
4. Expand the managed objects in the console tree to find the computer that contains the new message queue.
5. Select the MSMQ node for the computer. A list of message queues hosted on the computer will be displayed in the contents pane on the right side of the MMC.

Figure 28.3 shows the MMC used to display the message queues currently created on a domain controller.

FIGURE 28.3

Using MSMQ to view the status of message queues on a server.

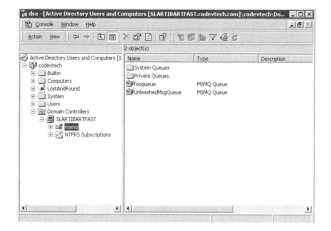

Opening an Existing Queue

Before messages can be written to or read from a message queue, the process that wants access to the queue must obtain a handle to the message queue. When a process uses MQCreateQueue to create a new message queue, a handle to the new message queue is returned to the caller.

There are two ways to retrieve a handle to a public queue. The first step in each of these methods is to obtain the format name that describes the message queue. After the format name has been determined, you can call MQOpenQueue to open the message queue and retrieve a handle to the queue. You can obtain a message queue's format name in these two ways:

- If you have the computer and queue names, call the MQPathNameToFormatName function to determine the queue's format name.
- If you have an instance value GUID for the message queue, call the MQInstanceToFormatName function to obtain the format name.

Alternatively, you can enumerate the set of message queues that meet a certain set of criteria. In order to search for message queues in this manner, you use three functions:

- MQLocateBegin. Defines the query used to search for message queues
- MQLocateNext. Retrieves the results for a message queue query
- MQLocateEnd. Ends a message queue query

After you've determined the format name for a message queue, the queue is opened by calling the MQOpenQueue function:

```
HANDLE hQueue = NULL;
DWORD dwAccess = MQ_RECEIVE_ACCESS;
DWORD dwShareMode = MQ_DENY_NONE;
HRESULT hr = MQOpenQueue(wszFormat,
                         dwAccess,
                         dwShareMode,
                         &hQueue);
```

The following four parameters are passed to MQOpenQueue:

- The format name of the message queue.
- The type of access needed to the message queue. MQ_PEEK_ACCESS specifies that messages can be viewed but not removed from the queue. MQ_RECEIVE_ACCESS specifies that messages can be viewed and optionally removed from the queue. MQ_SEND_ACCESS specifies that messages may be sent to the queue.
- The share mode for the message queue. MQ_DENY_NONE allows access to the message queue by other processes. MQ_DENY_RECEIVE_SHARE prevents other processes from opening the message queue for reading. MQ_DENY_NONE must be used when opening the pipe for sending messages.
- The address of a HANDLE variable that will receive the message queue handle if the function call succeeds.

Sending Messages over a Message Queue

Messages are sent over a message queue using the MQSendMessage function:

```
HRESULT hr = MQSendMessage(hQueue,
                           &g_msgProps,
                           NULL);
```

The MQSendMessage function has three parameters:

- A handle to the message queue that will carry the message.
- The address of an MQMSGPROPS structure that defines properties for the message to be sent.
- A pointer to a constant or object that specifies the transaction characteristics that are to be applied to the message. NULL is used if the message is not part of a transaction.

Listing 28.3 contains a console mode application that opens an existing message queue and uses MQSendMessage to place a message into the queue. The source code in Listing 28.3 can be found on this book's CD-ROM as part of the SendQueueMsg project.

LISTING 28.3   SENDING A MESSAGE TO A MESSAGE QUEUE

```c
#define _WIN32_WINNT 0x0500
#include <windows.h>
#include <mq.h>
#include <wchar.h>

void HandleError(LPCWSTR strTitle, HRESULT hr);
void GetQueueNameFromUser();
void GetMsgFromUser();
void InitMessageProps();

#define MAX_PROPS  5
#define MAX_FORMAT 256
#define MAX_BUFFER 512

// Global data used by the example
WCHAR    g_szComputerName[MAX_BUFFER];
WCHAR    g_szQueueName[MAX_BUFFER];
WCHAR    g_szQueuePath[MAX_BUFFER * 2];
WCHAR    g_szMessageBody[MAX_BUFFER];

// Data structures used for the message queue.
MQMSGPROPS       g_msgProps;
PROPVARIANT      g_rgMsgPropVar[MAX_PROPS];
MSGPROPID        g_rgMsgPropID[MAX_PROPS];
HRESULT          g_rgMsgResults[MAX_PROPS];
WCHAR            g_szFormat[MAX_FORMAT];

int wmain()
{
    GetQueueNameFromUser();

    // Get the format name of the queue
    DWORD cbFormat = MAX_FORMAT;
    HRESULT hr = MQPathNameToFormatName(g_szQueuePath,
                                        g_szFormat,
                                        &cbFormat);
    if(FAILED(hr))
    {
        HandleError(L"Format Name Failed", hr);
        return 0;
    }

    // Open a handle to the message queue
    HANDLE hQueue = NULL;
    DWORD dwAccess = MQ_SEND_ACCESS;
    DWORD dwShareMode = MQ_DENY_NONE;
    hr = MQOpenQueue(g_szFormat,
                     dwAccess,
```

28

USING MSMQ

continues

LISTING 28.3   CONTINUED

```
                        dwShareMode,
                        &hQueue);
    if(FAILED(hr))
    {
        HandleError(L"Open Queue Failed", hr);
        return 0;
    }

    InitMessageProps();

    do{
        GetMsgFromUser();
        hr = MQSendMessage(hQueue,
                           &g_msgProps,
                           NULL);
        if(FAILED(hr))
            HandleError(L"MQSendMessage", hr);

    }while(SUCCEEDED(hr)&&lstrcmpi(L"Q",g_szMessageBody) != 0);

    MQCloseQueue(hQueue);
    return 0;
}

// Initialize message properties
void InitMessageProps()
{
    DWORD cbMsgProps = 0;

    g_rgMsgPropID[cbMsgProps] = PROPID_M_BODY;
    g_rgMsgPropVar[cbMsgProps].vt = VT_VECTOR|VT_UI1;
    g_rgMsgPropVar[cbMsgProps].caub.pElems = (BYTE*)g_szMessageBody;
    g_rgMsgPropVar[cbMsgProps].caub.cElems = sizeof(g_szMessageBody);
    cbMsgProps++;

    g_rgMsgPropID[cbMsgProps] = PROPID_M_LABEL;
    g_rgMsgPropVar[cbMsgProps].vt = VT_LPWSTR;
    g_rgMsgPropVar[cbMsgProps].pwszVal = L"Test Msg";
    cbMsgProps++;

    g_rgMsgPropID[cbMsgProps] = PROPID_M_DELIVERY;
    g_rgMsgPropVar[cbMsgProps].vt = VT_UI1;
    g_rgMsgPropVar[cbMsgProps].bVal = MQMSG_DELIVERY_RECOVERABLE;
    cbMsgProps++;

    g_msgProps.cProp = cbMsgProps;
    g_msgProps.aPropID = g_rgMsgPropID;
    g_msgProps.aPropVar = g_rgMsgPropVar;
```

```
        g_msgProps.aStatus = g_rgMsgResults;
}


// Error handling routine
void HandleError(LPCWSTR strTitle, HRESULT hr)
{
    LPVOID lpMsgBuf;

    DWORD dwRet = FormatMessageW(FORMAT_MESSAGE_ALLOCATE_BUFFER|
                        FORMAT_MESSAGE_FROM_SYSTEM,
                        NULL,
                        hr,
                        MAKELANGID(LANG_NEUTRAL, SUBLANG_DEFAULT),
                        (LPWSTR)&lpMsgBuf,
                        0,
                        NULL);
    if(dwRet == 0)
    {
        // Can't find error text, display HRESULT instead.
        lpMsgBuf = LocalAlloc(LPTR, 42);
        if(lpMsgBuf)
        {
            wsprintf((LPWSTR)lpMsgBuf,
                    L"HRESULT = 0x%X",
                    hr);
        }
    }
    MessageBoxW(NULL,
                (LPCWSTR)lpMsgBuf,
                strTitle,
                MB_OK | MB_ICONINFORMATION);
    LocalFree(lpMsgBuf);
}


// Collect computer and queue names from the user.
void GetQueueNameFromUser()
{
    do{
        wprintf(L"Computer name for the message queue:");
        _getws(g_szComputerName);
        wprintf(L"Name of the message queue:");
        _getws(g_szQueueName);

    }while(!lstrlen(g_szComputerName) || !lstrlen(g_szQueueName));

    wsprintf(g_szQueuePath,
            L"%s\\%s",
            g_szComputerName,
            g_szQueueName);
}
```

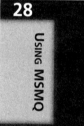

28

USING MSMQ

continues

LISTING 28.3   CONTINUED

```
// Get a message from the user
void GetMsgFromUser()
{
    do{
        wprintf(L"Message to be sent (Q to quit):");
        _getws(g_szMessageBody);

    }while(!lstrlen(g_szMessageBody));
}
```

In Listing 28.3, SendQueueMsg.cpp begins by requesting the message queue path from the user, as was done earlier in Listing 28.2. Next, MQPathNameToFormatName is used to generate the format name for the message queue. The format name is used to open the message queue with the MQOpenQueue function.

Next, the initial properties for the message are defined in the InitMessageProps function. InitMessageProps defines three properties for the message:

- The message body is defined as the contents of the global g_szMessageBody Unicode string.

- The message label is defined as "Test Msg".

- The message delivery type is set to MQ_RECOVERABLE, which specifies that the message must be backed up onto disk storage until it's successfully delivered.

These properties are defined in arrays of PROPVARIANT and MSGPROPID. The addresses of these arrays are placed in a global MQMSGPROPS structure that will be passed as a parameter in a call to MQSendMessage. The user is then prompted for messages to be placed in the message queue, with MQSendMessage called for each message. The last message sent by the user has a message body that consists of the Unicode string "Q" to mark the end of the series of messages.

The messages currently stored in the message queue can be displayed using the Active Directory Users and Computers MMC snap-in, as shown in Figure 28.4.

FIGURE 28.4

Using MSMQ to view messages stored in a message queue.

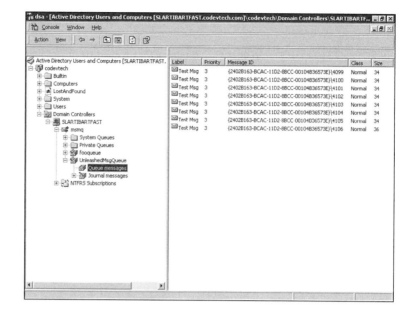

Receiving Messages from a Message Queue

Messages are read from a message queue using the MQReceiveMessage function:

```
DWORD dwAction = MQ_ACTION_RECEIVE;
HRESULT hr = MQReceiveMessage(hQueue,
                              0,           // Timeout, in msecs.
                              dwAction,
                              &g_props,
                              NULL,
                              NULL,
                              NULL,
                              NULL);
```

The MQReceiveMessage function has eight parameters:

- A handle to the message queue that messages will be read from.

- The amount of time the calling thread will wait for a message, in milliseconds. A value of 0 specifies that there is no timeout.

- The type of action that should be performed in order to receive a message from the queue. A value of MQ_ACTION_RECEIVE specifies that the first message in the queue should be read and removed from the queue. A value of MQ_ACTION_PEEK_CURRENT specifies that the first message should be read but not removed from the queue. A value of MQ_ACTION_PEEK_NEXT is used with a message cursor to scroll through messages located in the message queue.

- The address of an MQMSGPROPS structure that carries properties for the message read from the queue.

- The address of an OVERLAPPED structure that's used when asynchronous reads are performed from the message queue. This value is NULL when messages are read synchronously.

- The address of a callback function that's used when messages are read asynchronously from the message queue. This value is NULL when messages are read synchronously.

- A handle to a message cursor. NULL is used if no message cursor is used.

- A pointer to a constant or object that specifies the transaction characteristics to be applied to the message. NULL is used if the message is not part of a transaction.

Listing 28.4 contains a console mode application that opens an existing message queue and uses MQReceiveMessage to read all the messages waiting in the queue. This source code is part of the RcvQueueMsg project, which can be found on the CD-ROM that accompanies this book.

LISTING 28.4   READING MESSAGES FROM A MESSAGE QUEUE

```
#define _WIN32_WINNT 0x0500
#include <windows.h>
#include <mq.h>
#include <wchar.h>

void HandleError(LPCWSTR strTitle, HRESULT hr);
void GetQueueNameFromUser();
void InitMessageProps();

#define MAX_PROPS  2
#define MAX_FORMAT 256
#define MAX_BUFFER 512

// Global data used by the example
WCHAR    g_szComputerName[MAX_BUFFER];
WCHAR    g_szQueueName[MAX_BUFFER];
WCHAR    g_szQueuePath[MAX_BUFFER * 2];
WCHAR    g_szMessageBody[MAX_BUFFER];


// Data structures used for the message queue.
MQMSGPROPS      g_msgProps;
PROPVARIANT     g_rgMsgPropVar[MAX_PROPS];
MSGPROPID       g_rgMsgPropID[MAX_PROPS];
HRESULT         g_rgMsgResults[MAX_PROPS];
WCHAR           g_szFormat[MAX_FORMAT];

int wmain()
```

```
{
    GetQueueNameFromUser();

    // Get the format name of the queue
    DWORD cbFormat = MAX_FORMAT;
    HRESULT hr = MQPathNameToFormatName(g_szQueuePath,
                                        g_szFormat,
                                        &cbFormat);
    if(FAILED(hr))
    {
        HandleError(L"Format Name Failed", hr);
        return 0;
    }

    // Open a handle to the message queue
    HANDLE hQueue = NULL;
    DWORD dwAccess = MQ_RECEIVE_ACCESS;
    DWORD dwShareMode = MQ_DENY_NONE;
    hr = MQOpenQueue(g_szFormat,
                     dwAccess,
                     dwShareMode,
                     &hQueue);
    if(FAILED(hr))
    {
        HandleError(L"Open Queue Failed", hr);
        return 0;
    }

    InitMessageProps();

    do{
        //GetMessage
        ZeroMemory(g_szMessageBody, sizeof(g_szMessageBody));
        DWORD dwAction = MQ_ACTION_RECEIVE;
        hr = MQReceiveMessage(hQueue,
                              0,           // Timeout, in msecs.
                              dwAction,
                              &g_msgProps,
                              NULL,
                              NULL,
                              NULL,
                              NULL);
        if(FAILED(hr))
        {
            HandleError(L"MQReceiveMessage", hr);
            break;
        }
        // If a message body was returned, print it.
        if(g_rgMsgPropVar[0].ulVal != 0)
        {
```

28

USING MSMQ

continues

LISTING 28.4   CONTINUED

```
            wprintf(L"Message:\n%s\n", g_szMessageBody);
        }
        else
        {
            wprintf(L"Message received without a message body\n");
        }

    } while(SUCCEEDED(hr) && lstrcmpi(L"Q", g_szMessageBody) != 0);

    MQCloseQueue(hQueue);
    return 0;
}

// Initialize message properties
void InitMessageProps()
{
    // Retrieve the size of the message body
    DWORD cbProps = 0;
    g_rgMsgPropID[cbProps] = PROPID_M_BODY_SIZE;
    g_rgMsgPropVar[cbProps].vt = VT_UI4;
    cbProps++;

    // Retrieve the message body
    g_rgMsgPropID[cbProps] = PROPID_M_BODY;
    g_rgMsgPropVar[cbProps].vt = VT_VECTOR|VT_UI1;
    g_rgMsgPropVar[cbProps].caub.pElems = (BYTE*)g_szMessageBody;
    g_rgMsgPropVar[cbProps].caub.cElems = sizeof(g_szMessageBody);
    cbProps++;

    g_msgProps.cProp = cbProps;
    g_msgProps.aPropID = g_rgMsgPropID;
    g_msgProps.aPropVar = g_rgMsgPropVar;
    g_msgProps.aStatus = g_rgMsgResults;
}

// Error handling routine
void HandleError(LPCWSTR strTitle, HRESULT hr)
{
    LPVOID lpMsgBuf;

    FormatMessageW(FORMAT_MESSAGE_ALLOCATE_BUFFER|
                FORMAT_MESSAGE_FROM_SYSTEM,
                NULL,
                hr,
                MAKELANGID(LANG_NEUTRAL, SUBLANG_DEFAULT),
                (LPWSTR)&lpMsgBuf,
                0,
                NULL);
    MessageBoxW(NULL,
                (LPCWSTR)lpMsgBuf,
```

```
                    strTitle,
                    MB_OK ¦ MB_ICONINFORMATION);
        LocalFree(lpMsgBuf);
    }

    // Collect computer and queue names from the user.
    void GetQueueNameFromUser()
    {
        do{
            wprintf(L"Computer name for the message queue:");
            _getws(g_szComputerName);
            wprintf(L"Name of the message queue:");
            _getws(g_szQueueName);

        }while(!lstrlen(g_szComputerName) ¦¦ !lstrlen(g_szQueueName));

        wsprintf(g_szQueuePath,
                L"%s\\%s",
                g_szComputerName,
                g_szQueueName);
    }
```

In Listing 28.4, RcvQueueMsg.cpp begins by requesting the message queue path from the user. Then the queue is opened just as it was in the previous example.

Next, the properties to be retrieved for the incoming message are defined in the InitMessageProps function. InitMessageProps defines two properties to be retrieved:

- The size of the message body buffer.
- The buffer that will contain the message body. This is defined as a global g_szMessageBody Unicode string.

These properties are defined in arrays of PROPVARIANT and MSGPROPID. The addresses of these arrays are placed in a global MQMSGPROPS structure that will be passed as a parameter in a call to MQReceiveMessage.

Closing a Message Queue Handle

After you've finished using a message queue handle, you must close the message queue and release the handle by calling the MQCloseQueue function:

```
HRESULT hr = MQCloseQueue(hQueue);
```

MQCloseQueue has one parameter: the message queue handle that you're releasing. As is the case with other message queue functions, MQCloseQueue returns an HRESULT.

Closing the queue does not delete the queue or erase any messages waiting for delivery. MQCloseQueue simply releases your connection with the message queue.

Deleting a Message Queue

When a message queue is no longer needed, you should remove it from Active Directory by calling the MQDeleteQueue function:

```
HRESULT hr = MQDeleteQueue(g_szFormat);
```

The MQDeleteQueue function has one parameter: the format name for the message queue to be deleted.

Listing 28.5 contains a console mode application that uses MQDeleteQueue to erase a message queue. The source code is part of the DeleteQueue project, which can be found on the CD-ROM that accompanies this book.

LISTING 28.5   DELETING A MESSAGE QUEUE FROM ACTIVE DIRECTORY

```c
#define _WIN32_WINNT 0x0500
#include <windows.h>
#include <mq.h>
#include <wchar.h>

void HandleError(LPCWSTR strTitle, HRESULT hr);
void GetQueueNameFromUser();

#define MAX_FORMAT 256
#define MAX_BUFFER 512

// Global data used by the example
WCHAR    g_szComputerName[MAX_BUFFER];
WCHAR    g_szQueueName[MAX_BUFFER];
WCHAR    g_szQueuePath[MAX_BUFFER * 2];
WCHAR    g_szFormat[MAX_FORMAT];

int wmain()
{
    GetQueueNameFromUser();

    // Get the format name of the queue
    DWORD cbFormat = MAX_FORMAT;
    HRESULT hr = MQPathNameToFormatName(g_szQueuePath,
                                        g_szFormat,
                                        &cbFormat);

    if(FAILED(hr))
    {
        HandleError(L"Format Name Failed", hr);
        return 0;
    }

    hr = MQDeleteQueue(g_szFormat);
    if(SUCCEEDED(hr))
```

```
                MessageBox(NULL, g_szQueuePath, L"Queue Deleted", MB_OK);

        return 0;
}

// Collect computer and queue names from the user.
void GetQueueNameFromUser()
{
        do{
            wprintf(L"Computer name for the message queue:");
            _getws(g_szComputerName);
            wprintf(L"Name of the message queue:");
            _getws(g_szQueueName);

        }while(!lstrlen(g_szComputerName) || !lstrlen(g_szQueueName));

        wsprintf(g_szQueuePath,
                L"%s\\%s",
                g_szComputerName,
                g_szQueueName);
}

// Error handling routine
void HandleError(LPCWSTR strTitle, HRESULT hr)
{
        LPVOID lpMsgBuf;

        DWORD dwRet = FormatMessageW(FORMAT_MESSAGE_ALLOCATE_BUFFER|
                            FORMAT_MESSAGE_FROM_SYSTEM,
                            NULL,
                            hr,
                            MAKELANGID(LANG_NEUTRAL, SUBLANG_DEFAULT),
                            (LPWSTR)&lpMsgBuf,
                            0,
                            NULL);
        if(dwRet == 0)
        {
            // Can't find error text, display HRESULT instead.
            lpMsgBuf = LocalAlloc(LPTR, 42);
            if(lpMsgBuf)
            {
                wsprintf((LPWSTR)lpMsgBuf,
                        L"HRESULT = 0x%X",
                        hr);
            }
        }
        MessageBoxW(NULL,
                    (LPCWSTR)lpMsgBuf,
                    strTitle,
                    MB_OK | MB_ICONINFORMATION);
        LocalFree(lpMsgBuf);
}
```

In Listing 28.5, `DeleteQueue.cpp` starts by gathering the message queue computer and queue names from the user and converting the message queue pathname into a format name. The `MQDeleteQueue` function is called to delete the message queue from the system.

A Message Queue Client Written in Visual Basic

Visual Basic can also be used to write MSMQ applications. As an example of how VB is used in a client-side application, the CD-ROM that accompanies the book includes MSMQSendMsg, a simple VB client that can interact with the C++ examples presented earlier in this chapter.

This VB example takes advantage of three ActiveX objects that are part of the MSMQ object library:

- `MSMQMessage`. Represents a message sent through a message queue
- `MSMQQueueInfo`. Represents the properties associated with a message queue
- `MSMQQueue`. Represents an instance of an open message queue

In order to use any of the MSMQ ActiveX objects, you must add a reference to the MSMQ object library. Select References from the Project menu to display the References dialog box. Check the Microsoft Message Queue Object Library item, as shown in Figure 28.5.

FIGURE 28.5

Adding a reference to the MSMQ object library.

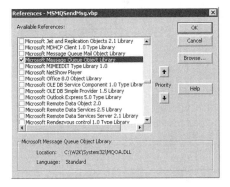

The main form, frmMain, used in the MSMQSendMsg project is shown in Figure 28.6. The form has two command buttons and two textbox controls.

FIGURE 28.6

The main form used by MSMQSendMsg.

The properties for the controls used in frmMain are provided in Table 28.1.

TABLE 28.1   PROPERTIES FOR CONTROLS IN FRMMAIN

Control	Name	Index	Caption
Button	cmd	0	&Close
Button	cmd	1	&Open
TextBox	txt	0	
TextBox	txt	1	

Listing 28.6 contains the source code for the frmMain form.

LISTING 28.6   SENDING MESSAGES TO A MESSAGE QUEUE USING VISUAL BASIC

```
Option Explicit

' Variables needed to interact with the message queue
Dim msmqInfo As New MSMQQueueInfo
Public msmqDest As MSMQQueue


Private Sub cmd_Click(Index As Integer)

    Dim fQueueOpen As Boolean

    If Index = 0 Then
        ' Close application
        End
    Else
        ' Open queue
        fQueueOpen = OpenMessageQueue(txt(0).Text, txt(1).Text)
    End If

    If fQueueOpen Then
        If msmqDest.IsOpen Then
            ' Display form
            frmMsg.Show vbModal
        End If
    End If
```

continues

28

USING MSMQ

LISTING 28.6 CONTINUED

```
End Sub

Private Function OpenMessageQueue(strComputer As String, _
                                  strQueue As String) As Boolean

On Error GoTo errHandler
    OpenMessageQueue = False

    msmqInfo.PathName = strComputer & "\" & strQueue
    Set msmqDest = msmqInfo.Open(MQ_SEND_ACCESS, MQ_DENY_NONE)

    OpenMessageQueue = True
    Exit Function

errHandler:
    MsgBox "Couldn't open queue:" + Chr(13) + Err.Description _
            + Chr(13) + "Error code: " + Hex(Err.Number)

 End Function


Private Sub Form_Unload(Cancel As Integer)

    Set msmqInfo = Nothing
    Set msmqDest = Nothing

End Sub
```

Most of the work in frmMain is performed in the `OpenMessageQueue` function. The `PathName` property for `msmqInfo`, the `MSMQQueueInfo` variable, is set to the user-provided message queue path. The value of `msmqDest` is set to a reference to the message queue opened by calling `msmqInfo.Open`. After the message queue is successfully opened, a new form will be displayed that prompts the user to write one or more messages to the message queue.

The frmMsg form, shown in Figure 28.7, is used to collect messages from the user that are written to the message queue.

FIGURE 28.7

The message-handling form used by MSMQSendMsg.

The properties for the controls used in frmMsg are provided in Table 28.2.

TABLE 28.2 PROPERTIES FOR CONTROLS IN FRMMSG

Control	Name	Index	Caption
Button	cmd	0	&Close
Button	cmd	1	&Send
Button	cmd	2	&Quit
TextBox	txtMsg		

Listing 28.7 contains the source code for the frmMain form.

LISTING 28.7 SENDING MESSAGES TO A MESSAGE QUEUE USING VISUAL BASIC

```
Option Explicit

Dim msg As New MSMQMessage


Private Sub cmd_Click(Index As Integer)

    If Index = 0 Then
        End
    ElseIf Index = 1 Then
        msg.Label = "Test Message"
        msg.Body = txtMsg.Text
        msg.Send frmMain.msmqDest
    Else
        msg.Label = "Last Message"
        msg.Body = "q"
        msg.Send frmMain.msmqDest
        Unload Me
    End If

    txtMsg.Text = ""

End Sub


Private Sub Form_Unload(Cancel As Integer)
    Set msg = Nothing
End Sub
```

If the user clicks the Send button, properties are defined for msg, which is an instance of the MSMQMessage object. The message is sent to the message queue by calling msg.Send and passing the destination message queue as a parameter. If the user clicks Quit, a "Q" string is sent to the message queue, and the form is unloaded.

Summary

This chapter has discussed the Microsoft Message Queue Server, also known as MSMQ. The most commonly used properties and features of MSMQ were discussed, such as how the ability for messages to be sent and received between clients might be disconnected from the network. Several examples were also provided in both C/C++ and Visual Basic.

Cluster Server

This chapter discusses Microsoft Cluster Server, which enables multiple computers to be joined together into a single virtual computer. Clusters improve the availability of critical resources by providing facilities to move failed applications to other computers in the cluster.

This chapter discusses how you can write applications that are "cluster-aware" and can take advantage of services offered by Microsoft Cluster Server. You must have Windows 2000 Advanced Server in order to run the examples in this chapter.

Microsoft Cluster Server Architecture

Microsoft Cluster Server, or MSCS, enables you to join multiple computers together to form a cluster. A *cluster* is a group of machines that appears to be a single server to clients of the cluster. Applications that run on the cluster tend to increase their availability to clients, because they can run on any machine in the cluster. The current release of MSCS supports clusters with two nodes; future releases will support larger clusters.

Applications, disk drives, IP addresses, and other server properties are registered with MSCS as *cluster resources*. When a cluster node fails, MSCS will move resources running on the failed node to a surviving node. Each cluster resource registers other resources that it depends on. Here are some examples of resources that an application might depend on:

- Other applications or services
- Hardware (such as disk drives)
- Network interfaces

If an application that a resource depends on becomes unavailable, the application is moved to another node in the cluster. Moving an application from one node to another is known as *failover*.

In addition, cluster-aware applications are monitored by the cluster service to ensure that they remain available. If an application fails due to an internal fault, the cluster service will failover the application to another node in the cluster.

Resources are placed into cluster objects known as *groups*. A group contains one or more cluster resources that failover together. An example of a group used on all clusters is a virtual server. A virtual server includes IP address and network name resources. Client computers can connect to the virtual server using the virtual server's IP address and computer name. If the node currently hosting the virtual server fails, a failover occurs, moving the virtual server to another node.

Cluster Server Hardware

Using the MSCS clustering service requires specific hardware that's used to support communication between nodes in the cluster. Although you can create a cluster using readily available components, Microsoft supports MSCS on hardware platforms that have been certified as part of its Hardware Compatibility List program. A list of certified cluster configurations can be viewed at

`www.microsoft.com\hwtest\hcl`

The physical architecture of a cluster is shown in Figure 29.1.

FIGURE 29.1

Hardware used in a Windows 2000 MSCS cluster.

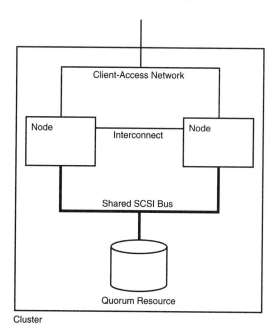

Nodes in a cluster share a storage bus that contains information about the cluster. Storage devices on the shared bus are each owned by only one node at a time. One device on the shared bus is designated as the cluster's *quorum device*—the node that owns the quorum device has controlling ownership over the cluster.

Nodes in a cluster are usually connected to two networks:

- A private network, sometimes called an *interconnect*, which is used for private communication between nodes. Clusters that have two nodes typically use a crossover cable to connect their network interface cards. In the future, when MSCS supports more than two nodes, larger clusters will require a hub.
- A client access network, which provides access to the cluster for clients.

Clients that connect to a cluster do not require any special hardware or software.

MSCS Software Components

A cluster is made up of a number of software components. The major software components in a Windows 2000 cluster are shown in Figure 29.2.

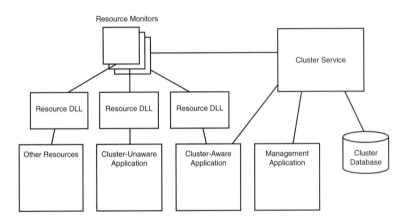

FIGURE 29.2

The major software components in a Windows 2000 MSCS cluster.

As shown in Figure 29.2, here are the major software components in a cluster:

- *Cluster service.* Must run on every node that participates in the cluster. The cluster service is composed of several smaller components that control communication with the network, maintain the cluster database, control failover, and perform other similar activities.
- *Management applications.* Programs that control the cluster or cluster-aware applications.
- *Cluster-aware applications.* Programs written to take advantage of MSCS. They may be able to detect that they're running in a cluster, or they may have features that enable them to be more manageable in a clustered environment.

- *Cluster-unaware applications*. Programs that are oblivious to MSCS. These applications are manageable by the cluster, but they won't be as available as an application that can interact with the cluster. You can transform an application that's unaware of the cluster into a cluster-aware application by writing a custom resource type.

- *Cluster database*. Currently implemented through the Win32 Registry. The cluster database stores configuration information about the cluster. More information about the cluster database is provided later in the section titled "Using the Cluster Database."

- *Resource DLLs*. Used by the cluster service to manage one or more resources. Resource DLLs are discussed in more detail in the section titled "Understanding Resource DLLs."

- *Resource monitors*. An isolation layer for the cluster service that's used to interact with resource DLLs. Resource monitors are discussed in more detail in the section titled "Understanding Resource Monitors."

Using the Cluster Database

The cluster database is used to store configuration information about the cluster. Cluster-aware applications also use the cluster database to store state and property data. When a failover occurs, the application that becomes active can retrieve a copy of the current state and property information from the cluster database.

Changes to the cluster database are automatically replicated to other nodes in the cluster. Changes are transactional, so you can be sure that the changes have been made to all nodes. The cluster database is routinely tested, or *checkpointed*, by the cluster service in order to ensure consistency.

The preferred method for accessing the cluster database is to use control code functions and property lists. Using code functions and property lists is discussed later in the section titled "Using Cluster Object Management APIs."

NOTE

Do not attempt to use Win32 Registry functions to access the cluster database directly. Your changes will not be properly replicated to other nodes, and you may destroy the cluster.

29

CLUSTER SERVER

Understanding Resource DLLs

Every resource managed by the cluster service is managed through a resource DLL. Resource DLLs are used by the cluster service to start, stop, and manage failover of resources in the cluster. In order to manage your cluster resource or application, you have two choices:

- You can use the Generic Application or Generic Service resource DLLs included with MSCS.
- You can create your own custom resource type and manage your resource through a custom resource DLL.

Creating a custom resource type will result in the best overall performance when running on a cluster, because the resource DLL can actively manage the resource on behalf on the cluster service.

Understanding Resource Monitors

The resource monitor sits between the cluster service and a resource DLL. The resource monitor is an executable that has the responsibility of managing one or more in-process resource DLLs. Without the resource monitor acting as an isolation layer, a poorly written resource DLL could take down the entire clustering service. As it is, a resource DLL can, at most, interrupt service for other resource DLLs that share the same resource monitor.

Using the Cluster Administrator, additional resource monitors can be used to manage resources in the cluster. This is typically done for debugging purposes or to isolate resource DLLs that are untrusted or suspected of being faulty.

Cluster Startup and Recovery

When a cluster node is started, it immediately looks for a cluster to join. It begins by searching for an existing cluster by using the private interconnect to communicate with other cluster nodes. If an existing cluster is found, the node will join the cluster and retrieve a copy of the cluster database.

Applications can run on a cluster in two modes:

- *Active/Passive*. The application runs on one cluster node and is marked as passive on other nodes.
- *Active/Active*. The application runs on each node in the cluster.

Most cluster-aware applications today run in Active/Passive mode. When an application runs in Active/Passive mode, two copies of the application are installed. When a failover occurs, the previously passive copy of the application becomes active, and the active application becomes passive.

When an application runs in Active/Active mode, two instances of the application may run on one node, although the typical case is for each node to run one copy of the application. This configuration enables one virtual server to appear to enjoy twice the capacity of a single server.

When an application runs in Active/Active mode, two copies of the application are passive, and two copies of the application are active.

In both Active/Active and Active/Passive modes, clients connect to the server in the same way. Clients attach to the application through the cluster's virtual server, and they have no need to know which particular instance of the application they're using. When a failover occurs, the clients are disconnected from the server and must attempt to reconnect in order to gain access to the application again.

Using Clustering APIs

Three categories of APIs are used with MSCS:

- Cluster Object Management APIs
- Resource DLL APIs
- Cluster Administration Extension DLL APIs

These API groups are discussed in the following sections.

Using Cluster Object Management APIs

Six types of cluster objects are managed through the Cluster Object Management API functions:

- Groups
- Nodes
- Resources
- Resource types
- Networks
- Network interfaces

Given these six types of cluster objects, there are also several ways for these objects to be managed:

- With control code functions and control codes.
- With the CClusPropList class.
- Through the cluster database APIs.
- Through direct manipulation of the cluster object using an object-specific function call.
- By manipulating the Win32 System Registry. (Although possible, this method is not recommended by Microsoft, because you're bypassing controls and facilities that are built into the cluster service.)

Using Control Code Functions and Control Codes

The preferred way to manage a resource is to use the cluster object control code functions. Control code functions are preferred because they allow the cluster service to notify resource DLLs of events that occur due to the requested function. This is especially true of functions that impact the cluster database.

Each cluster object type has a separate control code function:

- ClusterGroupControl. Manages a cluster group.
- ClusterNetworkControl. Manages a cluster network.
- ClusterNetInterfaceControl. Manages a network interface.
- ClusterNodeControl. Manages a node in the cluster.
- ClusterResourceControl. Manages a resource in the cluster. This function cannot be called from a resource DLL because it will cause a deadlock.
- ClusterResourceTypeControl. Manages a cluster resource type. This function cannot be called from a resource DLL because it will cause a deadlock.

> **NOTE**
>
> A resource DLL is not allowed to call the ClusterResourceControl or ClusterResourceTypeControl functions, because a deadlock will result. A resource DLL is not allowed to call these functions, even if the target resource is handled by a different DLL.

All the control code functions have similar parameters. The `ClusterGroupControl` function is declared as follows:

```
DWORD WINAPI ClusterGroupControl(HGROUP   hGroup,
                                 HNODE    hHostNode,
                                 DWORD    dwControlCode,
                                 LPVOID   lpInBuffer,
                                 DWORD    cbInBufferSize,
                                 LPVOID   lpOutBuffer,
                                 DWORD    cbOutBufferSize,
                                 LPDWORD  lpcbBytesReturned);
```

The `ClusterResourceTypeControl` function has eight parameters:

- A handle to the group to be managed. This handle is retrieved by calling the `OpenClusterGroup` function. Other cluster control functions accept different types of handles as their first parameters.

- A handle to the cluster node that's to perform the function. If NULL is passed as this parameter, the node that currently owns the group will handle the function. A node handle is opened with the `OpenClusterNode` function.

- A control code that represents the task to be performed. Information about control codes is discussed later in this section.

- A pointer to a buffer containing input information, if required; otherwise, NULL is passed as this parameter.

- The size of the input buffer, in bytes.

- A pointer to a buffer containing output information, if required; otherwise, NULL is passed as this parameter.

- The size of the output buffer, in bytes.

- A pointer to a DWORD that contains the size of the data actually stored in the output buffer. If this information isn't provided, you can pass NULL as this parameter.

Control code functions accept a control code as one of function's parameters. Because there are dozens of possible control codes, they aren't individually discussed in this chapter. For a thorough list of all possible control codes, consult the Platform SDK documentation.

Control codes are classed as either internal or external. An external control code is used by an application to manage a cluster object. An internal control code is used by the cluster service to notify a resource DLL that an event has occurred.

Control codes follow a specific naming convention:

```
CLUSCTL_OBJECT_FUNCTION
```

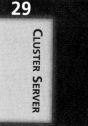

29

CLUSTER SERVER

For example, to retrieve the name of a group, you use the `CLUSCTRL_GROUP_GET_NAME` control code. To retrieve the name of a resource, you use the `CLUSCTRL_RESOURCE_GET_NAME` control code. Here are some examples of control codes used with cluster resources:

- `CLUSCTL_RESOURCE_SET_PRIVATE_PROPERTIES`. Sets the value of a cluster resource's private property
- `CLUSCTL_RESOURCE_ENUM_PRIVATE_PROPERTIES`. Enumerates the names of private properties that belong to the resource
- `CLUSCTL_RESOURCE_GET_PRIVATE_PROPERTIES`. Retrieves the value of a private property that belongs to a resource

Using `CClusPropList` to Retrieve Properties

Manipulating cluster object properties is rather difficult using the MSCS API functions. However, it's greatly simplified with the `CClusPropList` class, which is generated by the Visual C++ 6.0 Cluster Resource Type Wizard.

The `CClusPropList` class is derived from the MFC `CObject` class and is automatically added to all resource type projects. This class is not documented, and it isn't part of the standard MFC class library distribution. If you need to use this class outside a wizard-generated project, use the wizard to create a resource type project and then manually copy the `proplist.cpp` and `proplist.h` files from the wizard-generated project into the project that requires them.

The `CClusPropList` class has the following public member functions:

- `Proplist`. Returns a pointer to the internal `CLUSPROP_BUFFER_HELPER` member variable that contains the property list.
- `PbProplist`. Returns a pointer to the byte array contained in the property list's internal `CLUSPROP_BUFFER_HELPER` variable.
- `CbPropList`. Returns the size of the property list.
- `Cprops`. Returns the number of properties stored in the property list.
- `AddProp`. Adds a property to the property list. There are four overloaded versions of this method; each version handles a specific data type.
- `AllocPropList`. Increases the size of the property list to a specified minimum value.
- `DwGetNodeProperties`. Retrieves properties from a cluster node object.

- DwGetGroupProperties. Retrieves properties from a cluster group object.
- DwGetResourceProperties. Retrieves properties from a cluster resource object.
- DwGetResourceTypeProperties. Retrieves properties from a cluster resource type object.
- DwGetNetworkProperties. Retrieves properties from a cluster network object.
- DwGetNetInterfaceProperties. Retrieves properties from a cluster network interface object.

The DwGet*Xxx* functions return properties of all types through a PVOID out parameter, contrary to the name, which might lead you to believe that only DWORD values are returned. Each of these functions requires you to pass a control code with the function, specifying the type of property to be retrieved.

Direct Management of Cluster Objects

In addition to control code functions and control codes, cluster objects may be managed directly by API functions. Each type of cluster object has a set of management functions. When either a control code function or a management function may manage a cluster object, it's preferable to use the control code.

Most cluster management functions require a cluster handle as a parameter. The OpenCluster function returns a handle to a cluster:

```
HCLUSTER hclus = OpenCluster(L"ZAPHOD");
```

OpenCluster has one parameter: the name of the cluster to be opened. If NULL is passed as this parameter, a handle to the local cluster is returned. If the cluster cannot be found, or if an error occurs, NULL is returned. This function can be used to determine whether an application is running on a machine that belongs to a cluster.

A cluster handle must be closed when it's no longer needed. To close a cluster handle, use the CloseCluster function:

```
BOOL fClosed = CloseCluster(hclus);
```

The CloseCluster function takes a cluster handle as its only parameter. If an error occurs while the handle is closing, CloseCluster returns FALSE.

Using cluster object direct management functions, you can create instances of the various cluster object types, open handles to cluster objects, and delete resources from the cluster. For a complete list of the functions used to manage cluster objects directly, consult the Platform SDK.

Direct Management of the Cluster Database

In general, it isn't recommended that an application manage the cluster database directly. In most cases, an application should use control code functions or direct management functions when working with a cluster. Direct access to the cluster database does not result in notification messages being sent to resource DLLs that may be affected by the change.

Because the cluster database is implemented on top of the Windows 2000 System Registry, the functions used for managing the cluster database are similar to Windows 2000 Registry functions.

The top-level key in the cluster database is retrieved using the `GetClusterKey` function:

```
HKEY hKeyRoot = GetClusterKey(hclus, KEY_READ);
```

The `GetClusterKey` function has two parameters:

- A handle to the cluster that hosts the cluster database.
- One or more access flags that indicate the level of desired access to the cluster database. Cluster database functions use the same flags as Win32 System Registry functions.

If `GetClusterKey` is successful, it returns the top-level key in the cluster database; otherwise, it returns `NULL`.

Similar functions exist to retrieve the top-level keys for other cluster object types:

- `GetClusterGroupKey`. Opens the root key for a specified cluster group object
- `GetClusterNetInterfaceKey`. Opens the root key for a specified cluster network interface object
- `GetClusterNetworkKey`. Opens the root key for a specified cluster network object
- `GetClusterNodeKey`. Opens the root key for a specified cluster node object
- `GetClusterResourceKey`. Opens the root key for a specified cluster resource object
- `GetClusterResourceTypeKey`. Opens the root key for a specified cluster resource type object

To open a subkey in the cluster database, use the `ClusterRegOpenKey` or `ClusterRegCreateKey` function. `ClusterRegOpenKey` is similar to the `RegOpenKeyEx` function, except that `ClusterRegOpenKey` is used to open an existing key in the cluster database, instead of the Registry:

```
LONG WINAPI ClusterRegOpenKey(HKEY    hKey,
                              LPCWSTR lpszSubKey,
                              REGSAM  samDesired,
                              PHKEY   phkResult);
```

The ClusterRegOpenKey function has four parameters:

- A handle to a currently open key in the cluster database
- A Unicode string that contains the name of the subkey to be opened
- One or more Registry access flags that indicate the level of desired access to the cluster database
- A pointer to an HKEY that will contain the subkey if the function succeeds

The ClusterRegOpenKey function returns ERROR_SUCCESS if successful and a Win32 error code upon failure.

If the key does not exist, the ClusterRegOpenKey function fails. The ClusterRegCreateKey function can also be used to open an existing key in the cluster database. Like ClusterRegOpenKey, ClusterRegCreateKey opens an existing key in the cluster database. Unlike ClusterRegOpenKey, the ClusterRegCreateKey function will return a handle to a newly created key if the key doesn't exist:

```
LONG WINAPI ClusterRegCreateKey(HKEY hKey,
                    LPCWSTR lpszSubKey,
                    DWORD dwOptions,
                    REGSAM samDesired,
                    LPSECURITY_ATTRIBUTES lpSecurityAttributes,
                    PHKEY phkResult,
                    LPDWORD lpdwDisposition);
```

The ClusterRegCreateKey function has seven parameters:

- A handle to a currently open key in the cluster database.
- A Unicode string that contains the name of the subkey to be opened.
- An option flag for the database key. There are currently two values defined for this parameter: REG_OPTION_VOLATILE specifies that the key is not saved if the system is restarted, and REG_OPTION_NON_VOLATILE specifies that the key is saved if the system is restarted.
- One or more Registry access flags that indicate the level of desired access to the cluster database.
- A pointer to a security descriptor to be used for the new key. You can specify NULL to use the default security descriptor.
- A pointer to an HKEY that will contain the subkey if the function succeeds.
- A pointer to a DWORD that will be set to one of two values: REG_CREATED_NEW_KEY, if a new key was created in the cluster database, or REG_OPENED_EXISTING_KEY, if an existing key was opened.

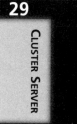

29

CLUSTER SERVER

The `ClusterRegCreateKey` function returns `ERROR_SUCCESS` if successful and a Win32 error code upon failure.

To retrieve a value from the cluster database, use the `ClusterRegQueryValue` function:

```
LONG WINAPI ClusterRegQueryValue(HKEY     hKey,
                                 LPCWSTR lpszValueName,
                                 LPDWORD lpdwValueType,
                                 LPBYTE  lpbData,
                                 LPDWORD lpcbData);
```

The `ClusterRegQueryValue` function has five parameters:

- A handle to a currently open key in the cluster database.
- A Unicode string that contains the name of the value to be retrieved.
- A pointer to a DWORD that will be filled with the type of the value. This value can be set to NULL if the type is already known.
- A pointer to a buffer that will be filled with the value retrieved from the cluster database.
- A pointer to a DWORD that contains the size of the buffer passed in the preceding parameter. If the function succeeds, the DWORD will contain the size of the data stored in the previous parameter.

If `ClusterRegQueryValue` succeeds, the function returns `ERROR_SUCCESS`; otherwise, a Win32 error code is returned.

To set a value in the cluster database, use the `ClusterRegSetValue` function:

```
DWORD WINAPI ClusterRegSetValue(HKEY     hKey,
                                LPCWSTR lpszValueName,
                                DWORD   dwType,
                                CONST BYTE* lpbData,
                                DWORD   cbData);
```

The `ClusterRegSetValue` function has five parameters:

- A handle to a currently open key in the cluster database
- A Unicode string that contains the name of the value to be set
- A DWORD variable that specifies the type of the value
- A pointer to the value to be stored in the cluster database
- The size of the value passed in the previous parameter

If `ClusterRegSetValue` succeeds, the function returns `ERROR_SUCCESS`; otherwise, a Win32 error code is returned.

To close a key that has been opened, use the `ClusterRegCloseKey` function:

```
LONG WINAPI ClusterRegCloseKey(HKEY hKey);
```

There are also cluster database functions that support removing keys, enumerating values, and other operations. In general, these functions work exactly like the equivalent Win32 System Registry functions. For more information about these functions, consult the Platform SDK documentation.

Resource DLL APIs

Resource DLLs communicate with a resource monitor and cluster service through two sets of interfaces:

- Entry point functions, which are implemented in the resource DLL to handle requests from MSCS
- Callback functions, which are called from your custom resource DLL back to MSCS

These functions are discussed in the following sections.

Resource DLL Entry Point Functions

Resource DLL entry point functions are used by the cluster service and resource monitor to send requests to the resource DLL. The resource DLL is expected not only to act on these requests but also to execute them in a timely manner.

A major constraint when trying to start, failover, or managing a cluster is the amount of time used by resource DLLs. In order to increase the availability of clusters, Microsoft recommends that resource DLLs return in 300 milliseconds *or less* when handling a resource DLL entry function.

This time limit is expected to apply to the upper bound of your processing time, which is not necessarily the optimal case. If your resource DLL needs to access devices on the network, or if it makes a Windows API call, it could easily be blocked for much longer than the 300 millisecond boundary. In order to complete within the 300 millisecond time constraint, a resource DLL will usually need to use a worker thread to perform much of the actual work.

There are 10 entry point functions implemented by all resource DLLs:

- `Startup`. The only resource DLL entry point function that's actually exported by the DLL. This function returns a pointer to a `CLRES_FUNCTION_TABLE` structure, which contains the addresses of the other entry point functions supported by the DLL. The resource monitor calls startup only once.

29

CLUSTER SERVER

- Open. Called when the resource monitor wants to begin working with a resource. The resource should be offline when this function is called; if it isn't offline, the resource DLL should force the resource into an offline state. The resource DLL should also initialize any data structures that will be required by the resource.

- Online. Called by the resource monitor to request that the resource be brought online. This function always requires that work be done in a worker thread—it's difficult to imagine any nontrivial resource that can be consistently brought online in less than 300 milliseconds.

- LooksAlive. Called periodically by the resource monitor to test the status of the resource DLL. The resource DLL is expected to perform an inexpensive check of the resource and return the status of the resource DLL. Performance is considered to be more important than accuracy in this case; if your resource DLL cannot complete this task in 300 milliseconds, it should use a worker thread to perform the test and return a cached value from the previous test. You can prevent this function from being called altogether by using an event handle, which is discussed in the next section, "Replacing LooksAlive with an Event Handle."

- IsAlive. Called by the resource monitor periodically to test the status of the resource DLL. Unlike LooksAlive, this function call cannot be optimized away. Also, a resource DLL is expected to perform a thorough test of the resource's functionality. As with LooksAlive, if a resource DLL cannot complete this task in 300 milliseconds, it should use a worker thread to perform the test and return a cached value from the previous test.

- Offline. Called to force the resource offline. This can be due to a failover or due to a normal shutdown request.

- Close. Called to remove the resource from the cluster. Implementations of this function typically require a worker thread in order to satisfy the 300-millisecond time limitation. The resource DLL should ensure that the resource is offline. If necessary, the resource should be forced offline using the Terminate function. Any resources that have been allocated to the resource must be freed in this function.

- Terminate. Called by the resource monitor or other functions to force an immediate shutdown of the resource. If this function is called, your resource DLL must forcibly release resources owned by the resource and return within 300 milliseconds. This is the only function that's reentrant—it can be called at any time, even when the resource DLL is processing an Open or Online function.

- ResourceControl. Called to ask the resource to handle a resource control code. Some control codes must be handled by the resource; others are usually handled by the resource monitor.

- `ResourceTypeControl`. Called to ask the resource to handle a resource type control code. Some control codes must be handled by the resource; others are usually handled by the resource monitor.

Two additional entry point functions are called for resource DLLs that are used for quorum resources:

- `Arbitrate`. Called after `Startup` and `Open`. This function requests that the resource attempt to gain control over the quorum resource.

- `Release`. Called to request that the resource release its arbitration over the quorum resource.

Examples of entry point functions are provided in the form of an example in the section titled "The High Availability Quote Cluster Resource Type."

Replacing `LooksAlive` with an Event Handle

To prevent `LooksAlive` from being called constantly, a resource DLL can provide an event handle back to the cluster service when the resource is placed online. The cluster service will monitor the event handle instead of calling `LooksAlive`; the resource DLL is expected to signal the event handle if the resource fails.

Resource DLL Callback Functions

Resource DLLs use two callback functions to notify the cluster service about events that are occurring in the resource DLL. Pointers to these functions are passed to the resource DLL as parameters when the `Startup` entry point function is called:

- `LogEvent`. A pointer to this function is passed to the resource DLL as a `PLOG_EVENT_ROUTINE` parameter in the `Startup` entry point function.

- `SetResourceStatus`. A pointer to this function is passed to the resource DLL as a `PSET_RESOURCE_STATUS_ROUTINE` parameter in the `Startup` entry point function.

`LogEvent` is called by the resource DLL to place error and event information into the cluster service's debug log:

```
(pLogEvent)(hResource,
            LOG_INFORMATION,
            L"An interesting event\n");
```

The `LogEvent` function has three parameters:

- A handle that identifies the resource that's creating the log entry. This parameter is passed to the resource DLL as a parameter when the `Startup` entry point function is called.

- A value that defines the level of the log entry. Possible values for this parameter are discussed in the following list.

- A Unicode text string that will be placed in the debug log.

The following four values are used to define the level of the debug log entry:

- LOG_INFORMATION. The log entry is provided for informational purposes.

- LOG_WARNING. The log entry refers to a possible failure.

- LOG_ERROR. The log entry refers to a fault that's isolated to a single component.

- LOG_SEVERE. The log entry refers to a fault that involves multiple components and may have compromised the entire system.

SetResourceStatus is called by the resource DLL to update the current status of a resource:

```
pSetResourceStatus(hResource,
                    &resStatus);
```

The SetResourceStatus function must be called to update the status of the resource in cases where the resource DLL has returned ERROR_IO_PENDING to indicate that a function could not be completed within the 300-millisecond time limit. The SetResourceStatus function has two parameters:

- A handle that identifies the resource that's creating the log entry. This parameter is passed to the resource DLL as a parameter when the Startup entry point function is called.

- A pointer to a RESOURCE_STATUS structure that contains information about the state of the resource.

The RESOURCE_STATUS structure is defined as follows:

```
typedef struct _RESOURCE_STATUS
{
    CLUSTER_RESOURCE_STATE  ResourceState;
    DWORD                   CheckPoint;
    DWORD                   WaitHint;
    HANDLE                  EventHandle;
}RESOURCE_STATUS, *PRESOURCE_STATUS;
```

The RESOURCE_STATUS structure has four member variables:

- ResourceState. The current state of the resource. Possible values for this member are discussed in the following list.

- CheckPoint. A counter that's initially set to zero and then incremented for each new call to SetResourceStatus.

- WaitHint. Not currently used.

- EventHandle. An event handle that will be signaled by the resource DLL if the resource fails.

The ResourceState member variable is set to one of the following states:

- ClusterResourceOnline. The resource is online and available.

- ClusterResourceOffline. The resource is offline and unavailable.

- ClusterResourceFailed. The resource has failed.

- ClusterResourceOnlinePending. The resource DLL is in the process of bringing the resource online.

- ClusterResourceOfflinePending. The resource DLL is in the process of taking the resource offline.

In addition to the callback functions discussed earlier, a quorum resource DLL calls a third callback function: QuorumResourceLost. A pointer to this function is passed to a quorum resource DLL when the Arbitrate entry point function is called. The QuorumResourceLost function is used to notify the cluster service that the resource DLL has lost control of the quorum resource.

Cluster Administration Extension APIs

The Cluster Administrator supports extensions through COM interfaces. If you use the Visual C++ 6.0 Cluster Resource Type Wizard to create your resource extension, it will handle these interfaces for you. This section describes each of the interfaces exposed by Cluster Administrator; for more details, consult the latest Platform SDK documentation.

Interfaces Exposed by Cluster Administrator Extensions

The following interfaces are exposed by the Cluster Administrator extension and are called by Cluster Administrator:

- IWEExtendContextMenu. Adds items to a Cluster Administrator context menu.

- IWEExtendPropertySheet. Adds pages to a Cluster Administrator property sheet.

- IWEExtendWizard. Adds pages to the Cluster Administrator wizards used to create groups or resources.

- IWEExtendWizard97. Adds Wizard97-style pages to a Cluster Administrator wizard.

- IWEInvokeCommand. Runs a command invoked from a context menu.

29

CLUSTER SERVER

Interfaces Exposed by Cluster Administrator

The following interfaces are exposed by Cluster Administrator and are called by the extension DLL in order to gather information about a specific object or to add to the Cluster Administrator user interface:

- IWCContextMenuCallback. Called by the extension DLL to add an item to a Cluster Administrator context menu

- IWCPropertySheetCallback. Called by the extension DLL to add pages to a Cluster Administrator property sheet

- IWCWizardCallback. Called by the extension DLL to add pages to the Cluster Administrator wizards used to create groups or resources

- IWCWizard97Callback. Called by the extension DLL to add Wizard97-style pages to a Cluster Administrator wizard

- IGetClusterDataInfo. Returns information about a cluster

- IGetClusterGroupInfo. Returns information about a group

- IGetClusterNetInterfaceInfo. Returns information about a network interface

- IGetClusterNetworkInfo. Returns information about a network

- IGetClusterNodeInfo. Returns information about a cluster node

- IGetClusterObjectInfo. Returns information about a cluster object

- IGetClusterResourceInfo. Returns information about a cluster resource

- IGetClusterUIInfo. Returns information about the Cluster Administrator user interface

Registering a Cluster Administration Extension

There are four registration functions that must be exported by a Cluster Administrator extension DLL. These four interfaces are automatically created by the Visual C++ 6.0 Cluster Resource Type Wizard:

- DllRegisterCluAdminExtension. Registers the extension in the cluster database

- DllUnregisterCluAdminExtension. Removes the extension from the cluster database

- DllRegisterServer. Registers the extension's COM interfaces

- DllUnregisterServer. Unregisters the extension's COM interfaces

To register your extension DLL manually, use the `regcladm` command. `regcladm` automatically calls the proper registration functions inside the extension DLL. Here's how you invoke `regcladm` from a DOS command line:

```
regcladm <DLL path>
```

To specify a particular cluster, use the `/C` switch:

```
regcladm /CZaphod <DLL path>
```

To unregister the DLL, use the `/U` switch:

```
regcladm /U <DLL path>
```

A Cluster-aware Example

As an example of how you can create applications that use MSCS, the CD-ROM that accompanies the book includes a set of sample projects that are based on the named pipe examples from Chapter 26, "Pipes":

- ClusterQuote. A new version of the BardServ project that was developed in Chapter 26. ClusterQuote stores the name of the named pipe in the cluster database and returns status information to the resource DLL.

- QuoteClient. A new version of the named pipe client developed in Chapter 26. QuoteClient allows you to specify the computer name and the name of the named pipe, instead of hard-coding these values.

- HiAvQuote. A resource DLL for the ClusterQuote executable developed using the Visual C++ Cluster Resource Type Wizard.

- HiAvQuoteEx. A Cluster Administrator extension developed using the Visual C++ Cluster Resource Type Wizard.

The complete source code for these projects is located on the CD-ROM that accompanies this book.

The ClusterQuote Project

ClusterQuote is a console mode project that's similar to the BardServ project created in Chapter 26. In Chapter 26, BardServ was created to demonstrate a simple application that acted as a named pipe server. As with BardServ, clients connect to an instance of ClusterQuote and request a quote to be delivered over a named pipe.

29

CLUSTER SERVER

ClusterQuote has a few enhancements over BardServ:

- A client can request the current status of ClusterQuote by sending the string "Status" to the server. If ClusterQuote is running, it will respond with "Okay". This interaction will be used by the resource DLL to test the status of the server.

- A client can shut down an instance of ClusterQuote by sending the string "Terminate" to the server.

- ClusterQuote is not hard-coded to use a particular pipe name. It uses a command-line argument as the pipe name when creating a named pipe. The resource DLL will retrieve a private property from the cluster database and pass this value to ClusterQuote as a command-line parameter.

The QuoteClient Project

QuoteClient is a dialog box–based MFC project that's similar to the NPClient project presented in Chapter 26. Like NPClient, QuoteClient connects to a named pipe and requests a quote from the server (in this case, an instance of ClusterQuote).

QuoteClient works just like NPClient, with a few new features:

- A user of QuoteClient can specify the name of the remote computer as well as the named pipe that QuoteClient will connect to.

- A user of QuoteClient can request a status message from the server by clicking the Status button.

- A user of QuoteClient can request that the server shut down by clicking the Terminate button.

An example of QuoteClient running is provided in Figure 29.3.

FIGURE 29.3

QuoteClient is used to connect to an instance of ClusterQuote.

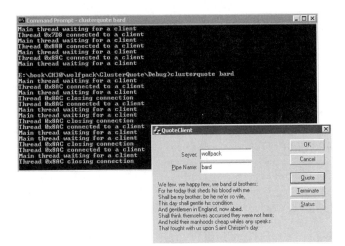

The High Availability Quote Cluster Resource Type

Although it's theoretically possible to create a cluster resource type by hand, it's much easier to use the Cluster Resource Type Wizard that's included with Visual C++ 6.0. This wizard will generate nearly complete projects for a resource DLL and a Cluster Administrator extension based on your input on two wizard pages.

Using Cluster Resource Type Wizard

The High Availability Quotes resource type was created using the Visual C++ Cluster Resource Type Wizard. Start by selecting the Cluster Resource Type Wizard from the Visual C++ Projects tab in the New dialog box. The first page of the Cluster Resource Type Wizard is shown in Figure 29.4.

FIGURE 29.4
The initial Cluster Resource Type Wizard page.

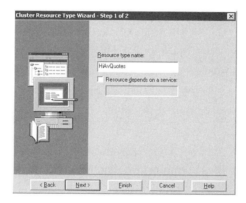

Three pieces of information are supplied in the first wizard page:

- The name of the cluster resource type.
- The name of a service, if any, that the resource depends on.
- For the HiAvQuotes project, the resource type name is High Availability Quotes. The resource type does not depend on a service.

The next Cluster Resource Type Wizard page is shown in Figure 29.5.

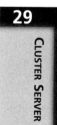

FIGURE 29.5

*The second
Cluster Resource
Type Wizard
page.*

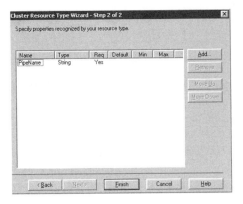

The second wizard page is used to define properties that are associated with the resource type. For HiAvQuotes, the only property is the PipeName property.

Each property has three attributes:

- The property name. This must be a valid C++ identifier.
- The property type. This value is selected from a drop-down list and is a type compatible with the cluster database. The PipeName property has the String type.
- A flag that indicates that the property is required in order to bring the resource online.

Clicking the Finish button on the second wizard page closes the Cluster Resource Type Wizard and displays the New Project Information dialog box. Close this dialog box to generate two skeleton projects:

- A resource DLL for the new cluster resource type. For the HiAvQuotes, this project is named HiAvQuotes.
- A Cluster Administrator extension for the new resource type. For HiAvQuotes, this project is named HiAvQuotesEx.

Writing Handlers for Resource DLL Entry Points

The skeleton resource DLL created by the wizard contains about 1,500 lines of C code that's largely complete. Areas that require you to add code are marked with // TODO: comments.

In the HiAvQuotes project that you'll find on the CD-ROM that accompanies this book, all changes that have been made to the wizard-generated code are marked with `// Hi-Av Quote` comments. Changes to the resource DLL include the following:

- Code was added to implement the resource-specific work needed in several of the resource DLL entry point functions. A list of the functions is provided in the following list.

- New worker threads were added to handle the `Offline` and `IsAlive` resource DLL entry point functions.

- A new variable that caches the value of the most recent `IsAlive` test was added. This value is returned in response to an `IsAlive` request, and the worker thread calculates a new value.

The following resource DLL entry point functions were modified:

- `Online`. Added code to create a worker thread and then return `ERROR_IO_PENDING`. The worker thread creates an instance of ClusterQuote.

- `LooksAlive`. Added code to test the process handle of the current instance of ClusterQuote and return `TRUE` if the process is still running.

- `IsAlive`. Added code to create a worker thread. While the worker thread performs an in-depth check, the function returns the result from the previous test. The worker thread connects to ClusterQuote and sends a "Status" string to the server. The worker thread then checks to make sure that ClusterQuote responds "Okay".

- `Offline`. Added code to create a worker thread and then return `ERROR_IO_PENDING`. The worker thread connects to ClusterQuote and sends a "Terminate" string to the server.

- `Terminate`. Added code to call `TerminateProcess`. This function is called only if the cluster service is not able to close the resource normally.

 Due to the vast amount of source code in this project, it's not presented here. However, the complete project can be found on this book's CD-ROM.

Installing the Resource Type in the Cluster

To register the resource DLL programmatically (for example, from a setup program), call the `CreateClusterResourceType` function. To register the Cluster Administrator extension, call the DLL's `DllRegisterCluAdminExtension` function to register the extension with Cluster Administrator and then call the DLL's `DllRegServer` function to register the extension with COM.

29

CLUSTER SERVER

To register the resource DLL manually, use the following command line:

```
CLUSTER restype "High Availability Quotes" -create -dllname:<DLL path>
```

As discussed earlier in the chapter, to register the Cluster Administrator DLL manually, use the following command line:

```
REGCLADM <DLL path>
```

Summary

This chapter has discussed Microsoft Cluster Server, also known as MSCS. You can use MSCS to make your mission-critical applications more available to clients as well as to increase the overall reliability of your network. This chapter also presented several examples, including a simple cluster-aware application and its associated resource DLL and Cluster Administrator extension DLL.

INDEX

U

W

mcp.com

The Authoritative Encyclopedia of Computing

Resource Centers
Books & Software
Personal Bookshelf
WWW Yellow Pages
Online Learning
Special Offers
Site Search
Industry News

▶ *Choose the online ebooks
that you can view from your
personal workspace on our site.*

About MCP   Site Map   Product Support

Turn to the *Authoritative* Encyclopedia of Computing

You'll find over 150 full text books online, hundreds of
shareware/freeware applications, online computing classes
and 10 computing resource centers full of expert advice
from the editors and publishers of:

- Adobe Press
- BradyGAMES
- Cisco Press
- Hayden Books
- Lycos Press
- New Riders

- Que
- Que Education & Training
- Sams Publishing
- Waite Group Press
- Ziff-Davis Press

mcp.com

The Authoritative Encyclopedia of Computing

Get the best information and learn about latest developments in:

- ■ Design
- ■ Graphics and Multimedia
- ■ Enterprise Computing and DBMS
- ■ General Internet Information
- ■ Operating Systems
- ■ Networking and Hardware
- ■ PC and Video Gaming
- ■ Productivity Applications
- ■ Programming
- ■ Web Programming and Administration
- ■ Web Publishing

When you're looking for computing information, consult the authority.
The Authoritative Encyclopedia of Computing at mcp.com.

Get **FREE** books and more...when you register this book online for our Personal Bookshelf Program

http://register.samspublishing.com/

 Register online and you can sign up for our *FREE Personal Bookshelf Program...*unlimited access to the electronic version of more than 200 complete computer books—immediately! That means you'll have 100,000 pages of valuable information onscreen, at your fingertips!

 Plus, you can access product support, including complimentary downloads, technical support files, book-focused links, companion Web sites, author sites, and more!

 And you'll be automatically registered to receive a *FREE subscription to a weekly email newsletter* to help you stay current with news, announcements, sample book chapters, and special events, including sweepstakes, contests, and various product giveaways!

 We value your comments! Best of all, the entire registration process takes only a few minutes to complete, so go online and get the greatest value going—absolutely FREE!

Don't Miss Out On This Great Opportunity!

Sams is a brand of Macmillan Computer Publishing USA.

For more information, please visit *www.mcp.com*

Copyright ©1999 Macmillan Computer Publishing USA

THE COMPREHENSIVE SOLUTION

Unleashed *takes you beyond the average technology discussions. It's the best resource for practical advice from experts and the most in-depth coverage of the latest information.* **Unleashed**—*the necessary tool for serious users.*

Building Enterprise Solutions with Visual Studio 6
G.A. Sullivan
0-672-31489-4
$49.99 USA/$71.95 CAN

Other Unleashed Titles

Oracle8 Server Unleashed
Joe Greene, et al.
0-672-31207-7
$49.99 USA/$70.95 CAN

Visual C++ 5 Unleashed, Second Edition
Viktor Toth
0-672-31013-9
$49.99 USA/$71.95 CAN

Active Server Pages 2.0 Unleashed
Stephen Walther, et al.
0-672-31613-7
$39.99 USA/$56.95 CAN

Sams Teach Yourself Visual C++ 6 in 21 Days
Davis Chapman
0-672-31240-9
$29.99 USA/$42.95 CAN

Sams Teach Yourself Visual InterDev 6 in 21 Days
Michael Van Hoozer
0-672-31251-4
$34.99 USA/$50.95 CAN

Sams Teach Yourself Visual Basic 6 in 21 Days
Greg Perry
0-672-31310-3
$29.99 USA/$42.95 CAN

Sams Teach Yourself Database Programming with Visual Basic 6 in 21 Days
Curtis Smith and Mike Amundsen
0-672-31308-1
$45.00 USA/$64.95 CAN

Visual InterDev 6 Unleashed
Paul Thurrott, et al.
0-672-31262-X
$49.99 USA/$71.95 CAN

Visual Basic 6 Unleashed
Rob Thayer
0-672-31309-X
$34.99 USA/$50.95 CAN

SAMS

www.samspublishing.com

All prices are subject to change.

What's on the Disc

The companion CD-ROM contains a lot of useful third-party software, plus all the source code from the book.

Windows 95/98 Installation Instructions

1. Insert the CD-ROM disc into your CD-ROM drive.
2. From the Windows 95 desktop, double-click the My Computer icon.
3. Double-click the icon representing your CD-ROM drive.
4. Double-click the icon titled START.EXE to run the program.

> **NOTE**
>
> If Windows 95 is installed on your computer, and you have the AutoPlay feature enabled, the START.EXE program starts automatically whenever you insert the disc into your CD-ROM drive.

Windows NT Installation Instructions

1. Insert the CD-ROM disc into your CD-ROM drive.
2. From File Manager or Program Manager, choose Run from the File menu.
3. Type `<drive>\START.EXE` and press Enter, where `<drive>` corresponds to the drive letter of your CD-ROM. For example, if your CD-ROM is drive D:, type `D:\START.EXE` and press Enter.

By opening this package, you are agreeing to be bound by the following agreement:

Some of the software included with this product may be copyrighted, in which case all rights are reserved by the respective copyright holder. You are licensed to use software copyrighted by the Publisher and its licensors on a single computer. You may copy and/or modify the software as needed to facilitate your use of it on a single computer. Making copies of the software for any other purpose is a violation of the United States copyright laws.

This software is sold as is without warranty of any kind, either express or implied, including but not limited to the implied warranties of merchantability and fitness for a particular purpose. Neither the publisher nor its dealers or distributors assume any liability for any alleged or actual damages arising from the use of this program. (Some states do not allow for the exclusion of implied warranties, so the exclusion might not apply to you.)